INDIAN AFFAIRS ANNUAL 2008

INDIAN AFFAIRS ANNUAL 2008

(In 9 Vols.)

Vol. 1

Chronology of Events

(01-04-2007 to 05-05-2007)

Shailendra Sengar

KALPAZ PUBLICATIONS

KALPAZ PUBLICATIONS
DELHI - 110052

Indian Affairs Annual 2008

Rs. 6300 (Set)

ISBN: 81-7835-693-7 (Set)
ISBN: 81-7835-694-5 (Vol. 1)

Published in 2008 in India by
Kalpaz Publications
C-30, Satyawati Nagar,
Delhi-110052
E-mail: kalpaz@hotmail.com
Phone : 9212729499

Laser Type Setting by: Quick Media, Delhi
Printed at : Singhal Print Media, Delhi

PREFACE

On completion of four years of the UPA government, the Prime Minister, Dr. Manmohan Singh, has released "Report to the people, 2008". In the foreword he says, "Four years ago the people of India charted a new course for themselves. They wanted a Government that would be a unifying expression of the collective will of all the people of India. They sought the politics of inclusion and the economics of inclusiveness. They wanted a Government that every Indian, irrespective of region, language, caste, community or creed, could say here is "Our Government". Building on the Flagship Programmes we launched, viz, the National Rural Employment Guarantee Programme, the National Rural Health Mission, the Jawaharlal Nehru National Urban Renewal Mission, Bharat Nirman, the expanded Sarva Siksha Abhiyan and the Mid-Day Meal Programme, the Food Security Mission and the Rashtriya Krishi Vikas Yojana, our Government has put in place an "architecture for inclusive growth". I assure you that these will be our guiding principles as we enter the final year of this term. We reiterate our commitment of the UPA Government to the principles and the goals of the National Common Minimum Programme. I sincerely hope, ladies and gentlemen, this Annual Report to the People will be read by one and all to get a better understanding of the work being done by our Government.

While Prime Minister Manmohan Singh kept mum on the Indo-US nuclear deal in his speech at the fourth anniversary celebrations of the UPA Government the "Report to the People: 2004-08" released by the PM had a passing reference to the issue. "Indo-US cooperation now spans a wide spectrum, including high technology, space, agriculture, education, trade and economic linkages, and there is a prospect of civil nuclear cooperation," is how the 63-page report describes the nuke deal. Pointing more towards outlays than outcomes, the report differentiates the UPA's aam aadmi claim from the NDA Government's "India Shining" promise.

In the face of unrelenting Left opposition to the Indo-US nuclear deal, the UPA Government's report card of its achievements in the last four years is largely silent on the pact. All that it says about the controversial deal is that there is "prospect of civil nuclear cooperation" with the US. The very brief mention comes in the section on "External Affairs", while the "Energy" part of the report gives it a complete miss. "Indo-US cooperation now spans a wide spectrum, including high technology, space, agriculture, education, trade and economic linkages and there is a prospect of civil nuclear cooperation," the report said while noting that there has been a transformation in Indo-US relations. Ironically, the report was brought out by Prime Minister Manmohan Singh, who has staked his prestige on the deal, which is his baby. This is perhaps reflective of the immense pressure on the Government from the Left allies to not operationalise the deal, which they claim will compromise the country's sovereignty and independent foreign policy. In the election year the policies and programmes of this government will judge by the people.

We are thankful to India's leading English dailies-*The Times of India, The Hindu, The Indian Express* and *The Hindustan Times* and Leading News Agencies-*PTI and UNI* as we were immensely benefited by their detailed and comprehensive coverage of day-to-day of Indian Affairs.

I take this opportunity to thank my associates Md. Salim Ansari, Dalbir Singh and Ahtesham Ahmad, who prepared the index of events with great care for the benefit of the readers.

—Shailendra Sengar

INDIAN AFFAIRS ANNUAL INDEX

EVENTS
(April 2007 to March 2008)

4404, 4405, 4409, 4458, 4480, 4595, 4596, 4597, 4598, 4606, 4608, 4667, 4676, 4698, 4699, 4700, 4764, 4769, 4772, 4782, 4786, 4787, 4814, 4843, 4849, 4851, 4937, 5040, 5081, 5094, 5108, 5113, 5114, 5126, 5133, 5167, 5192, 5198, 5211, 5233, 5247, 5259, 5321, 5322, 5324, 5368, 5376, 5389, 5394, 5450, 5461, 5498, 5521, 5544, 5560, 5565, 5570, 5584, 5614, 5616, 5624, 5632, 5645, 5647, 5696, 5742, 5743, 5786, 5805, 5815, 5820, 5835, 5845, 5905, 5931, 5938, 5970, 6012, 6028, 6034, 6035, 6065, 6075, 6143, 6148, 6197, 6273, 6315, 6316, 6317, 6319, 6400, 6522, 6525, 6568, 6651, 6652, 6653, 6654, 6807, 6808, 6812, 6867, 6873, 6883, 6900, 6904, 6972.

Defence

144, 170, 182, 186, 205, 206, 256, 290, 306, 309, 323, 326, 338, 351, 357, 358, 369, 428, 436, 473, 497, 550, 580, 600, 604, 645, 647, 648, 649, 650, 696, 714, 790, 796, 797, 798, 799, 801, 802, 803, 804, 805, 866, 867, 868, 873, 876, 877, 951, 1055, 1056, 1057, 1095, 1096, 1097, 1098, 1099, 1100, 1101, 1103, 1104, 1119, 1143, 1150, 1151, 1157, 1158, 1160, 1162, 1178, 1180, 1189, 1200, 1274, 1309, 1329, 1335, 1364, 1394, 1396, 1398, 1405, 1418, 1435, 1436, 1437, 1449, 1474, 1497, 1509, 1539, 1554, 1566, 1586, 1592, 1596, 1606, 1619, 1642, 1648, 1650, 1657, 1671, 1687, 1691, 1692, 1709, 1715, 1721, 1729, 1749, 1755, 1802, 1806, 1823, 1897, 1918, 1939, 1943, 1992, 2029, 2031, 2041, 2051, 2053, 2069, 2078, 2087, 2112, 2125, 2142, 2156, 2180, 2224, 2228, 2245, 2256, 2300, 2301, 2311, 2325, 2333, 2377, 2391, 2422, 2426, 2527, 2528, 2529, 2530, 2553, 2580, 2581, 2604, 2605, 2606, 2607, 2701, 2722, 2738, 2739, 2779, 2787, 2796, 2797, 2799, 2801, 2802, 2803, 2804, 2805, 2806, 2807, 2808, 2844, 2851, 2852, 2854, 2861, 2862, 2870, 2943, 2948, 2990, 3010, 3011, 3019, 3020, 3046, 3047, 3049, 3051, 3086, 3203, 3204, 3205, 3281, 3325, 3359, 3363, 3383, 3394, 3395, 3423, 3465, 3483, 3485, 3498, 3511, 3532, 3544, 3545, 3548, 3550, 3560, 3565, 3577, 3579, 3597, 3603, 3612, 3617, 3618, 3626, 3670, 3690, 3691, 3710, 3750, 3752, 3759, 3806, 3816, 3819, 3839, 3842, 3859, 3884, 3887, 3888, 3889, 3893, 3894, 3897, 3925, 3929, 3932, 3933, 3934, 3955, 4010, 4035, 4044, 4073, 4095, 4102, 4110, 4111, 4141, 4149, 4166, 4255, 4256, 4329, 4331, 4332, 4333, 4352, 4364, 4374, 4384, 4398, 4408, 4439, 4446, 4487, 4525, 4526, 4527, 4528, 4529, 4530, 4531, 4532, 4533, 4534, 4603, 4623, 4624, 4625, 4626, 4627, 4628, 4631, 4683, 4711, 4712, 4716, 4744, 4788, 4794, 4795, 4797, 4798, 4799, 4815, 4883, 4884, 4885, 4886, 4887, 4893, 4968, 4973, 4990, 4991, 4995, 5001, 5019, 5026, 5028, 5034, 5071, 5082, 5090, 5092, 5105, 5111, 5117, 5124, 5141, 5142, 5148, 5169, 5180, 5189, 5218, 5222, 5234, 5242, 5243, 5257, 5275, 5276, 5281, 5300, 5302, 5304, 5320, 5327, 5341, 5350, 5372, 5380, 5387, 5398, 5406, 5437, 5450, 5453, 5555, 5577, 5584, 5603, 5604, 5617, 5629, 5634, 5645, 5671, 5676, 5678, 5679, 5698, 5702, 5746, 5772, 5787, 5791, 5792, 5806, 5840, 5882, 5894, 5895, 5916, 5921, 5954, 5957, 5969, 5974, 5988, 5989, 6025, 6044, 6052, 6074,

1204, 1206, 1212, 1217, 1219, 1223, 1230, 1233, 1235, 1237, 1239, 1241, 1247, 1248, 1275, 1280, 1294, 1306, 1316, 1325, 1331, 1361, 1366, 1372, 1373, 1381, 1408, 1431, 1452, 1453, 1454, 1467, 1469, 1478, 1479, 1480, 1502, 1519, 1520, 1530, 1567, 1588, 1598, 1614, 1620, 1624, 1629, 1649, 1662, 1665, 1699, 1714, 1718, 1719, 1744, 1750, 1761, 1765, 1775, 1779, 1780, 1791, 1794, 1826, 1827, 1838, 1842, 1844, 1845, 1855, 1857, 1866, 1884, 1896, 1898, 1903, 1913, 1915, 1920, 1922, 1928, 1935, 1983, 1985, 1988, 1989, 2003, 2012, 2025, 2043, 2056, 2092, 2095, 2118, 2126, 2128, 2134, 2139, 2145, 2173, 2202, 2203, 2226, 2234, 2270, 2271, 2272, 2273, 2287, 2314, 2328, 2365, 2372, 2387, 2424, 2455, 2458, 2460, 2461, 2481, 2516, 2538, 2632, 2635, 2653, 2654, 2655, 2656, 2664, 2666, 2713, 2718, 2738, 2740, 2747, 2763, 2825, 2858, 2883, 2892, 2914, 2925, 2937, 2942, 2943, 2968, 2971, 2978, 3057, 3058, 3059, 3067, 3070, 3071, 3072, 3085, 3087, 3120, 3154, 3192, 3201, 3222, 3228, 3229, 3235, 3240, 3241, 3244, 3261, 3264, 3267, 3286, 3305, 3317, 3331, 3361, 3363, 3397, 3428, 3430, 3450, 3466, 3467, 3470, 3478, 3497, 3535, 3570, 3593, 3597, 3627, 3643, 3650, 3658, 3673, 3725, 3729, 3738, 3750, 3764, 3766, 3768, 3789, 3811, 3828, 3843, 3850, 3856, 3891, 3903, 3905, 3916, 3926, 3936, 3947, 3958, 3963, 3979, 4033, 4050, 4069, 4071, 4089, 4132, 4164, 4169, 4184, 4186, 4199, 4229, 4251, 4275, 4276, 4277, 4278, 4279, 4280, 4303, 4307, 4424, 4438, 4442, 4448, 4476, 4479, 4493, 4511, 4512, 4536, 4551, 4571, 4601, 4625, 4645, 4648, 4651, 4652, 4653, 4654, 4655, 4656, 4657, 4681, 4703, 4737, 4743, 4766, 4771, 4792, 4817, 4818, 4819, 4820, 4821, 4824, 4837, 4844, 4847, 4850, 4900, 4901, 4905, 4906, 4907, 4908, 4909, 4910, 4911, 4924, 4966, 4983, 4999, 5032, 5037, 5052, 5056, 5062, 5077, 5078, 5107, 5108, 5120, 5127, 5129, 5133, 5139, 5158, 5182, 5186, 5219, 5237, 5269, 5279, 5282, 5283, 5317, 5319, 5336, 5358, 5389, 5394, 5398, 5403, 5428, 5430, 5435, 5451, 5463, 5469, 5498, 5509, 5510, 5511, 5516, 5521, 5534, 5554, 5570, 5576, 5579, 5581, 5582, 5584, 5586, 5591, 5596, 5606, 5621, 5651, 5665, 5681, 5683, 5685, 5689, 5692, 5693, 5697, 5701, 5703, 5716, 5741, 5761, 5770, 5816, 5823, 5824, 5837, 5854, 5897, 5939, 5958, 5963, 5982, 5984, 5986, 6020, 6037, 6049, 6095, 6134, 6148, 6153, 6154, 6155, 6159, 6175, 6185, 6188, 6237, 6248, 6258, 6265, 6266, 6268, 6273, 6329, 6333, 6359, 6374, 6375, 6376, 6401, 6419, 6445, 6449, 6459, 6460, 6461, 6462, 6476, 6478, 6492, 6507, 6509, 6559, 6567, 6585, 6593, 6599, 6613, 6631, 6660, 6664, 6684, 6710, 6714, 6723, 6724, 6725, 6726, 6727, 6728, 6730, 6735, 6780, 6785, 6794, 6810, 6819, 6834, 6841, 6845, 6847, 6848, 6849, 6850, 6852, 6870, 6871, 6875, 6880, 6927, 6939, 6981, 6993, 7023, 7026.

Environment

10, 13, 17, 29, 38, 47, 61, 75, 115, 116, 118, 120, 206, 212, 219, 233, 249, 346, 371, 410, 422, 470, 477, 485, 493, 505, 531, 536,

6644, 6687, 6731, 6738, 6778, 6780, 6900, 6969, 6977, 7001, 7018, 7034.

Labour

19, 132, 152, 166, 168, 196, 217, 251, 260, 269, 341, 446, 447, 489, 492, 493, 505, 517, 518, 519, 535, 548, 565, 677, 699, 729, 740, 742, 743, 773, 806, 807, 808, 809, 810, 811, 812, 853, 914, 915, 916, 977, 993, 1001, 1004, 1064, 1066, 1067, 1068, 1106, 1146, 1148, 1164, 1166, 1170, 1182, 1200, 1212, 1217, 1222, 1230, 1247, 1280, 1285, 1294, 1306, 1347, 1366, 1408, 1431, 1453, 1480, 1495, 1501, 1502, 1506, 1507, 1565, 1567, 1588, 1598, 1645, 1656, 1662, 1699, 1718, 1735, 1755, 1761, 1779, 1857, 1884, 1896, 1910, 1913, 1928, 1965, 1983, 1985, 2003, 2095, 2118, 2128, 2149, 2159, 2160, 2174, 2270, 2271, 2272, 2273, 2345, 2424, 2537, 2538, 2575, 2600, 2645, 2653, 2654, 2656, 2666, 2679, 2715, 2736, 2740, 2747, 2766, 2845, 2874, 2892, 2937, 3057, 3058, 3059, 3192, 3201, 3233, 3244, 3331, 3444, 3448, 3461, 3466, 3530, 3619, 3643, 3673, 3730, 3764, 3811, 3834, 3856, 3862, 3878, 3891, 3896, 3916, 3937, 3959, 3996, 3999, 4000, 4071, 4103, 4132, 4164, 4184, 4251, 4268, 4275, 4276, 4277, 4278, 4279, 4280, 4289, 4303, 4307, 4493, 4511, 4512, 4513, 4551, 4650, 4651, 4652, 4654, 4655, 4656, 4657, 4707, 4709, 4737, 4743, 4817, 4818, 4819, 4820, 4821, 4905, 4906, 4907, 4908, 4909, 4910, 4911, 4966, 5002, 5015, 5041, 5056, 5077, 5078, 5096, 5107, 5127, 5140, 5158, 5182, 5282, 5362, 5369, 5376, 5390, 5403, 5469, 5491, 5516, 5613, 5651, 5665, 5837, 6045, 6156, 6163, 6185, 6188, 6251, 6265, 6266, 6268, 6359, 6374, 6375, 6376, 6403, 6459, 6460, 6461, 6462, 6478, 6613, 6631, 6660, 6701, 6723, 6724, 6725, 6726, 6727, 6773, 6819, 6843, 6845, 6847, 6848, 6849, 6850, 6852, 6871, 6882.

Law

1564, 1569, 1707, 1711, 1721, 1761, 1789, 1824, 1837, 1869, 1875, 1882, 1893, 1900, 1905, 1956, 1968, 2051, 2064, 2095, 2107, 2177, 51, 77, 80, 95, 107, 111, 166, 188, 220, 224, 239, 268, 311, 333, 334, 424, 496, 497, 500, 502, 510, 547, 577, 580, 606, 608, 633, 640, 642, 643, 673, 676, 725, 727, 728, 764, 780, 834, 840, 864, 887, 949, 975, 977, 1013, 1027, 1043, 1045, 1076, 1078, 1118, 1138, 1237, 1333, 1334, 1361, 1425, 1463, 1507, 1518, 1533, 1550, 2265, 2268, 2269, 2285, 2350, 2364, 2391, 2429, 2459, 2464, 2465, 2467, 2468, 2533, 2534, 2535, 2545, 2573, 2601, 2607, 2688, 2689, 2728, 2748, 2749, 2750, 2790, 2838, 2850, 2899, 2901, 3028, 3072, 3126, 3131, 3132, 3133, 3134, 3168, 3189, 3190, 3191, 3230, 3243, 3255, 3282, 3343, 3354, 3380, 3400, 3417, 3421, 3440, 3444, 3453, 3464, 3482, 3495, 3499, 3543, 3564, 3587, 3590, 3600, 3630, 3649, 3651, 3671, 3674, 3694, 3702, 3738, 3764, 3797, 3877, 3886, 3933, 3961, 4007, 4017, 4058, 4072, 4101, 4107, 4134, 4169, 4239, 4240, 4242, 4243, 4268, 4283, 4292, 4307, 4308, 4340, 4406, 4415, 4437, 4486, 4516, 4579, 4671, 4680, 4809, 4845, 4846, 4895,

4334, 4335, 4336, 4337, 4345, 4346, 4351, 4352, 4353, 4354, 4365, 4375, 4378, 4400, 4412, 4416, 4419, 4427, 4433, 4434, 4435, 4436, 4438, 4443, 4448, 4449, 4450, 4451, 4452, 4453, 4454, 4455, 4463, 4464, 4476, 4511, 4512, 4515, 4517, 4518, 4525, 4526, 4527, 4528, 4529, 4530, 4531, 4532, 4533, 4534, 4535, 4536, 4537, 4538, 4539, 4540, 4541, 4566, 4567, 4568, 4569, 4577, 4579, 4580, 4581, 4592, 4593, 4608, 4610, 4611, 4612, 4613, 4614, 4615, 4616, 4617, 4618, 4621, 4622, 4630, 4633, 4637, 4639, 4640, 4641, 4643, 4644, 4645, 4659, 4660, 4671, 4674, 4675, 4687, 4689, 4692, 4699, 4700, 4701, 4702, 4703, 4721, 4731, 4735, 4738, 4739, 4740, 4741, 4742, 4743, 4762, 4763, 4765, 4768, 4777, 4793, 4794, 4797, 4798, 4799, 4802, 4803, 4804, 4805, 4806, 4807, 4809, 4810, 4811, 4812, 4813, 4817, 4818, 4819, 4820, 4821, 4824, 4825, 4826, 4827, 4847, 4848, 4855, 4871, 4872, 4878, 4879, 4880, 4881, 4889, 4890, 4891, 4892, 4896, 4898, 4899, 4912, 4913, 4914, 4915, 4916, 4917, 4918, 4919, 4920, 4921, 4928, 4929, 4930, 4931, 4935, 4936, 4937, 4938, 4939, 4967, 4973, 4976, 4994, 4996, 4998, 4999, 5000, 5004, 5005, 5006, 5007, 5008, 5010, 5011, 5012, 5015, 5016, 5081, 5196, 5296, 5298, 5360, 5600, 5615, 5651, 5773, 5779, 5825, 5836, 5921, 6001, 6056, 6061, 6069, 6072, 6073, 6077, 6078, 6080, 6083, 6084, 6085, 6086, 6088, 6091, 6095, 6112, 6115, 6116, 6118, 6119, 6120, 6121, 6122, 6123, 6124, 6125, 6126, 6127, 6128, 6129, 6130, 6135, 6136, 6137, 6138, 6139, 6140, 6141, 6152, 6153, 6155, 6156, 6157, 6160, 6161, 6175, 6195, 6206, 6217, 6218, 6219, 6220, 6221, 6222, 6223, 6224, 6225, 6226, 6227, 6228, 6229, 6230, 6237, 6238, 6239, 6240, 6241, 6250, 6258, 6259, 6265, 6266, 6268, 6271, 6272, 6274, 6275, 6276, 6278, 6280, 6287, 6295, 6304, 6306, 6307, 6311, 6328, 6331, 6340, 6343, 6345, 6346, 6347, 6351, 6352, 6353, 6354, 6355, 6356, 6358, 6359, 6360, 6361, 6362, 6364, 6365, 6366, 6368, 6370, 6371, 6372, 6373, 6386, 6428, 6433, 6445, 6446, 6449, 6459, 6460, 6461, 6462, 6469, 6470, 6471, 6472, 6476, 6479, 6482, 6484, 6485, 6487, 6491, 6493, 6507, 6516, 6519, 6520, 6524, 6529, 6545, 6546, 6547, 6548, 6550, 6551, 6552, 6553, 6554, 6563, 6565, 6566, 6567, 6569, 6571, 6572, 6573, 6574, 6575, 6576, 6577, 6579, 6583, 6588, 6589, 6590, 6593, 6594, 6596, 6613, 6630, 6636, 6637, 6638, 6639, 6651, 6652, 6653, 6654, 6665, 6666, 6668, 6673, 6674, 6675, 6676, 6677, 6678, 6681, 6682, 6687, 6688, 6689, 6693, 6694, 6696, 6697, 6698, 6710, 6711, 6722, 6723, 6724, 6725, 6726, 6727, 6738, 6739, 6740, 6741, 6742, 6743, 6745, 6746, 6749, 6753, 6759, 6764, 6765, 6766, 6767, 6768, 6774, 6783, 6790, 6792, 6793, 6798, 6803, 6804, 6805, 6811, 6812, 6813, 6816, 6824, 6825, 6826, 6827, 6846, 6853, 6856, 6857, 6858, 6859, 6861, 6862, 6863, 6864, 6865, 6866, 7012, 740, 742, 743, 744, 754, 759, 760, 761, 764, 765, 766, 774, 775, 781, 792, 793, 794, 814, 817, 818, 819, 820, 835, 836, 866, 867, 868, 885, 887, 888, 890, 898, 899, 900, 901, 908, 909, 910, 913, 914, 915, 916, 919, 920, 921, 922, 923, 924, 930, 931, 932, 933, 935, 942, 949, 954, 955, 956, 957, 973, 974, 975, 977, 978, 979, 982, 984, 985,

3865, 3891, 3903, 3926, 3954, 3962, 4069, 4071, 4123, 4162, 4168, 4169, 4247, 4317, 4424, 4464, 4484, 4540, 4547, 4638, 4708, 4727, 4743, 4813, 4837, 4841, 4867, 4879, 4896, 4906, 4924, 4932, 4973, 5008, 5012, 5112, 5129, 5315, 5353, 5370, 5384, 5406, 5430, 5449, 5451, 5482, 5498, 5510, 5527, 5570, 5581, 5586, 5591, 5642, 5683, 5705, 5709, 5788, 5795, 5823, 5856, 5889, 5915, 5958, 5975, 5982, 5986, 6027, 6045, 6059, 6068, 6073, 6099, 6118, 6136, 6149, 6251, 6266, 6270, 6310, 6371, 6401, 6446, 6497, 6528, 6545, 6552, 6582, 6626, 6639, 6640, 6679, 6734, 6768, 6780, 6840, 6880, 6887, 6909, 6924, 6957, 6970, 7014, 7046, 7048.

PMGSY

21, 24, 40, 41, 42, 43, 44, 69, 208, 267, 304, 344, 787, 821, 825, 936, 937, 1174, 1201, 1212, 1223, 1293, 1413, 1427, 1646, 1653, 1665, 1675, 1734, 1772, 1873, 2189, 2454, 2457, 2561, 2635, 2718, 2942, 3157, 3273, 3292, 3447, 3570, 4900, 4915, 4998, 5509, 5697, 5984, 6297, 6336, 6375, 6415, 6513, 6558, 6822, 6963, 6970, 6978.

Power

6, 14, 37, 51, 55, 108, 126, 132, 133, 137, 143, 148, 149, 175, 224, 229, 232, 246, 248, 262, 280, 286, 300, 304, 317, 321, 366, 367, 372, 374, 379, 382, 386, 397, 416, 426, 445, 470, 491, 492, 506, 556, 571, 601, 625, 638, 669, 722, 752, 776, 780, 844, 859, 870, 886, 890, 901, 917, 960, 999, 1031, 1032, 1053, 1116, 1131, 1132, 1140, 1142, 1166, 1167, 1178, 1217, 1222, 1224, 1241, 1252, 1254, 1266, 1267, 1270, 1275, 1282, 1284, 1287, 1296, 1299, 1304, 1336, 1345, 1362, 1363, 1385, 1389, 1396, 1414, 1424, 1427, 1446, 1460, 1466, 1477, 1505, 1537, 1542, 1555, 1560, 1583, 1584, 1593, 1615, 1621, 1636, 1660, 1663, 1667, 1687, 1689, 1690, 1708, 1744, 1778, 1799, 1806, 1814, 1846, 1863, 1886, 1897, 1909, 1919, 1922, 1940, 1943, 1954, 1961, 1973, 1985, 1993, 2013, 2019, 2032, 2039, 2051, 2055, 2080, 2094, 2096, 2105, 2107, 2116, 2121, 2132, 2141, 2177, 2186, 2193, 2206, 2213, 2231, 2241, 2247, 2266, 2277, 2279, 2280, 2281, 2292, 2309, 2358, 2365, 2373, 2383, 2393, 2441, 2442, 2446, 2452, 2461, 2462, 2503, 2509, 2510, 2512, 2513, 2514, 2547, 2554, 2578, 2615, 2636, 2639, 2655, 2664, 2666, 2685, 2698, 2716, 2742, 2744, 2745, 2786, 2810, 2829, 2831, 2832, 2843, 2863, 2869, 2892, 2905, 2918, 2920, 2938, 2944, 2955, 2956, 2957, 2958, 2959, 2969, 2978, 2991, 2996, 3007, 3008, 3025, 3031, 3036, 3037, 3038, 3092, 3100, 3105, 3116, 3122, 3137, 3154, 3164, 3165, 3166, 3167, 3178, 3194, 3215, 3228, 3229, 3237, 3257, 3268, 3271, 3287, 3291, 3304, 3306, 3344, 3347, 3351, 3363, 3376, 3380, 3389, 3413, 3415, 3431, 3433, 3434, 3494, 3499, 3513, 3524, 3553, 3571, 3577, 3589, 3592, 3593, 3601, 3603, 3606, 3608, 3672, 3681, 3700, 3709, 3724, 3739, 3749, 3770, 3786, 3789, 3797, 3817, 3854, 3899, 3904, 3910, 3927, 3953, 3965, 3977, 4001, 4007, 4014, 4016, 4017, 4023, 4028, 4036, 4043, 4072, 4114, 4130, 4138, 4142, 4156, 4162, 4173, 4186,

Prime Minister

2938, 2939, 2940, 2998, 3031, 3089, 3090, 3091, 3121, 3123, 3156, 3170, 3171, 3172, 3173, 3223, 3263, 3314, 3336, 3358, 3368, 3373, 3424, 3455, 3458, 3480, 3505, 3536, 3546, 3574, 3578, 3599, 3689, 3700, 3708, 3793, 3798, 3857, 3931, 3944, 3945, 3946, 3953, 4036, 4077, 4135, 4147, 4190, 4192, 4221, 4238, 4344, 4357, 4390, 4399, 4400, 4401, 4402, 4418, 4467, 4468, 4473, 4475, 4661, 4687, 4688, 4689, 4690, 4691, 4749, 4858, 4874, 4935, 4936, 4937, 5037, 5061, 5070, 5081, 5084, 5097, 5098, 5137, 5162, 5205, 5217, 5228, 5241, 5253, 5258, 5262, 5364, 5381, 5416, 5420, 5454, 5488, 5511, 5514, 5557, 5574, 5580, 5601, 5642, 5645, 5654, 5711, 5749, 5755, 5757, 5759, 5776, 5836, 5846, 5847, 5869, 5911, 5932, 5982, 5993, 6009, 6022, 6083, 6084, 6085, 6086, 6088, 6090, 6091, 6092, 6094, 6095, 6096, 6097, 6098, 6136, 6201, 6202, 6317, 6494, 6555, 6610, 6617, 6665, 6666, 6702, 6758, 6808, 6863, 6944, 6990, 6991, 7029, 7035.

Rajiv Gandhi Gramin Vidutikaran Yojana

3105.

Rajya Sabha

139, 368, 419, 420, 421, 423, 425, 426, 436, 439, 444, 447, 448, 458, 465, 466, 494, 495, 497, 498, 499, 501, 503, 541, 584, 585, 586, 587, 589, 590, 591, 592, 593, 594, 595, 598, 600, 601, 603, 604, 607, 609, 612, 613, 615, 617, 618, 619, 620, 621, 622, 623, 627, 628, 629, 630, 640, 642, 643, 644, 645, 657, 659, 660, 679, 680, 682, 683, 684, 688, 689, 691, 697, 700, 708, 716, 717, 718, 719, 720, 723, 724, 725, 727, 728, 732, 745, 746, 755, 756, 757, 758, 777, 778, 779, 782, 783, 784, 785, 789, 797, 799, 802, 803, 804, 805, 807, 808, 809, 811, 812, 813, 821, 827, 828, 829, 830, 831, 837, 838, 842, 843, 844, 846, 847, 848, 870, 871, 903, 907, 909, 911, 925, 926, 927, 928, 946, 961, 962, 964, 965, 966, 967, 968, 969, 972, 977, 990, 991, 993, 994, 995, 996, 997, 1012, 1013, 1014, 1017, 1021, 1024, 1025, 1026, 1028, 1046, 1047, 1049, 1051, 1055, 1056, 1057, 1058, 1059, 1060, 1061, 1062, 1064, 1065, 1066, 1067, 1068, 1074, 1086, 1117, 1118, 1121, 1123, 1124, 1125, 1128, 1129, 1130, 1131, 1144, 1146, 1334, 1344, 1417, 1425, 1479, 1530, 1545, 1563, 1644, 1654, 1770, 1809, 1821, 1901, 1905, 1909, 1917, 1922, 1926, 1940, 1956, 1985, 1986, 2061, 2136, 2220, 2265, 2268, 2269, 2278, 2279, 2280, 2281, 2283, 2284, 2285, 2287, 2288, 2290, 2291, 2292, 2293, 2294, 2295, 2296, 2297, 2312, 2315, 2329, 2330, 2331, 2332, 2352, 2353, 2363, 2364, 2371, 2376, 2393, 2394, 2395, 2398, 2401, 2402, 2403, 2416, 2418, 2421, 2422, 2439, 2444, 2471, 2472, 2473, 2474, 2475, 2476, 2479, 2480, 2482, 2512, 2513, 2514, 2515, 2516, 2517, 2533, 2534, 2535, 2536, 2543, 2544, 2545, 2563, 2564, 2566, 2567, 2568, 2569, 2581, 2582, 2583, 2584, 2585, 2600, 2601, 2604, 2605, 2606, 2607, 2610, 2616, 2631, 2632, 2653, 2654, 2656, 2676, 2677, 2678, 2679, 2681, 2682, 2684, 2687, 2690, 2691, 2692, 2693, 2694, 2695, 2696, 2698, 2699, 2700, 2701, 2734, 2735, 2746, 2753, 2754, 2755, 2758, 2760, 2763, 2764,

3267, 3305, 3308, 3316, 3331, 3339, 3341, 3361, 3400, 3442, 3446, 3476, 3525, 3543, 3573, 3580, 3585, 3587, 3594, 3620, 3621, 3621, 3702, 3712, 3764, 3769, 3785, 3797, 3800, 3830, 3839, 3909, 3920, 3937, 3953, 3959, 3984, 3995, 3997, 4052, 4093, 4131, 4137, 4203, 4230, 4241, 4251, 4258, 4266, 4276, 4278, 4287, 4296, 4298, 4302, 4306, 4309, 4310, 4318, 4326, 4338, 4343, 4351, 4362, 4368, 4378, 4404, 4415, 4423, 4424, 4429, 4453, 4461, 4493, 4513, 4516, 4535, 4538, 4561, 4567, 4586, 4593, 4595, 4618, 4619, 4631, 4644, 4649, 4662, 4671, 4680, 4686, 4723, 4724, 4727, 4728, 4730, 4733, 4743, 4749, 4773, 4802, 4806, 4807, 4818, 4832, 4840, 4849, 4862, 4863, 4865, 4870, 4871, 4872, 4891, 4899, 4900, 4905, 4911, 4932, 4941, 4942, 4943, 4954, 4964, 4966, 4972, 4974, 4978, 4985, 4989, 4998, 5002, 5020, 5056, 5061, 5075, 5077, 5078, 5081, 5099, 5103, 5107, 5132, 5153, 5155, 5229, 5237, 5291, 5298, 5299, 5325, 5338, 5343, 5409, 5428, 5439, 5454, 5472, 5497, 5508, 5512, 5564, 5570, 5586, 5592, 5600, 5609, 5613, 5618, 5642, 5645, 5651, 5665, 5687, 5687, 5697, 5726, 5773, 5780, 5791, 5816, 5824, 5834, 5837, 5888, 5897, 5905, 5921, 5929, 5933, 5968, 5983, 5984, 5985, 5987, 5994, 6019, 6027, 6041, 6064, 6077, 6082, 6101, 6132, 6146, 6155, 6162, 6184, 6186, 6231, 6242, 6244, 6245, 6250, 6272, 6285, 6317, 6323, 6328, 6335, 6343, 6365, 6370, 6373, 6389, 6410, 6421, 6440, 6443, 6446, 6449, 6450, 6451, 6453, 6458, 6459, 6461, 6469, 6470, 6471, 6476, 6495, 6497, 6498, 6521, 6523, 6531, 6532, 6558, 6561, 6566, 6569, 6582, 6584, 6591, 6591, 6592, 6600, 6613, 6623, 6630, 6640, 6650, 6652, 6659, 6681, 6683, 6686, 6687, 6688, 6708, 6709, 6711, 6785, 6817, 6820, 6837, 6839, 6845, 6847, 6854, 6879, 6882, 6884, 6909, 6914, 6924, 6929, 6943, 6970, 6973, 6988, 7006, 7018, 7045, 7052.

Statistics and Programme Implementation

185, 446, 628, 1836, 1848, 2648, 2927, 3252, 3371, 3821, 3861, 4888, 5703, 5754, 6159, 6562.

Steel

6, 59, 132, 148, 177, 248, 277, 307, 321, 355, 384, 385, 417, 492, 521, 570, 571, 691, 759, 776, 845, 850, 861, 869, 970, 1028, 1087, 1120, 1131, 1141, 1177, 1207, 1234, 1283, 1432, 1464, 1536, 1560,, 1629, 1634, 1660, 1679, 1730, 1769, 1794, 1844, 1885, 1904, 1910, 1937, 1969, 1998, 2009, 2055, 2076, 2104, 2105, 2126, 2187, 2197, 2214, 2355, 2423, 2472, 2485, 2502, 2541, 2555, 2585, 2716, 2746, 2849, 2910, 2946, 2968, 3011, 3106, 3226, 3251, 3276, 3278, 3291, 3344, 3364, 3365, 3388, 3396, 3413, 3441, 3444, 3445, 3467, 3468, 3492, 3608, 3646, 3661, 3672, 3709, 3726, 3797, 3840, 3860, 3907, 3944, 3953, 3974, 3994, 4046, 4072, 4103, 4125, 4185, 4200, 4208, 4357, 4419, 4461, 4473, 4601, 4672, 4692, 4703, 4737, 4745, 4747, 4854, 4897, 4922, 4949, 5003, 5037, 5041, 5075, 5137, 5209, 5220, 5271, 5350, 5372, 5380, 5480, 5514, 5551, 5575, 5629, 5630, 5636, 5648, 5672, 5711, 5747, 5809, 5831, 5832, 5888, 5936, 5993, 6087, 6095, 6158, 6160, 6161, 6190, 6193, 6209, 6285, 6318, 6392, 6591, 6691, 6758, 7000, 7008, 7056.

UNION CABINET

1. **Dr. Manmohan Singh**

Prime Minister and also in-charge of the Ministries/ Departments not specifically allocated to the charge of any Minister viz.:

(i) Ministry of Personnel, Public Grievances & Pensions;
(ii) Ministry of Planning;
(iii) Department of Atomic Energy;
(iv) Department of Space;
(v) Ministry of Coal. and
(vi) Ministry of Environment and Forests.

2. **Shri Pranab Mukherjee**
   Minister of External Affairs.
3. **Shri Arjun Singh**
   Minister of Human Resource Development.
4. **Shri Sharad Pawar**
   Minister of Agriculture and Minister of Consumer Affairs, Food & Public Distribution.
5. **Shri Lalu Prasad**
   Minister of Railways.
6. **Shri A.K. Antony**
   Minister of Defence
7. **Shri Shivraj V. Patil**
   Minister of Home Affairs.
8. **Shri A.R. Antulay**
   Minister of Minority Affairs.
9. **Shri Sushilkumar Shinde**
   Minister of Power
10. **Shri Ram Vilas Paswan**
    Minister of Chemicals & Fertilizers and Minister of Steel.
11. **Shri S. Jaipal Reddy**
    Minister of Urban Development.
12. **Shri Sis Ram Ola**
    Minister of Mines.

13. **Shri P. Chidambaram**
Minister of Finance.
14. **Shri Mahavir Prasad**
Minister of Micro, Small and Medium Enterprises.
15. **Shri P.R. Kyndiah**
Minister of Tribal Affairs.
16. **Shri T.R. Baalu**
Minister of Shipping, Road Transport & Highways.
17. **Shri Shankersinh Vaghela**
Minister of Textiles.
18. **Shri Vayalar Ravi**
Minister of Overseas Indian Affairs and Minister of Parliamentary Affairs.
19. **Shri Kamal Nath**
Minister of Commerce & Industry.
20. **Shri H.R. Bhardwaj**
Minister of Law & Justice.
21. **Shri Sontosh Mohan Dev**
Minister of Heavy Industries & Public Enterprises.
22. **Prof. Saif-ud-din Soz**
Minister of Water Resources.
23. **Shri Raghuvansh Prasad Singh**
Minister of Rural Development.
24. **Shri Priyaranjan Dasmunsi**
Minister of Information & Broadcasting.
25. **Shri Mani Shankar Aiyar**
Minister of Panchayati Raj and Minister of Development of North Eastern Region. .
26. **Smt. Meira Kumar**
Minister of Social Justice & Empowerment.
27. **Shri Murli Deora**
Minister of Petroleum & Natural Gas.
28. **Smt. Ambika Soni**
Minister of Tourism and Minister of Culture.
29. **Shri A. Raja**
Minister of Communications and Information Technology.
30. **Dr. Anbumani Ramdoss**
Minister of Health & Family Welfare.
31. **Shri Kapil Sibal**
Minister of Science & Technology and Minister of Earth Sciences.
32. **Shri Prem Chand Gupta**
Minister of Corporate Affairs.

MINISTERS OF STATE (INDEPENDENT CHARGE)

1. **Shri Oscar Fernandes**
   Minister of State (Independent Charge) of the Ministry of Labour & Employment.
2. **Smt. Renuka Chowdhury**
   Minister of State (Independent Charge) of the Ministry of Women & Child Development.
3. **Shri Subodh Kant Sahay**
   Minister of State (Independent Charge) of the Ministry of Food Processing Industries.
4. **Shri Vilas Muttemwar**
   Minister of State (Independent Charge) of the Ministry of New and Renewable Energy
5. **Kumari Selja**
   Minister of State (Independent Charge) of the Ministry of Housing and Urban Poverty Alleviation.
6. **Shri Praful Patel**
   Minister of State (Independent Charge) of the Ministry of Civil Aviation.
7. **Shri G.K.Vasan**
   Minister of State (Independent Charge) of the Ministry of Statistics & Programme Implementation.
8. **Dr. M. S. Gill**
   Minister of State (Independent Charge) of the Ministry of Youth Affairs & Sports.

MINISTERS OF STATE

1. **Shri E. Ahammed**
   Minister of State in the Ministry of External Affairs.
2. **Shri B.K. Handique**
   Minister of State in the Ministry of Chemicals & Fertilizers and Minister of State in the Ministry of Mines.
3. **Smt. Panabaka Lakshmi**
   Minister of State in the Ministry of Health & Family Welfare.
4. **Dr. Shakeel Ahmad**
   Minister of State in the Ministry of Home Affairs..
5. **Shri Rao Inderjit Singh**
   Minister of State in the Ministry of Defence.
6. **Shri Naranbhai Rathwa**
   Minister of State in the Ministry of Railways.
7. **Shri K.H. Muniappa**
   Minister of State in the Ministry of Shipping, Road Transport & Highways.

8. **Shri Kantilal Bhuria**
   Minister of State in the Ministry of Agriculture and Minister of State in the Ministry of Consumer Affairs, Food & Public Distribution.
9. **Shri Shriprakash Jaiswal**
   Minister of State in the Ministry of Home Affairs.
10. **Shri Prithviraj Chavan**
    Minister of State in the Prime Minister's Office and Minister of State in the Ministry of Personnel, Public Grievances and Pensions.
11. **Shri Taslimuddin**
    Minister of State in the Ministry of Agriculture and Minister of State in the Ministry of Consumer Affairs, Food & Public Distribution.
12. **Smt. Suryakanta Patil**
    Minister of State in the Ministry of Rural Development and Minister of State in the Ministry of Parliamentary Affairs.
13. **Shri Md. Ali Ashraf Fatmi**
    Minister of State in the Ministry of Human Resource Development.
14. **Shri R. Velu**
    Minister of State in the Ministry of Railways.
15. **Shri S.S. Palanimanickam**
    Minister of State in the Ministry of Finance.
16. **Shri S. Regupathy**
    Minister of State in the Ministry of Environment and Forests.
17. **Shri K. Venkatapathy**
    Minister of State in the Ministry of Law & Justice.
18. **Smt. Subbulakshmi Jagadeesan**
    Minister of State in the Ministry of Social Justice & Empowerment.
19. **Shri E.V.K.S. Elangovan**
    Minister of State in the Ministry of Textiles.
20. **Smt Kanti Singh**
    Minister of State in the Ministry of Tourism and Minister of State in the Ministry of Culture.
21. **Shri Namo Narain Meena**
    Minister of State in the Ministry of Environment & Forests.
22. **Shri Jay Prakash Narayan Yadav**
    Minister of State in the Ministry of Water Resources.
23. **Dr. Akhilesh Prasad Singh**
    Minister of State in the Ministry of Agriculture and Minister of State in the Ministry of Consumer Affairs, Food & Public Distribution.
24. **Shri Pawan Kumar Bansal**
    Minister of State in the Ministry of Finance and Minister of State in the Ministry of Parliamentary Affairs.

25. **Shri Anand Sharma**
    Minister of State in the Ministry of External Affairs.
26. **Shri Ajay Maken**
    Minister of State in the Ministry of Urban Development.
27. **Shri Dinsha J. Patel**
    Minister of State in the Ministry of Petroleum & Natural Gas.
28. **Shri M.M. Pallam Raju**
    Minister of State in the Ministry of Defence.
29. **Shri Ashwani Kumar**
    Minister of State in the Department of Industrial Policy & Promotion, Ministry of Commerce & Industry.
30. **Shri Jairam Ramesh**
    Minister of State in the Department of Commerce, Ministry of Commerce & Industry and Minister of State in the Ministry of Power.
31. **Shri Chandra Sekhar Sahu**
    Minister of State in the Ministry of Rural Development.
32. **Smt. D. Purandeswari**
    Minister of State in the Ministry of Human Resource Development.
33. **Shri M.H. Ambareesh**
    Minister of State in the Ministry of Information & Broadcasting.
34. **Smt. V. Radhika Selvi**
    Minister of State in the Ministry of Home Affairs.
35. **Shri V. Narayanasamy**
    Minister of State in the Ministry of Parliamentary Affairs and Minister of State in the Ministry of Planning.
36. **Shri Santosh Bagrodia**
    Minister of State in the Ministry of Coal.
37. **Shri Raghunath Jha**
    Minister of State in the Ministry of Heavy Industries & Public Enterprises.
38. **Dr. Rameshwar Oraon**
    Minister of State in the Ministry of Tribal Affairs.
39. **Shri Jyotiraditya Madhavrao Scindia**
    Minister of State in the Ministry of Communications and Information Technology.
40. **Shri Jitin Prasada**
    Minister of State in the Ministry of Steel.

The Report to the People
of
UPA GOVERNMENT
2004–2008

FOREWORD

Prime Minister

The presentation of an Annual Report to the People by the Government of the United Progressive Alliance has set a new standard for accountability and transparency in governance.

Over the past four years the UPA Government has offered an annual update on the implementation of the National Common Minimum Programme. These reports, taken together with this year's, show that the UPA Government has so far been able to implement substantially the commitments made in the NCMP.

Building on the initiatives taken during the first three years, especially the launch of our Flagship Programmes, namely, Bharat Nirman, National Rural Employment Guarantee Programme, National Rural Health Mission, Jawaharlal Nehru National Urban Renewal Mission, modified Sarva Shiksha Abhiyan with expanded Mid-Day Meal Programme, the Government has put in place an "architecture for inclusive growth" during its four years in office. The 11th Five Year Plan, launched during the year, is based on this architecture.

The central vision of the 11th Five Year Plan is to trigger a development process that ensures broad-based improvement in the quality of life of our people, especially the poor, the Scheduled Castes, the Scheduled Tribes, Other Backward Classes and Minorities. The Plan also seeks to ensure more regionally balanced development.

In meeting these objectives our Government has given high priority to revitalization of agriculture, the empowerment of our farmers and the modernization of the rural economy. Several initiatives, listed in this Report, have been taken to reverse the neglect of agriculture in the period 1996-2004. We have improved the terms of trade for agriculture, in particular by increasing the minimum support price for foodgrains, increased investment in irrigation, agricultural research and rural infrastructure and have launched the Rashtriya Krishi Vikas Yojana, with an allocation of Rs. 25,000 crores for the 11th Five Year Plan. These initiatives along with the National Food Security Mission and the National Policy for Farmers will facilitate a turnaround of the agricultural economy. I am confident that this will also enable us to return to a regime of moderate inflation.

Our Government has made determined efforts to accelerate the pace of development while maintaining reasonable price stability. Control of inflation has been a priority concern. The Government ensured that the rate of inflation was brought down from around 6% in 2003-2004 to a little over 3% in the years 2004-2005 and 2005-2006. An upward pressure on prices since 2007 has been wholly on account of the steep increase in global commodity prices, especially oil prices. The sharp escalation in oil prices and in the price of metals, especially steel, and foodgrains has impacted our domestic economy. The Government has taken several measures to deal with this challenge. Controls have been imposed on commodity exports, tariffs have been reduced to encourage cheaper imports, fiscal and monetary policy initiatives have been taken by the authorities and, wherever needed, administrative measures are being taken to discourage speculation and hoarding.

While supply side and demand side measures will have their salutary impact on the price level, a normal monsoon and public recognition of the Government's determination to reverse the recent spurt in inflation will also help alter the state of expectations. The Indian economy is on a high growth path and I am confident that we will be able to increase production and satisfy the growing demands of our people and at the same time keep a check on prices.

The focus of the 11th Five Year Plan is education. India is a nation of young people. I sincerely hope the initiatives we have taken in the field of education will unleash the creative potential of all our people. We have increased investment in education with the twin objectives of widening access to education and promoting excellence. Special emphasis is being laid on the empowerment through education of scheduled castes, scheduled tribes, other backward classes and minority communities and women. Our Government has also taken important initiatives in the fields of health care, urban development and the modernization of infrastructure. All these have been stated in detail in this Report.

I am also happy to note that during this year we have extended the National Rural Employment Guarantee Programme to all rural districts across the country. This programme will make a major contribution to softening the harsh edges of extreme poverty in rural India. I urge State Governments to ensure proper and transparent implementation of the NREGA.

The UPA Government has worked hard to make our growth process socially inclusive and regionally balanced. The North Eastern region, Jammu & Kashmir and other backward regions have received special attention. At the same time, it has also worked to make the Indian economy more globally competitive. The external profile of our economy has become more robust and has contributed to an improvement in India's global standing. It has also enabled us to reach out to our neighbours and increase economic cooperation with the countries of South Asia, South East Asia, Indian Ocean Region and Africa.

Our foreign policy has been guided by our desire to create an external environment conducive to peace and stability in our region, ensure India's accelerated economic development and safeguard our national security and our energy security. We have given the highest priority to strengthening close political, economic, social and cultural relations with our immediate and extended neighbourhood, all major powers as well as our partners in the developing world and Non-Aligned Movement.

India today enjoys an enhanced profile in the international arena as a model of stable, liberal, plural and secular democracy and a rapidly growing economy with the ability and capability to play a larger international role.

I reiterate the commitment of the UPA Government to the principles and the goals of the National Common Minimum Programme. I sincerely hope this Annual Report to the People will be read by one and all to appreciate the work being done by our Government.

May 22, 2008. Manmohan Singh

INDIAN AFFAIRS ANNUAL 2008

Chronology of Events

(01-04-2007 to 05-05-2007)

1. (1-4-2007) NEW DELHI : The Press Council of India (PCI) received 600 complaints between April 01, 2006 and January 25, 2007. Of these, the Press had filed 164 cases while 436 were filed against the Press. The Council disposed of 404 cases during this period. The total disposal during 2006-07 is expected to reach the 654 mark. The Council initiated also a process of consultation and dialogue with press/media Council and similar bodies in different parts of the world for active encouragement to preservation of the press freedom and promotion of its standards and ethics worldwide.

2. (1-4-2007) NEW DELHI : 'Employment News' the much popular journal of Publications Division touched a weekly circulation of 6.5 lakh copies, during 2006-07. During the first six months of the year, revenue generated stood at Rs. 25.63 crore which is a significant improvement over the corresponding period last year. The total revenue generated in 2005-06 was Rs. 41.10 crore. As a step towards reaching to youth in Jammu & Kashmir and North-Eastern Region, Employment News is sending free copies to libraries, educational institutions and Government offices in North-East and J&K regions. The Publications Division published 75 titles during the period April-December 2006 in English, Hindi and other regional languages. Some of the important titles released during this period are: 5000 years of Indian Architecture, The Story of India's Struggle for Freedom, A Career for You, Upbhokta Samrakshan Adhiniyam Aur Upbhokta Adhikar, Krantikari Mahilayein, Sangeet Bachchon Ke Liye, Jallianwala Bagh, Lehron Ka Kahar, Great Men and Women of India, Kalpana Chawla etc.

3. (1-4-2007) NEW DELHI : Shri V. N. Kaila has taken over as new Controller General of Accounts here today. Shri Kaila belongs to the 1971 batch of the Indian Civil Accounts Service. Before becoming CGA, he was holding the post of Principal Chief Controller of Accounts, CBEC. Shri Kaila succeeds Shri S.W. Oak who has demitted office of CGA on superannuation. A hard-working and innovative officer, Shri Kaila has several important projects to his credit. He has also served as an Adviser to the Finance Ministries of the Governments of Lesotho and Peoples' Democratic Republic of Laos. Controller General of Accounts is the principal Accounts Adviser to the Government of India and is responsible for establishing and maintaining a technically sound management accounting system. He prepares a critical analysis of expenditures, revenues, borrowings and the deficit for the Finance Minister every month. He also prepares annual Appropriation Accounts and Union Finance Accounts for presentation to the Parliament. CGA exercises the powers of the President under Article 150 of the Constitution and Central Pension Accounting Office, the Chief Controller of Accounts and the Pay and Accounts Offices of the Central Government perform their payment, accounting and internal audit functions under his overall guidance. Receipt accounting, which covers tax revenues to the extent of Rs. 4.66 lakh crores in 2006-07, is also carried out by this organization.

4. (1-4-2007) NEW DELHI : BJP Vice President Shri Mukhtar Abbas Naqvi today said that the BJP will launch an aggressive election campaign to totally root out the "Tamancha, Tijori, Tushtikaran Raj" (Lawless, Corrupt, Appeasement Government) of Mulayam Singh Yadav in Uttar Pradesh. Shri Naqvi said that the Mulayam, Singh Yadav Government in Uttar Pradesh has completely looted the people of the state and filled its party coffers to the brim, reduced Uttar Pradesh to a state of penury, and simultaneously supported mafia and unlawful elements in the state by giving them a free hand to terrorize the common people. The net result is that besides the common people, even the duty bound and neutral police and administrative machinery of the' state has become helpless before these unlawful elements. The Samajwadi Party's policy of appeasement touched its peak when they declared the anti national and terrorist organization SIMI as a nationalist organization. During the last three years various terrorist organizations have spread and strengthened their net in 34 districts of the state. Moreover, there is a competition between the Samajwadi Party, BSP and Congress Party to lead the pack in opposing Vande Mataram. Shri Naqvi added that the release of the BJP's Election Manifesto in Lucknow tomorrow will mark the beginning of the party's aggressive and effective election campaign for the seven phases of polling in the state. Shri Naqvi said that BJP President Shri Rajnath Singh and former Chief Minister Shri Kalyan Singh will address election rallies in virtually every assembly segment of the state. While Shri Rajnath Singh will address about 209 rallies and meetings in 28 days, Shri Kalyan Singh will address 230 in 30 days. Shri Naqvi added that senior BJP leader Shri L K Advani will address 120 rallies and meetings in 20 days, Dr. Murli Manohar Joshi will participate in the election campaign for 10 days and Smt Sushma Swaraj will address various rallies in different parts of the state over 14 days. Shri Jaswant Singh, Shri M Venkaiah Naidu, Shri Arun Jaitley, Shri Yashwant Sinha, Shri Mukhtar Abbas Naqvi, Shri Kalraj Mishra, Shri Vinay Katiyar, Shri Gopinath Munde and Shri Anant Kumar will also address rallies and meetings in various parts of the state. Shri Naqvi said that the Chief Ministers of BJP ruled states Shri Narendra Modi, Shri Shivraj Singh Chauhan,

Smt Vasundhara Raje Scindia, Shri B C Khanduri, Dr. Raman Singh and Deputy Chief Minister Shri Sushil Modi will address over 100 rallies and meetings in various parts of the state. Shri Naqvi added that the BJP's Members of Parliament and senior leader Shri Shatrughan Sinha, Smt Hema Malini, Shri Vinod Khanna, Shri Navjot Singh Siddhu will address over 200 rallies and meetings in various parts of the state. The leaders of the alliance partners Shri Sharad Yadav, Chief Minister of Bihar Shri Nitish Kumar and President of Apna Dal Shri Sone Lal Patel, alongwith Shri L K Advani, Shri Rajnath Singh and Shri Kalyan Singh will participate in over three dozen joint rallies. Shri Naqvi said that the BJP as part of its alliance left 16 seats for the JD(U) and 36 seats for the Apna Dal. The BJP is contesting the balance 351 seats in the state. Therefore the BJP led alliance is contesting all 403 seats to the state assembly. Shri Naqvi said that the BJP is determined to end the "Tamancha, Tijori, Tushtikaran Raj" of Mulayam Singh Yadav in the state, and is working with the objective to establish a secure, prosperous and well administered government in Uttar Pradesh.

5. (1-4-2007) NEW DELHI: Union Minister and Lok Jan Shakti Party president Ram Vilas Paswan on Saturday warned of social unrest across the country if the reservation for Other Backward Classes in higher educational institutions was delayed further. The country could witness the kind of reaction Tamil Nadu saw over the past couple of days. Addressing a press conference here, Mr. Paswan said there was no point in convening an all-party meeting to discuss the situation arising out of the Supreme Court order staying the implementation of 27 per cent reservation for OBCs in higher educational institutions run by the Centre as "all political parties had already spoken out in favour of such a move." However, he did express support for the unanimous resolution adopted by the Tamil Nadu Assembly asking for a joint session of Parliament to discuss the court order. As for the Supreme Court's observation on the outdated data based on which the reservation was proposed, the Minister said the basis of this move was not the 1931 Census alone but the Mandal Commission list which was finalised after considerable effort in the 1990s. He said reservation should not be delayed further on the premise of inadequate data, but the Government should ask for OBC data to be collected in the next decadal census.

6. (1-4-2007) NEW DELHI : The Prime Minister's Awards for Excellence in Public Administration for the year 2005-06 are being awarded to Shri Rajeev Chawla, IAS, Secretary, Government of Karnataka and Shri R.S. Pandey, IAS Secretary, Ministry of Steel (Former Chief Secretary of Nagaland). Shri Chawla receives the award for implementing "Bhoomi", a computerized land records system for delivery, updating and safe storing of land records in Karnataka. Bhoomi enables citizens to access their land records easily and ensures transparency in the management of these records. On line access and creation of electronic database of land records has obliterated the need for manual rewriting and updating of land records, Mr. Pandey has won the award for his initiative in enabling participation of the user community in the management of public institutions and services in the State of Nagaland as Chief Secretary of Nagaland. Mr. Pandey conceptualized and implemented the programme to involve user communities in fields like education, health and power. The increased attendance and enrolment at schools, improved availability of doctors and increase in treatment of patients and improved collection of electricity revenues as well as reduced power theft testified to the efficacy of the initiatives taken. It may be recalled that Prime Minister Dr. Manmohan Singh announced the institution of the Prime Minister's Awards for excellence in Public Administration on Civil Services Day, April 21st, 2006. These Awards will be given away on 21st April, 2007, Civil Services Day.

7. (1-4-2007) NEW DELHI : Air Marshal JK Gupta has been appointed as Director General (Medical Service) Air. He has taken over the charge from Air Mshl HK Maini today at Air HQ (RKP) New Delhi. Air Marshal J K Gupta an alumni of Armed Forces Medical College, Pune was commissioned on 15 Jan 1970. With more than 37 years of service, he will be occupying the highest chair that a medical officer in IAF can aspire. His innate interest in Aviation and the aviator urged him to specialize in Aviation Medicine in 1975. Since then he has had a very successful career as a specialist and a friend of the aviator. This is borne out of his long stints at the institute of Aerospace Medicine at Bangalore, where he contributed not only in Research and Medical Evolution but was recognized by Bangalore University and later Rajiv Gandhi University of Health Sciences as Professor in Aerospace Medicine. During his tenure with DGCA he represented the country in a number of ICAO Medical Conferences. The Air Officer has commanded prestigious institutes like Air Force Central Medical Establishment, Delhi and Command Hospital Air Force, Bangalore. Preceding these assignments he has served as Principal Medical Officer (PMO) Eastern Air Command, South Western Air Command & Training Command.

8. (2-4-2007) NEW DELHI : A festival of Russian films got underway in New Delhi today. Inaugurating the Festival, the Minister of Information and Broadcasting Shri Priya Ranjan Dasmunsi said that the time-tested relations between India and Russia, which culminated into a strategic partnership, remain unique in International relations. The participation of delegations from India and Russia in the International Film Festivals at each other's countries, have gone a long way in boosting our ties in the field of cinematographic cooperation. A Russian Film Festival on such an occasion reminds us of cooperation by way of joint productions such as "Pradesi", "Sohni Mahiwal" and "Richi-Ticki-Tawi". Indians have adored Russian masters of world cinema such as Eisenshtein, Tarkovsky, Bondarchuk, and others and their great classics. This festival will go a long way in further consolidating bilateral friendship between the two countries, the Minister added. Mr. Vyacheslav I. Trubnikov, Russian ambassador to India, who was the chief guest at the event, in his remarks said that Indo-Russia diplomatic relations began prior to

India's Independence. This festival is a landmark in commemorating the longstanding and time-tested friendship in the fields of cinema, art and culture. He said that Indian Film Industry always has had a considerable presence in the Moscow Film Festival.

9. (2-4-2007) NEW DELHI : Government of India have announced the sale (re-issue) of "7.55 percent Government Stock, 2010" under Market Stabilization Scheme for a notified amount of Rs. 6,000 crore (nominal). The Government Stock will be sold through price based auction using multiple price method. The auction will be conducted by the Reserve Bank of India, Mumbai Office, Fort, Mumbai on April 4, 2007 (Wednesday). Up to 5% of the amount notified for the sale of stock is reserved for allotment to eligible individuals and Institutions on non-competitive basis as per the Scheme for Non-Competitive Bidding Facility in the Auction of Government Securities. Bids in the prescribed form obtainable from the Regional Director, Reserve Bank of India, Mumbai Office (Public Debt Office), Fort, Mumbai-400 001 and RBI website www.rbi.org.in should be submitted to that Office on April 4, 2007. The NDS members should submit competitive as well as non-competitive bids in electronic format using Primary Market Operation (PMO) module of NDS. All bids should be submitted by 12.30 P.M. The result of the auction will be announced on April 4, 2007 and payment by successful bidders will be during banking hours on April 5, 2007 (Thursday).

10. (2-4-2007) NEW DELHI : India and the United States renew the agreement on environment cooperation. Both the countries signed a memorandum of understanding (MOU) to renew their commitment to work cooperatively on environmental issues in New Delhi today. It was signed by Minister of Environment and Forests, Mr. A. Raja. And the U.S. Environmental Protection Agency (EPA) Administrator Stephen L. Johnson. It focuses on four priorities namely air quality, water quality, toxic chemicals and waste and the management of environmental agencies. Administrator Stephen L. Johnson expressed the view that renewing this MOU will strengthen EPA's vital collaborations with India in order to continue to accelerate the pace of environmental progress in both nations. Today's renewed commitment builds on significant accomplishments during the first five years of the memorandum of understanding. Through collaboration with the Pune Municipal Corporation and the California Air Resources Board, the city developed a comprehensive air quality management plan that is currently being replicated in six cities throughout India. Additionally, the U.S. Environmental Protection Agency is working with Pune and the state of Maharashtra to demonstrate the effectiveness of using technology to reduce air pollution from diesel buses and auto-rickshaws.

11. (2-4-2007) NEW DELHI : Shri S. Chandrasekaran has assumed the charge of the post of Technical Member (Patents), Intellectual Property Appellate Board (IPAB), Chennai on 2nd April, 2007. With the appointment of Technical Member (Patents), the provisions of Patents Act related to IPAB, set up on 15th September

2003, now stands operationalised. The Intellectual Property Appellate Board is now fully functional for hearing the appeals against the orders of the Registrar of Trade Marks, Geographical Indications as well as the Controller of Patents.

12. (2-4-2007) NEW DELHI : At the 13th Summit of South Asian Association for Regional Cooperation (SAARC) in Dakha in November 2006, the Prime Minister Dr. Manmohan Singh had already laid the foundation stone for pushing this grouping forward in every sector. In his speech he said "Let us agree all South Asian Countries would provide to each other reciprocally transit facility to Third world countries, not only connecting one another but also connecting the larger Asian neighbourhood, to the Gulf, Central Asia and in the South East Asia. India which borders each of the members of the South Asia, is willing to do so". The Prime Minister also expressed concern over SAARC not being able to achieve the set targets and goals since its inception about 22 years ago.

13. (2-4-2007) NEW DELHI : The Annual Plan for Gujarat for the year 2007-08 was finalized at a meeting, here today, between the Deputy Chairman Planning Commission, Shri Montek Singh Ahluwalia and the Chief Minister of Gujarat, Shri Narendra Modi. Plan size for the current year was agreed at Rs. 16000 crores. This includes additional Central assistance of Rs.90 crores for projects of special importance to the State. The Deputy Chairman, Planning Commission, complemented the State for economic reforms and working towards creating investor friendly environment. He said the State government has successfully introduced public / private partnership in social sector. While appreciating the progress recorded in human development, it was pointed out that more focused attention was needed to address problem of malnutrition and high gender differential in education. He said fiscal performance as well as plan realization during Tenth Plan period was good. The State government has spent more than budget estimates in the last fiscal and hopefully it would repeat performance during current financial year. Besides being revenue surplus for two consecutive years, it has also achieved fiscal deficit of 2.51 per cent for 2006-07. Achievements in the agriculture sector despite natural calamities were appreciated.

14. (2-4-2007) NEW DELHI : Indian Naval ships, which are on an overseas deployment to Southeast and Fareast Asia, received distress call from Shipping Corporation of India Ship 'MV Maharashtra' while on transit from Singapore to Japan. The beleaguered ship, in position 270 nautical miles northeast of Ho Chi Minh city, was on passage from Tianjin, China to Bander Imam Khomeini in Iran and was without any power supply due to failure of her Main Diesel Alternators. Attempts by the crew of the merchant vessel to restore the power supply were unsuccessful. On receipt on distress message, INS Rana was promptly despatched to provide necessary assistance to the vessel at 0700 h (Indian Standard Time) today morning. The ship reached the area at 0830 h (Indian Standard Time) and a technical team comprising 10 naval personnel were transferred by helicopter and boat to the merchant vessel for rendering assistance. The Naval team quickly rectified the diesel alternators enabling restoration of power supply on board the merchant ship. During the defect rectification, it was also observed that the fuel tanks supplying the diesel fuel to the alternators were contaminated. Supply of fresh fuel was essential to ensure uninterrupted power supply.

15. (2-4-2007) NEW DELHI : Top Central and State officials of agriculture ministries and agriculture scientists are gathering in New Delhi tomorrow to chalk out strategy for maximizing farm production in the coming Kharif season. The two-day National Conference on Agriculture for Kharif Campaign-2007 will be inaugurated by Agriculture Secretary, Dr. P.K. Mishra. Besides all Divisions and Departments of the Agriculture Ministry, ICAR, State agriculture universities and related Ministries/Departments are participated in this Campaign. While making preparations for the ensuing Kharif season and finding ways to remove bottlenecks, the Campaign strategy will be fine-tuned with the goal of 4% growth in the agriculture sector in the XI Plan. For this, detailed Sector-wise and State-wise analysis has been done and sectors and States identified for focused attention. For example, horticulture, livestocks and fisheries sectors have been identified with potential for more than 4% per annum growth. Similarly, States such as Madhya Pradesh, Orissa, Rajasthan, Maharashtra, Andhra Pradesh, Uttar Pradesh, Tamil Nadu and Karnataka are seen to have potential for increase in productivity of pulses and oilseeds. These will be discussed with individual States during the Kharif Campaign and specific strategies arrived at. Areas that will find focus in the Campaign include revamping horticulture (National Horticulture Mission), quality seed production of pulses and oilseed crops (ISOPOM) quality seed production of other crops (Seed Bank Scheme), quality control of inputs, and strengthening extension network (ATMA). The Campaign will also review the availability of inputs vis-a-vis their requirement in the coming crop season. The assessments of fertilizer availability made earlier in Zonal Meetings will be validated after discussion with individual States.

16. (2-4-2007) NEW DELHI : Shri Mahabir Prasad, Union Minister for Small Scale Industries and Agro and Rural Industries, urged the State Governments to take the benefit of the Package for Micro, Medium and Small Enterprises announced by the Centre recently. Inaugurating a Conference on "Small and Medium Enterprises-Past, Present and Future" jointly organized by PHD Chamber of Commerce and Industry and Konrad-Adenauer Foundation of Germany here today the Minister said, as per the commitment of the National Common Minimum Programme (NCMP), the Central Government announced this Package. He said the Package included loan, assistance for cluster-based development, assistance for entrepreneurial development and quality enhancement, marketing assistance, empowerment of women entrepreneurs etc. The Minister further stated that the MSMEs sector contribute to 39 per cent of the GDP and 34 per cent of exports from India. In the first four years of the Tenth Plan, the annual growth rate of this sector has been 8.87 per cent. He expressed the hope that Micro, Small and Medium Enterprises Development Act, 2006 would go a long way to develop this sector substantially and take it to a greater height. Dr. Chandrapal, Secretary, Small Scale Industries and Agro and Rural Industries, Mr. Bernd Muetzelburg, Ambassador of Germany to India and Dr. Michael Fuchs, MP and Chairman of the Parliamentary Group for Medium-sized Businesses of Germany also spoke on this occasion.

17. (2-4-2007) NEW DELHI : A delegation of Adventure Tour Operators Association today called on Minister of Tourism and Culture Smt. Ambika Soni at her office. The delegation was led by Sh. Ajeet Bajaj who unfurled the Indian Flag at the South Pole on January 26, 2007. Sh. Bajaj has the distinction of becoming the first Indian to ski to the South Pole and North Pole. During their half an hour meeting the delegation members discussed with the Minister ways and means to promote the adventure tourism in the country with special emphasis on mountaineering. Smt. Soni said Adventure Tourism activity in the country has reached a high level of participation. The Ministry accordingly issued a set of safety guidelines covering adventure activities that are land, air and water based. These guidelines addressed issued of not only merely the safety of the tourists but also the quality of the adventure experience. It also addresses the issues of minimizing impacts on the fragile environment in which these activities are generally conducted. Sh. Ajeet Bajaj, who came back from the South Polar expedition in February 2007, said after the meeting that it is the spirit of adventure in him that has taken him to all these remote inhospitable terrains.

18. (2-4-2007) NEW DELHI : In the last decade, India has made significant strides in the financial sector. Some of the important developments are strengthening of banks, deregulation of interest rates and competition in the banking system; development of the government securities market; infrastructure for trading, particularly in the equity market with the move to electronic trading; novation at the clearing corporation, T+2 rolling settlement, dematerialized settlement, demutualization of stock exchanges and derivatives trading. This raises expectations about how Mumbai can play a bigger role in the global market for financial services so that India's institutions get integrated with global institutions and economies in terms of provision of financial services. In recognition of this, as announced in Budget 2005-06, Government appointed a High Powered Expert Committee on Mumbai as an International Financial Centre. The Committee included senior representatives of Government and heads of several financial and market institutions.

19. (2-4-2007) NEW DELHI : More than Rs. 26 crore were paid as maternity benefits to eligible women workers under the Maternity Benefit Act, 1961 and the Employees State Insurance Act 1948 during 2004. The benefit was availed by 38,474 women workers. According to the annual returns filed with Labour Bureau, the maximum maternity benefit of Rs. 21,02 crore was paid under the Employees State Insurance Act to 20,515 women workers claiming the maternity benefit. The number of women workers who claimed maternity benefits under this Act was the highest in Tamil Nadu (5,609) constituting 27.34% of the total eligible workers, followed by Karnataka with 23.94%, Maharashtra with 14.47% and Kerala with 12.12%. The highest amount of maternity benefit of over Rs. 5.30 crore was paid in Tamil Nadu. The percentage of women claiming maternity benefits to the total number of women workers employed in factories under the Maternity Benefits Act was the highest in Jammu & Kashmir (4.5%), followed by West Bengal (4.2%) and Maharashtra (2.8%).

20. (2-4-2007) NEW DELHI : The Ministry of Rural Development has sanctioned Rs. 37.21 crore to the State Government of Bihar towards second instalment of funds against the allocation of Rs. 18571.00 lakh (Rs. 16557.00 lakh as original allocation and Rs.2014.00 lakh as additional allocation) made for the Government of Bihar after deducting Rs.5536.50 lakh on account of less State share under Accelerated Rural Water Supply Programme (Normal) of Rajiv Gandhi National Drinking Water Mission, during the year 2006-07. Up to 15 per cent of funds released under this sanction may be utilized for Operation & Maintenance and up to 5 per cent of funds may be spent for taking sustainability measures. States have been requested to delegate powers for management of Rural Water Supply Schemes through the Panchayati Raj Institutions (PRIs) as per the Constitution of India. As such Operation and Maintenance of the completed RWS Scheme should be transferred to the PRIs. No expenditure shall be incurred on taking water quality problems form the present release, as there is a separate allocation for the purpose. This release is being made for execution/completion of schemes to provide safe drinking water facilities to rural habitations and schools under the Centrally Sponsored ARWSP. Priorities set in ARWSP guidelines and through other instructions issued from time to time shall be followed for coverage of rural habitations and rural schools.

21. (2-4-2007) NEW DELHI : The Ministry of Rural Development has released Rs. 90.00 crore as part payment of first instalment for Phase VI of Pradhan Mantri Gram Sadak Yojana (PMGSY) to Rajasthan Rural Road Development Authority (RRRDA), which is the autonomous agency for receiving funds under the programme. The grant is towards the Plan expenditure and will be subject to the conditions laid down from time to time in the guidelines of the PMGSY and supplementary directions. The Pradhan Mantri Gram Sadak Yojana aims to provide all-weather basic access to about 1.72 lakh habitations of population of 500 or more (250 or more in Hill States (including North East), desert and tribal areas). PMGSY roads are constructed to high technical standards and backed by 5 year maintenance contracts. The construction cost is fully borne by the Government of India as a Centrally sponsored Scheme, while the State Governments are responsible for providing maintenance funds.

22. (2-4-2007) NEW DELHI : The Ministry of Rural Development has released grants-in-aid of Rs.9.50 lakh as Second instalment to West Champaran DRDA in

Bihar towards Restoration of cut on account of State Short Release of Central share of funds under the 'Swarnjayanti Gram Swarojgar Yojana' (SGSY) during the year 2006-07. Funds amounting to Rs.87.10 lakh as second instalment has also been released to Munger DRDA of Bihar under the same scheme. The amount should be utilized on the Programme as per approved guidelines of SGSY. The funding pattern will be 75:25 by the Centre and the State. The State Govts/DRDAs/ZPs are also to ensure to submit the report of State and District Levels Vigilance & Monitoring Committee meeting held during current year by March 31, 2007, otherwise Ist instalment during the next year will be held up. The State Government should release its share within one month of the date of release of the Central assistance. Under SGSY, assistance is given to the poor family living below the poverty line for taking up self-employment. It actively promotes group approach by organising the rural poor into Self-Help Groups.

23. (2-4-2007) NEW DELHI : The Ministry of Rural Development has released Rs.76.30 lakh as additional instalment of the central share under the 'Swarnjayanti Gram Swarojgar Yojana' (SGSY) during the year 2006-07 to North Tripura DRDA of Tripura. The amount should be utilized on the Programme as per approved guidelines of SGSY. The funding pattern will be 75:25 by the Centre and the State. The State Govts/DRDAs/ZPs are also to ensure to submit the report of State and District Levels Vigilance & Monitoring Committee meeting held during current year by March 31, 2007, otherwise Ist instalment during the next year will be held up. The State Government should release its share within one month of the date of release of the Central assistance. Under SGSY, assistance is given to the poor family living below the poverty line for taking up self-employment. It actively promotes group approach by organising the rural poor into Self-Help Groups.

24. (2-4-2007) NEW DELHI : The Ministry of Rural Development has released Rs. 90 crore as part payment of first instalment of Phase-VI as Grants-in-aid to the MADHYA PRADESH RURAL ROADS DEVELOPMENT AUTHORITY (MPRRDA), which is the Autonomous Agency for receiving the funds for the programme under Pradhan Mantri Gram Sadak Yojana (PMGSY). The grant is towards the Plan expenditure and will be subject to the conditions laid down from time to time in the guidelines of the PMGSY and supplementary directions. PMGSY was launched in December 2000 as a 100 per cent Centrally Sponsored Scheme with a target of connecting every habitation that has a population of more than 1000 within the next three years and every habitation with a population of more than 500 by the year 2007 *i.e.* by the end of the 10th Five Year Plan through good all-weather road. A sum of Rs.20,400.70 crore has been released to the States/UTs towards the programme and up to December 2006, 35,868 roadworks covering a length of 1,07,569.08 Kms. have been completed.

25. (2-4-2007) NEW DELHI : The Ministry of Rural Development has sanctioned Grants-in-aid to two districts of Uttar Pradesh, viz. Basti (Rs.9.02 lakh-as Restoration of Second instalment) and Balia (Rs. 7.46 crore-as second instalment after deducting an amount of Rs.0.13 lakh on account of less expenditure under SC/ST), as central assistance for the implementation of the Sampoorna Grameen Rozgar Yojana (SGRY) during the year 2006-07. The grant is towards plan expenditure and will be utilized for approved items of works subject to the conditions laid down in the SGRY Guidelines. The expenditure on implementation of the programme with regard to cash component is to be shared on 75:25 basis between the Central and the State Government respectively. The first instalment during the year 2007-08 under the scheme will be released after receiving the details of the Meetings held by the Vigilance and Monitoring Committee at the District and State level in 2006-07. The Sampoorna Grameen Rozgar Yojana (SGRY) is a Centrally Sponsored Scheme (CSS) to provide additional wage employment to the rural areas as also food security, alongside the creation of durable community assets, socio-economic infrastructure in the rural areas. Under the Scheme, foodgrains is provided every year, free of cost to the State Governments and Union Territory Administration. The payment of food grains is made by the Ministry of Rural Development to the Food Corporation of India (FCI) directly.

26. (2-4-2007) NEW DELHI : The Minister of Tourism and Culture Smt. Ambika Soni has said that various sensitivities and the plurality of cultural contexts will have to be taken into account while including new forms in the Representative List of the Intangible Cultural Heritage. Inaugurating the UNESCO experts meeting on the Intangible Cultural Heritage Convention here today, she said proactive measures meant to safeguards these forms are necessary at the national and international level. She said vulnerable forms should receive priority in matters of financial support but at the same time, regional equity and adequate representation too has to be ensured while selecting forms for financial assistance under the Convention. Smt. Soni said India which is home to an exuberance of intangible cultural expressions has welcomed and enthusiastically ratified the Convention. She said the Convention on Intangible Cultural Heritage is an opportunity to do justice to posterity by ensuring the continued existence and rejuvention of cultural expressions, which might have, if left unattended, disappeared forever. UNESCO has adopted the Convention for the Safeguarding of Intangible Cultural Heritage in 2003. India has ratified this Convention. India is also on the Intergovernmental Committee that decides on the implementation aspects of the Convention.

27. (3-4-2007) NEW DELHI : With a view to increase availability of cement and moderate prices, the Government has exempted imports of Portland Cements (other than white cements) from countervailing duty (in lieu of excise duty) and the special additional duty of customs of 4% vide notification no.53/2007-Customs dated 3.4.2007 with immediate effect. Cement prices have been rising in the course of last one year. The average price of cement has risen from Rs.165 per 50 Kg. bag in January 2006 to Rs.209 per 50 Kg. Bag in February 2007 and to Rs.220 per 50 Kg. Bag in March 2007. The Government, with a view to keep prices of cement in check, had fully exempted basic customs duty on Portland cements in January 2007. However, cement prices continue to be high. The cement industry was requested to moderate prices in the interest of the consumer. However, The industry is of the view that prevailing high prices are a consequence of a demand-supply mismatch. It is expected that the present move will improve supply situation in the country. Government has already invited cement manufacturers to come forward with proposals to moderate the price of cement. Government expects that the cement manufacturers, in the larger interests of consumers and for checking inflation, will take appropriate measures for moderating cement prices.

28. (3-4-2007) NEW DELHI : The Union Public Service Commission has recommended 32 more candidates to fill up the remaining posts based on Civil Services Examination, 2005. These candidates will be communicated by the Department of Personnel and Training directly. The result of the Civil Services (Main) Examination, 2005 was declared on 8th May, 2006/6th June, 2006 recommending 425 candidates in order of merit for appointment to IAS, IFS, IPS and Central Services Group 'A' and Group 'B' on the basis of the results of Civil Services (Main) Examination, 2005 against 457 vacancies. The Commission had, in accordance with the Civil Services Examination Rules, 2005, maintained a consolidated Reserve List of 64 candidates ranking in order of merit below the last recommended candidate under respective category.

29. (3-4-2007) NEW DELHI : The Ministry of Women and Child Development has requested the State Governments to involve Panchayats and other local bodies to identify orphan and destitute children so that they can be provided proper care and placed for adoption. Launching the redesigned website of Central Adoption Resource Agency (CARA) here today, the Minister said that the work has already been started to simplify and streamlined adoption procedure and to make it more transparent. She added that Government has planned integrated child protection scheme for the development and welfare of the children, adoption could also contribute in these efforts by providing family care and homely environment to the destitute children. On the occasion chairman of the CARA, Shri J.K. Mittal briefed the media persons about the new initiatives planned by his Organization. Secretary, Women and Child Development, Smt. Deepa Jain Singh was also present during the presentation of the website. The website of CARA can be accessed on www.adoptionindia.nic.in and it has been redesigned for the purpose of providing adequate information to all associated /partner agencies and prospective adoptive parents. It contains information on existing Guidelines on Adoption, provides link to procedure to be followed in case of in-country and inter-country adoption separately, action plan for the year 2007-08. In addition to the above, the updated list of Recognized Placement Agencies in India and Foreign Agencies enlisted by CARA is also available on the website. The Central Adoption Resource Agency (CARA) is an Autonomous Body under the Ministry of Women & Child

Development, Government of India. Its mandate is to find a loving and caring family for every orphan/destitute/ surrendered child in the country.

30. (3-4-2007) NEW DELHI : A cheque for Rs.12.4 crore was presented here today to Shri Kamal Nath, Union Minister of Commerce and Industry, by Shri Sanjiv Batra, Chairman & Managing Director, MMTC Limited, towards 25% interim dividend declared by the company for fiscal 2006-07 in its Board meeting held on 7th March, 2007. MMTC, the largest international trading company of India, with a net worth of over Rs.925 crore and zero long-term debt shall be achieving its highest ever turnover of over Rs.23000 crore and a net profit after tax of about Rs.120 crore during financial year 2006-07. The impressive performance is indicative of the success of strategic initiatives taken by the company and reflects the value creation through effective combination of goods, services and investment. The broad based growth in all business lines, debt free capital structure with adequate cash reserves and a sound net worth provides robust base for company's future growth. MMTC has recently commissioned 15 MW wind farms in Karnataka which have started producing electricity. MMTC has also drawn ambitious business plans to expand its role as a trade organizer and facilitator by venturing into newer areas such as free trade warehousing zones, development of a cold chain, entering into long-term strategic alliances for energy inputs and enlarging existing franchisee network to provide outlets for its 'SANCHI' brand silverware besides entering into iron ore and coal mining. The company would continue to pursue these efforts for achieving consistent growth in future and strengthen its base further, so as to provide value-added services and sustainable returns to its stakeholders.

31. (3-4-2007) NEW DELHI : The Five Federations belonging to Indian Railways congratulated Shri J.P. Batra, Chairman, Railway Board on his election as Chairman, International Union of Railways (UIC) at a function held here today. The five federations are All India Railwaymen's Federation (AIRF), National Federation of Indian Railwaymen (NFIR), All India RPF Association (AIRPFA), Indian Railway Promote Officers Federation (IRPOF) and Federation of Railway Officers Associations (FROA). It may be recalled that Shri J.P. Batra was unanimously elected as Chairman, International Union of Railways at the meeting held in Paris last year, for a period of two years. He is the first non-European to be elected as Chairman.

32. (3-4-2007) NEW DELHI : The BJP delegation led by Shri Rajiv Pratap Rudy, National Spokesperson and Incharge Goa Elections, alongwith Shri Balbir Punj, National Secretary and other central functionaries met the Chief Election Commissioner Shri N. Gaopalaswamy in New Delhi today. The delegation demanded early declarations of Goa State Assembly Elections. During the inter action the Chief Election Commissioner made it clear that they are not going to interfere with the State Panchayat polls as already notified and that the state Assembly elections will only take place after the conclusion of the Panchayat polls. With this clarification the National Spokesperson Mr. Rudy said that with the active and timely intervention of the BJP, the uncertainty and doubts prevailing in the State of Goa have been dispelled. However, he added that the Chief Election Commissioner took a serious note of the large-scale transfers and posting being undertaken by the State Government as also of the large-scale announcements of development schemes and various others poll sops. The Hon'ble Election Commission assured that all precautions would be taken to prevent and over lapping of the state elections in the state while and also taking into account the possibility of early monsoons.

33. (3-4-2007) KOCHI: A Division Bench of the Kerala High Court on Monday said the remark made by Local Self-Government Minister Paloli Mohammed Kutty in a speech in Kozhikode on January 30 was outrageous and amounted to contempt of court. The court said the Minister could mitigate the damage done to the judicial system to some extent if an unconditional apology was tendered to the public in general, to regain the confidence the public have in the system. The Bench of acting Chief Justice K.S. Radhakrishan and Justice M. N. Krishnan observed that "we are prima facie of the view that the words spoken by the Minister are scurrilous abuse and so grave and have a tendency to shake the basic structure of the judicial system and (are) likely to undermine the deep-rooted faith and respects for our courts among the general public, thereby diminishes the confidence of the people in our judicial system."

34. (3-4-2007) NEW DELHI : The MCD General Elections-2007 are scheduled to be held on 5th April 2007. The Central Government offices will not be closed on the day on which the MCD elections are to be held but as per the prescribed guidelines, the Central Government employees who are bona-fide voters and desire to exercise their franchise may be offered reasonable facility, subject to normal exigencies of services, either by coming late to office or being allowed to leave office early or a short absence on that day by their Ministries/Departments.

35. (3-4-2007) NEW DELHI : In a competitive globalised economy comparative advantage often lies with those who can innovate and deliver cost effective solutions. If the Information Technology Industry was responsible for the present growth of India, then the future of India lies in the growth of the bio-medical industry. Globalization brings with it increasing threats to health including SARS, Avian Flu, HIV/ AIDS, Humanitarian Emergencies and Bio-terrorism. These and other threats to health know no boundaries as in an age of wide spread global trade and travel, new and existing diseases can cross national borders and threaten our collective security. The importance of dialogues and experience sharing among experts worldwide can therefore be lost on none. Only strong collaboration amongst both developing and developed nations, increased information sharing and robust public health systems and surveillance can enable us to contain the threats to international health security. At a more basic level the promotion of health is a fundamental value by itself, a vital public good and a basic human right. Instruments such as the Human Development Index have forced governments to redefine development. The importance of Universal access to health including water, sanitation and nutrition are essential to a balanced development. India has both substantial achievements as well as a daunting unfinished agenda in the health sector. Longevity in the country has more than doubled since Independence in 1947; Infant Mortality Rate has fallen by 70% points; Malaria has been contained; Small pox and Guinea worm have been completely eradicated and Leprosy and Polio are nearing elimination. In the preceding 5 years over 500, 000 deaths have been averted due to the up scaling of the Directly Observed Treatment Short Course (DOTS). The Indian doctors are comparable to the best in the world and the country provides world class facilities for performing sophisticated procedures at a fraction of the cost of similar procedures in much of the developed world.

36. (3-4-2007) NEW DELHI : The Union Minister of Shipping, Road Transport and Highways, Thiru T.R. Baalu has approved a sum of Rs. 3549.86 lakh for road repair works in the various stretches on National Highway in the state of West Bengal. Of the above sum, an amount of Rs. 1224.58 lakh has been sanctioned for widening and strengthening of existing intermediate lane to two-lane carriageway from km 72/8 to km 75/0 and from km 88/0 to 95/0 (9.2 km) of NH-117 in the district of South 24-Panrganas, West Bengal. This road serves as main connector from the State capital Kolkata to number of important places of historical importance as well as emerging places of Trade and Commerce like Amtala, Falta-Export processing Zone, Raichak, Diamond Harbour, Kulpi-River Port, Kakdwip, Namkhana, Bakkhali-tourist spot and Fazerganage which is already declared as Heritage town. Further, an amount of Rs. 960.07 lakh has been sanctioned for widening and strengthening of existing intermediate lane to two-lane carriageway from km 205/2 to km 215/5 of NH 60 in the district of Bankura of the state. This road is negotiating through an area of poor sub-grade soil condition, frequent road-side unplanned development causing obstruction to the drainage of water, road side ponds whose water tables are of same level or higher than road top in some cases. Therefore, it is necessary the roads should be strengthened and improved. An amount of Rs. 1365.21 lakh has also been sanctioned for strengthening the existing weak two lane pavement from km 136/638 to km 142/0 and from km 142/0 to 151/353 in the district of Paschim Midnapur of the state. This stretch connects important areas like Jhargram, Kolaikunda Airbase, Chichera Check post, Kharagpur town etc. in West Bengal. This stretch suffers from capacity constraint as well as structural deficiency so far as thickness of the flexible pavement is concerned with progressively increasing and varied traffic on this stretch. In view of this, the strengthening of the proposed stretch has been necessitated.

37. (3-4-2007) NEW DELHI : Public Sector Satluj Jal Vidyut Nigam Limited plans a gross energy generation of 6720 million units with an expected revenue realization of Rs.1403 crore during the year 2007-08 from its 1500 MW Nathpa

Jhakri Hydro Power Station. A Memorandum of Understanding (MoU) to this effect was signed between Shri Anil Razdan, Secretary Power, Govt. of India and Shri H.K. Sharma, CMD, SJVNL on March 31, 2007 at New Delhi in the presence of Shri Rakesh Nath, Chairman, Central Electricity Authority, Shri A.K. Kutty, Joint Secretary (Hydel) and senior officers of the Ministry of Power. The energy generation shall however be subject to 15% mandatory discharge release in the river Satluj as per notification of the Govt. of Himachal Pradesh, and also the availability of water as per the 90% dependable year design water inflows. The parameters will be subject to change in line with the reduction in the river water inflow, if any observed during the year 2007-08. The MoU includes targets of construction of the 412 MW Rampur HE Project. As per the targets specified, the Kunni adit of Rampur Project is scheduled to be completed in May 2007 followed by Goshai adit in December 2007 and the Kazo adit in February 2008. The MoU also provides for excavation of 900 meters of the 15 Kms. long Head Race Tunnel by February 2008. The Electro Mechanical Works of this project are planned to be awarded in August 2007 as per the terms of the MoU. The MoU further spells out schedules for submission of Detailed Project Reports (DPR) of other projects viz 700 MW Luhri HE Project in August 2007, 36 MW Jakhol Sankari HE Project in January 2008 and 34.5 MW Naitwar Mori HE Project in August 2007.

38. (3-4-2007) NEW DELHI : The sustained high growth rate of merchandise exports at more than 20 per cent during the last four years is more than twice the current growth of Gross Domestic Product (GDP). "This has been possible as a result of stable policy framework provided by the Trade Policy and a continuous, conscious & concerted effort by the Government to reduce trade barriers, bring down transaction costs and facilitate a favourable international environment", notes the Annual Report of Ministry of Commerce & Industry (Department of Commerce) which was released recently. After crossing the landmark figure of US $ 100 billion in 2005-06, exports in the current year touched US $ 89 billion during the first three quarters (April-December 2006). During the last few years, the rising competitiveness of some of the sectors like engineering goods (auto parts) and high commodity prices (petroleum and metals) have been the driving force for high sustained growth of exports. The Annual Report mentions the several benefits that accrue from the Special Economic Zones (SEZs). The SEZ policy aims at generating greater economic activity and employment by providing a stable, transparent and efficient policy framework for establishment and running of SEZs. The main objectives of the SEZ Act are; generation of additional economic activity, promotion of exports of goods and services, promotion of investment from domestic and foreign sources, creation of employment opportunities and, development of infrastructure facilities. So far, formal approval has been granted to 234 SEZ proposals and in-principle approval to 162 SEZ proposals. Investment of the order of Rs.1,00,000 crore including FDI of US $ 5-6 billion is expected by end of December 2007 leading to creation of direct employment of 5 lakh jobs. Out of the 234 formal approvals, notifications have already been issued in respect of 63 SEZs. IN the 63 notified SEZs which have come up after 10th February 2006, investment of Rs.13,435 crore has already been made in less than one year. These SEZs have, so far, provided direct employment to 18457 persons.

39. (3-4-2007) NEW DELHI : Kharif Campaign-2007 started today with a call to harness growth potential in all possible areas to ensure 4% per year growth in the agriculture sector. Opening the two-day conference for Kharif Campaign, in which Central and State officials and experts will chalk out strategy for the coming kharif season and beyond, Agriculture Secretary, Dr. P.K. Mishra asked the States to prepare Action Plans targeting specific issues and start implementing them quickly. The Ministry has identified areas needing special focus, viz. food security, production of pulses and oilseeds, ensuring availability of quality seeds, revamping extension system and development of horticulture. Focus will also be on improving productivity of rainfed areas, as these constitute over 60% of the total farm area in the country, he said. Dr. Mishra informed that State-wise, region-wise and agro climatic zone-wise detailed studies show that 4.1% per year growth is achievable during the Eleventh Five Year Plan. He mentioned that this year's budget has enhanced the outlays for agriculture, irrigation, development of land resources, and production of quality seeds. Fertilizer Secretary, Dr. J.S. Sarma informed that stocks of 20 lakh tonnes of urea, 11 lakh tonnes of DAP and 14 lakh tonnes MoP are available for the kharif season which, supplemented by indigenous production, will be sufficient to meet the requirement of the kharif season. He asked the States to prepare district and month wise plans and follow them rigorously so that no localized shortages occur in any part of the country. The Centre will ensure that 75% of the requirement for any month will be available at the beginning of the month and the rest 25% by 15th of the month. Besides, buffer stock are being maintained in different States and movements and availability of fertilizer up to district level are being monitored very closely through on-line Fertilizer Management System, Dr. Sarma added. Secretary, Animal Husbandary Dairying and Fisheries, Ms. Charusheela Sohoni called upon the States to pay attention to fodder production. This, she said, is especially important because the livestock sector constitutes 27% to the agricultural income, provides subsidiary income to farmers and has potential to grow at a fast rate.

40. (3-4-2007) NEW DELHI : The Ministry of Rural Development has released Rs. 48.42 crore as part payment of second instalment of Phase-IV for the projects under Pradhan Mantri Gram Sadak Yojana (PMGSY) to West Bengal State Rural Development Agency (WBSRDA), which is the autonomous agency for receiving funds under the programme in the State. The grant is towards the Plan expenditure and will be subject to the conditions laid down from time to time in the guidelines of the Pradhan Mantri Gram Sadak Yojana and supplementary directions. PMGSY was launched in December 2000 as a 100 per cent Centrally Sponsored Scheme with a target of connecting every habitation that has a population of more than

1000 within the next three years and every habitation with a population of more than 500 by the year 2007 *i.e.* by the end of the 10th Five Year Plan through good all-weather road. A sum of Rs.20,400.70 crore has been released to the States/UTs towards the programme and up to December 2006, 35,868 roadworks covering a length of 1,07,569.08 Kms. have been completed.

41. (3-4-2007) NEW DELHI : The Ministry of Rural Development has released Rs. 80.00 crore as part payment of first instalment for Phase-V and Rs.20.00 crore as part payment of second instalment of the ADBI assisted projects-RRSIP-Batch-II under Pradhan Mantri Gram Sadak Yojana (PMGSY) to Chhattisgarh Rural Road Development Agency (CGRRDA), which is the autonomous agency for receiving funds under the programme. The grant is towards the Plan expenditure and will be subject to the conditions laid down from time to time in the guidelines of the PMGSY and supplementary directions. The Pradhan Mantri Gram Sadak Yojana aims to provide all-weather basic access to about 1.72 lakh habitations of population of 500 or more (250 or more in Hill States (including North East), desert and tribal areas). PMGSY roads are constructed to high technical standards and backed by 5 year maintenance contracts. The construction cost is fully borne by the Government of India as a Centrally sponsored Scheme, while the State Governments are responsible for providing maintenance funds.

42. (3-4-2007) NEW DELHI : The Ministry of Rural Development has released Rs.103.00 crore as part payment of second instalment for Phase V of Pradhan Mantri Gram Sadak Yojana (PMGSY) to Assam State Road Board (ASRB), Guwahati which is the autonomous agency for receiving funds under the programme. The grant is towards the Plan expenditure and will be subject to the conditions laid down from time to time in the guidelines of the PMGSY and supplementary directions. The Pradhan Mantri Gram Sadak Yojana aims to provide all-weather basic access to about 1.72 lakh habitations of population of 500 or more (250 or more in Hill States (including North East), desert and tribal areas). PMGSY roads are constructed to high technical standards and backed by 5 year maintenance contracts. The construction cost is fully borne by the Government of India as a Centrally sponsored Scheme, while the State Governments are responsible for providing maintenance funds.

43. (3-4-2007) NEW DELHI : The Ministry of Rural Development has released Rs. 27 crore as part payment of second instalment of Phase-IV of Grants-in-aid to the Mizoram Rural Roads Development Agency (MRRDA), which is the Autonomous Agency for receiving the funds for the programme under Pradhan Mantri Gram Sadak Yojana (PMGSY). The grant is towards the Plan expenditure and will be subject to the conditions laid down from time to time in the guidelines of the PMGSY and supplementary directions. PMGSY was launched in December 2000 as a 100 per cent Centrally Sponsored Scheme with a target of connecting every habitation that has a population of more than 1000 within the next three years and every habitation with a population of more than 500 by the year 2007 *i.e.* by the end of the 10th Five Year Plan through good all-weather road. A sum of Rs.20,400.70 crore has been released to the States/UTs towards the programme and up to December 2006, 35,868 roadworks covering a length of 1,07,569.08 Kms. have been completed.

44. (3-4-2007) NEW DELHI : The Ministry of Rural Development has released Rs. 70.47 crore as second instalment of Phase-IV of Grants-in-aid to the Andhra Pradesh State Rural Roads Development Agency (APSRRDA), which is the Autonomous Agency for receiving the funds for the programme under Pradhan Mantri Gram Sadak Yojana (PMGSY). The grant is towards the Plan expenditure and will be subject to the conditions laid down from time to time in the guidelines of the PMGSY and supplementary directions. PMGSY was launched in December 2000 as a 100 per cent Centrally Sponsored Scheme with a target of connecting every habitation that has a population of more than 1000 within the next three years and every habitation with a population of more than 500 by the year 2007 *i.e.* by the end of the 10th Five Year Plan through good all-weather road. A sum of Rs.20,400.70 crore has been released to the States/UTs towards the programme and up to December 2006, 35,868 roadworks covering a length of 1,07,569.08 Kms. have been completed.

45. (3-4-2007) NEW DELHI : The Rural Development Ministry has invited proposals from civil society organizations/professional institutions that are engaged with the issues and processes of NREGA (National Rural Employment Guarantee Act) for undertaking the tasks of capacity building of local rural communities in selected districts under the Act. Organizations selected will be assigned a district each and the tasks will have to be undertaken from the village to the district level for six months at the beginning. The selected organisations will undertake social mobilization and awareness generation campaign through door to door contact, village conventions and personal contact programmes to enable the local community exercise their rights under NREGA and claim entitlements, like apply for job card and employment, ensure appropriate wage remuneration, participate in village level planning, avail of work site facilities and enforce employment allowance. The campaign is also meant to enforce transparency and accountability, like the use of Right to Information Act, and help to understand and scrutiny vital records such as muster rolls, measurement books, Job cards, do social audit and enforce grievance redresal. They will impart training to NREGA workforce, members of Village Vigilance and Monitoring Committee, members of Gram Panchayat and Gram Rozgar Sewak on NREGA procedures and their respective roles as part of the capacity building exercise. Interested organizations are required to apply with their profile of work, proposals for tasks and their choice of district. The proposal should also include strategy, timeline and cost. Organizations applying must have at least five years work experience with rural communities and an institutional presence in the concerned State/District and knowledge of local language.

46. (3-4-2007) NEW DELHI : The Appointments Committee of the Cabinet has approved the following secretary level appointments: Shri S.K. Arora, IAS (AP, 1971) presently Secretary, Ministry of Information & Broadcasting as Secretary, Ministry of Youth Affairs & Sports. Ms. Asha Swarup, IAS (HP, 1973) presently Special Secretary and Financial Adviser, Department of Commerce, Ministry of Commerce and Industry as Secretary, Ministry of Information & Broadcasting.

47. (4-4-2007) NEW DELHI : The following is the text of the opening remarks of External Affairs Minister, Shri Pranab Mukherjee at the press conference held soon after the conclusion of 14th SAARC Summit, here today: "We have just concluded a very successful, indeed a landmark, 14th SAARC Summit. Let me briefly go over some of the main points. For the first time in its history, SAARC expanded its membership to welcome Afghanistan as its eighth member. Again, for the first time, five Observers from outside the region attended the Summit, which also decided to give a similar status to Iran. The expansion of SAARC and the developing external linkages are indicative of the high level of maturity that SAARC has reached as an organization. The Summit adopted a comprehensive and forward-looking New Delhi Declaration, which sets out the core principles underlining our collective vision of an interconnected South Asia where there is a free flow of goods, services, people and ideas. At the Retreat this morning, the Leaders agreed to make tangible progress in the next six months on four issues that affect the daily lives of our people. These include water (including flood control), energy, food and the environment. They decided to work with international agencies to develop and implement viable cross-border regional projects in these four sectors, which address our peoples' basic needs. The Leaders also decided to designate 2008 as the "SAARC Year of Good Governance".

48. (4-4-2007) NEW DELHI : The first Meeting of the Empowered Committee of the National Capital Region Planning Board was held under the Chairmanship of Secretary, Urban Development Ministry, Shri M. Ramachandran in New Delhi today. Chief Secretary of Haryana, Additional Chief Secretary of Rajasthan besides senior officials from the Government of Uttar Pradesh, and Government of National Capital Territory of Delhi and other officials from the Central Government Departments, attended the meeting. The meeting discussed issues relating to unrestricted movement of buses, taxis and auto rickshaws within the National Capital Region, use of CNG fuel to reduce pollution levels in the towns of National Capital Region, opening large number of CNG Pump Stations in the NCR as well as improving connectivity in the National Capital Region both by extension of Metro to satellite towns around NCT of Delhi as well as better framework of roads in preparation for the forthcoming Commonwealth Games-2010. The Empowered Committee also decided to set up a Committee of Transport Secretaries under the aegis of NCR Planning Board to work out a common framework for seamless traffic and to develop a draft for a common multi-lateral agreement.

49. (4-4-2007) NEW DELHI : The term of the Liberhan Ayodhya Commission of Inquiry has been extended by three months up to 30th June, 2007. The Commission is inquiring into the destruction of the Ram Janma Bhoomi-Babri Masjid structure at Ayodhya on 6th December 1992.

50. (4-4-2007) NEW DELHI : Following is the text of the address of the Prime Minister, Dr. Manmohan Singh, at the concluding session of 14th SAARC Summit here today: "It is my proud privilege to extend my profound appreciation and gratitude to your Excellencies for the immense cooperation you have all extended to me. The Declaration adopted today is comprehensive and forward-looking. It gives SAARC a wider mandate to promote peace and development in our region, including through greater connectivity-in trade, in the movement of people and through the flow of ideas. During this Summit we had the honour of admitting Afghanistan to take its due place in the comity of SAARC. We also had the privilege of welcoming Observers for the first time. They are among our major civilisational neighbours and economic partners. This manifests our common desire for SAARC to be outward looking and engaged with the world community; to be a springboard for exploiting the vast physical and intellectual resources of South Asia. Our Summit has agreed to operationalise the SAARC Development Fund; establish the South Asian University; create a SAARC Food Bank; and, set up the SAARC Arbitration Council. The cooperation and accommodation that have characterized our deliberations and negotiations show that our countries are ready for a transformation of SAARC into an effective instrument of regional cooperation.

51. (4-4-2007) NEW DELHI : Smt. Jayanti Natrajan talked about the posters put up by the Indian National Congress with the main theme for the Assembly Elections in Uttar Pradesh. The posters depict the main theme and the fundamental principles in the party's campaign in Uttar Pradesh. The consistent stand of the Indian National Congress for secularism, and fight against communalism, the highest integrity in public life, principled politics, a politics that is based fundamentally upon the welfare of the people, a commitment to the maintenance of law and order and all-round development are the most fundamental tenets of our campaign. The first poster therefore says: Hamari ladai garibi aur berojgari ke khilaf; so the main battle will be against poverty and unemployment. Hamari ladai sampradaikta or annyay ke khilaf; we will continue our commitment to fight against injustice and communalism in every form. Hamari ladai jaat-paat aur bhed-bhav ke khilaf; we will continue to fight for social justice and against differences of any kind. Hamari ladai beimaani aur bhrashtachar ke khilaf; we feel very strongly that corruption and lack of integrity are fundamental to the deterioration of governance in the state of Uttar Pradesh and we will go to the people on the basic slogan that they should vote for the Indian National Congress if they want to vote against corruption and the lack of integrity. Hamari ladai apradh aur arajakta ke khilaf; we all know the total deterioration of law and order in Uttar

Pradesh, we all know that we have said from this very platform time and again that the most horrific incidence of deteriorating law and order continue to take place in Uttar Pradesh in places like Nithari where even the Chief Minister has not cared to visit and we would like to go to the people to say that if they want to root out this lawlessness, they should cast their vote for the Indian National Congress. Hamari ladai asuoolon ki rajniti ke liya; we stand for principles of secularism of a secular government and of principled politics and we would like the people to vote for us on these grounds. Hamari ladai Uttar Pradesh ke saaman ke liya; the slogan speaks for itself. Hamari ladai yuvaon ke sapnoo ke liya; we want to reach out to the youth whose voice is not heard, whose plea for development and the share in the progress of the nation has gone unheeded by the present Uttar Pradesh government, so we reach out to the youth of Uttar Pradesh. Sabko ajmaa liya, in sab se achhaa to Congress ka zamana tha; we all know that all experiences of crime, of law and order problem, of all other issues that the people of Uttar Pradesh have experienced under this government was much better when the Indian National Congress was in power, in government in Uttar Pradesh. There are two more posters in Urdu. To a question that the popular slogan of "Congress ka haath Aam Aadmi ke Saath" is missing in these posters, Smt. Natarajan said that every single poster deals with issues relating with the 'Aam Aadmi'. When you talk about politics of principles, when you talk about lack of law and order and wanting to improve it, when we talk about a secular government, when we talk about the development of Uttar Pradesh, the dreams of youth, every single thought is for the 'Aam Adami'. The entire campaign and the principles and intensions of the Indian National Congress are focused towards the 'Aam Admi'. To a question that the other day your spokesperson was talking of caste-based census and you are talking of no 'jaat-paat', Smt. Natarajan said that we are totally committed to the principles of social justice. Regarding the caste census, the facts are all very clear. There is one judgement of the Supreme Court in the Indira Sahani case and the nine-judge bench of the Supreme Court which upheld the 27 percent reservation for OBC in employment and we have the latest judgement of the Supreme Court which is by a two-judge bench where while there has been no criticism of reservation as such, the Hon'ble Supreme Court has asked the govt. to supply the data on what basis the OBCs have been identified and therefore this is a very complicated issue.

52. (4-4-2007) NEW DELHI : Central Government issued Notification No.15/2007-Service Tax dated 04.04.07 under section 11C of the Central Excise Act, 1944, exempting levy of service tax, for the period from 01.04.2000 to 04.02.04, on 60% of the gross amount charged for taxable services provided by tour operators, operating under a contract carriage permit issued by the appropriate transport authority, for transport of passengers from one place to another (other than services provided in relation to package tours). Representations were received from transport operators / bus owners operating regular point to point transport of passengers between different cities or towns under contract carriage permit issued by the appropriate transport authority that they had been asked to pay service tax on 100% of the gross amount charged by them with effect from 01.04.2000, whereas service tax should be charged only on the commission earned. Notification No.2/2004-ST dated 05.02.04 was issued prescribing abatement of 90% from gross value in respect of taxable service other than packaged tours. Abatement of 60% from gross value has been available since 09.07.04 vide notification No.8/2004-Service Tax dated 09.07.04 and not prior to that date. The Central Government has decided to extend the benefit of abatement of 60% from gross value in respect of the above mentioned taxable services to the past period also *i.e.* from 01.04.2000 to 04.02.04.

53. (4-4-2007) NEW DELHI : 'In the hands of a beggar a coconut shell serves as his begging bowl, in the hands of an artist it turns into a thing of beauty, it provides the humble housewife with a brightly burning fire to cook her simple fare, it lets the chemist unlock its secrets and yields a dozen new things. Such is the coconut shell, a versatile part of the world's most versatile tree the coconut palm...' Dr. W. R. N. Nathanael. Under the expert hands of an artisan not just the Coconut shell but coconut leaf midribs, coconut wood, coconut spathe, coconut stipule husk are all turned into all sort of handicrafts and utility articles! There was a time when coconut shell was seen as either a poor man's bowl or for domestic fire wood. Of course there were limited diversified products of coconut shell like the coconut shell ladle and spoons. But the latest diversified products from coconut has been unheard. Artisans who found dearth of wood with dwindling forests, have found a new expression through this medium.

54. (4-4-2007) NEW DELHI : National Sample Survey Organisation report is the third in the series of seven reports based on employment-unemployment data of the NSS 61st round. The report provides statistics on literacy, attainment of general and technical education, current attendance in educational institutions etc. The survey covered the whole of the Indian Union except certain areas in Jammu & Kashmir, and Andaman and Nicobar Islands which remained inaccessible throughout the year. The key findings of the Report are as below. The Government is seized of the incidence of high women illiteracy in certain parts of the country.

55. (4-4-2007) NEW DELHI : Smt. Asha Swarup today assumed office as Secretary, Information & Broadcasting. She took over from Shri S.K. Arora who has been shifted to Ministry of Youth Affairs and Sports. A 1973 batch IAS officer of the Himachal Pradesh Cadre, Smt. Swarup was Special Secretary and Financial Advisor for the Department of Commerce and Ministry of Textiles. During her career, Smt. Swarup has held prestigious assignments such as Joint Secretary in the Ministries of Rural Development, Human Resource Development and Youth Affairs & Sports. As the state level, she was chairperson, HP State Electricity Board & Principal Secretary (Power) besides holding other crucial portfolio such as Principal Secretary (Home & Vigilance) and Principal Secretary (Health & Family Welfare).

56. (4-4-2007) NEW DELHI : The National Commission for Enterprises in the Unorganized Sector (NCEUS), set up by the Government of India as an advisory body and a watchdog for the informal sector, under the Ministry of Small Scale Industries and Agro and Rural Industries, has proposed to recommend the formation of a National Fund designed to meet the multi purpose needs of both enterprises and workers in the unorganized sector. Addressing a Press Conference here today the Chairman of the Commission, Dr. Arjun Sengupta said that the tasks proposed to be handled by the Fund were extensive as the sector needed a holistic approach for its development taking into account all essential needs covering finance, technology, raw material, marketing, infrastructure, skill and entrepreneurship and would cover both farm and non-farm sectors and also rural and urban areas. The Commission's findings show that forty per cent of the workers in the unorganised agricultural and non-agricultural sector are wage workers and sixty per cent are self-employed. Among the self-employed, the overwhelming majority are own account or assisting family workers and only 1.15 % (among non-agricultural workers) are employers. Dr. Sengupta said that the vast majority of the self-employed in the unorganised sector themselves worked under poor conditions and the productivity of their enterprises was low. Measures to protect the livelihood of the self-employed workers and to promote the productivity of the unorganised enterprises, will not only have an impact on the condition of the self-employed, but also on the condition of the unorganised wage workers who work in the unorganised enterprises. Thus, regulation of the condition of work of wage workers needs to go hand in hand with the protection and promotion of livelihood of the self-employed workers and enhancing the growth and productivity of the unorganised sector enterprises.

57. (4-4-2007) NEW DELHI : Human resources are central to advancing health. With the launch of the Health Workforce Decade (2006-2015), the World Health Day 2006 and World Health Report acknowledge the contribution and importance of health workers to health and development. Health workforce is an integral part of national and international health systems. In India, health workforce and Human Resources for Health (HRH) issues remain among the most complex and difficult areas to modify as we strive to reform the health sector and improve its performance. The National Rural Health Mission also seeks to address some of these challenges. Planning and developing human resources is crucial to expand health sector across various schemes and programmes. Recognizing this, the Ministry of Health & Family Welfare in collaboration with WHO Country Office for India is organizing a two-day National Workshop on Human Resources for Health on 5-6 April, 2007 at India Habitat Centre, New Delhi which will be inaugurated by the Union Minister for Health & Family Welfare, Dr. Anbumani Ramadoss. The workshop seeks to identify and agree on priorities for coordinated action in improving HRH policy and practice. The workshop has the objective of enhancing the understanding of successful approaches towards development of workforce development and HRH. This include sharing of best practices, strategies and the evidence base and achieving consensus amongst key stakeholders on a strategy for building up, nurturing and managing human resources in health sector. The participants of the workshop include representatives from various stakeholder groups' in health and allied fields viz. policy makers & programme managers from the Centre and select states, other ministries, academic institutions, professional councils, professional associations, civil society and development partners. It is envisaged to provide a platform for these groups to deliberate and bring forth recommendations on various issues related to Human Resources for Health.

58. (4-4-2007) NEW DELHI : Third North East Business Summit is being organized on April 10-11, 2007 in New Delhi. This is a joint event of the Department of Development of the North East (DoNER) and the Indian Chamber of Commerce (ICC) to showcase the strengths of the Northeastern region and to present significant business opportunities. Recognising the imperative need to promote the competitive advantage of the region, the ICC has launched a major initiative to help the process of economic development of the region in active collaboration with the Department for Development of North Eastern Region. Two Business Summits were earlier held in Mumbai in July 2002 and New Delhi in January 2004. The present summit is being organized with the prime objective of exposing the rich potential of the region to the prospective investors in India and abroad. Several Union Ministers, Chief Ministers of North-Eastern States and other stake holders are expected to participate in the present Summit which will be inaugurated by Dr. Manmohan Singh, Hon'ble Prime Minister of India. A press conference is being organized on April 09, 2007 at 12.30 p.m in Shastri Bhavan in order to brief the press before the start of the meeting.

59. (4-4-2007) NEW DELHI : Production of finished carbon steel has registered an increase of 10.1% during April-February 2007 (*i.e.* in eleven months) as compared to the corresponding period last year. The production rose from 40.237 to 44.300 million tonnes (mt.) during the period. Export of the finished carbon steel has also shown an increase of 9.3% during this period rising from 3.934 to 4.300 mt. During April 2006 to February, 2007 Steel Authority of India Limited (SAIL) produced 11.402 mt. of saleable steel registering an increase by 5 per cent in comparison to 10.910 mt. produced last year. However, the production of hot metal marginally declined from 13.328 to 13.215 mt. while the production of crude steel remained the same during the said period. For the month of February, 2007 SAIL produced 0.993 mt. of saleable steel against the target of 0.954 mt. with 104% capacity utilisation. The Public Sector National Mineral Development Corporation (NMDC) produced 23.79 mt. of iron ore during the first 11 months compared to 20.41 mt. during the same period in the previous fiscal, registering a rise of 16.6 per cent. During February 07, the Company mined 2.94 mt. ore as against the target of 2.04 mt. with 144% capacity utilisation.

60. (4-4-2007) NEW DELHI : Ministry of Rural Development is implementing various poverty alleviation and rural development programmes having special components for women with earmarked funds to ensure the flow of adequate resources for the coverage of women. Under National Rural Employment Guarantee Act (NREGA), during the year 2006-07, a total of 5,365.38 lakh persondays (up to January, 2007) were generated and out of which 2,113.06 lakh persondays were generated for women which is 39.38% of the total employment generated under the scheme. Under Sampoorna Grameen Rozgar Yojana (SGRY), 605.13 lakh persondays were created for women which is 26.07% of the total employment generated (2,320.76 lakh persondays) under the programme. The number of women swarozgaris assisted under Swarnjayanti Gram Swarozgar Yojana (SGSY) up to Jan., 2007, is 4,20,412 which is 60.01% of the total swarozgaris (7,00,605) assisted under the Yojana. During 2006-07, under Indira Awas Yojana (IAY), 8,95,236 number of dwelling units were completed up to Jan., 2007, out of which 5,54,277 (61.91%) houses were allotted in the name of women and 1,88,781 (21.09%) jointly in the name of both husband and wife.

61. (4-4-2007) NEW DELHI : The Union Minister of Shipping Road Transport and Highways Thiru T.R. Baalu has called upon the Major Ports to brace themselves for the challenges ahead and strive hard for developing the Indian ports to meet the growing demands of country's burgeoning export-import needs in the coming years. Inaugurating a day-long Seminar on the "Consolidated Port Development Plan" organized by the Indian Ports Association, Thiru Baalu said that the Indian economy is now irreversibly on a path of growth leading to its integration with the global economy and in the process, we have to develop our infrastructure that meets international standards, especially the ports and roads to provide the environment for facilitating this growth. Speaking on the occasion, Thiru Baalu said that we need the Port Business Plans to look beyond our immediate commitments, to lay down a structured road map to guide us in the long term, not only for fulfilling the emerging demands but also for proactive engagement in tapping the potential for a share in the maritime activities, with particular focus on and around our neighbourhood. The Minister hoped that the national perspective is expected to be provided in the Consolidated Port Development Plan prepared by the Port of Rotterdam Authority, who have coordinated the preparation of Business Plans for Major Ports. Thiru Baalu also hoped that the insights provided by the plans would enable us to prepare for the future.

62. (4-4-2007) NEW DELHI : The Ministry of Rural Development has sanctioned Grants-in-aid amounting to Rs 9.60 lakh as restoration of second instalment to Jaisalmer District of Rajasthan under central assistance for the implementation of the Sampoorna Grameen Rozgar Yojana (SGRY) during the year 2006-07. The grant is towards plan expenditure and will be utilized for approved items of works subject to the conditions laid down in the SGRY Guidelines. The expenditure on implementation of the programme with regard to cash component is to be shared on 75:25 basis between the Central and the State Government respectively. The Sampoorna Grameen Rozgar Yojana (SGRY) is a Centrally Sponsored Scheme

(CSS) to provide additional wage employment to the rural areas as also food security, alongside the creation of durable community assets, socio-economic infrastructure in the rural areas. Under the Scheme, foodgrains is provided every year, free of cost to the State Governments and Union Territory Administration. The payment of food grains is made by the Ministry of Rural Development to the Food Corporation of India (FCI) directly.

63. (4-4-2007)THIRUVANANTHAPURAM: Minister for Water Resources N. K. Premachandran on Tuesday challenged Tamil Nadu Chief Minister M. Karunanidhi's contention that the Central Water Commission (CWC) had not recommended the construction of a new dam at Mullaperiyar. Producing photocopies of the documents signed by Tamil Nadu Special Officer for Inter-State Waters A. Mohanakrishnan in December 1979, the Minister said the Commission had indeed proposed a new dam 1,300 feet downstream of the present dam. He also produced copy of a location map of the new dam site prepared in 1979. The Tamil Nadu Chief Minister had questioned Chief Minister V. S. Achuthanandan's statement at a press conference in Delhi that the proposal for new dam had been made by the CWC. Mr. Premachandran said the proposal for a new dam was one of the three main recommendations of the Commission.

64. (4-4-2007) NEW DELHI : The Ministry of Rural Development has sanctioned an amount of Rs.12.19 lakh to the State Government of Goa as extended first instalment for undertaking IEC & HRD activities relating to National Rural Drinking Water Quality Monitoring & Surveillance Programme (NRDWQM&SP) under Rajiv Gandhi National Drinking Water Mission (RGNDWM) during the year 2006-07. Out of these, an amount of Rs.2.73 lakh for IEC activities and remaining Rs.9.46 lakh should be utilized for HRD activities as per the guidelines. The funds for undertaking these activities are to be transferred to Community & Capacity Development Unit established in the State. This release is for plan expenditure. The funds are to be utilized for the purpose for which it is released and as per the terms and conditions. The release is on the basis of norms for each activity as per the guidelines.

65. (4-4-2007) NEW DELHI : Pakistan Prime Minister, Mr. Shaukat Aziz called on the Prime Minister, Dr. Manmohan Singh, here today. The two leaders discussed a wide range of bilateral issues including trade, energy, banking, air connectivity and other issues. Prime Minister Aziz assured Dr. Singh that Pakistan would take early action to return fishing boats seized from Indian fishermen to their owners. The two leaders also agreed to review the status of each other's citizens held prisoners in the two countries. They agreed to increase air connectivity between India and Pakistan. They also agreed to continue the ongoing discussions on the Iran-Pakistan-India gas pipeline. Mr. Aziz said Pakistan is ready to export cement to India taking advantage of the duty reduction announced by the Government. Mr. Aziz also informed the Prime Minister that Pakistan was issuing more visas to Sikh Yatris coming from across the world to visit Sikh shrines in Pakistan. Prime

Minister Aziz thanked Dr. Singh for the financial support given to the families of the victims of the Samjhauta train incident. He complemented Prime Minister Singh for the successful and efficient conduct of the SAARC summit. He also expressed satisfaction at the content of the discussions at the summit.

66. (4-4-2007) NEW DELHI : The Ministry of Rural Development has sanctioned Rs. 25.49 lakh to the State Government of Meghalaya as extended first instalment for undertaking IEC and HRD activities relating to National Rural Drinking Water Quality Monitoring and Surveillance Programme during the year 2006-07. Out of these, an amount of Rs.7.49 lakh for IEC activities and remaining Rs.18.00 lakh for HRD activities as per the guidelines under Rajiv Gandhi National Drinking Water Mission (RGNDWM). The funds for undertaking these activities are to be transferred to Community & Capacity Development Unit established in the State. This release is for plan expenditure. The funds are to be utilized for the purpose for which it is released and as per the terms and conditions. The release is on the basis of norms for each activity as per the guidelines.

67. (4-4-2007) NEW DELHI : The Ministry of Rural Development has sanctioned an amount of Rs.5.46 crore to the State Government of Bihar as extended first instalment for undertaking IEC & HRD activities relating to National Rural Drinking Water Quality Monitoring & Surveillance Programme (NRDWQM&SP) under Rajiv Gandhi National Drinking Water Mission (RGNDWM) during the year 2006-07. Out of these, an amount of Rs.299.89 lakh for IEC activities and remaining Rs.246.48 lakh should be utilized for HRD activities as per the guidelines. The funds for undertaking these activities are to be transferred to Community & Capacity Development Unit established in the State. This release is for plan expenditure. The funds are to be utilized for the purpose for which it is released and as per the terms and conditions. The release is on the basis of norms for each activity as per the guidelines.

68. (4-4-2007) NEW DELHI : The Ministry of Rural Development has sanctioned an amount of Rs.7.77 crore to the State Government of Andhra Pradesh as extended first instalment for undertaking IEC & HRD activities relating to National Rural Drinking Water Quality Monitoring & Surveillance Programme (NRDWQM&SP) under Rajiv Gandhi National Drinking Water Mission (RGNDWM) during the year 2006-07. Out of these, an amount of Rs.223.20 lakh for IEC activities and remaining Rs.553.61 lakh should be utilized for HRD activities as per the guidelines. The funds for undertaking these activities are to be transferred to Community & Capacity Development Unit established in the State. This release is for plan expenditure. The funds are to be utilized for the purpose for which it is released and as per the terms and conditions. The release is on the basis of norms for each activity as per the guidelines.

69. (4-4-2007) NEW DELHI : The Ministry of Rural Development has released Rs. 40.00 crore as grants-in-aid for a value of Rs.18.80 as Balance Payment of first instalment for Phase-IV and Rs.21.20 crore as part payment of second instalment for Phase-IV under the Pradhan Mantri Gram Sadak Yojana (PMGSY) to the Tripura Rural Road Development Agency (TRRDA), which is the autonomous agency for receiving funds under the programme. The grant is towards the Plan expenditure and will be subject to the conditions laid down from time to time in the guidelines of the PMGSY and supplementary directions. The Pradhan Mantri Gram Sadak Yojana aims to provide all-weather basic access to about 1.72 lakh habitations of population of 500 or more (250 or more in Hill States (including North East), desert and tribal areas). PMGSY roads are constructed to high technical standards and backed by 5 year maintenance contracts. The construction cost is fully borne by the Government of India as a Centrally sponsored Scheme, while the State Governments are responsible for providing maintenance funds.

70. (4-4-2007) NEW DELHI : The Ministry of Rural Development has sanctioned Grants-in-aid amounting to Rs.1.57 crore to Jabalpur District of Madhya Pradesh as Restoration of Second instalment as central assistance for the implementation of the Sampoorna Grameen Rozgar Yojana (SGRY) during the year 2006-07. The grant is towards plan expenditure and will be utilized for approved items of works subject to the conditions laid down in the SGRY Guidelines. The expenditure on implementation of the programme with regard to cash component is to be shared on 75:25 basis between the Central and the State Government respectively. The first instalment during the year 2007-08 under the scheme will be released after receiving the details of the Meetings held by the Vigilance and Monitoring Committee at the District and State level in 2006-07. The Sampoorna Grameen Rozgar Yojana (SGRY) is a Centrally Sponsored Scheme (CSS) to provide additional wage employment to the rural areas as also food security, alongside the creation of durable community assets, socio-economic infrastructure in the rural areas. Under the Scheme, foodgrains is provided every year, free of cost to the State Governments and Union Territory Administration. The payment of food grains is made by the Ministry of Rural Development to the Food Corporation of India (FCI) directly.

71. (4-4-2007) NEW DELHI : The Government is finalizing new National Urban Housing and Habitat Policy to tackle housing shortage in the country. Addressing a two-day National Conference on 'Affordable Housing for All'here today, the Minister of State (Independent Charge) Housing and Urban Poverty Alleviation, Kumari Selja said that the new Policy is based on the feedback from the Sectoral developments since 1998. She said that promotion of sustainable cities through adequate provisions of housing and related infrastructure is the need of the hour. Expressing concern over the wide gape in urban housing and infrastructure, the Minister said that over Rs. 4,00,000 crore are needed for housing alone and a large amount is needed for infrastructure also. She said that arrangements of this magnitude of funds were not possible within budgetary allocation of Central and State Governments. Kumari Selja said that the proposed policy recognizes the key role which all actors; public, private and the cooperative sectors need to play in meeting the housing shortage. It envisages a facilitative role for the state and a direct and proactive role for the other players. The Minister said that there was a shortage of about 24.71 lakh houses at the beginning of 11th Plan and the gap is expected to increase to 26 million at the end of 11th Plan. Underlining the importance of real sector in the housing sector, she said there is a great significance of real estate in the housing development and development of the economy. The Indian economy has shown impressive growth rate of GDP over 9%, the real sector in the country is also booming. The rapid urbanization will continue to fuel the real estate boom in India, she added. The function is being organized by National Real Estate Development Council and aims to bring all stakeholders on one platform and share and deliberate upon the issues, concerns and opportunities in housing sector, to reduce the widening gap between housing demand and supply in the country and make housing affordable for all, especially the low income and economically weaker sector in the society.

72. (5-4-2007) NEW DELHI : The President of India has been pleased to appoint the following: 1. Shri B.L. Joshi, Lt. Governor of the National Capital Territory of Delhi to be the Governor of Meghalaya with effect from the date he assumes charge of his office. 2. Shri Katteekal Sankaranarayanan, Governor of Nagaland, to discharge the functions of the Governor of Arunachal Pradesh, in addition to his own duties, during the absence, on leave, of Shri Shilendra Kumar Singh, Governor of Arunachal Pradesh with effect from the date he assumes charge of his office. 3. Shri Tejendra Khanna as the Lt. Governor of National Capital Territory of Delhi with effect from the date he assumes charge of his office.

73. (5-4-2007) NEW DELHI : The outstanding balance of 13.05 per cent Government Stock, 2007 is repayable at par on April 22, 2007 and no interest will accrue thereon from the said date. April 22, 2007 being Sunday the repayment shall be made on April 21, 2007. In the event of a holiday being declared on April 21, 2007 by any State Government under the Negotiable Instruments Act, 1881, the Loan will be repaid by the paying offices in that State on the previous working day. To facilitate repayment of the Loan on the due date, holders may tender the securities, duly discharged, at the Public Debt Offices, Treasuries/Sub-Treasuries and branches of State Bank of India and its Associate Banks (at which they are enfaced/registered for payment of interest) 20 days in advance of the due date for repayment. Full details of the procedure for receiving the discharge value may be obtained from any of the aforesaid paying offices.

74. (5-4-2007) NEW DELHI : Government of India have announced the sale (re-issue) of "7.38 per cent Government Stock, 2015" for a notified amount of Rs. 6,000 crore (nominal). Government of India have also announced the sale (re-sale) of "8.33 per cent Government Stock, 2036" for a notified amount of Rs.4,000 crore (nominal). Both the Government stocks will be sold through price based auctions using multiple price method. The auctions will be conducted by the Reserve Bank of India, Mumbai Office, Fort, Mumbai on April 12, 2007 (Thursday). Up to 5 per cent of the notified amount of the sale of both the stocks will be allotted to eligible individuals and Institutions as per the Scheme for Non-Competitive Bidding Facility in the Auction of Government Securities. Both the Stocks will be eligible for "When Issued" trading in accordance with the guidelines issued by the Reserve Bank of India in its circular No.RBI/2006-07/178 dated November 16, 2006. Bids in the prescribed form obtainable from the Regional Director, Reserve Bank of India, Mumbai Office (Public Debt Office), Fort, Mumbai-400 001 and RBI website www.rbi.org.in should be submitted to that Office on April 12, 2007. The NDS members should submit competitive as well as non-competitive bids in electronic format using Primary Market Operation (PMO) module of NDS. All bids should be submitted by 12.30 p.m. The result of the auctions will be announced on April 12, 2007 and payment by successful bidders will be during banking hours on April 13, 2007 (Friday).

75. (5-4-2007) NEW DELHI : The Chief Minister of Andhra Pradesh Dr.YSR Reddy formally announced the nationwide launch of 5 per cent Ethanol Blended Petrol (EBP) Programme at Hyderabad today. Shri Murli Deora, Minister of Petroleum and Natural Gas presided over the function which was also attended by several dignitaries including Union Minister of Urban Development Shri S. Jaipal Reddy and Minister State for Petroleum and Natural Gas Shri Dinsha Patel, among others. This initiative is part of the UPA Government's commitment to put in place policies to enhance the country's energy security. The launch of the programme marks a significant step in the direction of utilizing alternative renewable and environment friendly sources of energy like ethanol, to supplement the hydro-carbon resources of the country. The EBP Programme of the Ministry of Petroleum and Natural Gas is primarily based on indigenously produced ethanol from sugarcane molasses which besides augmenting fuel availability in the country, also helps sugarcane growing farmers with better returns. Ethanol is further environment friendly as it enhances combustion of petrol resulting in lower emission of pollutants. To implement the programme nationwide, Ministry of Petroleum and Natural Gas had earlier notified 20 States and 4 Union Territories to implement EBP Programme with effect from 1.11.2006 leaving aside J&K, North East Sikkim, Andaman & Nicobar and Lakshadweep where ethanol cannot be made available for logistic reasons.. So far, tenders to procure Ethanol from indigenous producers have been finalized in the States of Andhra Pradesh, Uttar Pradesh, Bihar, Delhi, Jharkhand, Goa, Karnataka, Maharashtra and Tamil Nadu. The state of Andhra Pradesh has been covered first time. EBP is being supplied in Andhra Pradesh, Uttar Pradesh, Delhi, Goa, Karnataka, Maharashtra and Tamil Nadu. It is expected that EBP supplies would commence in Bihar and Jharkhand shortly.

76. (5-4-2007) NEW DELHI : An international seminar on Renewable Energy begins at Solar Energy Centre (SEC), Gwal Pahari in Haryana from ninth of this month. SEC is the centre of excellence for the development and promotion of sola energy technologies under the ministry of New and Renewable Energy Sources The centre also has national facilities for Research and Development Technology testing and training. The two week seminar will share India's programmes in renewable energy which are largest in the world. It will cover all the aspects o renewable energy including resource assessment, technologies, policy and implementing mechanism. Scientists, experts from SEC and MNRE, academics research organizations and representatives from industries will participate in it

77. (5-4-2007) NEW DELHI : In exercise of the powers conferred by clause (1) of Article 222 of the Constitution of India, the President, after consultation with the Chief Justice of India, is pleased to transfer Shri Justice Virender Singh Judge of the Punjab and Haryana High Court as a Judge of the Jammu and Kashmi High Court and to direct him to assume charge of his office in the Jammu & Kashmir High Court on or before 20th April, 2007. Ministry of Law and Justice (Department of Justice) New Delhi, Chaitra 15, 1928 /April 5, 2007.

78. (5-4-2007) NEW DELHI : The Empowered Group of Ministers (EGOM) on Special Economic Zones (SEZs) met here today and discussed various issues relating to SEZs. It decided, inter-alia, to lift the current freeze on SEZs, with tighter rules and prescribed a ceiling on the size of SEZs, which has now been fixed at an upper limit of 5000 hectares. Shri Kamal Nath, Union Minister of Commerce & Industry, also indicated that a comprehensive rehabilitation policy was being finalised and that it would include employment to at least 1 person from each displaced family.

79. (5-4-2007) NEW DELHI : The Central Government vide Notification no. 53/2007 Customs dated 3.4.2007 exempted Portland cement from Countervailing duty (CVD) and Special Additional duty. The CVD in respect of such exempted cement is Rs.350 per metric tonne for cement of declared retail sale price not exceeding Rs.190 per 50 kg bag. For higher priced cement, the excise duty is Rs 600/-per metric tonne.

80. (5-4-2007) NEW DELHI : In exercise of the powers conferred by clause (1) of Article 224 of the Constitution of India, the President is pleased to appoint Shri Amjad Ahtesham Sayed to be an Additional Judge of Bombay High Court, for a period of two years with effect from the date he assumes charge of his office. Ministry of Law and Justice (Department of Justice) New Delhi, Chaitra 15, 1928 /April 5, 2007.

81. (5-4-2007) NEW DELHI : On the occasion of the World Health Day, 7th April, the Ministry of Health & Family Welfare has launched a website on Healthy India (www.healthy-india.org). The website aims to provide people with information on health promotion and encourage them to adopt healthy lifestyles. In his message to the people on the launch of the website, the Union Minister for Health & Family

Welfare, Dr. Anbumani Ramadoss urged every individual to access this site and make the best use of the information available.

82. (5-4-2007) NEW DELHI : Hon'ble Mr. Arefaine Berhe, Minister of Agriculture of Eritrea called on Shri Kanti Lal Bhuria, Minister of State for Agriculture here today. Welcoming the delegation Shri Bhuria said the visit would pave the way for further cooperation in agri-sector between the countries. The Minister expressed the country's willingness to send agricultural scientists to Eritrea. He also hoped that Eritrean students could benefit from the vast network of agriculture institutes in India. The Eriteran Minister reiterated the long history of cooperation in agriculture between the countries and expressed the hope that cooperation will extend to other areas like fisheries and tourism.

83. (5-4-2007) NEW DELHI : The supply of urea to the States has surpassed the target during the month of February 2007. About 19.44 lakh Metric Tonnes (MT) of urea was despatched to the States against the target of 15.33 lakh MT making the availability of urea to the tune of about 27.65 lakh MT for the month. The availability of urea was satisfactory in all the States. With the sale of 111.61 lakh MT urea during Rabi 2006-07 upto February 2007 as compared to the sale of 100.54 lakh MT in the corresponding period of the previous year, the rise in sale has gone up by about 11.01 per cent. The availability of the decontrolled fertilizers *i.e.* DAP and MOP during this month had been 10.62 lakh MT and 4.14 lakh MT respectively, which was also adequate to meet the demand of the States.

84. (5-4-2007) NEW DELHI : The Films Division produced 24 documentary/ short fiction/video films during April-December, 2006. Out of these, 22 films were produced departmentally and two films through independent producers. The Division released 9791 prints of 39 films in the theatrical circuits from 1.4.06 to 30.11.06. 188 informative and educative films have been digitized, 480 films transferred on High Definition tapes and 825 films transferred on international tracks (transferred on DVD) during this period. The Division earned a total revenue of Rs. 398.68 lakh during the period under reference. The Division produced biographical films on eminent personalities such as, Dr. Ram Manohar Lohia, BR Chopra, Dagar Brothers and Salil Chowdhury. Another ten biographical films on the undernoted personalities are under production. Pt. Ram Narayan, Husnalal Bhagatram, Late Shri K. R. Narayanan-Former President of India, Sankaradeva-A life larger than life (films on Sankaradeva-a multifarious genius of 15th century from Assam, Shri Gopal Swaroop Pathak, Satguru Ramsinghji and Kuka Movement, Mubarak Begum, Naushad Ali, Rajashree Bhagyachandra of Manipur and Pt. Shiv Kumar Sharma.

85. (5-4-2007) NEW DELHI : Army Chief Gen JJ Singh inaugurated the Reunion of the Maratha Light Infantry (MARATHA LI) here today. The four day Reunion is being held at the Regimental Centre located here, which also is the training centre and 'home' to the Maratha soldiers. On arrival Gen JJ Singh was presented a Guard of honour. This is the 13th Reunion since the country attained its independence. It is organized twice a decade and serves as an opportunity for retired officers to meet the present generation and reminiscence their nostalgic memories and also pass on their experiences. Approximately 225 serving and Retired Officers, Retired Foreign Officers and 500 Junior Commissioned Officers and Other Ranks are participating in the celebrations. Besides them, widows and parents of martyrs who sacrificed their lives for the cause of the nation have also been invited. The history of the Maratha Regiment, spanning over two hundred years, has been written in blood and sweat, with deeds of great valour and sacrifice. The 1st Battalion of the Maratha Light Infantry was raised in 1768 and from then on, the Regiment has grown from strength to strength. The Regiment has the unique distinction of being affiliated with both Indian Navy (INS-MUMBAI) and Indian Air Force (20 AF Sqn-Sukhoi). Gen JJ Singh, who is also the Colonel Commandant of the MARATHA LI, while addressing the officers and men of the Regiment complemented them on their excellent performance in operations and safeguarding the frontiers of the nation. The Army Chief also released a first day cover to commemorate the event. The first day cover displays the sketch of Chhatrapati Shivaji Maharaj. Incidentally, the war cry of this regiment is "Bol Shri Chhatrapati Shivaji Maharaj ki Jai".

86. (5-4-2007) NEW DELHI : Health workers are the heart of the health system, they are the most visible face of health delivery system as they are directly involved in providing care to the population. Addressing the National Workshop on Human Resources for Health in New Delhi, the Minister for Health & Family Welfare, Dr. Anbumani Ramadoss said that human resources are central to managing and delivering health services. The health needs of communities are fast changing with changing morbidity patterns, emergence of newer diseases and increasing use of technology in health care. In India, we are facing stiff challenges with containing communicable diseases and maternal and child morbidity on one hand and are faced with threats like HIV/AIDS and raising incidence of non-communicable diseases on the other hand. This is a complex situation calling for multi-pronged approaches. Planning for management of personnel in health systems is a critical issue in all these efforts. He further said that while there is need for a strong and adequate health force, suitably trained to deliver varied services, we, like many other countries, are faced with issues like shortages & uneven distribution of health personnel. Absent personnel means unmanned health facilities and hence services to the community. We require an increasing number of medical and paramedical personnel to effectively improve healthcare services. The severe shortages in specializations like anesthesia, obstetrics & gynecology, pediatrics etc. needs to be addressed. We are also facing the problem of concentration of health personnel in urban areas leaving vast tracts of rural population in need of basic health services and a requirement of these groups of personnel. Attracting and retaining health personnel in the already created facilities is one of the biggest challenges of our health system. To address this, different approaches have been tried including providing incentives for doctors posted in rural areas, compulsory rural posting as well as developing a cadre of community health workers. Community health workers have taken various forms in different programmes; there is need to review and learn from these experiences and enhance current programmes. Efforts are needed to strike a balance between doctors and these health workers for delivering primary health care services; services of these personnel are to be utilized optimally, he added. The two-day Workshop being organized by the Ministry in collaboration with WHO, Country office for India seeks to identify and agree on priorities for coordinated action in improving the Human Resources for Health (HRH) Policy and practice. The problem of shortages and distribution of health manpower so as to enhance the effectiveness of the health system will also be addressed at the workshop.

87. (5-4-2007) NEW DELHI : The Ministry of Rural Development has sanctioned Rs. 3467.83 lakh to the State Government of Orissa towards restoration of cut imposed while releasing second instalment of funds against the original allocation of Rs.9212.00 lakh made for the Government of Orissa under Accelerated Rural Water Supply Programme (Normal) of Rajiv Gandhi National Drinking Water Mission, during the year 2006-07. Up to 15 per cent of funds released under this sanction may be utilized for Operation & Maintenance and up to 5 per cent of funds may be spent for taking sustainability measures. States have been requested to delegate powers for management of Rural Water Supply Schemes through the Panchayati Raj Institutions (PRIs) as per the Constitution of India. As such Operation and Maintenance of the completed RWS Scheme should be transferred to the PRIs. No expenditure shall be incurred on taking water quality problems form the present release, as there is a separate allocation for the purpose. This release is being made for execution/completion of schemes to provide safe drinking water facilities to rural habitations and schools under the Centrally Sponsored ARWSP. Priorities set in ARWSP guidelines and through other instructions issued from time to time shall be followed for coverage of rural habitations and rural schools.

88. (5-4-2007) NEW DELHI : The Ministry of Rural Development has sanctioned Rs. 1330.85 lakh to the State Government of Meghalaya towards additional release under Accelerated Rural Water Supply Programme (Normal) of Rajiv Gandhi National Drinking Water Mission, during the year 2006-07. Up to 15 per cent of funds released under this sanction may be utilized for Operation & Maintenance and up to 5 per cent of funds may be spent for taking sustainability measures. States have been requested to delegate powers for management of Rural Water Supply Schemes through the Panchayati Raj Institutions (PRIs) as per the Constitution of India. As such Operation and Maintenance of the completed RWS Scheme should be transferred to the PRIs. No expenditure shall be incurred on taking water quality problems form the present release, as there is a separate allocation for the purpose. This release is being made for execution/completion of schemes to provide safe drinking water facilities to rural habitations and schools under the Centrally Sponsored ARWSP. Priorities set in ARWSP guidelines and through other instructions issued from time to time shall be followed for coverage of rural habitations and rural schools.

89. (5-4-2007) NEW DELHI : UNESCO meeting of experts on Intangible Cultural Heritage (ICH) Convention concluded here yesterday. The three-day meeting was attended by 25 experts from 22 countries. Criteria for inscription on the Representative List was discussed. Discussions were held on ICH elements that are viable and ICH elements that are fully viable. ICH not in need of safeguarding and ICH in need of safeguarding were also discussed. ICH in need of urgent safeguarding and ICH in need of extremely urgent safeguarding also figured in the talks. The experts agreed to discuss further Representative List of the ICH of humanity and list of ICH in need of urgent safeguarding. The next meeting of the experts will be held in Chengdu, China in May this year. UNESCO has adopted the Convention for the Safeguarding of Intangible Cultural Heritage in 2003. India has ratified this Convention. India is also on the Intergovernmental Committee that decides on the implementation aspects of the Convention. The Intangible Heritage Convention seeks to protect, safeguard and regenerate intangible cultural expressions, which include oral traditions, belief systems, folklore, traditional knowledge systems and art forms. Prior to the adoption of the Convention, UNESCO had a practice of declaring important forms of Intangible Cultural Expressions as 'Masterpieces to Humanity'. Under this scheme, three forms-Kutiyattam, Vedic Chanting and Ramlila-from India have been declared as masterpieces. However, with the convention becoming operational, the practice of such declaration as Masterpieces will be discontinued. Instead, the Convention provides for a Representative List of 'Intangible Heritage'.

90. (5-4-2007) NEW DELHI : The Ministry of Rural Development has released grant-in-aid of Rs. 98.93 lakh to DRDA Kishanganj in Bihar towards second instalment of Central Share of funds under 'Swarnjayanti Gram Swarojgar Yojana' (SGSY) during the year 2006-07. Lakhisarai DRDA of Bihar has also been granted funds of Rs. 86.49 lakh as first instalment. An amount of Rs.33.39 crore to 26 DRDAs in Bihar towards Restoration of cut on account of excess O.B. as on 1.4. 2006 as per Annexure has also been released under the scheme. The amount should be utilized on the Programme as per approved guidelines of SGSY. The funding pattern will be 75:25 by the Centre and the State. The State Govts/DRDAs/ZPs are also to ensure to submit the report of State and District Levels Vigilance & Monitoring Committee meeting held during current year by March 31, 2007, otherwise Ist instalment during the next year will be held up. The State Government should release its share within one month of the date of release of the Central assistance. Under SGSY, assistance is given to the poor family living below the poverty line for taking up self-employment. It actively promotes group approach by organising the rural poor into Self-Help Groups.

91. (5-4-2007) NEW DELHI: "India and Pakistan will press ahead with a proposed gas pipeline from Iran," an official Pakistani statement said after talks between Prime Ministers Manmohan Singh and Shaukat Aziz here on Wednesday morning. Reaffirming their commitment to sincerely and seriously pursue the project, the release said, "They [the two leaders] expressed satisfaction over the progress made so far in the technical-level talks among the three sides." According to the statement, Dr. Singh agreed that Pakistan would be provided with periodic status reports on the probe into the February 19 firebombing of the Samjhauta Express as most of the victims were Pakistanis. "The Indian Prime Minister reiterated the Government of India's determination to pay compensation to the victims of the terrorist incident," the release said after delegation-level and one-to-one talks between the two leaders. While an official Indian statement said the two leaders discussed a wide range of issues including trade, energy, banking and air connectivity, the Pakistani side was more specific. The two leaders "agreed on granting permission to their respective banks to open branches and increasing air links between the countries," the Pakistani release stated.

92. (5-4-2007) NEW DELHI : The Ministry of Rural Development has sanctioned Rs. 1.22 crore to the State Government of Gujarat towards second instalment of funds against the total approved cost of Rs. 355.07 lakh for Computerization project of Rajiv Gandhi National Drinking Water Mission (RGNDWM) for the year 2006-07. This grant is being provided under revised MIS guidelines during the year 2006-07. With this, the total release has become Rs. 229.17 lakh. This release is subject to the guidelines laid down in the programme. A half yearly progress report of implementation of Computerisation project of RGNDWM is to be regularly sent to Rajiv Gandhi National Drinking Water Mission.

93. (5-4-2007) NEW DELHI : The Ministry of Rural Development has sanctioned Rs. 954.19 lakh to the State Government of Mizoram towards additional release under Accelerated Rural Water Supply Programme (Normal) of Rajiv Gandhi National Drinking Water Mission, during the year 2006-07. Up to 15 per cent of funds released under this sanction may be utilized for Operation & Maintenance and up to 5 per cent of funds may be spent for taking sustainability measures. States have been requested to delegate powers for management of Rural Water Supply Schemes through the Panchayati Raj Institutions (PRIs) as per the Constitution of India. As such Operation and Maintenance of the completed RWS Scheme should be transferred to the PRIs. No expenditure shall be incurred on taking water quality problems form the present release, as there is a separate allocation for the purpose. This release is being made for execution/completion of schemes to provide safe drinking water facilities to rural habitations and schools under the Centrally Sponsored ARWSP. Priorities set in ARWSP guidelines and through other instructions issued from time to time shall be followed for coverage of rural habitations and rural schools.

94. (5-4-2007) NEW DELHI : The Ministry of Rural Development has sanctioned Rs. 33.65 crore to the State Government of Arunachal Pradesh towards additional release under Accelerated Rural Water Supply Programme (Normal) of Rajiv Gandhi National Drinking Water Mission, during the year 2006-07. Up to 15 per cent of funds released under this sanction may be utilized for Operation & Maintenance and up to 5 per cent of funds may be spent for taking sustainability measures. States have been requested to delegate powers for management of Rural Water Supply Schemes through the Panchayati Raj Institutions (PRIs) as per the Constitution of India. As such Operation and Maintenance of the completed RWS Scheme should be transferred to the PRIs. No expenditure shall be incurred on taking water quality problems form the present release, as there is a separate allocation for the purpose. This release is being made for execution/completion of schemes to provide safe drinking water facilities to rural habitations and schools under the Centrally Sponsored ARWSP. Priorities set in ARWSP guidelines and through other instructions issued from time to time shall be followed for coverage of rural habitations and rural schools.

95. (5-4-2007) NEW DELHI : A Joint Conference of Chief Ministers and Chief Justices of High Courts is being held on Sunday (8th April, 2007) on the theme "Administration of Justice on Fast Track. " The Prime Minister, Dr. Manmohan Singh, will inaugurate the Conference. The Chief Justice of India, Justice Shri K.G. Balakrishnan and the Minister of Law and Justice, Shri H.R. Bhardwaj will also address the Conference. The Conference, besides taking stock of the implementation of various decisions taken at the previous such conference held on March 11, 2006 will focus on strengthening and modernization of the delivery of justice system. The Conference will discuss augmentation and expansion of infrastructure of the courts such as buildings, equipments, software knowledge, resources including human resources facility. There is already a Centrally Sponsored Scheme for development of infrastructure in judiciary, which includes construction of court building and accommodation for judges and judicial officers covering High Courts and subordinate Courts. The expenditure under the scheme is shared by the State and Central Government on 50:50 basis. As per the information collected by the First National Judicial Pay Commission, every State has been providing less than 1% of the budget for subordinate judiciary except Delhi which has provided 1.03%. During the Tenth Plan, the allocation was Rs. 700 crore constituting 0.078% of the total plan outlay of Rs. 8,93,183 crore. It has been observed that these allocations have been inadequate to meet the requirements of the judiciary. Another issue to figure at the Conference is regarding the enhancement of the strength of judges and disposal of arrears in courts. As per available statistics, there are about 2.85 crore cases, both civil and criminal, pending in High Courts and Subordinate Courts. In order to clear this average backlog would require an immediate improvement in judge-population ratio by increasing the number of judges as well as introduction of new technology to help in speedy justice. The sanctioned strength of judges of the High Courts was 725 and working strength was 597 as on March 1, 1997 leaving 128 vacancies. Similarly, with 11,767 working strength of Subordinate Judges there were 2710 vacancies. Based on the disposal of cases in 2006, average disposal per judge comes to 2374 cases in High Courts and 1346 cases in Subordinate Courts. Applying this average the country will require 1539 High Court Judges and 18,479 Subordinate Judges to clear the backlog in one year. The requirement would come down to 770 more High Court Judges and 9,239 more Subordinate judges if the arrears alone have to be cleared in the next two years. One of the ways to ease the backlog would be to introduce functioning of the existing courts in two shifts. This would considerably reduce the burden on resources as the same infrastructure would be used for second shift. In Gujarat 30 evening courts have already started functioning and they disposed off 16,153 cases between 14th and 27th December 2006.

96. (5-4-2007) NEW DELHI : According to "India Science Report", published in 2005, based on a survey sponsored by Indian National Science Academy (INSA) and carried out by National Council of Applied Economic Research (NCAER), the proportion of the students enrolled in science courses has gone up from 28.8% of the population in 1995-96 to 34.6% in 2003-04. As part of the exercise towards developing the National Curriculum Framework-2005, the NCERT set up a National Focus Group on 'Teaching of Science', to deliberate on the issues of science education in the country. The recommendations of the National Focus Group were considered during the formulation of the National Curriculum Framework. Further, the Ministry of Human Resource Development, had constituted a Task Force under the Chairmanship of Prof. M.M. Sharma for basic scientific research in Universities. Details of the recommendations of the above mentioned Task Force are at Annexure-I. In order to build scientific research institutions of the highest standards in which teaching and research at the undergraduate and post-graduate levels will be undertaken in an integrated manner, Ministry of Human Resource Development has set up two Indian Institutes of Scientific Education and Research (IISERs) at Kolkata and Pune and the third IISER is being set up at Mohali in Punjab. Ministry of Science and Technology has also a scheme namely 'Innovation in Science Pursuit for Inspired Research (INSPIRE)' incorporating measures such as scholarship, summer camps with science icons and assured income for the a hand holding and safety net mechanism for identifying and nurturing youth with talented in science so that they take up research as a career. This integrated approach provides aptitude and talent for research.

97. (5-4-2007) NEW DELHI : The Minister of Tourism and Culture Smt. Ambika Soni will be on a two day visit to Andhra Pradesh from 6th April, 2007 to review tourism and culture projects in the State. Accompanied by the senior officials of the Ministry of Tourism and Culture and Archaeological Survey of India, Smt. Soni will inaugurate a Paryatak Bhavan, visit Salarjung museum and Qutabshahi Tomb and Shilparaman to inspect the work of Shilpasandhya. She will also inaugurate a rural tourism project at Pochampalli before returning to Delhi on 7th evening.

98. (6-4-2007) NEW DELHI : The leaders of the UPA Coordination Committee along with the Left Parties met and reviewed the situation arising out of the judgement of the Supreme Court in respect of the Central Educational Institutions (Reservation in Admission) Act 2006. It was resolved that the Government will take all appropriate steps to ensure that the reservation for OBCs to the extent of 27 per cent becomes operational from this academic session. Government will also consult other political parties.

99. (6-4-2007) NEW DELHI : The Prime Minister of Nepal, Rt. Hon'ble Girija Prasad Koirala today returned to Nepal after attending the 14th SAARC Summit, here. On behalf of Government of India, the Union Water Resources Minister, Prof. Saif-ud-din Soz bid formal farewell to the Hon'ble Prime Minister of Nepal at the ceremonial lounge of IGI airport. Prof. Soz recalled the close ties between India and Nepal and thanked Shri Koirala for visiting India to attend the SAARC Summit. Shri Koirala congratulated Government of India for smooth conduct of the Summit. Prof. Soz also had the honour of receiving the Prime Minister of Nepal on his arrival at IGI airport on April 1, 2007.

100. (6-4-2007) NEW DELHI : Doordarshan has drawn a detailed plan for digitizing its holdings of approximately 70,000 hours of programme on analogue video tapes in its Central Archives. 1400 hours of programmes have already been digitized and DD Archives so far released 51 titles in the market. 600 hours of programmes have been identified for the DD MTNL Broadband Video on demand project. These are exclusive content relating to culture, travel, personalities, historical places, health, fitness, lifestyles, crafts etc. The future comprehensive plan in this regard includes, Digital migration, Facilitating Broadband convergence, Commercial exploitation of the holdings, Preparing DVDs/CDs/VCDs to provide more flexibility of viewing and listening to the connoisseurs, Creating interest of learners and young practitioners of Indian culture in these programmes and Making the recordings of performances of our great artists available to cultural institutions in India and abroad.

101. (6-4-2007) NEW DELHI : The Central Board of Film Certification (CBFC) issued a total of 10551 certificates during the year 2006, as against 7417 during 2005. 3454 certificates were issued to celluloid films and 7097 certificates to video films during this period. These consisted of 1091 Indian feature films (celluloid), and 336 foreign feature films (Celluloid). In the Indian feature films category, the highest number 245 was of Telugu films. 223 Hindi films were certified whereas Tamil language films were at the third slot with 162. Films in Malayalam, Bhojpuri, Kannada and Marathi language were next with 77, 76, 75 and 73 certifications respectively. Out of 1636 Indian feature films (Celluloid & Video) certified during the period, 1130 were granted "U" certificates, 270 "UA" certificates, and 236 "A" certificates. Similarly, of the 1080 foreign feature films certified in the year, 460 were granted "U" certificates, 269 "UA" certificates, and 351 "A" certificates.

The Board certified a total of 7242 Indian short films during the period January to December, 2006, of which 6717 were granted "U" certificates, 359 "UA" certificates, 165 "A" certificates. A total of 7097 certificates were issued to video films. Of these, there were 545 Indian feature films, 744 foreign feature films, 5494 Indian short films, 235 foreign short films, 75 Indian and 4 foreign films belonging to the "Others" category (long films other than feature).

102. (6-4-2007) NEW DELHI : In some sections of the Press, recently modified 'Dredging Policy' of this Department has been subject to some comments. In order to put the records straight the following clarifications are given: 1. The provision for a right of first refusal extended to the Indian companies owning Indian flag dredgers is different from the concept of 'purchase preference' policy of the Government which is applicable only to PSUs. This right of first refusal is available to both private and public sector enterprises. This has been introduced to provide a level playing field to the Indian dredging companies vis-a-vis their foreign competitors. While in the macro-economic perspective, the forces governing the policy trade-off between higher procurement cost and protection to domestic enterprises have perhaps changed in favour of India during the recent years, this is not completely true in case of the dredging sector. The sector remains dominated by a handful of international players and the capacity of Indian flag dredgers remains low warranting the continuation of intervention from the Government to help build greater domestic capability in dredging, including the public sector enterprise. So far as the right of refusal being available to a bidder within 10% of lowest valid bid is concerned, it is clarified that the contract will be awarded to the person exercising the right of refusal only if he matches the lowest bid. 2. In some cases where dredging is to be undertaken, the cost of dredging offered by competitive bidders is far above the estimated cost and sometimes unreasonably exorbitant. It has been felt, therefore, that in such situation the government should entrust the work to public sector undertakings whose cost could be determined normatively so as to avoid the bidders to take undue advantage of the pressing dredging needs of Indian ports and other organizations. The intention in stipulating this is to keep an option open so that bidders offering exorbitant cost do not unduly burden customer organizations with unreasonably higher cost. Department of Shipping, M/o Shipping, Road Transport and Highways Dated 6th April, 2007.

103. (7-4-2007) LUCKNOW: The first phase of the Uttar Pradesh Assembly elections will be held on Saturday in 62 constituencies spread across 13 districts, including Etawah, home district of Chief Minister Mulayam Singh. Mr. Singh is in the fray in Bhartana there. For this reason alone, Etawah had emerged as the symbol of political change in Uttar Pradesh, if there has to be one, which would be known only on May 11. Since the political parties hit the campaign trail, Etawah had emerged as the epicentre of campaigning. Ever since the campaign began, Etawah had attracted the attention of all parties. It was Bahujan Samaj Party leader

Mayawati who first addressed a rally in Etawah. She was followed by Bharatiya Janata Party president Rajnath Singh. Congress MP Rahul Gandhi addressed a rally in Bhartana on April 3 and conducted a roadshow. The next day Congress president Sonia Gandhi was in Etawah, as was Railway Minister Lalu Prasad. Though according to political observers here, the Chief Minister is likely to win from Bhartana and his brother, Shivpal Singh Yadav, from Jaswantnagar, which was once represented by Mr. Singh, the same cannot be said of the chances of other SP candidates in the Lakhna, Bidhuna, Ajitmal and Auraiya constituencies. In fact, the onslaught by the Congress, the BJP and the BSP appears to have given the Chief Minister anxious moments. He is reported to be spending the nights in Etawah after finishing the campaign in other parts. The organisation in-charge of the Uttar Pradesh Congress Committee, Satyadeo Tripathi, who belongs to Etawah, expressed an apprehension that the SP would use all the tricks in the trade to prevent its defeat here. With 14 constituencies, Kanpur and Kanpur Dehat are the other important districts going to the polls in the first phase. Jan Morcha alliance president Raj Babbar's political prestige is at stake in Agra. He has been camping in Agra for the past 20 days to ensure the victory of the Jan Morcha and alliance candidates. In the 2002 Assembly polls, the SP won in 24 constituencies, the BJP in 16, the BSP in 14, the Congress in 4, the Rashtriya Lok Dal in two and the Rashtriya Kranti Party and Independent in one each of the 62 constituencies going to the polls on Saturday. For the first phase, 657 companies of the Central paramilitary force would be deployed at 16,000 polling stations and around 9,000 polling centres. Chief Electoral Officer Anuj Kumar Bishnoi said that in some places the Central forces would be assisted by the Provincial Armed Constabulary. Mr. Bishnoi said no booth capturing would be allowed and those places have been identified where the weaker sections were not allowed to cast their votes. He added that the persons who intimidated them have also be identified. He said Deputy Election Commissioner J.P. Prakash would move in a chopper and conduct surprise checks.

104. (7-4-2007) NEW DELHI : The Prime Minister, Dr. Manmohan Singh, gave away Indian Police Medals for Meritorious Service to Special Protection Group (SPG) Officers announced on Independence Day 2006 and Republic Day 2007. The awards were presented at a function to commemorate the 22nd Raising Day of SPG, here today. Following is the text of the Prime Minister's Address on the Occasion: I am delighted once again to be here this morning to attend the 22nd Raising Day of this elite organization, the Special Protection Group. I would like to compliment you on completing yet another year of successful and highly satisfying service despite difficult and trying conditions. I would also like to extend my warm greetings to all officers and personnel who have won medals and trophies in recognition of their meritorious services and for their excellence in different professional fields of endeavour. I take this opportunity to extend my warm felicitations to all officers and staff of the SPG and their families. It is a matter of pride and satisfaction for all of us that in the last twenty-two years of its existence, SPG has developed into a formidable force, displaying a very high degree of professionalism and the most outstanding commitment to its truly onerous responsibilities. We are all justly proud that our country has a committed, well-trained Force for the security of the highest political leadership of the country. The informative and wonderful film, which I understand is a home production, is yet another proof of your commitment to excellence through upgradation of skills. It is heartening to note that the organization is not resting on its laurels, but is constantly gearing up to meet newly emerging future challenges. The constant goal of infusing fresh ideas and new concepts highlights your forward-looking approach. I would like to compliment the Mr. Wanchoo, Director and all ranks for making a determined effort to keep SPG prepared for all future threats.

105. (7-4-2007) NEW DELHI : BJP President Shri Rajnath Singh thanked voters of Delhi for giving BJP resounding victory and congratulated the Delhi Pradesh BJP leaders and worker for its comprehensive victory in the recently held elections to the Municipal Corporation of Delhi. Shri Rajnath Singh said that BJP victory is a clear indication of the complete rejection by the people of Delhi of the so called "Aam Admi" policies of the Congress Party which are nothing more than hollow promises used only for electoral posturing. Shri Rajnath Singh said that under the Congress Party, the people of Delhi have been severely impacted by poor governance and anti-people policies including unprecedented price rise of every essential commodity, lack of proper civic amenities such as good quality roads, sewerage, garbage collection and above all high levels of corruption. With this result, the citizens of Delhi have not only conclusively rejected the policies of the Congress Party in Delhi but are also taking the lead in indicating the future trend of electoral results expected across the country, he added. The BJP President said that the party will live upto the expectations of the people of Delhi and ensure that they get a responsible and responsive government that will solve all their problems and make the city a world class capital.

106. (8-4-2007) NEW DELHI : The Prime Minister, Dr. Manmohan Singh has laid foundation stone for 2nd Bridge over river Brahmaputra, in Guwahati today. Following is the text of the Prime Minister's address on the occasion: It gives me immense happiness to be here on this auspicious day. We are in the presence of a mighty and sacred river, the River Brahmaputra. This river is the lifeline of the people of Assam. This new bridge over Brahmaputra will serve the people of Assam as well as the States of Meghalaya, Tripura, Mizoram, Manipur, Nagaland and Arunachal Pradesh. It will provide a new path towards progress and prosperity. The people of Assam and the North Eastern region have a special place in our hearts and minds. The UPA Government is committed to the rapid development of this region. The government of Shri Tarun Gogoi has been working tirelessly for the last six years to push this state forward in its race to catch up with the rest of the country. The second bridge over the Brahmaputra river is part of the

East-West corridor, which would connect the North East Region with the rest of the country. At the same time, a high speed highway from Silchar to Srirampur is being constructed in Assam at an investment of Rs 6000 crores.

107. (8-4-2007) NEW DELHI : The Prime Minister, Dr. Manmohan Singh has called for harmonious functioning of the judiciary, legilature and the executive. Inaugurating the Joint Conference of Chief Ministers and Chief Justices of High Courts on the theme 'Administration of Justice on Fast Track' here today, the Prime Minister said that each organ of the state must respect the roles and functions of the other and powers accorded to each must be exercised cautiously. He said "Courts have played a salutary and corrective role in innumerable instances. They are highly respected by our people for that. At the same time, the dividing line between judicial activism and judicial over-reach is a thin one..... All organs, including the judiciary, must ensure that the dividing lines between them are not breached." The Prime Minister also called upon the Supreme Court to take lead in framing rules for screening Public Interest Litigation (PIL) "so that only genuine PILs with a justiciable cause of action based on judicially manageable standards are taken up. This will also ensure consistency in judicial pronouncements", he said. Acknowledging the great utility of PILs in initiating corrective action, Dr. Singh said, "PILs cannot become vehicles for settling political or other scores. We need standards and benchmarks for screening PILs". Expressing concern over the huge pendency and backlog of cases in courts, the Prime Minister said that there is an urgent need to improve the disposal of cases. He said that the states and the High Courts have to execute and implement a time bound exercise for filling up vacancies. "I am sure once the unfilled vacancies are filled up there would definitely be reduction in the arrears", he added. He highlighted the initiatives taken by the Government in providing support for the Fast Track Courts, drawing up of a Plan for infrastructure development in terms of construction of courts etc. and the steps taken for computerization and application of information and communication technology to the judiciary. He expressed the hope that with these measures the position regarding delays and backlogs would improve. The Prime Minister also expressed concern over all States not having set up family courts. The Chief Justice of India, Justice Shri K.G. Balakrishnan in his keynote address spoke about the process of judicial review, its purpose and desirability. He mentioned that in a country governed by a rule of Law every decision must be made under the rule of law. He said "The superior judiciary not only decide civil and criminal cases but the judicial review safeguards civil and political rights of individuals and sometime define and control the powers of every organ of the state". He spoke about legitimate and responsible criticism of the judiciary and the judicial responsibility and independence that was associated with judicial functioning. Justice Shri Balakrishnan said that judicial review sometimes creates tension between the judge, the legislative and the executive branch. He said "such tension is natural and to some extent desirable".

108. (8-4-2007) NEW DELHI : The Minister of State for Commerce, Shri Jairam Ramesh is leading a multi-sectoral Indian delegation to Azerbaijan and Uzbekistan from April 10-16th, 2007 to boost bilateral economic relationships covering both investment and trade. In Baku, Shri Ramesh will sign the first-ever agreement with Azerbaijan for establishing the India-Azerbaijan Intergovernmental Commission on Trade, Economic, Scientific and Technological Cooperation. Along with the Managing Director of ONGC Videsh, he will also pursue India's interests for oil and gas exploration in Azerbaijan. ONGC Videsh has identified some promising prospects which it would like to develop, Azerbaijan having re-emerged as a major oil-rich country with the commissioning of the Baku-Tbilisi-Ceyhan pipeline that links Azerbaijan, Georgia and Turkey and is the world's second longest oil pipeline connecting rich Caspian Sea oil reserves with the Mediterranean Sea. Azerbaijan also having vast resources of minerals and metals, senior officials from MMTC and the National Mineral Development Corporation (NMDC) are accompanying Shri Jairam Ramesh, to explore the possibilities of entering into a Memorandum of Understanding for cooperation in the mineral sector with the Azerbaijan Government. BHEL has executed a major project for supply and installation of power generators. Indian pharmaceutical companies are also building their presence in Azerbaijan. The Minister of State's visit is expected to provide a fillip to these efforts. In Tashkent, Shri Ramesh will chair the Seventh Session of the India-Uzbekistan Intergovernmental Commission. Accompanied by senior officials of GAIL, Ministry of Petroleum & National Gas, he will pursue with the Uzbek government the projects identified by GAIL for investment in Uzbekistan in petrochemicals, LPG and city gas distribution. In addition, GAIL has identified 4 natural gas exploration and production blocks as prospective ones in Uzbekistan on which it would like to move forward, Uzbekistan being one of the top natural gas producing countries in the world. ONGC Videsh is also interested in investing in gas fields in Uzbekistan.

109. (8-4-2007) NEW DELHI : Doordarshan has approved a scheme for establishment of a network of VSAT (Very Small Aperture Terminals) at 70 places all over the country with a central hub at Delhi with a view to strengthening the newsgathering facilities. Action for procurement of VSAT has already been initiated. Establishment of the VSAT network would enable feeding of news from the 70 places to National/Regional News Units through satellite. This network would also enable voice/data communication among the places, where VSAT are set up. Doordarshan's proposal for a pilot project in HDTV has been recently approved. As part of this project, facility for field production in HDTV is envisaged to be set up at Delhi in 2007 08.

110. (8-4-2007) NEW DELHI : The Bharatiya Janata party has decided to organise protest demonstration in all the state capitals on 9th April (Monday), demanding immediate withdrawal of 2nd FIR against its president Shri Rajnath Singh. Party President Shri Rajnath Singh will court arrest in Lucknow tomorrow as FIR has registered against him in the wake of CD controversy in Uttar Pradesh. Shri L.K. Advani, Shri M. Venkaiah Naidu, Smt. Sushma Swaraj, Arun Jaitley, Yashwant Sinha and other leaders will be present on the occasion in Lucknow. This is a protest against the 2nd FIR filed against the Party President by State Election Office under the influence of local administration. This has happened despite party's explanation to the Chief Election Commissioner that the controversial CD was not a part of official campaign material and had been withdrawn. 2nd FIR against the Party President is a malicious design of Samajwadi Party and other psuedo secularist parties. It is worthwhile to note that the same action was not initiated against Shri Lalu Prasad Yadav who used a Godhra CD in Bihar Election for divisive politics. Recently notices have been issued to Shri Sharad Pawar for violation of code of conduct by declaring sugar package and to Shri Mulayam Singh Yadav for castist appeal. But no FIR is registered against them. Earlier no FIR was registered against either Sonia Gandhi for using State Aircraft during Chhattisgarh Assembly Election, or Lalu Prasad Yadav for distributing cash during Bihar Assembly campaign. Call of action against BJP by other parties is a worst type of appeasement politics.

111. (8-4-2007) NEW DELHI : The Prime Minister, Dr. Manmohan Singh, inaugurated the Conference of Chief Ministers and Chief Justices of High Courts on "Administration of Justice on Fast Track", here today. The Chief Justice of India, Hon'ble Justice Shri K.G. Balakrishnan, the Union Minister for Law and Justice, Shri H.R. Bhardwaj, Minister of State for Law and Justice, Shri Venkatapathy, Judges of the Supreme Court, Chief Justices of the High Courts, Chief Ministers of the States were among the dignitaries who participated in the function. Following is the text of the Prime Minister's address on the occasion. "I feel privileged to be once again at this very important conference of Chief Ministers and Chief Justices of our High Courts. These are important and useful opportunities for representatives of the executive, the legislature and the judiciary to interact, both formally and informally. Apart from discussing various issues on the agenda, I hope each one of you will use this opportunity to gain a better understanding and appreciation of the other's concerns and preoccupations. In this way this conference would be an important asset in mutual comprehension. Unless the three wings of the State understand each other better, they will not be able to function effectively in the interests of our nation and our people at large. The three wings have well defined roles and functions under our Constitution. However, all the wings have a common goal-which is the fulfillment of the hopes of the founding fathers of our Republic and as spelt out so clearly in our magnificent Constitution. Therefore, conferences such as these give us an opportunity to discuss contemporary issues which have a bearing on the organs of the State, particularly those issues where the interface between the organs is large. In last year's Conference I had an opportunity to share some of my views on judicial reforms and e-governance. Our Government accords high priority to judicial reforms. The National Common Minimum Programme envisages judicial and legal reforms as one of the thrust areas in promoting good governance. In that direction, my Government has already undertaken certain initiatives. It has amended the Procedural Laws with a view to improving the Criminal Justice System. 'Plea Bargaining' has been introduced in the Criminal Procedure Code. I must place on record here my very sincere appreciation of the fulsome support and cooperation our Government has received from the leadership of our judiciary in this regard. Both former Chief Justices of the Supreme Court and the present Chief Justice have shown great commitment to judicial reform and I thank them for this. Our Government places special emphasis on professionalism in investigation and prosecution as well as providing protection to our citizens, particularly women, against arbitrary harassment from the police. There is a bill now before Parliament that seeks to amend the Criminal Procedure Code to deal with the problem of witnesses turning hostile. It also seeks to provide legal rights and compensation to victims. It will also facilitate the use of modern techniques in investigation. The Bill will make summary trial mandatory in cases with imprisonment up to 3 years.

112. (9-4-2007) NEW DELHI : The Deputy Prime Minister and Minister of Public Infrastructure, Land Transport and Shipping of Mauritius, H.E. Dr. Ahmed Rashid Beebeejaun held a meeting with the Union Minister of Shipping, Road Transport and Highways, Thiru T.R. Baalu here today. The meeting paved the way of both sides exploring future areas of cooperation in the Shipping and Road infrastructure sectors. During the meeting, the two sides agreed to work together towards development of efficient transportation in two countries. The Mauritian Deputy Prime Minister is on a six-day visit to India on the invitation of Thiru T.R. Baalu. Thiru Baalu briefed the visiting Deputy Prime Minister about the progress made by India in the Road and Shipping Sector and also about the introduction of public-private partnership in these sectors. Thiru Baalu informed his Mauritian counterpart that several Indian Companies operating in the infrastructure sector have the resources and required technical know-how which could be of benefit to Mauritius in the development of its physical infrastructure.

113. (9-4-2007) NEW DELHI : With the arrival of SAARC Car Rally vehicles at Colombo port this morning, the Sri Lankan leg of the 30-day long Rally is all set for an early morning flag-off tomorrow. The vehicles were shipped from Mumbai to Colombo by the Indian Navy vessel, INS Shardul. After the flag-off by SAARC leaders at Delhi on April 3, the convoy had reached Mumbai on April 5, making night halts at Jaipur and Udaipur on the way. The Rally cars were brought to the Mumbai port and set sail for Colombo on April 6 under the supervision of Indian Navy. Continuing the series of business events scheduled to coincide with the rally, a workshop on 'Promotion of Intra-SAARC Tourism' was organized today by the Federation of Chambers of Commerce and Industry of Sri Lanka, here. The Deputy Minister of Tourism, Government of Sri Lanka, Mr. Faizer Mustafar was the chief guest on the occasion. Addressing the delegates,

Shri Mustafar called for greater cooperation between SAARC countries in jointly projecting the region as an attractive tourist destination. The 'Incredible India' tourism promotion campaign of Government of India was widely cited as a success story during the deliberations and it was felt that other SAARC countries too should consider similar campaigns for promotion of tourism. With the vehicles having arrived, the rally participants were accorded a ceremonial welcome in the evening. It was followed by a cultural programme showcasing the rich cultural diversity of Sri Lanka, also known as the 'Pearl of Indian Ocean'. On day 27 of the Rally tomorrow, the convoy would start from Colombo and halt at Tissamaharama for the night.

114. (9-4-2007) NEW DELHI : Union Finance Minister, Shri P. Chidambaram has approved 13 Foreign Direct Investment proposals recommended by Foreign Investment Promotion Board (FIPB) in its meeting held on 29th March, 2007. The approval amounts to Rs. 476.6837 crore. The proposals relate to Ministries/ Departments, namely, Commerce, Information & Broadcasting, Information Technology, Telecommunications and Economic Affairs. The major investment proposals pertain to the Ministry/Departments of Commerce, Information & Broadcasting and Economic Affairs.

115. (9-4-2007) NEW DELHI : The Indian Food industry-both primary and processed-are posed for a rapid growth. India has the potential to become a reliable outsourcing partner in the food sector given its strengths in the primary food sector. The Indian Food sector is estimated to be worth over US$200 billion and is expected to grow to US$ 310 billion by FY 2015. It also contributes to a major part of the retail basket. The US$ 6.11 billion food retail sector is also growing at a hefty 9 per cent. FDI in India, in this segment has exceeded US$ 3 billion. Indian food brands are now increasingly finding prime self-space in the retail chains across the US and Europe. The recently enacted Food Safety and Standards Act provides a major opportunity to India for revisiting its Food Regulatory regime to ensure that the Indian consumers get high quality, safe food as well as create a conducive, industry friendly environment to enable a faster growth of the Indian food industry. The food business is growing beyond borders in the new WTO regime, nations are replacing their Tariff barriers with more complicated Non-Tariff Barriers and Quality and Safety considerations have acquired centre stage with an ascending importance of the role of Standards and Conformity assessment. Different perceptions of different countries on these issues creates considerable frictions and often conflicts in accepting each countries' Standards, testing methodologies and inspection results. Therefore, it is imperative to harmonize country specific Food Regulatory regimes with the benchmarks set by well established international bodies like CODEX and SPS and TBT agreement assured under WTO. To maximize opportunities and to meet the challenges of the rapidly changing global food regulatory practices, both the Indian Food companies as well as Food service providers need to be conversant with globally emerging food safety, quality and initiatives influencing business and trade. In order to address the above issues, the Confederation of Indian Industry (CII) in cooperation with the Food and Agriculture Organization of the United Nations (FAO) is organizing a two-day International Food Regulatory Summit, 2007 "Aligning India to the World" from 10-11 April, 2007 in New Delhi. The Summit will inaugurate by the Union Minister for Health & Family Welfare, Dr. Anbumani Ramadoss.

116. (9-4-2007) NEW DELHI : Ministry of Women and Child Development released today a study on Child Abuse conducted with the help of UNICEF, Save the Child and a Delhi based NGO, PRAYAS. Releasing the report, the Smt. Renuka Chowdhury, Minister for Women and Child Development said that the gravity of the situation demands that the issue of child abuse be placed on the national agenda. The Ministry on its part has taken measures such as the enabling legislation to establish the National and State Commissions for Protection of Rights of the Child, the Integrated Child Protection Scheme, the draft Offences against Children Bill etc. These are a few important steps to ensure protection of children of the country. But clearly, this will not be enough, the government, civil society and communities need to complement each other and work towards creating a protective environment for children. The momentum gained needs to enhance further discussion on the issue amongst all stakeholders and be translated into a movement to ensure protection of children of this country. The Minister said that the aim of the study was to develop a dependable and comprehensive understanding of the phenomenon of child abuse, with a view to facilitate the formulation of appropriate policies and programmes meant to effectively curb and control the problem of child abuse in India. The National Study on Child abuse is one of the largest empirical in country studies of its kind in the world. This study also complements the UN Secretary General's Global study on violence against Children, 2006. The initiative of the Ministry to conduct this study was supported by UNICEF and Save the Children. A Delhi based NGO, Prayas was contracted to design and conduct the research and submit a preliminary report. After the submission of the preliminary report, the MWCD appointed a core Committee to review the complete data, analyze the findings and produce the final report along with recommendations. The study has provided revealing statistics on the extent and magnitude of various forms of child abuse-an area by and large unexplored. The study has also thrown up data on variations among different age groups, gender variations, state variations and variations within evidence groups. The findings will help to strengthen the understanding of all stakeholders including families, communities, civil society organizations and the state.

117. (9-4-2007) NEW DELHI : Congress Spokesman Shri Devender Dwivedi said that the scene in Uttar Pradesh has taken an ugly turn in the past few days in the manner of which the events have unfolded themselves have brought out into sharp contrast the attempt by the BJP to communalise the electoral scene by trying to inflame passions and adopt the campaign style which is going to be divisive. Beginning with the release of the controversial video CD, the contents of which are so pernicious that even very responsible people have chosen to take risk of printing them and publishing them by taking the responsibility that they are doing so in public interest. The Congress Party approached the Election Commission with the notice of the Election Commission about the nature and the content of the CD. The Election Commission has started its hearing today. We also were aghast and surprised when we went there that it was a casual proceedings in which all the parties which had either were issued notice or which had approached the Election Commission like BJP, Congress, CPM and Mayawatiji's party and since whatever papers had been given by us and the BJP wanted to respond, we wanted to respond to what BJP had said about which we do not know anything. So they have been adjourned for day-after. The delegation consisted of Shri Kapil Sibal, Shri Ashok Gehlot, Shri Narayanswami and the secretary of the AICC, Shri Ranji Thomas and myself. Today, we saw the two faces of the BJP. One in Delhi and one in Lucknow. That was the double role that BJP had been playing in national politics. Here was Shri Arun Jaitely complying with the notice of the Election Commission and seeking to explain the case of the BJP in the CD and simultaneously having disowned the CD, having dis-attached itself from the CD. The president of the party against whom there was no arrest warrant, no police case filed, pitted up an ugly drama. The former Deputy Prime Minister, the president of the party presenting themselves unwanted adequacies, the sole purpose of which was to undo the act of withdrawal for the CD and withdraw was technical. In pursuance of the suo moto taken by the Election Commission whereby they have been asked why they should not be de-recognised and why criminal proceedings should not be initiated? At one end you are withdrawing while on the other you want to send the message to the party ranks that luckily we stand by the contents, that is the message on which we are going to fight the elections. In cutting long story short, the CD is intended to inflame passions, create hatred and feelings of enmity and favouring different sections of the society. Seeking to malign the Muslims by creating doubts about their loyalty, about their commitment to the constitution. Let nobody be fooled that their tap brass of the party were not associated. This was conceived by them, it was conceptualized by them, it was choreographed by them such are the contexts if you only see, almost everybody is participating, everybody is speaking and everybody is a part of that. And then suddenly, as a party of well-designed drama, can you imagine that a party which has governed this country for five years doesn't know that Election Commission would take note of it and issue notice suo moto.

118. (9-4-2007) NEW DELHI : Ministry of Women and Child Development released today a study on Child Abuse conducted with the help of UNICEF, Save the Child and a Delhi based NGO, PRAYAS. Releasing the report, the Smt. Renuka Chowdhury, Minister for Women and Child Development said that the gravity of the situation demands that the issue of child abuse be placed on the national agenda. The Ministry on its part has taken measures such as the enabling legislation to establish the National and State Commissions for Protection of Rights of the Child, the Integrated Child Protection Scheme, the draft Offences against Children Bill etc. These are a few important steps to ensure protection of children of the country. But clearly, this will not be enough, the government, civil society and communities need to complement each other and work towards creating a protective environment for children. The momentum gained needs to enhance further discussion on the issue amongst all stakeholders and be translated into a movement to ensure protection of children of this country. The Minister said that the aim of the study was to develop a dependable and comprehensive understanding of the phenomenon of child abuse, with a view to facilitate the formulation of appropriate policies and programmes meant to effectively curb and control the problem of child abuse in India. The National Study on Child abuse is one of the largest empirical in country studies of its kind in the world. This study also complements the UN Secretary General's Global study on violence against Children, 2006.

119. (9-4-2007) NEW DELHI : Several programmes are being organized all over the country to celebrate the 150th year of India's First War of Independence. The celebrations are a "National Tribute" to the martyrs who lost their lives for the cause of Independence of our country from the clutches of the British raj. A National Youth Action Plan for the commemoration of 1857 has been worked out in the 'National Workshop on 1857, India's First War of Independence' on May 8 and 9, 2006. This workshop was held under the leadership of Minister of Youth Affairs and Sports Mani Shankar Aiyar. Nehru Yuva Kendra Sangathan (NYKS) an autonomous organization under the Ministry of Youth Affairs and Sports, Government of India, is carrying out the initiatives of the commemoration plan.

120. (9-4-2007) NEW DELHI : A Committee has been constituted for spot appraisal relating to recurring mortality of lions in and around the Gir National Park and Wildlife Sanctuary in Gujarat. National Tiger Conservation Authority, a statutory body under the Ministry of Environment and Forests today announced the composition and the terms of reference of the Committee. It will consider the fact that the only last world population of the highly endangered Asiatic lions (Panthera leo persica) is present in the this habitat. The Regional Deputy Directors (Wildlife) Ms. Meeta Banerjee, Western Region and Shri Santosh Tiwari, Northern Region will be Members of the Committee. This three Member Committee will have Shri Pramod Krishnan, Joint Director (Wildlife), Ministry of Environment and Forests as Member Convener: The Committee will give appraisal of protection strategy in vogue vis-a-vis mortality of lions during the last three years (natural / disease / poaching), resource dependency of local people on Gir habitat and steps taken towards redressing park people interface conflicts and fostering coexistence, managerial constraints in this area and possibility of restorative management in crucial corridor linkages around Gir to prevent insularization of the lion population. The Committee will also recommend measures to improve the situation. Dr. Rajesh Gopal, Member Secretary of the National Tiger Conservation Authority informed in New Delhi today that the Committee may co-opt State officials as required and submit its report within 30 days from today.

121. (9-4-2007) NEW DELHI: Expressing serious concern over judicial interventions, Prime Minister Manmohan Singh on Sunday said that in the guise of judicial activism, the judiciary must not over-reach itself. Inaugurating a conference of Chief Ministers/Law Ministers of various States and Union Territories and Chief Justices of High Courts, the Prime Minister said: "Courts have played a salutary and corrective role in innumerable instances. They are highly respected by our people for that. At the same time, the dividing line between judicial activism and judicial over-reach is a thin one." Without indicating any particular judgment or order, Dr. Singh said "as an example, compelling action by authorities of the State through the power of mandamus is an inherent power vested in the judiciary. However, substituting mandamus with a takeover of the functions of another organ may, at times, become a case of over-reach. These are all delicate issues, which need to be addressed cautiously. All organs, including the judiciary, must ensure that the dividing lines between them are not breached. This makes for a harmonious functioning." Earlier, Chief Justice of India K.G. Balakrishnan, said: "Judicial review to determine constitutionality of a legislation and to review the executive decision sometimes creates tension between the judge and the legislative and the executive branch. Such tension is natural and to some extent desirable. Of course, the judicial review of legislative and administrative actions has given rise to some criticism of the way in which the courts are functioning. Like any other public institution, the judiciary can be subjected to fair criticism if and when occasion demands but if the criticism is illegitimate and irresponsible, it may lead to incalculable damage to the institution of the judiciary." Dr. Singh said the judiciary, the executive and the legislature had an obligation both to our Constitution and to our people, to work in harmony.

122. (9-4-2007) NEW DELHI : The two day Kharif Campaign Conference 2007-08 was concluded on 4th April 2007. Within the Conference, the Ministry of Agriculture proposed its strategy to achieve 4% agricultural growth in the Eleventh Plan period for consideration and deliberation by states and other participants. The conference was chaired by Dr. P.K.Mishra, Secretary (Agriculture & Cooperation). The Conference was also addressed by Dr. J.S. Sarma, Secretary, Department of Fertilizers and Ms. Charusheela Sohoni, Secretary, Department of Animal Husbandry, Dairy and Fisheries. It was attended by the policy makers, scientists, administrators and researchers. The participants in the two days Conference included State Agriculture Production Commissioners/Agriculture Secretaries, Vice-Chancellors of State Agriculture Universities, Officers of various departments/organizations of Central Government such as DAC, Department of Space, India Meteorological Department, National Horticulture Board, Indian Council of Agricultural Research, Department of Fertilizers, Planning Commission and others. Dr. S.M. Jharwal, Principal Adviser, DAC, welcomed the participants to the two days Conference. He referred to the Approach Paper for the 11th Plan, approved by the National Development Council and Draft National Policy for Farmers based on the recommendations of National Commission for Farmers, and highlighted the need to translate their recommendations into an action plan. In his inaugural address, Secretary (DAC) stated that agriculture is at a cross road but there are immense opportunities. He stressed on the need for achieving 4% growth in agriculture and allied sectors. He referred to the constraints which the agriculture sector is facing like agrarian distress, agricultural risks, spatial and temporal climatic aberrations and vulnerability for food security. He also referred to the problems of land degradation, soil nutrient deficiency, imbalanced use of fertilizers, depleting water resources which need urgent attention. He highlighted the need for concerted efforts to revamp the seed management system, agriculture extension system and development of horticulture sector. He stressed that there is need now for preparing an action plan which could be implemented in medium term for identified areas such as food security, production of pulses and oilseeds, availability of quality seeds, extension system, horticulture sector and the present Conference should come up with a road-map for revitalizing the agriculture sector and enhancing income of farmers.

123. (9-4-2007) NEW DELHI : The Ministry of Rural Development has sanctioned Rs. 401.77 lakh to the State Government of Sikkim towards additional release under Accelerated Rural Water Supply Programme (Normal) of Rajiv Gandhi National Drinking Water Mission, during the year 2006-07. Up to 15 per cent of funds released under this sanction may be utilized for Operation & Maintenance and up to 5 per cent of funds may be spent for taking sustainability measures. States have been requested to delegate powers for management of Rural Water Supply Schemes through the Panchayati Raj Institutions (PRIs) as per the Constitution of India. As such Operation and Maintenance of the completed RWS Scheme should be transferred to the PRIs. No expenditure shall be incurred on taking water quality problems form the present release, as there is a separate allocation for the purpose. This release is being made for execution/completion of schemes to provide safe drinking water facilities to rural habitations and schools under the Centrally Sponsored ARWSP. Priorities set in ARWSP guidelines and through other instructions issued from time to time shall be followed for coverage of rural habitations and rural schools.

124. (9-4-2007) NEW DELHI : The Ministry of Rural Development has released second instalment of the Central share towards Restortion of cut on account of late submission under the 'Swarnjayanti Gram Swarojgar Yojana' (SGSY) during the year 2006-07 to DRDA Ri-Bhoi (Rs.12.00 lakh) & DRDA West Khasi Hills (Rs. 39.27 lakh) of Meghalaya; and Rs.4.51 lakh to DRDA West Siang of Arunachal

Pradesh. An amount of Rs. 16.91 lakh has been released towards restoration of cut on account of excess o.b. as on 1.4.2006 to DRDA South Tripura of Tripura and Rs. 5.97 to Gangtok DRDA of Sikkim under SGSY during 2006.07. Release of Additional instalment of central share for implementation of SGSY during 2006-07 has also been released to Dhalai DRDA (Rs. 51.91 lakh) of Tripura and DRDA Mamit-Aizwal (Rs.5.98 lakh) of Mizoram under the scheme. Grant-in-aid as first instalment of central share amounting to Rs. 13.71 lakh to South Garo Hills DRDA of Meghalaya; Rs. 22.80 lakh to DRDA Mon of Nagaland; Rs. 26.42 lakh to DRDA Thoubal & Rs. 16.50 lakh to DRDA Ukhrul of Manipur has also been released under the scheme. The Ministry has also released second instalment of funds under SGSY to DRDA East Khasi Hills (Rs.51.96 lakh) of Meghalaya and DRDA Kiphire (Rs.10.85 lakh) of Nagaland under the scheme. The amount should be utilized on the Programme as per approved guidelines of SGSY. The funding pattern will be 75:25 by the Centre and the State. The State Govts/DRDAs/ZPs are also to ensure to submit the report of State and District Levels Vigilance & Monitoring Committee meeting held during current year by March 31, 2007, otherwise Ist instalment during the next year will be held up. The State Government should release its share within one month of the date of release of the Central assistance.

125. (9-4-2007) NEW DELHI : The Ministry of Rural Development has sanctioned an amount of Rs.3.33 crore to the State Government of West Bengal as extended first instalment for undertaking IEC & HRD activities relating to National Rural Drinking Water Quality Monitoring & Surveillance Programme (NRDWQM&SP) under Rajiv Gandhi National Drinking Water Mission (RGNDWM) during the year 2006-07. Out of these, an amount of Rs.233.34 lakh for IEC activities and remaining Rs.99.81 lakh should be utilized for HRD activities as per the guidelines. The funds for undertaking these activities are to be transferred to Community & Capacity Development Unit established in the State. This release is for plan expenditure. The funds are to be utilized for the purpose for which it is released and as per the terms and conditions. The release is on the basis of norms for each activity as per the guidelines.

126. (9-4-2007) NEW DELHI : BJP spokesperson Shri Rajiv Pratap Rudy today said that the demand for action against the BJP by the Congress Party, SP, BSP and Left Front is a result of their rising despondency and frustration on seeing the ground realities change in Uttar Pradesh and the growing public mood in favour of the BJP. Shri Rudy reiterated that the so called CD which was inadvertently released was withdrawn much before the intervention of the Election Commission. In fact the BJP should be credited for initiating timely and prompt action against the person responsible for the purported action and for pre-empting any use or circulation of the CD. However, the action initiated against the BJP National President Shri Rajnath Singh and the lodging of an FIR against him in such haste clearly indicates towards the existence of prejudicial action. Shri Rudy said that statement of Mr. Kapil Sibal asking the BJP National President to retire from politics shows the Congress Party's shallow attitude and growing desperation. The recent surge and victory of the Bharatiya Janata Party in the assembly polls in Punjab, Uttarakhand and the recent MCD elections in Delhi has not only made the Congress Party completely clueless on issues but has also left it searching for an effective poll agenda. In this context, the Congress Party is working on a devious design to distract the people from the real issues of price rise, appeasement, national security and good governance. Shri Rudy added that it is time for the Congress Party to close shop as several recent actions of the UPA coalition government at the centre clearly shows the redundancy of the Congress leadership. While making the demand for derecognizing the BJP, Mr. Sibal is failing to actually assess the fact that it is the Congress Party which has been outrightly dismissed by the people's mandate in the recent elections and it is the Congress which is faced with the real prospect of being completely derecognized by the people of India. Shri Rudy condemned Mr. Sibal's recent remark that BJP President Shri Rajnath Singh was resorting to theatrics. He said that before Mr. Sibal makes any such absurd remarks about the BJP President, he should not fail to remember that it is the Congress Party which has created a remote power centre that is compromising the position of the Prime Minister and is itself engaged in actively playing theatrics with the "Aam Aadmi".

127. (9-4-2007) NEW DELHI: A Congress party delegation will meet the Election Commission here on Monday to demand the de-recognition of the Bharatiya Janata Party (BJP) for releasing the controversial compact disc. The Commission has sought the views of the complainants, various political parties, including the BJP, before deciding on the show-cause issued to the BJP as to why it should not be de-recognised for violating the Model Code of Conduct. The former Prime Minister, V.P. Singh, and Bahujan Samajwadi Party leader Mayawati will also give oral representations before the Commission on the issue. Talking to reporters here on Sunday, Union Science and Technology Minister Kapil Sibal said the Congress delegation was of the opinion that any national political party that sought to create ill will between different communities could not be part of the democratic process. Besides Mr. Sibal, the delegation will comprise several senior leaders, including M.L. Vohra and Ashok Gehlot.

128. (9-4-2007) NEW DELHI : The Ministry of Rural Development has sanctioned an amount of Rs.2.98 crore to the State Government of Chhattisgarh as extended first instalment for undertaking IEC & HRD activities relating to National Rural Drinking Water Quality Monitoring & Surveillance Programme (NRDWQM&SP) under Rajiv Gandhi National Drinking Water Mission (RGNDWM) during the year 2006-07. Out of these, an amount of Rs.67.18 lakh for IEC activities and remaining Rs.231.32 lakh should be utilized for HRD activities as per the guidelines. The funds for undertaking these activities are to be transferred to Community & Capacity Development Unit established in the State. This release is for plan expenditure. The funds are to be utilized for the purpose for which it is released and as per the terms and conditions. The release is on the basis of norms for each activity as per the guidelines.

129. (9-4-2007) NEW DELHI : External Affairs Minister Shri Pranab Mukherjee has been reviewed by a team of specialists at Army Hospital (R&R), early this morning. He had a sound sleep yesterday and continues to remain active and cheerful. A fresh series of investigations, including CT and MRI head, and CT chest were done and these ruled out any bony or internal injuries. His vital parameters continue to be within normal limits. He has a lacerated wound scalp, which is clean and has nine sutres. Apart from this, there are no other bony or soft issue injuries. Shri Pranab Mukherjee is able to walk around and is progressing well. He is expected to be discharged from the hospital tomorrow. Gen JJ Singh, Chief of Army Staff called on the Minister this morning.

130. (9-4-2007) NEW DELHI : Government of India, Ministry of Health & Family Welfare has proposed amendment to the Drugs and Cosmetics Rules, 1945 for registration of cosmetic products for the purpose of their import into the country. A Gazette Notification, GSR 63(E) dated 2/2/2007, has been published inviting objections and suggestions from the public within 45 days for the consideration of the Government. The comments, if any, should be addressed to the Secretary, Health, Ministry of Health & Family Welfare, Nirman Bhawan, New Delhi-110011 for the consideration of the Government. Ministry of Health & Family Welfare, Department of Health New Delhi, April 9, 2007; Chaitra 19, 1928

131. (9-4-2007) NEW DELHI : The UPSC has declared the results of Engineering Services Examination, 2006. On the basis of written part of the examination held in June, 2005, 1010 candidates have qualified for the interview (Personality Test) for admission to Civil Engineering, Mechanical Engineering, Electrical Engineering and Electronics & Telecom. Engineering. Of these, 194 are from Other Backward Classes, 116 from Scheduled Castes, 44 from Scheduled Tribes and 15 from Physically Challenged category.

132. (9-4-2007) NEW DELHI : The Prime Minister, Dr. Manmohan Singh today laid the Foundation Stone of the Rs. 5460 crore Petrochemical Project of Brahmaputra Cracker and Polymer Limited (BCPL). This marks a significant step in the direction of setting up the petrochemical project in Assam, which is expected to be completed in 2011 *i.e.* 60 months from the date of approval. The dignitaries present on the occasion include Lt. Gen. (Retd.) Ajai Singh, PVSM, AVSM, Governor of Assam, Shri Tarun Gogoi, Chief Minister, Assam, Shri Murli Deora, Union Minister of Petroleum and Natural Gas, Shri Ram Vilas Paswan, Union Minister of Chemicals and Fertilizers and Steel, Shri Sontosh Mohan Dev, Union Minister of Heavy Industries and Public Enterprises, Shri B K Handique, Union Minister of State for Chemicals and Fertilizers and Parliamentary Affairs and Shri Dinsha Patel, Union Minister of State for Petroleum and Natural Gas. Also present were Shri Prithibi Majhi, Minister of Planning and Development, Labour and

Employment and Tea Tribes Welfare, Assam, Shri Pradyut Bordoloi, Minister of Power, Industries and Commerce, Assam and Shri Sarbananda Sonowal, Member of Parliament, Dibrugarh were also present on the occasion. Brahmaputra Cracker and Polymer Limited, is a Joint Venture company promoted by GAIL (India) Limited with 70 per cent equity stake. The remaining 30 per cent equity will be shared equally among OIL, NRL and Govt. of Assam. The company is implementing the project to setup an integrated Petrochemical Complex at Lepetkata, District Dibrugarh. The site has been identified by the Govt. of Assam and necessary Environmental clearance has been obtained. Towards contributing to the industrial development of the region, the project is expected to give a boost to further investments in downstream plastic processing industries and allied activities with a potential for substantial direct ant indirect employment generation. The Government of Assam has agreed to grant Exemption from Entry tax on capital goods, Exemption from Works Contract Tax during construction and Sales Tax / VAT exemption on feed stock and products for 15 years from the date of commencement of production.

133. (9-4-2007) NEW DELHI : The Minister of State for Commerce, Shri Jairam Ramesh is leading a multi-sectoral delegation to Azerbaijan and Uzbekistan from April 10-16 2007 to boost bilateral economic relationships covering both investment and trade. In Baku, Shri Ramesh will sign the first-ever agreement with Azerbaijan for establishing the India-Azerbaijan Intergovernmental Commission on Trade, Economic, Scientific and Technological Cooperation. Along with the Managing Director of ONGC Videsh, he will also pursue India's interests for oil and gas exploration in Azerbaijan. ONGC Videsh has identified some promising prospects which it would like to develop, Azerbaijan having re-emerged as a major oil-rich country with the commissioning of the Baku-Tbilisi-Ceyhan pipeline that links Azerbaijan, Georgia and Turkey and is the world's second longest oil pipeline connecting rich Caspian Sea oil reserves with the Mediterranean Sea. Azerbaijan also having vast resources of minerals and metals, senior officials from MMTC and the National Mineral Development Corporation (NMDC) are accompanying Shri Jairam Ramesh, to explore the possibilities of entering into a Memorandum of Understanding for cooperation in the mineral sector with the Azerbaijan Government. BHEL has executed a major project for supply and installation of power generators. Indian pharmaceutical companies are also building their presence in Azerbaijan. The Minister of State's visit is expected to provide a fillip to these efforts. In Tashkent, Shri Ramesh will chair the Seventh Session of the India-Uzbekistan Intergovernmental Commission. Accompanied by senior officials of GAIL, Ministry of Petroleum & National Gas, he will pursue with the Uzbek government the projects identified by GAIL for investment in Uzbekistan in petrochemicals, LPG and city gas distribution. In addition, GAIL has identified 4 natural gas exploration and production blocks as prospective ones in Uzbekistan on which it would like to move forward, Uzbekistan being one of the top natural gas producing countries in the world. ONGC Videsh is also interested in investing in gas fields in Uzbekistan.

134. (9-4-2007) NEW DELHI : Ministry of HRD has convened a two-day conference of State Education Ministers (April 10-11) in New Delhi. The conference will deliberate on issues concerning the entire gamut of education such as elementary, secondary, higher and technical education so that maximum possible progress can be achieved during the XIth Plan in the education sector in terms of access, equity, quality and efficiency. The recent initiatives of the Central Government for the XI Plan such as the extension of Mid-Day Meal Scheme to the upper primary stage and increasing the Central Plan outlay for Secondary Education, bulk of which will go as assistance to State Governments are some of the areas where Centre would look forward to the feedback from the States. The Department of School Education and Literacy has drawn up an elaborate list of agenda items which include, Universal Elementary Education (UEE), improving achievement levels of children in elementary and secondary schools, steps to be taken by States to meet their enhanced share under Sarva Shiksha Abhiyan (SSA) in the XIth Plan and bridging the existing gap in the participation and achievement rates of disadvantaged groups(girls, Scheduled Castes and Scheduled Tribes, minorities and the differently-abled, etc.) The Higher Education department will interact with the State Governments on improving the quality of higher education, especially in State-funded colleges and Universities; establishing polytechnics in districts which have no polytechnic at present as well as strengthening the infrastructure of polytechnics in special identified districts; e-networking of the institutions of higher learning; maximizing the use of ICT including EDUSAT to widen access and improve quality of education; work relating to authentication of educational certificates and special emphasis on education of minorities disadvantaged sections of the society including SC/ST/OBCs and women. Senior officials from the ministry of HRD and the Planning Commission, apart from senior functionaries from the autonomous organizations/subordinate office under the ministry such a NCERT, CBSE, KVS, Department of Adult Education, UGC, AICTE, IGNOU etc., will also participate in the deliberations. The General Body meeting of NCERT, which comprises the Education Ministers from all the States, will also be held on the second day of the conference. The current conference is in the line of similar Conference of State Ministers of Higher Education organized in Bangalore in January 2005 as well as the meetings of the Central Advisory Board on Education (CABE), held later in the same year.

135. (9-4-2007) NEW DELHI : The Prime Minister, Dr. Manmohan Singh, laid the foundation stone of Brahmaputra Cracker & Polymer Limited (Petrochemicals Project) at Lepetkata, Dibrugarh in Assam today. The Governor of Assam, Lt. Gen (Retd.) Ajai Singh, Chief Minister Shri Tarun Gogoi, Union Cabinet Ministers, Shri Ram Vilas Paswan, Shri Murli Deora, Shri Sontosh Mohan Deb, Shri B.K. Handique were among the dignitaries present on the occasion. Following is the text of the Prime Minister's speech at the occasion: "I am always happy to be here in my adopted home state of Assam! My heart fills with joy and pride each time I come to Assam and see the faces of hope. It gives me even greater pleasure when I come here to associate myself with a development project of profound importance. I came to this area of Assam over a year ago to lay the foundation stone of an important coal mining project at Ledo in Tinsukia. I am now particularly happy to be here today to lay the foundation of the Assam Gas Cracker Project.

136. (9-4-2007) NEW DELHI : Delhi Development Authority to go for online computerization to provide efficient services to the citizens of Delhi. The Authority has decided to computerize all the operations and functions of the organization under computerization programme called, Integrated Management System, IMS. The system will automate all functions and operations of the DDA and usher in a new era in the working of the Authority and will be of immense benefit to the citizens of Delhi. The online computerization will improve the citizen interface, increase transparency in DDA operations, bring out efficiency in processing papers and provide speedy information access. For the DDA, the computerization will provide effective information management system, help decision making, provide seamless information flow between various departments of the Authority, help re-engineer various processes, improve information reliability, and will connect all DDA offices through state of art networking infrastructure. The Delhi Development Authority awarded the work of complete online computerization to M.S Birlasoft Limited, which is a leading provider of information technology, services in both onshore and offshore organizations. Birlasoft's services include application development, support and maintenance, enterprise application implementation, integration, infrastructure management and quality assurance and testing.

137. (9-4-2007) NEW DELHI : Central Water Commission (CWC) under Ministry of Water Resources is monitoring storage position of 76 important reservoirs spread all over the country, of which as many as 31 reservoirs have significant hydro-power benefits with installed capacity of more than 60 MW each. The combined live storage in these 76 reservoirs at the beginning of monsoon *i.e.* 1st June, 2006 was 22 per cent of their designed capacity and stood at 39 per cent of the designed capacity as on 29th March 2007. The present storage is 106 per cent of the last year's storage and 140 per cent of last 10 years average storage during the same period. Out of these 76 reservoirs there are presently 15 reservoirs where this year's storage is 80 per cent or less than the average of previous 10 years and in the remaining 61 reservoirs the storage is more than 80 per cent of the average of previous 10 years. In order to derive the best possible benefits from the available water, Central Water Commission is keeping in touch with the Department of Agriculture and Cooperation and providing information of the weekly storage position to the Crop Weather Watch Group for evolving suitable crop strategies and also apprising the situation to various Departments and Ministries involved in Water Resources Planning. Basinwise storage position as on 29th

March' 07 is as follows: The storage position in eleven basins namely Indus, Ganga, Tapi, Mahi, Sabarmati, Krishna, Rivers of Kutch, Godavari, Cauvery and Neighbouring East Flowing Rivers, Mahanadi and Neighbouring East flowing Rivers and West Flowing rivers of South is better than average of previous 10 years. Out of 31 reservoirs with significant hydro potential, 6 reservoirs have storage build up less than the average of last 10 years capacity and no reservoir has negative storage *i.e.* less than MDDL.

138. (10-4-2007) NEW DELHI : The Urban Development Minister, Shri S. Jaipal Reddy has said that transparency is one way to reducing corruption and increasing the level of efficiency. Speaking at the launch of the Integrated Management System for a complete online computerization of the Delhi Development Authority here today, Shri Reddy said that computer is a wonderful tool, which enables government and governance as a transparent system. He said that the Integrated Management System would streamline the information in the Authority. The Minister stated that the UPA Government has laid great stress on e-governance and the integrated management system at the DDA will be an example to other organizations not only in Delhi but also in the country. Earlier, the Minister lauded the role played by the DDA in keeping the capital city green. Shri Reddy expressed happiness stating that there is no complaint against the Authority with regard to transparency, impartiality and non-partisanship in the recent land auctions. Speaking on the occasion, the Vice Chairman of the DDA, Shri Dinesh Rai said that the Integrated Management System would not only improve the image of the organization but also bring about transparency in the DDA. By launching Integrated Management System, the DDA aims to provide efficient services to the citizens of Delhi. Under this system all the operations and functions of the DDA will be computerized and automated. The Integrated Management System will improve the citizen interface and improve public image, increase transparency in DDA operations, increase efficiency in processing of papers and will help access information by citizens. Because of the Integrated Management System, DDA will have effective management information systems in place, have effective decision making, have seamless information flow between various departments, have improved information reliability, will connect all DDA offices through state of art networking infrastructure. The Information Management System will have broad scope for integrating areas like planning, architecture, land management, landscaping horticulture, engineering, housing, finance, land disposal, personnel management etc.

139. (10-4-2007) NEW DELHI : Prof. M.S. Swaminathan and Dr. (Smt.) Kapila Vatsyayan have been nominated to the Rajya Sabha. Prof. Swaminathan has been nominated against the vacancy caused due to the retirement of a nominated member, while Dr. Vatsyayan has been nominated against the casual vacancy caused by resignation in her earlier capacity as member of the Rajya Sabha, till the remainder of her term *i.e.* 15th February 2012.

140. (10-4-2007) NEW DELHI : A one-year Work Plan in pursuance of the Memorandum of Understanding (MOU) on Bilateral Cooperation between the Office of the Controller General of Patents, Designs and Trade Marks (CGPDTM) and the European Patent Office (EPO) was signed here today by Dr. Ajay Dua, Secretary, Department of Industrial Policy & Promotion (DIPP), Ministry of Commerce & Industry and Professor Alain Pompidou, President of the European Patent Office, in the presence of Shri Kamal Nath, Minister of Commerce & Industry. The Work Plan includes programmes for Human Resource development, Automation and Data Exchange between the two offices. The EPO is a top level Patent Office in the world and has a Membership of 31 countries. It is an important International Patents Search Authority and International Preliminary Examining Authority under the Patent Cooperation Treaty (PCT). An important component of the cooperation programme which will run from mid-2007 to mid-2008 is the provision for training at the European Patent Office for 10 senior patent examiners from India; and training by 3 EPO experts of 20 to 30 patent examiners in India.

141. (10-4-2007) NEW DELHI : Shri R.K. Das will be the new Director General of the Central Industrial Security Force (CISF). Shri Das, a 1970 batch Uttar Pradesh Cadre IPS officer, is currently holding the post of Special Director, Intelligence Bureau.

142. (10-4-2007) NEW DELHI : The second bridge over the Brahmaputra is part of the East-West corridor, which would connect the North East Region with the rest of the country. At the same time, a high speed highway from Silchar to Srirampur is being constructed in Assam at an investment of Rs 6000 crores. The mighty and sacred river, the Brahmaputra, is the lifeline of the people of Assam. A new bridge over Brahmaputra will serve the people of Assam as well as the States of Meghalaya, Tripura, Mizoram, Manipur, Nagaland and Arunachal Pradesh. It will provide a new path towards progress and prosperity. The UPA Government is committed to the rapid development of the North East Region. This project is scheduled to be completed by December 2008. It will reduce the overall travel time and distance between the North East region and rest of India.

143. (10-4-2007) NEW DELHI : The Government has unveiled far reaching plans to encourage and attract investments in the North East Region. The Minister of Development of North Eastern Region, Mr. Mani Shankar Aiyar emphasized on North East as a great investment destination. He was addressing the 3rd North-East Business Summit in New Delhi today. Talking on the issue of security in the North-East he said that it is a wrong perception to view the entire Northeast as insurgency infested. Mr. Aiyar said that barring a few pockets the security situation in the entire Northeast was most conducive to business. Mr. Aiyar highlighted the new North-East Industrial and Investment Policy (NEIIP) which has some unique features. This policy was unveiled on 31st March, 2007 and it is a exclusive policy relating to all areas of North-East. The policy is valid for the next 10 years.

However, any body who wishes to take advantage of this policy will get the advantage for the next 10 years from the date of him/her adopting the policy. This policy has virtual tax exemption which means that there will be no income tax for 10 years and no Excise Duty except on some health harming substances like tobacco, gutka etc. Mr. Aiyar also indicated the government's intention to have cold storages at 5 major air ports in the Northeast region to promote business. The Minister outlined an infrastructure building programme including the transport and air travel segment. He said that as against 226 air links in the North-East region at present the government plans to increase the air links to over 500 in the next 2 years. He said that as against the Central money flow of Rs.80,000 crores in the North-East in the 10th Plan, the expected fund flow in the 11th Plan will be Rs.1,20,000 crores. The Minister appealed to the private industry to generously invest in the business ventures in power, tourism, food processing, handicrafts and other industries in this region to encourage employment generation, local area development and to economic power to the people. The Chief Guest for the 3rd North-East Business Summit is Mr. Bhairon Singh Shekhawat, Vice President of India. The other dignitaries present at the inaugural session were Shri Gegong Apang, Chief Minister of Arunachal Pradesh, Shri Tarun Gogoi, Chief Minister of Assam, Shri Okram Ibobi Singh, Chief Minister of Manipur, Dr. D.D.Lapang, Chief Minister of Meghalaya, Lt.Gen (Retd) M.M. Lekhera, Governor, Mizoram, Shri Neiphiu Rio, Chief Minister of Nagaland, Shri Pawan Chamling, Chief Minister of Sikkim and Shri Tapan Chakravorty, Minister (Industry) Tripura. Delegations from Thailand, Nepal, Bangladesh and other countries are also attending the summit. An exhibition is also being organized to showcase the products of North-Eastern States and to facilitate business to business contact. The 2 day summit will conclude on 11th April, 2007.

144. (10-4-2007) NEW DELHI : The first India—US Defence Joint Working Group meeting was held in New Delhi today. The meeting was co-chaired by Shri S Banerjee, Director General (Acquisition), Ministry of Defence and Shri Richard P Lawless, Deputy Under Secretary of Defence (Asian and Pacific Affairs), US Department of Defence. The discussions were held in the most cordial and friendly atmosphere. The Joint Working Group was envisaged in the New Framework for India-US Defence Relationship, signed by the then Defence Ministers of India and US, Shri Pranab Mukherjee and Mr. Donald Rumsfeld, in June 2005. The Defence Joint Working Group conducts midyear review of the work overseen by the Defence Policy Group, which is the apex dialogue mechanism for the India-US defence relationship.

145. (10-4-2007) NEW DELHI : Inaugurating the first International Food Regulatory Summit 2007 on the theme "Aligning India to the World" in New Delhi, the Minister for Health & Family Welfare, Dr. Anbumani Ramadoss said that India has recently enacted a new Food Safety and Standards Act which provides an excellent opportunity to India to have a relook at its Food Regulatory regime and bring about wide ranging improvements for ensuring safety and quality in Food Value Chains-from farm to fork. Shri Piruz Khambata, Chairman, CII National Committee on Food Processing, Dr. Daniel Gustafson, Representative of FAO (UN) for India and Bhutan, Shri Abhiram Seth, Chairman CII Expert Group on Food Regulatory Affairs, Dr. Naresh Trehan, Chairman, CII National Committee on Healthcare, Mr. Ezzeddine Boutrif, Chief Food Quality and Standards Service, Nutrition and Consumer Protection Division, FAO also spoke in today's Summit.

146. (10-4-2007) NEW DELHI : Government of India, Ministry of Health & Family Welfare has proposed a clubbed notification (on different rules and schedules as mentioned in the notification) to the Drugs and Cosmetics Rules, 1945, vide Gazette Notification, GSR 62 (E) dated 2/2/2007, which includes the proposed amendments of Schedule E, rule 75-A, 78-A, rule 94, rule 96, Form 17-A, Form 35, Schedule K and Schedule S. The draft amendments have been published in the Gazette in order to obtain objections and suggestion from the public within 45 days for the consideration of the Government. The comments, if any, should be addressed to the Secretary, Health, Ministry of Health & Family Welfare, Nirman Bhawan, New Delhi-110011.

147. (10-4-2007) NEW DELHI : 52nd Railway Week function organized by the Railway Board was held here today. Shri Satish Kumar Vij, Member Engineering, Railways Board who was the Chief Guest on the occasion gave away the Running Shield Merit Certificates and Cash Awards to the officers and staff of Railway Board for the best performances for the year 2006-07. Speaking on the occasion, Shri Vij said that it was due to the untiring efforts and dedication of the railwaymen that today Indian Railways has made remarkable progress in achieving important goals and targets. He congratulated the award winners for putting in their best performance and hoped that they would rededicate themselves to produce better results in the future. The Running Efficiency Shield, Merit Certificates plus Cash Awards of Rs. 4,000/-each for maintaining high standard of efficiency, prompt disposal of cases and punctuality was jointly begged by ERB-II and E(G) Branches. In Addition, four more branches were also given merit certificates plus cash award of Rs. 2,000/-each. A total 109 officers and staff of Railway Board were given merit certificates and cash prizes of Rs. 2,000/-each for their outstanding services during the year 2006-07. Artistes and outstanding sports persons of Railway Board who excelled in the Inter-Railway, Inter-Ministry and All India Civil Services Competitions were also felicitated with cash awards, appreciation letters and souvenirs on the occasion. Also present on the occasion among others were Member Electrical, Shri Ramesh Chandra, Member Mechanical, Shri R.K.Rao and Secretary, Shri Mathew John of Railway Board. President's address at the annual function of Indian Music Academy, New Delhi.

148. (10-4-2007) NEW DELHI : The Public Sector, Metallurgical and Engineering Consultants, MECON, under the Ministry of Steel has bagged contracts for 2 x

500 MW Power Plant in Tamil Nadu, being promoted jointly by the Neyveli Lignite Corporation (NLC) and the Tamil Nadu Electricity Board. MECON will provide detailed engineering and consultancy from concept to commissioning for two units of 500 MW each to be set up at Tuticorin. This is for the first time that MECON will provide consultancy for power projects of 500 MW capacity. Earlier MECON had also provided similar service to the NLC for their 2 x 210 MW expansion programme which was successfully completed in 2003. Some of its other well known clients include National Aluminum Company (NALCO), Damodar Valley Corporation (DVC), Tamil Nadu Electricity Board (TNEB), besides private sector companies like Jindal Steel & Power, Bhushan Steel and Adhunik Group. In an effort to enable it to offer state of the art technology, MECON has signed a cooperation agreement with internationally renowned consultancy organisation, M/s AF-Enprima of Finland for joint working in power sector consultancy in India.. With the business in power sector rising, MECON is preparing a road map to develop its Strategic Business Unit further. The power plant division at Ranchi is being augmented with more resources and latest design softwares to facilitate better and timely services to the valued customers.

149. (10-4-2007) NEW DELHI : The Vice President of India Shri Bhairon Singh Shekhawat has said that there are multiple problems of poverty, unemployment and inadequacy of physical and economic infrastructure leading to a feeling of alienation from the mainstream in the North Eastern Region. Unfortunately, some parts have problems of militancy and violence. Delivering inaugural address at the "3rd North-East Business Summit" organized by the Ministry for the Development of the North-East region and the Indian Chamber of Commerce here today, Shri Shekhawat said that holistic development of the North East assumes urgency and seriousness, as the country just cannot afford to neglect a region which has potential to contribute enormously to the nation's development. Shri Shekhawat has said that a new North East Industrial and Investment Promotional Policy, 2007 has been put in place effective from April 1. This policy provides enhanced financial and fiscal incentives. This policy also extends these benefits to the units in the services sector, biotechnology and power generation. He hoped that this liberal policy framework would be found attractive enough by our entrepreneurs to make substantial investments in the N-E Region.

150. (10-4-2007) NEW DELHI : BJP National Vice President Shri Mukhtar Abbas Naqvi today said that where as the focus of BJP is to stop Terrorism, Corruption, Price Rise and Appeasement, pseudo-secular brigade is focusing only on stopping BJP. Shri Naqvi said that worried and unnerved by the progressive victorious nationalist march of BJP, the pseudo secular quartet comprising the Congress, Samajwadi, BSP and Left Front parties have come together to seek ban and de-recognision of BJP. This is happening because they have realised that the people of the country have rejected their policies and are wholesomely supporting the nationalist principles of the BJP. Shri Naqvi said the BJP has already recorded electoral victories in Punjab, Uttarakhand and Delhi on the issues of terrorism, corruption, price rise and appeasement. These issues are also relevant in Uttar Pradesh where the BJP is confident of attaining complete majority on its own. Shri Naqvi said that the parties who are trying to restrict the BJP by using the excuse of an unauthorised CD, are well aware that the BJP is firmly committed on all nationalist issues that affect the common people and the people have also accepted this. As a result of this, the Congress, SP, BSP and Left Front are trying to divert the people from the real issues and are instead raising only artificial issues. Shri Naqvi said that the anti-BJP parties have from the very beginning been trying to divert the people of Uttar Pradesh from the real issues. That's why sometimes the Congress raises the Babri Masjid issue, while the SP speaks about Madarsas and Urdu teachers, the BSP is trying to project itself as the sole benefactor of the Muslims and all the parties are in a race to fight the elections only on caste and communal issues. Shri Naqvi said that the pseudo secular brigade has got unnerved and is worried after seeing the impressive electoral victories of the BJP in Punjab, Uttarakhand and Delhi, and now is realising that the atmosphere has also become favourable for the BJP in Uttar Pradesh. However, their strategy of trapping the BJP in the name of the so called CD has backfired on them and they are instead trying to find an escape route for themselves in the name of secularism. Shri Naqvi said that even today the BJP's key issues for Uttar Pradesh are the removal of misgovernment, terrorism, corruption, price rise and appeasement, but for the Congress, SP, BSP and Left Front the only issue is stopping the BJP. Shri Naqvi said that the BJP workers are visiting each and every house in Uttar Pradesh with a "Do or Die" spirit to expose and give a befitting reply to the nefarious anti-BJP campaign of the pseudo secular quartet comprising the Congress, SP, BSP and Left Front.

151. (10-4-2007) NEW DELHI : A meeting of District Collectors from 45 high malaria endemic districts in 11 States is scheduled on 11th April, 2007 at 11.00 A.M. at Vigyan Bhawan, New Delhi under the Chairmanship of Hon'ble Minister for Health & Family Welfare, Dr. Anbumani Ramadoss. The participants will deliberate on the malaria situation and operational constraints and devise strategic District Action Plans for effective prevention and control of malaria. They include the District Collectors of following 45 high Plasmodium falciparum endemic districts from 11 states, Secretaries, Directors and officials from the respective State Health Departments, partner institutions, the WHO, World Bank, etc. Since there are many high risk districts in Orissa, a separate meeting of Collectors of 20 districts is proposed to be held later in Bhubaneshwar. List of participating States/Districts: Andhra Pradesh (Visakhapatnam and East Godavari); Assam (North Cachar, Karbi Anglong, Nagaon, Lahimpur, Kokrajhar, Goalpara, Morigaon and Hailakandi); Chhattisgarh (Dantewada, Jagdalpur, Kanker, Jashpur, Ambikapur, Korea and Raigarh); Jharkhand (West Singhbhum, Simdega, Gumla, Dumka, Sahebganj, East Singhbhum and Lohardagga); Madhya Pradesh (Jhabua, Mandla, Panna, Gwalior and Chindwara); Maharashtra (Gadchiroli); Meghalaya (East

Khasi Hills and East Garo Hills); Mizoram (Colasib, Aizawl, Mamit and Lunglei); Orissa (Mayurbhanj, Keonjhar, Angul and Sundergarh); Tripura (Kailashahar (North Tripura), Dhalai and Udaipur (South Tripura); and West Bengal (Purulia and Jalpaiguri). Despite effective tools and technologies and support for malaria control, certain constraints in relation to programme management at the level of implementation still exists. Therefore, there is an urgent need for strategic micro-planning with package of focused interventions with proven effectiveness that can generate the greatest impact in the high risk areas.

152. (10-4-2007) NEW DELHI : An agreement between the Federations of Port and Dock Workers and the Management benefiting 66000 thousand Port and Dock workers was signed here today in the presence of Thiru T.R. Baalu, Union Minister of Shipping, Road Transport and Highways. Shri N. K. Raghupati, Vice Chairman of Indian Ports Association alongwith the Chairmen of Major Port Trusts signed the Agreement on behalf of the Management while leaders of five major federations signed on behalf of the employees. Shri A..K. Mohapatra, Secretary, Shipping was also present on the occasion. It may be recalled that on an initiative taken by Thiru T.R. Baalu, the Government has recently approved the new Productivity Linked Reward Scheme for the employees of Major Port Trusts and Dock Labour Boards, which will replace the earlier Productivity Linked Reward Scheme. The PLR shall be paid annually on the basis of the productivity and performance of the Major Ports on three parameters viz. average turn round time of ships, average ship berth day output and unit cost of handling. The new scheme envisaged under the Agreement signed today, will be applicable from the year 2002-03 onwards and will remain operative upto the year 2009-10. The scheme also envisages the payment of the difference between the PLR payable and the adhoc PLR paid for the years 2002 to 2006. With the signing of the settlement today, the way has been paved for the joint withdrawal of reference from the National Industrial Tribunal, thereby finally, settling the long-pending issue relating to the payment of PLR. It may be recalled that a joint reference was made to the National Industrial Tribunal, Mumbai through Ministry of Labour for settling the issue connected with payment of PLR in October 2002. The leaders of the Federations present during the signing ceremony welcomed the new agreement and applauded the positive approach adopted by Thiru T.R. Baalu in this regard. Thiru Baalu hoped that the new agreement would pave the way for further improving the efficiency of major ports and would help in achieving higher port productivity. The representatives who signed the Agreement included Shri S.R. Kulakarni of All India Dock & Port Workers Federation, Dr. Shanti Patel of All India Dock & Port Workers Federation (W), Shri P.K. Samantray of Indian National Port & Dock Workers Federation, Shri V.V. Rama Rao of Port, Dock Water Front Workers Federation of India and Shri S. Chakravorty of Water Transport Workers Federation of India. Thiru Baalu has already approved the release of the PLR arrears to the approximately 66000 Port and Dock employees and workers. The expenditure to be incurred for this payment of arrears is likely to be to the tune of Rs. 31 Crores.

153. (10-4-2007) NEW DELHI : India and Australia have signed an MoU to foster cooperation between the two countries in the field of Biotechnology. Under the MoU signed by the Department of Biotechnology, Government of India and Department of Education Science &Training, Government of Australia, an Indo-Australian Biotechnology Fund has been set up. The Fund consists of six million Australian dollars from the Australian Government with a matching Indian grant over five years. The overall objective of the Fund is to develop and support collaborative research activities, which draw upon complementary science and technology strengths in India and Australia. It will support Indian and Australian scientists, from both the public and private sector, for collaborative and leading edge science and technology in order to contribute to the economic, social and environmental well being of both countries. In the first round following priority areas have been identified-Biomedical devices and implants, stem cells, vaccines/ medical diagnostics, transgenic crops, Nutraceuticals and functional foods; and Bioremediation. A Joint-Biotechnology Committee, comprising senior experts from both countries constituted to oversee the joint programme, met in New Delhi on 14th March 2007 and considered applications received in the priority areas.

154. (10-4-2007) NEW DELHI : Shri Arjun Singh, Human Resource Development Minister has said that an educated skilled, healthy empowered people are an asset and the challenge before us is to ensure that each and every citizen of India is an asset. Shri Singh was inaugurating the Conference of State Education Minister here today. Ministry of HRD has convened a two-day conference of State Education Ministers (April 10-11) in New Delhi. The conference will deliberate on issues concerning the entire gamut of education such as elementary, secondary, higher and technical education so that maximum possible progress can be achieved during the XIth Plan in the education sector in terms of access, equity, quality and efficiency. The recent initiatives of the Central Government for the XI Plan such as the extension of Mid-Day Meal Scheme to the upper primary stage and increasing the Central Plan outlay for Secondary Education, bulk of which will go as assistance to State Governments are some of the areas where Centre would look forward to the feedback from the States.

155. (10-4-2007) NEW DELHI : The Ministry of Rural Development has released grant-in-aid of Rs. 5.99 lakh to the District Rural Development Agency in Pondicherry towards Restoration of cut on account of excess O.B. as on 1.4. 2006 of funds under 'Swarnjayanti Gram Swarojgar Yojana' (SGSY) during the year 2006-07. The amount should be utilized on the Programme as per approved guidelines of SGSY. The funding pattern will be 75:25 by the Centre and the State. The State Govts/DRDAs/ZPs are also to ensure to submit the report of State and District Levels Vigilance & Monitoring Committee meeting held during current year by March 31, 2007, otherwise Ist instalment during the next year will be held up. The State Government should release its share within one month of the date of release of the Central assistance. Under SGSY, assistance is given to the poor family living below the poverty line for taking up self-employment. It actively promotes group approach by organising the rural poor into Self-Help Groups.

156. (10-4-2007) NEW DELHI : The Ministry of Rural Development has released grant-in-aid of Rs. 42.69 lakh to DRDA Baramulla in Jammu & Kashmir towards Restoration of cut on account of excess O.B. as on 1.4. 2006 and late submission of Central Share of funds under 'Swarnjayanti Gram Swarojgar Yojana' (SGSY) during the year 2006-07. The amount should be utilized on the Programme as per approved guidelines of SGSY. The funding pattern will be 75:25 by the Centre and the State. The State Govts/DRDAs/ZPs are also to ensure to submit the report of State and District Levels Vigilance & Monitoring Committee meeting held during current year by March 31, 2007, otherwise Ist instalment during the next year will be held up. The State Government should release its share within one month of the date of release of the Central assistance. Under SGSY, assistance is given to the poor family living below the poverty line for taking up self-employment. It actively promotes group approach by organising the rural poor into Self-Help Groups.

157. (10-4-2007) NEW DELHI : The Ministry of Rural Development has sanctioned Rs. 3.61 crore to the State Government of Punjab as extended first instalment for undertaking IEC and HRD activities relating to National Rural Drinking Water Quality Monitoring and Surveillance Programme (NRDWQM&SP) during the year 2006-07. Out of these, an amount of Rs.64.84 lakh for IEC activities and remaining Rs.295.82 lakh for HRD activities as per the guidelines under Rajiv Gandhi National Drinking Water Mission (RGNDWM). The funds for undertaking these activities are to be transferred to Community & Capacity Development Unit established in the State. This release is for plan expenditure. The funds are to be utilized for the purpose for which it is released and as per the terms and conditions. The release is on the basis of norms for each activity as per the guidelines.

158. (10-4-2007) NEW DELHI : The Ministry of Rural Development has sanctioned Rs. 1180.18 lakh to the State Government of Tripura towards additional release under Accelerated Rural Water Supply Programme (Normal) of Rajiv Gandhi National Drinking Water Mission, during the year 2006-07. Up to 15 per cent of funds released under this sanction may be utilized for Operation & Maintenance and up to 5 per cent of funds may be spent for taking sustainability measures. States have been requested to delegate powers for management of Rural Water Supply Schemes through the Panchayati Raj Institutions (PRIs) as per the Constitution of India. As such Operation and Maintenance of the completed RWS Scheme should be transferred to the PRIs. No expenditure shall be incurred on taking water quality problems form the present release, as there is a separate allocation for the purpose. This release is being made for execution/completion of schemes to provide safe drinking water facilities to rural habitations and schools under the Centrally Sponsored ARWSP. Priorities set in ARWSP guidelines and through other instructions issued from time to time shall be followed for coverage of rural habitations and rural schools.

159. (10-4-2007) NEW DELHI : The Ministry of Rural Development has sanctioned an amount of Rs.2.99 crore to the State Government of Orissa as extended first instalment for undertaking IEC & HRD activities relating to National Rural Drinking Water Quality Monitoring & Surveillance Programme (NRDWQM&SP) under Rajiv Gandhi National Drinking Water Mission (RGNDWM) during the year 2006-07. Out of these, an amount of Rs.126.14 lakh for IEC activities and remaining Rs.172.66 lakh for HRD activities should be utilized as per the guidelines. The funds for undertaking these activities are to be transferred to Community & Capacity Development Unit established in the State. This release is for plan expenditure. The funds are to be utilized for the purpose for which it is released and as per the terms and conditions. The release is on the basis of norms for each activity as per the guidelines.

160. (10-4-2007) COLOMBO : The SAARC Car Rally started the Sri Lankan leg of the Rally amidst much festivity and traditional dances this morning from the capital city of Colombo. The Rally was flagged off by the Hon'ble Prime Minister of Sri Lanka, Mr. Ratnasiri Wickramanayake. Before the flag-off, the Hon'ble Prime Minister was presented the SAARC Car Rally flag signed by all rally participants. Mr. Wickramanayake welcomed the coming together of all SAARC countries to hold the first SAARC Car Rally and conveyed his good wishes for the Sri Lankan leg. The Rally travelled over 300 km down south from Colombo today to reach the resort town of Tissamaharama for the night halt. It's a picturesque route dotted with tourist resorts and travels all along the coast with the road almost touching the sea at some points. The Government of Sri Lanka has made elaborate traffic and security arrangements for smooth run of the Rally, complete with police escort and air cover by Sri Lankan Air Force helicopters. The first halt for the Rally today was the coastal town of Galle, well known for the remnants of the 17th century Portuguese built fort. Amidst the ruins of Galle fort, the participants got a first hand experience of the traditional handicrafts and folk dances of Sri Lanka. The convoy touched the southern-most point of Sri Lanka before visiting the ancient Katargama religious complex, one of the most revered pilgrimage destination in Sri Lanka for Buddhists, Hindus as well as Muslims, with an over 2000 year-old history. The evening before, the Foreign Minister of Sri Lanka. H. E. Mr. Rohitha Bogollagama welcomed the rally participants at Colombo and said that Prime Minister Dr. Manmohan Singh's initiative to hold a SAARC Car Rally is a well thought approach to give a definite fillip to connectivity in the SAARC region. The smooth passage of the rally vehicles through the borders of SAARC countries demonstrates that if SAARC Governments cooperate, intra-SAARC connectivity can be greatly enhanced, resulting in greater intra-SAARC trade and tourist arrivals, he stressed. On day

28, which is day two of the SAARC Car Rally in Sri Lanka, the convoy is scheduled to travel through some of the most picturesque tea plantations on way to Candy.

161. (11-4-2007) NEW DELHI : The Ganguly Committee which was set up in November 2006 to draft/review course structure for full-time and distance education programmes in respect of Health Facility Planning & Designing and Healthcare Engineering & Management submitted its report to the Union Health & Family Welfare Minister, Dr. Anbumani Ramadoss today. The Committee has recommended starting these two highly multi-disciplinary programmes as 'Master's in Health Facility Planning & Designing" and Master's in Healthcare Engineering & Management. Both these courses will be started in the PGI, Chandigarh. The Committee also recommended starting similar courses for middle managers in states at Polytechnic and IIT level. Such training facilities/courses are being developed for the first time in South East Asia and India has the potentiality of becoming a 'knowledge hub'. Due to fast changing medical technology hospital buildings require constant changes and hence constant research in designs, building technologies, new materials, space utilization sustainability, green concepts and applications. Efficiently run hospitals will contribute a lot in medical tourisms. It is hoped that these programmes being the first in South East Asia will also help in certified Healthcare manpower export. Healthcare Engineers are important adjunct of Hospital Administrations and inter-disciplinary approach will help patient care, hospital environs and quality of life of patients. The Committee has strongly recommended that these courses be started in 2007. India has ambitious plants to expand healthcare facilities at all levels. The Corporate and Private Sector Hospitals are being built. However, during exercise of establishing 6 new AIIMS type Institutes and upgrading 13 Medical Colleges, a serious difficulty was experienced in locating qualified Hospital Architects and Hospital Engineers. Also the Management of Hospital Engineering Services including building, plants, machinery, equipments require high calibre engineers for efficient running of hospitals. These are micro-specialties in wider areas of public health. The Ministry of Health & Family Welfare plans to advise states to develop Health Engineering Courses at Master's, Post-Diploma and Technician level.

162. (11-4-2007) NEW DELHI : The Minister for Development of North East Region, Shri Mani Shankar Aiyar outlined the key areas to be developed in North East Region in order to enhance economic development and investment in the region. Speaking on the concluding day, of the 3rd North East Business Summit, Mr. Aiyar chalked out the areas of potential collaboration between India and Thailand. The Minister of Commerce of Thailand, Mr. Krirk-Krai Jirapaet was the chief guest in this Session. Mr. Aiyar said that the development of the NE Region cannot happen unless and until the neighbouring countries are recognized and joint effort is made for progress. He said that in the last 30 years Thailand has done remarkable amount of development and there is no reason why NE

Region cannot do the same? He said the geographical and bio-diversity features of Thailand and NE India are very similar. Mr. Aiyar said that Thailand has made excellent forays in road construction and it would be of great advantage to the NE Region if Thailand can partner in this area. He said that Government intends to spend $15 billion on road construction in NE in the next 5 years. Mr. Aiyar said that the second area of collaboration of Thailand could be river transport segment. He said that with Thailand's cooperation all three rivers *i.e.*, the Brahmaputra, the Barak and the Kaladan can be made navigational to aid trade and transport. Mr. Aiyar said that third area of cooperation could be the natural rubber industry. He said that the given potential of NE it is possible that in future this Region accounts for 80 percent of India's natural rubber production. The DoNER Minister said that the Thai and NE silk is also very similar and a collaboration is possible in this area also. He said that to promote partnership in trade, investment, technology and entrepreneurship between the people of NE and Thailand an institute will be set up in NE to teach the Thai language. The two-day summit which concluded today saw participation of representatives of Government, business people and other delegates.

163. (11-4-2007) NEW DELHI : President, Shri APJ Abdul Kalam conferred five Kirti Chakras and twenty three Shaurya Chakras to armed forces / paramilitary personnel and civilians for displaying conspicuous gallantry, indomitable courage and extreme devotion to duty at a solemn ceremony in Rashtrapati Bhawan, New Delhi today. The President also conferred twelve Param Vishisht Seva Medals, one Bar to Ati Vishisht Seva Medal, twenty nine Ati Vishisht Seva Medals to senior officers of the Armed Forces for distinguished service of an exceptional order.

164. (11-4-2007) NEW DELHI : The President Dr. APJ Abdul Kalam, awarded Kirti Chakras to Col Gurbir Singh Sarna and Maj James Thomas-both martyrs, here today. The gallantry awards were received by Mrs. Jasleen Kaur and Mrs. Nitha James, respectively. Eight Shaurya Chakras were also awarded posthumously and received by the next of kin of martyrs. These are Lt. Col Vinay Rao Chauhan, Capt. Shashi Bhushan Singh, Naib Subedar Raj Bahadur, CHM Sarabjit Singh, Naik Gurjant Singh, Sepoy Satnam Singh, Rifleman HB Singh, and Gunner Ranjeet Singh. Col GS Sarna was commanding 29 Rashtriya Rifles and was martyred in a gallant action against militants in Pattan District (J&K) on 23 Dec. 2006. Maj James Thomas of 10 Sikh Light Infantry laid down his life fighting the militants in Poonch District (J&K) on 28 Jan 2006. All those awarded Shaurya Chakras posthumously lost their lives in J&K expect Rifleman HB Singh of 7 Assam Rifle who was laid down his life in the North East. Amongst other awardees, the seniormost to receive Param Vishisht Seva Medal is Lt. Gen Aditya Singh, Southern Army Commander. Lt. Gen Paramjit Singh, DGDS and Lt. Gen RK Mehta, Military Advisor in UN HQ at New York are amongst other awardees for this recognition. Ten Shaurya Chakras, and 15 Ati Vishisht Seva Medals have also been awarded to serving Army personnel.

165. (11-4-2007) NEW DELHI : Shri Murli Deora, Minister of Petroleum & Natural Gas has called upon the dealers of petroleum products (petrol & diesel) to call off their proposed agitation and a call to close retail outlets. He expressed hope that the dealers will appreciate that the strike serves nobody's cause and leads to totally avoidable inconvenience to the customers. At a meeting with the representatives of the Federation of All India Petroleum Traders (FAIPT), here today, Shri Deora pointed out that the Government has always been sympathetic to their genuine demands. It may be recalled that the concerted efforts of Shri Murli Deora resulted in Maharashtra Government recently effecting substantial reduction in the sales tax on petrol and diesel which addressed a long pending demand of the retail dealers in Maharashtra. He said that Government will endeavour to take a decision on the demand of the FAIPT for increase in commission on petrol and diesel by 1st May after consultation with Oil Marketing Companies (OMCs). Regarding the issue of raising stock variation ceiling, the representatives of the federation were informed that a study by Indian Institute of Petroleum (IIP) has already been commissioned to study the impact of different climatic conditions in India on petrol and diesel stocks. The IIP will be submitting its report by middle of July which will be examined expeditiously for appropriate decision. The issue of stock variation requires in-depth and serious scientific studies before effecting any change in the present norms. The meeting was attended by Shri A.K. Badhwar, President, FAIPT and other representatives of the FAIPT. The Minister of State for Petroleum & Natural Gas Shri Dinsha Patel and senior officers of the Ministry were also present.

166. (11-4-2007) NEW DELHI : India and Kuwait has signed a Memorandum of Understanding on Labour, Employment and Manpower Development. The MoU was signed by Shri Vayalar Ravi, Minister of Overseas Indian Affairs with Sheikh Sabah Al-Khaled Al-Hamad Al-Sabah, Minister of Social Affairs and Labour of Kuwait during his visit to Kuwait from April 7-10, 2007. The MoU provides for further strengthening of cooperation between the two countries in the area of labour employment and manpower development. It sets out various parameters governing the welfare of the workers in the private sector in line with the laws and regulations of the host country. It provides a mechanism for settlement of labour disputes. The MoU addresses issues relating to the protection and welfare of workers not covered under the Kuwaiti Labour Law. The document provides for the constitutions of a Joint Working Group by early next year to further study ways and means of improving the conditions of the workers, including skills upgradation and addressing issues of mutual concern. The Joint Working Group will meet in each other's country alternately every six months. Shri Ravi also had extensive discussions with Sheikh Sabah Al-Khaled Al-Hamad Al-Sabah. The focus of discussions was on the presence of the large Indian community in Kuwait and related issues. Bilateral, regional and international developments of mutual interest were also touched upon during the discussions. The distinguished leaders of the State of Kuwait appreciated the role and contribution of the Indian community in Kuwait towards Kuwait's welfare and development. Mr. Ravi met with a wide cross-section of the Indian community, both collectively and individually. He discussed issues of concern affecting the welfare of the large Indian community. One of the major issues related to the situation in the region of Abbassiya, which was taken up with the leadership of Kuwait and with of Farwaniya. The Minister was assured that adequate steps would be taken to ensure the safety and security of the community in this area. The Indian community in Kuwait numbers around 550,000. He also invited Sheith Sabah Al-Khaled Al-Hamad Al-Sabah, Minister of Social Affairs and Labour of the State of Kuwait to visit India.

167. (11-4-2007) NEW DELHI : National Rural Employment Guarantee Act (NREGA) during the first year of its implementation in 200 districts has generated 72.93 crore persondays of employment on 6.68 lakh works. 40.76% of employment opportunities were availed by women, 37.72% by members of ST and 24.7% by SC. Under the programme, 1.83 crore households were provided with employment up to February 2007. The amendment to the Schedule I of the Act has further expanded the scope of works which can now be taken up in the lands of individual beneficiaries. The amendment to the Schedule II has permitted starting of the new work with 10 workers relaxing the earlier limit of 50 workers. The focus of the programme remained on water conservation and harvesting. In a recently held workshop on Experience Sharing in New Delhi with the participation of selected District Programme Coordinators (DPCs) from every State, several best practices and innovations adopted in the implementation of NREGA were discussed at length and some of them have been identified for adoption in the newly added 113 NREGA districts. Some such practices are printing the main provisions of NREGA and RTI Acts and telephone numbers of key district functionaries on the cover page of job cards, payment of wage through Post Offices and Banks and colour codes for copies of master rolls at Gram Panchayat, Block and District level as a precaution against tampering. Further, holding of Panchayat Vikas Utsav in clusters of 4-5 Panchayats and involvement of Self-Help Groups from BPL families in awareness creation, implementation of works and social audit process have also been encouraged. The Ministry of Rural Development in an Orientation Workshop held here has advised the DPCs from the newly added districts to follow such practices in the implementation of the programme for better results.

168. (11-4-2007) NEW DELHI : Labour figures in the Concurrent List in the Constitution. Thus, both Centre and States can legislate and enforce labour laws. There are 43 central labour laws enacted by the Central Government concerning different aspects of labour. 12 of these laws are enforced by the Central Government, 16 by both Centre and the State Governments and 15 laws by the State Governments. There are also about 91 state labour laws enacted and enforced by the State Governments in their respective domain.

169. (11-4-2007) NEW DELHI : A meeting of District Collectors of High Malaria Endemic Districts was inaugurated today by the Union Minister for Health &

Family Welfare, Dr. Anbumani Ramadoss. Shri Naresh Dayal, Secretary (H&FW), Dr. R.K. Srivastava, DGHS and other senior officials of the Ministry were also present at the meeting. In his address, the Minister said that the office of the District Collector is the cornerstone of the district administration as well as the success of all programmes including disease control programmes is largely determined by the initiative and enterprise of the District Collector. We have made the District Collector the Chairman of the District Health Society for this very reason including timely release of funds. For control of malaria, therefore, I need not underline your leadership role and responsibility, but I would like to urge your personal involvement and driving force in boosting up the district health setup for malaria control. There is ample evidence that anti-malaria programmes have been successful only because of the wholehearted cooperation extended by the district administration.

170. (11-4-2007) NEW DELHI : One Cheetah helicopter of Indian Air Force crashed near Amar Post in Central Siachen Glacier this morning. Both the pilots suffered fatal injuries. The helicopter had taken off from Siachen base camp and was on a routine flying mission. A court of inquiry has been ordered to investigate the incident. The Defence Minister Shri A K Antony has conveyed his heart-felt condolences to the bereaved families. The Government has deeply appreciated the cooperation extended by the Pakistan authorities in aerial and ground based rescue operations.

171. (11-4-2007) NEW DELHI : Shri Kamal Nath, Union Minister of Commerce & Industry, had a bilateral meeting with Mr. Krirk-krai Jirapaet, Minister of Commerce of Thailand here today. The discussions covered review of bilateral trade and bilateral investments, with both the Ministers underlining the scope for substantially stepping up the level of two-way trade, which stood at US $ 2.2 billion in 2005-06 (comprising US $ 1 billion worth of India's exports to Thailand and India's imports from Thailand valued at US $ 1.2 billion). India's exports to Thailand registered a growth of almost 20% over the previous year, while imports from Thailand increased by about 39%. With regard to investments, while several major Indian companies have invested in Thailand, in the post-liberalisation era, Thailand too had emerged as an important investor in India with foreign direct investment (FDI) inflows of about US $ 77.6 million from August 1991 to December 2006. Thailand now ranks 27th largest investor in India and the 3rd largest from the ASEAN region, after Singapore and Malaysia. There is a Framework Agreement for establishing a Free Trade Area (FTA) between India and Thailand which was signed by the two governments in October 2003 in Bangkok, covering goods, services and investment and areas of cooperation. The Framework Agreement also provides for a Early Harvest Scheme (EHS) under which common items of export interest to the sides have been agreed for elimination of tariffs on a fast track basis. The tariff concessions on 82 items of EHS list have been implemented with effect from 1/9/2004 with the signing of the Protocol between India and

Thailand in August 2004 in New Delhi. India Thailand Trade Negotiating Committee (TNC) has been constituted to carry forward the programme of negotiations as per the Framework Agreement. Nine meetings of the TNC have been held so far. During these meetings, discussions are being held on the texts of the Agreement on Trade in Goods, Services and Investment and also on the Rules of Origin for the FTA.

172. (11-4-2007) NEW DELHI : Following is the text of Finance Minister, Shri P. Chidambaram's speech delivered at 32nd Annual Conference of International Organisation of Securities Commissions at Mumbai today: "I am happy that the Securities and Exchange Board of India has the honour to host the 32nd Annual Conference of the International Organisation of Securities Commissions (IOSCO). On behalf of the Government of India, may I extend a warm welcome to the delegates to this conference? May I also congratulate SEBI, and its Chairman, for the excellent arrangements made for the conference? Many years ago, I was advised that, at a dinner, one should speak well but not too wisely and eat wisely but not too well. A conference of capital market regulators is more challenging than a sumptuous dinner. It is the only market that I know that will react to the arch of an eyebrow or a meaningful cough. I wonder if I should speak to you wisely or well or do neither. Nevertheless, I shall do my best. The protection of the interests of the investors and the promotion and development of the securities market are inseparable twin objectives. These twin objectives are paramount for the securities market regulator; all other objectives are secondary and subordinate to these two. Other stakeholders-while they may be driven by the profit motive-also have the obligation to secure these twin objectives. No securities market is an island. Thanks to global flows of capital, the working of the capital market in a country-especially any precipitous rise or fall-has an effect upon other capital markets in the region as well as elsewhere in the world. Good regulation, therefore, is no longer a mere national 'public good'; it has a global dimension and it must be regarded as a global 'public good'.

173. (11-4-2007) NEW DELHI : Assam, Bihar, West Bengal, Uttar Pradesh and Orissa are more prone to floods almost every year. Other states like Arunachal Pradesh, Andhra Pradesh, Maharashtra, Meghalaya, Tripura, Chattisgarh, Himachal Pradesh, Gujarat, Karnataka, Kerala, Madhya Pradesh, Punjab and Rajasthan are also affected by floods/drainage congestion occasionally. During the financial year 2006-07, an amount of Rs.81.337 crore has been released to various State Governments by the Union Government under various plan schemes related to Flood Management. A National Water Policy has been adopted in 2002 which also deals with Flood Control and Management aspects; which envisages preparation of Master Plans for each flood prone basin, providing adequate flood cushion in water storage projects, construction of flood protection works like embankments and dykes and also non-structural measures such as flood forecasting and warning, flood plain zoning and flood proofing for the minimization of losses, as the measures for the effective flood management. As per provisions of the National Water Policy each State Government has to formulate a State Water Policy with an operational action plan.

174. (11-4-2007) NEW DELHI : The total approximate earnings of Indian Railways on originating basis during the financial year 2006-07 were Rs. 62484.02 crore compared to Rs. 53644.74 crore during the same period last year, registering an increase of 16.48 per cent. The total goods earnings have gone up from Rs. 36302.39 during fiscal 2005-06 to Rs. 42074.90 crore during 2006-07, an increase of 15.90 per cent. The total passenger revenue earnings during April '06-March '07 were Rs. 17230.53 crore compared to Rs. 15398.56 crore during the same period last year, registering an increase of 11.90 per cent. The revenue earnings from other coaching amounted to Rs. 1737.36 crore during April '06-March '07 compared to Rs. 1223.04 crore during the same period last year, an increase of 42.05 per cent. The total sundry earnings have gone up from Rs. 720.75 crore during April '05-March '06 to Rs. 1441.23 crore during April'06-March'07, an increase of 99.96 percent. The total approximate number of passengers booked during the financial year 2006-07 were 6352.07 million compared to 5932.10 million during the same period last year, showing an increase of 7.08 per cent. In the suburban and non-suburban sectors, the number of passengers booked during April'06-Marh'07 were 3517.61 million and 2834.46 million compared to 3331.89 million and 2600.21 million during the same period last year, an increase of 5.57 per cent and 9.01 per cent respectively.

175. (11-4-2007) NEW DELHI : Among the six basic principles of governance underlying the National Common Minimum Programme (NCMP) of the Government, sustained "economic growth in a manner that generates employment" has a pride of place. The NCMP also describes the small scale industries as "the most employment-intensive segment". The small scale industries of India (including the tiny industries and small scale service and business entities) have a long history of promoting economic growth that is employment-oriented and spatially widespread, and hence inclusive. This is thus rightly called the segment which provides employment next only to agriculture. A simple analysis shows that the employment intensity of the segment (registered units) is 1 person for every 1.49 lakh of rupees invested in fixed assets, as against 1 person per Rs. 5.56 lakh in the large organised sector. And, the rate of growth of employment in this segment is well above that of the population of India (1.5 per cent) or, that in the large industries segment (0.85 per cent). The contribution of this segment to the economic sinews of the nation is no less significant. Nearly 39 per cent of the gross manufacturing output and 34 per cent of the exports of India arise from these enterprises. During the last four years of the Tenth Plan, the output of the segment has recorded a real growth rate of 8.87 per cent annually. Over six thousand products manufactured by these include several sophisticated items used in high technology areas like nuclear power, missile and space programmes, information technology, biotechnology, etc. The level of exports by this segment also testifies to its overall competitiveness in the global markets. Yet, the segment does not constitute a homogeneous universe and a large majority of the units faces several challenges.

176. (11-4-2007) NEW DELHI : The Union Tourism Secretary Shri A.K. Mishra has urged the North-Eastern States to promote Bed and Breakfast Scheme wherever practicable and enable the local communities to receive visitors and plan for development of their tourist attractions. He was speaking at the 3rd North-East Business Summit here today where various stake holders discussed opportunities in the tourism sector in the North-East. Shri Mishra said the Union Tourism Ministry has been consistently providing more than 10% of its budgetary outlay for development of tourism in North-East. He said in the year 2005-06, more than Rs. 100 crore was released as against the ceiling of Rs. 79 crore and, the release during the recently concluded 2006-07 was Rs. 110 crore against the ceiling of Rs. 83 crore. Shri Mishra said the region is being projected as a destination through domestic and international media campaigns aggressively. He said the Central Government has encouraged participation of the North-Eastern Region in major domestic and international fairs and festivals. The space in Indian Pavilion at these festivals is being provided free of cost. The presence of the North-East in prestigious events like WTM-London and ITB-Berlin was impressive. Shri Mishra said that his ministry is conscious that the existence of restrictive measures such as Protected Area Permits (PAP)/Restricted Area Permits (RAP)/Inner Line Permits (ILP) is a major constraint. He said, the issue of relaxation of these artificial constraints to tourism has been taken up with the Home Ministry which, in turn, has asked for the views of the State Governments. He said, it will help matters if the State Governments can send their response quickly. He said, while promotion of tourism is necessary for economic development, at the same time we should not be unmindful of the adverse impact that mass tourism would have on fragile ecosystems of the region. Therefore, the emphasis should be on promotion of responsible and controlled tourism and not mass tourism. Shri Mishra said, there is great scope for developing niche tourism products such as River, Tea, Wildlife, Adventure, Heritage and Eco-tourism in the region. He said, we have something to learn from Bhutan in this regard-the way it has promoted limited but high value tourism.

177. (11-4-2007) NEW DELHI : The Chemicals and Fertilisers Ministry will provide Rs. 2138 crore capital subsidy to the Assam Gas Cracker Project, the foundation of which was laid by the Prime Minister Dr. Manmohan Singh at Lepetkata in Dibrugarh district on Monday. Out of this Rs. 60 crore has been provided for subsidy in this year's budget for the Ministry. The total subsidy amount to be provided by the Government is expected to be over Rs. 3,000 crore. The Ministry of Chemicals and Fertilisers will also monitor the implementation of the project through a high-powered committee led by the Secretary, Department of Chemicals and Petrochemicals. The Minister of Chemicals, Fertilisers and Steel

Shri Ram Vilas Paswan has urged the management of the joint venture project to implement the project in 50 months instead of the proposed 60 months and make it internationally competitive by bringing in world class state-of-the-art technology. He said over one lakh people will get employment opportunity in industries associated with this project and other spill over benefits of industrial development like infrastructure and transport will be there. He said better educational and health opportunities will also benefit the local population and improve their living standards. Shri Paswan said, the project will need 1108 acres of land, of which, 542 acres have been provided by the State government. The Minister urged the State government to make available the remaining required land expeditiously and fulfil other commitments. He also urged the State government to take appropriate steps to create atmosphere for industrialisation. He said, the Bramhapuram Valley Fertiliser Corporation at Namrup has improved its performance and production has increased, which has helped the farmers of the North-Eastern region through timely availability of fertilizer. Shri Paswan said the UPA Government under the leadership of Prime Minister Dr. Manmohan Singh has taken a number of path-breaking steps. He said, Public Sector Undertakings like HOCL, HIL, FACT and BPCL under the Ministry of Chemicals and Fertilisers have been revived. These undertakings were on the verge of closure after becoming sick. Besides, efforts are on to reopen the HFC/FCI plants and rehabilitate IDPL and MFL.

178. (11-4-2007) NEW DELHI : The Ministry of Rural Development has sanctioned Rs. 2.01 crore to the State Government of Haryana as extended first instalment for undertaking IEC and HRD activities relating to National Rural Drinking Water Quality Monitoring and Surveillance Programme(NRDWQM&SP) during the year 2006-07. Out of these, an amount of Rs.60.50 lakh for IEC activities and remaining Rs.140.70 lakh for HRD activities as per the guidelines under Rajiv Gandhi National Drinking Water Mission (RGNDWM). The funds for undertaking these activities are to be transferred to Community & Capacity Development Unit established in the State. This release is for plan expenditure. The funds are to be utilized for the purpose for which it is released and as per the terms and conditions. The release is on the basis of norms for each activity as per the guidelines.

179. (11-4-2007) NEW DELHI : An amount of Rs.1.88 crore to the State Government of Jharkhand as extended first instalment for undertaking IEC & HRD activities relating to National Rural Drinking Water Quality Monitoring & Surveillance Programme (NRDWQM&SP) under Rajiv Gandhi National Drinking Water Mission (RGNDWM) during the year 2006-07 has been granted by the Ministry of Rural Development. Out of these, an amount of Rs.84.56 lakh for IEC activities and remaining Rs.103.61 lakh for HRD activities should be utilized as per the guidelines. The funds for undertaking these activities are to be transferred to Community & Capacity Development Unit established in the State. This release is for plan expenditure. The funds are to be utilized for the purpose for which it is released and as per the terms and conditions. The release is on the basis of norms for each activity as per the guidelines.

180. (11-4-2007) NEW DELHI : Rajiv Gandhi National Drinking Water Mission (RGNDWM) grant-in-aid amounting to Rs.1.00 crore has been sanctioned by the Ministry of Rural Development to the State Government of Himachal Pradesh as extended first instalment for undertaking IEC & HRD activities relating to National Rural Drinking Water Quality Monitoring & Surveillance Programme (NRDWQM&SP) during the year 2006-07. Out of these, an amount of Rs.22.16 lakh for IEC activities and remaining Rs.78.39 lakh should be utilized for HRD activities as per the guidelines. The funds for undertaking these activities are to be transferred to Community & Capacity Development Unit established in the State. This release is for plan expenditure. The funds are to be utilized for the purpose for which it is released and as per the terms and conditions. The release is on the basis of norms for each activity as per the guidelines.

181. (12-4-2007) NEW DELHI : After covering nearly a 1000 km in the last three days, the SAARC Car Rally today completed the Sri Lankan leg of the Rally and returned to Colombo from Kandy. The route provided a glimpse of the amazing contrast in landscapes that Sri Lanka has been blessed with. While the picturesque Colombo-Tissamaharama coastal road is dotted with numerous beach resorts, the winding road through the tea estates of Nuwara Eliya is a unique experience. After the night halt at Tissamahara lake resort, the Rally headed for Nuwara Eliya, a beautiful hill station with numerous tea estates, on day 28. The rally was received at Kandy by the Hon'ble Governor of Kandy and taken to Sri Dalada Maligawa, also called the Temple of the Tooth. It houses Sri Lanka's most important Buddhist relic-a sacred tooth of Lord Buddha. The Temple is one of the most important centres of pilgrimage for Buddhists. The rallyists were permitted to pay their respects at the sanctum sanctorum, a rare privilege. On day 29, the Rally started from Kandy and headed for Anuradhapura, the ancient capital city of Sinhalese kings. The huge Sri Maha Bodhi tree here is the oldest historically authenticated tree in the world, having been tended by an uninterrupted succession of guardians for over 2000 years. The tree has grown from a sapling brought from Bodhgaya in India. The convoy reached Colombo in the evening and received a warm welcome. With this, the journey of the Rally cars came to an end, after driving over 9000 km through six SAARC countries. Although the Rally will officially end on day 30 at Male, only the rally participants (and not the rally cars) will go to Maldives tomorrow as a symbolic gesture.

182. (12-4-2007) NEW DELHI : The Prime Minister has conveyed his felicitations to all those associated with the successful test launch of Agni-III Missile here today. He called it, "an impressive illustration of the indigenous capacity developed by our scientists and technologists in mastering strategic high technologies essential for maintaining the nation's defence and security".

183. (12-4-2007) NEW DELHI : The Centre is quite hopeful of achieving the procurement target of 15 million tonnes of wheat this season. Citing recent procurement figures, Union Minister of State for Food and Public Distribution, Dr. Akhilesh Prasad Singh today said that latest figures of Haryana show that Government agencies have been able to procure upto 94% of the market arrivals whereas it is around 85% for Punjab. The total procurement till April 11, 2007 in Haryana is 4,26,538 MT against market arrival of 4,52,120 MT. In Punjab, the total procurement is 2,34,621 MT against the market arrival of 2,75,289 MT. The procurement have been almost 96% in Haryana and about 90% in Punjab in the last few days against a relatively sluggish rate in the 1st week of April. This also dispels the notion that the private parties are able to procure the largest chunk of the market arrivals as compared to the Government Agencies. Dr. Singh attributed the increase in procurement to the government's decision of giving an attractive bonus of Rs. 100 above the MSP and the recent government's decision to ban futures trading in rice and wheat, the benefit of which was mainly going to speculators. According to Dr. Singh, the government was keeping a close watch on the situation and would take all necessary measures to ensure that the procurement targets were reached.

184. (12-4-2007) NEW DELHI : The Conference of the State Education Ministers (April 10-11) was convened in New Delhi. This meeting with State Education Ministers coincided with the commencement of the XIth Plan, and the main objective of the conference was to jointly take stock and to plan ahead so that to achieve maximum possible progress during the XIth Plan in the education sector in terms of access, equity, quality and efficiency. Prime Minister Shri Manmohan Singh has recently stated, "For too long we have viewed the size of our population as an economic and social liability. However, an educated skilled, healthy empowered people are an asset. The challenge before us is to ensure that each and every citizen of India is an asset." We live in the era of Globalization. Liberalization and privatization are held out as the keys to economic progress. However, we are clear in our mind that when more than 40% of our population is in the age group of 6-24 and when education has been identified as the most crucial element in the national developmental effort, the role of the government in providing education has necessarily to increase and not diminish.

185. (12-4-2007) NEW DELHI : The Quick Estimates of Index of Industrial Production (IIP) with base 1993-94 for the month of February 2007 have been released by the Central Statistical Organisation of the Ministry of Statistics and Programme Implementation. The General Index stands at 252.4, which is 11.0% higher as compared to the level in the month of February 2006. The cumulative growth for the period April-February 2006-07 stands at 11.1% over the corresponding period of the pervious year. 2. The Indices of Industrial Production for the Mining, Manufacturing and Electricity sectors for the month of February 2007 stand at 168.3, 271.2, and 192.5 respectively, with the corresponding growth rates of 6.3%, 12.3% and 3.3% as compared to February 2006. The cumulative growth during April-February, 2006-07 over the corresponding period of 2005-06 in the three sectors have been 4.9%, 12.1% and 7.2% respectively, which moved the overall growth in the General Index to 11.1%. 3. In terms of industries, as many as fifteen (15) out of the seventeen (17) industry groups (as per 2-digit NIC-1987) have shown positive growth during the month of February 2007 as compared to the corresponding month of the previous year. The industry group 'Wood and Wood Products; Furniture and Fixtures' have shown the highest growth of 128.9%, followed by 27.4% in 'Basic Metal and Alloy Industries' and 16.1% in 'Cotton Textiles'. On the other hand, the industry group 'Jute and Other Vegetable Fibre Textiles (except cotton)' have shown a negative growth of 88.0% followed by 2.2% in 'Metal Products and Parts, except Machinery and Equipment'. 4. As per Use-based classification, the Sectoral growth rates in February 2007 over February 2006 are 10.4% in Basic goods, 18.2% in Capital goods and 13.7% in Intermediate goods. The Consumer durables and Consumer non-durables have recorded growth of 1.6% and 9.7% respectively, with the overall growth in Consumer goods being 7.6%. 5. Alongwith the Quick Estimates of IIP for February 2007, the indices for January 2007 have undergone the first revision and those for November 2006 have undergone the second (final) revision in the light of the updated data received from the source agencies. There are no significant revisions in the indices for November 2006 and January 2007. 6. Statements giving Quick Estimates of the Index of Industrial Production at Sectoral, 2-digit level of National Industrial Classification (NIC)-1987 and by Use-based classification for the month of February 2007, along with the growth rates over the corresponding month of previous year, including the cumulative indices and growth rates, are enclosed.

186. (12-4-2007) NEW DELHI : The Defence Minister Shri AK Antony has congratulated the Defence Scientists on the successful flight-test of the Intermediate Range Ballistic Missile Agni-III from the Wheeler Island, off the coast of Orissa this morning. Shri Antony spoke to the DRDO Chief Shri M Natarajan and the Mission Director Shri Avinash Chander over telephone and told them that the nation is proud of the achievement of the scientists. Shri Antony said what really gladdens his heart is that the scientists were not deterred by the partially unsuccessful test of Agni-III last year and put their heart and soul into making today's test an unqualified success. He said today's success also strengthens our view that the Indian Scientists have the ability to design and develop critical and strategic systems through indigenous efforts. Shri Antony also stated that the country has matured in missile technology and is today at par with many other developed countries. He said, Agni-III has confirmed India's strategic capability for minimum credible deterrence.

187. (12-4-2007) NEW DELHI : The Union Cabinet today gave its approval for introduction of a Bill titled "The Gram Nyayalayas Bill, 2007" with certain consequential changes, in the Parliament in the ensuing session of Parliament and also to incur necessary recurring expenditure from the Consolidated Fund of India to the tune of Rs. 324.29 crores per annum towards the establishment of the Gram Nyayalayas. The Government of India and the State Governments will share the recurring expenditure for first three years. The Bill seeks to provide for the establishment of Gram Nyayalayas for every Panchayat at intermediate level or for a group of contiguous Panchayats at intermediate level throughout the country except the State of Jammu and Kashmir. However, proposed legislation will come into force in a State on such date as may be notified by the Central Government and different dates may be notified for different States. The Gram Nyayalaya will be the lowest court of subordinate judiciary in a State and shall be in addition to the regular civil and criminal courts. The Gram Nyayalayas will exercise both civil and criminal cases of a simple nature as specified in the Schedule to the proposed legislation. The Gram Nyayalaya will be presided over by a Nyayadhikari who shall be qualified to be eligible to be a Judicial Magistrate first class and shall be appointed by the State Government in consultation with the Chief Justice of the High Court concerned. The Nyayalaya will follow summary procedure in criminal cases and a simple procedure having regard to the principles of natural justice in civil cases. This legislation will reduce considerable number of pending cases in subordinate judiciary. It will give a system of judiciary which will be less expensive, free from protracted procedural wrangles, quick and available at the grassroots level, accessible to the common man and render justice to him as enshrined in article 39A of the Constitution.

188. (12-4-2007) NEW DELHI : The Union Cabinet today gave its approval for signing of the Agreement in order to facilitate the transfer of foreign convicted prisoners to their home countries and prisoners of Indian origin are brought to India to serve the remaining part of their sentence. Earlier, there was no legal provision either in the Code of Criminal procedure, or any other law, under which foreign prisoners could be transferred to the country of their origin to serve the remaining part of their sentence; nor was there a provision for the transfer of prisoners of India origin convicted by a foreign court to serve their sentence in India. This Agreement would enable the prisoners to be near their families and would help in the process of their social rehabilitation.

189. (12-4-2007) NEW DELHI : The Cabinet Committee on Economic Affairs today gave its approval for: (i) Inclusion of 780 km of National Highways in Bihar for upgradation as four lane highways under NHDP Phase-IIIA over and above the approved length of 4035 km under NHDP Phase IIIA on the condition that the procedure for clearance for PPPAC would be followed. With this inclusion, total length of National Highways to be upgraded under NHDP Phase III would be 4815 km. (ii) Implementation (four laning) of 780 km of National Highways on BOT (Toll) mode at an estimated cost of Rs.6782 crore including cost of land acquisition, utility shifting, rehabilitation and resettlement, consultancy, etc. within the ceiling of 40% of viability gap funding (grant) in accordance with implementation mechanism. (iii) As some of the sections (such as Mokama-Muker Section of NH-80, Muzzafarpur-Sonbarsa Section of NH-77, Motihari-Raxaul Section of NH-28A and Forbesgenj-Jogbani Section of NH-57A) approved to be taken up on BOT (Toll) have very low traffic volume and probably higher maintenance cost than the toll collected in these sections, it is likely that there will be no response to bids for BOT (Toll) projects. In that event, CCEA gave approval to take up these sections [unviable on BOT (Toll) mode] on BOT (Annuity) mode without any further clearance from CCEA, if no response to the bids on BOT (Toll) is received, after at least two advertisements. Upgradation of existing road will improve traffic safety and provide faster movement of vehicles with improved riding quality and time. This will lead to reduction in vehicle operating cost and significant reduction in fuel consumption for the vehicle resulting in energy conservation. This will also provide linkage to other corridors of high density / Economic importance / tourism / pilgrimage centres in the state of Bihar.

190. (12-4-2007) NEW DELHI : The Union Cabinet today gave its approval for signing the Agreement in the field of Vaccine Research by India and International Institute of Vaccine, Seoul, Korea. International Vaccine Institute (IVI), with headquarters at Seoul, South Korea is an autonomous organization set up at the initiative of the united Nations Development Programme under the Vienna Convention of 1969. IVI is an international centre of research, training & technical assistance for vaccine production in developing countries. The Agreement shall encourage cooperation between India and the international Vaccine Institute. By the agreement, India could offer a place on Board of Trustees, and would be able to play a role in formulation of international policy related to vaccines. Signatories to the IVI Establishment Agreement as of March 2002 are Republic of Korea, China, Brazil, Egypt, Pakistan, Netherlands, Sri Lanka, Sweden, Bangladesh, Bhutan, Ecuador, Indonesia, Israel, Jamaica, Kazakhstan, Kyrgyzstan, Lebanon, Malta, Mongolia, Myanmar, Nepal, Oman, Panama Papua New Guinea, Peru, Philippines, Romania, Senegal, Tajikistan, Thailand, Turkey, Uzbekistan, Vietnam and World Health Organization. The signing of the Agreement does not have any financial implication for the Government of India. On the other hand, it will give opportunities for inputs to the direction and priorities of IVI, which would be beneficial to India.

191. (12-4-2007) NEW DELHI : The Cabinet Committee on Economic Affairs today gave its approval for award of 3 sub-projects for Four Laning of Khalghat-MP / Maharashtra border section of NH-3 (total 82.8 kms), Hazaribagh-Ranchi section of NH-33 (total 71.16 km) and Rohtak-Hissar section of NH-10 (total 89.36 km). Total projected cost excluding land acquisition of the 3 sub-projects are amounted to Rs.549 crore, 524 crore and 543 crore respectively.

192. (12-4-2007) NEW DELHI : The Cabinet Committee on Economic Affairs today gave its approval for undertaking the Project for Rs.557.0 crore for providing

4 lane NH Connectivity to the proposed International Container Transshipment Terminal (ICTT) at Vallarpadam, Cochin, Kerala using cess funds. This project has been undertaken as per commitment given to the Licensee of ICTT. Being a first Container Transshipment Terminal in India, considerable savings in transshipment cost currently incurred via third country ports (Colombo) are expected. The Project will be implemented by NHAI and is to be completed within a period of 30 months and will be commencing from April, 2007.

193. (12-4-2007) NEW DELHI : The Union Cabinet today gave its approval for signing of a MoU on cooperation in the fields of Agriculture and allied sectors with Uganda. The Agreement will be signed during the upcoming proposed visit of Minister of State for Agriculture to Uganda and Rwanda. MoU will be valid for a period of five (5) years from the date of signatures and will automatically be renewed for a subsequent period of five years. MoU will promote further bilateral cooperation through joint activities and exchanges in the areas of agricultural activities and also through exchange of scientific delegations and experts between the two countries.

194. (12-4-2007) NEW DELHI: Union Human Resource Development (HRD) Minister Arjun Singh on Wednesday said the Government would approach the Supreme Court in a couple of days as part of its steps to ensure that reservation for Other Backward Classes (OBCs) in higher education institutions under the Centre becomes operational from the coming academic session. Responding to questions on the situation arising out of the interim order staying the implementation of OBC reservation, Mr. Singh said: "We will file a petition in the next couple of days but I cannot say what our prayer will be." To a question on the impact of the stay on admissions, he said: "I hope the court will take into consideration the case of the students affected by the interim order."

195. (12-4-2007) NEW DELHI : The Cabinet Committee on Economic Affairs, on the recommendations of the CACP, today gave its approval for the fixation of Minimum Support Price (MSP) of TD-5 grade of Jute ex-Assam for 2007-08 season at Rs.1055 per quintal. The approved MSP for TD-5 grade of jute ex-Assam for the year 2007-08 is higher by Rs.55 per quintal over the prices approved by the Government for the year 2006-07. The corresponding minimum support price for other varieties and grades of raw jute across locations be fixed keeping in view, apart from normal market price differentials, the aggregate scores assigned to different grades. The Jute Corporation of India will continue as the Central nodal agency to undertake price support operations and the losses incurred, if any, will be reimbursed by Government of India. The enhancement of MSP will protect the interest of Jute growers through assured remunerative prices.

196. (12-4-2007) NEW DELHI : The Union Cabinet today gave its approval to the MoU signed between India and UAE in the field of Manpower. The MoU was signed on 13th December, 2006 during the visit of the Labour Minister of the UAE, H.E. Dr. Ali Bin Abdulla Al-Kaabi to India. Although we have bilateral labour agreements with Qatar and Jordan, there was no such bilateral arrangement with the UAE so far. A bilateral agreement or MoU is especially important in the case of countries like the UAE since the local labour laws do not cover the workers in the informal sector. The Cabinet's decision would benefit the Indian workers especially the un-skilled, semi-skilled and skilled workers. The MoU has come into effect immediately and will be valid for 4 years. It will automatically extend by another 4 years each time thereafter unless either of the parties notifies its intention to terminate it.

197. (12-4-2007) NEW DELHI : At a function organized by the Army Wives Welfare Association (AWWA) at the Army Public School here today, the Chief of the Army Staff General JJ Singh, released the Teachers Manual and Guide and the Army Pre Schools Ready Reckoner. The event marks a paradigm shift with the training of teachers as well as imparting education to pre school children through a process of standardization, innovation and creativity. It also marks simultaneous implementation of the curriculum in 250 schools of the army, benefiting 40,000 children and improving the professional skills of 1800 teachers. With dedicated support from NCERT, Mrs. Anupama Singh, President AWWA, Mrs. Vibha Parthasarathy and Mrs. Anjali Arora have been actively involved in this project. Speaking on the occasion Gen JJ Singh said that wards of Army personnel who are posted from one location to another would benefit immensely from standardisation of syllabus and teaching methodologies. He also lauded the efforts of AWWA to take a lead in this direction and synchronise the expertise of NCERT, eminent educationists and teachers to achieve this standardisation.

198. (12-4-2007) NEW DELHI : Union Minister for Statistics & Programme Implementation, Shri G. K. Vasan today called upon the Statisticians to develop a strong data base on various socio-economic parameters to help the Central and State Governments in developing planning and policy formulation. Inaugurating the two-day Conference of Central and State Statistical Organization on "Training of Trainers" for 64th Round of National Sample Survey he said Core Statistics critical to the development of economy should be identified to evolve national policies and priorities relating to the statistical system. He said the Statistical system is being re-engineered to produce reliable and timely data on all important aspects to guide the development strategy. Statistical advice has more reliable and timely solutions than committee of experts. To formulate effective policies and programmes for eliminating poverty, the Statistical System need to provide reliable data base for estimating the incidence of poverty in different regions, he said. Mr. Vasan said the subjects for 64th Round have been picked up keeping in mind the priorities of Government and objectives of the Eleventh Five Year Plan. Beginning from 1st July, 2007, the National Sample Survey would cover expenditure in education, migration, employment & unemployment and consumer expenditure. The subjects would provide sound data base for taking evidence based policy decisions in these critical sectors in conjunction with the objectives and priorities of the Central Government. The Chairman of the National Statistical Commission, Prof. S.D. Tendulkar said the collection of statistics act is being amended to bring even the socio-economic survey under the ambit of the Act. The initiative would fail in achieving the objective unless investigators have the skill to establish rapport with the respondents and collect quality data. He said a comprehensive survey on education is being carried out after a gap of over ten years. New items of information have been included in the survey instruments to capture information on drop outs, frequency of migration from one institute to another, number of courses simultaneously pursued and great stagnation. The Survey would contribute significantly to understanding education scenario in the country. He said drop out from the education system despite governmental intervention including Sarva Shiksha Abhiyan is a major cause of concern. Data would also be collected on seasonal migration or movement in search of employment to enlighten planners on the socio-economic implications of this dimension. Dr. Pronab Sen, Chief Statistician of India said that the era of liberalization has ushered in significant structural changes in the economy which need to be captured by the Statistical system. Consequent changes in the role and responsibility of NSS in meeting these demands has been most pertinent issue.

199. (12-4-2007) NEW DELHI : The Ministry of Minority Affairs is formulating a number of schemes during the current financial year (2007-08) for the benefit of minority communities. Out of an allocation of Rs.500 crore, a sum of Rs.310 crore has been provided for the proposed schemes, namely Pre-Matric scholarship, Post-Matric scholarship, Multi Sectoral Development Programme and Grant-in-Aid to State Channelising Agencies (MCAs) engaged in national Minorities Development Finance Corporation (NMDFC) programmes. Under the Pre-Matric Scholarship programme for minorities 80,000 school going children up to class X will be benefited. The scheme is meant to provide quality education, reduce the financial burden of parents in supporting school education and enable students complete education up to secondary level. Rs.80 crore has been allocated for this purpose during 2007-08. 75,000 scholarships will be provided under Post-Matric Scholarship Programme for persuing Technical and Vocational Courses for classes XIth and XIIth and also for general courses at Undergraduate and Post-graduate levels. An outlay of Rs.100 crore has been made under the programme during the current financial year. Under the Multi Sectoral Development Programme for Minorities in selected minority concentration districts, Rs.120 crore has been provided to address the development deficits in the identified districts. Grant-in-Aid to the tune of Rs. 10 crore will be provided to State Channelising Agencies (SCAs) implementing the National Minorities Development & Finance Corporation (NDMFC) Programmes for strengthening their infrastructure, manpower and resources. Further, a sum of Rs.190 crore has been provided for the ongoing schemes of Ministry like Grant-in-Aid to Maulana Azad Education Foundation (MAEF), Coaching and Allied schemes for economically weaker sections of the minorities, Research/Studies, Monitoring and Evaluation of development schemes and Merit cum Means Scholarship for professional and technical courses during the current year.

200. (12-4-2007) NEW DELHI : The first meeting of the Indo-Brazil joint working group was held here for organizing of the weeks of Indian culture in Brazil and Brazilian culture in India. It was proposed during the meeting that the Cultural Festival of Brazil in India will take place during the months of January-March, 2008 and Cultural Festival of India in Brazil in July-September, 2008. Both sides agreed to hold Visual Art Exhibitions, display of performing arts, academic exchanges and seminars and Food Festivals during the Cultural Festivals. Sangeet Natak Academy, Lalit Kala Academy, Sahitya Academy, the National School of Drama, National Museum, Ministry of Information and Broadcasting, ITDC will actively participate in the Cultural Festivals. It was proposed to hold the next meeting of the JWG in Brazil in August-September, 2007 whereby the Indian side could also see the venues at Brazil. The probable cities where the cultural festival could travel in Brazil are Sao Paulo, Brasilia, Rio and Salvador. The Brazilian festival in India is proposed to be held in New Delhi and some of the events could possibly be taken to some other cities also like Mumbai, Kolkata and Chennai.

201. (12-4-2007) NEW DELHI : Indian Railways have carried 728.41 million tonnes of revenue earning freight traffic against the target of 726.00 million tonnes during the financial year 2006-07. The freight carried shows an increase of 61.21 million tonnes over the freight traffic of 667.20 million tonnes actually carried during the corresponding period last year, an increase of 9.17 per cent. During the month of March 2007, the revenue earning freight traffic carried by Indian Railways was 72.05 million tonnes. There is an increase of 5.86 million tonnes over the actual freight traffic of 66.19 million tonnes actually carried by the Indian Railways during the same period last year, an increase of 8.85 per cent.

202. (12-4-2007) NEW DELHI : Rs.1353 crore have been released as the first instalment of central assistance for the projects under the Jawaharlal Nehru National Urban Renewal Mission during 2006-07. Out of the approved projects, 64 are for water supply, 39 for sewerage, 39 for road and flyovers, 27 for drainage and 20 for solid waster management. 205 projects have been approved involving a total cost of Rs. 17,000 crore. These projects will get central assistance of about Rs. 8300 crore. 62 cities have prepared city development plans, 49 cities have signed Memorandum of Agreement with the Urban Development Ministry with regard to reform agenda and implementation schedule. 28 cities and Union Territories have submitted their detailed project reports with regard to submission Urban Infrastructure and Governance. Rs. 1184 crore have been released as first instalment of central assistance for projects under the Urban Infrastructure Development Scheme for Small and Medium Towns, UIDSSMT during 2006-07. 328 projects have been approved for 274 towns involving a total cost of Rs. 4204.62 crore. The Government will release 3382.36 crore as central grant for the projects during the implementation period. Secretary, Urban Development Ministry Shri M.Ramachandran took a review meeting of the progress of the JNNURM projects with the senior officials of his Ministry. The Government is giving top priority to drinking water, sewerage, drainage and solid waste management schemes in mission cities. Shri Ramachandran convened a meeting of all States and UT secretaries of Urban Development in Kochi on 14th of April 2007. The meeting will discuss issues including capacity building at States and City levels, monitoring and implementation of JNNURM projects, urban infrastructure development schemes for small and medium towns, community participation, new technologies in sewerage and solid waste management, resource mobilization for urban local bodies, measures to improve urban governments, reduction in water wastage and initiatives to improve public transport in cities.

203. (12-4-2007) NEW DELHI : Vice President, Shri Bhairon Singh Shekhawat has said that it is not easy to craft a healthcare strategy for 26 crores of poor people who are inhabiting the margins of the society, facing formidable problems of inadequate nutrition, unhygienic conditions and accompanying health hazards. Therefore, problems of food security, safe drinking water and adequate sanitation are some of the key areas of priority in the rural healthcare system. Our mission should be to serve the poor and the deprived and to help them in enjoying their fundamental right to live, not simply to live but to live with dignity. Every citizen of the country has a right to have access to affordable healthcare so that he or she can lead a dignified life. Shri Shekhawat while inaugurating Smt. Radhikabai Meghe Memorial College of Nursing Building and the Auditorium at Wardha this morning said that given India's size, its limited resources and vast segment of poor people living below the poverty line, it is certainly not an easy task to put in place a dependable public healthcare system. We need to constantly harness the resources of the private sector and the civil society to supplement the government's efforts and to meet the ever-expanding demand for medical care. Our Panchayati Raj Institutions, properly empowered, have the potential to bring about an effective rural healthcare system. Participation of the people, in managing and overseeing the functioning of the health sector, especially in rural areas can be an important factor in improving the health sector. He said that healthcare is a crucial component in promoting the quality of life of the people. Good health of the people is not only a desirable goal but also an essential investment in human resource development. Our achievement in healthcare during last six decades is, no doubt, a story of some great successes. Significant improvements have been achieved in several key health indicators, besides sizeable increase in the life span of our people. We have developed life saving drugs and medical devices for curing many chronic diseases, besides reasonably improving the health infrastructure.

204. (12-4-2007) NEW DELHI : It is imperative to augment facilities for Cancer treatment as it has now become one of the ten leading causes of death. It is estimated that over 7 lakh new cases of cancer and 3 lakh deaths occur annually due to cancer. Nearly 15 lakh patients require facilities for diagnosis, treatment and follow-up at a given time. With the commissioning of the Linear Accelerator, this Medical Institute will be able to provide qualitative cancer treatment to the poor in this backward region of Vidarbha. While commissioning in indigenously built Linear Accelerator in Mahatma Gandhi Institute of Medical Sciences at Wardha this afternoon, Shri Shekhawat said that for a long time he has been committed to the cause of cancer care and treatment. When he was Chief Minister of Rajasthan in the year 1992, he had motivated the people, gathered in large numbers for the Mahavir Jayanti celebrations, to generously donate for setting up a cancer hospital in Jaipur. There was a spontaneous response to his appeal and more than Rs. 40 lakhs were collected on the spot. A plot of Government land was allotted. The project was completed in record time. Today, the Bhagawan Mahavir Cancer Hospital is doing an excellent service. He has been visiting this Hospital every year on his birthday to spend some time with the cancer patients. This Hospital is a glowing example of public-private partnership model in the area of cancer treatment. Shri Shekhawat said that there is a great need for an affordable healthcare for the poor. In our country where about 26 % people are still below the poverty line, this is certainly a formidable challenge. It is of crucial importance that we evolve a comprehensive agenda for improving medical and healthcare services which are inclusive of coverage of the poor and the deprived sections. He believes that key to an affordable and reliable healthcare system lies in the intelligent integration of all systems of medicines-Allopathy as well as Unani, Homoeopathy, Ayurveda and Yoga. We need to formulate a policy based on utilizing the best elements which reflect the strength of traditional and modern systems for ensuring affordable universal healthcare. Also, with the use of information technology, we should deepen the reach of medical facilities even upto the remotest areas. He appreciated that this Institute has always been engaged in enriching the community oriented healthcare. He hopes that this Institute will also be evolving a suitable model of universal healthcare particularly to make access to basic health services affordable to the poor and the deprived. After reaching the Institute, he garlanded the portraits of Mahatma Gandhi and Dr. Sushila Nayar. Mr. D. S. Mehta, President, Kasturba Health Society in his welcome speech gave a brief account of the activities of the Institute. After this programme, Shri Shekhawat left for Bangalore.

205. (12-4-2007) NEW DELHI : Ministry of Water Resources has requested other Central Ministries/Departments of Railways, Defence, Posts, Telecommunications, Central Public Works Department and National Highways Authority of India to provide roof top rain water harvesting structures in the buildings under their control. To promote roof top rain water harvesting in rural areas, Ministry of Water Resources is implementing a demonstrative scheme through Non-Government Organizations under which funding is provided for construction of roof top rain water harvesting structures for collection of rain water for drinking and use in toilets constructed for girls' in Girls' Schools in the states.

The Central Ground Water Authority (CGWA) has directed the Chief Secretaries of the concerned States to take all measures to adopt artificial recharge to ground water/promote rain water harvesting in all the Over-exploited areas falling under their jurisdiction and ensure inclusion of roof top rain water harvesting in the building bye-laws. CGWA has issued directions to Group Housing Societies, Industries, Farm Houses, etc. in the notified areas of Delhi, Faridabad, Gurgaon and Ghaziabad and other areas of NCT Delhi where ground water table is below 8 metres from ground surface, to adopt rain water harvesting system. CGWA promotes rain water harvesting and artificial recharge of ground water by conducting mass awareness/training programmes throughout the country involving Central/State Governments/Non-Government Organizations/Voluntary Organizations/Resident Welfare Associations/Educational Institutions/Industries and Individuals. So far, the CGWA has conducted 207 training programmes and 290 mass awareness programmes. During 2006-07, 26 mass awareness programmes and 32 training programmes have been conducted.

206. (12-4-2007) NEW DELHI : Indian scientists today achieved a major milestone in missile technology when they successfully conducted the flight test of the Intermediate Range Ballistic Missile (IRBM)-AGNI III from the Wheeler Island, off the coast of Orissa at 10.50 this morning. The 16 meter long missile weighing 48 tonnes, lifted off successfully from its Rail Mobile Launcher System leaving a trail of orange and yellow smoke. The missile which has a range of more than 3000 kms is capable of carrying a pay load of 1.5 Tonnes. The trajectory of AGNI III is computed by the onboard computer system based on the launch and target coordinates. During the flight the missile has no communication with the ground systems and is autonomous and fully 'intelligent' to reach its designated target. With this success, the design team is happy that the problems faced in the previous attempt on July 09 last year has been fully understood and solved. The entire flight path of approx 15 minutes duration validated all mission objectives primarily to establish the performance of the two stage propulsion in flight and the flex nozzle control system being attempted by DRDO scientists for the very first time. The flight was tracked from ground stations at Dhamra, ITR, Balasore, Port Blair and two Indian Naval ships in the Indian Ocean. Shri M Natarajan, Scientific Advisor to Raksha Mantri made a specific reference to the achievement of high degree of self reliance in AGNI III, as most of the sub systems have been developed within the country with the synergy between DRDO-Industry (both Public and Private sector) and Academia. As per the Mission Director, Shri Avinash Chander, many "firsts" have been established by this launch, which includes the Flex Nozzle Controls of Rocket Motor during powered phase, specially developed composite propellant with high specific impulse for the rocket. Guidance and Control with built in fault tolerant avionics, withstanding of severe aero thermal environment experienced during the Re-entry phase and coordinated mission management. The Defence Minister Shri AK Antony has congratulated the defence scientists on the successful launch and for achieving another important milestone in self-reliance in this critical strategic system. He also stated that India has matured in the missile technology area and was definitely at par with many other developed countries. AGNI III has confirmed India's Strategic capability for minimum credible deterrence. Today's historic event was witnessed by Shri Pallam Raju, Raksha Rajya Mantri, Shri M Natarajan, SA to RM and a host of senior officials of Ministry of Defence and Services.

207. (12-4-2007) NEW DELHI : Under 'Swarnjayanti Gram Swarojgar Yojana' (SGSY), grant-in-aid amounting to Rs. 5.52 lakh has been released to Dakshin Dinajpur DRDA of West Bengal by the Ministry of Rural Development towards Restoration of cut on account of excess O.B. as on 1.4. 2006 during the year 2006-07. The amount should be utilized on the Programme as per approved guidelines of SGSY. The funding pattern will be 75:25 by the Centre and the State. The State Govts/DRDAs/ZPs are also to ensure to submit the report of State and District Levels Vigilance & Monitoring Committee meeting held during current year by March 31, 2007, otherwise Ist instalment during the next year will be held up. The State Government should release its share within one month of the date of release of the Central assistance. Under SGSY, assistance is given to the poor family living below the poverty line for taking up self-employment. It actively promotes group approach by organising the rural poor into Self-Help Groups.

208. (12-4-2007) NEW DELHI : Under Pradhan Mantri Gram Sadak Yojana (PMGSY), the Ministry of Rural Development has released Rs. 200.00 crore as part payment of first instalment for Phase VI of grants-in-aid to Rajasthan Rural Road Development Authority (RRRDA), which is the autonomous agency for receiving funds under the programme. The grant is towards the Plan expenditure and will be subject to the conditions laid down from time to time in the guidelines of the PMGSY and supplementary directions. The Pradhan Mantri Gram Sadak Yojana aims to provide all-weather basic access to about 1.72 lakh habitations of population of 500 or more (250 or more in Hill States (including North East), desert and tribal areas). PMGSY roads are constructed to high technical standards and backed by 5 year maintenance contracts. The construction cost is fully borne by the Government of India as a Centrally sponsored Scheme, while the State Governments are responsible for providing maintenance funds.

209. (12-4-2007) NEW DELHI : The State Government of Madhya Pradesh has been sanctioned an amount of Rs. 7.39 crore as extended first instalment for undertaking IEC and HRD activities relating to National Rural Drinking Water Quality Monitoring and Surveillance Programme (NRDWQM&SP) during the year 2006-07 under Rajiv Gandhi National Drinking Water Mission (RGNDWM). Out of these, an amount of Rs.178.97 lakh for IEC activities and remaining Rs.559.86 lakh for HRD activities as per the guidelines. The funds for undertaking these activities are to be transferred to Community & Capacity Development Unit established in the State. This release is for plan expenditure. The funds are to be utilized for the purpose for which it is released and as per the terms and conditions. The release is on the basis of norms for each activity as per the guidelines.

210. (12-4-2007) NEW DELHI : An amount of Rs.1.05 crore has been granted to the State Government of Jammu & Kashmir as extended first instalment for undertaking IEC & HRD activities relating to National Rural Drinking Water Quality Monitoring & Surveillance Programme (NRDWQM&SP) under Rajiv Gandhi National Drinking Water Mission (RGNDWM) during the year 2006-07 by the Ministry of Rural Development. Out of these, an amount of Rs.30.57 lakh for IEC activities and remaining Rs.74.75 lakh for HRD activities should be utilized as per the guidelines. The funds for undertaking these activities are to be transferred to Community & Capacity Development Unit established in the State. This release is for plan expenditure. The funds are to be utilized for the purpose for which it is released and as per the terms and conditions. The release is on the basis of norms for each activity as per the guidelines.

211. (12-4-2007) NEW DELHI: The Bharatiya Janata Party on Wednesday strongly objected to the presence of Election Commissioner Navin Chawla in the hearing of the complaints seeking its de-recognition following the release of the controversial compact disc in Uttar Pradesh with communal overtones. On April 9, the Election Commission had granted time to the BJP to submit its replies to the complaints filed by various political parties and posted the matter for hearing on Wednesday. When the matter was taken up by Chief Election Commissioner N. Gopalaswami and Commissioners Mr. Chawla and S.Y. Qureshi, the BJP objected to Mr. Chawla's participation in the proceedings and presented an application demanding that he should recuse himself from hearing the case. The Commission granted time to the complainants till Thursday to respond to the BJP's application. Briefing reporters BJP spokesman Ravi Shankar Prasad said, "Being a quasi-judicial proceeding, the party submitted a petition before the Commission against the presence of a Member [Mr. Chawla] against whom 205 NDA MPs had made a representation before the President, A.P.J. Abdul Kalam. Another petition against him is pending before the Supreme Court.

212. (12-4-2007) NEW DELHI : Vice President of India, Shri Bhairon Singh Shekhawat has said that the biggest challenge we face today is the integration of leprosy cured persons into the society's mainstream. A large number of leprosy affected people after they are cured, remain poor and live below the poverty line. They do not have any access to basic amenities like education, healthcare, shelter and remunerative employment. They are denied their fundamental right of life with dignity. If we provide tangible facilities and support systems to the leprosy cured persons, they also can lead a life with dignity. They are willing to work hard, stand on their own feet and prove themselves as useful members of society. He has seen this happening at Sarthak Manav Kendra in Jaipur, Rajasthan and several such centres in different parts of the country. Their productivity is manifested in a wide range of activities such as handlooms; handicrafts, poultry, cow-shed, spare parts production, garment production, shops and enterprises, and the like. The civil society organisations and the business houses should come forward towards creating more and more such opportunities for the cured people to work. And, alongside, care should be taken to provide their children good education and upbringing so that they become capable of making their presence felt in the fast changing economic environment. Shri Shekhawat while presenting the International Gandhi Award instituted by Gandhi Memorial Leprosy Foundation for the year 2006 to Mr. Yohei Sasakawa at Wardha this morning, said that Mr. Sasakawa is an exceptional man of our times in the field of leprosy eradication. Shri Shekhawat said that a visit to Wardha is a pilgrimage for those who cherish our freedom and uphold the Gandhian values of service and sacrifice, care and compassion, equality and human dignity. Shri Shekhawat said that our efforts should be directed towards post-leprosy elimination operations, which will be more social, economic and humane and less medical. We have a long way to go in this direction. Leprosy eradication, in all its dimensions, still continues to be an unfinished task. Let us pool our collective efforts to stamp out leprosy and its ugly manifestations from our midst. He was confident that in this mission, persons like Mr. Sasakawa will continue to show us the way. Shri Shekhawat said that the progress made in the field of leprosy is not just statistics alone. Advances made in alleviating psychological and social suffering are truly immense. Now, thanks to the untiring and dedicated work by people like Mr. Sasakawa, we can say with a measure of certainty that society's perception towards leprosy is changing considerably. The stigma attached to leprosy is far less now. People have gradually accepted that leprosy is a curable and a non-contagious disease.

213. (13-4-2007) NEW DELHI : As part of its strategy to keep the prices of essential commodities under check, Government has moderated customs duty on edible oils in the past. In addition, the tariff values have also been kept frozen at July, 2006 levels. Keeping in view the high prices of edible oils, Ministry of Finance, Government of India has decided to further reduce the customs duty on specified edible oils as under: a. Crude palm oil, crude palmolein and other fractions of crude palm oil from 60% to 50%; b. Refined Bleached Deodorized (RBD) palm oil, RBD palmolein and other refined palm oils from 67.5% to 57.5%; c. Notification No.58/2007-Customs to this effect has been issued today by the Central Board of Excise and Customs. Reduction in customs duty will reduce the landed cost of these oils, and is expected to soften the domestic prices of edible oils. The tariff values for the palm group of oils will also continue to remain frozen at July, 2006 levels.

214. (13-4-2007) NEW DELHI : Minister for Rural Development, Dr. Raghuvansh Prasad Singh called upon the State Rural Development Secretaries to ensure full and timely utilization of funds of all the rural development schemes, so that their benefits reach to the poorest of the poor in rural areas. Since the review meeting is taking place at the beginning of a new financial year and the 11th Plan, it assumes a greater significance to set the pace for the future development, the Minister said. He was addressing a 'Two day Performance Review Committee meeting', organized by the Ministry in New Delhi today. The outlay for the 1st year of the 11th plan for the Ministry of Rural Development is Rs.41,060 crores as against a provision of Rs.31, 444 crores for the previous year (2006-07) which marks an increase of about 30%. The releases for 10th Plan period itself was Rs 1,14068 crores as against outlay of Rs 76,774 crores which means 48.6% increase in releases as against the outlay. In this backdrop, the Minister appealed to the State secretaries that the trend of recording significant higher achievements during the 10th Plan period should also be continued during the 11th Plan. The Minister also highlighted the need for online reporting by the DRDAs. Minister also asked all the States to make special efforts so as to finalise the BPL list within a period of two months. He said except Arunachal Pradesh, Chattisgarh, Jharkhand, Madhya Pradesh, Punjab, Uttarakhand, Uttar Pradesh and Andaman & Nicobar Islands, no other State has finalized the new BPL list. Dr. Raghuvansh Prasad Singh expressed a serious concern in this regard and emphasized the need for its immediate preparation and wide publicity. He said the Ministry will take further strict measures in terms of linking the BPL list preparation with release of funds. In his opening address, Dr. Subash Pani, Secretary (RD) emphasized that since additional districts have been brought under the ambit of the National Rural Employment Guarantee Programme, there is a need for sharing of good practices and developing customized communication according to the stakeholders' need. He also underlined the importance of online monitoring of all RD Schemes to ensure that physical and financial outcomes are fast tracked and chartered as per the road map set. Over the two days, scheme-wise review of funds released and financial and physical achievements for 2006-07, action plan for 2007-08 and issues on a state-wise basis were discussed.

215. (13-4-2007) NEW DELHI : An expert committee under the chairmanship of Mr. Nasser Munjee, Chairman, Development Credit Bank, has submitted its Report to the Minority Affairs Minister today. The Committee was set up on the advice of Shri Deepak Parekh, Chairman, HDFC Bank to consider and suggest an Action Plan for improving the strategy and operational performance of the National Minorities Development and Finance Cooperation (NMDFC). NMDFC has the main objective of promoting economic development of poorer sections of minority communities and provides term loans, educational loans and micro-finance through State Channelising Agencies (SCA). It also provides micro finance through NGOs. Since its inception from September, 1994, it has disbursed a total loan amount of Rs.900 crore covering about 3 lakh beneficiaries. NMDFC needs to further expand its scale of operation considering the size of the envisaged target groups and to make a perceptible impact on the quality of life of the disadvantaged sections amongst the minorities. One of the main constraints that the NMDFC faces in the operation of its scheme is the weak infrastructure of the most of SCAs.

The Committee was set up to look into the problems of its operational constraint and device a suitable Action Plan and strategy.

216. (13-4-2007) NEW DELHI : The centenary celebrations of Matheran Light Railway (1907-2007) will be held at Matheran Railway Station near Mumbai on 15th April, 2007. The Matheran Light Railway will be completing 100 years of its existence on this day. The highlights of the function include the flagging off the steam train, release of special postal cover and display of an exhibition besides visits of VIPs. It may be mentioned here that an application for declaration of Matheran Light Railway as world heritage site will be made to UNESCO, Paris during the current year.

217. (13-4-2007) NEW DELHI : Come April 14 and streets and bye lanes in the cities and hamlets outside villages all over India flutter with a riot of luxurious blue. Wheels of Ashok Chakra shine everywhere. Busts in every nook and corner and the life size statues on pedestals either indicating the right path with a finger or holding books, come to life again. Rare are such adoration seen for a national icon. More than hundred years ago a star had shown on the horizon of India and its light is becoming bright and bright as days and years pass. Dr. Babasaheb Ambedkar is the name. True icon of modern India and messiah of the downtrodden. Photographs, banners, posters, hoardings, huge cut-outs and welcome gates adorn Babasaheb's photograph in full splendour with a halo and Bhagvan Buddha's images on the backdrop on this day. The boy of a Subhedar Major who was presented with a copy of the life of Buddha by Keluskar Dada, a scholar from Western Universities, whom Shahu Maharaj mentioned as "your own leader", a revolutionary who fought to change the oppressive features of his ancient religion, a crusader for the unalienable rights of Dalits, a scholar par excellence who wrote the magnum opus "Who were Shudras" the Labour Member, architect of Indian Constitution and the one who brought back the glory of Buddha's teaching to the forgotten land and above all Baba of his own people-Babasaheb Ambedkar symbolizes all this and much more. A lover of books Babasaheb's scholarly career began with his M. Phil dissertation "Castes in India", and continued till death knocked on his door. His political career was launched under the able support of Shahu Maharaj of Kolhapur then spearheading the Non Brahmin Movement in Maharashtra. This Maharaja of people, who even addressed textile mill workers' public rallies in Central Mumbai, had hardly any match amongst the heads of the princely states in India then. Unfortunately the collaboration lasted for a short period first because of Ambedkar's choosing to take doctoral studies in London School of Economics and then by the death of Maharaja himself in 1922. After returning back and being part of the Bombay Legislative Assembly Dr. Ambedkar started satyagrahas against the practice of untouchability at religious and public places including Mahad lake and Kalaram Mandir at Nasik-an example of organizing public force and teaching followers a vast array of technics of protest in public arena. He taught his people to get themselves educated, to organize themselves and to wage a fight for achieving their goals. His was a democratic battle against the dark forces who thwarted the very implementation of the legislative measures passed by Bombay province to throw open the public sources of water to the entire citizenry.

218. (13-4-2007) NEW DELHI : A news item "Rubber Hartal on April 16" appeared in a section of the press, in which it was reported that Union Government is to allow import of Natural Rubber from Thailand at a reduced import duty. It is clarified that there is no such move by the Union Government. During the India-Thailand Trade Negotiating Committee Meeting which took place on 3-5 April 2007 in New Delhi and India Thailand Minister level bilateral meeting which took place on 11th April 2007 in New Delhi, Thailand side requested for market access for Natural Rubber. The Indian side while taking note of the request, made no commitment, whatsoever, for reduction of tariff on Natural Rubber.

219. (13-4-2007) NEW DELHI : Indian mangoes will enter the US market this season and the first export consignment of Indian mangoes for USA is expected to leave later this month. Both India and the United States had expressed happiness over this market opening for a major Indian agricultural product at the Sixth Ministerial level meeting of the US-India Trade Policy Forum (TPF) which was held here today under the chairmanship of Shri Kamal Nath, Union Minister of Commerce and Industry and Ms. Susan Schwab, United States Trade Representative (USTR). The progress made by the US and India on key bilateral issues was reviewed at the meeting. USTR Ms. Schwab and Shri Kamal Nath also announced the formation of a Private Sector Advisory Group of prominent US and Indian trade experts who will provide strategic recommendations and insights into the US-India Trade Policy Forum. "The U.S.-India Trade Policy Forum is a critical instrument for advancing bilateral trade and fostering investment. It is our hope that Private Sector Advisory Group will infuse our very productive existing dialogue with new ideas to enhance the bilateral trade and investment environment", Ms. Schwab said. Shri Kamal Nath said: "The Private Sector Advisory Group being an independent think tank would prove to be a valuable channel for giving the private sector perspective and a new dimension to the ongoing dialogue which will provide fillip to US India bilateral trade and investments." Membership of the Private Sector Advisory Group includes key voices in the United State and India on international economic and trade policy. US representatives include: Ambassador Carla A. Hills, & Co; Mr. C. Fred Bergesten, Director of the Pete G. Peterson Institute for International Economics (IIE) Mr. John J. Castellani, President of the Business Roundtable; and Mr. Ron Somers, President of the U.S. India Business Council.

220. (13-4-2007) NEW DELHI : ISRO, along with Astronautical Society of India (ASI), will select 50 Indian students who will be sponsored as Student Delegates to the International Astronautical Congress (IAC-2007), which is being hosted by

ASI and ISRO at Hyderabad, during September 23-28, 2007. The congress is organised by the International Asronautical Federation in cooperation with the International Academy of Astronautics and International Institute of Space Law. It is a prestigious International Space Event attended by about 2000 delegates from Space Agencies, industries, academia and international organisations. Students studying in 11th and 12th Standard/Pre-University, undergraduate students who have already completed their first year in Science, Engineering or Law Courses and post graduate students of science, engineering and law will be eligible for selection.

221. (13-4-2007) NEW DELHI : Army Commanders Conference, is scheduled to be held from 16 to 20 Apr. 2007 at New Delhi. The conference will be chaired by Army Chief, Gen JJ Singh. During the Conference, operational review of the situation in J&K and the NE, to incl. modernization and capability building, operational readiness and training will be carried out. Other activities of the Army will also be reviewed and wherever required directions will be issued to carry out midcourse corrections. The Conference will commence with the address by Hon'ble Raksha Mantri to the Army Commanders on 16 Apr. 07. A large number of important issues have been slated for discussions. A review of the training for primary tasks and important administrative matters will be discussed. Detailed discussion in particular will be carried out on "Value Based Leadership" to evoke a deliberate in house introspection. The scope of 'Asymmetric Warfare in Indian Context' will be deliberated upon. Other important issues slated for discussions are the steps to be taken at ground level for 'Improvement in Promotion/ Service Conditions of personnel Below officer Rank including update on VIth CPC, Appraisal System team & Redress Mechanism' and a review of the policy on 'Strategy for an Integrated Approach towards Peacekeeping Operations'. A well thought out strategy and road map to IVth Mil World Games Oct. 07' will also be presented. COAS Sports Trophy will also be presented on this occasion.

222. (13-4-2007) NEW DELHI : In a unique ceremony, Armed Forces officers including senior doctors and other dignitaries are to pledge their organs for donation on 14 Apr. 2007 at Army Hospital (R&R). Amongst others, Ms. Nikita Anand and Ms. Gul Panag, both former Miss India, Mrs. Shyama Chona, Principal DPS, RK Puram, New Delhi, Mr. Ajit Bajaj, the first Indian to conquer North & South poles and eminent media personality Col Ajai Shukla, are to pledge their organs. On the same day another unique initiative is being launched by the Army doctors in the form of Armed Forces organ Retrieval and transplantation Authority (AORTA). AORTA aims to increase awareness of organ donations, organ retrieval and transplantation. The efforts of this Authority will be coordinated by Col (Dr.) AK Seth, an eminent super Specialist who has vast experience of organ transplantation. Very recently Maj Vipin Chaudhary took the noble step of agreeing to donate the organs of his mother, who breathed her last following brain hemorrhage at Army Hospital (R & R). The liver was transplanted, for the first time, at Army

Hospital Research & Referral into a serving soldier, one kidney into a serving officer, another kidney into an 18 year old and two eyes into suitable recipients. This selfless gesture affected the lives of five families and served as an inspiration to others. To acknowledge the noble deed done by Maj Chaudhary, he is being felicitated during the ceremony. On this occasion Lt. Gen Saibal Mukherjee, Director General Medical Service (Army) will be the Chief Guest.

223. (13-4-2007) NEW DELHI : The Government has anounced that all Central Government offices including industrial establishments will remain closed on Saturday, the 14th April 2007 on account of the birthday of Dr. B.R. Ambedkar.

224. (13-4-2007) NEW DELHI : Shri Abhishek Singhvi said that the Congress Party deplores the subversion and distortion of India's electoral process by the use of devious and deceptive electoral tricks which are not only criminal offences but totally unconstitutional. India is rightly proud of its democratic traditions and shines forth as an exception amongst the wrecks and ruins of constitutionalism which litter the South Asian landscape. Parties like the BJP and the SP are a blot on India's proud secular democratic heritage. Whether it is BJP's CD, whether it is BJP's communally provocative advertisements or it is the CD's alleged to be used by the SP, they strike at the root of India's basic structure, its secular ethos and its inclusive spirit. Both these parties have decided to stop fighting electoral battles by the rules of the game. They want power by hook or by crook and more by crook than by hook. They have tried to deceive, mislead, provoke, confuse, confound, corrupt and fool the electorate, by false propaganda, and inflammatory material, all designed to divide, inflame, and create internal conflict. In so doing, they show their ignorance of India's syncretic culture, its pluralistic humanism and its humanistic pluralism. We have no doubt that the electorate of UP will see through this cheap gimmickry, this diabolical subversion of democracy and this obvious disrespect for our secular Constitution and for rule of law. Parties like the BJP and the SP need no major political adversary- they have already converted the sober and balanced voter of UP into a collective political opponent, as the second phase of elections propels the Congress to yet another great performance in western U.P. today. To a question that with defeat from Maharashtra, Punjab, Uttarakhand and Delhi, have the people rejected Congress policies? Shri Singhvi said that there are some principles which are unchangeable. Secularism not creating communal divides, not making provocative statements are non-negotiable. They are not dependent on electoral success or defeat, at least that is the Congress Party's philosophy. I am sure it is not the philosophy of many of our opponents and we intend to stick by that philosophy irrespective of electoral verdicts. I do not think that the public of India has any hiatus or any dichotomy between that philosophy and voting. Temporary election victories and defeats apart this is the basic structure of India's constitutional sprit and we shall stand by it and not be shaken by its simple verdict here and there. To a question that these defeats are due to Dr. Manmohan Singh policies, Shri Singhvi said that prior to the recent elections in this year we have won several elections which perhaps you have not noticed. Since this year there have been elections where there have been close verdicts in some places and we bow down to that. The point is not to allocation of blame to a single individuals, that is certainly wrong. The point is that we have to fight and that is the basic point I am repeating. We have to fight these electoral battles by the rules of the game. To a question that the Congress Party is on a losing spree, what is wrong? Shri Singhvi said that I completely deny the very premise of your question, what connection does the losing spree have with the communal, divisive politics of people like the SP and the BJP. The electoral defeats are a part of a political process and we take them seriously. We are having great and detailed internal study. It could be a mixture of so many factors. There is off course a factor which we cannot deny and that is the basic truth of Indian politics in several areas which is cyclical and anti incumbency. Surely that has worked and that is not meant as an excuse. It is not meant as a justification. It is only given as a partial explanation. Now that does not mean that we will sit back and expect anti incumbency to repeat itself against us. We will take strong correctives steps and that process is still already on. To a question that Indian democracy does not have responsible Opposition, Shri Singhvi said that I don't think that we at least talk of a responsible Opposition in terms of numbers. When we talk of a responsible Opposition you are giving weight only to the second word Opposition and I am giving equal weight to the two words, responsible and Opposition. Certainly, winning elections is not a reflection of responsibility if you win elections for a example with the kind of nonsense they are depicting on CDs, I leave it to you to judge whether you can call them not only a responsible Opposition but at all a responsible entity. I think responsibility comes from maturity and maturity comes from knowledge of India's past and a participation in India's evolution. To a question that Congress Party candidate was appealing to the minority community in Uttar Pradesh election campaign, was is correct? Shri Singhvi said that appealing to vote is not objectionable.

225. (13-4-2007) NEW DELHI : The President, Dr. A.P.J. Abdul Kalam in his message on the occasion of Vaisakhi, which is being celebrated tomorrow, has said: "On the occasion of Vaisakhi, I extend my greetings and good wishes to all my people, particularly to those engaged in cultivation and agriculture. This harvest festival is an occasion to remember our farmers who sweat and toil in the fields to bring us good harvests and happiness to our homes. On this day, let us pledge to work to develop our rural communities so that our mission of a developed India touches the remotest parts of the country and everybody is benefited leading to prosperity of the nation."

226. (13-4-2007) NEW DELHI : Under 'Swarnjayanti Gram Swarojgar Yojana' (SGSY), grant-in-aid amounting to Rs. 2.78 lakh has been released to Navasari DRDA of Gujarat by the Ministry of Rural Development towards Restoration of cut on account of excess O.B. as on 1.4. 2006 during the year 2006-07. The amount should be utilized on the Programme as per approved guidelines of SGSY. The funding pattern will be 75:25 by the Centre and the State. The State Govts/DRDAs/ZPs are also to ensure to submit the report of State and District Levels Vigilance & Monitoring Committee meeting held during current year by March 31, 2007, otherwise Ist instalment during the next year will be held up. The State Government should release its share within one month of the date of release of the Central assistance. Under SGSY, assistance is given to the poor family living below the poverty line for taking up self-employment. It actively promotes group approach by organising the rural poor into Self-Help Groups.

227. (13-4-2007) NEW DELHI : Grant-in-aid amounting to Rs. 1.10 crore has been released to 3 DRDAs of Andhra Pradesh, namely Cuddapah (Rs.0.04 lakh), Karimnagar (Rs.20.71 lakh) & Visakhapatnam (Rs.89.12 lakh) by the Ministry of Rural Development towards Restoration of cut on account of excess O.B. as on 1.4. 2006 during the year 2006-07 under 'Swarnjayanti Gram Swarojgar Yojana' (SGSY). The amount should be utilized on the Programme as per approved guidelines of SGSY. The funding pattern will be 75:25 by the Centre and the State. The State Govts/DRDAs/ZPs are also to ensure to submit the report of State and District Levels Vigilance & Monitoring Committee meeting held during current year by March 31, 2007, otherwise Ist instalment during the next year will be held up. The State Government should release its share within one month of the date of release of the Central assistance. Under SGSY, assistance is given to the poor family living below the poverty line for taking up self-employment. It actively promotes group approach by organising the rural poor into Self-Help Groups.

228. (13-4-2007) NEW DELHI : The manufacturing sector in India grew by a record 12.3% in February 2007, while the cumulative industrial growth in the 11-month period, *i.e.* April 06 to February 07 has been 11.1% over the corresponding period of the previous year. This is the first time that Industrial growth has crossed the 11% mark in the last decade. Shri Kamal Nath, Union Minister of Commerce and Industry, has said that the record manufacturing growth is significant in the context the high priority being accorded by the government to manufacturing as a source of employment generation. Meanwhile, foreign direct investment (FDI) inflows (equity only) in February 2007 amounted to US $ 698 million, compared to only US $ 127 million in February 2006, a huge increase of 450%. Cumulatively, from April 2006 to February 2007, an amount of US$ 11.89 billion have come in equity, compared to US$ 4.31 billion during the 11 months of the previous year. This marks a growth of 176% in dollar terms in FDI inflows into India cumulatively. As per the Quick Estimates of Industrial Production, manufacturing sector grew by 12.3% in February 2007. As a result, during April 2006 to February 2007, there was a 12.1% rate of growth in the Manufacturing Sector during the 11-month period. "This augurs well for the beginning of the 11th Plan, which aims to achieve a growth of 12% per annum in Manufacturing during the entire Plan period", Shri Kamal Nath said.

229. (13-4-2007) NEW DELHI : Under the scheme of Research and Development (R&D) of the Ministry of Water Resources, the budget allocations in the last three years were Rs. 6.00 crore for 2004-05, Rs. 10.00 crore for 2005-06 and Rs. 14.96 crore for 2006-07. Various research organizations and academic institutions are provided assistance for taking up research in specific areas of water resources. The support is provided by way of grants to academic/research organizations. The scheme also has a component for providing assistance for organization of workshops/ symposiums/seminars etc. on important issues related to water resources and mass awareness programmes. The research activities are primarily undertaken by premier organizations of the Ministry of Water Resources *i.e.* Central Water and Power Research Station, Pune, Central Soil and Materials Research Station, New Delhi, National Institute of Hydrology, Roorkee and Central Ground Water Board. The scheme for Research and Development is to provide incentive to various academic and research organizations which helps in addressing specific issues, The overall objectives of R&D are not adversely affected as the major activities related to research are undertaken by premier research institutes. Various measures like examination of proposal by Indian National Committees, monitoring of the progress, evaluation of reports etc. are taken by the Ministry to ensure timely utilization of funds earmarked to research judiciously.

230. (13-4-2007) AHMEDABAD: All the Indian Institutes of Management (IIMs) have decided to defer the publication of the final admissions list to their two-year post-graduate management programme from Thursday till April 21 in deference to the wishes of the Union Human Resource Development (HRD) Ministry. Speaking on behalf of the six IIMs, Bakul Dholakia, Director, IIM-Ahmedabad, said, "This is the maximum stretch we can give to the Government without disrupting the beginning of the next academic year."

231. (14-4-2007) NEW DELHI : Importers and Exporters operating through the Delhi Air Cargo Customs experienced certain difficulties in filing their documents through ICEGATE for the last one week. Consequently, documents were filed through the Service centres of CMC, creating an additional pressure on these centres. On 9th April, 2007, the service centres were unable to transfer documents to the ICES, thus aggravating the problem of filing of documents. With regard to these problems, Member (Customs), CBEC has clarified that NIC has rectified the problems relating to the Service centres by the evening of 10th April, 2007. CMC and the Customs department deployed additional staff to work overtime to clear the backlog of the shipments. The problems relating to ICEGATE were resolved and by 11th April, the exporters/importers were able to file their documents through ICEGATE. The import shipments were normalized by 13th evening, and the export shipments are expected to stabilize by this afternoon. The Delhi Air Cargo Complex on an average handles 1000 import shipments and about 1800 export shipments per day. Sixty five percent of the documents are filed through the ICEGATE and remaining are filed through the Service centres. ICEGATE is the gateway, which allows remote filing of the Shipping Bills and Bills of Entry.

232. (14-4-2007) THANJAVUR: Communal forces took advantage of the Congress Party's failure in the recent elections, as the party deviated from its original ideology, Union Agriculture Minister Sharad Pawar has said. Speaking at a function got up in connection with the merger of the Tamil Nadu Jananayaga Congress with the Nationalist Congress Party (NCP) here on Friday, Mr. Pawar stressed the need to strengthen secular forces in the country. Congress under the leadership of Kamaraj, Mahatma Gandhi and Jawaharlal Nehru worked for the welfare of the party workers and the common man. But the present Congress was not supporting the party workers, he claimed. Congress was away from power for the past 40 years in Tamil Nadu and the leadership had not taken any step to capture power in the State. The party leaders were visiting Dravida Munnetra Kazhagam office and not the Congress office. "I am not saying that Congress leaders should not have any relationship with the DMK which is an alliance partner, but before visiting the DMK office they should visit Sathyamoorthy Bhavan and talk to Congress workers," Mr. Pawar said. The NCP was floated eight years ago and it had representation in 11 State Assemblies. In Tamil Nadu also, it would soon make its presence soon, Mr. Pawar said. The NCP wanted to take up the cause of farmers and it was also committed to the welfare of Backward Class, SC and ST.

233. (14-4-2007) NEW DELHI : The Vice President of India, Shri Bhairon Singh Shekhawat has said that by effectively influencing the course of socio-economic and human development, voluntary organisations can become the conduits for growth and development at the grass root level. Inaugurating the Silver Jubilee Celebrations of Shri Kshethra Dharmasthala Rural Development Project in Karnataka this morning, he expressed the hope that these Organisations can become catalysts for good governance, helping full participation of the poor and the marginalized in the developmental process. Shri Shekhawat said that voluntary actions for socially useful purposes have been a tradition in our society. This project is one such success story of voluntary initiative which has mad a major impact in the development of this region, besides empowering the poor and marginalized sections. He hoped that with its dedicated service, this project can provide them right opportunities and enabling environment thus creating a social miracle which we all have been waiting for. Shri Shekhawat said that our public programmes aimed at ameliorating the conditions of the poor ought to be effectively implemented, benefiting the targeted beneficiaries. Needs and aspirations of the poor and the deprived can be met only when the public administration becomes people-oriented, with a focus on the welfare of the common man. Corruption tends to create mal-administration and in the process the concerns and priority of the poor get relegated to the background. Reforms in public governance are fundamental to any strategy towards alleviation of poverty, he added.

234. (14-4-2007) NEW DELHI : In a unique ceremony, Armed Forces officers including senior doctors and other dignitaries pledged their organs for donation at Army Hospital (R&R), here today. Amongst others, Ms. Nikita Anand and Ms. Gul Panag, both former Miss India, Mrs. Shyama Chona, Principal DPS, RK Puram, New Delhi, Mr. Ajit Bajaj, the first Indian to conquer North & South poles and eminent media personality Col Ajai Shukla, also pledged their organs. Another unique initiative was also taken by the Army doctors in the form of launching Armed Forces Organ Retrieval and Transplantation Authority (AORTA). AORTA aims to increase awareness of organ donations, organ retrieval and transplantation. The efforts of this Authority will be coordinated by Col (Dr.) AK Seth, an eminent super Specialist who has vast experience of organ transplantation. Very recently Maj Vipin Chaudhary took the noble step of agreeing to donate the organs of his mother, who breathed her last following brain hemorrhage at Army Hospital (R & R). The liver was transplanted, for the first time, at Army Hospital Research & Referral into a serving soldier, one kidney into a serving officer, another kidney into an 18 year old and two eyes into suitable recipients. This selfless gesture affected the lives of five families and served as an inspiration to others. To acknowledge the noble deed done by Maj Chaudhary, he was felicitated during the ceremony. On this occasion Lt. Gen Saibal Mukherjee, Director General Medical Service (Army) lauded the efforts of the Army Hospital and all others who are associated with these initiatives.

235. (14-4-2007) NEW DELHI : Indo-Japan trade and economic relations are moving on to a new trajectory with major new initiatives such as the Delhi-Mumbai Industrial Corridor (DMIC) being given concrete shape and the Economic Partnership Agreement (EPA) negotiations between the two countries getting underway. This was indicated by Shri Kamal Nath, Union Minister of Commerce and Industry and Mr. Akira Amari, Minister of Economy, Trade and Industry of Japan at an interactive session with business representatives, which was jointly organised here this afternoon by the Department of Industrial Policy & Promotion (DIPP), Ministry of Commerce and Industry and the Confederation of Indian Industries (CII). In a presentation made on the occasion, Dr. Ajay Dua, Secretary (DIPP), outlined the key features of the Delhi-Mumbai Industrial Corridor, which would pass through 6 states of India (viz., Haryana, Delhi, Uttar Pradesh, Rajasthan, Gujarat and Maharashtra). The dedicated freight corridors were planned along Delhi-Mumbai in phase-I and along Delhi-Kolkata routes in phase-II. The project would double employment potential in India; triple industrial output; and quadruple exports from the regions covered by the Project in 5 years, he said. The Project would involve development of industrial infrastructure such as upgradation of all industrial clusters in the corridor together with promotion of 10-12 new ones; improvement of physical infrastructure including upgradation of 5-6 airports, setting up of 2 greenfield ports in Gujarat and Maharashtra and augmenting rail and port connectivity, he added. Shri Kamal Nath hailed Japan's role as the largest contributor of ODA (Overseas Development Assistance) to India and stressed that the Delhi-Mumbai Industrial Corridor project as well as the EPA negotiations would significantly enhance bilateral trade and economic ties. He also reiterated India's support to Japan's proposal for an East Asian Economic Region (ASEAN + 6). Mr. Amari in his address referred to the series of measures initiated since the visit of Prime Minister Dr. Manmohan Singh to Japan in December 2006 to strengthen Indo-Japan relations. The DMIC, he said, was extremely important as it would accelerate Japanese investment in India, rapidly develop India's infrastructure sector including industrial parks, roads, ports, rail connectivity etc., along the routes and facilitate exports from the regions covered by the Corridor. He said that he would come to India with a large business delegation in July, ahead of Prime Minister Shinzo Abe's visit to the country.

236. (14-4-2007) NEW DELHI: The Election Commission has sought a status report from the Uttar Pradesh Chief Electoral Officer on the issue of the controversial CD released by the Bharatiya Janata Party. In a communication to the CEO, the Commission sought particulars of the first information reports filed against the BJP leaders responsible for the release of the CD. In case the CD was still in circulation, it should be seized and the Commission informed of the action taken. The direction was a sequel to the demands made by the Congress and the CPI(M) on Thursday that the Commission issue administrative instructions to stop the distribution and circulation of the controversial CD.

237. (14-4-2007) THIRUVANANTHAPURAM: CPI(M) State secretary Pinarayi Vijayan said here on Friday that the party would explore all legal options available to it to face the Kerala High Court decision to proceed against Local Self-Government Minister Paloli Mohammed Kutty in the contempt case. Reacting to the High Court decision here on Friday, Mr. Vijayan said given the manner in which the Court had handled the case all along, there was nothing surprising about the High Court's decision to proceed against Mr. Mohammed Kutty. He also firmly ruled out of the possibility of Mr. Mohammed Kutty resigning. The CPI(M) leader contended that all resignations in the past over observations made by Courts related to corruption charges. The former Forest Minister K. P. Viswanathan had to resign because of his alleged links with the forest mafia and the former Food and Civil Supplies Minister K.K. Ramachandran because of the adverse findings of the Lok Ayukta.

238. (14-4-2007) NEW DELHI : The Prime Minister, Dr. Manmohan Singh, has greeted the Nation on the auspicious occasion of Vaisakhadi and Bahag Bihu. In a message, the Prime Minister said that these festivals are occasions to celebrate the indomitable spirit of the Indian farmer. They symbolise hope even as they mark the culmination of hard work and solid determination of our farmers to move ahead on the path of progress. May Vaisakhdi and Bahag Bihu usher in peace, prosperity and happiness for all, the Prime Minister added.

239. (15-4-2007) NEW DELHI : India and Azerbaijan have agreed to cooperate in several areas including oil & gas sector and Indian companies are set to play a greater role in the development of Azerbaijan's rapidly expanding oil and gas industry. This was the result of a meeting last week between the President of Azerbaijan, Mr. Ilham Aliyev and the visiting Minister of State for Commerce, Shri Jairam Ramesh at Baku. At the end of a 45-minute discussion, Mr. Aliyev consented to ONGC Videsh and SOCAR, the state-owned oil and gas exploration company of Azerbaijan starting talks for cooperation for ONGC Videsh's investments in hydrocarbon-rich Azerbaijan. ONGC Videsh has already invested close to $ 5 billion in 15 countries around the world, half of which is in Russia alone and that ONGC Videsh has much to offer to Azerbaijan, particularly in fields where production is declining. Mr. Aliyev sought India's assistance in enhanced oil recovery and deep sea drilling. Shri Ramesh also offered GAIL's expertise in gas-based petrochemicals and city-gas distribution. To begin with, ONGC Videsh and GAIL will participate in the Caspian Sea Oil and Gas Exhibition being held in Baku, June 3-4, 2007. Shri Ramesh also briefed the President of India's interests in exploring for gold in Azerbaijan, particularly since India is now the world's largest importer of gold. MMTC and NMDC will work with their Azerbaijani counterparts to identify specific areas where prospecting and appraisal work can be undertaken. Mr. Aliyev also expressed deep appreciation for India's offer to help establish a centre for education and training in IT in Baku. The President agreed with the observations made by Shri Ramesh that India's great strength lies in skills training and human resource development, particularly in management, law and science and technology. Of the 100 Azeri students who are to be sent abroad for higher education this year, it is expected that 20 will come to India.

240. (15-4-2007) NEW DELHI : Uzbekistan has agreed to open technical talks with GAIL for enabling the Indian company to start exploration activity in natural gas in the gas-rich Central Asian country. This materialised after meetings between the Prime Minister of Uzbekistan, Mr. Savkit Mirziyayev and the visiting Minister of State for Commerce, Shri Jairam Ramesh on April 13, 2007 at Tashkent. India has also offered to help establish a training institute for gas technology in Tashkent, along the lines of the Jawaharlal Nehru IT Centre in the Uzbek capital that was inaugurated by the Prime Minister, Dr. Manmohan Singh last year. GAIL has identified 4 specific blocks for gas exploration. So far Russia, China and South Korea have invested in gas exploration in Uzbekistan. Shri Jairam Ramesh was accompanied in his meetings with the Prime Minister of Uzbekistan and other senior ministers by Shri Mukund Chaudhury, Managing Director of CLC Textiles which has recently invested $ 81 million in cotton spinning and yarn in Uzbekistan. A further investment of $ 40 million is planned by CLC Textiles over the next two years. The Uzebk Prime Minister appreciated the operations of CLC Textiles and expressed Uzbekistan's keenness for similar investments by Indian companies in pharmaceuticals and leather. Shri Jairam Ramesh promised to talk to Indian companies in this regard soon. Shri Jairam Ramesh also conveyed to the Uzbek

Prime Minister, India's interest in exploring for gold in gold-rich Uzbekistan since India is now the world's largest importer of gold. The Uzbek government has agreed to consider a proposal from MMTC/ National Mineral Development Corporation (NMDC) for gold exploration but wants this proposal to include value-addition investments in Uzbekistan itself, like in gold jewellery. MMTC and NMDC will now formulate a proposal for submission to the Uzbek government in the next 30 days. The Uzbek Prime Minister underscored the special cultural and political relationship that exists between India and Uzbekistan. He also mentioned the great personal regard and respect that the President of Uzbekistan has for Dr. Manmohan Singh whom he has known personally for over a decade and a half. He felt that the time was now ripe for taking the bilateral economic relationship to a whole new level and that Shri Jairam Ramesh's visit will contribute significantly to this.

241. (16-4-2007) NEW DELHI : The Prime Minister's assertion of Rahul Gandhi as the future of either UP or the country, is not only preposterous but is the worst kind of Prime Ministerial sycophancy stemming from the politics of dynasty. What else can be expected from a man who has been reduced to the position of a regent by the dynasty, which expects him to keep the seat warm until the crown prince is ready. The Prime Minister has not only once again shown his utter irresoluteness by this eulogy of Rahul, he has also insulted democracy in which it is up to the people to decide who their future leader should be. Dynasty is the antithesis of democracy and people of the country are the sovereign judge in selecting their leader and future. The recent remarks of Rahul Gandhi also expose his limited family World Vision. His statement that the freedom struggle is the achievement of his family is an insult to the great freedom struggle, revolutionaries and freedom fighters. His assertion that the division of Pakistan was also his family achievement is also absurd and has proved a diplomatic disaster. The Congress may defend him but let the Ministry of External Affairs validate his statement. His earlier statement about demolition of the disputed structure in Ayodhya also betrays the same mindset. If Rahul Gandhi wants to take credit for certain things by ignoring the contribution by others then he has to take the blame for partition of India and the creation of Pakistan, for the creation of POK, for allowing Pakistan to hand over Aksai Chin to China, for imposing emergency and destroying democracy, for promoting Bhindranwale, for the IPKF misadventure in Sri Lanka, for promoting and protecting Mr. Quotrochhi, for the Sikhs' massacre in 1984 and for disastrous Nehruvian economic policies which led to many of the maladies of the country. The eulogy of a man who does not see beyond his family, and does not recognize their own Prime Ministers Shri Lal Bahadur Shastri and Shri Narsimha Rao is undemocratic and condemnable.

242. (16-4-2007) NEW DELHI : Shri Priya Ranjan Das Munshi, Minister for Information & Broadcasting, has condemned the attack on Star TV. In a statement here today, Shri Das Munshi said: "I have learnt about the attack on Star TV by members of a Hindu fundamentalist group. The concerned State Government should take firm action and book the culprits for justice immediately. This is an assault on democracy and the fundamental rights of the media, which I strongly condemn".

243. (16-4-2007) NEW DELHI : Taking a common stand after assessing the progress of negotiations in the Doha Round of the World Trade Organisation (WTO) at this critical juncture, Shri Kamal Nath, Minister of Commerce & Industry and Mr. Bo Xilai, Chinese Commerce Minister have agreed that the major issue holding back and impeding the progress in Round is the lack of movement by the developed countries in terms of early removal of distortions caused by huge subsidies and significant market access barriers in developed countries. "Unless the outcome of the negotiations upholds the proposals of developing countries resulting in real and effective reduction of trade distorting domestic support coupled with meaningful disciplines, substantial improvement in market access by developed countries and eliminations of all form of export subsidies the aspirations of the developing countries, as built in the mandate, will not be fulfilled", they categorically said in the India-China Joint Ministerial Statement which was issued in Beijing today. Mr. Bo Xilai and Shri Kamal Nath met in Beijing on 16th April 2007 to compare notes and exchange views in order to review the progress of negotiations on the Doha Development Agenda (DDA) of the WTO and to safeguard the common interests of developing country Members in the future course of negotiations. Mr. Kamal Nath briefed Minister Bo Xilai about the discussions in the G-4/G-6 meetings in Delhi on April 12, 2007. They recalled the commitment of the two countries expressed in the Joint Declaration issued during the state visit of the President of the People's Republic of China in November 2006 to strengthen the cooperation of the two countries in the WTO and safeguard the legitimate rights and interests of the developing countries. Reaffirming their support for an open, fair, equitable, transparent and rule-based multilateral trading system and their determination to coordinate with other members of the WTO, especially the developing countries, in order to ensure placing the development dimension at the heart of this Round, the two Ministers expressed their sincere hope for achieving an expeditious conclusion of the Doha Development Round based on full realization of the development goals as mandated in the Doha Declaration, the Framework Agreement of July 2004 and the Hong Kong Declaration.

244. (16-4-2007) NEW DELHI : Central Board of Excise and Customs (CBEC), Department of Revenue issued Notification no. 31/2007-Cus (N.T), here today, notifying tariff values of edible oils and brass scrap (all grades) as shown in the Table below. The tariff values of six palm group oils and crude soyabean oil remain unchanged. However, tariff value of brass scrap (all grades) has been lowered.

245. (16-4-2007) NEW DELHI : Government of India have announced the sale (re-issue) of "7.55 percent Government Stock, 2010" under Market Stabilization

Scheme for a notified amount of Rs. 3,000 crore (nominal). The Government Stock will be sold through price based auction using multiple price method. The auction will be conducted by the Reserve Bank of India, Mumbai Office, Fort, Mumbai on April 18, 2007 (Wednesday). Up to 5% of the amount notified for the sale of stock is reserved for allotment to eligible individuals and Institutions on non-competitive basis as per the Scheme for Non-Competitive Bidding Facility in the Auction of Government Securities. Bids in the prescribed form obtainable from the Regional Director, Reserve Bank of India, Mumbai Office (Public Debt Office), Fort, Mumbai-400 001 and RBI website www.rbi.org.in should be submitted to that Office on April 18, 2007. The NDS members should submit competitive as well as non-competitive bids in electronic format using Primary Market Operation (PMO) module of NDS. All bids should be submitted by 12.30 P.M. The result of the auction will be announced on April 18, 2007 and payment by successful bidders will be during banking hours on April 19, 2007 (Thursday). Department of Economic Affairs, Ministry of Finance New Delhi: Chaitra 26, 1929; April 16, 2007.

246. (16-4-2007) NEW DELHI : The Annual Plan for Andhra Pradesh for the year 2007-08 was finalized, here today, at a meeting between Deputy Chairman, Planning Commission Shri Montek Singh Ahluwalia and the Chief Minister of Andhra Pradesh Dr. Y.S. Rajasekhara Reddy. The Plan outlay was agreed at Rs.30500 crores. This includes one time Central assistance of Rs.150 crores to the State for special programmes in the Animal Husbandry sector. In his opening remarks, Deputy Chairman, Planning Commission, complemented the State Government for significantly improving the growth rate and following a development process having focus on inclusive growth. He said Plan realization as well as outlay was moving in the right direction. Efforts made to improve performance in agriculture, power and health sector were appreciated. It was pointed out that National Rural Employment Guarantee Programme was very well executed by the State and many other States were trying to follow it. In the power sector transmission and distribution losses have substantially come down. The State was advised to have more focus on horticulture and animal husbandry. Deputy Chairman, Planning Commission, said that the Commission was concerned about the slow execution of Central schemes. He said States should come forward in pointing out difficulties in the execution of these schemes so that steps can be taken to make guidelines flexible. He said the Planning Commission would shortly initiate regional consultations aimed at having in-depth discussions with the States on priorities for the Eleventh Plan.

247. (16-4-2007) NEW DELHI : Rural Development Ministry has released an amount of Rs.1.60 lakh, being 20% of the cost of the project to the Development Facilitators, New Delhi by way of final instalment for conducting a study on assessment of the implementation of Rural Housing in the State of Madhya Pradesh and Tamil Nadu under Indira Awas Yojana (IAY). Rural Housing is a part of the Bharat Nirman programme. Under Indira Awaas Yojana, 60 lakh houses are to be constructed within the time frame of 2005 to 2009. Out of which, 23.68 lakh houses have been constructed during 2005-06 and 2006-07 (up to Feb., 2007) and 9.14 lakh houses are under construction. In a major initiative to impart transparency to the selection process 'permanent waitlist' is being prepared for selection of beneficiaries under IAY. During 2006-07, the States which have achieved more than 75% targets are-Andhra Pradesh, Assam, Goa, Jammu & Kashmir, Jharkhand, Madhya Pradesh, Nagaland, Sikkim, Uttarakhand, West Bengal and Lakshadweep. The States which have achieved more than 50% but less than 75% are-Arunachal Pradesh, Bihar, Chhattisgarh, Gujarat, Haryana, Himachal Pradesh, Karnataka, Kerala, Mizoram, Orissa and Uttar Pradesh. The States which have achieved less than 50% are-Maharashtra, Meghalaya, Punjab, Rajasthan, Tamil Nadu, A&N Islands, D&N Haveli, Pondichery, Tripura and Daman & Diu.

248. (16-4-2007) NEW DELHI : The Metallurgical & Engineering Consultants (India) Limited (MECON Ltd.), the Ranchi based engineering consultancy outfit is a public sector undertaking under the Ministry of Steel. It was set up to reduce dependence on foreign engineering consultants by building indigenous capability in design & engineering. During its existence of past four decades, besides executing varied type engineering/consultancy assignments, MECON has been a pioneer in acquiring and assimilating newer technologies for various sectors of the Indian Industry. MECON is also the first engineering and consultancy organisation in India to receive the ISO 9001 certification. It is one of the premier multi disciplinary design, engineering, consultancy and contracting organization in the field of iron & steel, chemicals, refineries & petrochemicals, power, roads & highways, water management, ports & harbours, gas & oil, pipelines, non-ferrous, mining, general engineering and other related/diversified areas with extensive overseas experience.

249. (16-4-2007) NEW DELHI : Kumari Selja, Minister of State for Housing & Urban Poverty Alleviation was unanimously elected as President of the Governing Council of UN Habitat at the 21st Governing Council meeting of the UN-Habitat at Nairobi for a two year term. This is the highest recognition India has received at the UN-Habitat with this two year term as President of the Governing Council till date. Kumari Selja succeeds Mr. Petr Kopriva, from the Czech Republic. UN-Habitat is an important organ of the UN system responsible for dealing with all issues relating to human settlements. It is mandated by the UN General Assembly to promote socially and environmentally sustainable towns and cities with the goal of providing adequate shelter for all. As the Minister of Housing & Urban Poverty Alleviation, Kumari Selja has taken significant initiatives for creating enabling and facilitating environment for effective delivery of housing and related infrastructure facilities in the rapidly urbanizing town and cities of India, with specific focus on the under-privileged and the economically weaker sections of the society. Formulation of New National Housing and Habitat Policy, National

Slum Policy, National Policy on Street Vendors etc. are some of the recent initiatives taken to address the concerns of the urban poor and slum dwellers with an inclusive approach for sustainable, safer and healthier cities besides specific focus on provision of basic services to the urban poor with security of tenure at affordable costs, improved housing, water supply and sanitation through the Jawaharlal Nehru National Urban Renewal Mission (JNNURM). She also holds the position of Chairperson of the Bureau of the Asia Pacific Ministers Conference of Housing and Urban Development (APMCHUD) and also represents Asia in the Commonwealth Local Government Forum's Conference.

250. (16-4-2007) NEW DELHI : National Water Development Agency (NWDA) has sought an outlay of Rs. 241 crore for the 11th Five Year Plan. Out of the 30 links identified for preparation of feasibility reports under National Perspective Plan for Water Resources Development (16 Peninsular and 14 Himalayan), NWDA has prepared feasibility reports (FRs) for 14 links under Peninsular Component and 2 under Himalayan Component (Indian portion only). The implementation of Interlinking of rivers depends upon the consensus and cooperation of the States. Consensus has been arrived for one priority link namely Ken-Betwa for which Government of Madhya Pradesh. Uttar Pradesh and Government of Indian signed a tripartite MoU on 25th August 2005 for preparation of Detailed Project Report (DPR). NWDA has incurred expenditure amounting to Rs. 19.7 crore for 2003-04, Rs. 21.3 crore for 2004-05 and Rs. 17 crore for 2005-06 for carrying out various studies pertaining to Inter basin water transfers including preparation of DPR of Ken-Betwa link. The expenditure is not booked State-wise by NWDA. The Ministry of Water Resources (erstwhile Ministry of Irrigation) and Central Water Commission (CWC) formulated a National Perspective Plan (NPP) for Water Resources Development in 1980 envisaging inter-basin transfer of water from surplus basins to deficit basins/areas for optimum utilization of water Resources. The NPP comprises two components, namely, Himalayan Rivers Development Component and Peninsular Rivers Development Component. National Water Development Agency (NWDA) was set up under the Ministry of Water Resources in 1982 for carrying out various technical studies to establish the feasibility of the proposals of NPP.

251. (16-4-2007) NEW DELHI : The Central Government has notified 8 subordinate offices of the Employees Provident Fund Organisation, working under the aegis of the Labour & Employment Ministry, whereof 80 per cent of the staff have acquired working knowledge of Hindi. The notification has been issued under the Official Languages (Use for the Official Purposes of the Union) Act, 1976. The notified offices are Regional Provident Fund Offices at Bangalore, Gantur and South Delhi, Sub-regional Providient Fund Offices at Raichur and Maysur in Karnataka, Vashi and Akola in Maharashtra and Kollam in Kerala. In addition, Zonal Training Institute, Western Region, Ujjain has also been notified for the 80 per cent staff having acquired the working knowledge of Hindi.

252. (16-4-2007) NEW DELHI : Prof. Ved Prakash, the Vice Chancellor of the National University of Educational Planning and Administration (NUEPA) has said that the data gathered by the District Information System of Education (DISE) is heavily used by the Researchers and thus has facilitated their work. On the occasion of the release of the District Report Cards: 2005-06 here today, he said this data is presently available for primary level and there is now need to have similar data for the Secondary level. He said the Department of Education and Planning in collaboration with the Human Resource Develop Ministry is making data for Secondary level education. He said that it has been made mandatory for the states to check data authenticity. Prof. Ved Prakash also said that an Education Development Index has been developed for Primary and Upper Primary levels and the states have been ranked as per this index.

253. (16-4-2007) NEW DELHI : Ministry of Agriculture, Department of Animal Husbandry, Dairying & Fisheries has banned fishing by all deep sea fishing vessels in the Exclusive Economic Zone of India from 15th April to 31st May, 2007 (both days inclusive) along east coast and from 15th June to 31st July, 2007 (both days inclusive) along west coast. All maritime States/UTs and other concerned are informed through this press release to note the decision of the Central Government.

254. (16-4-2007) NEW DELHI : Grants-in-aid amounting to Rs. 3.00 lakh has been released to Chaubisee Vikas Sangh (NGO) as 3rd and final instalment of Central Assistance for setting up RBC at Meham, District Rohtak in Haryana by the Ministry of Rural Development. The grant is towards the Plan expenditure and will be utilised for approved items of works as per the project proposal submitted by the concerned grant-receiving agency and approved by Government of India for setting up Rural Building Centre. The Grants receiving Agency shall keep a separate account of its activities and submit Utilisation Certificate supported by Audited statement of Account of the funds released for the purpose along with completion certificate. The Agency will also have to submit quarterly progress report on the implementation of the project.

255. (16-4-2007) NEW DELHI : The Ministry of Rural Development has released Grants-in-aid amounting to Rs. 3.00 lakh to the Purba Hailakandi Development Council as 3rd and final instalment of Central Assistance for setting up Rural Building Centre (RBC) at Bashdor, District Hailakandi in Assam. The grant is towards the Plan expenditure and will be utilised for approved items of works as per the project proposal submitted by the concerned grant-receiving agency and approved by Government of India for setting up the Rural Building Centre. The Grants receiving Agency shall keep a separate account of its activities and submit Utilisation Certificate supported by Audited statement of Account of the funds released for the purpose along with completion certificate.

256. (16-4-2007) NEW DELHI : The Defence Minister Shri AK Antony has called upon the Armed Forces to reduce revenue expenditure, while utilizing more funds for capital acquisitions and modernisation. Addressing the Army Commanders' Conference here today, Shri Antony called upon the top brass to embrace austerity and shun profligacy to ensure optimum and efficient utilization of funds. He suggested the Forces may adopt the motto of "Service with Simplicity". "We have been allotted an enhanced budget for the current financial year. We need to ensure optimum and efficient utilization of funds. Our Armed Forces would do well to embrace austerity and shun profligacy. I would like the slogan of our Armed Forces to be "Service with Simplicity". The emphasis should be more on reducing revenue expenditure, while utilizing more funds for capital acquisitions and modernisation", he said. The Defence Minister spoke on a wide range of issues relating to the security situation in the country and in the region. He said, the situation in Jammu and Kashmir is by and large under control. The violence has been brought down to a large extent by effective operations by our Security Forces, along the Line of Control as well as in the hinterland. The policy of the Security Forces of 'Iron Fist with Velvet Glove', as enunciated in the recently released doctrine on sub-conventional operations, is paying dividends. Shri Antony said, the cease fire along the Line of Control is holding. Though various political and diplomatic developments and initiatives on both sides have increased the levels of expectancy, there is no change in Pakistan's support to cross-border terrorism in Jammu and Kashmir. This remains a cause of concern to us, he said. Referring to the Indo-Pak talks, he said, Islamabad will have to put an end to cross-border terrorism for the dialogue to be successful. Shri Antony said, Pakistan has continued to increase its defence budget and receive military assistance from various countries. "Although we wish to continue the talks process with Pakistan, it is imperative for us to keep a close watch on various developments and maintain constant vigil", he said.

257. (16-4-2007) NEW DELHI : Shri Satyavrat Chaturvedi said that the elections in Uttar Pradesh has reached a very interesting and important stage. Our national leaders have campaigned across the state and Shri Rahul Gandlli has been a great source of attraction and inspiration to the youth of Uttar Pradesh which has come to support actively the Congress Party's campaign .The amount of support that we are getting and the response that we are getting from the people has created a sort of uproar in some of the political parties and their leaders who otherwise thought that the Congress Party was a non-issue in this election in the beginning. To a question whether raking up history of the 1971 war was correct, Shri Chaturvedi said that all political parties and their leaders, including Congress and Rahul Gandhi, when they campaign for their party in the elections, it is but very natural that they would like to highlight. The achievements of their party and their political leaders and Congress is not the only one. Don't you think there are people who are talking about the achievements of Kanshi Ram, there are others who are talking about the achievements of Atal Behariji, and there others who are talking about Lohiaji .If they can talk about them, why cant the Congress leader talk about his own party's achievements and its leader's achievements .so we are trying to go to the people and convince them from our past achievements and show them a way for the future. To a question on Rahul Gandhi's statements on dismemberment of Pakistan and on the dynasty role, Shri Chaturvedi said that when Rahul Gandhi talked about dismemberment of Pakistan he referred to what happened as a result of the 1971 war that Pakistan thrusted upon us and that is part of the history. We may not have intended to do that but that was the ultimate result and if that was the ultimate result and yes, of course he referred to it as one of its achievements. Let me in the first place read out exactly what he said. Because I have seen the reports in the newspapers and each paper has written about his statement in his own way. So let us see exactly as to what he said. This statement was in Hindi and which goes like" Gandhi pariwar ne jo thana usea haashil bhi kiya, chayhe wo aazadi ho, chayhe wo aazadi ka mudda ho ya Pak ka vibhajan ho athva desh ko ekkishvin sadi main Ie jane ki pehal ka ho, hamney har jaghe agwai ki". This is exactly what he said. Now, when he talks about the dismemberment of Pakistan, he talks about the fact of the history. So the fact of the history is that the war that was thrusted upon India during 1971 by Pakistan and there were early morning bombardments at various places in India and ultimately as a result of this war Pakistan got dismembered and Bangladesh was born. To a question on dynasty role, Shir Chaturvedi said that when it comes to Congress Party there is always a reference and acquisition of dynasty politics being played. What about others, I have a list of all the political leaders and let me go and read it out to you. Shri Chaturvedi read out the names of political leaders of other parties and their relatives who also were in active politics begin with the name of relatives of Shri Atal Behariji. To a question of only highlighting his family members by Rahul Gandhi, Shri Chaturvedi said that you have misread his statement, whether it is referred in reference to the freedom struggle or this or the latter part, the leader of the organization always stands in the forefront, whether it is criticism, he faces the flak, or it is the credit but it is the entire organization.

258. (16-4-2007) NEW DELHI : The Belarus Interior Minister, Mr. Vladimir Naumov met the Union Home Minister, Shri Shivraj Patil here today. The two leaders expressed satisfaction over the current level of understanding between the two countries and expressed the desire to further strengthen the bilateral relations. During the meeting, various issues including those relating to security were discussed. Shri Patil informed the visiting Minister that India has suffered a lot due to terrorism, but has been able to contain the menace. He expressed satisfaction over the fact that there is growing international realization now about the need to contain terrorism. The Union Home Minister also briefed the Belarus Interior Minister about the working of his Ministry, particularly in the sphere of Centre-State relations. Shri Patil accepted Mr. Naumov's invitation to visit Belarus. The meeting lasted about 45 minutes.

259. (16-4-2007) NEW DELHI : The total live storage of 76 important reservoirs in different parts of the country is 46.354 billion cubic metre (BCM), which is

13.9 BCM or 43% more than the average of last 10 years storage. It is 3.381 BCM more than the last year's storage too. Of the 76 reservoirs monitored by the Central Water Commission, 61 are having more than 80% of normal storage as on April 12, 2007. As per Weekly Weather Watch Group Report, the total area coverage of wheat has been significantly higher. The area this year is 284.969 lakh hectare as against 266.970 lakh hectare in the corresponding period of 2005-06. Higher coverage has been reported from Bihar, Gujarat, Haryana, Karnataka, Madhya Pradesh, Rajasthan and Uttar Pradesh. The crop condition is normal. Sowing of rabi rice is in progress in many states. The total coverage so far is 41.010 lakh hectare. The area coverage of coarse cereals has been higher at 67.193 lakh hectare against last year's 63.091 lakh hectare. Pulses cover 142.246 lakh hectare which is 4.594 lakh hectare more than that of last year.

260. (16-4-2007) NEW DELHI : The Security Printing Press, Hyderabad will continue to be a public utility service for another six months from April 17, 2007. The Security Printing Press, Hyderabad was declared a public utility service under the Industrial Disputes Act, 1947 for six months with effect from October 17, 2006. According to a notification issued by the Ministry of Labour and Employment, this has been done in public interest. The employees in this industry, as a result, would among other things be required to give notice to their employer six weeks in advance of proceeding on strike so that conciliatory proceedings could be started. During the conciliatory proceedings and seven days after their completion, the employees cannot go on strike.

261. (17-4-2007) NEW DELHI : The Government has decided that officers holding honorary ranks of Field Marshal of the Army and Marshal of the Air Force would be entitled to an upgraded pay and emoluments package along with certain other facilities in keeping with the rare honour attached to these ranks. The upgraded package would become effective from the date of holding of these ranks, as a mark of the country's deep appreciation of the invaluable services rendered. With this decision Field Marshal SHFJ Manekshaw and Marshal of the Air Force Arjan Singh, would be entitled to the same scale of pay as a Chief of the Service, along with a Special Pay. Residential accommodation or House Rent Allowance in lieu and Leave Travel Concession would also be admissible to both the dignitaries as per rules applicable to the Chief of Service. Other facilities such as Staff Officer, a nominated Staff Car, Medical facilities, and an official Hospitality allowance would also be made available. The dignitaries would also be extended the status of State Guest on visit to any state.

262. (17-4-2007) NEW DELHI : Following is the statement issued by the Power Ministry: "It has been reported in a section of the press that Secretary, Ministry of Power has stated that the Power Finance Corporation (PFC) which is the nodal agency for bidding for Ultra Mega Power Projects has sought clarification on the low tariff of Sasan Power Project through M/s Ernst and Young. However, the clarifications that have been sought do not relate to tariff. The procedure of allotment of Ultra Mega Power Projects seeks to attain market determined tariffs. Tariff issues are handled in the CERC and the PFC has been trying to obtain the lowest possible tariffs for the power procurers. This clarification had been given to the PTI last evening itself."

263. (17-4-2007) NEW DELHI : The guidelines for publication of newspapers and periodicals dealing with news and current affairs and publication of facsimile editions of foreign newspapers have been partially amended. As per the amended Clause 4(iv) pertaining to basic conditions/obligations of the guidelines, "the entity shall be liable to intimate the names and details of any foreigners/NRIs proposed to be employed/engaged in the entity either as consultant (or in any other capacity) for more than 60 days in a year, or, as regular employees. The entity shall be liable to dispense with the services of such persons if not found security cleared subsequently." Earlier, the clause read as "all entities shall obtain prior clearance of the Ministry of Information & Broadcasting of any foreigners/NRIs proposed to be employed/engaged in the new entity either as consultants (or in any other capacity) for more than 60 days in a year, or, as regular employees."

264. (17-4-2007) NEW DELHI : India's Civil Services have a proud record of contribution to national integration and development for which our whole nation has to be grateful to them. Central Civil Services are the backbone of the governance structure of our nation. They have played a vital role in the task of nation building, right from the time we achieved independence, to the present day. It was Sardar Vallabhbhai Patel's vision that the Civil Service should strengthen cohesion and national unity. He wanted a strong and vibrant federal administrative system in which the All India Services would play an important role. True to his conviction, the Civil Services have provided the framework for the administration of the country. The values of integrity, impartiality and merit remain the guiding principles of Civil Services and that is as it should be. Sardar Patel advised young officers at the dawn of Independence in 1947: "Above all I would advise you to maintain to the utmost the impartiality and incorruptibility of administration. A Civil Servant cannot afford to, and must not, take part in politics. Nor must he involve himself in communal wrangles. To depart from the path of rectitude in either of these respects is to debase public service and to lower its dignity. Similarly no service worth the name can claim to exist if it does not have in view the achievement of the highest standard of integrity."

265. (17-4-2007) NEW DELHI : Air Chief Marshal Fali Homi Major PVSM AVSM SC VM ADC, Chief of the Air Staff 'flagged off' the IAF Platinum Jubilee Celebrations Mountaineering Expedition Team to Mt Cho Oyu today in an impressive ceremony at Air HQ (Vayu Bhawan), New Delhi. Mt. Cho Oyu, the sixth highest peak in the world will be attempted by a team of fifteen air warriors from the North West route in China in Apr.-May 07. Expedition to Mt. Cho Oyu is part of the major events planned as Indian Air Force celebrates its Platinum Jubilee. The team led by Wg Cdr RC Tripathi VM will leave for the expedition on 19 Apr. 07. Mt. Cho Oyu stands astride the Nepal/Tibet border, just 30 miles West of Mt. Everest. The climb route is from Tibetan side of the Nangpa La pass which used to be old trading route to Nepal. The expedition team will be entering Tibet via Kathmandu and Lhasa and thereafter driving over the Tibetan Plateau to the North side of the mountain. From the last roadhead, a three days approach march would lead to the Base Camp. The team will establish three higher camps after the advance base camp before attempting the final summit push some time by end of May 2007. Earlier, IAF created history in the mountaineering fraternity by hosting the tricolour on top of Everest on 30 May 2005. The air warriors of the Indian Air Force (including lady officers) have been pursuing mountaineering activity as a part of adventure for more than three decades. Today Indian Air Force has a nucleus of qualified mountaineers ready to take on the challenge of climbing any peak in the world. The Air Chief encouraged the mountaineers and told them that not only did they have the blessings of the Air Force-the whole Nation was behind them and wished them all success.

266. (17-4-2007) NEW DELHI : Shri Murli Deora, Minister of Petroleum & Natural Gas is leaving tomorrow on a seven-day official visit to three oil and gas rich countries-Syria, Algeria and Egypt for further expanding the growing cooperation between India and these countries in the oil and gas sector. Other members of the delegation are, Petroleum Secretary Shri M.S. Srinivasan, CMD ONGC Shri R.S. Sharma, IOC Chairman Shri S. Behuria, GAIL CMD Dr. U.D. Choubey and EILCMD Shri M. Rohatagi. In the first leg of his visit Shri Deora will be reaching Damascus, Syria tomorrow afternoon and would lead the Indian delegation during official meeting with his counterpart Minister of Oil & Natural Resources Mr. Soufian Allaw. He is expected to call on the President of Republic of Syria besides meeting the Deputy Prime Minister for Economic Affairs. In addition to the ONGC holding interests in two properties (OVL's 60% in Exploration Block XXIV and ONGC's 33% jointly with CNPCI in a producing field), Indian companies would be looking at the possibility of utilizing next round of bidding for exploration blocks in 2007. In the downstream area, EIL is interested in examining revamping jobs of Hayan and Banias refinery. Indian oil's proposal for construction of 6.5MMTPA refinery at Deir Ez Zor is likely to be discussed. Further, Indian side would offer GAIL's expertise in developing city gas projects in Syria benefiting from highly successful Indian experience of city gas project implementation in Delhi and Mumbai. The delegation would arrive in Algeria on 20th April in the afternoon. A delegation level talk will be co-chaired by Shri Deora and his counterpart Mr. Chakib Khelil, Minister of Energy & Mining of Algeria next day. The agreed minute of the meeting is likely to be signed by the two Ministers on 22nd April. Shri Deora also expected to call on the President of Algeria. The visit would be utilized for creating positive atmosphere for Indian E&P companies to pursue opportunities in the next round of bidding for blocks by the Algerian Minister of Energy & Mines. OVL proposes to jointly bid with the Algerian National Oil Company, Sonatrach for which OVL has an MoU in place with Sonatrach along with one for jointly bidding with Iraq. OIL and GAIL are also pursuing E&P opportunity in Algeria. In the down stream sector, possibilities of securing Liquefied Natural Gas (LNG) supplies for Petronet LNG, GAIL and IOC would be explored besides IOC's interests in gas based petrochemical projects. Opportunities for Indian Oil PSUs in City Gas Distribution Projects would also be taken up during the visit.

267. (17-4-2007) NEW DELHI : The Prime Minister is to inaugurate a National Conference on Rural Roads on May 23, 2007 in New Delhi. He will also release the document "Rural Roads Plan : Vision-2025", prepared by the M/o rural Development for future development on rural roads in the country, on the occasion. The conference organized by the Ministry of Rural Development will have a series of technical sessions in which the stakeholders would share their experience about development of rural roads. Around 1500 key experts from the Central and State Governments, Financial Institutions, R & D institutions, Field Engineers from States, Consultants, Machinery Manufacturers and Private Sector Construction Agencies are expected to participate in the conference. A technical exhibition to exhibit various materials and machinaries and to showcase the achievements in the flagship rural roads development programme has also been planned during the conference. Pradhan Mantri Gram Sadak Yojana (PMGSY) is implemented by Ministry of Rural Development with the objective of providing all weather connectivity to habitations of 500 plus in the plain areas and 250 or more in the hill states, desert areas and tribal areas of the country. Under PMGSY, more than one lakh km of road has been completed so far and work is in progress in respect of projects covering another one lakh kilometer. Under Bharat Nirman, a time bound goal has been set to provide connectivity to 66,802 habitations of the country by 2009 with 1.46 lakh km of new link roads. Further, 1.94 lakh km of existing routes and major rural link roads are targeted to be upgraded/ renewed within the same time frame to ensure full farm to market connectivity. Since its launch in Dec., 2000, the programme has not only set standards and benchmarks for technical aspects of rural road construction but has also introduced a host of good practices for effective project management.

268. (17-4-2007) NEW DELHI : Shri Milon Kumar Banerji has been re-appointed as Attorney General of India. A notification issued in this regard by the Ministry of Law and Justice here said, " The President is pleased to re-appoint Shri Milon Kumar Banerji, Senior Advocate as Attorney General for India for a period of two years with effect from 5th June 2007." The three-year tenure of Shri Banerji as Attorney General is to expire on June 4, 2007. Born on September 27, 1929, Shri Banerji earlier served as Attorney General of India from November 1992 to July 1996.

269. (17-4-2007) NEW DELHI : Banking Industry will continue to be a public utility service for another six months from April 17, 2007. The industry was declared a public utility service under the Industrial Disputes Act, 1947 for six months with effect from October 17, 2006. According to a notification issued by the Ministry of Labour and Employment, this has been done in public interest. The employees in this industry, as a result, would among other things be required to give notice to their employer six weeks in advance of proceeding on strike so that conciliatory proceedings could be started. During the conciliatory proceedings and seven days after their completion, the employees cannot go on strike.

270. (17-4-2007) SHAJAHANPUR: The Central and State leadership of the Congress has stoutly defended Rahul Gandhi's statement on the Nehru-Gandhi family's role "in dividing Pakistan" as a valid historical assessment, but the reaction among the party's rank and file in Uttar Pradesh does not reflect the same conviction. On the contrary, sections of the Congress support base admit that they are a bit bewildered by the political points being made the young leader, though his presence in the campaign has indeed enthused them. Scores of Congress workers that this correspondent met between Badayun and Shajahanpur, the campaign trail hit by Rahul Gandhi over the weekend, were unable to decipher or elucidate the political purpose of Rahul Gandhi's comment on the division of Pakistan. "One cannot make out why he brought in this element to highlight the political determination of the Nehru family," said Veerender Kashyap of Dataganj, who had travelled around 30 km and waited for more than five hours to see and hear "Rahul Baba" at Badayun. This Youth Congress worker was of the view that Rahul Gandhi should have focused more on the "extreme sacrifices that the Nehru-Gandhi family had made in the interests of the nation." That, he felt, would have touched an emotional chord with the masses in general and dormant party workers in particular. A veteran Congress activist from Bareilly, who wished to remain anonymous, perceived shades of the Rajiv Gandhi brand of soft Hindutva politics in Rahul Gandhi's statement. "A claim that the Congress had actively worked for the division of Pakistan would certainly appeal more to a section of sectarian Hindus. Rajiv Gandhi had also tried to win this segment over in the mid-eighties by supporting the construction of a Ram temple in Ayodhya and overseeing the Shilanyas (laying of foundation stone) for the same."

271. (17-4-2007) NEW DELHI : Farm commodity prices monitored by the Department of Consumer Affairs have generally remained steady or declined at the 18 monitoring centres over the week ending April 10, 2007. Prices of wheat at retail level remained steady at 16 out of 18 centres. The price declined at Lucknow and Ahmedabad. The Government has notified extension of duty free imports of wheat till 31st December, 2007. Retail price of sugar remained steady over the week across most of the centres, decreased at Agartala, Bhubaneshwar and Shillong, and increased only at Chennai. Prices of gram dal and tur dal have generally remained steady across all the monitoring centres. Over 48 thousand tonne of imported pulses have arrived at Indian ports out of 2.25 lakh tonne contracted by STC (1,00,000 T), Nafed (70,000 T), PEC (29,000 T) and MMTC (26,000 T). At Delhi, as on 10.4.07, prices of rice, onion and mustard oil were holding steady for one week; those of wheat and atta, sugar and milk for one month; of vanaspati for 6 months; and price of salt was steady for one year. Prices of loose tea and potato declined & those of gram dal and tur dal increased over the week.

272. (17-4-2007) NEW DELHI : The Home Minister, Shri Shivraj Patil has stressed the need for accelerating the process of computerization of police stations in the country. Speaking at the Investiture Ceremony of the National Crime Records Bureau (NCRB) here today, he said that proper plans would have to be drawn up for the purpose. He expressed confidence that the Central and State Governments would be in a position to spare the necessary funds for the purpose. Training of police personnel will also be necessary and the facilities available outside the police setup may also be used for the purpose. The Home Minister said that proper systems have to be put in place to collect information about crimes from every nook and corner of the country and collate, store, analyse and use it in a scientific manner. Speaking on the occasion, the Union Home Secretary, Shri Madhukar Gupta expressed happiness over the fact that NCRB has continued to maintain world-class norms of operations and called upon the organization to continuously strive for further excellence. The Home Minister presented the Indian Police Medals for meritorious service to Shri Darwan Singh Sajwan, Jt. Assistant Director and Shri Chet Narayan Kumar, retired Deputy Superintendent (Records). The Khan Bahadur Azizul Haque rolling shield for the top merit holder of the All India Board Examination for Fingerprint Experts for 2006 was given to Shri Ranbir Singh, Sub Inspector, Finger Prints Bureau, Haryana. The Home Minister also handed over the renewed ISO 9001:2000 Certification, given by the Bureau of Indian Standards, to the Director of NCRB, Shri Sudhir Awasthi. The Minister of State for Home, Shri S. Regupathy was among those presented on the occasion. NCRB was established in 1986 under the Ministry of Home Affairs with the primary mandate of functioning as a clearing house of information on crime and criminals and collecting and processing crime statistics. Over a period of time, the NCRB has taken up the implementation of national projects on police computerization and crime and criminal information systems and is striving to assist the State Governments and other police agencies in setting up of data banks for ensuring availability of correct, complete and reliable information on crime and criminals.

273. (17-4-2007) NEW DELHI : In Arunachal Pradesh, National Rural Employment Guarantee Act (NREGA) during 2006-07 was initially launched in one district and has further been extended to 2 more districts during the current financial year. During the first year of its implementation, 0.17 lakh households demanded employment and all of them have been provided employment. The number of person day of employment provided in the State is 4.53 lakh. The average person days of employment provided in a district stands at 4.53 lakh compared to the national average of 36.47 lakh person days. Of them, 30.02% are provided to women and 100% to members of ST. The employment provided was on 496 works, of which 397 number of works have been completed. The average number of works taken up in a district is 496 against the national average of 3,581. The average number of households provided employment in a district of the State is 16,926, while the National Average stands at 91,685. An amount of Rs. 12.11 crore was released to the State during 2006-07. Up to January 2007, Rs.2.21 crore was utilized, which is 18.27% of the total availability. The expenditure on wages stood at 98.90%, material at Nil% and on administration 1.09% was spent. The average expenditure on a district came out to be Rs. 2.21 crore compared to the National average of Rs. 35 crore.

274. (17-4-2007) NEW DELHI : In Andhra Pradesh, National Rural Employment Guarantee Act (NREGA) during 2006-07 was launched in 13 districts and has further been extended to 6 more districts during the current financial year. During the first year of its implementation, 19.15 lakh households demanded employment and all of them have been provided employment. Moreover, 46 thousand households have completed the 100 days of guaranteed employment provided in the Act up to February 2007. The number of person days of employment provided in the State is 548.23 lakh. The average person days of employment provided in a district stands at 42.17 lakh compared to the national average of 36.47 lakh person days. Of them, 53.59% are provided to women, 30.31% to SC and 12.62% to ST. The employment provided was on 1,78,844 works, of which 55,757 number of works have been completed. The average number of works taken up in a district is 13,757 against the national average of 3,581. The average number of households provided employment in a district of the State is 1,47,325, while the National Average stands at 91,685. An amount of Rs. 999.61 crore was released to the State during 2006-07. Up to February 2007, Rs.512.53 crore was utilized, which is 46.25% of the total availability. The expenditure on wages stood at 87.76%, material at 0.89% and on administration 11.35% was spent. The average expenditure on a district came out to be Rs. 39.43 crore compared to the National average of Rs. 35.00 crore.

275. (17-4-2007) NEW DELHI : The Union Minister for Shipping, Road Transport & Highways Thiru T.R.Baalu, received an interim dividend cheque of Rs. 192,26,33,955/-(Rs. 192.26 crore) from the Chairman & Managing Director of Shipping Corporation of India (SCI), Shri S. Hajara, here today. Shri A.K.Mohapatra, Secretary (Shipping), was also present on the occasion. The Shipping Corporation of India (SCI) declared an Interim Dividend of 85% for the year 2006-07. This dividend amount of Rs.192.26 crore, reflects the earnings on the 80.12% shareholding of the Government of India in the SCI. It may be recalled that the SCI has declared a net profit of Rs. 729.93 crore for the nine months ending on 31.12.2006, during the financial year 2006-07. The Shipping Corporation of India, is the largest shipping company in India and has a share of about 35% of the total Indian tonnage. SCI is the first Indian shipping company to enter the LNG transportation business as partner in a joint venture, comprising of SCI, Mitsui

OSK Lines, NYK Line and K-Line. This consortium is already operating 2 LNG tankers, which carries LNG for Petronet for its Dahej project. This consortium has successfully bid and won the tender for construction, ownership and 25 years of operation of the 3rd LNG tanker required by Petronet LNG Limited for its expansion project at Dahej. SCI has also formed a joint venture company with Forbes Gokak Ltd. & Sterling Investment Corporation Pvt. Ltd. for owning and operation of chemical carriers. This JVC has placed already orders for 4 nos. Chemical Carriers of about 13,000 dwt each. SCI has also initiated an Integrated End-to-End IT system and M/s Tata Consultancy Services (TCS) was selected as IT partner for the same. The project would be implemented in two phases. During the Phase-I, TCS would study the IT requirements of SCI and prepare the IT blueprint and roadmap for implementation, which would be completed in 4 months, which is nearing completion. In the Phase-II, which is the implementation phase, the solutions identified in phase I would be implemented as per the roadmap and this is expected to be completed in 18 to 24 months. SCI has also implemented a company-wide quality management system based on the international standards ISO 9001:2000. As a part of the implementation, the Company has conducted the internal audit, pre-assessment audit and final certification audit.

276. (17-4-2007) NEW DELHI : Vice President, Shri Bhairon Singh Shekhawat has said that to realize our full potential in the game of football, we need to build world class sports infrastructure in rural and tribal areas. We need to identify talent in schools and catch them young for rigorous training. We should provide playing fields and all other sports facilities in all Colleges and Schools. Shri Shekhawat while addressing a Special Congress organised to celebrate the 70th anniversary of All India Football Federation in New Delhi this afternoon said that he himself used to play football in his school days and he loves it as it is the game of common man. He has been in public life for over 50 years. All these years he has enjoyed playing the game of politics, like football, always in the service of the common man. He has always believed in playing a fair game in sportsman's spirit. Therefore, in his long innings he always won friends and never made enemies. He hoped that if many more sports persons join politics, it will improve our system. Shri Shekhawat said that when AIFF is celebrating its 70th Anniversary, it is opportune to introspect as to how we can give Indian Football a new thrust and upswing. He is happy that some serious steps are already on the anvil. About two years back, he had laid the foundation of Football House of India. This project was funded by FIFA. He hoped that President of FIFA, who was present there, would help in setting up some other such projects. He thanked AFC President for providing two Vision Asia projects for Delhi and Manipur. Such projects will not only provide big fillip and support to football in India, but will also go a long way in building amongst the youth a new culture and ethos of brotherhood, understanding, harmony and peace. He believes that this is certainly a very effective way to build a better world of shared values of mutual trust and care. Shri Shekhawat complemented Mr. Dasmunsi for having organized, in his capacity as President of AIFF, this Special Congress. He hoped that it will contribute to firm up and launch new projects of powerful kinetic energy that would generate a new momentum for kicking Indian football high in the global arena. Shri Priyaranjan Dasmunshi, President, AIFF and Union Minister for Parliamentary Affairs welcomed the guests. Mr. Joseph Sepp Blatter, President, FIFA and Mr. Mohammed Bin Hammam, President, AFC also spoke on the occasion. Both said that Football in India has great potential and they would provide full assistance. Shri Praful Patel, Vice President, AIFF and Union Minister for Civil Aviation thanked the guests.

277. (17-4-2007) NEW DELHI : The Railways have generated Rs.41754.85 crore of revenue earnings from freight traffic during April 2006-March 2007 as compared to Rs. 35534.69 crore during the corresponding period last year, registering an increase of 17.50 per cent. Railways carried 728.41 million tonnes of freight traffic during April-March 2007 as compared to 667.20 million tonnes carried during the corresponding period last year, an increase of 9.17 per cent. The Net Tonne Kilo Metres (NTKM) went up from 439596 million during April-March 2006 to 475046 million during April-March 2007, an increase of 8.06 per cent. The earnings from freight traffic during the month of March 2007 was Rs. 4100.55 crore, compared to Rs. 3550.46 crore during the corresponding period last year showing an increase of 15.49 per cent. Railways carried 72.07 million tonnes (MTs) of freight traffic during the month as compared to 66.19 million tonnes of freight traffic during the corresponding period last year, registering an increase of 8.88 per cent. The Net Tonne Kilo Metres (NTKM) went up from 43564 million during the month of March 2006 to 46009 million during March 2007, an increase of 5.61 per cent. Of the total earnings during the month of March 2007, Rs. 1566.87 crore came from transportation of 31.12 million tonnes of coal, followed by Rs. 333.55 crore from 3.97 million tonnes of foodgrains, Rs. 371.00 crore from 7.09 million tonnes of cement, Rs. 243.61 crore from 3.08 million tonnes of petroleum oil and lubricant (POL), Rs. 256.26 crore from 3.67 million tonnes iron ore for exports, Rs. 179.65 crore from 2.85 million tonnes of fertilizers, Rs. 213.32 crore from 1.99 million tonnes of iron & steel for steel plants, Rs. 183.29 crore from 5.00 million tonnes of raw material for steel plants and Rs. 753.00 crore from 13.30 million tonnes of other goods.

278. (17-4-2007) NEW DELHI : Shri Dvendra Dwivedi said that the Congress Party expresses its anguish and grave concern at the manner on which the BJP in the past few days has injected hate based political rhetoric and misplaced confrontatism into the election campaign in Uttar Pradesh and political discourse at the national level. The BJP has taken recourse to what it is best at: Communalizing the nation's politics; distorting history and falsifying facts and belittling and denigrating the contribution that the Congress Party and the Nehru family have made to the making of modern India. The outrageous tone in the attacks on Shri Rahul Gandhi and yesterday on Prime Minister Manmohan Singh for his laudatory comments about Shri Rahul Gandhi's future as a leader are in tune with the BJP's standard politics. The history of the rich contributions that the members of the Nehru family have made during the course of freedom struggle and nation building is also in a substantive measure the political biography of the resurgent India. Between themselves, Mr. Nehru and Mrs. Indira Gandhi provided stewardship to the new nation state for a good thirty three years and the five years of Mr. Rajiv Gandhi's memorable leadership make it thirty eight years of a historical legacy which has no parallel in democratic history. During this period they received massive political and electoral support from the Indian people. This lent legitimacy to their leadership and to the institutions of democracy. The three leaders along with other stalwarts laid the foundations of the Indian state defined the contours and content of the foundational principles of our democracy, strengthened the secular order, made India economically self reliant and preserved India's unity, integrity and sovereignty. In the process the nation witnessed the sacrifice of the lives of Indiraji and Rajivji. Theirs is legacy of which the entire nation is proud. For the BJP to use the term Dynasty for that heritage is to betray intellectual bankruptcy and to do violence to history. Shri Rahul Gandhi was fully justified in bringing that legacy to the collective memory of the people of Uttar Pradesh and also the country. The pathological hatred of the Sangh Parivar against the Nehru family and the Congress Party was central to its politics during the life time of Mr. Nehru, Mrs. Indira Gandhi and Rajiv Gandhi. Now Smt. Sonia Gandhi and Rahul Gandhi are its targets. Besides, the outrageous and intemperate attack yesterday on Prime Minister Manmohan Singh borders on being vituperative and abusive and violates even modicum of norms of decency and political civility. It is a part of an ongoing attack on the Prime minister and his person which reflects the BJP's desperation and its failure to reconcile to the defeat at the hustings. The BJP's record in obstructing parliamentary proceeding in the past three years including the debate on the budgets and customary address to the President sadly brings out its innate disrespect for our constitutional scheme. For the BJP to say that the Prime Minister is trying to impose Shri Rahul Gandhi on the people of Uttar Pradesh is ludicrous and reflects an authoritarian mindset. The future leader of UP and India will be, as always, decided by people. The speeches of Shri Rahul Gandhi in essence have reflected his commitment to secularism, a liberal and tolerant India and the welfare of the people of Uttar Pradesh.

279. (17-4-2007) NEW DELHI : India and Belarus have signed a Programme of Cooperation in the field of Culture, Arts, Education, Mass Media and Press for 2007-2009. It was signed by the Minister of Tourism and Culture Smt. Ambika Soni and Foreign Minister of Belarus, Sergei Martynov here last evening. According to the programme both the countries will exchange information on international music, dance and folklore festivals in the field of culture to be held in their respective countries. They will also invite specialists in the field of culture and artists to participate in international events to be held both in India and in Belarus. Both the countries will collaborate in exchanging audio and video in the field of performing arts. They will exchange artistic exhibitions and encourage establishing direct links and exchanges between the cultural establishments and artistic educational institutions. Both the countries will encourage collaboration between Indian and Belarusian governmental establishments of cinematography and explore possibility of signing a co-production agreement. The countries will organise cinema weeks in both the countries and will take part in International Film Festivals held in both the countries. Both the countries will promote establishing direct cooperation between educational institutions of both the countries to implement joint scientific research works, exchange probationers, professors, teachers and students on a parity basis. Both the countries will explore the possibility of mutual exchange of visits of journalists and mass media experts.

280. (18-4-2007) NEW DELHI : Shri Kamal Nath, Minister of Commerce & Industry, launched the UN-ESCAP's annual Economic and Social Survey of Asia and the Pacific 2007 at a global media launch here today.Releasing the Survey, the Minister noted that "the publication finds that apart from the remarkable performance in IT services, India is rapidly emerging as a force in manufacturing exports, with capital-intensive products featuring prominently". Speaking on the occasion, Shri Kamal Nath said he was pleased to note that this year's survey drew particular attention to the ascendancy of India of economic powerhouse. UN-ESCAP's analysis indicates that India's contribution to global growth has nearly doubled in the last two decades. As a result, India is now the world's fourth largest economy in terms of purchasing power parity. "Furthermore, the enormous trade potential between India and China is highlighted as one of the key phenomena in coming years. There has already been a four-fold increase in trade since 2002, and the still comparatively low absolute value promises dramatic room for future increase", he observed. Mr. Kim Hak-Su, Under Secretary General of the United Nations and Executive Secretary of UN-ESCAP, made a presentation of the Survey and Ms. Shalini Dewan, Director, United Nations Information Centre, also spoke on this occasion.

281. (18-4-2007) NEW DELHI : The Chief Minister of Maharashtra, Mr. Vilas Rao Deshmukh led a delegation from Maharashtra to appraise the Prime Minister regarding the Babhali Project on Godavari river. There was representation made earlier on the project to the Prime Minister by an All Party Delegation from Andhra Pradesh. After hearing representations from both sides, the Prime Minister has directed the Union Water Resources Minister, Mr. Saifuddin Soz to discuss the matter with both State Governments and facilitate an amicable solution.

282. (18-4-2007) NEW DELHI : The term of the Legislative Assembly of Goa is normally due to expire on 11th June, 2007. By virtue of its powers, duties and functions under Article 324 read with Article 172(1) of the Constitution of India, Section 15 of Representation of the People Act, 1951, the Commission is under a constitutional mandate to hold general election to constitute the new Legislative

Assembly in the State at anytime within a period of six months before the expiry of its present term.

283. (18-4-2007) NEW DELHI : The Minister of State for External Affairs, Shri Anand Sharma will launch the 8th World Hindi Conference (WHC) logo and website, in New Delhi tomorrow. The Conference is scheduled to be held in New York from July 13 to 15, 2007. The inaugural ceremony of the Conference will be held at UN Headquarters. It will be followed by an academic session on 'Hindi in the UN' at the same venue. The programme of the Conference includes other academic sessions, cultural programmes, exhibitions etc. A well-equipped media centre will be set up for use of media persons and appropriate arrangements for briefings are being made at the venue. Registration of delegates for the 8th WHC will commence soon. A steering Committee comprising of 33 non-official and 14 official members has been constituted under the Chairmanship of Minister of State, Shri Anand Sharma for the 8th WHC. 11 Sub-committees have been formed to deliberate on various aspects of the conference and submit their recommendations to the Steering Committee for consideration and approval. In New York, an Organising Committee has been formed under the chairmanship of Dr. Navin Mehta, Chairman, Bharatiya Vidya Bhavan, New York, which is the associate organization for organising the Conference. Indian Ambassador in USA is the Patron, and Consul General of India in New York, the Advisor of the Committee. The beginning of World Hindi Conferences was made more then 30 years ago under the patronage of then Prime Minister, Smt. Indira Gandhi when the first World Hindi Conference was held under the auspices of Rastrabhasha Prachar Samiti, Wardha in Nagpur from 10-12 January 1975. Six Conferences have been held since then, the last one in Suriname in June 2003. Ministry of External Affairs is the nodal Ministry for organizing these Conferences.

284. (18-4-2007) NEW DELHI : The Prime Minister has sanctioned an ex-gratia of Rupees one lakh from the Prime Minister's Relief Fund to Master Ankit of Faridabad, aged seven years, who was kidnapped and escaped from his kidnappers. Master Ankit exhibited bravery under extreme stress leading to ensuring the arrest of the kidnappers. The Prime Minister has also approved taking over of the cost of immediate medical assistance. The Prime Minister has further approved provision of assistance for artificial limb through the All India Institute of Medical Sciences, New Delhi. The ex-gratia would be kept in a fixed deposit in the name of the child, with interest income for use of his parents and the amount would be given to the child on his attaining 18 years of age.

285. (18-4-2007) NEW DELHI : Shri U.C.D. Shreni, President, Institution of Railway Electrical Engineers (IREE) and Additional Member (Electrical), Railway Board called on the Union Minister of State for Railways, Shri Naranbhai J. Rathwa here today and presented him with a paper on the decisions taken at the International Seminar on Energy Efficient Electrical System in Rail Sector-A

Vehicle for Turn Around held in January 2007 in New Delhi. Out of 36 papers presented at this Seminar, 14 papers were presented by experts from Japan, Switzerland, France, Sweden, Germany and USA.

286. (18-4-2007) NEW DELHI : Population growth along with limited fresh water sources has made good quality water a precious commodity today. Towards the alleviation of acute shortage of fresh water in the costal areas and Island territories of India, National Institute of Ocean Technology (NIOT), Chennai, an autonomous body under the Ministry of Earth Sciences has undertaken to establish low temperature thermal desalination plants to generate the fresh water from the sea surface water (28-30 0C) and cold deep sea water (9-12 0C). By flash evaporating the warm sea water under low pressure and condensing the water vapour with the cold sea water potable water is produced. This was revealed by Shri Kapil Sibal, Union Minister for Science and Technology & Earth Sciences at a press conference in New Delhi today. After successful trials in the laboratory and an experiment on a moored barge off Tuticorin in 400 m water depth, a land based plant was commissioned at Kavarati in Lakshadweep which is continuously generating good quality water since May 2005. So far more than 5 crore litres of water has been produced. The availability of high quality fresh water has drastically reduced dysentery and other such diseases. Buoyed with this success, eight more such units are being set up on other islands of Lakshadweep. Towards achieving large capacity plants suitable for mainland requirements an experimental floating desalination plant of one million litre per day capacity working on low temperature thermaldesalination plant has been commissioned for the first time ever in the world at a location 40 km offshore Chennai. The most complex part of the process is the drawal of cold water from the ocean which requires a long pipe of 1 m diameter made up of HDPE. HDPE pipes of such diameter are manufactured in the length of 12 m and these have to be fused together to make a 600 m long pipe weighing 100 tonnes. Since the density of the pipe is almost equal to saline water, it floats in the water and hence, heavy weight has to be attached at one end of the pipe to make it straight to reach the depth of 600 m where cold temperature of 9-12 0C is available. The deployment and connection of this pipe to the barge is a very challenging work, especially with limited offshore facility available in the country. The 600 m pipe was assembled at Ennore port, then towed to the site and connected vertically below the barge 'Sagar Shakti'. The barge is moored to a single point mooring in deep waters. Having generated that quantity of water, the next difficult task is its storage and transportation from 40 km offshore point to the shore. For this purpose, water bags of special material have been designed which can hold and carry 2 lakhs litres of fresh water. Since fresh water is lighter than the sea water, it floats and very little power is required to tow it to the shore.

287. (18-4-2007) NEW DELHI : Under the Swarnjayanti Gram Swarozgar Yojana (SGSY), a total of 24,13,176 Self Help Groups (SHGs) were formed in the rural areas during the year 2006-07. The number of Swarozgaries assisted stood at 74,03,737 comprising of 41,31,949 SHG swarozgaries and 32,71,788 individual swarozgaries. Subsidy worth Rs.5,401.98 crore and credit to the tune of Rs.10,705.16 crore were also distributed during the year. The per capita investment was Rs.21,818. The main feature of the SGSY is mobilization of rural poor to organize them into Self Help Groups and bring the assisted BPL families above the poverty line. It is a credit-cum-subsidy scheme where credit is a critical component and subsidy is only an enabling element. Participatory approach is adopted in the selection of key activities and emphasis is on development of activity clusters to ensure proper forward and backward linkages. The strengthening of groups is done through Revolving Fund Assistance (RFA). Training of beneficiaries in Group processes and Skill Development are the integral part of the project. Moreover, marketing support with stress on market research, upgradation/diversification of products, packaging, creation of market facilities, is also provided. There is also a provision for development of infrastructure to provide the missing critical link. 20% funds (in case of NE State 25%) are earmarked for infrastructure development. The other features include an active role of NGOs in formation and capacity building of SHGs. Focus is also on Vulnerable Groups *i.e.* SC, ST, Women and the Disabled. Besides, 15% funds are earmarked for time bound programmes to bring specific number of BPL families above the poverty line. The Scheme was launched on 1st April, 1999 and is the largest Self-Employment Programme of the Ministry of Rural Development. The funds under the programme are shared between Centre and the States in the ratio of 75:25.

288. (18-4-2007) NEW DELHI : In Bihar, the National Rural Employment Guarantee Act (NREGA) was initially launched during 2006-07 in 23 Districts and has further been extended to 15 more Districts in the current financial year. A total of 12.64 lakh households demanded employment and 12.56 of them were provided employment up to Feb.'07. The number of person day of employment provided in the State is 370.44 lakh. The average person days of employment provided in a district stands at 16.11 lakh compared to the national average of 36.47 lakh person days. Of them, 16.52% are provided to women, 46.44% to SC and 2.41% to members of ST. The employment was provided on 49,956 works, out of which 22,971 works have been completed. The average number of works taken up in a district stood at 2,172 against the national average of 3,581. The average number of households provided employment in a district of the State was 54,623, while the National Average stands at 91,685. An amount of Rs. 485.81 crore was released to the State during 2006-07. Up to February 2007, Rs. 557.66 crore was utilized, which is 48.08% of the total availability. The expenditure on wages stood at 55.48%, material at 43.90% and on administration 0.006% was spent. The average expenditure on a district came out to be Rs. 24.25 crore compared to the National average of Rs. 35 crore.

289. (18-4-2007) NEW DELHI : In Assam, the National Rural Employment Guarantee Act (NREGA) was initially launched during 2006-07 in 7 districts and has further been extended to 6 more districts in the current financial year. A total of 7.16 lakh households demanded employment and 6.98 of them were provided employment up to Feb.'07. The number of person day of employment provided in the State is 471.97 lakh. The average person days of employment provided in a district stands at 67.42 lakh compared to the national average of 36.47 lakh person days. Of them, 33.23% are provided to women, 9.02% to SC and 47.08% to members of ST. The employment was provided on 12,659 works, out of which 7260 works have been completed. The average number of works taken up in a district stood at 1808 against the national average of 3,581. The average number of households provided employment in a district of the State was 99,751, while the National Average stands at 91,685. An amount of Rs. 239.71 crore was released to the State during 2006-07. Up to February 2007, Rs. 460.88 crore was utilized, which is 64.31% of the total availability. The expenditure on wages stood at 65.01%, material at 33.50% and on administration 1.48% was spent. The average expenditure on a district came out to be Rs. 65.84 crore compared to the National average of Rs. 35 crore.

290. (18-4-2007) NEW DELHI : The Defence Secretary Shri Shekhar Dutt today handed over a cheque of back wages of over Rs. 1,16,00,000/-to Field Marshal S H F J Manekshaw at the Military Hospital in Wellington. This is in connection with Government's decision that officers holding honorary ranks of Field Marshal of the Army and Marshal of the Air Force would be entitled to salary and emoluments package alongwith several other facilities in keeping with rare honours attached to these ranks. These back wages will be effective from Jan 01, 1973, when Gen Manekshaw took up the Field Marshal rank and from this month onwards he will get the enhanced salary. When asked by the Field Marshal Manekshaw whether any imposition of tax on his new salary structure, the Defence Secretary replied that if at all tax has to be imposed it will be at the minimum. He said he will try to exempt it from tax deduction. Shri Dutt also conveyed the greetings from the President and Supreme Commander of Armed Forces Dr. A P J Abdul Kalam and handed over the message of the Prime Minister Dr. Manmohan Singh. Field Marshal Manekshaw is now undergoing treatment at the Military Hospital, Wellington.

291. (18-4-2007) NEW DELHI : BASANT SARAS Fair-2007, organized by the Ministry of Rural Development, as part of the ongoing Regional SARAS sequel, is going on in Dilli Haat and to continue till April 23, 2007. The Fair is one of the efforts of the Ministry to assist rural artisans and beneficiaries under SGSY to sell their products in the city market. A total of about 400 artisans from 22 States and one Union territory are participating in the Fair. Some stalls have been allotted to CAPART (Council for Advancement of People's Action & Rural Technology) and TRIFED (Tribal Cooperative Marketing Development Federation of India

Limited). The Ministry provides Rs.25 lakh for Regional SARAS Fairs in metros and Rs.20 lakh in major cities in the country. During 2006-07, 23 Regional SARAS Fairs were organized besides the IITF SARAS Fair. There was a sale of Rs. 17 crore in these Fairs against the total expenditure of Rs.6.48 crore. About 25 thousand rural Swarozgaris have been benefited by these Fairs since 2003-04. The Ministry of Rural Development has taken several steps for creation of marketing infrastructure in Delhi to sell the products of rural artisans. Rural Development Pavilion located at Pragati Maidan is being renovated for construction of 39 permanent stalls for giving them to the States on rotation basis. Renovation work has been assigned to NBCC and the construction work is to start immediately. A space measuring 398.89 sq.mt. at Rajiv Gandhi Crafts Bhavan on Baba Kharag Singh Marg, New Delhi has been hired for running SARAS Gallery. DDA has allotted 2 acres of land at Jasola, near Apollo Hospital for construction of a marketing complex. The Ministry has also taken action for purchase of 44 stalls at Dilli Haat, Pitampura from DT & TDC. Setting up of a National Rural Products Marketing Agency (NRPMA) is also on the anvil.

292. (18-4-2007) NEW DELHI : The Minister for Rural Development, Dr. Raghuvansh Prasad Singh has said that marketing support will be provided to rural products under SGSY through Fairs like BASANT SARAS. He was speaking after a visit to the Dilli Haat, late in the evening yesterday. Expressing satisfaction on the progress of the formation of Self Help Groups (SHGs) under the Swarnajayanti Gram Swarozgar Yojana (SGSY) in Tamil Nadu, Andhra Pradesh, Gujarat, Maharashtra, U.P. and Uttrakhand, he said efforts would be made to extend the SHG cover to all the BPL families in the country during the 11th Plan. So far, 25 lakh SHGs have been formed in the country, he added. The fortnight long BASANT SARAS Fair, organized by the Ministry of Rural Development, is going on at the Dilli Haat in New Delhi from April 10, 2007. A total of about 400 artisans from 22 States and One Union Territory are participating in the fair.

293. (18-4-2007) NEW DELHI : Shri Abhishek Singhvi said that with each passing phase of the Uttar Pradesh elections we find the stamp of defeat on the incumbent govt. of Mulayam Singh Yadav and the SP. There have been three defeats in each of the three phases and we have no doubt that the remaining four phases will constitute a political 'chautha' for this party (a political end for this party). Each phase is no less than a tortuous phase, each phase constitutes a new nail in the political coffin of the SP. We believe that the SP lost the political battle, lost the human battle, lost the moral battle many times over. It lost the battle when Nithari happened. It lost the battle when the largest number of people with civil antecedents are found to have found the place in that party. It lost the battle when Apex Court stigmatized it for survival by buying MLAs and buying votes. It lost the battle when it did things like Lucknow allotments. It lost the battle when the Election Commission reversed many hundreds of transfers of so-called favourite and biased officers deliberately, strategically placed by this party for electoral gains. We have here very strange combination of parties which cross-fertilize and support each other—the SP and the BJP. Did you not find it strange that there was hardly a whimper, hardly a whisper of protest on a distorted, communal, anti-constitutional, illegal CD circulated by the BJP, of the BJP, by the BJP, for the BJP and yet the SP hardly lodges a whimper of protest. This shows the collusion. At one end of the spectrum you have the SP, at the other end you have yet a another example of the true face and character of the BJP. The BJP's true face and character has been illustrated yet again by another example hardly two hours ago when a sitting Member of Parliament from Gujarat, of the Lok Sabha, has been detained at the airport on the charge of travelling with a lady, on his own wife's passport when the lady does not happen to be his wife. This is fairly a serious matter, no doubt it requires detailed criminal investigation but I would like you to appreciate the scope and the magnitude of this. It involves several offences of a very serious nature. It involves forgery, it involves impersonation, it involves false misrepresentation, it may involve immigration racket whereby monies are paid to a passport holder to facilitate safe passage for a illegal traveller or an immigrant. Although we have no doubt that separate investigations will establish guilt. One should not forget that the lady travelling with Abu Salim, Ms. Monika, had been arrested for a similar offence. This is the true face, the true character, the true nature of the SP at one end, of the BJP at the other end and it is this character and face which keeps coming to the fore time and again. And it is this character and face which the electorate of UP is bound to deliver a stinging defeat. To a question that the Congress Party has left out BSP from accusation from its UP election campaign, Shri Singhvi said that we will decide whom to attack when and if we attack one it does not mean that we are supporting the other. But certainly the incidents in the last two hours are more important and whether you like it or not, they are the two very serious incidents which you have before you. To a question that will the BJP MP be expelled from the House, Shri Singhvi said that I am not here to prescribe remedies and I would request to you not to dilute the seriousness of the offence.

294. (18-4-2007) NEW DELHI : Inaugurating the Orientation and Capacity Building workshop for the CEOs of State Medicinal Plant Boards on "Strategies for Conservation and Cultivation of Medicinal Plants" in New Delhi today, the Minister of State for Health & Family Welfare, Smt. Panabaka Lakshmi said that our strategies and action plans should focus not only on conserving and enriching the existing medicinal plants biodiversity in the forest areas but promote cultivation of medicinal plants through farmers. This two pronged approach will not only ensure that medicinal plants that are collected by tribals and other forest dwellers for their livelihood are made available to the AYUSH industry but also that the farmers are able to cultivate medicinal plants as an alternative crop. The two-day workshop has been organized by the National Medicinal Plants Board in collaboration with Foundation for Revitalization of Local Health Traditions (FRLHT). Besides Mrs. Anita Das, Secretary in Department of AYUSH, Mr.

Sajwan, Chief Executive officer, National Medicinal Plants Board and Dr. Darshan Shankar from the FRLHT, Bangalore were also present at the workshop.

295. (18-4-2007) NEW DELHI : Shri Kamal Nath, Union Minister of Commerce and Industry, will announce the Annual Supplement to the Foreign Trade Policy here tomorrow. All stakeholder inputs have been taken into account in fine-tuning the elements of the Annual Supplement 2007 to the Foreign Trade Policy (2004-09) through consultations, including in the Board of Trade. The first-ever comprehensive Foreign Trade Policy (FTP) was announced by Shri Kamal Nath on 31st August, 2004 with a five year framework (2004-09), which took an integrated view of the overall development of India's foreign trade with a two-fold objective of (a) doubling India's percentage share of global merchandise trade by 2009; and (b) acting as an effective instrument of economic growth by giving a thrust to employment generation. India's merchandise exports since the announcement of the Policy in August 2004 have gone up significantly. India's exports crossed the landmark figure of US $ 100 billion in 2005-06. India's merchandise exports increased from US $ 53 billion in 2002-03 to US $ 103 billion in 2005-06. Exports in the current year touched US $ 109 billion during April 2006 to February 2007, showing a growth of 22.95%.

296. (19-4-2007) NEW DELHI : Pakistan Tourism Minister, Ms. Nilofar Bakhtiar today paid a courtesy visit to Tourism and Culture Minister Smt. Ambika Soni. Ms. Bakhtiar is currently in New Delhi to participate in the South Asian Tourism and Travel Expo (SATTE). During their 40 minutes meeting both the leaders discussed tourism related matters. The visiting dignitary complemented Smt. Ambika Soni on the Incredible India campaign and lauded successful participation of India at recently concluded ITB-Berlin. Smt. Soni welcomed the initiatives of Pakistan in promoting tourism specially steps taken by them to grant visa on arrival to the nationals of 24 countries. The Pakistan Minister was greatly appreciative of the India's initiative with regard to the 'Bed and Breakfast' scheme which will not only supplement the room numbers but will also provide experimental tourism to both domestic as well as foreign tourists. She enquired in details about the guidelines of the scheme and stated that she would explore the possibilities of launching the similar initiative in her own country. Smt. Soni stated that the Composite Dialogue between the two countries would go a long way in boosting the ties and people to people contact between India and Pakistan. Both the leaders felt that there is a tremendous tourism potential in both the countries which should be tapped.

297. (19-4-2007) NEW DELHI : The first session of the Indian-Greek Joint Commission on tourism was held here recently. The Indian delegation was led by Shri Sanjay Kothari, Additional Director General, Ministry of Tourism and the Greek delegation was headed by Mrs. Esthir Vitali, Director General of Tourist Promotion of the Greek Ministry of Tourism. It was agreed to establish a programme to exchange visits of tour operators, travel agents, hospitality organizations and travel media personnel to motivate consumers in both countries to travel to the other country. The importance of interaction between the private stakeholders of the two countries was stressed to develop better understanding of the tourism products in India and Greece. It was agreed by both sides to participate in tourism fairs/exhibitions held in each other's country to promote their destinations/tourism products. Both sides informed each other about the investment opportunity available in their countries in the tourism sector. It was agreed that growing opportunities in tourism sector should be showcased to attract investments from the private stakeholders of the two countries. It was agreed by both sides to establish an exchange programme for students and faculties to enhance cooperation by developing partnership programmes between leading academic institutions and educational organizations as well as tourism schools in the tourism sector of both countries. The Greek side expressed its readiness to invite five students of Schools Tourism Professions from India to visit Greece during the summer of 2007 for a three month on the job training in selective, luxury and 'A' category Greek hotels. Both sides expressed willingness to assist the NTO's/Tourism Boards of each other's country in carrying out promotion and marketing activities to increase the tourism traffic including beach, adventure and aqua tourism between the two countries.

298. (19-4-2007) NEW DELHI : The third meeting of the Joint Working Group on tourism was held here today. The Indian delegation was led by Additional Director General (Tourism) Shri Sanjay Kothari and the Egyptian delegation was headed by Chairman Egyptian Tourism Authority, Mr. Amir El Ezabi. Both sides exchanged views on the economic, social and political importance of tourism for their respective countries and expressed the need for cooperation in the field of tourism. During the talks both the delegations gave an over view of the tourism sector in their respective countries and underlined its importance for employment and growth. It was viewed by both sides that increase in the flow of tourism would further enhance bilateral relations between the two countries. It was agreed to establish a programme to exchange visits of tour operators and travel media to motivate consumers in both countries to travel to the other country. Both sides informed each other about the investment opportunities available in their countries in the tourism sector. It was agreed that growing opportunities should be showcased to attract investments from the private stakeholders. Egyptian side was briefed on the facilities available in India for Human Resource Development in travel and hospitality sector. It was agreed by both sides to establish an exchange programme for students and faculties to enhance cooperation by developing partnership programmes between leading academic institutions in the tourism sector of both countries. Both sides expressed willingness to assist the NTO's/Tourism Boards of each other's country in carrying out promotion and marketing activities to increase the tourism traffic between the two countries. Both the countries agreed to formulate an action plan for promotion and marketing of their destinations in each other's country.

299. (19-4-2007) NEW DELHI : India and Germany will set up a Joint Working Group for cooperation in agriculture and allied sectors. The Working Group will meet twice a year. The proposal emerged at a discussion between Shri Sharad Pawar, Minister of Agriculture and H.E. Mr. Gerd Muller, Parliamentary State Secretary in the Ministry of Food, Agriculture and Consumer Protection of Germany here today. Shri Pawar suggested that areas like agro-processing, farm research, animal breeding have vast potential for bilateral cooperation. A number of reforms have been initiated in the agri-marketing sector to promote corporate investment in the sector. The Minister said the country is looking forward to more proposals for cooperation in the agri-business. He also drew the attention to the difficulties being faced by the country in the market access for our agricultural products in Europe and Germany owing to difference in standards. At the delegation level discussions held earlier Dr. P.K. Mishra, Secretary, Department of Agriculture and Cooperation informed that tremendous emphasis is being laid on increasing investment in rural infrastructure and improving productivity in agriculture. Other key areas include diversification of high value crops, strengthening post-harvest infrastructure, linking agriculture to markets and agro-products. Specific areas discussed relate to cooperation in the field of agriculture research, food processing, animal husbandry, development of plant varieties, seeds and planting material, farm machinery and marketing of agricultural products.

300. (19-4-2007) NEW DELHI : It has been reported in some sections of the media that a large number of taxpayers are awaiting refunds from the Income Tax department for up to three years. These reports are factually incorrect and based on incomplete appraisal of facts. The Income Tax department has already issued over 43 lakh refund cheques amounting to over Rs.39,000 crore during fiscal 2006-07. The amount of refund issued during fiscal 2005-06 was over Rs.29,000 crore. Thus there is an increase of about 33% in the amount of refund issued during 2006-07 compared to 2005-06. In first two weeks of April 2007 alone, refunds amounting to Rs.1,834 crore have been issued. In order to speed up the issue of refunds and make the procedure error-free, a pilot Refund Banker Scheme was launched on 24th January 2007 by the Finance Minister in select Commissionerates in Delhi and Patna. Under this scheme, over 30,000 refunds have been issued in Delhi and Patna through the ECS or as paper refunds. In most cases, refunds have reached the taxpayers or have been credited to their bank account electronically within 15 days of processing. Processing of tax returns takes time. The Income Tax department receives over 3.20 crore tax returns. Administratively, time of 4 months is taken to complete the electronic processing of returns. Sometimes, delays take place due to lack of manpower, connectivity, power failure, etc. These issues are being addressed separately. While processing tax returns, it is observed that many taxpayers do not furnish all the details as required. The bank account details or ECS code are not furnished or are inaccurate / incomplete. Sometimes, addresses of taxpayers change and no intimation to this effect is given to the department. Due to these factors also refunds are delayed. Taxpayers are, therefore, advised to file their tax returns with due care and caution. A Tax Return Preparer Scheme has also been launched to help small and medium taxpayers file their returns.

301. (19-4-2007) NEW DELHI : Four more FM radio channels have been commissioned during March 2007 taking the total of private FM radio channels in the country to 58. The new channels are: Ananda Offset at Kolkata, H.T. Music at Bangalore, Singla Property and Puran Multimedia at Hissar. The Government received a sum of over Rs. 4.56 crore as annual fee from these private FM radio broadcasters.

302. (19-4-2007) NEW DELHI : The long range forecast for the 2007 Southwest monsoon (June to September) by the India Meteorological Department (IMD) says that the rainfall for the country as a whole is likely to be 95% of the long period average with a model error of ± 5%. This is based upon the newly-adopted statistical forecast system. IMD will update the above forecast in June 2007 as a part of the second stage forecasts. Separate forecasts for the July rainfall over the country as a whole and seasonal (June-September) rainfall over the four geographical regions of India also will be issued. India Meteorological Department has been adopting a two-stage forecast strategy for the southwest monsoon rainfall for the past four years. The first long range forecast for the southwest monsoon season (June-September) rainfall is issued in April using the 8 parameter models and the forecast update is issued in June based on the 10 parameter models.

303. (19-4-2007) NEW DELHI : The Payment of Bonus Act, 1965 provides for payment of bonus to persons employed in an establishments or industry employing 20 or more persons, to do any skilled, unskilled, manual, supervisory, managerial, administrative, technical or clerical work. The bonus is paid on the basis of profits or production or productivity and for matters connected therein. The Act provides for payment of a minimum bonus of 8.33%. The Act is not, however, applicable to government employees who are covered under the Ad-hoc Bonus Scheme administered by the Department of Expenditure.

304. (19-4-2007) NEW DELHI : The Ministry of Rural Development has released Rs. 25.11 crore to M/s. National Hydroelectric Power Corporation Ltd. for implementation of 91 road work packages in Bihar under Pradhan Mantri Gram Sadak Yojana (PMGSY) for the year 2007-08. The grant is towards the Plan expenditure and will be subject to the conditions laid down from time to time in the guidelines of the PMGSY and supplementary directions. PMGSY was launched in December 2000 as a 100 per cent Centrally Sponsored Scheme with a target of connecting every habitation that has a population of more than 1000 within the next three years and every habitation with a population of more than 500 by the year 2007 *i.e.* by the end of the 10th Five Year Plan through good all-weather road. A sum of Rs.20,400.70 crore has been released to the States/UTs towards the programme and up to December 2006, 35,868 roadworks covering a length of 1,07,569.08 Kms. have been completed.

305. (19-4-2007) NEW DELHI : National Rural Employment Guarantee Act (NREGA) was initially launched in 11 districts of Chhattisgarh and another 4 Districts have been added in the year 2007-08. In the State 11.91 lakh households have demanded employment and 11.60 households have been provided employment up to Feb.,07. The average number of households provided employment in a district of the State is 1,05,459, while the national average is 91,685 households. In the State 0.54 lakh household have completed the 100 days guarantee of employment provided in the Act. The number of person days of employment provided in the State is 600.82 lakh. The average person days of employment provided in a district is 54.62 lakh compared to the national average of 36.47 lakh person days. The employment was provided on 12, 942 works, out of which 7260 works have been completed. The average number of works taken up in a district stood at 2482 against the national average of 3,581. An amount of Rs. 701.31 crore has been released to the State during 2006-07. Against this, the utlisation up to February 2007, is Rs. 552.40 crore, which is 67.84% of the total availability. The expenditure on wages is 64.94%, material is 34.11% and on administration is 0.96%. The average expenditure of a district in the State is Rs. 50.22 crore compared to the National average of Rs. 35 crore. The Act provides that 1/3rd of the employment provided should be to women. In the State 37.43% person days of employment has been provided to women, 11.8% to SC and 46.63% to ST. A visit to the State by the National Level Monitors in December, 2006 & January 2007 has revealed that more than 70% of the works pertain to water & soil conservation and that Coordinated Grievance Redressal Mechanism has been developed in some districts like Bilaspur, Rajnandgaon and Kawardha.

306. (19-4-2007) NEW DELHI : The Defence Minister of New Zealand Mr. Phil Goff called on Defence Minister Shri AK Antony here today. Both the leaders discussed matters of mutual interest and Defence Cooperation. The talks were held in a very cordial atmosphere.

307. (19-4-2007) NEW DELHI : In a parliamentary democracy like ours political decision-maker is supreme, but officials play a pivotal role, both in implementing the decision and giving it a measure of legitimacy. It therefore, becomes incumbent for the bureaucracy to help the political leadership to tackle a crisis and also help in policy formulation. The relationship is intertwined. If the political leader has scaled down from the lofty heights that the freedom movement and the early years placed him, the bureaucrat too has departed from the high qualities of being a "steel frame" during the British era to "cast iron frame". All of it is true, and all of it needs to be placed in a perspective to be understood and appreciated, if one is to scrutinize the country's governance. The assessment needs to be done in the context of the changing relationship and the respective roles in the new century where opportunities have grown and so have the challenges.

308. (19-4-2007) NEW DELHI : The Kazakhstan companies have expressed interest in import of textiles from India, mainly home textiles. They have also expressed interests in training of textile engineering and design students from Kazakhstan in India. This was conveyed to the Union Minister of Textiles, Shri Shankersinh Vaghela during his recent visit to Kazakhstan with a High Level Delegation. During his visit, the Minister had meetings with representatives of Chamber of Commerce and Industry of Kazakhstan and the Light Industry Association of Kazakhstan at Almaty, Governor of South Kazakhstan Region at Shymkent, the Foreign Minister, the Minister of Industry and Trade and the Agriculture Ministers of Kazakhstan Republic at Astana. The delegation also visited the Special Economic Zone for development of textile cluster 'Ontustik (SEZ), Shymkent. Tashkent, Uzbekistan is very close to Shymkent and Uzbekistan, a part of the former Soviet Republics in Central Asia, is India's prominent trading partner among the Central Asian Republics. Shri Vaghela also visited Tashkent, Uzbekistan. The Indian Ambassador in Uzbekistan briefed him about the possibilities of textile cooperation with that country. Shri Vaghela also visited the Shri Lal Bahadur Shastri Memorial in Tashkent. Kazakhstan is India's largest trading partner among the Central Asian Republics. Though the current volume of textile trade between the two countries is low, there are enormous possibilities of increasing bilateral trade and cooperation in the textile sector between the two countries. The visit was successful in boosting the bilateral cooperation with these two important CIS countries.

309. (19-4-2007) NEW DELHI : Vice Admiral Raman P Suthan, AVSM VSM will assume command of the premiere Eastern Naval Command, one of the two operational commands of the Indian Navy on 30 Apr. 07. Vadm Suthan takes over from Vice Admiral A K Singh, who retires that day. The Eastern seaboard has gained prominence in the recent past and this is witnessed by the increasing engagement with immediate regional neighbours like Bangladesh, Indonesia, Malaysia, Myanmar, Singapore, Thailand and other states of South East Asia. The Eastern Fleet is on overseas deployment and the ships have just completed a visit to China and Japan to exercise with their ships. All this is in consonance with the 'Look East Policy' of our country. Also, the coming days would see Indian Navy exercising with US Fleet in the Bay of Bengal. Admiral Suthan takes over the Eastern Naval command after two years stint in Delhi. He took over his present appointment as Deputy Chief of the Naval Staff on 24 Jul 06 when "Operation-Sukoon" (evacuation of civilians) from Beirut to Larnaca was in full swing. The prompt response by the Indian Navy has won admiration, the world over. The Admiral was born on 14 Aug 1949. He is an alumnus of the National Defence Academy, Khadakvasala and was commissioned in the Indian Navy in July 1970. He saw action early in life as the Navigating Officer of INS Kavaratti, which took active part in Eastern Fleet operations off erstwhile East Pakistan in 1971. After specialisation in Navigation and Direction, he has held various staff, instructional, operational and command appointments. The Flag Officer is a graduate of the prestigious Defence Services Staff College, Wellington. During his long and illustrious career, Vice Admiral Raman P Suthan has commanded five ships of different size and capabilities. His other important assignment at sea includes Fleet Navigation Officer of Eastern Fleet. As Flag Officer, he has been Flag Officer Commanding Eastern Fleet, one of the two sword arms of the Navy.

310. (19-4-2007) NEW DELHI : The Ministry of Rural Development has already released Rs.203.09 crore to Punjab for implementation of various rural development programmes. Rural Development Minister, Dr. Raghuvansh Prasad Singh in a letter further assured the Chief Minister of Punjab, Shri Parkash Singh Badal that requisite Central share of funds under SGRY, DRDA and IAY will be released on receipt of complete proposals from the State. The Chief Minister of Punjab has issued strict instructions to the State Department of Rural Development and Panchayats to send immediately complete proposals relating to all these programmes for availing the balance funds under these schemes.

311. (19-4-2007) NEW DELHI : A day long Conference of Chief Secretaries is being organized here tomorrow by the Department of Administrative Reforms & Public Grievances. The Conference will be inaugurated by the Cabinet Secretary and will deliberate on the issues pertaining to Internal Security, food security, Sarva Shiksha Abhiyan, National Rural Health Mission, improving business climate and strategy for improving governance. The conference serves the twin purpose of assessing the performance of different states over a period of time, as also, appraisal of the progress made in respect of various flagship programmes of different nodal Ministries of the Government of India. Over a period of time this has proved to be a useful platform to deliberate upon critical issues like-law and order, education, health, employment and rural development. Not only this, such a conference proves useful in sorting out issues constraining speedy implementation of centrally sponsored and central sector schemes.

312. (19-4-2007) NEW DELHI : Announcing a record high of FDI (equity) inflows in India while announcing the Annual Supplement to the Foreign Trade Policy (2004-09) here today, Shri Kamal Nath, Minister of Commerce & Industry, said: "I must mention here about the robust growth in our Foreign Direct Investment. A liberal Trade Policy has a direct effect on FDI flows and the two are closely inter-related. The year 2006-07 has seen our FDI equity inflow go up to almost US$ 16 billion from US$ 5.5 billion in the previous year-almost tripling of the inflows in one year. The last three years of our Government has seen a staggering 725% increase in FDI inflows-up from US$ 2.22 billion in 2003-04 to US$ 16 billion in 2006-07! In line with the international practice of including the retained earnings reinvested, our FDI touches US$ 19 billion in 2006-07, constituting 2.3%

of our GDP. This is about 6.8% of the gross capital formation or gross investment in the economy. I am sure, you would agree, that this is quantum jump compared to only 0.5% of GDP and about 1.5% of gross investment three years ago. The directional flow of FDI into manufacturing and export of goods and services is contributing immensely to our export efforts".

313. (19-4-2007) NEW DELHI : Responding to the demand of the status holders, Shri Kamal Nath, Minister of Commerce & Industry, has re-christened them as Export House (earlier known as One Star Export House), Star Export House (earlier known as Two Star Export House), Trading House (earlier known as Three Star Export House), Star Trading House (earlier known as Four Star Export House), and Premier Trading House (earlier known as Five Star Export House). They will be granted such status on achieving aggregate exports of Rs.20 crore, Rs.100 crore, Rs.500 crore, Rs.2500 crore and Rs.10000 crore respectively over a period of four years.

314. (19-4-2007) NEW DELHI : The Union Cabinet today gave its approval for signing the Bilateral Investment Promotion Agreement with the Hellenic Republic. This Agreement will increase the investment flow between India and the Hellenic Republic. Till 13th March, 2007 India have signed with 63 countries on Bilateral Investment Promotion Agreements.

315. (19-4-2007) NEW DELHI : The Union Cabinet today gave its approval for undertaking legislation for amendment of Indian Boilers Act, 1923 (3 of 1923) The amendments in the Act will modify the outdated provisions of the present Act which was enacted in 1923 for inspection of boilers during use and will provide for the inspection of boilers during manufacture / erection, operations and maintenance of boilers in line with the present technological developments throughout the world. It will help in creating competition for inspection of boilers during manufacture, erection and commissioning so that delays are avoided. It will also indicate clearly powers of the Central Boilers Board. It will help in minimizing and preventing accidents and loss of human life from boiler related accidents. It will provide for adequate trained manpower and laboratory facilities for inspection of boilers during manufacture and use. It will bring in uniformity of standards of inspection and avoid the Inter-State disputes. The Amendment Bill will again be moved to Parliament along with the modifications.

316. (19-4-2007) NEW DELHI : The Union Cabinet today gave its approval to move the new amended Bill in the parliament for its consideration and adoption for repealing the existing Carriers Act, 1865 and enacting the new Bill namely the Carriage by Road Bill, 2005. The new legislation would cater to the present day requirements of trade and transportation in road transport sector. After the Bill is passed by Parliament, Presidential assent would be obtained on the Bill, Legislation will be notified in the Gazette of India. Thereafter, Rules will be framed in accordance with the requirements under the Act.

317. (19-4-2007) NEW DELHI : The Union Cabinet today gave its approval for carrying out the Amendments on the basis of recommendations of the Standing Committee to the State Bank of India (Subsidiary Banks Laws) Amendment Bill, 2006 introduced in the Lok Sabha on 22nd May, 2006 with a view to enhance flexibility of the Boards of Directors, improve corporate governance and provide power to the Boards of the subsidiary banks to frame regulations. The amendments would bring the operations of subsidiary banks in tune with the changed scenario and modern business practices.

318. (19-4-2007) NEW DELHI : CAPART, an autonomous body under the aegis of Ministry of Rural Development is initiating a pilot project in Bihar to promote Information Communication Technology (ICT) to rural masses. A central studio has been set up at Consultancy-Cum-Guidance Centre at Bania in Muzaffarpur district and is being connected to one remote site at Serukahin Panchayat in Kanti block of district Muzaffarpur. CAPART has recently introduced a Village Knowledge Centre (VKC) Scheme to render distant services from a single window point to rural masses especially in remote areas of the country through modern ICT. The knowledge centre will be connected to a central studio using technologies viz WiMax/VSAT/leased line. There will be live interactive sessions in real time by the central speaker with audience at remote villages to disseminate information on any subject of interest to the rural communities. The purpose of setting up of a VKC is to bring access to a range of services, content and information to people living in remote villages or areas. The Hon'ble Minister of Rural Development, Dr. Raghuvansh Prasad Singh, is inaugurating the centre on 22nd April.

319. (19-4-2007) NEW DELHI : Grant-in-aid amounting to Rs.8.48 lakh has been released by the Ministry of Rural Development to the Lakshadweep District Rural Development Agency towards the second instalment of Central Share for the year 2006-07 under DRDA Administration. The funding pattern under the scheme is 75:25 between Centre and the State. The utilization of funds is to be in accordance with the DRDA administration guidelines and the release of the second instalment during 2007-08 is subject to the fulfillment of all the conditions as per the DRDA Administration guidelines.

320. (19-4-2007) NEW DELHI : The Ministry of Rural Development has sanctioned Rs. 26.38 lakh of Grants-in-aid to the Tumkur District Rural Development Agency (DRDA) of Karnataka towards the second instalment of Central Share for the year 2006-07 under DRDA Administration. The funding pattern under the scheme is 75:25 between Centre and the State. The utilization of funds is to be in accordance with the DRDA administration guidelines and the release of the second instalment during 2007-08 is subject to the fulfillment of all the conditions as per the DRDA Administration guidelines.

321. (19-4-2007) NEW DELHI : The Prime Minister, Dr. Manmohan Singh, chaired a special meeting to review progress of infrastructure projects in Orissa.

The meeting reviewed implementation of road, railway, port, power, coal, steel, mining and forest land development projects. In his opening remarks the Prime Minister said that the Central Government would take all steps needed to promote development in Orissa. He assured the Chief Minister that procedural delays and inter-ministerial issues will be addressed and the State's interests protected. The review meeting was extremely fruitful and helped identify the problems with respect to various infrastructure projects, it fixed responsibility for taking next steps, it fixed time lines for taking decisions and implementing them and it directed the State Government and the respective Central Ministries to carry forward the discussions at the earliest. The State Government assured the Central Government that issues pertaining to POSCO will be addressed to the satisfaction of all and that through persuasion of stake holders the project will be taken forward. The meeting was attended among others by the Union Finance Minister, the Deputy Chairman Planning Commission, the Principal Secretary to PM and Twelve Secretaries to Government of India from concerned Ministries. This is the second meeting that the Prime Minister has chaired with a State Chief Minister and with senior Central Government officials to review development projects in a State. The Prime Minister had chaired a similar meeting on Jammu & Kashmir last year. The Prime Minister will be convening similar meetings with other State Governments to review the implementation of infrastructure projects and clear bureaucratic hurdles. The Chief Minister of Orissa Mr. Naveen Patnaik thanked the Prime Minister for taking the initiative and organizing the meeting.

322. (19-4-2007) NEW DELHI : The Annual Replenishable Ground Water Resources of the country have been reassessed as 433 Billion Cubic Metres (BCM) and the Net Annual Ground Water Availability is estimated as 399 BCM. Existing Gross Ground Water Draft as on March, 2004 for all uses is 231 BCM year. The Stage of Ground Water Development is 58 per cent. The development and tapping of ground water comes under the purview of the State Governments as water being a state subject. As assessment was carried out jointly by the Central Ground Water Board (CGWB) and the State Ground Water Departments on the State-wise and Union Territory-wise details of annual replenishable ground water resources, net ground water availability, existing gross ground water draft for irrigation, drinking and industrial uses and stage of ground water development as on March 2004. In the State of Delhi, Haryana, Punjab and Rajasthan and UTs of Daman & Diu and Pondicherry, the annual ground water draft is more than the net annual ground water availability. This has resulted in over-exploitation of ground water resources in these States/UTs.

323. (20-4-2007) NEW DELHI : India and Germany today agreed to increase defence cooperation in a number of areas including exchange of expertise in peace-keeping operations, exchange of experience in disaster management, etc. In the first Indo-German High Defence Committee meeting held in New Delhi today, the Federal State Secretary for Defence of Germany Dr. Peter Eickenboom assured India to provide transfer of technology in armament procurement and joint development of armament platforms wherever possible. He also said that Germany shares India's security perspectives and recognizes the growing importance of India in regional stability and peace. Germany has also assured India that it will be an open and reliable partner in all areas of defence cooperation. The Indian side at the talks was led by Shri Shekhar Dutt, Defence Secretary. This was the first meeting at the level of defence secretary after the signing of bilateral defence agreement between the two sides in September last year during the visit of the then Defence Minister Shri Pranab Mukherjee to Germany.

324. (20-4-2007) NEW DELHI : Shri B. K. Handique, Minister of State for Parliamentary Affairs and Chemicals & Fertilizers gave away prizes to the winners of the 9th Youth Parliament Competition, 2005-2006 for Jawahar Navodaya Vidyalayas today. The students of Jawahar Navodaya Vidyalaya, Veleru, Distt. Krishna (Andhra Pradesh) bagged the first prize. Merit Trophies were awarded to seven schools for winning top positions in their respective regions. These Jawahar Navodaya Vidyalayas are: Bringkhera, Distt. Muktsar, Punjab (Chandigarh Region), Shankar Nagar, Biloli, Distt. Nanded, Maharashtra, (Pune Region), Monacherra, Assam (Shillong Region), Pauta, P.O. Chandwar, Jharkhand (Patna Region), Pichhore, Near Darba, Madhya Pradesh (Bhopal Region), Saindwar, Distt. Bijnor, Uttar Pradesh (Lucknow Region) and Kherli, Distt. Dausa, Rajasthan (Jaipur Region). 84 schools took part in the competition at the regional level. In his remarks, Shri Handique said, the Youth Parliament Competitions help promote habits of discipline, qualities of leadership, awareness of social problems and the democratic means of solving them. Such training of our younger generation plays a vital role in inculcating democratic spirit in them, he added. Ministry of Parliamentary Affairs have been organizing Youth Parliament competitions for Jawahar Navodaya Vidyalayas for the past nine years. In 1988, a separate National Youth Parliament Scheme for Kendriya Vidyalayas was introduced as a part of the celebrations of 40 years of India's Independence and Pandit Jawaharlal Nehru's birth centenary. The Youth Parliament Scheme aims at inculcating among the younger generation the spirit of self-discipline, tolerance of diverse opinion, righteous expression of views and other virtues of democratic way of life. Besides, the scheme also acquaints the students with the practices and procedures of Parliament, techniques of discussion and debate and develops in them the quality of leadership. Teams of judges, which included MPs/Ex-MPs along with officers of the Ministry of Parliamentary Affairs evaluated these competitions. Shri P. K. Mishra, Secretary, Ministry of Parliamentary Affairs, in his opening remarks said that such competitions promote democratic values/outlook among the students. It helps them understand the procedures/nuances of parliamentary democracy and the role of discussion and consensus building in resolving issues.

325. (20-4-2007) NEW DELHI : India is all set to export rice seeds to Brazil for the first time. This has been made possible due to efforts made by officials of the Department of Agriculture & Cooperation alongside Agricultural & Processed Food Products Export Development Authority (APEDA) and Ministry of Agriculture, Livestock and Food Supply (MAPA) of the Republic of Brazil, who have successfully negotiated a plant health protocol for the purpose. The next step would be issuance of a phytosanitary notification by MAPA, Brazil as per the agreed protocol, following which rice seed exports could commence. While technical discussions on the matter have been continuing for some time, the two sides agreed on the protocol for export of rice seeds from India to Brazil during the meeting of the Working Group on Plant Health issues being held at New Delhi from 16th to 20th April 2007, the Working Group having been set up under the auspices of the bilateral Memorandum of Understanding on Plant Health issues signed between the two countries in September 2006 during the visit of the Prime Minister of India to Brazil.

326. (20-4-2007) NEW DELHI : In Ships Rana and Ranjit under the command of Capt. LV Sarat Babu and Captain DM Sudan respectively, visited Qingdao from 12 to 15 Apr. 07 during the course of the ships Overseas Deployment (RAJDOOT 01/07) to the North Pacific Region. The ships visit to Qingdao, China coincided with the concurrent visit of INS Mysore, Jyoti and Kuthar under the operational command of Rear Admiral Ravinder Kumar Dhowan, AVSM, YSM to Yokosuka, Japan. On arrival at Qingdao harbour the ships were welcomed by Her Excellency Mrs. Nirupama Rao, Ambassadress of India to China, Vice Admiral R P Suthan, Deputy Chief of Naval Staff and Rear Admiral Su Shiliang, Commander North Sea Fleet (NSF) of PLA Navy. A first day postal cover commemorating the first visit of Indian Naval ships to Qingdao was also released on this occasion. During the welcome address Rear Admiral Su Shiliang, Commander North Sea Fleet and H.E. Mrs. Nirupama Rao, Ambassadress of India highlighted the strategic significance of Indo-China relations. These views were echoed during the formal interaction between Vice Admiral RP Suthan, Rear Admiral Shu Shiliang and the Commanding Officers of the Indian Naval ships. The Navys' role in the expanding military / diplomatic ties as well as 'Building Bridges of Freindship' between India and China was clearly evident during the ships stay in Qingdao. A reception was hosted for the PLA Navy officers and Defence Attaches of Australia, South Korea, Germany, Brazil, Japan, France and the US on board Rana on 13 Apr.

327. (20-4-2007) NEW DELHI : Government of India have announced the sale (re-issue) of "8.07 per cent Government Stock, 2017" for a notified amount of Rs.6,000 crore (nominal) through a price based auction using multiple price auction method. The auction will be conducted by the Reserve Bank of India, Mumbai Office, Fort, Mumbai on April 27, 2007(Friday). Up to 5% of the notified amount of the sale of the stock will be allotted to eligible individuals and Institutions as per the Scheme for Non-Competitive Bidding Facility in the Auction of Government Securities. Bids in the prescribed form obtainable from the Regional

Director, Reserve Bank of India, Mumbai Office (Public Debt Office), Fort, Mumbai-400 001 and RBI website www.rbi.org.in should be submitted to that Office on April 27, 2007. The NDS members should submit competitive as well as non competitive bids in electronic format using Primary Market Operation (PMO) module of NDS. All bids should be submitted by 12.30 P.M. The result of the auction will be announced on April 27, 2007 and payment by successful bidders will be during banking hours on April 30, 2007 (Monday). The Stocks will be eligible for "When Issued" trading in accordance with the guidelines on "When Issued transactions in Central Government Securities" issued by the Reserve Bank of India vide circular No.RBI/2006-07/178 dated November 16, 2006.

328. (20-4-2007) NEW DELHI : Cabinet Secretary, Shri B.K. Chaturvedi has said that Public Service Delivery needs to be more citizen-centric and e-governance needs to be more rural oriented. While inaugurating one-day long Conference of Chief Secretaries here today, Shri Chaturvedi also added that for this the common service centres are to be extended to the rural areas. Shri Chaturvedi while setting the agenda of the Conference underlined few thrust areas that needed attention. He said, the Public Service Delivery can be improved only if the corruption is minimized with transparency in and simplification of the existing procedures and systems. He also underlined the importance of accountability, which cannot be feasible without fixed tenures of the officers. For this, he spoke of the amendment in All India Services Rules, which is pending notification from the States. Earlier welcoming the participants, Secretary Department of Administrative Reforms & Public Grievances and Pensions and Pensioners' Welfare, Smt. Rajni Razdan said our public services have to constantly upgrade their competence and acquire new skills to fully optimize the emerging opportunities. Governance, she said in the changed scenario, has to be transparent, professionally managed, citizen-centric and sensitive to the changing needs of time. This Conference, organized by the Department of Administrative Reforms & Public Grievances, Government of India, deliberated on the issues relating to internal security, food security, Sarva Shiksha Abhiyan, National Rural Health Mission, Improving Business Climate and Strategy for improving Governance.

329. (20-4-2007) NEW DELHI : The total approximate earnings of Indian Railways on originating basis during the period 1st April-10th April 2007 were Rs. 1800.30 crore compared to Rs. 1616.10 crore during the same period last year, registering an increase of 11.40 per cent. The total goods earnings have gone up from Rs. 1073.87 crore during 1-10 April 2006 to Rs. 1187.08 crore during 1-10 April 2007, showing an increase of 10.54 per cent. The total passenger revenue earnings during the period 1-10 April 2007 were Rs. 541.89 crore compared to Rs. 483.99 crore during the same period last year, an increase of 11.96 per cent. The revenue earnings from other coaching amounted to Rs. 51.57 crore during this period compared to Rs. 41.20 crore during the same period last year, an increase of 25.17 per cent. The total sundry earnings have gone up from Rs. 17.04 crore during 1-10 April 2006 to Rs. 19.76 crore during 1-10 April 2007, showing an increase of 15.96 per cent. The total approximate number of passengers booked during the period 1-10 April 2007 were 185.59 million compared to 173.93 million during the same period last year, showing an increase of 6.70 per cent. In the suburban and non-suburban sectors, the number of passengers booked during 1-10 April 2007 were 105.93 million and 79.66 million compared to 99.97 million and 73.96 million during the same period last year, registering an increase of 5.96 per cent and 7.71 per cent respectively.

330. (20-4-2007) NEW DELHI : Essential parameters in elementary education, enrolment, reduction in the dropout rates, the pass percentage as well as the attendance of the teachers in the primary schools marked a quantum rise in Nagaland between 2002 to 2004. So also is the case in the efficiency of the village health service delivery system measured in terms of number of child and adult patients visiting health centres in rural Nagaland, improvement in the staff attendance, visit of the medical officers and even in the staff attitude. All this is reflected in a report by the UNICEF on the impact assessment of cummunitisation of public institutions and services in Nagaland. The unique scheme for involving the community was conceived under the stewardship of the then Chief Secretary of the State Shri R. S.Pandey and was launched after the passage of an Act namely Nagaland Communitisation of Public Institutions and Services Act in 2002. Initially, the scheme focused on three very important areas : Elementary education, Grass root health services and Electricity management. The experiment evolved from the need to revitalize the massive welfare infrastructure and vast network of delivery services set up by the government which had become ineffective and dysfunctional. It is based on the philosophy of communitisation as an alternative to privatization as well as management by government. This philosophy attempts to combine the best of both approaches by substituting the private profit motive with enlightened collective self interest. It holds among other tenets, that when the empowered are not adequately motivated to perform, it makes sense to empower the motivated. In a sense it was an attempt to reinvent the welfare state,

331. (20-4-2007) NEW DELHI : Shri Kamal Nath, Union Minister for Commerce & Industry, while addressing two separate interactive sessions on the Annual Supplement to the Foreign Trade Policy with Federation of Indian Chamber of Commerce & Industry (FICCI) & Confederation of Indian Industry (CII) here today stated that agricultural exports including fruits and vegetables will be the next area for growth for Indian exports. "Our great area in future will be in the field of agriculture exports", he said. The Minister highlighted the need to strengthen the infrastructure in the post-harvest stage to benefit from the opportunities in this area. Shri Nath informed that the Government is looking at the possibility of setting up Food Parks and would provide the necessary assistance in this regard. He also referred to his recent visit to China and pointed out the great potential for agro-exports that China may provide. "I have taken upon myself that in the next few months Chinese markets will open to the Indian agricultural exports", Shri Nath said. The Minister also pointed out the significance of the record US dollar 16 billion Foreign Direct Investment (FDI) recorded in 20006-07 and said the country would continue to attract more investments. "I have targeted FDI for 2007-08 at US dollar 25 billion", he said. Responding to questions from the industry representatives, he agreed that a lot needs to be done to improve the infrastructure and the Government was committed to address the issue. To a question pertaining to the Governments policy on Special Economic Zones (SEZs), Shri Nath stated that the real issue in SEZs is not the number of SEZs but the number of units set up in the SEZs. He stated that since it was not possible to have mega-sized SEZs in India as in case of China it is therefore necessary that India has a higher number of SEZs to bring about rapid industrialization and to give momentum to exports. "If we have limits on the size of SEZs, we cannot limit the number of SEZs", he said. The Minister reiterated that the Government is committed to ensure that land acquisition for the purpose of SEZs is done in a fair and transparent manner. Meanwhile, Shri Kamal Nath announced that the Ministry would hold two open houses in the coming days at which the exporters and the industry representatives could discuss their specific concerns and problems if any, related to the Foreign Trade Policy Supplement announced yesterday before the necessary notifications are issued.

332. (20-4-2007) NEW DELHI : The All-India Consumer Price Index for Agricultural and Rural Labourers (Base 1986-87 = 100) remained stationary during March 2007 at 392 points for Agricultural Labourers and 393 points for Rural Labourers. The rise and fall in index varied from state to state. In case of Agricultural Labourers 11 states reflected an increase in indices ranging between 1 to 7 points while in eight states the indices went down by 1 to 3 points. It remained stationary in one state. In case of Rural Labourers, 12 states reflected an increase ranging between 1 to 7 points, in seven states the indices fell by one to three points while in one state the index remained constant. Assam experienced a sharpest increase of 7 points each in respect of Agricultural Labourers and Rural Labourers. The rise has been mainly due to increase in the prices of Rice, Fish Fresh, Vegetables & Fruits, Pan Leaf, Supari and Country Liquor. On the other hand, the indices in respect of Himachal Pradesh, Kerala and Tamil Nadu for Agricultural Labourers and Andhra Pradesh, Kerala and Tamil Nadu in respect of Rural Labourers recorded the maximum decrease of 3 points each mainly due to decrease in the prices of Wheat Atta, Jowar, Onions, Dry Chillies, Tamarind, Vegetables & Fruits, Gur and Pan Leaf. Rajasthan with 423 points for Agricultural Labourers and Punjab & Rajasthan with 422 points for Rural Labourers figured at the top of the index table.

333. (20-4-2007) NEW DELHI : In exercise of the powers conferred by clause (1) of Article 217 of the Constitution of India, the President is pleased to appoint

(i) Smt. Justice Vasanti Anil Naik (ii) Shri Justice Jagmohansingh Hakamsingh Bhatia, (iii) Shri Justice Ravindra Chandrakant Chavan and (iv) Smt. Justice Roshan Shamim Dalvi, Additional Judges of the Bombay High Court, to be Judges of the Bombay High Court, in that order of seniority, with effect from the dates they assume charge of their respective offices. Ministry of Law and Justice (Department of Justice) New Delhi, Chaitra 30, 1929 /April 20, 2007.

334. (20-4-2007) NEW DELHI : In exercise of the powers conferred by clause (1) of Article 217 of the Constitution of India, the President is pleased to appoint (i) Shri Justice Shiv Narayan Dhingra, (ii) Shri Justice Sunder Lal Bhayana, (iii) Shri Justice Jatinder Mohan Malik, (iv) Smt. Justice Reva Khetrapal, (v) Shri Justice Sri Niwas Aggarwal and (vi) Shri Justice Pravesh Kumar Bhasin, Additional Judges of the Delhi High Court, to be Judges of the Delhi High Court, in that order of seniority, with effect from the dates they assume charge of their respective offices. Ministry of Law and Justice (Department of Justice) New Delhi, Chaitra 30, 1929 /April 20, 2007.

335. (20-4-2007) NEW DELHI : India and Syria has identified a number of projects and key areas for further enhancing cooperation in the hydrocarbon sector spanning across exploration & production, refinery modernization and new projects, development of gas infrastructure including city gas projects, marketing, training of Syrian technicians and engineers etc. This was agreed at a meeting between Shri Murli Deora, Minister of Petroleum & Natural Gas and his counterpart Mr. Sufian Al-Alao, Minister of Petroleum & Mineral Resources of Syria at Damascus late yesterday evening. Shri Deora while elaborating recent developments in Indian oil and gas sector at the delegation level talks, emphasized the need for greater cooperation between two countries. His counterpart Mr. Al-Alao also reciprocated the sentiments. At the end of the meeting agreed minutes were signed by Petroleum Secretary Shri M.S. Srinivasan from Indian side and Dr. Eng. Hassan Zaienab, Dy. Minister Petroleum & Mineral Resources from Syrian side. Syria has agreed to work closely together with Indian companies, and to consider the request of Indian side for allocating blocks on preferential basis in the spirit of mutually beneficial relationship. Further, Syria would provide information to Indian companies about 7 off-shore blocks proposed for bidding later this year. ONGC extended offer of assistance to Syrian Petroleum Company(SPC) for increased oil recovery/enhanced oil recovery (IOR/EOR) from their heavy oil fields through techniques such as in-situ combustion, gas and water injection, slim hole drilling, side tracking, production system optimization, etc. ONGC will also assist SPC in data interpretation pertaining sub-surface activities. ONGC's offer for EOR/IOR projects could help in arresting Syrian oil production decline which fell from about 6,00,000 barrels per day(bd) in 2002 to about 4,00,000 bd at present. ONGC emphasized that they have world class training facilities in India and can train Syrian engineers and personnel in areas like Reservoir Management, Data Interpretation, 3 D Seismic Survey for greater coverage of exploration acreages in Syria, etc. In refining sector, IOC and EIL conveyed their interests in participating in different opportunities in Syria. EIL specifically expressed interest in participating in the upcoming Banias Refinery upgradation project for providing PMC services as well as the new Refinery projects. Syrian side agreed to provide details of the project, companies working on the tender for Banias Refinery Upgradation project for maximizing gasoline and gas oil production. Syria will further send the project plans and other terms and conditions proposed for setting up new Refineries through JV route with Venezuela (Capacity:1,40,000 bd); JV with China (Capacity: 70,000 bd); new refinery with share-holding by Kuwaiti Financial company (1,40,000 bd).

336. (20-4-2007) NEW DELHI : National Rural Employment Guarantee Act (NREGA) was initially launched in 2 districts of Haryana and another 2 Districts have been added in the year 2007-08. In the State 44 Thousand households have demanded employment and all of them have been provided employment up to Feb.,07. The average number of households provided employment in a district of the State is 21,887, while the national average is 91,685 households. Besides, three thousand household have completed the 100 days guarantee of employment provided in the Act. The number of person days of employment provided in the State is 19.66 lakh. The average person days of employment provided in a district is 9.83 lakh compared to the national average of 36.47 lakh person days. The employment was provided on 1238 works, out of which 462 works have been completed. The average number of works taken up in a district stood at 619 against the national average of 3,581. An amount of Rs. 31.29 crore has been released to the State during 2006-07. Against this, the utlisation up to February 2007, is Rs. 26.41 crore, which is 58.01% of the total availability. The expenditure on wages is 71.66%, material is 27.06% and on administration is 1.28%. The average expenditure of a district in the State is Rs. 13.21 crore compared to the National average of Rs. 35 crore. The Act provides that 1/3rd of the employment provided should be to women. In the State 31% person days of employment has been provided to women and 58.98% to members of SC.

337. (20-4-2007) NEW DELHI : The Tourism and Culture Minister Smt. Ambika Soni has called for better air, train and bus connectivity to promote tourism in the SAARC Region. Addressing the inaugural session of the 14th Annual South Asian Travel and Tourism Exchange (SATTE) here today she said South Asia is witnessing unprecedented economic changes and for enhanced growth rates in the region, the need for greater connectivity in terms of rail, road and air is important. She said all members of the SAARC must collectively commit to making travel easier in the region. Smt. Soni said people to people contact and connectivity are the best ways to have harmonious relationship and peace in the region. She said efforts should be made to work on Tourist Circuits which will take people to atleast two to three countries. The Minister said tourism has kept pace with the overall rate of growth of the economy in India. In the last five years, foreign tourist arrivals have grown by 78% and foreign exchange earnings have increased by 122%. She said although in rare terms the figures may be small as compared to many of countries in the neighborhood, what is important is that we have taken up on ourselves the challenge to unleash the full potential of the tourism sector. She said tourism has multiplier effect on the economy as the biggest employment generator and every year the sector is said to be creative two to three million jobs-both direct and indirect. Listing the various initiatives taken by the Government in the tourism sector with the objective of providing visitors to India with a world class experience, Smt. Soni said an Advance Passenger Information System and Long Term Visas are on the anvil to facilitate tourists. Foreign investment in the tourism sector is encouraged and overseas investors are allowed to invest upto 100% equity on repatriation basis. She said India is focusing on promotion of niche segments and innovative concepts such as Rural Tourism, Medical Tourism, Conference & Convention, Cruise Tourism, Golf Tourism, Luxury Trains, wedding and Honeymoon Tourism.

338. (20-4-2007) NEW DELHI : The Annual Conference of Relief Commissioners/ Secretaries (Disaster Management) of States and Union Territories to review the status of preparedness for the South-West Monsoon will be held here on Monday. About 40 Central Ministries/ Departments/ Organizations which render Emergency Support functions in the wake of natural calamities will participate in the Conference, organized by the Ministry of Home Affairs. Key Central Organizations such as the India Meteorological Department, Central Water Commission, Ministries of Defence and Health & Family Welfare are likely to make presentations detailing the Early Warning and Preparatory and Logistic support to be rendered by them in the wake of various natural disasters. The Union Home Secretary, Shri Madhukar Gupta will inaugurate the Conference. A preparatory meeting to discuss and finalize various issues to be taken up in the Annual Conference was held on the 13th of this month under the chairmanship of Secretary (Border Management) in the Ministry of Home Affairs, Shri U.N. Panjiar. Representatives of the States and those of the Central Ministries took part in the meeting.

339. (20-4-2007) NEW DELHI : To promote greater cooperation between the U.S. and Indian aviation sectors, the U.S. Trade and Development Agency (USTDA), in cooperation with the Indian Ministry of Civil Aviation (MoCA), the Airports Authority of India (AAI), Directorate General of Civil Aviation (DGCA), the U.S. Federal Aviation Administration, U.S. Department of State, U.S. Department of Commerce, U.S. Transportation Security Administration, American Association of Airport Executives (AAAE), International Association of Airport Executives (IAAE) and the MITRE Corporation will sponsor a high-level U.S.-India Aviation Partnership Summit. The event will take place at New Delhi, India, April 23-25, 2007. The objective of the summit is to generate discussions between the U.S. and Indian aviation sector regarding industry growth opportunities and challenges. Moreover, the summit will help build the long-term strategic and commercial relationship between U.S. and Indian aviation sectors in addressing, among other issues, air traffic management, airspace utilization and U.S.-India commercial collaboration in new airborne systems. The purpose of the summit is to promote trade and provide exposure to technical, managerial and strategic planning approaches as India adopts integrated and automated air traffic control and management systems. These systems will focus on safety, capacity, efficiency and security management for future air transport systems.

340. (20-4-2007) NEW DELHI : An Egyptian tourism delegation led by Mr. Amr El Egaby Chairman, Egyptian Tourism Authority called on Minister of Tourism and Culture Smt. Ambika Soni here today. During their half-an-hour meeting, the Egyptian side lauded the Incredible India Campaign and efforts of the Union Tourism Ministry to spread social awareness about preservation and cleanliness of cities and historical monuments for domestic tourists. Smt. Ambika Soni recalling the age old historical and cultural relations between the two countries said there is a tremendous potential in India and Egypt to promote places of historical importance and tourist destinations in each other's country. Mr. Amr El Egaby said his country would be happy to know the process how Forts and Havelis have been converted into Heritage Hotels in India. He also offered Egyptian expertise in the field of monument preservation. The Egyptian side also suggested twinning of the cities between India and Egypt as the two countries have many similarities on historical destinations. Smt. Soni welcomed the idea and said to step forward in this direction profiles of different cities should be provided to each other to identify the right matches. Earlier, the third meeting of the Joint Working Group on tourism was held between India and Egypt here yesterday. It was viewed by both sides that increase in the flow of tourism would further enhance bilateral relations between the two countries. It was agreed to establish a programme to exchange visits of tour operators and travel media to motivate consumers in both countries to travel to the other country. Both sides informed each other about the investment opportunities available in their countries in the tourism sector. It was agreed that growing opportunities should be showcased to attract investments from the private stakeholders. Egyptian side was briefed on the facilities available in India for Human Resource Development in travel and hospitality sector. It was agreed by both sides to establish an exchange programme for students and faculties to enhance cooperation by developing partnership programmes between leading academic institutions in the tourism sector of both countries. Both sides expressed willingness to assist the NTO's/Tourism Boards of each other's country in carrying out promotion and marketing activities to increase the tourism traffic between the two countries. Both the countries agreed to formulate an action plan for promotion and marketing of their destinations in each other's country.

341. (20-4-2007) NEW DELHI : The Uranium industry has been declared as a public utility service under the Industrial Disputes Act, 1947 for six months with immediate effect. The Labour Ministry in a notification issued here today said that this has been done by the Central Government in public interest. The employees in this establishment, as a result, would among other things be required to give notice to their employer six weeks in advance of proceeding on strike so that conciliatory proceedings could be started. During the conciliatory proceedings and seven days after their completion, the employees cannot go on strike.

342. (20-4-2007) NEW DELHI : The Ministry of Rural Development has sanctioned Rs. 30.97 lakh of Grants-in-aid of Central Share for the year 2006-07 under Administration to the Udhampur (Rs.21.64 lakh) District Rural Development Agency (DRDA) of Jammu & Kashmir towards the first instalment and as second instalment to Baramula DRDA(Rs. 9.33 lakh). The funding pattern under the scheme is 75:25 between Centre and the State. The utilization of funds is to be in accordance with the DRDA administration guidelines and the release of the second instalment during 2007-08 is subject to the fulfillment of all the conditions as per the DRDA Administration guidelines.

343. (20-4-2007) NEW DELHI : The average annual rainfall of the country is about 1170 mm. However, there is very high temporal and spatial variation in rainfall. With a view to conserve water, several water resources development projects have been taken up in the country. There has been considerable progress in respect of water resources development in India since independence through major, medium and minor irrigation schemes and multipurpose projects. The live storage capacity of the completed dam projects is estimated to be 213 Billion Cubic Metre (BCM) which was only about 15.6 BCM at the time of independence. Besides, as per present assessment, the total estimated storage capacity of the various projects under construction is about 76 BCM. Further, the State Governments have identified various other schemes for investigation and planning and the estimated storage for such schemes is about 108 BCM. The average annual precipitation is estimated as 4000 Billion Cubic Metre (BCM) in the country. After accounting for the natural process of evaporation etc. the average annual water availability is assessed as 1869 BCM. It is estimated that owing to topographic, hydrological and other constraints, the utilizable water is 1123 BCM. Rest of the water could be considered to be flowing down to sea. Government of India is providing central assistance to the State Governments through various schemes, programmes, such as Accelerated Irrigation Benefits Programmes (AIBP); Command Area Development and Water Management (CADWM) Programme; National Project for Repair, Renovation and Restoration of Water Bodies directly linked to Agriculture etc. It also encourages rainwater harvesting and recharge to groundwater for conservation of water. Several measures for development and management of water resources are undertaken by the respective States Governments which include creation of storages, restoration of water bodies, rain water harvesting, artificial recharge to ground water and adoption of better management practices etc. State Governments conceive, plan and implement major, medium and minor schemes (both surface and ground water) for utilization of water resources.

344. (20-4-2007) NEW DELHI : Pradhan Mantri Gram Sadak Yojana (PMGSY) was launched in December 2000 as a 100 per cent Centrally Sponsored Scheme with a target of connecting every habitation that has a population of more than 1000 within the next three years and every habitation with a population of more than 500 by the year 2007 *i.e.* by the end of the 10th Five Year Plan through good all-weather road. A sum of Rs.20,400.70 crore has been released to the States/ UTs towards the programme and up to December 2006, 35,868 roadworks covering a length of 1,07,569.08 Kms. have been completed. The Ministry of Rural Development has released Rs. 19.39 crore as balance payment of second instalment of Phase-IV as Grants-in-aid to the MIZORAM RURAL ROADS DEVELOPMENT AGENCY (MRRDA), Aizawl, which is the Autonomous Agency for receiving the funds for the programme under PMGSY. The grant is towards the Plan expenditure and will be subject to the conditions laid down from time to time in the guidelines of the PMGSY and supplementary directions.

345. (20-4-2007) NEW DELHI : National Rural Employment Guarantee Act (NREGA) was initially launched in 6 districts of Gujarat and another 3 Districts have been added in the year 2007-08. In the State 1.79 lakh households have demanded employment and all the households have been provided employment up to Feb.,07. The average number of households provided employment in a district of the State is 25,536, while the national average is 91,685 households. In the State 0.08 lakh household have completed the 100 days guarantee of employment provided in the Act. The number of person days of employment provided in the State is 84.57 lakh. The average person days of employment provided in a district is 14.09 lakh compared to the national average of 36.47 lakh person days. The employment was provided on 7,409 works, out of which 2,796 works have been completed. The average number of works taken up in a district stood at 1,235, against the national average of 3,581. An amount of Rs. 67.44 crore has been released to the State during 2006-07. Against this, the utlisation up to February 2007, is Rs. 68.68 crore, which is 57.59% of the total availability. The expenditure on wages is 62.39%, material is 14.85% and on administration is 22.76%. The average expenditure of a district in the State is Rs. 11.45 crore compared to the National average of Rs. 35 crore. The Act provides that 1/3rd of the employment provided should be to women. In the State 52.51% person days of employment has been provided to women, 6.65% to SC and 61.04% to ST. A visit to the State by the National Level Monitors in December, 2006 & January 2007 has revealed that Grievance Redressal Mechanism has been set up.

346. (21-4-2007) NEW DELHI : This year's focus on Earth Day is 'A call for action on Climate Change'. Addressing a Press Conference Union Minister of Science & Technology and Earth Sciences, Shri Kapil Sibal, called for a need to look into possible large scale and sudden changes in the earth's living environment due to global warming and climate change in the coming years. India has contributed significantly, both in term of leadership and pursuit of scientific quest in the field of environmental conservation, technological development and mitigation factors, which are leading to climate change. Development of cleaner and eco-friendly technology is a priority area of the Ministry. Low Temperature Thermal Desalination (LTTD) is one such innovation, which the scientists at the National Institute of Technology (NIOT), Chennai, an autonomous R & D Institute under the Ministry have developed. The people of Lakshdweep islands are now getting the benefit of this technology. NIOT has recently successfully tested a one million liter capacity LTTD plant and soon it will be going for a higher capacity cost effective desalination plant, which can run on commercial scale. Celebration of 'Earth Day' has its beginning in 1970. The issue was raised by Senator Gaylord Nelson of Wisconsin, USA, in response to wide spread environmental degradation. He called for an 'Environmental Tech-in' or 'Earth Day' to be held on April 22. It is now observed each year by more than 500 million people and National Governments in over 175 countries. The main purpose to celebrate Earth Day is to promote environmental citizenship and progressive action by steering environmental awareness around the world. Creation of the Ministry of Earth Sciences and an Earth Commission by bringing together the domains of Oceans and Atmospheric Sciences is a major step of the Government of India. Ministry of Earth Sciences has also taken positive steps to bring a greater focus on the environmental issues specially keeping in view the concerns raised by the scientists on climate change in recent times. Oceans and atmosphere together actually play a much greater role in Indian sub-continent than perceived earlier, whether it is monsoon or tropical cyclones. Efforts have been stepped up to understand the climate and climate change processes. An advanced weather prediction and forecasting will help in minimizing human misery and environmental degradation, which arises due to vagaries of weather.

347. (21-4-2007) NEW DELHI : Shri Arjun Singh, Minister for Human Resource Development received a report containing recommendations for introduction of Modern Education in Madarsas and setting up of a Central Madarsa Board from Justice M.S.A Siddiqui, Chairman of the National Commission for Minority Educational Institutions. The Commission was established through an Ordinance in November 2004 and started receiving petitions/representations from February 2005 onwards. The educational backwardness of the Muslim community has been brought to the notice of the Commission by various sources. The Commission recognized that the educational backwardness of the Muslim community has become a matter of unprecedented national concern, calling for significant remedial initiatives. Modernizing and upgrading Madarsa education, besides prioritizing Muslim-majority areas for educational development, is arguably the most critical task in this regard. The need to establish a Central Madarsa Board for the coordination and standardization of system of education and also for its integrated development and mainstreaming was examined in detail in a series of consultations held by this Commission with educationists, religious scholars and eminent citizens associated with Madarsa education. In order to elicit a wider spectrum of opinions and to facilitate a free interaction on the subject of introduction of modern education in Madarsas and the need to set up an autonomous body like Central Madarsa Board, a national consultation of the prominent spiritual leaders, educationists, intellectuals and religious scholars was held on 3rd December, 2006, in New Delhi which was inaugurated by Shri Arjun Singh, Minister for Human Resource Development. It turned out to be one of the best attended and keenly participated exercises of its kind in which every one felt free to express their views without fear or favour. An overwhelming majority of participants endorsed the idea of setting up a Central Madarsa Board so as to standarise and mainstream Madarsa education, which has become a crying need today. Eminent scholars of Barelvi School of thought, Ahle Hadis, Dawoodi Bohras, Imam Shefai's Sect, Nadvatul Ulma, Lucknow and a section of Deoband School of thought represented by Sheikhul Hadis and president of Tanzeem Ulma-e-Hind, Hazrat Maulana Anzar Shah Kashmiri have supported the proposal for establishment of a Central Madarsa Board. In an interview published in ALMI SAHARA (Urdu Weekly) dated 16th December, 2006, Maulana Syed Rabe Hasmi Nadvi, Rector Nadwat-ul-Ulma, Lucknow, and President of All India Muslim Personal Board has also supported the proposal.

348. (22-4-2007) NEW DELHI : Protest march carrying pro Pakistani Lashkar–e–Taiba flags, shouting slogans in favour of Pakistan in Kashmir Valley by LeT militants is a serious development and Govt. of India should take immediate action against the protestors. This is a direct challenge to national security. Pro-Pakistani Militant action is a result of soft policy adopted by the Prime Minister and UPA government, towards the challenge of terrorism. The Kashmir situation is worsening day by day because of this soft policy of government. Pro-Pakistani Slogans is a threat to national security. BJP always stands for policy of zero tolerance for issues concerning danger to national security. The whole Kashmir issue is the result of Nehruvian blunder of giving separate status to Jammu and Kashmir. This separate status is now converting into full-fledged separatism. Initiatives like roundtable conference have no meaning unless this threat is addressed squarely. The whole peace efforts and negotiations in Kashmir should be focused on security angle. Unfortunately the government is discussing the formula of autonomy, self-rule, demilitarization as proposed by Pakistan President Gen. Pervez Musharraf. India in the process has lost initiative created during the NDA regime.

349. (21-4-2007) NEW DELHI : The Union Minister of Shipping, Road Transport and Highways, Thiru T.R. Baalu has said that the stake-holders including the Central Government, State Governments and others who have passion for road safety need to come together and play active role in promoting road safety. He was speaking at the 10th meeting of the National Road Safety Council being held in Coimbatore in Tamil Nadu today. Besides the Centre, the Council has representatives from the States, State Police Departments, State Transport Department and from the NGOs working in the field of road safety etc. The

Council brings all the stake-holders on one platform to exchange ideas, share initiatives taken by them in encouraging road safety with the ultimate aim to reduce road accidents and fatalities. Speaking on the occasion, Thiru Baalu emphasised the need to give a fillip to the e-governance in the transport sector with a view to mitigate the problems being faced by the people as well the enforcement agencies. He told the Council that the Union Government has already finalised the policy issues by way of Central assistance in the form of software development and its transfer to the States. However, he added that somehow, the actual pace of implementation by the State Governments by way of Smart Card based Driving Licences, Registration Certificates for motor vehicles has not been quite encouraging. He urged the Ministers-in-charge of Transport attending the Council meeting and also the State officials to implement the new initiatives of the Government in their respective States. The Minister also asked the States to effectively enforce the provisions of the Motor Vehicle Act about overloading. He said that road infrastructure is severely damaged by tendency of plying vehicles with overloading and the damage caused to the roads is disproportionate to the gains, if any. He requested all State Governments to take effective steps in this regard.

350. (21-4-2007) NEW DELHI : The Prime Minister, Dr. Manmohan Singh, today inaugurated the South Asian Inter-Faith Harmony Conclave organised by the Inter Faith Harmony Foundation of India in collaboration with the Indian Council for Cultural Relations [ICCR]. The Chief Minister of Delhi, Smt. Sheila Dikshit, Dr. Karan Singh, DG, ICCR, Shri Pawan Verma, religious leaders from various faiths from the SAARC countries were among dignitaries present at the Conclave. Following is the text of the Prime Minister's Address on the Occasion: "I am truly delighted to be here at this very important gathering. Let me begin by recalling the great and wise words of that great son of India whose message of religious harmony in India resonates even to this day and, I believe, will do so for all times to come. I refer to the remarks of Swami Vivekananda at the World's Parliament of Religions, held in Chicago in September, 1893. Swamiji spoke of our civilisational tradition of accepting the greatness of all religions. He said very aptly, "We believe not only in universal toleration, but we accept all religions as true." This is a simple but exceedingly important idea. It was not religious "tolerance" that Swamiji valued, as much as religious "harmony". Of course, harmony requires tolerance, but harmony is more than mere tolerance. There can be tolerance of an unequal, but there can be harmony only among equals. Harmony requires mutual respect. One can be tolerant of another, without being respectful. This cannot produce harmony. True harmony, I believe, is based on mutual respect and regard. Hence, I prefer the concept of religious harmony rather than just religious tolerance. I agree with what Swami Vivekananda that what makes our civilization great is the fact that it is based on the idea of the coexistence of faiths-Sarva Dharma Sambhava. This notion implies that we have equal respect for all Dharmas, for all faiths. Elaborating this idea Swami Vivekananda used the metaphor of many rivers flowing into one mighty ocean. He quoted from an ancient hymn to say: "As the different streams having their sources in different places all mingle their water in the sea, sources in different tendencies, various though they appear, crooked or straight, all lead to Thee."

351. (22-4-2007) NEW DELHI : Yet another flight trial of the land version of the Supersonic Cruise Missile Brahmos-the fourteenth one to be precise, has been successful. The trial of the 290 Km range of the missile was carried out at Chandipur-on-Sea, Balasore in Orissa today. The complete test was carried out by Army personnel in the presence of Lt. Gen BS Pawar, Commandant, School of Artillery, Major General VK Chaturvedi, Additional Director General Artillery, and a host of other senior Army officers. Emphasis was laid on the ability of the supersonic missile to carry out a number of exacting maneuvers during its flight towards a pre-determined target-point. Lt. Gen Pawar expressed complete satisfaction at the missile's performance especially in its display of additional capabilities and meeting all other mission objectives. The Defence Minister, Shri AK Antony congratulated Dr. Sivathanu Pillai, CEO, BRAHMOS and Chief Controller R&D, the scientists from DRDO and the specialists from Russia for today's successful flight trial by the Army. Earlier accepted by the Navy for its warship, the Indian Army will be the second major customer inducting this missile in its arsenal this year.

352. (22-4-2007) NEW DELHI : Shri Murli Deora, Minister of Petroleum & Natural Gas today called on the Prime Minister of Algeria Mr. Abdelaziz Belkhadem. In the hour long meeting Shri Deora conveyed India's strong desire to strengthen the friendly relations between India and Algeria particularly in oil & gas sector. He informed that India is keen to have an arrangement to purchase LPG from Algeria on term contract basis besides pursuing opportunities in other areas of hydrocarbon sector for mutual benefit. Algeria has large exportable surplus of LPG while India is a large importer of the product. Mr. Abdelaziz Belkhadem emphasised the need for forging strategic relations in hydrocarbon domain in the backdrop of long standing friendship between the two countries. He fondly recalled his meeting with the two former Prime Ministers of India late Smt Indira Gandhi and late Shri Rajiv Gandhi in 1983 at Kolkata during Congress conclave. Mr. Chakib Khelil, Minister of Energy and Mines, Algeria was also present. Other members of Indian delegation who attended the meeting are Petroleum Secretary Shri MS Srinivasan, CMD ONGC Shri R S Sharma, Chairman IOC Shri S Behuria, CMD GAIL Dr. U D Choubey, CMD EIL and Shri M Rohatgi. Shri Murli Deora will call on the President of Algeria later in the evening. Earlier during delegation level talks, Shri Deora recounted the close ties between the two countries and expressed the hope that present discussions will lead to expanding hydrocarbon cooperation between the two countries. He referred to the presence of Engineers India Limited (EIL) in Algeria for the past 25 years. Mr. Chakib Khelil gave a comprehensive insight into the structure of the hydrocarbon, Electricity and Mining sectors in Algeria. He informed that Algeria aims exporting 85 billion cubic metres of gas by the year 2010 up from about 62 billion cubic metres with 50% being supplied as LNG. He also highlighted plan to expand pipeline capacity to supply gas to Europe. GAIL expressed their interest to participate in a major project on the anvil, the envisaged Trans-Sahara gas pipeline project linking Nigeria to Algeria and onwards to the European market through existing pipeline network. The Company also offered pursuing equity in LNG infrastructure and in CNG projects in Algeria for which thay are prepared to work closely with the local agencies. In upstream sector India conveyed that Indian oil PSUs are open for joint bidding with NOCs of Algeria in their upcoming Seventh Round of Bidding during 2007. ONGC expressed interest in working jointly with Sonatrach through the two MOUs already signed with them. The leading upstream company of India also offered to give training to the Algerian oil sector personnel in diverse areas covering reservoir management, seismic studies, etc. Indian companies would pursue working with Naftec for identifying prospective refining projects for participation by Indian companies and offering PMC services, etc. IOC offered to work together with Algerian companies in the areas of Refinery upgradation, setting up of new refineries, bitumen formulations, consultancy services pertaining to process units commissioning, etc. Algeria's current refining capacity of 500,000barrels per day(bd) is being increased with a new refinery in the South to be commissioned shortly alongwith construction of another refinery of 100,000 bd capacity at Skikda by 2009 and one more refinery by 2011.

353. (23-4-2007) NEW DELHI : Mr. Mohamed Hosni Mubarak, President of the Arab Republic of Egypt received Mr. Murli Deora, Minister for Petroleum and Natural Gas of India this morning. During the call, Mr. Deora delivered a message to President Mubarak from Dr. Manmohan Singh, Prime Minister of India. President Mubarak reiterated his support to the traditional relations of friendship and cooperation between India and Egypt and noted with satisfaction that high-level bilateral ministerial exchanges in the past few months had imparted renewed impetus to the Indo-Egyptian relationship. President Mubarak also expressed confidence that, besides deepening cooperation in the oil and gas sector, Shri Deora's visit would strengthen the contacts at the political plane and promote better understanding between the two countries. Conveying the greetings and good wishes of the people and leadership of India to the people and leadership of Egypt, Shri Deora emphasized that India attached priority to its relations with Egypt and was appreciative of Egypt's role in the region. He expressed optimism that the multi-faceted relations existing between India and Egypt would be further reinforced with the continuing expansion of economic and commercial ties. Shri Deora also apprised President Mubarak about the discovery of significant reserves of oil in the North Ramadan oil field by OVL in partnership with IPR Red Sea Inc. earlier this month. Shri Deora, who arrived in Cairo yesterday evening on an official visit (22-25 April), is scheduled to hold detailed discussions on cooperation in the oil and gas sector with the Minister of Petroleum of Egypt, Mr. Amin Sameh Fahmy later today. The itinerary also includes a meeting with the Minister of Trade &

Industry, Mr. Rachid Mohammed Rachid. The Indian delegation led by Mr. Deora includes Petroleum Secretary Shri M.S. Srinivasan and the Heads of India's main public sector oil and gas companies namely, Oil & Natural Gas Corporation (ONGC); Indian Oil Corporation (IOC); Gas Authority of India Limited (GAIL); and, Engineers India Limited (EIL).

354. (23-4-2007) NEW DELHI : A 12 member media delegation from China called on Tourism and Culture Minister Smt. Ambika Soni here today. During an hour interaction with the visitors Smt. Soni recalled the visit of Chinese President in November, 2006 and Chinese Foreign Minister's visit to India in February, 2007. She said this is a India-China Friendship Year Through Tourism and both the countries are committed to increase tourists inflow in each other's country. She said Incredible India Website has been launched in Chinese and her Ministry has also translated tourism related material into Chinese language. Smt. Soni said to attract tourists from Asia, Buddhist Circuit in India is being promoted in a big way and a special train has also been introduced. India is soon opening a tourist office in Shenghai. When asked about the new tourism products and infrastructure development, the Minister said her Government is committed to increase availability of hotel rooms in the country before the 2010 Commonwealth Games and efforts are on to build budget hotels. She said 6.5 billion US $ investment is in the pipeline in hotels. The Minister said visas will be made easily available. She said India is promoting adventure tourism, rural tourism, Tea tourism, shopping tourism, medical tourism and food tourism to attract foreigners as well as domestic tourists. The representatives in the Media Delegation were from Beijing Daily, CPPCC Journal, Jiefang Daily, Fujian Journalists' Association, All-China Journalists' Association, Ningxia General Station of Radio & TV, China Taxation News, Shijiazhuang Daily, Information Office of the State Council and China Press Journal.

355. (23-4-2007) NEW DELHI : National Mineral Development Corporation Ltd. (NMDC), incorporated in 1958, is a Government Undertaking under the Ministry of Steel. Since inception it is involved in the exploration of wide range of minerals including iron ore, copper, rock phosphate, limestone, dolomite gypsum, bentorite, magnerite, diamond, tin, tungsten, graphite, beach sands etc. Hyderabad based NMDC is India's single largest iron ore producer and exporter. In the wake of expansion and investment plans announced by steel producers securing raw material has become the major concern. NMDC which was originally exporting its entire product has shifted its focus to domestic steel industry, supplying as much as 90% of its iron ore production to domestic market. Having backup of an ISO 9001 certified Research & Development Centre NMDC undertakes product and technology development missions related to ore and minerals.

356. (23-4-2007) NEW DELHI : A three-day India-US Aviation Partnership Summit was inaugurated by the Minister for Civil Aviation, Shri Praful Patel, here today. Also present at the inauguration were the Administrator, Federal Aviation

Administration (FAA), Ms. Marion Blakey, the Secretary, Civil Aviation, Shri Ashok Chawla and the Deputy Director of the US Trade and Development Agency (USTDA), Ms. Leocadia Zak. The objective of the Summit is to encourage high level discussions between the US and the Indian Aviation Sectors regarding Industry growth challenges. It is expected to help in building long term strategy and commercial relationship between the two countries to address important issues like air traffic management, air-space utilization and commercial collaborations in new airborne systems. The Summit is designed to promote trade, shared technical managerial and strategic planning approaches to adept integrated automatic air traffic control and management systems focusing on safety, capacity, efficiency and security for future air transport systems. Speaking on the occasion, the Minister of Civil Aviation, Shri Praful Patel said that in the last three years the US India relationship in Civil Aviation has been building on a new note and partnership which will be ever lasting. Aviation, he said, is a catalyst in bringing about integration of all countries of the world. In India, Aviation was very peripheral till recently. It was a means of transport of the elite only. However, now with the Government opening up to change and adoption of good practices across the globe, Civil Aviation has not only become a mode for mass transportation but also a catalyst for equitable growth, providing connectivity to every corner of the country, leading to growth in employment and giving a boost to the economy. Mr. Patel said that India for the next ten years would enjoy a compounded growth of about 25% in the aviation sector, which will be sustained for the next 10 to 15 years. The reason for this he said was the liberalization of the regime and the proactive bilaterals which have minimized restrictions in the free flow of passengers. Speaking about the United States the Minister said that It is only with the USA that India enjoys total Open Skies-"which shows that we want to take the US Indian relationship to a much greater height, and what better way than in the field of Aviation". The Minister also added that India can not rest with what it has. It has to integrate its expertise with the good practices of leading countries like the USA. Of the billion strong population of India, less than one percent fly once a year. If this could be increased to nominal 10% people who fly once a year, the Minister predicted that at least a thousand planes would be required in the country. This, he said would require both physical and technical infrastructure. However, the Government alone would not be doing this in India. It was looking forward to Public, Private, Partnership (PPP) for the growth of this sector. The Government was looking forward to liberalizing the sector, to change the air traffic pattern and redistributing air traffic across the country.

357. (23-4-2007) NEW DELHI : Vice Admiral Anup Singh will be taking over as the Indian Navy's new Deputy Chief on 26 Apr. 07. He relieves Vice Admiral RP Suthan who is proceeding to Vishakhapatnam as Flag Officer Commanding-in-Chief of the Eastern Naval Command. Vice Admiral Anup Singh was commissioned in the Indian Navy on 01 Jul 1973. A specialist in Navigation and Direction, he has held a mix of operational and staff appointments. He has recently reported at New Delhi, on promotion, after relinquishing his appointment as the Flag Officer Commanding, Western Fleet. As the Fleet Commander, he had led Operation Sukoon, the evacuation of civilians from war torn Lebanon in July 2006 in what came to be the largest post-Independence civilian-evacuation operation undertaken by the Indian Navy. He has also held command and staff appointments afloat and ashore including Assistant Controller of Carrier Projects and Warship Production and Acquisition at Naval Headquarters, Chief Instructor (Navy), Defence Services staff College, Wellington and Chief of Staff, Western Naval Command. The Flag Officer is a recipient of the Ati Vishisht Seva Medal and the Nao Sena Medal. A keen sportsman and adventurer, he was the Sailing Master of the first ever square-rigged Sail Training vessel 'Varuna' in 1981-82. He also skippered the Naval Yacht 'Samudra' for the Pacific Crossing during her round the world voyage in 1989. As the Deputy Chief of the Naval Staff, he will be heading the 'Operations' branch of the Navy, including foreign cooperation.

358. (23-4-2007) NEW DELHI : The Chief Minister of Jammu & Kashmir Shri Ghulam Nabi Azad today called on the Minister of Civil Aviation, Shri Praful Patel to discuss the upgradation and modernization of the Airports in the State of Jammu & Kashmir. Also present on the occasion were Shri F.H. Major, Chief of Air Staff, Shri Ashok Chawla, Secretary, Ministry of Civil Aviation, Dr. K. Ramalingam, Chairman, Airport Authority of India (AAI) and the other senior officials of the Civil Aviation Ministry. The meeting discussed in detail the development works taken up at the Jammu Airport which belongs to the Ministry of Defence (IAF) and a Civil Enclave is maintained there by the AAI. Jammu has seen an unprecedented growth in aircraft movement which has gone up from 36 per week in 2004-05 to the current figure of 168 per week. This growth has made it necessary to expand the terminal building to cope with the traffic growth, expand the Apron to accommodate more aircraft and to extend the runway to cater to bigger aircraft. AAI has drawn up plans to extend the runway from 6000 ft. to about 9000 ft. to cater to operations of AB-320/B-737-800 type of aircraft. AAI in coordination with BCAS has also approved plans for modification of car park area at civil enclave to ensure stringent security measures before permitting the departing passengers into the terminal building and also proper segregation of arriving/departing passengers, VVIP/VIP/General/Staff vehicles etc. Plans are also being finalized to improve and modify the Terminal Building for better space utilization to meet the needs of growing number of airline operators and passengers and also a separate administrative complex. The Ministry of Civil Aviation, the Indian Air Force and the State Government today have agreed to take up and resolve these issues at the earliest. All concerned will soon be meeting in Jammu to review on site the problems & find the necessary solutions for the upgradation of the Jammu Airport. The meeting also discussed the status of the development work being done at the Srinagar Airport which was declared an International Airport by the Government of India on 11th March, 2005. The work is targeted to be completed by 2008. This Airport also belongs to the Ministry of Defence (IAF) where AAI maintains a Civil Enclave for handling Civil domestic operations as well as limited International Haj operations. Besides, the meeting also discussed the development work that is to be carried out in the Leh Airport and the possibilities of starting runway operations in areas like Kishtwar and Poonch in J&K.

359. (23-4-2007) NEW DELHI : The Centre has provided support to State Governments by releasing a sum of Rs. 168.59 crore for taking up necessary flood management activities during the last one year. Ministry of Water Resources has proposed increased allocation for flood management of Rs. 20,100 crore as against Rs. 5417 crore in Xth plan. The Working Group has recommended State Plan Outlay of Rs. 10,200 crore and Central Plan Outlay of Rs. 10,750 crore. Total outlay during Xth Plan was of the order of Rs. 4619 crore in State Plan and about Rs. 1355 crore in Central Plan. The Centre has stressed that works of flood control and drainage in North Bihar (that requires cooperation with Nepal as well) and prevention of erosion in Padma-Ganga and Bhagirathi flood control will be completed expeditiously. It further stresses that a flood-prone area development programme will be surged and the Central Government will fully support flood control works in inter-state and international rivers.

360. (23-4-2007) NEW DELHI : National Rural Employment Guarantee Act (NREGA) was initially launched in 20 districts of Jharkhand and another two Districts have been added in the year 2007-08. In the State 8.69 lakh households have demanded employment and of them 8.46 lakh households have been provided employment up to December, 06. The average number of households provided employment in a district of the State is 42,320, while the national average is 91,685 households. Besides, 16 thousand households completed the 100 days guarantee of employment provided in the Act. The number of person days of employment provided in the State is 308.14 lakh. The average person days of employment provided in a district is 15.41 lakh compared to the national average of 36.47 lakh person days. The employment was provided on 42,571 works, out of which 15,836 works have been completed. The average number of works taken up in a district stood at 2,129 against the national average of 3,581. An amount of Rs. 549.49 crore has been released to the State during 2006-07. Against this, the utlisation up to December, 06 is Rs. 369.59 crore, which is 40.42 % of the total availability. The expenditure on wages is 58.68%, material is 39.97% and on administration is 1.34%. The average expenditure of a district in the State is Rs. 18.48 crore compared to the National average of Rs. 35 crore. The Act provides that 1/3rd of the employment provided should be to women. In the State 34.67% person days of employment has been provided to women, 24.07% to SC and 40.35% to ST. A visit to the State by the National Level Monitors in December, 2006 & January 2007 has revealed that NGOs have been assigned task of creating awareness in villages particularly to Job card holders and in some districts convergence with Janashri Bima Yojana of LIC has been initiated.

361. (23-4-2007) NEW DELHI : National Rural Employment Guarantee Act (NREGA) was initially launched in 2 districts of Himachal Pradesh and another two Districts have been added in the year 2007-08. Up to February, 07, 62 thousand households demanded employment and out of them 59 thousand households have been provided employment in the State. The average number of households provided employment in a district of the State is 29,506 while the national average is 91,685 households. Besides, eight thousand households have completed the 100 days guarantee of employment provided in the Act. The number of person days of employment provided in the State is 23.07 lakh. The average person days of employment provided in a district is 11.54 lakh compared to the national average of 36.47 lakh person days. The employment was provided on 8094 works, out of which 3725 works have been completed. The average number of works taken up in a district stood at 4047 against the national average of 3,581. An amount of Rs. 42.08 crore has been released to the State during 2006-07. Against this, the utlisation up to February 2007, is Rs. 29.22 crore, which is 51.77% of the total availability. The expenditure on wages is 55.21%, material is 44.05% and on administration is 0.74%. The average expenditure of a district in the State is Rs. 14.61 crore compared to the National average of Rs. 35 crore. The Act provides that 1/3rd of the employment provided should be to women. In the State 10.51% person days of employment has been provided to women and 29.74% to SC and 22.49% to members of ST.

362. (23-4-2007) NEW DELHI : In Jammu & Kashmir the National Rural Employment Guarantee Act (NREGA) was initially launched in 3 districts of the State and another two Districts have been added in the year 2007-08. Up to, December, 2006, 59 thousand households have demanded employment and all of them have been provided employment in the State. The average number of households provided employment in a district of the State is 19,769 while the national average is 91,685 households. Besides, 12 thousand households have completed the 100 days guarantee of employment provided in the Act. The number of person days of employment provided in the State is 10.68 lakh. The average person days of employment provided in a district is 3.56 lakh compared to the national average of 36.47 lakh person days. The employment was provided on 1102 works, out of which 368 works have been completed. The average number of works taken up in a district stood at 367 against the national average of 3,581. An amount of Rs. 37.76 crore has been released to the State during 2006-07. Against this, the utlisation up to December, 2006, is Rs. 12.17 crore, which is 24.4% of the total availability. The expenditure on wages is 62.23%, material is 35.71% and on administration is 2.06%. The average expenditure of a district in the State is Rs. 4.06 crore compared to the National average of Rs. 35 crore. The Act provides that 1/3rd of the employment provided should be to women. In the State 9.77% person days of employment has been provided to women and 5.9% to SC and 18.82% to members of ST.

363. (23-4-2007) NEW DELHI : The Union Minister of Shipping, Road Transport & Highways Thiru T.R. Baalu has constituted a high powered Committee today under the Chairmanship of Chairman, Cochin Port Trust to assess and advise the Port Authorities and also to review the security preparedness of the Ports, Shipyards and other allied installations in the country. This follows an anonymous threat call in writing received by the Chairman, Chennai Port Trust on Saturday, the 21st April. Thiru Baalu visited the premises of the Chennai Port to review the security measures taken by the Port Authorities in the wake of threat call. The Port Chairman informed the Minister that the security level of the Port has been suitably upgraded. Secretary, Department of Shipping, Shri A.K. Mohapatra also accompanied the Minister during this visit. The Minister was in Chennai after the Road Safety Council Meeting concluded in Coimbatore yesterday. Apart from the Chairman of Cochin Port Trust, the Committee consists of representatives from the Chennai, Paradeep, Jawaharlal Nehru and Mumbai Port Trusts. In a separate meeting held today in Chennai, Thiru Baalu reviewed the pace of implementation of the Sethusamudaram Ship Channel Project with concerned agencies.

364. (23-4-2007) NEW DELHI : The Prime Minister Dr. Manmohan Singh, had a review meeting with the Scientific Advisory Council on Saturday, 21st April 2007. The meeting was attended by Shri Kapil Sibal, Minister for S&T and Earth Sciences. The Chairman of the Scientific Advisory Council to the Prime Minister, Professor C.N.R. Rao, made a presentation of the progress made on various fronts. Some of the major accomplishments in the last two years arising from the deliberations of the Scientific Advisory Council are the establishment of the new Indian Institutes of Science Education and Research, establishment of Earth Commission, setting up of the empowered Committee on University Education, creation of J.C. Bose and Ramanujam Fellowships to reward talented scientists etc. The proposal to set up the National Science Engineering and Research Board responsible for funding of scientific research in the country is expected to be submitted to the Parliament soon. Based on the recommendation of the Scientific Advisory Council to the Prime Minister, Home Ministry is organizing a national agency for forensic science. The restructuring of the Indian Council of Medical Research (ICMR) is being undertaken by Mr. Ramdoss, Minister of Health to ensure that medical research and education get adequate support and are also properly directed in the years to come. There was discussion on some of the important issues being examined at present by the Scientific Advisory Council. One of them pertained to the bureaucratic impediments in governing scientific institutions, particularly the appointment/promotion of scientists. A proposal to establish an appropriate institutional mechanism for promoting technology innovation and management was discussed. Other important issues discussed included the need for a knowledge TV channel in the country making use of public-private partnership and the need for a national science & technology commission. The Prime Minister commended the progress made by the Council on various fronts and the positive results that have emerged. He urged the Council to proceed with its good work and to come out with appropriate recommendations related to several other important aspects of S&T in the country.

365. (23-4-2007) NEW DELHI : Iron deficiency anemia is the commonest medical disorder in pregnancy, adversely affecting maternal and fetal health. Despite several national programmes targeted at control and treatment of anemia during pregnancy, the success has not been as anticipated, since the majority of women present late. Poor nutritional status and anemia in pregnancy have consequences that extend over generations. Girls born underweight are at risk of producing small, premature infants themselves. Adolescent anemia is easy to diagnose and easy to treat. Yet it is rampant and not being identified. Majority is not even aware of Hb or iron resulting in colossal economic and public health costs. Appropriate anemia control programme for adolescents do not exist in any country. Keeping this in mind 12 by 12 initiative is being launched in the country today with an overall objective of ensuring that every child by the age of 12 years has haemoglobin of 12g%. This innovative initiative is jointly being taken by Ministry of Health & Family Welfare, Govt. of India; WHO; FOGSI and UNICEF along with other partners. Awareness and correction of iron deficiency anemia during adolescence will go a long way in improving health of the future parents. Anemia is a silent epidemic; however it is a preventable condition. 12 by 12 initiative for controlling adolescent anemia is an implementable, effective and sustainable nation building exercise with far reaching benefits in terms of safe motherhood and healthier future generations.

366. (23-4-2007) NEW DELHI : Power Finance Corporation Ltd. (PFC) has transferred Coastal Gujarat Power Ltd. (CGPL), the Special Purpose Vehicle established to develop Mundra Ultra Mega Power Project to the selected bidder namely Tata Power Company Ltd. The transfer of documents were exchanged between PFC and Tata power Company Ltd. at a brief function held in the presence of Union Minister of Power Shri Sushilkumar Shinde, Secretary, Ministry of Power, and Chief Secretaries and Energy Secretaries of the beneficiary States and other State Governments. With this, Mundra Ultra Mega Power Project to be located in Gujarat has become the first project under the UMPP initiative to be transferred to the bidder. Earlier Tata Power Company Ltd. emerged as the successful bidder through tariff based competitive bidding process by submitting the lowest tariff bid of Rs. 2.26 per unit (levelized tariff for 25 years with first year tariff at the rate of Rs. 1.91 per unit). The Mundra Project (5x800 MW) is to be based on imported coal. The project would use Super Critical Technology with a view to achieve higher levels of fuel efficiency, which results in saving of fuel and lower green-house gas emissions. The identified beneficiary states in terms of allocation of power from the proposed project are Gujarat (1900 MW), Maharashtra (800 MW), Punjab (500 MW), Haryana (400 MW) and Rajasthan (400 MW). Recognizing the fact that economics of scale leading to cheaper power can be secured through development of large size power projects, the Government has taken an initiative for facilitating the development of a few Ultra Mega power Projects of about 4000 MW capacity each under tariff based competitive bidding route using super critical technology. These projects are to be awarded to developers on Build, Own, Operate (BOO) basis. The size of these projects being large, they will meet the power needs of a number of states through transmission of power on regional and national basis. For the implementation of this initiative, PFC has been identified as nodal agency. Under this prestigious initiative, nine projects with an estimated investment of about Rs. 1,50,000 crores have been identified. Bidding in respect of 2 projects has been completed and bidding process in respect of another 2 projects is currently on.

367. (23-4-2007) NEW DELHI : The Union Power Minister, Shri Sushil kumar Shinde today inaugurated a conference of the Chief Secretaries and Power/Energy Secretaries of all States and Union Territories to discuss various power related issues. Addressing the delegates the Minister pointed out that the entire country is looking towards this sector with a lot of hope and some amount of desperation. He said the recent growth rate of the Indian economy at 8-10 per cent has placed the country amongst the front runners in the world. If this rate of economic growth is to be sustained, our responsibility in the power sector assumes critical importance not only have we to close the gap in terms of the present energy shortages but expand capacity at a rate commensurate with the overall growth rate of the economy. Shri Shinde said that an ambitious plan to add a generation capacity of more than 70,000 MW in the next 5 years has been envisaged. Transmission network expansion and associated distribution augmentation to match this expansion is also planned. He disclosed that a Working Group constituted to prepare power sector plan for the next five years has estimated that an investment of about more than rupees ten lakh crores will be required for the envisaged expansion in power sector during the years 2007-2012. Out of this, about Rs. 4,10,000 crores will be required for utility based generation and IPPs. Another Rs. 4,27,000 crores of investment is estimated in transmission, distribution and rural electrification segments. The Minister said that two more Ultra Mega Power Projects, one coastal and one pit-head are under bidding process. There are four more such projects for which bidding process would be started soon. The model of SPV adopted in the UMPP initiative addresses the difficulties earlier faced by investors in initial project development activities.

368. (23-4-2007) NEW DELHI : The Prime Minister, Dr. Manmohan Singh, released a collection of Parliamentary speeches of Maulana Syed Asad Madani, at the Fida-e-Millat Seminar on "Hazarat Maulana Syed Asad Madani : Life and Contribution", here today. The Union Home Minister, Shri Shivraj Patil was among those present at the function. Following is the English rendering of the Prime Minister's speech delivered in Urdu on the occasion:-"I have great pleasure releasing this collection of Parliamentary Speeches of Maulana Syed Asad Madani. He was a fine product of our freedom struggle and composite culture. He was deeply religious and spiritual and at the same time had a modern, secular and progressive outlook. All his activities as a private person and a public figure reflected the values he inherited from our struggle for independence and the shared heritage of our people professing diverse faiths. The Maulana was a staunch advocate of pluralism and secularism and dedicated his life to defend our common ethos and composite culture. His speeches in the Rajya Sabha present to us a modern mind, a patriotic and nationalist mind. Maulana Syed Asad Madani was a nation-builder. In his farewell speech in the Rajya Sabha in March 1994 he stated "It is my earnest desire to see India as a developed country." His vision of India as a developed country went beyond GNP and other indicators of economic growth. It included in its scope the triumph of democratic ideals of liberty, equality and fraternity and substantial advancement of socio-economic conditions of all sections of society. In his vision of a developed India he wanted that the minorities, weaker sections of society and women enjoy equality and equality of opportunity.

369. (23-4-2007) NEW DELHI : The Annual Conference of Relief Commissioners/ Secretaries (Disaster Management) of States and Union Territories to review the status of preparedness for the South-West Monsoon began here this morning. Inaugurating the Conference, the Union Home Secretary, Shri Madhukar Gupta stressed the need to put in place Standard Operating Procedures (SOPs) to deal with various situations which are required to be handled during disasters. These SOPs may relate to rescue operations, supply of foodgrains, etc. He said that this is essential to respond immediately and effectively to disaster situations. Some simulation exercises should also be undertaken to identify gaps in coordination, planning, etc. The Union Home Secretary also drew the attention of the gathering towards the importance of prevention and mitigation aspects of disaster management. In his keynote address, Secretary (Border Management) in the Ministry of Home Affairs, Shri U.N. Panjiar called upon the States to introduce systems to facilitate quick information management and prompt alerting of the concerned authorities. He also urged the States to set up their search and rescue teams and provide them specialized training and necessary equipment so that these teams could cater to the needs not only of the concerned state but also other states during the crisis period. Central Ministries/ Departments/ Organizations which render emergency support functions in the wake of natural calamities are also participating in the one-day Conference, organized by the Ministry of Home Affairs. Key Central Organizations such as the India Meteorological Department, Central Water Commission, Ministries of Defence and Health & Family Welfare will make presentations detailing the Early Warning and Preparatory and Logistic support to be rendered by them in the wake of various natural disasters.

370. (23-4-2007) NEW DELHI : Launching the "Twelve by Twelve (12 by 12) Initiative-Making Pregnancy Safer-Targeting Anemia Eradication during Adolescence" in New Delhi, Union Minister for Health & Family Welfare, Dr. Anbumani Ramadoss said that this unique campaign of '12 by 12 initiative' initiated by Prof. Suneeta Mittal is focusing on adolescent children with an aim of sensitizing the youth to the importance of anemia prevention and optimal haemoglobin level for good physical and mental performance, with a hope that in the long-run when these children enter parenthood there will be fewer complications and lesser maternal and prenatal morbidity and mortality. The function was also attended by Dr. N.K. Ganguly, DG (ICMR), Dr. P. Venugopal, Director, AIIMS, Dr. D.K. Latief, Director, FCC, WHO SEARO, Dr. Marzio Babille, Chief, Health, UNICEF, Dr. Pankaj Desai, President, FOGSI and Dr. Suneeta Mittal, Chief Coordinator of the programme.

371. (24-4-2007) NEW DELHI : The participants at the Third Round Table Conference welcomed the continuation of the process of a wide ranging dialogue initiated by the Prime Minister in February, 2006, and carried forward in Srinagar in May 2006. It was acknowledged that this had helped evolve a better understanding of the issues and problems that affect the lives of the people of Jammu & Kashmir. It had produced an environment in which the citizens of all parts of the State could hope to lead a life of dignity, self-respect and fulfillment without fear of war, and want or exploitation and discrimination. 2. The members expressed their appreciation for the sincere efforts made by the Working Groups established at the end of the Second Round Table Conference and observed that the recommendations made by the first four Groups which had submitted their reports could very substantially contribute to the objectives of the dialogue process. 3. The Conference gave in principle endorsement to the approach suggested by the Working Group on Confidence Building Measures across Segments of Society in the State viz. strengthening human rights protection; improving relief and rehabilitation of widows, orphans and other victims of militancy and violence; and preserving the rich and diverse cultural landscape of the State. It appreciated the concerns expressed by the Working Group regarding the rights of all minorities in J&K, and the urgent need to facilitate the return of Kashmiri Pandits to their hearth and homes. It urged the State/Central Government to take all possible initiatives towards this end, and also to resolve, in a time bound manner, other long pending issues like rehabilitation of refugees from West Pakistan in 1947 and persons affected by the wars of 1965 and 1971. 4. The Conference applauded ongoing efforts to strengthen people to people contacts and promote trade and commerce across the LoC. It endorsed the recommendation of the II Group and need to further streamline these processes, and to expand and deepen such contacts and exchanges in the spheres of trade, tourism and various other walks of life. 5. The Conference endorsed the recommendations of Group III on Balanced Economic Development of Jammu & Kashmir and urged the Central and State Governments to take steps to carry them forward. To start with, these should be adequately integrated with the XI Plan. Issues requiring further consultations could be taken up in a time-bound manner through a suitable mechanism of the Central and the State Governments. It also takes note of the fact that the State Finance Commission and institutional structures have been set up to ensure balanced regional development. 6. The Round Table Conference fully endorsed the recommendations of Group IV on Good Governance and urged the State Government to operationalise them in right earnest in order to bring greater efficiency, transparency and accountability into the systems and processes of governance and to bring the Government closer to the people. 7. The Round Table Conference recognized that steps relating to a number of recommendations had already been taken but new initiatives still needed to be launched.

372. (24-4-2007) NEW DELHI : Shri Devendra Dwivedi said that the Uttar Pradesh elections have entered a critical phase in which, in the midst of much electoral rhetoric, the issues before the electorate are getting articulated. The Congress party during the campaign has substantially succeeded in setting the agenda for electoral discourse by adding ideological dimension to it. The party's campaign has centred around two themes: how much Uttar Pradesh has suffered in the past seventeen years on account of two political evils: communal politics and caste based politics and secondly, how important it has became for the state to return to the path of politics of moderation, politics of consensus and politics of development. The sectarian politics in Uttar Pradesh has disconnected U.P. from the mainstream of national politics which has weakened both politics of Uttar Pradesh and also national politics. The resort to communal and caste based politics has disfigured the face of democracy in the state, turned the clock of history backwards and has paved the way for a non–political route to power. Communal politics and caste based politics have changed the idiom of politics and the means of political mobilization. Ideology and political agenda have been replaced by caste and religion and democratic mobilization has been replaced by sectarian appeals and loyalties, thus changing the very rules of the democratic game. The concept of the citizen voter has been substituted by votes being sought as members of a caste or of a religion community. This has destroyed the very basis of representative democracy and is seeking to change a single electorate into multiple electorates. This retrograde development has fragmented politics, prevents free expression of popular will, weakened civil society, affected social harmony and brought about political instability and crises of governance in Uttar Pradesh. The BJP is seeking to create a Hindu vote bank by exploiting religious beliefs and symbols and by creating a bias against the Muslims. By misusing religion for achieving narrow political ends, the BJP has denigrated religion and delegitimated politics. The BJP's aim is to change the concept of majority into religious majoriterianism which strikes at the very roots of constitutional democracy. Like the BJP, SP and BSP also are practicing vote bank politics by appealing to caste-based exclusivist loyalties. Social justice was a principal goal of freedom movement and nation building and has been the centre piece of the Congress policies since independence. The SP and BSP, however, have used social justice as the basis for caste-based mobilization which has deepened the existing social divides and led to polarization on the basis of the castes. The leaders of these parties have sought personal empowerment to the total neglect of the empowerment of the masses. Over and above all this, the BJP and the Samajwadi party have developed a vested interest in deepening communal polarization at the time of elections. In the ongoing elections, the BJP and the SP are providing aid and comfort to each other. The Congress party has succeeded in focusing the people's attention on the immense harm done to the state by the practitioners of this brand of politics. The main thrust of the Congress party's message as articulated by Shri Rahul Gandhi is that if UP has to rejoin the mainstream national politics and play its due role in the nation's affairs, it must reject hate politics and politics of caste polarization and instead vote for the Congress party's plank of an inclusive, liberal, secular society based on unity in diversity and its agenda for good governance, all round development and growth with equity.

373. (24-4-2007) SRIHARIKOTA: The Indian Space Research Organisation (ISRO) on Monday successfully made the first commercial launch of a foreign satellite through the Polar Satellite Launch Vehicle (PSLV-C8). Italian satellite, Agile, weighing 352 kg, was placed in a precise orbit about 550 km above the earth. The PSLV also carried an ISRO payload, Advanced Avionics Module (AAM), to establish the next generation computers, navigation, guidance, control and telemetry systems that will be used in future launch vehicles. It weighed 185 kg. ISRO Chairman G. Madhavan Nair called the mission "a 100 per cent success" and "a remarkable achievement." He said: "We have made a good entry into the launch business. I hope we will get more and more business opportunities in future. The contract [to launch the Italian satellite] came at a time when there was a complex, competitive environment." Italian Space Agency President Giovanni Bignami felt "thrilled" by the successful mission, which would mark "the beginning of a new stage of cooperation" between India and Italy in space endeavours. It has placed India "on a totally different footing"" in the launch market, he said. The PSLV's final countdown that lasted 48 hours and a half progressed without any hitch at the Mission Control Centre of the Satish Dhawan Space Centre at Sriharikota in Andhra Pradesh. At 3.30 p.m, the 44-metre tall, four-stage vehicle took off from the second launch pad. Without the firepower of the strap-on booster motors, the vehicle's ascent was a little slow in the beginning. But it soon gathered speed and the ascent was flawless. In the backdrop of a clear sky, it soared, emitting flames and thick white smoke. Soon the first stage jettisoned. All events, from ignition and jettisoning, occurred at the appointed time. After the third stage separated at 518 seconds, the fourth stage coasted on its velocity for about eight minutes. Then it came into life and 22 minutes after lift-off, it injected Agile into orbit at a velocity of about 25,000 km an hour. Applause filled the air. B.N. Suresh, Director of Vikram Sarabhai Space Centre (VSSC), Thiruvananthapuram, said it "altogether was a new mission for us." The VSSC built the vehicle.

374. (24-4-2007) NEW DELHI : In a two-day conference with the Chief Secretaries/Power Secretaries of the States and Union Territories, convened by the Ministry of Power on 23rd-24th April 2007 at New Delhi, various power sector issues were reviewed for stock taking as well as to chalk out a clear time bound road map for the future. The conference was inaugurated by the Union Minister for Power, Mr. Sushilkumar Shinde and Dr. Kirit S. Parikh, Member (Energy) Planning Commission was also present. Stressing the high priority accorded by the Government to timely capacity addition, the Union Power Minister, advised the states not to shy away from their primary responsibility for capacity addition, keeping in view the demand growth in the state. He made it abundantly clear that any slippages in the capacity addition programme would be clearly unacceptable as the states had to primarily gear up to meet their growing demands even though the central sector would make its share of contribution towards capacity addition. The deliberations focused upon the contentious issues currently being confronted by the power sector. The open forum provided a platform conducive for constructive resolutions on the 5 key themes deliberated upon-namely, reduction of losses by the distribution utilities, capacity addition road map for the XIth five year plan, open access in transmission & distribution, rural electrification and energy conservation. The issues related to reduction of losses by the distribution utilities and the capacity addition programme were intensively discussed and the Union Power Secretary made it unambiguously clear to the state governments that aggregate technical & commercial losses (AT&C losses) in excess of 15% by 2012, were clearly unacceptable. The state governments were asked to speed up their initiatives to achieve this figure. Another issue keenly assessed was the preparedness of the states for the XIth Plan power projects. During the review it emerged that 78,000 MW capacity addition must be targeted. Implementation plans year wise during the XIth Plan for a total capacity of 78,577 was firmed up with the states indicating a programmed schedule of 16,785MW, 7272MW, 15198MW, 16970MW and 22372MW over the next five years commencing 2007-08 to 2011-12. An additional shelf of 25,357MW projects has been proposed by the states whose viability would be scrutinized. Union Power Secretary urged that capacity addition roadmaps have to be drawn up for the immediate, medium (2-3 years) and long term (2012 & beyond) by the State Governments and shared with the Ministry of Power. The states were positive in their response and promised that they would tighten the schedules of the projects. However, the Union Power Secretary on a word of caution advised the states against delays on account of bunching of the projects. He further requested the states to ensure that the awards for these projects are placed by December 2007 so as to ensure that these projects fructify in the XIth plan itself. Chairman BHEL, who also attended the conference, confirmed that BHEL would have scaled up its manufacturing capacity from 6000 MW per annum to 10,000 MW per annum by 2008 and would further scale it upto 15000 MW by 2010 to meet the requirements of the power sector.

375. (24-4-2007) NEW DELHI : The Election Commission has announced today, the schedule for holding bye-elections to fill a number of casual vacancies in the Lok Sabha and State Legislative Assemblies including the vacancy from 9-Jamshedpur Parliamentary Constituency in Jharkhand. The work of special revision of electoral roll w.r.t. 1.1.2007 and preparation of photo electoral roll in two assembly segments *i.e.*, 48-Jamshedpur East and 49-Jamshedpur West of this 9-Jamshedpur PC is underway and cannot be completed before 25th July, 2007. The electoral rolls in other four assembly segments of this Parliamentary Constituency already stand revised w.r.t. 1.1.2007. The Commission after considering the matter has decided that the bye-election from 9-Jamshedpur PC should not be held now. The schedule for this bye-election will be announced in due course.

376. (24-4-2007) NEW DELHI : Awards were presented to the winners of the 19th National Photo Contest. The theme of this year's contest was 'Happiness'. Shri Bijoy Chowdhury from Hooghly and Shri Abhijit Nandi from Kolkata won the First Prize in the Black & White and Colour Section respectively. The Second Prize went to Shri Kailash Mittal in Black & White and Shri Nupur Kumar Roy in Colour. The 3rd Prize has been won by Shri Somenath Mukhopadhyay in Black &White and Shri Ashoke Kumar Ghosh in colour both from West Bengal. Ten consolation prizes were also awarded to commended photographs. Smt. Asha Swarup, Secretary, Ministry of I&B gave away the prizes. In her remarks, she said that watching the good photograph is a treat to the mind as it captures the mood of the subject. Smt. Asha Swarup hoped to have still better participation from all over the country in the coming years. She felt that photo clubs in the country could help promote this cause. The First Prize carries a cash award of Rs. 20,000/-, a Memento and a Citation. Second and Third Prize comprises of Rs. 15,000/-and Rs. 10,000/-respectively with a Memento and Citation. A total number of 2088 entries were received for the competition from 470 entrants from different parts of the country. A National Jury comprising of renowned and eminent photographers went through all the entries and selected a total number of 92 photographs for the exhibition, including to the award wining photographs. Speaking on the occasion, Smt. Stuti Kacker, Jt. Secretary, Ministry of I&B, said that photography is a fine art, which documents the events in a faithful manner. The digitization of Photo Division archives which houses nearly eight lakh photographs would make the access to these historic treasure available to the people at large, she added. Director, Photo Division, Shri D. Sengupta delivered the vote of thanks. An exhibition of select photographs from the contest was also inaugurated which will remain open till April 30, 2007. There is no entry fee for the Exhibition which is open to the public from 3.00 p.m. to 7.00 p.m. daily. Photo Division, Ministry of Information & Broadcasting organizes the contest to encourage photographers in the country, so that the talent in this field can be projected and given their due recognition. Each participant can send a maximum of four photographs.

377. (24-4-2007) NEW DELHI : As the clock clicked 1530 hours on April 23, 2007, the 44 meter tall PSLV-C-8 (Polar Satellite Launch Vehicle) blasted off from the Port town Sriharikota of Nellore district in Andhra Pradesh making every Indian proud that the country has now joined the select club of just five nations who can commercially launch satellites with indigenous technology. The Italian Satellite Agile piggy backed on Indian Advanced Avionics Module. The Italian satellite will in due course of time reach its designated celestial home. PSLV has been the work horse of Indian Space Research Organisation and all its ten launches have been copy-book success. The vehicle is now being fabricated to carry the Space Probe-Orbiter, which will be the keenly watched payload of Chandrayan, the ambitious Moon Mission of India. In its eleventh flight, conducted from Satish Dhawan Space Centre (SDSC) SHAR, Sriharikota, ISRO's Polar Satellite Launch Vehicle, PSLV-C8, successfully launched the 352 kg Italian astronomical satellite, AGILE, into a 550 km circular orbit, inclined at an angle of 2.5 degree to the equator.

378. (24-4-2007) NEW DELHI : Delivering the keynote address at the American Cancer Society's (ACS) "Leadership Training Programme on Community based Cancer Control" in New Delhi today, the Union Minister for Health & Family Welfare, Dr. Anbumani Ramadoss said that a dedicated National Programme for Tobacco Control will be instituted under the 11th Five Year Plan. Under this programme, a National Regulatory Authority (NRA) to monitor and regulate the effective implementation of tobacco control laws will be set up. The other vital components of the programme include a State/District level programme and setting up of tobacco testing laboratories for content regulation. A national level public awareness campaign highlighting the ill effects of tobacco use will also be launched under this programme. The function was also attended by Mr. Kevin Brady, Associate Vice-President and other Representatives of US Centres for Disease Control and Prevention (CDC) Foundation, Ms. Pat Felts, Dy. Chief Operating Officer, American Cancer Society (ACS), Dr. Shalini Vallabhan, Director, Asian Cancer Control Strategies, ACS and other Representatives of ACS, Ms. Stuti Kacker, Director, Indian Institute of Mass Communication, Representatives of GE Healthcare, John and Editha Kapoor Charitable Foundation and Ms. Bhavani Thyagarajan, Joint Secretary, Ministry of Health & Family Welfare.

379. (24-4-2007) NEW DELHI : Shri Vilas Muttemwar, Union Minister of State for New and Renewable Energy is a Member of a High Power Delegation for President's five-day State Visit to Strasbourg, France and Greece from today. He would accompany President during his Address to the European Parliament, International Space University at Strasbourg and meetings with other dignitaries. Renewable energy would feature prominently in discussions during these visits.

380. (24-4-2007) NEW DELHI : The Union Minister of Shipping, Road Transport & Highways Thiru. T.R. Baalu has said that setting up of an integral network of trauma care system to tackle road accident emergencies is absolutely crucial and should be addressed within a definite time frame. Thiru. Baalu was speaking at the joint meeting held today by the Ministries of Shipping, Road Transport & Highways and Health & Family Welfare to work out a plan of action for onward formulation of a scheme for trauma care facilities across the country in general and along the National Highways in particular. The meeting was co-chaired by the Union Minister of Health & Family Welfare, Dr. Anbumani Ramadoss. The Ministry of Health & Family welfare gave a presentation highlighting the details of the proposal drafted by them for trauma care facilities. It was brought out that 140 identified hospitals along and in the vicinity of the National Highways would be upgraded and strengthened by the central funding for trauma care purposes. The network of trauma care facilities is being planned to have four levels of trauma and emergency management viz., L-1, L-2, L-3 and L-4 levels. The-L1, L-2 and L-3 levels comprise different levels of trauma care management at State, City and Town/Village levels, respectively. The L-4 level comprises a matrix of ambulance facilities in the proposed network. Thiru. Baalu stated that his Ministry would work closely with the Ministry of Health & Family welfare to intensify the Government's efforts to provide immediate care to the victims of the road accidents on the National Highways across the country. Terming the problem of road accidents in India as critical, Thiru. Baalu said that in the year 2005 alone, 94,928 people died in 4.5 lakh accidents. Thiru. Baalu further stated that the Department of Road Transport & Highways and the National Highway Authority of India (NHAI) would consider providing fully loaded Ambulances with state of the art equipment, in addition to the ones already being provided under Ministry's schemes, to ensure that proper medical care is given to the accident victims in the 'Golden one hour' to save precious lives. Dr. Ramadoss while responding to Thiru. Baalu's observations, stated that the main requirement is of the trained manpower for running these trauma care centres and the Ministry of Health would help in all respects whether it is in the Public Private Partnership or a totally private venture along the National Highways. He said that the Ministry of Health would give all the technical assistance and the support required for developing and manning such trauma care centres along the Highways. He also mentioned that the Health Ministry has also designed a nine-month course for training of paramedics, who could be used for manning the Ambulances to be made available by the NHAI for the 4/6 lane stretches of Golden Quadrilateral (GQ) and would be located at an interval of 50 km. The two Union Ministers agreed to meet before the end of next month to finalise the finer details of the proposed network and broad details of the proposed Central Scheme.

381. (24-4-2007) NEW DELHI : At a time when nearly 40% of India's population is in the age group of 6-24 years and when education has been identified as the singular, most important element in the national developmental effort, the activities of the Ministry of Human Resource Development are of crucial importance. Policies, programmes and schemes of the Ministry, consequently, have been wrought keeping this in view. This Annual Report endeavours to present the highlights of what has been attempted in 2006-2007, to take stock of the present stage of major programmes and schemes and to give some indication of our proposals for the future. The National Policy on Education (NPE), 1986, as updated in 1992, envisages improvement and expansion of education in all sectors, elimination of disparities in access and laying greater access on improvement in the quality and relevance of education at all levels, including technical and professional education. It also emphasizes that education must play a positive and interventionist role in correcting social and regional imbalances, empowering women and in securing a rightful place for the disadvantaged, linguistic groups and minorities. With the vigorous implementation of the Sarva Shiksha Abhiyan (SSA) and the cooked Mid Day Meal (MDM Scheme), the number of out of school children has come down to less than 5% of the total population in the age group of 6 to 14 years *i.e.* from 4.4 crores in 2001-02 to 70 lakhs in 2006. The Mid Day Meal Scheme was revised in mid 2006. Under the revised scheme nutritional norms have been raised from the existing 300 calories and 8-12 grams of protein to minimum 450 calories and 12 grams of protein per child. To facilitate this, Central assistance towards cooking cost, has been raised from existing Rs. 1 to Rs.1.50 per child per school day with mandatory contribution of Re.0.50 per child by States, making the overall cost norm of Rs.2 per child per day. In the case of North-Eastern States, the sharing pattern is 90:10 between the Centre and States. Kasturba Gandhi Balika Vidyalaya Scheme, under which 1000 new schools have been approved in the year 2006, besides the 1180 approved earlier, provides residential education to girls predominantly belonging to the SC, ST, OBC and minority communities. Kendriya Vidyalayas (KVs), and Jawahar Navodaya Vidyalayas (JNVs) have been recognized as setting the standards for the secondary education in the country. 50 new KVs and 28 new JNVs have been approved in 2006-07, in addition to the 919 existing KVs and 539 JNVs.

382. (24-4-2007) NEW DELHI : Memorandum of Understanding (MoU) has been signed on 23rd April, 2007 between SATLUJ JAL VIDYUT NIGAM Ltd. (A joint venture of Govt. of India and Govt. of Himachal Pradesh) under the Ministry of Power and KONKAN RAILWAY CORPORATION Ltd. under the Ministry of Railways for providing Consultancy Services for Geotechnical Investigation and related Design Works for tunnels for J&K Project of Konkan Railway Corporation Ltd. Satluj Jal Vidyut Nigam Ltd. is appointed as Consultant to assist Konkan Railway Corporation Ltd. in this project. The MOU was signed through ShriVinod Kumar, E.D. (Project), KRCL and Shri Ramesh Chaudhary, DGM (Consultancy) of SJVNL in the August presence of Shri H.K. Sharma, CMD and Shri J.K. Sharma, Director (Civil) & other Sr. Officers of SJVNL and Shri Brajendra Kumar, Financial Advisor and Chief Accounts Officer (Project) of KRCL at New Delhi.

383. (24-4-2007) NEW DELHI : Dr. Raghuvansh Prasad Singh, the Rural Development Minister, while speaking at the National meet of NGOs of Rural India in New Delhi today, has said that the services of NGOs are being utilized for creation of awareness and conducting of social audit in the rural areas of various schemes run by his Ministry. He said there are more than 4000 NGOs in the country having their representatives at the Block, District, State and National level and they are rendering valuable services to the process of societal transformation and their transparent approach has given a new direction to the implementation of rural development programmes. The NGOs are to act as agents of implementing Right to Information Act, he said. The Minister also lauded the role of NGOs in the formation of Self Help Groups in the rural areas. The Minister highlighted the role of CAPART in the countrywide mobilization of NGOs. He informed that applications has been invited from the civil society organisations for creation of awareness and capacity building of rural communities in selected districts under the NREGA and so far 600 applications have been received. The awareness campaign is meant to create transparency and accountability like the use of Right to Information Act and help the beneficiaries to understand and scrutiny vital records such as muster rolls, measurement books, job cards, do social audit and enforce grievance The programme was also attended by Sh. M.V. Rajasekharan, Minister of State for Planning and Dr. Mohan Dharia, Chairman of CNRI. The three-day conference has been organised by the Confederation of NGOs of Rural India (CNRI).

384. (24-4-2007) NEW DELHI : Production of finished carbon steel in the country recorded 10.8 per cent growth during 2006-07. According to the provisional figures, total production stood at 49.35 million tonnes during April 2006 and March 2007 as against 44.544 million tonnes during 2005-06. Production of pig iron rose by 5.6 per cent during the year at 4.960 million tonnes compared to 4.695 million tonnes in the previous year. The country exported 4.75 million tonnes of finished carbon steel during the year. While exports went up by 6.1 per cent, imports rose by 6.5 percent. Total imports of finished carbon steel stood at 4.1 million tonnes during the year compared to 3.85 million tonnes in the previous year. Public sector Steel Authority of India Limited (SAIL) produced 12.581 million tones of saleable steel in FY 07 as against 12.051 million tonnes in the previous year. The Vizag Steel Plant produced 3.29 million tonnes of saleable steel during the year as against 3.237 million tonnes in FY 06. SAIL produced hot metal of 14.606 million tonnes in FY 07 compared to 14.603 million tonnes in the previous year.

385. (24-4-2007) NEW DELHI : The Prime Minister Dr. Manmohan Singh will honour 45 workers with 33 prestigious Prime Minister's Shram Awards for the year 2004 at Vigyan Bhawan in the capital on Friday (April 27, 2007). They will be decorated with Shram Bhushan, Shram Vir/Shram Veerangana and Shram Shree/Shram Devi awards in recognition of their distinguished performances, innovative abilities, outstanding contribution in the field of productivity and exhibition of exceptional courage and presence of mind. These workers are employed in the Departmental Undertakings & Public Sector Undertakings of the Central and State Governments and Private Sector Units employing 500 workers or more. The Private Sector, for the first time, has been brought within the ambit of Prime Minister's Shram Awards' Scheme. Also, the number of awards has been increased from 17 to 33. 29 awardees are from the public sector while 16 workers belong to the private sector. Some of them have bagged the awards jointly. No nomination was found suitable for the top most prestigious honour Shram Ratna Award but in lieu of Shram Ratna/Shram Bhushan Awards three additional Shram Vir/Shram Veerangana awards and one additional Shram Shree/Shram Devi Awards are being given. Shri S.P. Gupta, Chargeman in BHEL, Haridwar has been conferred with the second highest Shram Bhushan Award. It carries a cash award of Rs. 1,00,000/-and a 'Sanad'. Fifteen nominees have been selected for Shram Vir/ Shram Veerangana Awards. They include two women workers who have been awarded Shram Veerangana Awards. Each award carries a cash prize of Rs. 60,000/-and a 'Sanad'. The Shram Vir/Shram Veerangana Awardees are: Shri Satyawan Nayak, Bhilai Steel Plant, Bhilai; Shri M. Subramanian, BHEL, Tiruchirapalli; Shri M. Sudhakar Reddy, BHEL, Hyderabad; a team comprising S/Shri Bihari Lal Dhruw & Sunil Kumar Soni (jointly), from BHEL, Bhopal; Shri Mahi Pal Singh, BHEL, Haridwar; a team comprising S/Shri A.K. Kerketta & Trilochan Maharana (jointly), from Bhilai Steel Plant, Bhilai; Smt. Valluripalli Vijayalakshmi, DRDL, Hyderabad, DRDO (all from the public sector); Shri Kartik Kumar Mandal, TISCO, Jamshedpur; Shri Birajdar Prakash Vishvanath, Bajaj Auto Ltd., Aurangabad; Shri Chavan Subhash Ramdas, Bajaj Auto Ltd., Pune; Shri Kadam Vijay Bhikaji, Larsen & Toubro, Mumbai; Shri Sushil Kumar, Tata Motors Ltd., Lucknow; Shri Ram Kailash, Hindalco Ltd., Sonebhadra; Shri Mahadik Sampatrao Bhagawan, Bajaj Auto Ltd., Aurangabad; Mrs. Jaswant Kaur, TISCO, Jamshedpur (all from the private sector).

386. (24-4-2007) NEW DELHI : Following is the text of the opening remarks of the Prime Minister, Dr. Manmohan Singh, at the Third Round Table Conference on Jammu & Kashmir, here today: "I thank all of you for coming here today to participate in the third meeting of the Roundtable on Jammu & Kashmir. We began this process slightly over a year ago. We have met twice before in this format, once in New Delhi and once in Srinagar. This series of conferences is part of our collective effort to find consensual solutions to the problems of Jammu & Kashmir through a process of dialogue. On both occasions, we reaffirmed that violence had no place in a civilized society and that we should engage with a wide cross-section of political groups and civil society to forge a consensus on specific issues which affect the lives of the people of Jammu & Kashmir. We also realized that the process was not easy and would be a long one, requiring patience and fortitude. It is almost a year since we last met in Srinagar. However, a lot of work has been done since then. At the outset, I would like to reaffirm that Jammu & Kashmir continues to remain at the top of our government's agenda. While I have visited the Jammu & Kashmir several times and wide ranging initiatives are already being implemented to revitalize the economy of the State and to bring about improvements on many fronts, we need to continue to work closely together to further carry forward our efforts to build a new, peaceful and prosperous Jammu & Kashmir. I repeat the simple vision which guides me and which I have articulated to university students in Srinagar. It is a vision of a Naya Jammu, Kashmir and

Ladakh which is symbolized by peace, prosperity and people's power. Jammu and Kashmir has tremendous economic potential, the talent of its people is unparalleled, and its cultural diversity is unique. It can and must become a model of real empowerment of the people and comprehensive security for them. If this happens, Jammu and Kashmir will be an epitome of unity, peace and prosperity in diversity. The vision for Jammu and Kashmir is embodied in a broader vision for India and South Asia. A harmonious neighbourhood and a reconciliation with Pakistan are important to realize the vision of an India and South Asia free from the fear of war, want and exploitation. For this it is essential to resolve our differences and overcome the trust deficit that has cast a shadow on our relations. I and our government remain deeply committed to do everything necessary and possible to realize this vision.

387. (24-4-2007) NEW DELHI : The GSM segment has shown an increase of 6.1 million during the month of March 2007 and the fixed segment by 0.5 million. However, the CDMA segment declined by 2.8 million. Due to the reduction in the number of CDMA subscribers, the credit of net increase in the subscriber base thus became 3.8 million only. With this the total number of telephones in the country is now more than 206.8 million with teledensity 18.3% while it was 142.1 million with 12.74% during the corresponding period of last year registering a growth rate of 45%. In the GSM segment, Rajasthan telecom circle added more than 5.6 lakh subscribers in the GSM segment. Karnataka and U.P. (East) Telecom Circles have both added 4.7 lakh subscribers each. The growth of broadband connections improved further and at the end of February 2007, about 2.18 million broadband connections were provided and coverage of broadband connectivity by public sector service providers has reached 892 cities. Further, the total number of existing ISP licencees is 382. Under Bharat Nirman Programme, out of the 66,822 villages, so far 41706 villages have been provided with Village Public Telephones (VPTs). The remaining 25116 villages are to be covered by November, this year.

388. (24-4-2007) NEW DELHI : National Rural Employment Guarantee Act (NREGA) was initially launched in 12 districts of Maharashtra and another 6 Districts have been added in the year 2007-08. In the State 3.53 lakh households demanded employment whereas 3.85 lakh households have been provided employment up to February, 07. The average number of households provided employment in a district of the State is 32,079, while the national average is 91,685 households. Besides, 5 thousand households completed the 100 days guarantee of employment provided in the Act. The number of person days of employment provided in the State is 159.28 lakh. The average person days of employment provided in a district is 13.27 lakh compared to the national average of 36.47 lakh person days. The employment was provided on 10,892 works, out of which 5,324 works have been completed. The average number of works taken up in a district stood at 908 against the national average of 3,581. An amount of Rs. 192.36 crore had been released to the State during 2006-07. Against this, the utlisation up to February, 07 is Rs. 174.61 crore, which is 35.86% of the total availability. The expenditure on wages is 94.59%, material is 4.92% and on administration is 0.48%. The average expenditure of a district in the State is Rs. 14.55 crore compared to the National average of Rs. 35 crore. The Act provides that 1/3rd of the employment provided should be to women. In the State 37.07% person days of employment has been provided to women, 16.19% to SC and 40.88% to ST. A visit to the State by the National Level Monitors in December, 2006 & January 2007 has revealed wages rates are variable and depend upon the type of works.

389. (24-4-2007) NEW DELHI : In Madhya Pradesh, the National Rural Employment Guarantee Act (NREGA) was initially launched in 18 districts of State and another 13 districts have been added in the year 2007-08. Up to February, 07, 26.86 Lakh households demanded employment and out of them 26.61 Lakh households were provided employment in the State. The average number of households provided employment in a district of the State is 1,47,858 while the national average is 91,685 households. Besides, 3.09 households have completed the 100 days guarantee of employment provided in the Act. The number of person days of employment provided in the State is 1,711.77 lakh. The average person days of employment provided in a district is 95.05 lakh compared to the national average of 36.47 lakh person days. An amount of Rs. 1,869.54 crore has been released to the State during 2006-07. Against this, the utlisation up to February 2007, is Rs. 1570.99 crore, which is 74.73% of the total availability. The expenditure on wages is 63.41%, material is 35.37% and on administration is 1.22%. The average expenditure of a district in the State is Rs. 87.28 crore compared to the National average of Rs. 35 crore. The Act provides that 1/3rd of the employment provided should be to women. In the State 44.05% person days of employment has been provided to women and 16.72% to SC and 48.72% to members of ST. The employment were provided on 1,62,283 works, out of which 83,330 works have been completed. The average number of works taken in a district was 9,016 against the national average number of 3,581 works taken in a district. A visit to the State by the State level Monitors have revealed that Perspective Plan was prepared in consultation of Gram Sabha and according to need based works.

390. (24-4-2007) NEW DELHI : In Kerala, the National Rural Employment Guarantee Act (NREGA) was initially launched in 2 districts of State and another 2 districts have been added in the year 2007-08. Up to February, 07, 83 thousand households demanded employment and out of them 78 thousand households were provided employment in the State. The average number of households provided employment in a district of the State is 38,871 while the national average is 91,685 households. Besides, 40 households have completed the 100 days guarantee of employment provided in the Act. The number of person days of employment provided in the State is 10.85 lakh. The average person days of employment provided in a district is 5.43 lakh compared to the national average of 36.47 lakh person days. An amount of Rs. 31.79 crore has been released to the State during 2006-07. Against this, the utlisation up to February 2007, is Rs. 14.25 crore, which is 32.68% of the total availability. The expenditure on wages is 83.36%, material is 3.38% and on administration is 13.24%. The average expenditure of a district in the State is Rs. 7.12 crore compared to the National average of Rs. 35 crore. The Act provides that 1/3rd of the employment provided should be to women. In the State 65.22% person days of employment has been provided to women and 18.8% to SC and 13.36% to members of ST. A visit to the State by the State level Monitors has revealed that Training has been imparted to the PRIs, Administrative/ technical staff and VMC members.

391. (24-4-2007) NEW DELHI : In Karnataka, the National Rural Employment Guarantee Act (NREGA) was initially launched in 5 districts of State and another 6 districts have been added in the year 2007-08. Up to February, 07, 5.16 lakh households demanded employment and out of them 5.02 lakh households were provided employment in the State. The average number of households provided employment in a district of the State is 1,00,314 while the national average is 91,685 households. Besides, 24 thousand households have completed the 100 days guarantee of employment provided in the Act. The number of person days of employment provided in the State is 182.22 lakh. The average person days of employment provided in a district is 36.44 lakh compared to the national average of 36.47 lakh person days. The employment was provided on 16,885 works, out of which 8,=486 works have been completed. The average number of works taken up in a district stood at 3,377 against the national average of 3,581. An amount of Rs. 229.71 crore has been released to the State during 2006-07. Against this, the utlisation up to February 2007, is Rs. 205.04 crore, which is 67.14% of the total availability. The expenditure on wages is 59.25%, material is 39.45% and on administration is 1.30%. The average expenditure of a district in the State is Rs. 41 crore compared to the National average of Rs. 35 crore. The Act provides that 1/3rd of the employment provided should be to women. In the State 52.05% person days of employment has been provided to women and 32.88% to SC and 20.95% to members of ST.

392. (24-4-2007) NEW DELHI : Grant-in-aid amounting to Rs.11.95 lakh has been released by the Ministry of Rural Development to the Zunheboto District Rural Development Agency of Nagaland towards the second instalment of Central Share for the year 2006-07 under DRDA Administration. An amount of Rs. 27.15 lakh has also been released to DRDA Kohima (Rs.20.76 lakh) and DRDA Tuensang (Rs.6.39 lakh) of Nagaland towards second instalment Restoration 1 of Central Share for the year 2006-07 under DRDA Administration. The funding pattern under the scheme is 75:25 between Centre and the State. The utilization of funds is to be in accordance with the DRDA administration guidelines and the release of the second instalment during 2007-08 is subject to the fulfillment of all the conditions as per the DRDA Administration guidelines.

393. (25-4-2007) NEW DELHI : The Government is committed to increase credit flow to rural masses and all necessary steps will be taken to strengthen Regional Rural Banks (RRBs) assured the Finance Minister Shri P. Chidambaram while addressing the members of Parliamentary Consultative Committee attached to his Ministry in a meeting held here today. The Finance Minister informed the members that the process for structural consolidation of RRBs by amalgamating RRBs, sponsored by the same bank within a State, started two years back, has been completed in March 2007 (target was June 2007) with number of RRBs reduced to 96 from 196. As a result of amalgamation the number of RRBs making profits is increasing and they are in a position to provide better customer service with better infrastructure and pooling of experienced work force. The Minister informed the members that he has given directions for the appointment of General Managers to oversee the work of RRBs. Lok Adalats are being constituted which will help to settle a large number of NPAs. Shri Chidambaram told the members that the Government has adopted an aggressive Branch Expansion Policy and expects to cover all 80 uncovered districts within the current fiscal. The Government has also decided to extend Securitisation and Reconstruction of Financial Assets and Enforcement of Securitisation of Interest (SARFAESI) Act to loans advanced by RRBs and the notification in this regard will be issued shortly, informed the Minister. The suggestions given by the members during the meeting include, loans for agro-based industries, insurance cover for farming loans by RRBs, loans for cold-storage, food-processing and fishing etc., proper training for the employees, ATM facilities in rural areas, more powers to the Branch Managers, strengthening of Self-Help Groups, rebate for timely repayment of loans etc. Speaking on the occasion, the Minister stated that the RRBs are playing an important role in developing the rural economy. RRBs have issued 69 lakh Kisan Credit Cards (KCCs) which is 11% of total KCCs and have been advised by the government to increase the number of KCCs, he said. The RRBs have formed 7.4 lakh SHGs till 2005-06 making the access easier to the farmers. Addressing the concern expressed by the members, the Finance Minister told that the RRBs have been directed to lend more money to non-farming community also within the rural population.

394. (25-4-2007) NEW DELHI : Anemia has been recognized as one of the major public health problems in India. It occurs when the iron balance in the body is disturbed. Deficient intake of iron in our diet and/or low absorption and availability of iron from foods consumed is the principle cause of anemia. Iron requirement of the body increases when there is rapid growth as seen in pre-school age children and in adolescence. Though nutritional anemia affects all age and sex groups in India, it is particularly severe among pregnant women, lactating mothers, adolescent girls and pre-school age (1-5 yrs.) children. More than half of the pregnant women suffer from Anemia. 13% are severely anemic (haemoglobin levels below 7gm./dl.). One in five of all the maternal deaths are attributed to anemia during pregnancy. Nearly 70 million *i.e.* 60-70% of all children below 6 years suffer from varying degrees of anemia in our country. More than half of the adolescent girls (50-60%) are anemic. A countrywide survey for estimating Haemoglobin among women (15-49 yrs) and children (0-3 yrs) was done for the first time in 1998-99 as a part of the National Family Health Survey (NFHS-II). In National Family Health Survey (NFHS)-III (2005-06), Haemoglobin (Hb) estimation was done among ever-married women in the age group 15-49 years, pregnant women, ever married men and children in age 6-35 months, in all the States of the country. It was found that overall 56.1% of ever-married women had some degree of anemia while the overall prevalence of anemia among pregnant women was 57.8%. Anemia was more in Rural Areas *i.e.* 58.1%.

395. (25-4-2007) NEW DELHI : The 23rd Coordination Centre meeting will be held here tomorrow to review the naxal situation in the country. It will be chaired by the Union Home Secretary, Shri Madhukar Gupta. Chief Secretaries and Directors General of Police of the affected States have been invited to attend the meeting. Senior officers from various Ministries and Departments of the Central Government will also be present. The main focus of the security-related discussion will be on the States where the naxal problem is of long gestation and where noticeable incidents of violence have taken place. The meeting will also go into the implementation of the major developmental initiatives like the Backward Regions Grant Fund (BRGF), Panchayat (Extension to Scheduled Areas) Act 1996 (PESA), NREGP and the Scheduled Tribes and other Traditional Forest Dwellers (Recognition of Forest Rights) Act, 2006.

396. (25-4-2007) NEW DELHI : The Ministry of Small Scale Industries is organizing sensitisation/awareness programmes at various locations throughout the country through its field offices, *i.e.* the Small Industries Service Institutes (SISIs) to increase awareness about the Credit Linked Capital Subsidy Scheme (CLCSS) among the beneficiary/ prospective beneficiary units and other stakeholders. The Government has also proposed to organize more sensitisation programmes, especially in areas where no such programme has been conducted so far. In these programmes, the SISIs associate the nodal agencies *i.e.* the SIDBI and the NABARD, industry associations, State Government Department and Agencies, Banks and Financial Institutions, so as to make collective efforts in sensitizing the participants about all aspects of the CLCSS, including the operational and modalities issues. A Governing and Technology Approval Board under the chairmanship of the Secretary, SSI and ARI is already in place to monitor the progress made in the implementation of the CLCSS and to bring suitable policy changes to make the scheme more focused and result oriented. In order to ensure more effective flow of subsidy to the eligible beneficiaries and to reduce the average time lag between filing of the request and release of subsidy under the CLCSS, nine new nodal banks/agencies have been included in addition to the existing nodal agencies *i.e.* the SIDBI and the NABARD. These banks/agencies have also been requested to undertake sensitisation programmes/ awareness campaign for the successful implementation of the CLCSS.

397. (25-4-2007) LUCKNOW: Bahujan Samaj Party leader Mayawati on Tuesday hinted at the possibility of a Bharatiya Janata Party - supported Samajwadi Party (SP) government in Uttar Pradesh after the Assembly elections. The BJP's gesture may be reciprocated by the SP at the Centre, she claimed. The Samajwadi Party and the BJP had entered into a tacit understanding and this was reflected in selection of candidates in some constituencies. Like the BJP, the Congress was also interested in retaining power at the Centre. The Congress-led UPA Government's refusal to dismiss the State Government after the Supreme Court verdict on MLAs' defection was aimed at this, she said. Ms. Mayawati alleged that Chief Minister Mulayam Singh and SP general secretary Amar Singh were preparing to leave the country after the elections. Stating that only the BSP could dethrone the SP Government, she assured the voters that her government would free the State from "goonda raj" and strive for a "samta moolak samaj" (equitable society). Addressing an election meeting here, Ms. Mayawati alleged that crores of rupees, earned through bribes and commissions, were stacked in foreign banks during the SP rule. Exhorting the people to vote for the BSP to end the "jungle raj," she accused the BJP, the Congress and the Rashtriya Lok Dal of foisting the SP Government. Since the formation of the present Government, the State had become synonymous with lawlessness, poverty, unemployment and incidents such as the Nithari serial killings, the madrasa rape case and the Kavita Rani case. Ms. Mayawati assured the people that a BSP government would address all problems. She held the Congress responsible for the situation in the State, as it was in power in the State and at the Centre for 40 years. BSP national general secretary Satish Chandra Mishra cautioned the party's Brahmin supporters against the designs of other parties to split the Brahmin vote. Mr. Mishra said unlike other parties, the BSP had restored the pride and prestige of Brahmins.

398. (25-4-2007) NEW DELHI : In Orissa, the National Rural Employment Guarantee Act (NREGA) was initially launched in 19 districts of State and another 5 districts have been added in the year 2007-08. Up to February, 07, 13.21 lakh households demanded employment and out of them 13.08 lakh households were provided employment in the State. The average number of households provided employment in a district of the State is 68,861 while the national average is 91,685 households. Besides, 48 thousand households have completed the 100 days guarantee of employment provided in the Act. The number of person days of employment provided in the State is 626.61 lakh. The average person days of employment provided in a district is 32.98 lakh compared to the national average of 36.47 lakh person days. An amount of Rs. 762.30 crore has been released to the State during 2006-07. Against this, the utlisation up to February 2007, is Rs. 540.33 crore, which is 60.88% of the total availability. The expenditure on wages is 57.89%, material is 41.25% and on administration is 0.87%. The average expenditure of a district in the State is Rs. 28.44 crore compared to the National average of Rs. 35 crore. The employment was provided on 51,521 works, out of which 18,803 works had been completed. The average number of works taken up in a district stood at 2,712 against the national average of 3,581. The Act provides that 1/3rd of the employment provided should be to women. In the State 34.17% person days of employment has been provided to women and 24.18% to SC and 48.56% to members of ST. A visit to the State by the State level Monitors have revealed that demand for employment is monitored during weekly NREGA day at Block office and Grievance Redressal day in GP.

399. (25-4-2007) NEW DELHI : In Punjab, the National Rural Employment Guarantee Act (NREGA) was initially launched in 1 districts of State and another 3 districts have been added in the year 2007-08. Up to February, 07, 31 thousand households demanded employment and out of them 30,800 households were provided employment in the State. The average number of households provided employment in a district of the State is 30,868 while the national average is 91,685 households. Besides, two thousand households have completed the 100 days guarantee of employment provided in the Act. The number of person days of employment provided in the State is 13.68 lakh. The average person days of employment provided in a district is 36.44 lakh compared to the national average of 36.47 lakh person days. The employment was provided on 1,233 works, out of which 436 works have been completed. The average number of works taken up in a district stood at 1,233 against the national average of 3,581. An amount of Rs. 27.56 crore has been released to the State during 2006-07. Against this, the utlisation up to February 2007, is Rs. 22.20 crore, which is 58.05% of the total availability. The expenditure on wages is 60.70%, material is 38.19% and on administration is 1.11%. The average expenditure of a district in the State is Rs. 22.20 crore compared to the National average of Rs. 35 crore. The Act provides that 1/3rd of the employment provided should be to women. In the State 33.09% person days of employment has been provided to women and 70.03% to members of SC.

400. (25-4-2007) NEW DELHI : In Rajasthan, the National Rural Employment Guarantee Act (NREGA) was initially launched during 2006-07 in 6 districts and has further been extended to 6 more districts in the current financial year. A total of 11.46 lakh households demanded employment and all of them were provided employment up to February, 2007. The number of person day of employment provided in the State is 912.79 lakh. The average person days of employment provided in a district is 152.13 lakh compared to the national average of 36.47 lakh person days. Of them, 65.77% are provided to women, 15.57% to SC and 64.08% to members of ST. The employment was provided on 20,343 works, out of which 6,769 works have been completed. The average number of works taken up in a district are 33,905 against the national average of 3,581. The average number of households provided employment in a district of the State was 1,90,996, while the National Average stands at 91,685. An amount of Rs. 761.61 crore was released to the State during 2006-07. Up to February 2007, Rs. 593.34 crore was utilized, which is 69.3% of the total availability. The expenditure on wages is

76.83%, material is 22.12% and on administration 1.05% was spent. The average expenditure on a district is Rs. 98.99 crore compared to the National average of Rs. 35 crore.

401. (25-4-2007) NEW DELHI : In Meghalaya, the National Rural Employment Guarantee Act (NREGA) was initially launched during 2006-07 in 3 Districts and has further been extended to 3 more Districts in the current financial year. A total of 0.83 lakh households demanded employment and all of them were provided employment up to Feb.'07. The number of person days of employment provided in the State is 19.42 lakh. The average person days of employment provided in a district is 9.71 lakh compared to the national average of 36.47 lakh person days. Of them, 21.63% are provided to women, 0.09% to SC and 83.17% to members of ST. The employment was provided on 164 works, out of which 4 works have been completed. The average number of works taken up in a district stood at 82 against the national average of 3,581. The average number of households provided employment in a district of the State was 41,483, while the National Average stands at 91,685. An amount of Rs. 25.65 crore was released to the State during 2006-07. Up to February 2007, Rs. 16.06 crore was utilized, which is 62.17% of the total availability. The expenditure on wages stood at 85.93%, material at 12.68% and on administration 1.39% was spent. The average expenditure on a district came out to be Rs. 8.03 crore compared to the National average of Rs. 35 crore.

402. (25-4-2007) NEW DELHI : In Sikkim, the National Rural Employment Guarantee Act (NREGA) was initially launched in 1 district of the State and another 2 districts have been added in the year 2007-08. Up to February, 2007, 0.04 lakh households demanded employment and all of them were provided employment in the State. The average number of households provided employment in a district of the State is 3,969 while the national average is 91,685 households. The number of person days of employment provided in the State is 2.34 lakh. The average person days of employment provided in a district is 2.34 lakh compared to the national average of 36.47 lakh person days. An amount of Rs. 4.51 crore has been released to the State during 2006-07. Against this, the utlisation up to February 2007, is Rs. 2.50 crore, which is 55.36% of the total availability. The expenditure on wages is 79.73% and material is 20.27%. The average expenditure of a district in the State is Rs. 2.50 crore compared to the National average of Rs. 35 crore. The Act provides that 1/3rd of the employment provided should be to women. In the State 24.79% person days of employment has been provided to women, 0.73% to SC and 97.86% to members of ST.

403. (25-4-2007) NEW DELHI : In Tamil Nadu, National Rural Employment Guarantee Act (NREGA) during 2006-07 was launched in 6 districts and has further been extended to 4 more districts during the current financial year. During the first year of its implementation, 5.79 lakh households demanded employment and all of them have been provided employment. Moreover, 800 households have completed the 100 days of guaranteed employment provided in the Act up to February 2007. The number of person days of employment provided in the State is 151.18 lakh. The average person days of employment provided in a district is 25.20 lakh compared to the national average of 36.47 lakh person days. Of them, 82% are provided to women, 54.76% to SC and 2.68% to ST. The employment provided was on 6.010 works, of which 1,513 number of works have been completed. The average number of works taken up in a district is 1,002 against the national average of 3,581. The average number of households provided employment in a district of the State is 96,579, while the National Average stands at 91,685. An amount of Rs. 170.89 crore was released to the State during 2006-07. Up to February 2007, Rs.126.15 crore was utilized, which is 50.91% of the total availability. The expenditure on wages stood at 95.87% and on administration was 4.13%. The average expenditure on a district came out to be Rs. 21.02 crore compared to the National average of Rs. 35.00 crore. A visit by the National Level Monitors in December, 2006 and January 2007 has revealed that Job Cards are issued on time, Numbered and authenticated muster rolls are used at the work site and Record maintenance at the GP level is according to NREG Act and is updated in timely manner.

404. (25-4-2007) NEW DELHI : In Nagaland, the National Rural Employment Guarantee Act (NREGA) was initially launched in 1 district of the State and another 4 districts have been added in the year 2007-08. Up to January, 2007, 28 thousand households demanded employment and all of them were provided employment in the State. The average number of households provided employment in a district of the State is 27,800 while the national average is 91,685 households. The number of person days of employment provided in the State is 11.82 lakh. The average person days of employment provided in a district is 11.82 lakh compared to the national average of 36.47 lakh person days. An amount of Rs. 4.30 crore has been released to the State during 2006-07. Against this, the utlisation up to January 2007, is Rs. 13.28 crore, which is 89% of the total availability. The expenditure on wages is 58.16%, material is 39.39% and on administration is 2.45%. The average expenditure of a district in the State is Rs. 13.28 crore compared to the National average of Rs. 35 crore. The Act provides that 1/3rd of the employment provided should be to women. In the State 29.95% person days of employment has been provided to women and 100% to members of ST.

405. (25-4-2007) NEW DELHI : In Mizoram, the National Rural Employment Guarantee Act (NREGA) was initially launched during 2006-07 in 2 districts and has further been extended to 2 more districts in the current financial year. A total of 0.19 lakh households demanded employment and 0.06 of them were provided employment up to December, 2006. The number of person day of employment provided in the State is 2.37 lakh. The average person days of employment provided in a district stands at 1.19 lakh compared to the national average of 36.47

lakh person days. Of them, 33.08% are provided to women and 100% to members of ST. The employment was provided on 263 works, out of which 216 works have been completed. The average number of works taken up in a district stood at 132 against the national average of 3,581. The average number of households provided employment in a district of the State was 3,333, while the National Average stands at 91,685. An amount of Rs. 17.84 crore was released to the State during 2006-07. Up to December 2006, Rs. 10.28 crore was utilized, which is 40.02% of the total availability. The expenditure on wages stood at 96.65% and on administration 3.35% was spent. The average expenditure on a district came out to be Rs. 5.14 crore compared to the National average of Rs. 35 crore.

406. (25-4-2007) NEW DELHI : In Manipur, the National Rural Employment Guarantee Act (NREGA) was initially launched in 1 districts of State and another 2 Districts have been added in the current financial year (2007-08). The households demanding employment stood at 18 thousand and all of them were provided employment up to February, 07. The average number of households provided employment in a district of State is 17,880 against national average of 91,685 households. The number of person days of employment provided in the State is 8.26 lakh. The average person days of employment provided in a district is 8.26 lakh compared to the national average of 36.47 lakh person days. The employment was provided on 234 works, out of which 15 works have been completed. The average number of works taken up in a district stood at 908 against the national average of 3,581. An amount of Rs. 12.53 crore had been released to the State during 2006-07. Against this, the utlisation up to September, 2006 is Rs. 9.50 crore, which is 49.15% of the total availability. The expenditure on wages is 60% and material it stood at 40% while on administration nothing was incurred. The average expenditure of a district in the State is Rs. 9.50 crore compared to the National average of Rs. 35 crore. The Act provides that 1/3rd of the employment provided should be to women. In the State 40.07% person days of employment has been provided to women 16.19% and 100% to members of ST.

407. (25-4-2007) NEW DELHI : The Union Minister of Shipping, Road Transport and Highways, Thiru T. R. Baalu, reviewed the developmental plans and major schemes of the Directorate General of Lighthouses and Lightships here today. Thiru Baalu asked the Directorate Authorities to expedite the work on proposal of establishment of National Automatic Identification System (AIS) network. This system would ensure the proper tracking of any vessel entering in our coastal waters with a view to ensure safety and security of the vessels. This system will cover the main land coast line. It will have 85 Base Stations and a National Control Centre at Directorate General of Lighthouses and Lightships, New Delhi. The proposed AIS Network will be implemented by March, 2009 at an estimated cost of Rs.50 crore and would give a fillip to the security of Indian Coast. The Minister asked the authorities to work out the plans to develop Lighthouses with some value addition and, in this context, he pointed out that some of the Lighthouses in developed countries are major tourist spots. He further said that the country has lighthouses at picturesque locations which could be developed as excellent tourist spots. This step would also showcase the advances made by the shipping industry in the country, he said. The Minister also was informed that as per Safety of Life at Sea (SOLAS) Convention, as amended, it is mandatory for all ocean going ships/vessels of 300 Gross Registered Tonnage (GRT) and above to carry AIS Transponders for security and safety reasons. The coastal vessels of 500 GRT and above and all passenger liners are also required to carry AIS Transponder in near future. The Directorate General of Lighthouses has requested the Ministry to make it mandatory to carry transponders for vessels between 50 GRT and 300 GRT excluding small fishing vessels and fishing trawlers. To ensure the safety of the fishermen plying in the operational areas of the local lighthouses, the Minister announced the formation a Committee to have a critical look on all local lighthouses for improvement of their reliability and availability. The Committee, which has been asked to submit its report within six months, would be chaired by the Chief Hydrographer to the Government of India and it will interact with the local Maritime Boards and Ports. Thiru Baalu commended the work done by the Directorate in connection with the tsunami restoration in Andamans & Nicobars and in the areas of Tamil Nadu coast. The Minister was informed that Indira Point Lighthouse was restored and made operational by winching down men and material from the helicopter as the Lighthouse is now in a three metre deep waters and about 50 metre away from the shifted shoreline and difficult to approach. Thiru Baalu also reviewed the progress of work of Vessel Traffic Service in the Gulf of Kachchh.

408. (25-4-2007) NEW DELHI : Telecom companies account for over 19% of the complaints received by the National Consumer Helpline (NCH), followed by banks and insurance companies. The National Consumer Helpline forwards complaints to the telecom service providers for redressal. Of the six telecom companies, MTNL and Idea have been providing regular feedback to NCH on the complaints sent to them. NCH has proposed that a telecom ombudsman may be set up on the lines of banking and insurance ombudsmen. About 10% of the complaints received by NCH are against banks. Over 3% of the complaints relate to defective services provided by insurance companies. NCH has started transmitting complaints to various companies and track them on-line to facilitate speedy redressal of grievances. This is a voluntary approach and so far Standard Chartered Bank, HDFC Bank, HSBC Bank, Citibank, ING Vysya Bank, ABN Amro Bank, ICICI Bank, PNB, Canara Bank and Banking Ombudsman (New Delhi), LG, Samsung and MTNL have joined this system. NCH receives complaints against various service providers and guides consumers in finding solutions to problems related to products and services.

409. (25-4-2007) NEW DELHI : To give a fillip to the industrial development of North Eastern Region (NER), Department of Industrial Policy and Promotion

(DIPP) had announced North East Industrial Policy (NEIP) in 1997 which was valid till 31.3.2007. Similarly, there is an industrial policy and an excise duty exemption scheme for the State of Sikkim. A revised North East Industrial and Investment Promotion Policy, 2007 (NEIIPP, 2007) has come into effect from 01.04.2007 which inter alia, provides for excise duty exemption scheme for industrial units located in the North Eastern Region including Sikkim. Accordingly, a Notification has been issued today. As per the Notification, the exemption will be available for a period of ten years for new units and existing units undertaking substantial expansion, irrespective of their location in the North East or Sikkim. However, this exemption will not apply to specified goods namely, pan masala, cigarettes and other tobacco products, plastic carry bags of less than 20 microns and petroleum products produced by petroleum oil or gas refineries. Simultaneously, another notification has also been issued today to carry out certain amendments in the excise duty exemption schemes for the North Eastern region.

410. (26-4-2007) NEW DELHI : Based on the recommendations of Ad-hoc Group of Experts, the Union Cabinet today approved the following proposals : i) To empower the holding companies to transfer of assets, floating of fresh equity and disinvestments of shareholding in subsidiaries subject to the condition that the delegation would be in respect of subsidiaries set up by the holding company under the powers delegated to the Navratna and Miniratna CPSEs and further to the proviso that the public sector character of the concerned CPSE would not be changed without prior approval of the Government. ii) Budgetary support to implement Government sponsored projects of national interest and Government sponsored R&D projects should not disqualify CPSEs from retaining Navratna / Miniratna status. However, for such projects, investment decision will be taken by the Government and not by the CPSE concerned. iii) Chief Executive of the CPSE would be a member of the Search Committee for selecting Independent Directors for the concerned CPSE Board of Directors. This will lead to devolving greater managerial and commercial autonomy to successful profit making PSEs operating in a competitive environment as provided in the National Common Minimum Programme.

411. (26-4-2007) NEW DELHI : The Union Cabinet today approved a proposal that India Tourism Development Corporation Ltd. (ITDC) may be permitted to form a Joint Venture (JV) Company with Aldeasa of Spain and subscribe to 50% of the paid up equity capital of the JV company. The formation of the proposed JV company with Aldeasa would enable ITDC to effectively compete in the duty-free retail industry in India and also expand its business operations to locations outside the country. Aldeasa would bring on board a strong international brand name, state-of-the-art technology platforms, cutting-edge retailing practices as well as global sourcing and supply chain linkages.

412. (26-4-2007) NEW DELHI : The Union Cabinet today approved a proposal to pursue the Warehousing (Development and Regulation) Bill, 2005 pending in the Lok Sabha and to move certain amendments to this Bill based on the recommendations of the Department related Parliamentary Standing Committee.

413. (26-4-2007) NEW DELHI : The Union Cabinet today gave its approval for the introduction of the Collection of Statistics Bill, 2007 in the Parliament and for repealing the Collection of Statistics Act, 1953. It will help in facilitating better management of statistical data collection for more effective planning and policy formulation.

414. (26-4-2007) NEW DELHI : The Union Cabinet today gave its approval for the introduction of the Private Detective Agencies (Regulation) Bill 2007 in Parliament to regulate the Private Detective Agencies through a system of mandatory licensing. This legislation will ensure that they work within the ambit of legal framework and accountable to a regulatory authority.

415. (26-4-2007) NEW DELHI : The Union Cabinet today gave its approval for the setting up of Indian Institute of Space Science & Technology (IIST) with an initial investment of Rs. 270 crores and annual recurring cost of Rs. 40 crores. Indian Space Research Organization (ISRO) has been experiencing severe shortage of highly talented graduate and post-graduate Scientists and Engineers during the last few years to take up the challenges of R&D in the areas of Space Science & Technology. The setting up of Indian Institute of Space Science & Technology, similar to the IITs, will provide high quality undergraduate and postgraduate education in Space Technology and Science and Post Graduate & research programmes in Space Science & Technology and integrated Masters in Space Science with customized curriculum meeting with the high technology requirements of ISRO mitigating the problem of acute shortage of quality human resources for ISRO. Pending development of the regular campus of the Institute, the courses will commence from the academic year 2007-08 itself in an alternate campus in the premises of Vikram Sarabhai Space Centre, Thiruvananthapuram. The campus and other infrastructure facilities will be completed within 24 months. To enable close interaction with ISRO, the Institute will be located close to Vikram Sarabhai Space Centre and Liquid Propulsion Systems Centre in Thiruvananthapuram. The Institute will have an intake of 150-200 students per annum. The entire expenses of the course will be supported by ISRO in the form of scholarships / assistantships. All the high performing students coming out of this Institute would be absorbed into ISRO stream.

416. (26-4-2007) NEW DELHI : Charged particle accelerators have played a central role in enhancing our understanding of structure of matter-atoms, nucleus and sub-atomic particles. Bigger and bigger accelerators continue to be conceived and built to answer some of the most fundamental questions before us. Apart from their scientific importance, such activities have contributed to rapid technological advancement with many spin-offs. This was stated by Shri. Anil Kakodkar, Chairman, Atomic Energy Commission. He was delivering a talk at the ongoing conference on " Accelerator and Low Level Radiation Safety", a two-day event organized by the Inter University Accelerator Centre, IUAC, in New Delhi. Shri Kakodkar said that in addition to very high energy charged particles such high energy and high power accelerators have also led to major advances in sources of neutrons and electromagnetic radiation, thus broadening and improving the choices of probes for scientific investigations. He said, apart from their role in scientific research, accelerators are becoming increasingly important tools for medical diagnosis and treatment, sterility assurance of food and medical products, enhancement of shelf life of food and agricultural products, processing of industrial products and possibly in future energy production-as well as in incineration of radioactive waste. Referring to India's advanced capability in building accelerators of different kinds, Shri Kakodkar observed that our involvement and contributions at some of the accelerator based international projects have earned accolades. He said there is now an unprecedented interest on the part of our international partners to involve us in various international mega projects of this kind. On domestic front, he said, there is an ambitious programme for accelerator driven systems as well as on development of robust accelerators for various applications. Shri Kakodkar observed that such high energy machines, associated electromagnetic and neutron fields and induced radioactivity constitute a significant challenge in ensuring safety through design, associated engineered safety features and the operational discipline. While there are many similarities with safety issues associated with other technologies, there are also some specific accelerator technology related issues. He said that with enlargement of the programme, the number of people involved in this activity at various levels and in various disciplines is continuously increasing and therefore, there is a need not only for more clearer quantitative understanding of safety issues but also an enlightened and all-pervading safety culture.

417. (26-4-2007) NEW DELHI : Shri Murli Deora, Minister of Petroleum & Natural Gas visited Iran on April 25-26. During the visit, he called on President of Iran, Mr. Mahmoud Ahmadinejad and met his counterpart Oil Minister Mr. Kazem Vaziri Hamaneh at Tehran today. He also met Foreign Minister Mr. Manouchehr Mottaki. The visit was part of regular exchanges at high level between India and Iran. The Minister was accompanied by Secretary, Ministry of Petroleum & Natural Gas and the CMDs of ONGC, GAIL and EIL. During their discussions both the sides stressed on the traditional and friendly ties between the two countries. They recognized that the energy sector constitutes a key element in Indo-Iran commercial relations. In this regard, the discussions also covered the bilateral contract for supply of 5 million tonnes of LNG per annum from Iran to India signed in June 2005 apart from the proposed Iran-Pakistan-India gas pipeline project. The Minister of Petroleum & Natural Gas stressed the need for early implementation of the LNG contract and reiterated India's commitment to the gas pipeline project. The Minister also conveyed the growing interest and keenness of India's private sector to participate in Iran's economic development in sectors as diverse as cement, steel, fertilizers, pharmaceuticals and automobiles. President Mahmoud Ahmadinejad reassured Minister of Petroleum and Natural Gas that the Iranian side is also committed to the projects, which will be implemented to mutual satisfaction. In particular, the President advised the Iranian Oil Ministry to look at ways to ensure early implementation of the LNG contract. India also expressed interest in procuring an additional quantity of 2.5 million tonnes of LNG per annum.

418. (26-4-2007) NEW DELHI : Lt. Gen KS Katoch, Padma Bhushan, Military Cross, a veteran of the Indian Army who passed away on Wednesday, was cremated here today. A large number of serving and retired officers and other dignitaries paid their last respects to the distinguished officer. Born in 1915 at Srinagar, Lt. Gen Katoch was commissioned in September 1936 from IMA Dehradun. During his early years in the Army, he served with the Surrey Regiment and Frontier Force Rifles. In 1945, during World War II in Italy, he was awarded a Military Cross for his gallantry. He was awarded a Padma Bhushan in 1965. He commanded three infantry Divisions-two in J&K and one in the North East. He held the appointments of Director General Military Training and Adjutant General, before commanding a Corps in Srinagar. He retired as Vice Chief of Army Staff in 1970. He is survived by a son of and a daughter.

419. (26-4-2007) NEW DELHI : The Minister of State for Communications & Information Technology, Dr. Shakeel Ahmad, informed the Rajya Sabha today, in a written reply to a question by Shri Veer Pal Singh Yadav that Bharat Sanchar Nigam Limited (BSNL) is providing Global System for Mobile Communications (GSM) based cellular mobile service in all its Licensed Service Areas which comprise of whole of India except Delhi and Mumbai Metro City Service Areas. Dr. Ahmad further stated that GSM based Cellular Mobile Telephone Service being provided by BSNL in the country is working satisfactorily and is in general meeting the Quality of Service (QoS) parameters prescribed by Telecom Regulatory Authority of India (TRAI). The Minister further stated that the cellular mobile network of BSNL is being continuously optimized for its performance and mo and monitoring of the network has been strengthened by BSNL to ensure performance as per the QoS parameters prescribed by TRAI. BSNL is also augmenting its network for enhancing its coverage and improving QoS.

420. (26-4-2007) NEW DELHI : The Minister of State for Communications & Information Technology, Dr. Shakeel Ahmad, informed the Rajya Sabha today, in a written reply to a question by Shri Ramdas Agarwal and Shri Dara Singh that on an average, 6.00 million telephone subscribers are added each month, which is equivalent to addition of around 2 lakh subscribers per day. The Minister further stated that India has become the third largest telecommunication network in the world after China and USA. The total number of telephones provided in the country as on January 31, 2006 were 130.91 million as against the target of 250 million telephones by December 31, 2007 both in rural and urban areas together. As on march 2007, the total number of telephones are 206.83 million, he added.

421. (26-4-2007) NEW DELHI : The Minister of State for Communications & Information Technology, Dr. Shakeel Ahmad, informed the Rajya Sabha today, in a written reply to a question by Dr. Murli Manohar Joshi and Shri Raj Mohinder Singh Majitha that 81 clusters have been set up for expansion of telephone network in rural areas in the country. The Minister further stated that a scheme has been launched by the Government to provide support for setting up and managing 7871 infrastructure sites spread over 500 districts across these 81 clusters in the country for provision of mobile services including other Wireless Access Services like Wireless in Local Loop (WLL) using Fixed/Mobile terminals in the specified rural and remote areas, where there is no existing fixed wireless or mobile coverage. The telephone facility is proposed to be set up in all such areas by June 2008.

422. (26-4-2007) NEW DELHI : The 23rd meeting of the Coordination Centre was held here today to review the naxal situation in the country. It was chaired by the Union Home Secretary, Shri Madhukar Gupta. Chief Secretaries and Directors General of Police of the naxal-affected States took part in the deliberations. Representatives from the Planning Commission and Central Ministries of Tribal Affairs, Panchayati Raj, Rural Development and Forests & Environment were also present to discuss the developmental strategy for these States. The States were urged to keep a constant watch on the movement of naxal groups, their weaponry, training camps, hideouts, sources of weapons and funds, areas of current activity and areas in which they plan to spread violence and activity. The States were also asked to strengthen their security structures and intelligence gathering machinery and raise India Reserve Battalions. The need for police to adhere to the field-craft and Standard Operating Procedures was stressed. On the developmental front, the States were advised to review their Resettlement and Rehabilitation policies on a priority basis. The need to put special focus on implementation of Backward Regions Grant Fund (BRGF), Panchayat (Extension to Scheduled Areas) Act, 1996 (PESA), NREGP and 'The Scheduled Tribes and other Traditional Forest Dwellers (Recognition of Forest Rights) Act, 2006 was emphasised. State Governments were urged to fill vacancies in the Government at the bottom level of the district administration especially in rural and tribal areas through special recruitment drives to ensure that the developmental agenda of the Government was not neglected due to absence of grassroot machinery. Some of the major States affected by naxal violence like Chhatisgarh, Jharkhand, Orissa and Bihar made detailed presentations on their action plans to tackle the naxal menace and the steps taken and proposed to be taken by them. Progress of steps taken to fill up vacancies in police, fortify police stations, improve delivery mechanisms, etc. was intimated by the States. During the first three months of 2007, 395 naxal incidents took place as against 431 during the corresponding period last year. 209 people were killed in these incidents during the current year as against 212 in the corresponding period last year.

423. (26-4-2007) NEW DELHI : Development of sports infrastructure is an issue being given a lot of importance by the Government. Several methods to ensure the development are being implemented. One of them being private-Public Partnership. There are two existing schemes that focus on the Private-Public Partnership mode for the development of sports infrastructure in the country viz., the National Sports Development Fund Scheme and the State Sports Academy Scheme. Under the National Sports Development Fund Scheme, there is a provision to accept contributions from different entities, including corporates. On receipt of such contributions, the Government also contributes on a matching basis for augmenting the corpus. However, there has been negligible contribution by the corporate sector to NSDF. The objects of the fund include creation of sports infrastructure. The State Sports Academy Scheme involves a financing pattern in the ratio of 51:25:24 between the Private sponsor, the Central Government and the State Government. The Central Government contribution is restricted to 25% of the capital cost subject to a ceiling of Rs.218 lakhs; and 25% of the recurring costs subject to a maximum of Rs.17 lakhs per annum for a period of 3 years. The cost of the land is not included in the scheme and is required to be provided gratis by the State Government or the sponsor. Apart from this the Sports Authority of India has also developed extensive infrastructure for sports training which is being further expanded and upgraded. Emphasis is also being given for maximum utilization of the infrastructure created in different parts of the country for events such as the National Games, SAF Games, Afro-Asian Games, etc., and under the State Governments Schemes. All this is in addition to the proposed creation of State-of-the-art infrastructure in the context of the Commonwealth Games 2010 and Commonwealth Youth Games 2008. The Ministry of Youth Affairs & Sports is also considering the launching of a scheme-"Panchayat Yuva Khel Abhiyan" with the objective of developing basic sports infrastructure, and promoting games and sports activities, at the village/sub-district level, both as an essential ingredient of the development of the Youth and to significantly expand the catchment for sporting and nurturing of sports talent. Consultations are being held in this regard with all the stakeholders concerned with a view to finalizing the proposal. This information was given by Shri Mani Shankar Aiyar, Minister of Panchayati Raj, Youth Affairs & Sports and DoNER in the Rajya Sabha today in a written reply to a question by Shri Rajeev Chandrasekhar and Shri Motiur Rahman.

424. (26-4-2007) NEW DELHI : Congress Spokesman Shri Abhishek Singhvi said that the Gujarat govt. and the entire official machinery of Gujarat is in complicit, compromise and convicted at bar of public opinion in the murder of individuals in the name of encounters. When the Congress Party tried to raise that issue today in the Lok Sabha, on the first day of this part of the session, they were understandably shouted down, disrupted. In fact the greater the disruption, the greater is the reflection of obvious guilt by those who seek to support their counterpart in Gujarat. Please consider these shocking facts and although you know some of these, let me tell you from the basis of our enquiry, our reports which is based on strong factual cases but in any case if there is some discussion or doubt, it must go immediately to an independent enquiry so that the facts are established. A man and his wife came to Gujarat. They are picked up by the guardians of the law. The persons involved are of the rank extremely high, of the rank of DIG. Ultimately the man and his wife are taken to a farm house. The ostensible basis is a complaint from some trader in Rajasthan assisted by the official machinery in that nearby state. Both states of geographical contiguity, both states under a similar party, a similar government, a similar philosophy. On that basis and using influence and pressure, ultimately the man is disposed off. He is disposed off in the name of encounters but more importantly he is disposed off in the name of glorifying Mr. Modi because everybody who has to be punished in the name of wanting to hurt Mr. Modi, in the name of wanting to attack Mr. Modi. That is the fig leaf for this encounter. What is amazing is that his wife's whereabouts, body, existence in not known today. It is most distracting and unfortunate but we have reasons to believe that she was raped before being disposed off similarly. But we would want this to be established immediately by a detailed enquiry. But till today the whereabouts of the lady are unknown. When under ultimately the direction and guidance and control and monitoring of the Apex court, finally an enquiry starts, the enquiry is sought to be derailed. It is sought to be obstructed. It is sought to be digressed, delayed. Who does this? The principle actors of the guardians of law themselves. No less than the Home Minister of that state under the benevolent of that state, no less than the DIG of that state. No less than the senior police officials of that state. An enquiry is not allowed to go on, it is only the good fortune of this nation that the enquiry officer had persisted and given a written report, which you have seen or heard of partly, where the findings are damning, the findings are specific, the findings are categorical about the obstruction, who has some thing to hide, obviously those who have obstructed. This is extremely serious matter, not only because two human lives were lost, of course two human lives are not a large number for the Gujarat administration and two lives may have no meaning for the administration but two lives have vanished but worse than that it shows the mindset, the approach to governance. The police officer concerned is supposed to be the leader and actor in over 12 such so-called encounters.

425. (26-4-2007) NEW DELHI : The locations for all the major competition and training venues, Games Village and the major non-competition venue viz. International Broadcasting Centre (IBC)/Main Press Centre (MPC), have been agreed to between all the stakeholders. All the stakeholders have indicated their specific time lines with reference to key milestones, viz., finalization of detailed design and estimates, commencement of tendering process, award of work, commencement of work, completion of work and handing over to Organising Committee Commonwealth Games, 2010 (OC). It is expected that work on all the major sports venue infrastructure projects will commence between June-August, 2007 and the venues will be handed over to the OC by the end of 2009. Besides, the implementing agencies/stakeholders concerned are in the process of seeking clearances from various agencies for the Commonwealth Games, 2010 related projects. This is an on-going process and any objections/clarifications raised are being suitably addressed by the concerned parties. For expediting the required clearances, an Empowered Committee has been set up under the chairmanship of Chief Secretary, Government of NCT of Delhi with representatives from all the concerned agencies/authorities to facilitate speedy clearances in respect of the games related projects. Another Committee has been set up, under Ministry of Urban Development and Poverty Alleviation to deal with clearances pertaining to Delhi Urban Arts Commission (DUAC). Keeping in view the need for developing adequate tourist accommodation in the context of the Commonwealth Games, an inter-ministerial Task Force has been set up under the Ministry of Tourism (MoT) for monitoring and coordinating further action in this regard by all the agencies concerned. For expediting the Central Government's clearances in respect of hotels coming up in Uttar Pradesh, a Committee has been set up under Ministry of Youth Affairs and Sports. As regards financial approvals, Government has approved projects of Sports Authority of India for an amount of Rs.1000 crores (± 10%) for upgradation/creation of venue infrastructure; ungradation of tennis venue by All India Tennis Association at a cost of Rs.30 crores (± 15%) and expenditure budget of Organizing Committee of Rs.767 crores (± 15%) for 'Conduct of the Games". Expenditure Finance Committee has recommended proposal of Delhi Development Authority of Rs.325.00 crores (± 25%) for international zone etc. in the Games village and sports infrastructure. The Planning Commission has, in principle approved a proposal of the Government of NCT of Delhi for upgradation of the civic infrastructure in the context of the Commonwealth Games, including sports venues for two events, for an amount of Rs.770.00 crores. As per time lines provided by the implementing agencies, all the Commonwealth Games related projects are expected to be completed in time. In respect of the preparation of the Indian contingent for Commonwealth Games, 2010 with a view to improve performance, extensive discussions were held with all stakeholders, and it was decided that expenditure on preparation of teams should be subsumed within the existing schemes of the Ministry related to talent search, training, competition, etc. with suitable modifications and enhancements. Other requirements over and above these, are being assessed in consultation with each National Sports Federation based on which an action plan for each discipline will also be prepared, and the special needs would be met out of the National Sports Development Fund, Private Sponsorship, etc. This information was given by Shri Mani Shankar Aiyar, Minister of Panchayati Raj, Youth Affairs & Sports and DoNER in the Rajya Sabha today in a written reply to a question by Shri Rajeev Chandrasekhar.

426. (26-4-2007) NEW DELHI : Several initiatives are being taken to strengthen Local Self Government (Panchayati Raj). A national consensus is being evolved in respect of the Roadmap for Panchayati Raj through mutual consultation between the Centre and the States. Ministry of Panchayati Raj has convened Seven Round Tables of State Panchayati Raj Ministers with the Union Minister of Panchayati

Raj between July and December 2004. The deliberations centered on the 18 identified dimensions of Panchayati Raj ranging from the effective Devolution of the Functions, Finances and Functionaries to District Planning, Training and Capacity Building and IT-enabled e-governance. At the conclusion of each Round Table, nearly 150 action points comprised in the Compendium were unanimously adopted by all Panchayati Raj Ministers and referred to State Governments/UTs for taking necessary action. This has become a National Roadmap for effective Panchayati Raj. A Committee of Panchayati Raj Secretaries has been constituted to monitor the progress and implementation of these 150 Action Points. This Committee of Secretaries headed by the Secretary, Ministry of Panchayati Raj also services the Council of Panchayati Raj Ministers. The Committee of Secretaries has held seven meetings. The Council of Ministers has been convened twice, at Kochi, Kerala in August 2005 and at Bhubaneshwar, Orissa in June 2006, respectively. The first mandate of the Ministry of Panchayati Raj is to ensure conformity to the Constitutional provisions of Part IX of the Constitution read with Article 243 ZD of Part IXA relating to the District Planning Committees together with the Eleventh Schedule which sets out a list of 29 matters, to be considered by State Legislatures for devolution to the Panchayats. While the Ministry of Panchayati Raj must ensure conformity to these Constitutional provisions, the Constitution of India charges the States (not the Centre) with the responsibility for devolution. In other words, the processes and content of devolution of functions, finances and functionaries-the crux of Power to the Panchayats-are vested entirely in State Legislatures, reinforcing the inclusion of Panchayati Raj in the State List of the Seventh Schedule. This information was given by Shri Mani Shankar Aiyar, Minister of Panchayati Raj, Youth Affairs & Sports and DoNER in the Rajya Sabha today in a written reply to a question by Shri Brij Bhushan Tiwari and Shri Bhagwati Singh.

427. (26-4-2007) NEW DELHI : The Minister of State for Petroleum & Natural Gas Shri Dinsha Patel informed the Lok Sabha in a written reply today that ONGC's MoU targets for production of various products for the year 2007-08 include 29.04 Million Metric Tonne (MMT) of crude oil production, 25,050 Million Metric Standard Cubic Metre (MMSCM) of natural gas production and 3.245 MMT of value added products. He further said that OVL has a production target of 6.34 MMT of oil and 1.65 BCM of gas for the year 2007-08. ONGC Videsh Limited (OVL), a wholly owned subsidiary of Oil & Natural Gas Corporation Limited (ONGC) is engaged in overseas exploration and production of oil and gas to supplement the reserves of the parent company, ONGC. To secure more equity oil, OVL is pursuing acquisition of E&P assets in identified countries viz. Sudan, Iran, Iraq, Nigeria, Algeria, Egypt, Syria, Libya, Russia, Venezuela, Kazakhistan, Azerbaijan, Latin American countries and some African countries. Replying to another question Shri Patel informed that ONGC produced 26.049 MMT crude oil and 22442 MMSCM gas during 2006-07 against 24.404 MMT and 22574 MMSCM respectively in previous year.

428. (26-4-2007) NEW DELHI : During the last five years (2002-2006), 1007 scientists have left their jobs from DRDO due to increased opportunities available in private sectors The rate of attrition is marginally higher compared to private sector industries. There has been no substantial impact of such attrition on completion of DRDO projects. The deficiencies are made up through regular recruitments. A comprehensive proposal of incentives to arrest exodus of scientists has already been submitted by DRDO and is under active consideration by the Government. Comprehensive proposal has also been submitted to the Sixth Central Pay Commission. DRDO has adopted a dynamic approach for recruitment of talented people with desired competency. DRDO conducts campus interviews in reputed institutions, like Indian Institute of Technology and Indian Institute of Science, Bangalore. DRDO also recruits scientists through Scientists Entry Tests (SET) and fresh Ph. D scholars under Registration of Students with Scholastic Aptitude (ROSSA). Image building exercise has been strengthened to attract young talents. This information was given by the Defence Minister Shri AK Antony in a written reply to Shri Asaduddin Owaisi and Smt Sumitra Mahajan in Lok Sabha today.

429. (26-4-2007) NEW DELHI : The Minister of State for Petroleum & Natural Gas Shri Dinsha Patel informed the Lok Sabha in a written reply today that Iran-Pakistan-India gas pipeline project has been found to be feasible. Indian side had appointed Ernst & Young as the Financial Consultant and ILF, UK as the Technical Consultant for preparation of the pre feasibility report of Iran Pakistan India Pipeline Project. He added that the price of gas against the alternate fuel prices will determine the economic viability of the pipeline project. Iran has given a formula for determining gas price at the Iran-Pakistan border. Two other issues namely Transportation Tariff and Transit Fee are under discussion between India and Pakistan. Once these issues are decided, the price of gas at Pakistan-India border would be known and then, a decision on the purchase of gas through Iran-Pakistan-India Pipeline Project will be taken. The Minister pointed out that as per current indications, pipeline within Iran upto Iran-Pakistan Border will be laid and operated by an agency to be nominated by Iran. Iran has offered to sell gas at Iran-Pakistan Border and all responsibilities for the safety and security of the pipeline within Iran will vest with Iran. In the Pakistan Territory, out of 1035 KMs, 800 KMs pipeline will be carrying the gas for both Pakistan and India. The safety and security for the pipeline and gas within Pakistan would be provided by the Pakistan Government for which a Transit Fee would be levied. Discussions on all these issues are continuing. Shri Patel also said that it has been agreed that the pipeline proposed to be laid in Iran, Pakistan and India will be constructed as per the international standards incorporating all the safety features as per prescribed standards and specifications. It is envisaged to provide round-the-clock communication and supervisory control system all along the pipeline.

430. (26-4-2007) NEW DELHI : "Coffee drinkers at lower risk for Parkinson's" study. "Diets damage health" says biggest ever study. " Can coffee fight cancer?"

a study in Tokyo. "Eat slowly"-researchers in a medical college. The above are some of the findings we come across everyday in newspapers and magazines. Why so much importance is given to such research works and surveys? Since time immemorial the focus has been on having good health. Researchers, scientists and NGOs across the country work throughout the year to spread awareness among people. The Government on its part is too seized of the issue and has been taking various steps, both big and small to provide health for all. The awareness campaign is designed and devised in different ways to reach various classes of society, rich and the poor, the literate and the illiterate and so on.

431. (26-4-2007) NEW DELHI : National Minority Development & finance Corporation (NMDFC) provides financial assistance on concessional terms to minorities in the target group for pursuing self-employment. NMDFC provides term loans as well as micro credit through State Channeling Agencies (SCAs). Besides, NMDFC also provides micro credit to self-help groups (SHGs) through non-governmental organizations (NGOs). Details of State-wise and year-wise funds disbursed and beneficiaries covered under these schemes during the last three years, are given in the statements at Annexure I & II respectively. For 2007-08, the target of disbursement is Rs.120.60 crores covering 45,700 beneficiaries. This information was given by the Minority Affairs Minister, Shri A.R. Antulay in reply to a starred Question in the Lok Sabha today.

432. (26-4-2007) NEW DELHI : One of the terms of reference of the National Commission for Religious and Linguistic Minorities (NCRLM) relates to the issues raised in Writ Petition 180/04 and 94/05 filed in the Supreme Court and in certain High courts relating to para 3 of the Constitution (Scheduled Castes) Order, 1950 and the modalities of inclusion in the list of Scheduled Castes. This information was given by the Minority Affairs Minister, Shri A.R. Antulay in reply to an Unstarred Question in the Lok Sabha today.

433. (26-4-2007) NEW DELHI : In the context of the formulation of the Eleventh Five Year Plan (2007-2012), the Planning Commission constituted a Working Group on 'Empowering the Minorities', Dr. Zoya Hasan, Professor of the Jawaharlal Nehru University was the chairperson of the Working Group which had 27 other members. The working Group formed three sub-groups. Dr. Vimal Thorat was the chairperson of the sub-group on educational development. The submissions of these sub-groups were internal to the deliberations of the working Group and were taken into account while finalizing the report of the Working Group submitted to the Planning Commission. The Planning Commission has not finalized the Eleventh Plan as yet. This information was given by the Minority Affairs Minister, Shri A.R. Antulay in reply to a starred Question in the Lok Sabha today.

434. (26-4-2007) NEW DELHI : The Minister of Tourism and Culture Smt. Ambika Soni has said that FICCI had commissioned a study on "Positioning India as a Hub for Buddhist Tourism" and its report was released on 25th January, 2007.

According to this report, three distinct circuits of Buddhist tourism in India can be identified and promoted, which can aim to attract 0.25% (from the current level of 0.06%) of the world's Buddhist population by 2012, which is equivalent to about one million tourists, and this is a rise of 400% from the current annual base of about 200,000. The report also states that this would require marketing efforts, better connectivity as well as improvement of on-ground conditions in terms of better infrastructure and creation of other enabling issues like security, visa, permit conditions, etc. In a written reply in the Lok Sabha today she said, infrastructure upgradation of Buddhist circuits has been taken in a big way through identification of 22 important Buddhist sites throughout the country. Government of India has sanctioned 14 projects amounting to Rs. 57.22 crore for development of tourism infrastructure in 12 sites across different states. The infrastructure development has also been taken up through Japan Bank for International Cooperation (JBIC) for Ajanta-Ellora amounting to Rs. 299 crore. Government has also entered into an agreement for undertaking infrastructure development at Buddhist sites of Sarnath, Kushinagar, Kapilvastu, Shravasti and Sankisa in Uttar Pradesh with JBIC for a loan assistance of Rs. 395.63 crore for total project of Rs. 680 crore. Smt. Soni said a major campaign titled "Come to India-Walk with the Buddha" was launched in the Sough East Asian market and in Domestic market for promotion of Buddhist circuit. In addition, Buddhism has also been identified for tourism development in Bangladesh, Bhutan, India, Nepal & Sri Lanka through a common promotional campaign. She said the Ministry of Tourism has requested Ministries of Civil Aviation, Railways and Road Transport & Highways to take steps for improving connectivity to important tourist destinations in the country, including the Buddhist sites. The issues related to visa-on-arrival, electronic visa, advanced passenger system and permits have been taken up with the Ministry of Home Affairs.

435. (26-4-2007) NEW DELHI : Air India proposes to take Science/Engineering graduates as Cadet Pilots. This information was given by Minister for Civil Aviation, Shri Praful Patel in Lok Sabha today. Under the scheme, Science and Engineering graduates who have passed in First Class will be recruited as Cadet Pilots after they successfully go through the Written Test/Interview/Psychometric & Pilot Aptitude Test/Medical Test. This has been done considering the expansion plans of Air India and Air India Express. It is estimated that Air India requires a strength of about 1500 Pilots by the time all the aircraft are inducted into the fleet. Air India is in the process of selecting the Training Institute for this purpose. The Cadet Pilots will have to arrange their own finance/study loan for their flying training. The cost of obtaining Commercial Pilot Licence would be approximately Rs. 20 lakhs. They will also be required to sign a Contract to serve the company for a minimum period of seven years.

436. (26-4-2007) NEW DELHI : The Foreign Secretaries of India and Pakistan met in Islamabad on 13-14 March 2007 to initiate 4th round of the Composite

Dialogue. They discussed Peace and Security including CBMs and Jammu & Kashmir. On Peace and Security, they decided to expedite negotiations to conclude an Agreement on Prevention of Incidents at Sea, to fully observe the ceasefire, to conclude and sign an Agreement on Modalities for the Conduct of Quarterly Flag meetings at the sectors to be agreed upon, to conclude and sign a framework agreement on Speedy Return of Inadvertent Line Crossers, to conclude an agreement on No Development of New Posts and Defence Works along the LOC and propose drafts for new border control guidelines along the International Border. On Nuclear CBMs, the two sides decided to hold discussions on security doctrines. On Jammu and Kashmir, both sides agreed to ensure implementation of the already agreed Jammu and Kashmir related CBMs, to ensure operationalisation of truck service and to ensure operationalisation/ rationalisation of the five crossing points. On Siachen, they agreed that the Defence Secretaries of the two countries assisted by respective Directors General (Military Operations) would meet to hold talks. The two sides agreed to conclude a bilateral visa agreement and an agreement on consular access and also to revise the Protocol on Visits to Religious Places during the 4th round of the Composite Dialogue. On the prisoners issue the two sides agreed that the proposed Committee on Prisoners to ensure humane treatment and expeditious release of prisoners on both sides would be composed of four retired judges from each side. The above information was given by the Minister of External Affairs, Shri Pranab Mukherjee in written reply to a question in Rajya Sabha today.

437. (26-4-2007) NEW DELHI : A 3-day International Seminar on 'UN Peacekeeping: Challenges and Prospects' is being organised in New Delhi on April 26-28, 2007. This is one of the confidence building activities approved by the 13th ASEAN Regional Forum (ARF) Ministerial Meeting held in Kuala Lumpur in July 2006. All the Member States are participating in the Seminar. Apart from distinguished experts in the field from the Member States, representatives from DPKO, UNDP, ICRC, UNHCR are also participating in the deliberations. The participants will discuss peacekeeping challenges in 21st century; peacebuilding and security sector reforms; humanitarian dimensions of peacekeeping; capacity building for UN Peacekeeping; and training for peacekeeping. The seminar is being held at the Centre for UN Peacekeeping, a centre set up by the Government of India with an exclusive focus on UN Peacekeeping activities. Apart from discussions on UN Peacekeeping and related subjects, the Centre also has facilities for training military professionals from both India and abroad engaged in UN Peacekeeping. India had earlier organized ARF Seminar on "UN Peacekeeping: Best Practices and Lesson Learnt" in March 2002 and has been participating in peacekeeping related workshops and seminars organized under the aegis of ASEAN Regional Forum regularly. India has been member of ARF since 1996. The objective of the ARF is to enhance cooperative security through confidence building measures in Asia-Pacific Region. Peacekeeping is one of the important themes discussed in the ARF meetings.

438. (26-4-2007) NEW DELHI : The 14th SAARC Summit held in New Delhi on April 3-4, 2007 adopted a comprehensive and a forward-looking Declaration, to promote regional cooperation. It underlined the collective vision of the Heads of State/Government of SAARC countries of an interconnected South Asia where there was a free flow of people, goods, services and ideas. Based on the region's common history, geography and socio-cultural ties, it reiterated that the future of the people of South Asia was interlinked. When implemented, the decisions outlined in the Declaration will boost intra-regional trade and investment, enhance understanding through increased people-to-people contact and promote cultural exchanges and travel within the region.

439. (26-4-2007) NEW DELHI : The India-Bhutan Treaty of 1949 has been updated by both governments. The revised India-Bhutan Friendship Treaty was signed in New Delhi on 8th February 2007. The Treaty has come into force following the exchange of Instruments of Ratification between the two governments in Thimphu on 2nd March 2007. The updated India-Bhutan Friendship Treaty reflects the contemporary nature of India-Bhutan relations and lays the firm foundation for their future development in the 21st century. The Treaty will enable the further intensification of our historically close, special and mutually beneficial relations in areas such as trade and economic cooperation, hydropower, human resource development, cultural and people-to-people exchanges. The Treaty contains fresh provisions for consolidating and expanding our relations in these areas. The above information was given by the Minister of External Affairs, Shri Pranab Mukherjee in written reply to a question in Rajya Sabha today.

440. (26-4-2007) NEW DELHI : Minister of Tourism and Culture Smt. Ambika Soni has said that a National Survey of Manuscripts in the State of Rajasthan, alongwith a series of public awareness programmes, is being undertaken under joint auspices of National Manuscripts Mission under Ministry of Culture and Rajasthan State Archives. This survey which is being conducted in each of 32 districts of the State, aims at locating the manuscript collections in the State, both in institutional and private holdings. The Director, Rajasthan State Archives, is the State coordinator in respect of the Survey of manuscripts in the State of Rajasthan. In a written reply in the Lok Sabha today she said, an allocation of Rs. 30.13 lakh has been made for the survey of manuscripts in Rajasthan out of which, Rs. 15.07 lakh has been released. She said, manuscripts are not being collected under the National Survey. The survey aims at locating the manuscript repositories in the State and documenting and cataloguing them. At present, there is no proposal to publish the manuscripts located in the Survey.

441. (26-4-2007) NEW DELHI : Minister of Tourism and Culture Smt. Ambika Soni has said that there are 70 monuments in the Mehrauli Archaeological Park. Of this, 7 are protected as monuments of national importance by the Archaeological Survey of India. In a written reply in the Lok Sabha today, she said the Mehrauli

Archaeological Park is under the Delhi Development Authority. The Park is only partially protected by fencing/boundary wall. It is learnt that a Cultural Resource Management Plan for the Mehrauli Archaeoloigcal Park has been prepared and this has been approved by the Lt. Governor, Delhi. She said there is no proposal at present to protect other monuments of the Mehrauli Archaeological Park by the Archaeological Survey of India.

442. (26-4-2007) NEW DELHI : The Minister of Tourism and Culture Smt. Ambika Soni informed the Lok Sabha today that a sum of Rs. 121 crore had been incurred in 2006-07 in regard to Incredible India Campaigns both in the domestic and overseas markets. In a written reply she said, there has been a remarkable growth in recent years in regard to domestic tourist visits, foreign tourist arrivals and foreign exchange earnings through tourism to the country. As per the figures available, there has been an overall increase of 26.35% in domestic tourist visits between 2003 (309038335) and 2005 (390466880). The foreign tourist arrivals have increased by about 65% from a level of 2.38 million in 2002 to 3.92 million in 2005, while foreign exchange earnings have grown up by about 96% during the same period. In the year 2006, the foreign tourist arrivals have increased to 4.43 million registering an increase of 14.2% compared to the previous year. The Incredible India campaigns have won worldwide acclaim.

443. (26-4-2007) NEW DELHI : The Inter University Accelerator Centre (IUAC), formerly Nuclear Science Centre, New Delhi, has organized a two-day Conference on "Accelerator and Low Level Radiation Safety (ALLRS)" at the National Centre for Plant Genome Research (NCPGR), New Delhi. Inaugurating the event today Prof. B.L. Mungekar, Member, Planning Commission, stressed the importance of Ethics in Science and Technology. He also expressed concern over the lack of interest among students for basic sciences. The presidential address was delivered by Prof. B. Bhattacharjee, Member, National Disaster Management Authority. Around 150 researchers, faculty members and research students from about 30 universities, 10 colleges, 10 institutes and foreign participants including Prof. Syuichi Ban, Head, Radiation Science Centre, and Dr. Hiroshi Matsumura, High Energy Accelerator research Organisation (KEK), Japan; Dr. Jaya Ramanuja, Tyco Healthcare, USA; Prof. F. Hoyler, AcUSA-Aachen, Campus Julich, Germany and Dr. Abdul Malek and Dr. Hamid Khan, Bangaldesh, will share their research activities in various disciplines on one platform. Ninety research Papers on various aspects of "Accelerator and Low Level Radiation Safety (ALLRS)" would be presented. The deliberations and the interactions during the conference will help in augmenting the research activities and give a new direction to the young researchers.

444. (26-4-2007) NEW DELHI : The process of finalizing the revised guidelines is on following the Union Government's approval for revision in the guidelines for regularization of unauthorized colonies in Delhi. Unauthorized colonies fulfilling the prescribed conditions will be eligible for regularization. The Minister of State for Urban Development Shri Ajay Maken told Rajya Sabha today that the Government of National Capital Territory had invited applications from Societies and Associations of unauthorized colonies existing as on 31st March.2002, seeking regularization. He said that the Delhi government has received 1539 applications. Shri Maken stated that verification of these applications on site has been taken up through different agencies. The minister said that once regularized, as per the provisions of Master Plan, unauthorized regularized colonies would be covered by the Special Area Building Regulations to be framed for special area, unauthorized regularized colonies and village abadis. Owners in special area, unauthorized regularized colonies and village abadis shall register themselves with the local body within a period of four months indicating the existing extent of construction. Thereafter, a certificate of structural safety by qualified engineers shall be submitted within the next six months. Subject to height restriction of 15 meters, all buildings covered by such registration shall be exempted from punitive action till Special Area Building Regulations for these areas are notified or for a maximum three years, whichever is earlier. The concerned local bodies/agencies responsible for civic services will provide civic facilities as per their service plans and over a period of time, those colonies will be integrated into the planned development. In view of the legal and administrative issues involved, no time frame has been fixed at this stage.

445. (26-4-2007) NEW DELHI : National Aluminium Company Limited (NALCO), the flagship PSU of the Ministry of Mines, and India's largest manufacturer and exporter of alumina and aluminium has reported a 52.39% jump in net profit to Rs.2380.70 crore during the financial year 2006-07, from Rs.1562.20 crore achieved in previous year. According to un-audited financial results declared by the company, it has also achieved highest every turnover of Rs.6516.78 crore, recording an increase of 22.40% over the previous year's figure of Rs.5324.16 crore. The Company has achieved the highest-every metal sale of 3,56,616 tonnes in the financial year 2006-07. This represents an increase of 3.4% against the MOU target of 3,45,000 tonnes. The previous best sale was 3,53,841 tonnes in the year 2005-06. The Aluminium Smelter of the Company also achieved 104% capacity utilization during the year. Similarly, the company's 960 MW Captive Power Plant, located at Angul near the Smelter Plant, has achieved the highest-ever power generation of 5968 million units, the previous best being 5679 million units in 2005-06. The generation is also higher than the MoU target of 5714 million units. Besides, this two decade old coal-fired power plant of NALCO achieved the highest-ever plant load factor (PLF) of 79.3%, surpassing the decade-old 78.85% PLF achieved in 1993-94. Nalco has been pursuing the plans of continuous expansion of production capacity in order to strengthen its business and increase market share. Soon after completion of the 1st phase expansion, the company has now launched its 2nd phase expansion involving fresh investment of Rs. 5,100 crore. The present capacity of bauxite Mines will go up from 48 lakh tonnes to

63 lakh tonnes, Alumina Refinery from 15.75 lakh tonnes to 21 lakh tonnes, Aluminium Smelter from 3.45 lakh tonnes to 4.60 lakh tonnes per year and Captive Power Plant from 960 MW to 1200 MW. As part of business development strategy, Nalco is also actively exploring the possibilities of setting up joint venture projects abroad for making aluminium based on its surplus alumina to the tune of 1.2 million tonnes expected to be available once the 2nd phase expansion is complete. In order to meet the requirement of its expansion activities relating to captive power generation, Nalco has been allotted Utkal-E Coal; Block for mining of Coal. Environmental studies have been carried out and M/s CMPDI and M/s. RITES have been appointed consultants for various jobs.

446. (26-4-2007) NEW DELHI : The Department of Industrial Policy and Promotion (DIPP), Ministry of Commerce & Industry has constituted an Expert Committee to render technical advice for development of Service Price Index (SPI) and its related issues. The Committee will be chaired by Prof C.P.Chandrasekhar, Centre for Economic Studies and Planning, Jawaharlal Nehru University. Members of the Committee includes Dr. B.N.Goldar, Institute of Economic Growth, Dr. Nagesh Kumar, DG, Research & Information System for Developing Countries, Dr.Tarun Das, Institute of Integrated Learning in Management, DG, CSO, Ministry of Statistics and Programme Implementation, DG, NSSO, Ministry of Statistics and Programme Implementation, Principal Adviser, Department of Statistical Analysis & Computer Services (RBI), Shri Tejinder Singh Laschar, Senior Economic Adviser (DIPP), Senior Economic Adviser, Department of Economic Affairs (Ministry of Finance) & DG, Labour Bureau. Shri Manoranjan Senapaty, Economic Adviser, DIPP will be the Member Secretary. The terms of reference of the Expert Committee includes:-to provide guidance in the context of concept, methodology, scope/coverage, related aspects and other important issues for the Services Sector Index; to render technical advice for development of sector specific Service Price Index (SPI) and its related issues, keeping in view best international practices; to examine regular availability and sources of data for compilation of Service Price Index; to scrutinize the sector specific studies/survey results and suggest improvements and modifications; to oversee the inter-sectoral consistency/uniformity with international standard and best practices; to provide continuous guidance to the Office of the Economic Advisor in actual construction of the Index; to oversee the process of evolution of an integrated Service Price Index; to identify new priority sectors for inclusion in construction of the Service Price Index, as and when a need arises; to suggest institutional mechanism for collection of requisite data for the Services Sector Index and also its periodical updation; to suggest measures for capacity building and augmentation of infrastructural facilities in the Office of the Economic Adviser.

447. (26-4-2007) NEW DELHI : The Ministry of Housing & Urban Poverty Alleviation is already implementing an employment oriented Urban Poverty Alleviation Centrally sponsored scheme named Swarna Jayanti Shahari Rozgar

Yojana (SJSRY) on all India basis, with effect from 1.12.1997. The SJSRY strives to provide gainful employment to the urban unemployed and underemployed poor through, firstly, encouraging the setting up of self-employment ventures by those who have not studied beyond 9th standard and, secondly, by providing wage employment by utilizing their labour for construction of socially and economically useful public assets. This was stated by the Minister of State (Independent Charge) for Housing and Urban Poverty Alleviation, Kumari Selja in a reply to a question by Shri Syed Azeez Pasha in Rajya Sabha today. She further stated that the Scheme is being implemented on all India basis through States/UTs Government and every State/UT makes efforts to implement the scheme effectively. However, some States viz. Kerala, Andhra Pradesh, Karnataka, Uttar Pradesh, Haryana, Madhya Pradesh, Tamil Nadu, Maharashtra, West Bengal and Gujarat are performing better than rest of the States/UTs in the implementation of the scheme, she added.

448. (26-4-2007) NEW DELHI : In the proposed National Urban Housing and Habitat Policy-2007, there is a provision to earmark at all levels, including the New Public/Private housing colonies a portion of land at affordable rates for housing for the Economically Weaker Section and Low Income Group. This could be 10-15% land area to accommodate 20-25% dwelling units for Economically Weaker Section and Low Income Group. This was stated by the Minister of State (Independent Charge) for Housing and Urban Poverty Alleviation, Kumari Selja in a reply to a question by Smt. Supriya Sule in Rajya Sabha today.

449. (26-4-2007) NEW DELHI : Railtel, a Public Sector Undertaking under the Ministry of Railways, has set up Cyber Cafes at 17 selected Railway stations so far under franchise model on revenue sharing arrangements. Wi-Fi connectivity for laptop has also been provided in and around such cyber cafes at five stations namely Bangalore, Hyderabad, Howrah, Jaipur and Sealdah so far. This information was given by the Minister of State for Railways, Shri R.Velu in a written reply to a question in the Lok Sabha today.

450. (26-4-2007) NEW DELHI : The thrust areas identified on Indian Railways for development during the 10th Five Year Plan include, growth in freight and passenger traffic, capacity augmentation, technology upgradation & modernization, rationalization of rail tariff and participative project funding. During the 10th Plan period, the Railways have surpassed its targets for freight and passenger traffic and achieved annual growth rate of over 8 per cent in freight and 4.5 per cent in passenger traffic. As regards capacity expansion, over 900 kms. of new lines, 4400 kms. of gauge conversion, 1300 kms. of doubling have been completed during the same period. Further, nearly 1800 kms. of railway electrification and 24,000 kms. of track renewals have also been done. Railways have also surpassed the targets of diesel and electric loco production and of production of passenger coaches.

451. (26-4-2007) NEW DELHI : Indian Railways provide separate toilets for ladies and disabled friendly toilets are provided at A1, A&B category stations. Waiting rooms with bathing facilities are taken up for ladies at all A1 and A category stations over South Central Railway and 26 stations have already been provided with this facility on this Railway. Drinking water facility is available at all stations. Drinking water facility through Automatic Vending Machines is not an essential passenger amenity.

452. (26-4-2007) NEW DELHI : The Ministry of External Affairs had, through Rail India Technical & Economic Services (RITES), carried out a feasibility study for India-Myanmar rail link. The Report is currently under bilateral consultation. The likely expenditure as per the study on construction of new rail link between Jiribam-Moreh in India and Tamu-Kalay-Segyi in Myanmar is estimated to cost Rs. 4280 crore. The link will provide substantial benefit to bilateral trade between India and Myanmar. No specific timeframe has been set for these projects. North-South Transport Corridor promotes transport cooperation between the Member States. The Corridor would connect Ocean and Persian Gulf to Russia via Iran and the Caspian Sea. The Corridor pertaining to India is purely a shipping route from the west coast of India to Iran. The Corridor provides opportunities to enhance trade between India and Iran. This information was given by the Minister of State for Railways, Shri R.Velu in a written reply to a question in the Lok Sabha today.

453. (26-4-2007) NEW DELHI : Fog has been severe this year and rail services were affected. The punctuality of 742 trains was affected. At present, there is no technique ensuring normal visibility during foggy weather. However, a dependable on board train protection system can effectively improve running in foggy weather conditions. Train protection and warning system, which is a proven system is now being installed on two pilot sections of Indian Railways for preventing signal passing at danger. "Fog vision instrumentation" project is being developed under the "Technology mission on Railway Safety" programme jointly by Indian Institute of Technology (IIT) and Research Design and Standard Organisation. The aim of these projects is to help Driver to run trains at normal speed in foggy weather. Fog vision instrumentation trials using "Thermal Imager" Technique have not succeeded so far. Based on success of these projects further works will be considered. This information was given by the Minister of State for Railways, Shri R.Velu in a written reply to a question in the Lok Sabha today.

454. (26-4-2007) NEW DELHI : Thirty Mega Food Parks will be set up in different parts of the country and subsidy to the tune of Rs.50 crore would be provided to catalyse investment in these Mega Food Parks. This was indicated by the Minister of Food Processing Shri Subodh Kant Sahai, while jointly chairing a meeting with Shri Kamal Nath, Minister of Commerce & Industry, on Agro-Food Processing Parks here on Tuesday. Shri Kamal Nath underlined that the emergence of food retailing in the country has opened up the opportunities for setting up of Food Parks successfully, unlike in the past. However, the infrastructure for evacuation of the farm produce needs to be strengthened, he added. He remarked that "in future, the backend of the retail would be the Food Park and that the backend of Food Park would be the farmer". Shri Kamal Nath also recalled his recent meetings with the Chinese leaders and stated that the huge import of processed foods by China was an opportunity to be tapped. Shri Sahai explained that the new Mega Food Park would be set up on the basis of a feasibility study by a consultant who would also identify the private investor and form a Special Purpose /vehicle for the execution of the project. Shri Suvarathan, Secretary, Ministry of Food Processing Industries, made a presentation on the new scheme of Mega Food Parks. Shri Suvarathan explained the concept of Mega Food Park and emphasized the need to integrate the supply chain. The meeting was attended, among others, by Dr. Ajay Dua, Secretary, Department of Industrial Policy & Promotion (DIPP), senior officers from different ministries, agencies like Agricultural & Processed Food Products Export Development Authority (APEDA) and NAFED and representatives of industry including Shri Sunil Bharati Mittal. The discussions brought out the need for coordination among the schemes of the Ministry of Commerce & Industry like Assistance to States for Infrastructure Development for Exports (ASIDE) and Industrial Infrastructure Upgradation Scheme (IIUS) and the Mega Food Park Scheme of the Ministry of Food Processing. Dr. Ajay Dua stressed the need to coordinate the Scheme of IIUS and ASIDE with the Mega Food Park Scheme. Shri Rawat, Principal Secretary to Chief Minister of Madhya Pradesh, offered all support from the State Government for setting up a Mega Food Park in Madhya Pradesh in an agriculturally rich zone like Chhindwara. Both Bharati Group and M/s Haldirams expressed their interest in becoming anchor investors in the proposed Mega Food Park to be set up in Chhindwara.

455. (26-4-2007) NEW DELHI : Sustained efforts on the part of the Department of Agriculture & Cooperation, Ministry of Agriculture and APEDA aimed at meeting the US import plant health requirements for mango have finally borne fruit. The United States Department of Agriculture has finally decided to grant market access for Indian Mangoes, thus paving the way for commencement of mango exports from India to US. The first export consignment of Indian mango is being shipped from Mumbai to US on 26th April 2007. Initially, India will be exporting Alphonso, Banganpalli and Kesar, the early maturing mango varieties, while Langra, Chausa, Mallika, Dussheri and other varieties are proposed for exports in the latter part of the mango season. Exports of Indian mango to US, which was a long-standing Indian request and an unresolved bilateral phytosanitary issue, has finally come through only as a consequence of protracted negotiations between USDA and DAC officials and after USDA brought out Import Rules for Indian mango, prescribing irradiation phytosanitary treatment and is based on a mutually agreed treatment protocol which aims at assuring that there would be no risk of introduction of exotic plant diseases and pests into US. Opening of the

US market for Indian mango spells an excellent business opportunity for Indian mango producers and it is now for the Indian entrepreneurs, mango growers and trade associations to realize the fruits of the efforts of the Ministry of Agriculture.

456. (26-4-2007) NEW DELHI : Smt. Renuka Chowdhury, Minister for Women and Child Development Minister has said that women should be given the opportunity to rise to her fullest. They should not be treated only as vote banks but also should be given fair share in decision-making. Underlining role of women in the overall development of the society, she said that empowerment of women could ensure the development in right perspectives, addressing the 4th World Congress on Rural Women at Durban in South Africa today, Smt. Renuka Chowdhury stressed that decentralized and local self-governance hold the key to women's empowerment in the rural areas. Apprising of the developments in the area of women welfare in India, the Minister said that of the approximately 127 million women workers in India, 106 million are in the rural areas and 96 per cent of these are in the unorganised sector. Obviously, globalization and liberalization, the engines that are driving the economy, will impact on these women. There is increased volatility of employment leading to ejection of older women', the nature of women's work is changing with an increase in informal, self employed low-end service work; there is more unpaid work and with a decline in agriculture-related work, increasing migration of women leading to insecurity and exploitation. Smt. Chowdhury said that the Government's efforts have, therefore, been multi-pronged. Legislations protecting women from violence, recognizing daughters as coparceners and equal inheritors in ancestral property, guaranteeing 100days of wage employment in a year, providing minimum social security cover in terms of health benefits, etc., already exist or are in the pipeline. Smt. Chowdhury said that the women in India are in the process of shaking the grounds they send on. "Inevitably the process is not going to be an easy one since the ground they stand on is made up of the vested interest which have gained dubious legitimacy over centuries in a man's world". But the Indian women are determined a lot to attain their due place in the society, she added. The Minister said "real freedom is when a women can walk at midnight with her head held high. Freedom from poverty, hunger, disease, abuse and transgression of trade boundaries is what is required today".

457. (26-4-2007) NEW DELHI : The Ministry of Rural Development has sanctioned Rs. 31.81 crore to the State Government of Tamil Nadu towards part of first instalment of funds against the provisional allocation of Rs.19.09 crore made for the Government of Tamil Nadu under Accelerated Rural Water Supply Programme (Normal) of Rajiv Gandhi National Drinking Water Mission, during the year 2007-08. The allocation of funds is provisional and likely to be changed during the course of the year. As such the amount released as first instalment may not be treated as 50% of the allocation for 2007-08. Up to 15 per cent of funds released under this sanction may be utilized for Operation & Maintenance and up to 5 per cent of funds may be spent for taking sustainability measures. States have been requested to delegate powers for management of Rural Water Supply Schemes through the Panchayati Raj Institutions (PRIs) as per the Constitution of India. As such Operation and Maintenance of the completed RWS Scheme should be transferred to the PRIs. No expenditure shall be incurred on taking water quality problems form the present release, as there is a separate allocation for the purpose. This release is being made for execution/completion of schemes to provide safe drinking water facilities to rural habitations and schools under the Centrally Sponsored ARWSP. Priorities set in ARWSP guidelines and through other instructions issued from time to time shall be followed for coverage of rural habitations and rural schools.

458. (26-4-2007) NEW DELHI : Out of the total freight and passenger traffic carried by railways and roads, the roads carry 61 percent of freight and 85 percent of the passenger traffic. As per available data as on March 2002, out of the total road length in the country 35.6% was of single lane standard (excluding the roads constructed under Pradhan Mantri Gram Sadak Yojana and Jawahar Rozgar Yojana) and 52.6% was unsurfaced. This was stated by Shri K.H. Muniyappa, Minister of State for Road Transport and Highways in a reply to a question by Shri Ekanath K. Thakur in the Rajya Sabha today. He further stated that the Ministry is primarily responsible for the development and maintenance of the National Highways. The State Government concerned is responsible for roads other than National Highways. The Union Government has taken up several initiatives for improvement of National Highways including four laning, six laning and construction of expressways etc., under the various phases of National Highways Development Project (NHDP), Special Accelerated Road Development Programme in the North East Region (SARDP-NE). Apart from this, the National Highways are improved under the Annual Programme of the Ministry as per the traffic, inter-se priority and availability of funds, he added.

459. (26-4-2007) NEW DELHI : In West Bengal, the National Rural Employment Guarantee Act (NREGA) was initially launched in 10 districts of the State and another 7 districts have been added for the year 2007-08. The tally of households demanding employment in the State stood at 28.57 lakh and out of them 26.82 lakh were provided employment up to February, 07. The average number of households provided employment in a district of the State is 2,68,187, while the national average is 91,685 households. Besides, four thousand households completed the 100 days guarantee of employment provided in the Act. The number of person days of employment provided in the State is 345.79 lakh. The average person days of employment provided in a district is 34.58 lakh compared to the national average of 36.47 lakh person days. The employment was provided on 35,907 works, out of which 17,000 works have been completed. The average number of works taken up in a district stood at 3,591 against the national average of 3,581. An amount of Rs. 358.59 crore has been released to the State during 2006-07.

Against this, the utlisation up to February, 07 is Rs. 311.41 crore, which is 51.92% of the total availability. The expenditure on wages is 77.87%, material is 19.61% and on administration is 2.51%. The average expenditure of a district in the State is Rs. 31.14 crore compared to the National average of Rs. 35 crore. The Act provides that 1/3rd of the employment provided should be to women. In the State 19.66% person days of employment has been provided to women, 35.84% to SC and 17.79% to ST. A visit to the State by the National Level Monitors in December, 2006 & January 2007 has revealed that Job Cards are issued on time and wage seeker has the custody of Job Card. Entries regarding employment provided and wage paid is made on the card. Moreover, authenticated muster rolls are used at the worksite.

460. (26-4-2007) NEW DELHI : In Uttarakhand, the National Rural Employment Guarantee Act (NREGA) was initially launched in 3 districts of the State and another 2 districts have been added for the year 2007-08. The tally of households demanding employment in the State stood at 1.14 lakh and all of them were provided employment up to February, 07. The average number of households provided employment in a district of the State is 37,871, while the national average is 91,685 households. Besides, 100 households completed the 100 days guarantee of employment provided in the Act. The number of person days of employment provided in the State is 30.05 lakh. The average person days of employment provided in a district is 10.01 lakh compared to the national average of 36.47 lakh person days. The employment was provided on 6,323 works, out of which 3,075 works have been completed. The average number of works taken up in a district stood at 2,108 against the national average of 3,581. An amount of Rs. 39.10 crore has been released to the State during 2006-07. Against this, the utlisation up to February, 07 is Rs. 38.28 crore, which is 53.93 % of the total availability. The expenditure on wages is 60.04%, material is 37.90% and on administration is 2.05%. The average expenditure of a district in the State is Rs. 12.76 crore compared to the National average of Rs. 35 crore. The Act provides that 1/3rd of the employment provided should be to women. In the State 26.86% person days of employment has been provided to women, 25.39% to SC and 1.56% to ST. A visit to the State by the National Level Monitors in December, 2006 & January 2007 has revealed that water and soil conservation works constitute more than 70% of the work. Moreover, retired Government employees and prominent persons of villages identified as resource person to conduct social audit. Training is provided to them in Gram Sabha..

461. (26-4-2007) NEW DELHI : National Rural Employment Guarantee Act (NREGA) was initially launched in 22 districts of Uttar Pradesh. However, there is no addition of districts in the tally so far in the year 2007-08. In the State 25.09 lakh households have demanded employment and of them 24.11 lakh households have been provided employment up to December, 06. The average number of households provided employment in a district of the State is 1,09,595, while the national average is 91,685 households. Besides, 1.06 lakh households completed the 100 days guarantee of employment provided in the Act. The number of person days of employment provided in the State is 617.64 lakh. The average person days of employment provided in a district is 28.07 lakh compared to the national average of 36.47 lakh person days. The employment was provided on 71,781 works, out of which 29,335 works have been completed. The average number of works taken up in a district stood at 3,263 against the national average of 3,581. An amount of Rs. 569.15 crore has been released to the State during 2006-07. Against this, the utlisation up to February, 07 is Rs. 665.28 crore, which is 65.24 % of the total availability. The expenditure on wages is 58.86%, material is 39.72% and on administration is 1.42%. The average expenditure of a district in the State is Rs. 30.24 crore compared to the National average of Rs. 35 crore. The Act provides that 1/3rd of the employment provided should be to women. In the State 15.97% person days of employment has been provided to women, 58.86% to SC and 3.3% to ST. A visit to the State by the National Level Monitors in December, 2006 & January 2007 has revealed that One Panchayat Mitra for each GP, Two Junior Engineers for every GP have been deployed and the Programme Officer has also been deployed at the Block level. In addition, the District Perspective Plan has also been prepared.

462. (26-4-2007) NEW DELHI : National Rural Employment Guarantee Act (NREGA) was initially launched in one district of Tripura and another 2 Districts have been added in the year 2007-08. In the State 0.67 lakh households have demanded employment and all the households have been provided employment up to Feb., 07. The average number of households provided employment in a district of the State is 66,656, while the national average is 91,685 households. In the State 200 household have completed the 100 days guarantee of employment provided in the Act. The number of person days of employment provided in the State is 45.74 lakh. The average person days of employment provided in a district is 45.74 lakh compared to the national average of 36.47 lakh person days. The employment was provided on 2,415 works, out of which 2,312 works have been completed. The average number of works taken up in a district is 2,415, against the national average of 3,581. An amount of Rs. 19.15 crore has been released to the State during 2006-07. Against this, the utlisation up to February 2007, is Rs. 42 crore, which is 88.25% of the total availability. The expenditure on wages is 66.10%, material is 33.80% and on administration is 1.09%. The average expenditure of a district in the State is Rs.42 crore compared to the National average of Rs. 35 crore. The Act provides that 1/3rd of the employment provided should be to women. In the State 75.1% person days of employment has been provided to women, 17.14% to SC and 60.78% to ST.

463. (26-4-2007) NEW DELHI : A high-powered Pakistani business delegation led by Mr. Muhammad Naser Khan, President of Islamabad Chamber of Commerce & Industry called on Dr. Ashwani Kumar, Minister of State for Industry, here today. Apart from discussing various business issues, the delegation in particular requested the Minister to ensure that the visa regime for Pakistani businessmen to visit India should become more liberal. Dr. Kumar assured that the government is committed to strengthening trade and economic ties with Pakistan and would take all steps to facilitate the same. Dr. Kumar said that "great complementarities exist between the two countries and greater trade and cooperation in the sphere of industry would only make both economies more competitive". He emphasised that such visits would help to promote people to people contact would consolidate the desire and aspirations of the people of India and Pakistan to promote mutual goodwill and harmony between the two neighbours. The Pakistani delegation was accompanied by Shri Sanjay Bhatia, President PHD Chamber of Commerce & Industry. Two-way trade between India and Pakistan has reached a record figure of US $ 977.03 million (April-October 2006). This comprises India's exports to Pakistan valued at US $ 789.13 million and India's imports from Pakistan valued at US $ 187.90 million. India's imports from Pakistan have been growing at a steady pace-87% in 2005-06 and 86% in April-October (2006-07).

464. (26-4-2007) NEW DELHI : Following is the text of the President, Dr. A.P.J. Abdul Kalam's address at the Banquet hosted by the President of the Hellenic Republic, His Excellency Mr. Karolos Papoulias in Greece today : "I greatly appreciate your warm welcome and your kind words. I am happy to be in Greece, which has contributed so much to human civilisation. Greece is the crucible of democracy and India is the world's largest democracy. My visit has been a rewarding experience. The arrangements are excellent and the hospitality extended to me and my delegation most generous. The friendship and warm sentiments of the people of Greece have made our stay most memorable. Our exchanges in ancient times began well before Alexander's invasion in 326 BCE. Pythagorus is reported to have travelled to India in the sixth century BC. Socrates (469-399 BCE) had occasion to meet an Indian philosopher in Athens and was greatly moved by the latter's Upanishadic observation that humans-the Relative, could be properly understood only in the light of an understanding of the Divine-the Absolute. In more recent times, in the 18th century, Demetrius Galanos of Athens embraced India as his second motherland and breathed his last in his beloved Varanasi, proving himself to be one of the earliest and ablest pioneers of Indology. In modern times, both our countries have faced great challenges. We have secured freedom from colonial rule and fought against fascism in World War II. We share a deep commitment to democracy and have active civil societies. We both believe in the values of freedom, dignity and respect for the individual. We stand together to fight against terrorism for which we have zero tolerance. These shared values have helped us to understand each other's concerns and aspirations, paving the way for broad-based cooperation. Greece is an important member of the European Union, with which our relationship has grown stronger over the years and with which we have a strategic partnership. This is another important element in our relations.

465. (26-4-2007) NEW DELHI : The traffic density on Golden Quadrilateral (GQ) passing through Rajasthan is in the range of 10,000 to 50,000 Passenger Car Unit per day. The proposal for six-laning of the whole GQ including the stretch passing through Rajasthan has been approved by the Government under the National Highways Development Project (NHDP) Phase V and is targeted for completion by December 2012. The work is expected to commence during 2008-09. This was stated by Shri K.H. Muniyappa, Minister of State for Road Transport and Highways in a reply to a question by Shri Krishan Lal Balmiki in the Rajya Sabha today.

466. (26-4-2007) NEW DELHI : Wherever 4/6 laning works under National Highways Development Project (NHDP) are under implementation, their maintenance is carried out by the Contractors/ Concessionaire to keep them in traffic worthy condition, as part of their obligations under contract/ concession agreement. In case of the sections which have been identified under NHDP but 4/6 laning have not yet started, the maintenance of existing roads is carried out by NHAI, State Public Works Departments (PWDs)/ Border Road Organisation (BRO) through funds provided by the Ministry of Shipping, Road Transport and Highways. This was stated by Shri K.H. Muniyappa, Minister of State for Road Transport and Highways in a reply to a question by Shri Lalit Kishore Chaturvedi in the Rajya Sabha today.

467. (27-4-2007) NEW DELHI : Trade between India and Pakistan has shown enormous buoyancy and is expected to cross US $ 1.5 billion (US $ 1500 million) in 2006-07. Exports to Pakistan in April-December (2006-07) stood at US $ 980.33 million while imports were US $ 247.48 million during the same period. A business delegation led by Muhammad Nasir Khan, President of Islamabad Chamber of Commerce & Industry, called on Shri Kamal Nath, Union Minister of Commerce & Industry, here this evening and expressed hope that the economic ties between the two countries would strengthen in the near future to benefit both countries. Shri Kamal Nath highlighted the many benefits that could accrue to both India and Pakistan if trade relations improve, as it would make both countries more competitive in an increasingly globalised economy. He expressed hope that Pakistan would grant the much awaited most favoured nation status (MFN) to India and said that the segment of trade between two nations that currently took place through third countries would then be replaced by direct trade. The Pakistan delegation requested the Minister to ensure easing of visa regime for Pakistani businessmen by the Indian government. Shri Kamal Nath assured that Government of India was committed to strengthening economic ties with its neighbour and this issue would also be taken care of in due course. The main commodities of exports to Pakistan include sugar, dyes, plastic & petroleum products and cotton while main import items from Pakistan are petroleum & crude products, fruits & nuts (excluding cashew nuts), cotton yarn & fabrics and organic chemicals.

468. (27-4-2007) NEW DELHI : To improve access and increase the representation of the physically challenged persons in the Civil Services under the central government, the government has decided that any physically challenged person, selected on the standards as applicable to the non-disabled candidate of his category, will be counted over and above the quota fixed for physically challenged persons. This would be exactly on the lines as it happens for SC/ST/OBC candidates. It has also been decided that the physically challenged persons belonging to the General Category shall be eligible for seven attempts as against existing four attempts. The physically challenged persons belonging to the OBC Category and SC/ST category would continue to be eligible for seven and unlimited attempts respectively. Additional relaxation of 10 years in the upper age limit for physically challenged persons will be continued. The Government has also decided that while reservation for the three categories of disability (visual impairment, hearing impairment and locomotor disability or cerebral palsy) shall be made separately, the interchange in the vacancies among the three categories would be possible in case of non-availability of persons of a specified category. A specially constituted Medical Board with experts in the area will examine physically challenged persons so that fair, consistent reports are available. To ensure the full utilisation of quota for physically challenged persons, it has been decided to treat the backlogs with respect to physically challenged persons in the same way as backlogs for the SC/ST categories. Union Public Service Commission will recommend physically challenged candidates after ensuring that they meet the prescribed eligibility criteria in terms of abilities/disabilities for identified services where vacancy exists. The eligibility for availing reservation against the quota for physically challenged persons would be the same as described in the Persons with Disabilities Act, 1995. Specific eligibility criteria as set by the Government for identified services/posts would have to be met by physically disables candidates. The implementation of these decisions shall be with prospective effect.

469. (27-4-2007) NEW DELHI : The total approximate earnings of Indian Railways on originating basis during the period 1st April-20th April 2007 were Rs. 3667.21 crore compared to Rs. 3251.04 crore during the same period last year, registering an increase of 12.80 per cent. The total goods earnings have gone up from Rs. 2168.15 crore during 1-20 April 2006 to Rs. 2447.78 crore during 1-20 April 2007, showing an increase of 12.90 per cent. The total passenger revenue earnings during the period 1-20 April 2007 were Rs. 1089.74 crore compared to Rs. 976.97 crore during the same period last year, an increase of 11.54 per cent. The revenue earnings from other coaching amounted to Rs. 101.37 crore during this period compared to Rs. 82.65 crore during the same period last year, an increase of 22.65 per cent. The total sundry earnings have gone up from Rs. 23.27 crore during 1-20 April 2006 to Rs. 28.32 crore during 1-20 April 2007, showing an increase of 21.70 per cent. The total approximate number of passengers booked during the period 1-20 April 2007 were 368.81 million compared to 346.46 million during the same period last year, showing an increase of 6.45 per cent. In the suburban and non-suburban sectors, the number of passengers booked during 1-20 April 2007 were 208.72 million and 160.09 million compared to 197.10 million and 149.36 million during the same period last year, registering an increase of 5.90 per cent and 7.18 per cent respectively.

470. (27-4-2007) NEW DELHI : The second 500 MW unit of Stage-III (2x500 MW) Vindhyachal Super Thermal Power Project was commissioned by Union Power Minister, Shri Sushilkumar Shinde at Vindhyanagar in Madhya Pradesh thus taking total installed capacity of the station of 3260 MW and Vindhyachal becomes the largest power station of the country. With the commissioning of the unit, the total installed capacity of NTPC Limited has risen to 27404 MW. Shri Anil Razdan, Secretary, Power, Shri T. Sankaralingam CMD, NTPC, Shri R.C. Shrivastav, Director (HR), Shri K.B. Dubey Director (Projects), Shri J.Jha Regional Executive Director, West and Shri R.P. Gupta GM, NTPC Vindhyachal will also be present on the occasion. This Power Station has been rated as one of the top ten power stations of the country during the year 2005-06. The station has achieved a plant load factor of more than 92 per cent during the year 2006-07. 210 MW Unit (No. 3) of station has created a national record of continuous running for 559 days, during the year 2006-07 recipient of several national awards in the areas of quality, productivity, safety, Vindhayachal station has been accredited with ISO-14001 and ISO-9001 for environment protection and quality management. The foundation stone of NTPC Vindhayachal was laid by Late Prime Minister Smt. Indira Gandhi in the year 1982. The station with 6 units of 210 MW and 4 units of 500 MW is the largest power station of the country. States of Madhya Pradesh, Maharashtra, Chhattisgarh, Gujarat and Union Territories of Goa, Daman, Diu and Dadra Nagar Haveli are the major beneficiaries of the station. NTPC is India's largest power generation company, with 14 coal based, 7 gas based and 4 JV power stations. The company has now grown into a multi location and multi fuel company.

471. (27-4-2007) NEW DELHI : The Minister of Petroleum & Natural Gas returned early today after a successful four nation visit of Syria, Algeria, Egypt and Iran. The visit was marked by the highest level diplomatic parleys to explore opportunities for oil PSUs in upstream, mid and down streams of the petroleum sector as part of securing participation in assets/business opportunities towards larger national goal of ensuring enhanced energy security for the country. The highlight of the visit was meetings with top leadership of these countries including Presidents of Iran, Egypt and Algeria and Dy. P.M. of Syria apart from the meeting with Prime Ministers of Egypt & Algeria. The delegation level meetings co-chaired by the visiting Indian Petroleum Minister and his counterparts from various countries identified specific projects and areas of cooperation. Shri Deora was accompanied by Petroleum Secretary Shri M.S. Srinivasan and the CEOs of India's main public sector oil and gas companies namely, Oil & Natural Gas Corporation (ONGC); Indian Oil Corporation (IOC), Gas Authority of India

Limited (GAIL); and, Engineers India Limited (EIL). During his visit, Minister (P&NG) highlighted India's growing hydrocarbon needs to fuel its strong economic growth and pointed out to the synergy that exists between a large energy consuming developing economy like India and the hydrocarbon rich countries like Syria, Algeria, Egypt and Iran. In the course of the visit, Shri Deora delivered messages to the Presidents of Syria, Algeria and Egypt from Dr. Manmohan Singh, Prime Minister of India. Arriving in Syria on April 18, Shri Deora met the Deputy Prime Minister Mr. Abdullah Dardari and held delegation level talks with his counterpart Mr. Sufian Al-Alao, Minister of Petroleum & Mineral Resources of Syria at Damascus in which a number of projects and key areas were identified for further enhancing cooperation between the two countries in the hydrocarbon sector spanning exploration & production, refinery modernization and new projects, development of gas infrastructure including city gas projects, marketing, training of Syrian technicians and engineers, etc. Syria agreed to work closely together with Indian companies, and to consider the request of Indian side for allocating blocks on preferential basis and provide information to Indian companies about 7 off-shore blocks proposed for bidding later this year. ONGC expressed interest in participating in upcoming blocks jointly with Syrian Petroleum Company (SPC). The company extended offer of expert assistance to SPC for increased oil recovery/enhanced oil recovery (IOR/EOR) from their heavy oil fields to help in arresting Syrian oil production decline. Syria agreed to favourably look into ONGC's request for extending existing licence of the blocks in which ONGC has a share through the Al Furat Petroleum Company, for another 10 years.

472. (27-4-2007) NEW DELHI : The Anthropological Survey of India under its monumental research project People of India not only prepares a comprehensive list of the existing communities in India, but also studied the Human surface of India. There are 4635 communities in India which includes the Banjara community. The Union Ministry of Culture is already taking various steps to preserve the ethnic culture of Banjaras through the Anthropological Survey of India and the Indira Gandhi Rashtriya Manav Sangrahalaya (IGRMS). The Anthropological Survey of India have published the report on different communities including various scheduled castes, scheduled tribes, other backward classes and nomadic communities from different parts of the country with special reference to their lifestyle, culture, language and handicrafts including that of the Banjaras. The Indira Gandhi Rashtriya Manav Sangrahalaya has already carried out field work and developed a very important collection of the material culture and handicrafts of the Banjara style. The zonal Anthropological Museum in collaboration with the Shilpgram at Udaipur, Rajasthan has established one of the best museums having rich collection of the artifacts on the different communities of Rajasthan including the Banjaras. The I.G.R.M.S. has organized a number of presentations pertaining to crafts of Banjara people. The museum would further expand its activities based on the culture of this community in future years.

473. (27-4-2007) NEW DELHI : Gen Oscar Izurieta Ferrer, Commander-in-Chief of the Chilean Army is visiting to India from 29 Apr. to 03 May 07. He reciprocates the visit of the Army Chief, Gen JJ Singh in May, last year. Defence cooperation as a part of defence diplomacy, is an important tool to enhance national security in consonance with other key players. Of late, countries from South America have evinced keen interest in interacting with the Indian Army, especially due to the reputed training institutions and rich operational experience of the Indian Army, in conventional and sub-conventional warfare and UN Peace Keeping. This visit by the Chilean Chief carries forward the impetus given by the COAS' visit earlier and will open the doors for exchanging each other's expertise in respective areas of core competence. He will be visiting an Armoured Division, the Para Brigade, the National Defence College and the Siachen Battle School. In addition, Gen Izurieta will also be making Office Calls on the Defence Minister and the Service Chiefs. Discussions on enhancing defence cooperation in the fields of training/ courses, UN Peace Keeping, mountain warfare, sports and adventure activities and defence industry cooperation are likely during this visit. Recognizing the growing convergence and mutual concerns of both nations, an Indian Defence Attache has been deputed in Santiago last year. Chile too, is actively considering posting a resident Defence Attache in Delhi. The Attaches will further assist in coordinating and executing the agreed activities of defence cooperation.

474. (27-4-2007) NEW DELHI : The Department of Food & Public Distribution is closely monitoring the wheat procurement in Rabi Marketing Season in 2006-07. A record wheat crop of 737 lakh tonnes has been estimated this year and harvesting of wheat in Punjab and Haryana is in full swing. The Government agencies have procured 73.75 lakh tonnes of wheat for central pool. In Punjab and Haryana, the Government agencies have procured more than 90% of mandi arrivals. Even though the arrivals are slow than normal due to manual harvesting of wheat crop, the Government agencies have procured more than 90% of arrivals. There is no proposal before the Government for any bonus over and above the bonus of Rs. 100 quintal announced by the Government of India in 2007-08. Procurement by Government agencies will continue as long as farmers bring wheat to mandis and procurement centres. In States having weak mandi infrastructure like Uttar Pradesh and Bihar, FCI and State agencies have been directed to procure wheat through cooperative societies and sub-agents.

475. (27-4-2007) NEW DELHI : "April is the cruelest month..." might have been said by T.S. Eliot to begin his long poem Wasteland but in Matheran April is not only cool and soothing but also provides livelihood to many. Matheran 2637 feet high and just about 110 kms. away, with a population of about six thousand is the hill station located on the Western Ghats range about 120 kms. from Pune. Its proximity to the two cities makes it a popular week end gataway. Matheran in Marathi means "forest on top". It is famous for it's two feet mini narrow gauge heritage train from Neral Junction to Matheran.

476. (27-4-2007) NEW DELHI : The West Bengal Minister for Irrigation and Waterways Shri Subhas Naskar and Finance Minister, Dr. Asim Dasgupta called on Union Minister of Water Resources, Prof. Saifuddin Soz here today and discussed with him various issues related to river and water development projects in West Bengal and sought Central support and assistance for their speedy implementation for augmentation of irrigation potential in the State. Some of the major projects and problems that came up for detailed discussion were the concrete constructions on both sides of river Baghirathi in the district of Murshidabad; the Ganga and Padma erosion problems; the extension of jurisdiction of Farakka Barrage on Ganga-Padma Main-Stem and Teesta Barrage Project etc. The Ministers pleaded for declaring Teesta as a national project. Prof. Soz assured them of full Central support in various river and irrigation projects now under implementation in the State. As for Teesta river, the Union Minister told the visiting Ministers that the Centre was considering to determine a sound criteria declaring some rivers in the country as National River Projects for conservation and overall development.

477. (27-4-2007) NEW DELHI : Expert group to finalise rules for implementation of the Scheduled Tribes and other Traditional Fest Dwellers (Recognition of Forest Rights) Act, met today and had intensive discussion on various issues for operationalising the provisions. The group consisting of representatives from the field of environment, forest, wildlife, anthropology, tribal welfare and Central and State Ministries already had five meetings in this regard. The 29 members group headed by Shri S.R. Sankaran, former Rural Development Secretary to the Government of India also had consultations with the State Governments at Hyderabad, Pune, Ranchi, New Delhi and Shillong last month in order to take care of State-specific differences while framing the rules. It is now in an advanced stage of preparation of the draft rules and is expected to finalize the same shortly. The expert group was set up on 12th February, 07 and was asked to submit its recommendations within three months. The Scheduled Tribes and other Traditional Forest Dwellers (Recognition of Forest Rights) Act, 2006 passed by the Parliament during the last session and notified on 2nd January, 2007, represents a major paradigm shift in approach towards addressing the concerns for providing tenurial security, livelihood and traditional rights to the Scheduled Tribes and other Traditional dwellers who have been living in forests for generations without a legal protection. The Act recognizes and vests the forest rights and occupation in forest land in forest dwelling Scheduled Tribes and other traditional forest dwellers who have been residing in such forests for generations but whose rights could not be recorded and to provide for a framework for recording the forest rights so vested and the nature of evidence required for such recognition and vesting in respect of forest land.

478. (27-4-2007) NEW DELHI : To a question on the OBC issue and what is the Congress Party's stand, Shri Abhishek Singhvi said that the case is subjudice and the case does not have any connection with the issue of creamy layer. The next hearing is pending in the Supreme Court and our stand remains unchanged as far as Supreme Court is concerned. To a question on the large number of fake encounters taking place all over the country, Shri Singhvi said that let us be very clear that fake encounters have all been condemned. But unless you realize the gravity of the situation in Gujarat on this issue, you will be in fact diluting it. Let us take J&K for a moment. J&K is a high security, high sensitive state but even there, the moment there is any allegations of this kind, it is considered as a serious allegation and immediate enquiry and action is taken. In the North East, there is system for it of immediate enquiry but Gujarat is very different because it is obvious that it is state sponsored, it is state supported at least with direct or indirect means and support by different agencies of the state, to top it all the orders are from the Court. To a question that Mr. Sheikh himself was a criminal, Shri Singhvi said that let us be very clear that nobody is proclaiming the guilt or innocence of Mr. Sheikh. He can and should be punished if he is convicted. But now Modi's Government and Home Minister made sure that he is beyond punishment. To a question on the comments made by Azam Khan, Shri Singhvi said that those who make comments like that, dignify and exemplify the content of what they are commenting about. Obviously, such inhabitants of the gutter do not deserve a reply. To a question whether the Congress would like to move the Election Commission against Mr. Azam Khan, Shri Singhvi said that we do not want to give slightest importance to such insignificant beings.

479. (27-4-2007) NEW DELHI : The interest rates on advances have been deregulated by Reserve Bank of India (RBI) and banks are free to fix the rate of interest themselves with the approval of their Boards. Banks have been advised to fix their Bench-mark Prime Lending Rate (BPLR) after taking into account cost of funds, transaction cost, risk factor, margin and other overhead expenses. However, as per Model Education Loan Scheme, 2004, the banks are to charge interest on education loan up to Rs.4 lakh at BPLR and above Rs.4 lakh at BPLR+1 per cent. This information was given by Shri Pawan Kumar Bansal, Minister of State for Finance in reply to a question raised by Shri N.N. Krishnadas in Lok Sabha today.

480. (27-4-2007) NEW DELHI : Indian Banks' Association (IBA) has circulated the Model Education Loan Scheme, 2004 to all Scheduled Commercial Banks for implementation. The Scheme provides broad guidelines indicating, inter-alia, courses eligible for education loan. The specific complaints, if any, regarding non-sanctioning of education loan by banks for eligible courses to eligible and deserving candidates/students are investigated and remedial measures are taken. Information available from 15 Public Sector Banks indicates that banks are extending education loans to all eligible students applying for recognized courses including Nursing. This information was given by Shri Pawan Kumar Bansal, Minister of State for Finance in reply to a question raised by Shri A.V. Bellarmin in Lok Sabha today.

481. (27-4-2007) NEW DELHI : The Sixth Central Pay Commission has commissioned a study by Indian Institute of Management, Ahmedabad to examine the correct basis of pay increases and their relation, if any, to performance and productivity of the employees and examine the possibility of evolving a direct co-relation between performance related pay and delivery of services. The Commission has not given its recommendations for providing interim relief to Central Government employees. This information was given by Shri Pawan Kumar Bansal, Minister of State for Finance in reply to a question raised by Dr. M. Jagannath in Lok Sabha today.

482. (27-4-2007) NEW DELHI : A number of persons made multiple applications for PAN, giving particulars differently, resulting in issue of multiple PANS. With a view to cleaning the PAN database, it was decided to undertake an exercise of de-duplication of PAN. No case of harassment during the de-duplication exercise has come to government's notice. However, in a few cases difficulties in the issue of refunds due to duplication of PAN have been noted. Field offices of the Income Tax Department have been directed to complete de-duplication exercise in a time-bound manner. Further, the software in this regard has been enhanced so as to speed up the de-duplication process. This information was given by Shri S.S. Palanimanickam, Minister of State for Finance in reply to a question raised by Shri Chengara Surendran in Lok Sabha today.

483. (27-4-2007) NEW DELHI : The National Slum Development Programe include slum development activities such as upgradation and construction of new houses, water supply, sewerage, sanitation, solid waste management, drains, storm water drains, connecting roads, electrification, community halls, parks/open space development and provision of other related civic amenities. Monitoring is undertaken by State Level Steering Committee and Nodal Agencies. Periodic reports are also sent to the Government of India. Building Material Technology Promotion Council (BMTPC) is entrusted with the monitoring work at the central level in the Ministry. This was stated by the Minister of State (Independent Charge) for Housing and Urban Poverty Alleviation, Kumari Selja in a reply to a question by Shri G.M. Siddeswara in Lok Sabha today.

484. (27-4-2007) NEW DELHI : According to recent report of the Planning Commission based on National Sample survey Organization (61st round) data, the number of urban poor living below poverty line in urban areas has gone up between 1993-94 and 2004-05. This was stated by the Minister of State (Independent Charge) for Housing and Urban Poverty Alleviation, Kumari Selja in a reply to a question by Shri Balashowry Vallabhaneni in Lok Sabha today. She further stated that as per 2001 census report, the percentage of slum population to the total population of cities/towns reporting slums is 23.1%. Jawaharlal Nehru National Urban Renewal Mission (JNNURM) launched in December, 2005 aims at improvement in housing and provision of civic amenities in slums. The Basic Services to the Urban Poor (BSUP) programme aims at providing housing and basic amenities to the poor in 63 Mission cities. Similarly, programmes in non-mission cities are addressed by Integrated Housing & Slum Development

Programme (IHSDP). Under programmes for capacity building for urban poverty alleviation, NGOs are involved by National Resource Centres on Urban poverty and slums in capacity building of self help groups, community organizations, civil society groups etc. in community development, gender development, strengthening the voice of the poor etc., she added.

485. (27-4-2007) NEW DELHI : The Third Nirmal Gram Puraskar (NGP) distribution function will be held on May 4 at the Ambedkar Stadium in New Delhi. The President of India will be the chief guest at the awards ceremony. He is participating in the programme for the third consecutive time since 2004. The number of award winners has risen from 40 in 2005, 769 in 2006 to over 4000 in the current year. Applications for NGP were received from 9,745 Gram Panchayats, 120 Block Panchayats and 2 District Panchayats from 24 states during the year 2006-07. The applications received were initially scrutinized in the Department of Drinking Water Supply, Ministry of Rural Development, and then those were verified by Independent Monitoring Agencies in the field. Based on the recommendations received from the independent evaluators, the National Committee on Nirmal Gram Puraskar has selected 4,437 Gram Panchayats and Block Panchayats from 22 States for awards for the year 2007. The NGP has created a country wide enthusiasm and a competitive spirit amongst Gram Panchayats. As part of the Total Sanitation Campaign (TSC), the Nirmal Gram Puraskar (NGP) was announced on 2nd October 2003, as a national award instituted to honour, facilitate and encourage those Panchayati Raj Institutions, which have attained total sanitation in their respective area. A 'Nirmal Gram' is an "open defecation free" village with all houses, schools and anganwadis having sanitary toilets and community is aware of the importance of maintaining hygiene, good sanitation and clean environment. The NGP contributed in accelerating the pace of the Total Sanitation Campaign (TSC), which has been in operation since 1999. The TSC is currently operational in 572 districts with an outlay of Rs. 11,375 crore in which Central, State and community contributions are Rs.7,092 crore, Rs. 2,505 crore and Rs. 1,778 crore respectively. With sustained efforts and Government-people partnership, 3.19 crore household toilets, 9,997 community sanitary complexes, 3.57 lakh school toilets and 1.10 lakh Aganwadi toilets have been constructed and 6,856 Production Centres/ Rural Sanitary Marts (RSMs) have been set up in Gram Panchayats under TSC till March 2007. Under the TSC scheme, the target is to provide all household access to sanitary toilets by 2012. India has committed itself to achieving the 55% coverage of rural households by 2015 as per the Millennium Development Goals, it is, however, estimated that the target may be achieved earlier, by the end of 2009.

486. (27-4-2007) NEW DELHI : The Ministry of Rural Development has sanctioned Rs. 70.17 crore to the State Government of Rajasthan towards part payment of first instalment of funds against the provisional allocation of Rs.421 crore made for the Government of Rajasthan under Accelerated Rural Water

Supply Programme (Normal) of Rajiv Gandhi National Drinking Water Mission, during the year 2007-08. The balance amount of first instalment will be released after receipt of AG report for 2004-05. Up to 15 per cent of funds released under this sanction may be utilized for Operation & Maintenance and up to 5 per cent of funds may be spent for taking sustainability measures. States have been requested to delegate powers for management of Rural Water Supply Schemes through the Panchayati Raj Institutions (PRIs) as per the Constitution of India. As such Operation and Maintenance of the completed RWS Scheme should be transferred to the PRIs. No expenditure shall be incurred on taking water quality problems form the present release, as there is a separate allocation for the purpose. This release is being made for execution/completion of schemes to provide safe drinking water facilities to rural habitations and schools under the Centrally Sponsored ARWSP. Priorities set in ARWSP guidelines and through other instructions issued from time to time shall be followed for coverage of rural habitations and rural schools.

487. (27-4-2007) NEW DELHI : In reply to a question whether District Rural Development Agencies (DRDAs) are receiving funds directly from Union Government, Rural Development Minister, Dr. Raghuvansh Prasad Singh has said that DRDAs) are receiving 75% of the funds directly from the Union Government and 25% of funds are received from the State Governments and the funds are disbursed as per the approved standard accounting procedure. In response to another question whether in many states DRDAs have been placed under Zila Parishads, the Minister replied that the Guidelines of the "DRDA Administration" Scheme issued by Ministry of Rural Development do not prescribe merger of DRDAs with the Zila Parishads as a general policy. However, under the Guidelines, State Governments have been allowed flexibility to operate the DRDAs as a distinct unit. At present, the DRDAs have been merged with Zila Parishads/Zila Panchayats and a separate "DRDA Cell" has been created in the States of Madhya Pradesh, Kerala, West Bengal, Chhattisgarh, Karnataka, Maharashtra and Rajasthan.

488. (27-4-2007) NEW DELHI : A focused attention to development of rural infrastructure has been put in place by the Government through a time bound business plan under the name 'Bharat Nirman'. The critical areas of rural infrastructure, namely Irrigation, Rural Drinking Water, Rural Roads, Rural Housing, Rural Electrification, Rural Telephone Connectivity have been identified. Under Irrigation one crore ha. of additional irrigation will be created. Potable drinking water to 55,067 Uncovered Habitations (as per revised assessment), Slipped Back Habitations, Quality Affected Habitations and Rural Schools will be provided under Rural Drinking Water and all villages having a population of 1000 (500 in hilly/tribal areas) with road will be connected under Rural Roads. Under Rural Housing 60 lakh additional houses for the poor will be constructed. Remaining 1.25 lakh villages will be electrified and electricity connection to 2.3 crore households will be offered under Rural Electrification and Telephone Connectivity to remaining 66,822 villages will be given under Rural Telephone Connectivity. The Ministry of Rural Development is implementing three of the six components of Bharat Nirman *i.e.* Rural Roads, Rural Housing and Rural Drinking Water Supply. Since Bharat Nirman is a time bound action plan, the Government has already taken steps to address the issues of capacity of the State Level Agencies for implementing the various components and mobilization of resources. Further, in order to ensure that outlays result into outcomes a strict monitoring and vigilance mechanism has been put in place. The progress on the implementation of the various components of Bharat Nirman is being strictly monitored regularly at different levels with reference to well defined targets. This was stated by the Union Rural Development Minister, Dr. Raghuvansh Prasad Singh in the Lok Sabha today.

489. (27-4-2007) NEW DELHI : In reply to a question whether the Government has drawn up any programme to ensure employment to all by 2010 A.D., Rural Development Minister, Dr. Raghuvansh Prasad Singh said in the Lok Sabha today that in the Approach Paper to the 11th Five Year Plan, it is estimated that the labour force will increase by 65 million over and above the present backlog of 35 million unemployed on a typical day during the 11th Plan if it grows at the present rate and the female participation rate also rises at the pace observed during the period 1999-2005. He further informed that creation of 70 million new work opportunities has been included as one of the monitorable socio-economic targets for the 11th Five Year Plan. A National Rural Employment Guarantee Scheme (NREGS) has already been launched on 2nd February, 2006 in 200 districts of the country with the objective to enhance livelihood security in rural areas by providing at least 100 days of guaranteed wage employment in a Financial Year to every household whose adult members volunteer to do unskilled manual work. Another 113 districts have been notified under the scheme during the current financial year and 17 districts from Uttar Pradesh are to be notified after the State Legislative Assembly elections. This scheme is to be extended to all the districts of the country by 2009-10, the Minister also informed.

490. (27-4-2007) NEW DELHI : With effect from 1.3.2007, a duty of Rs. 300 per metric tonne has been imposed on exports of iron ore, all sorts. Exports of iron ore during March 2007 are more or less at par with the estimates. It is, however, too early to comment on whether exports of iron ore will be affected by this levy. Tax issues are decided by the Government taking into account various factors including revenue effect, need to preserve natural resources and profitability of the relevant industry. Government will take appropriate action, if considered necessary, after taking into account all relevant considerations. Shri S.S. Palanimanickam, Minister of State for Finance gave this information in reply to a question raised by Shri Suresh Kalmadi in Lok Sabha today.

491. (27-4-2007) NEW DELHI : PFC has released Bid Bonds of Rs. 120 Crs each received from the six bidders for the 4000 MW Mundra Ultra Mega Power

Project which was transferred to M/s. Tata Power Company Ltd. on 22.4.2007. The return of the Bid Bonds to Tata Power Company Ltd., Essar Power Ltd., Reliance Energy Gen. Ltd., Sterlite Industries (India) Ltd., Adani Enterprises Ltd. and Larsen & Tourbo Ltd. was announced immediately after M/s. Tata Power Company furnished the Performance Guarantee of Rs. 300 crs. PFC which is following up for Coastal Regulatory Zone (CRZ) clearance, forest clearance and acceptance of tariff by CERC announced that CRZ clearance has been accorded by MoEF on 25.4.2007. It is learnt that Forest Clearance which has been stuck up in the absence of constitution of the Forest Advisory Committee (FAC), is also likely to be resolved as Supreme Court has given time to MoEF upto 27.4.2007 to give its views on the inclusion of Independent Environmentalists on the Committee. Formal acceptance of tariff by CERC is also expected to be issued in a couple of weeks.

492. (27-4-2007) NEW DELHI : The Prime Minister Dr. Manmohan Singh honoured 45 workers with 33 prestigious Prime Minister's Shram Awards for the year 2004 here today at a function to inaugurate the 41st session of Indian labour Conference. They were decorated with Shram Bhushan, Shram Vir/Shram Veerangana and Shram Shree/Shram Devi awards in recognition of their distinguished performances, innovative abilities, outstanding contribution in the field of productivity and exhibition of exceptional courage and presence of mind. These workers are employed in the Departmental Undertakings & Public Sector Undertakings of the Central and State Governments and Private Sector Units employing 500 workers or more. Felicitating the awardees, Dr. Manmohan Singh said that their achievement should act as an inspiration for others to also work hard for the welfare of the people and the progress of our nation. The Private Sector, for the first time, has been brought within the ambit of Prime Minister's Shram Awards' Scheme. Also, the number of awards has been increased from 17 to 33. 29 awardees are from the public sector while 16 workers belong to the private sector. Some of them have bagged the awards jointly. No nomination was found suitable for the top most prestigious honour Shram Ratna Award. Shri S.P. Gupta, Chargeman in BHEL, Haridwar. was conferred with the second highest Shram Bhushan Award. It carries a cash award of Rs. 1,00,000/-and a 'Sanad'. Fifteen Shram Vir/Shram Veerangana awardees included two women workers who have been awarded Shram Veerangana Awards. Each award carries a cash prize of Rs. 60,000/-and a 'Sanad'. The Shram Vir/Shram Veerangana Awardees are: Shri Satyawan Nayak, Bhilai Steel Plant, Bhilai; Shri M. Subramanian, BHEL, Tiruchirapalli; Shri M. Sudhakar Reddy, BHEL, Hyderabad; a team comprising S/Shri Bihari Lal Dhruw & Sunil Kumar Soni (jointly), from BHEL, Bhopal; Shri Mahi Pal Singh, BHEL, Haridwar; a team comprising S/Shri A.K. Kerketta & Trilochan Maharana (jointly), from Bhilai Steel Plant, Bhilai; Smt. Valluripalli Vijayalakshmi, DRDL, Hyderabad, DRDO (all from the public sector); Shri Kartik Kumar Mandal, TISCO, Jamshedpur; Shri Birajdar Prakash Vishvanath, Bajaj Auto Ltd., Aurangabad; Shri Chavan Subhash Ramdas, Bajaj Auto Ltd., Pune; Shri

Kadam Vijay Bhikaji, Larsen & Toubro, Mumbai; Shri Sushil Kumar, Tata Motors Ltd., Lucknow; Shri Ram Kailash, Hindalco Ltd., Sonebhadra; Shri Mahadik Sampatrao Bhagawan, Bajaj Auto Ltd., Aurangabad; Mrs. Jaswant Kaur, TISCO, Jamshedpur (all from the private sector). Seventeen Workers were be conferred with Shram Shree/Shram Devi Awards. Among them are four women workers who were decorated with Shram Devi Awards. Each of these awards carries a cash prize of Rs. 40,000/-and a 'Sanad'. The Shram Shree/Shram Devi Awardees are, a team comprising S/Shri Murugan G., Ramachandra T., Chandrashekar H., and Mylarappa H.,(jointly) from BHEL, Bangalore; Shri D. Murugasatasaram, BHEL, Tiruchirapalli & Shri K. Rajendran, BHEL, Bangalore (jointly); Shri Mohammed Dastagir, Electronic Corporation of India Ltd., Hyderabad; a team comprising S/Shri Faheem Mohammed, Abhay Deshpande, Malkeet Singh, Rajesh Kumar Besra and Nagendra Kumar Yadav, (jointly) from Bhilai Steel Plant, Bhilai; a team comprising S/Shri T. Kamaraj and G. Pichu, (jointly) from BHEL, Tiruchirapalli; Shri K. Rajashekar and Shri T. Padmanabhachary, (jointly) from SAIL, Bhadravati; Shri Rajendra Vishnu Kasar, Rashtriya Chemicals and Fertilizers Ltd., Mumbai; Smt. V. Bhuvaneswari, Advance System Laboratory, DRDO, Hyderabad; Smt. Ravita Singh, Indian Telephone Industries, Mankapur (all from the public sector); Shri Suresh Prasad, Hindalco Ltd., Sonebhadra; Shri Hari Prakash Pandey, Jindal Steel and Power Ltd., Raigarh; Shri Mahesh Yashwantrao Sewlikar, Bajaj Auto Ltd., Aurangabad; Shri B. Sanmukh Rao, Indian Aluminium Co. Ltd., Orissa; Shri Rafiqulla Saheb Shaikh, Larsen & Toubro Ltd., Mumbai; Shri Dhiren Kumar Maher, Tata Chemicals Ltd., Gujarat; Mrs. Domini Murmu, TISCO, Jamshedpur; Mrs. Asha Hansda, TISCO, Jamshedpur (all from the private sector). The function was attended by the Union Labour Minister, Shri Oscar Fernandes, the Union Minister for Heavy Industries and Public Enterprises, Shri Santosh Mohan Dev, State Labour Ministers, representative of trade unions and industry and others.

493. (27-4-2007) NEW DELHI : The Prime Minister, Dr. Manmohan Singh, has called for creating an environment in which both Government and Private sector are encouraged to invest for promoting new employment. Seeking help of trade unions and business leaders in this regard, Dr. Singh said that by providing "an environment in which investors feel confident enough to invest, we will be able to generate more gainful employment and promote workers' welfare." Inaugurating the 41st Session of the Indian Labour Conference (ILC) here this morning, the Prime Minister said "I would like our trade union movement to be as committed to the task of generating new employment as it is to the responsibility of protecting the interests of those already working...... Our system of industrial relations should promote both growth of productivity and a fairer sharing of the gains resulting from rising productivity." He assured that the Government would work with trade unions and industry to ensure twin objectives of employment generation and workers' welfare. Referring to vital role of industrial modernisation and technical change in progress of countries like China, the Prime Minister said that the country has to be receptive to technological change and imperative of modernisation to remain competitive in an increasingly integrated global economy. At the same time, the Prime Minister added, the cost of modernisation and change should not be borne unduly by the working class. He said "It is our solemn duty to protect the interests of workers and of all those seeking work even as we manage change.......... Our industrial relations policy must be sensitive both to the need to absorb new technologies and ensure competitiveness of our firms as well as the need to create new employment opportunities and protect the interests of the working people." The Prime Minister said that the challenge before us is to increase the skilled workforce from the present 5% to about 50%, the norm in developed countries. He urged industry to involve itself in every aspect of skill development so that skill creation is demand driven and relevant to market opportunities. Earlier in his presidential address, the Minister of State for Labour and Employment (Independent Charge) Shri Oscar Fernandes said that the Government is working on setting up of a "National Mission for Skills". He said a Task Force on Skill Development under the Chairmanship of Dr. Tarun Das, Chief Mentor, CII, has been set up to recommend measures to meet the requirement of skilled manpower during the 11th Plan and beyond. Shri Fernandes urged the Conference to take a view on amending the Contract Labour (Regulation & Abolition) Act, 1970 to facilitate "outsourcing or prohibiting employment of Contract Labour in core activities and to mandate automatic absorption of existing contract labour." He said this is necessary in view of the diametrically opposite views held by the trade unions and the employers' organisations on dealing with contract labour issue. Referring to the strengthening of labour enforcement machinery, Shri Fernandes said that our ultimate oal is to minimize violation of labour laws.

494. (27-4-2007) NEW DELHI : The Government has proposed to introduce new schemes for Agro & Rural Industries for overall development of rural population. The new schemes are : Workshed-cum-Housing Scheme for Khadi Weavers and Artisans: This is a scheme exactly identical to the one under implementation in the Ministry of Textiles. Scheme for enhancement of productivity and competitiveness of Khadi Industry and Artisans: This aims to provide financial assistance to 200 of the 'A plus' and 'A' category Khadi institutions in a Public Private Partnership mode to increase value addition to Khadi product, readymade garments, muslin khadi, setting up of common facility centre, need based dying and printing facilities besides ensuring better wages to artisans along with skill upgradation. Package for developing infrastructure of Khadi institutions including nursing fund for weak institutions: This scheme envisages replacement of looms and charkhas for increasing production of khadi and to expand employment base. The scheme involves renovation of sales outlets also. Restructuring of Rural Employment Generation Programme: This scheme is going to be a comprehensive proposal which seeks to merge the major employment generation schemes viz. Pradhan Mantri Rozgar Yojana and Rural Employment Generation Programme. Rejuvenation, modernisation and technology upgradation for Coir Industry: The

Scheme has two components. First is the rejuvenation and modernisation part. Increasing the utilisation of husk, better conversion rate of husk into coir products and providing additional employment to around 50,000 workers per year are some of the targets. The second part is to promote 5 mega clusters, one each in Kerala, Tamil Nadu, Andhra Pradesh, Karnataka and Orissa. This information was given by the Minister of Small Scale Industries and Agro & Rural Industries, Shri Mahabir Prasad in a written reply to a question in Rajya Sabha today.

495. (27-4-2007) NEW DELHI : There is no specific reports to suggest that Indian small scale industries as a whole are affected due to competition from big industries and multi-national corporations (MNCs). However, from the fact that the annual rate of growth of production of the SSI sector has so far been consistently higher than that of the country's industrial sector as a whole, it can be inferred that the SSI sector has generally been able to face the competition in the market, including that from the big industries and MNCs. The Government has been following a policy of progressive de-reservation of items from the SSI list. Review of the list of such reserved items is a continuous process, during which creation of opportunities for higher investment, facilitating technological upgradation, improving quality, promoting exports and achieving economies of scale in manufacturing the said items are kept in mind. Allowing domestic competition to check large-scale imports of such reserved items is also an issue considered by the Government. To enhance the competitiveness of the SSI units vis-a-vis the big industries and MNCs, the Government has put in place several measures, which include assistance for technological upgradation, accessing markets, improved infrastructure, better availability of credit, facilities for training and capacity building of entrepreneurs, etc. This information was given by the Minister of Small Scale Industries and Agro & Rural Industries, Shri Mahabir Prasad in a written reply to a question in Rajya Sabha today.

496. (27-4-2007) NEW DELHI : The National Company Law Tribunal (NCLT) and the National Company Law Appellate Tribunal (NCLAT) have not been constituted as yet since the provisions of the Companies Act, 1956 consequent to the Companies (Second) Amendment Act, 2002 relating to setting up of the NCLT/NCLAT faced a legal challenge, and the matter is sub-judice on account of a Special Leave Petition (SLP) filed by the Central Government in the Supreme Court, following a ruling by the Madras High Court in the matter. Therefore, no time schedule for setting up of NCLT/NCLAT can be stated at present. This information was given by Shri Prem Chand Gupta, Minister of Company Affairs in reply to the questions raised by Shri Kuldeep Bishnoi in Lok Sabha today.

497. (27-4-2007) NEW DELHI : At present there are 4 New Line, 6 Gauge Conversion, 13 Doubling ongoing projects in North Eastern Railway. The projects are being progressed as per availability of resources. Delay in land acquisition, adverse law & order condition and failure of contractors are affecting the progress of works. A number of initiatives have been taken for generating additional resources through Public Private Partnership, cost sharing by State Government, funding through Ministry of Defence and National Projects etc. Funds have also been allocated through increased internal resource generation. At present, the internet website of North Eastern Railway is working satisfactorily through Railway's internet *i.e.* Railnet, the website address is www.ner.railnet.gov.in. The North Eastern Railway's website is also planned to be hosted on Government owned Centre for Railway Information System (CRIS) server. This information was given by the Minister of State for Railways, Shri R.Velu in a written reply to a question in the Rajya Sabha today

498. (27-4-2007) NEW DELHI : Railways do not have any surplus land. Railways have however 44,894 hectare of vacant land. Till such time, the land is required by Railways for its own operational use, the same is put to various short term uses like commercial licensing, plantation, Grow More Food scheme, etc. In addition where potential exists, commercial development of land will be undertaken through Rail Land development Authority (RLDA). By way of commercial utilization of Railway Land, Railways are expected to earn Rs. 500-Rs.600 core annually in the next two financial years. During the financial year 2006-07, (upto February, 2007) Railways has realized Rs. 307 crore approximately from land utilization. This information was given by the Minister of State for Railways, Shri R.Velu in a written reply to a question in the Rajya Sabha today

499. (27-4-2007) NEW DELHI : Jammu-Udhampur project has already been commissioned. Work is in progress on Udhampur-Srinagar-Baramulla project where overall progress is about 45 per cent. On this project, Kakapore-Budgam has been completed and Udhampur-Katra and balance on Qazigund-Baramulla are targeted for completion during 2007-08. Target for Katra-Qazigund section is under review in view of different geological conditions, adverse working conditions, forestry clearances and construction of bridges/tunnels involved. This information was given by the Minister of State for Railways, Shri R.Velu in a written reply to a question in the Rajya Sabha today.

500. (27-4-2007) NEW DELHI : The Company Law Board has a sanctioned strength of 9 Members including the Chairman and the Vice-Chairman. Presently, 4 Members, including the Chairman and the Vice-Chairman, are in position. The Government has already initiated the process of filling up two more posts in the CLB. This information was given by Shri Prem Chand Gupta, Minister of Company Affairs in reply to the questions raised by Shri Kuldeep Bishnoi in Lok Sabha today.

501. (27-4-2007) NEW DELHI : It is proposed to introduce Narasapur-Tirupati link service in conjunction with Machchilipatnam-Tirupati train. There is no proposal for introduction of superfast train between New Delhi-Secunderabad and between Visakhapatnam-Chennai. This information was given by the Minister of State for Railways, Shri R.Velu in a written reply to a question in the Rajya Sabha today.

502. (27-4-2007) NEW DELHI : The Government has received the Report of the Committee headed by Shri O.P.Vaish on Streamlining Prosecution Mechanism under the Companies Act, 1956 on 19.10.2005. The Report examines the types of cases filed under various provisions of the Companies Act, 1956 before the Courts and makes suggestions for expediting their disposal. The Report has been examined and instructions issued to the field offices of the Ministry for follow up of cases filed in relevant courts as per provisions of law. It is expected that such follow up would enable expeditious disposal of the cases in question. This information was given by Shri Prem Chand Gupta, Minister of Company Affairs in reply to the questions raised by Shri Braja Kishore Tripathy in Lok Sabha today.

503. (27-4-2007) NEW DELHI : With a view to improve dispensation of unreserved tickets in rural areas, a Gramin Ticket Booking Sevak (GTBS) scheme has been launched as a pilot project on East Central Railway. Gramin Ticket Booking Sevaks are authorized to collect Rs.0.50 per ticket from the passengers for the service provided by them. This scheme has not yet been extended to South East Central Railway. This information was given by the Minister of State for Railways, Shri R.Velu in a written reply to a question in the Rajya Sabha today.

504. (27-4-2007) NEW DELHI : This is further to our communications (No. F.14-40/2007-TS.H. dated the 5th April, 2007 and the 19th April, 2007). You (All Central Educational Institutions, as per list) are aware that the Hon'ble Supreme Court of India has by an Interim Order of the 29th March, 2007 stayed the operation of the Central Educational Institutions (Reservation in Admission) Act, 2006 so far as it relates to Section 6 thereof for the OBC Category; and the matter is now posted for hearing on the 8th May, 2007. In the light of the above, the offer of admissions for the ensuing academic session in Central Educational Institutions shall, until further communication, be limited to the approved intake that existed during the academic session 2006-07 as per the policy of reservation prevailing for that session. It is further clarified that no offers of admission shall be made until further communication, in respect of seats that are proposed to be expanded during the ensuing academic session. This issues with the approval of the Competent Authority.

505. (27-4-2007) NEW DELHI : In order to promote employment, the Prime Minister, Dr. Manmohan Singh has urged the trade unions and business leaders to create an environment in which both Government and the private sector are encouraged to invest. In his Inaugural Address at the 41st Session of Indian Labour Conference, here today, Dr. Singh observed that "if we can provide an environment in which investors feel confident enough to invest, we will be able to generate more gainful employment and promote also workers welfare." The Prime Minister stressed the need to increase the skilled labour force from about 5% at present to about 50%, which is the norm in developed countries. He declared that the Government would work with trade unions and industry to strengthen labour laws and to ensure that the twin objectives of employment generation and labour welfare are met. Dr. Singh gave away Shram Awards at the function which was attended by the Union Labour Minister, Shri Oscar Fernandes, the Union Minister for Heavy Industries and Public Enterprises, Shri Santosh Mohan Dev, State Labour Ministers, representatives of trade unions and industry and others. Following is the text of the Prime Minister's address on the occasion: "I am very happy to be here at this 41st Session of the Indian Labour Conference. I attach great importance to the deliberations of this conference. I would like this conference to create a climate congenial to good industrial relations in our country. Our Government is committed to working with labour and business communities to create a new era of inclusive and employment oriented economic growth. I urge you all to strengthen our hands in our efforts to speed up the process of social and economic development. I am particularly happy that on this occasion we are presenting the Shram Awards for the year 2004. I offer my warmest greetings and hearty congratulations to all the Award Winners. The Shram Awards recognise exemplary commitment and dedication to work. It is said that successful people are not different from others. They only do things differently. Our award winners today are normal ordinary people who have accomplished extraordinary achievements. Their single minded pursuit of excellence through creativity and hard work should be a source of inspiration to all their colleagues and comrades. These awards are therefore a way of expressing our gratitude and our appreciation. They should inspire others to also work hard for the welfare of our people and the progress of our nation. It is not a coincidence that this year we have chosen to present these Awards at the 41st Session of the Indian Labour Conference. It is our intention to give these Awards in the presence of the tallest leaders of our Trade Union Movement, Distinguished representatives of business and representatives of Central and State Governments. These three arms form the tripartite edifice of the industrial economy of our country and must work together for our nation to move forward. Each one of the three arms should feel proud that we have among our workers and employees exemplary achievers. Let us all celebrate their achievement together since we are all the beneficiaries of our nation's progress.

506. (28-4-2007) NEW DELHI : The Prime Minister, Dr. Manmohan Singh has said that we need a new social compact involving all stakeholders "to launch a nationwide movement of youth in sports". After inaugurating the Indian Olympic Bhawan, here today, Dr. Singh stressed the need to pay much greater attention to athletics and gymnastics, apart from popular games like cricket, football and hockey. He also urged the Indian Olympic Association to work closely with the Government, at the Centre and in the States, and 'unleash a new wave of sports consciousness and sports development.' The President of International Olympic Association Mr. Jacqus Rogge and the President of Indian Olympic Association, Shri Suresh Kalmadi were among those present. Following is the text of the prime Minister's remarks on the occasion. "I am delighted to associate myself with the inauguration of this Olympic Bhavan. I hope this Bhavan will provide a warm home for the hopes and aspirations of our sportspersons. India has been part of the Olympic movement for a long time. Our participation in the Olympic Games has been in consonance with our age old ethos of promoting friendship among people, understanding and peace through sports and the medium of games. The Olympic Games in fact do constitute one of the biggest peace movements in the world. As a country of young people, India has great potential in the world of sports and games. We are yet to fully harness the talent of our youth in this vast field. Especially in the areas of games that figure at the Olympics. Our performances in hockey and other disciplines of sports and games have to improve substantially to enable our sports persons win more Olympic medals. Suresh Kalmadi ji has referred certain financial issues. He has my assurance that our government will do all that is within our power to exploit the vast untapped potential that undoubtedly lies in this area. But it would not proper for me to comment on specific proposals having financial implications.

507. (28-4-2007) KOLKATA: Trinamool Congress leader, Mamata Banerjee, warned the State Government here on Friday against "playing with fire for which it will have to suffer the consequences" in the face of the continuing violence in Nandigram area of the State's Purbo Medinipur district. The patience of those who are being targeted by activists of the Communist Party of India [Marxist] is being stretched and the "State Government will be solely responsible if something untoward occurs", Ms. Banerjee said. "Violence has been raging in the Nandigram area over the past three days and even on Friday there were reports of firing and hurling of bombs by the CPI (M)," she added. "If there is a bloodbath in the area in the future, the Chief Minister will be responsible," she said. Ridiculing Buddhadeb Bhattacharjee's recent appeal to the Opposition to attend an all-party meeting to facilitate the restoration of normality in the area Ms. Banerjee said, "Such appeals are only a charade; he is talking of such meetings even as he is giving his approval to party cadres to fire on innocent people." She repeated her charge that the State Government had been "managing" the Centre and "doing away with all the evidence of victims" of the March 14 police firing at Nandigram. "The police has been directed to assist the CPI (M) cadres in their attack on the people" and the Untied Progressive Alliance government cannot absolve its responsibilities for the developments there "just because it is receiving the support of the CPI (M)." The situation at Nandigram was taking a communal turn with minorities under attack and "the Centre should understand the political implications", Ms. Banerjee said, adding that she would take her agitation to Delhi and stage a demonstration outside the residence of the Prime Minister along with the victims of rape if the Centre continued to remain silent. The State Congress leadership has appealed for peace to be restored in the area to ensure the safety of the people living there.

508. (29-4-2007) NEW DELHI : Central Adoption Resource Agency (CARA) a nodal body of the Union Government in the matters related to rehabilitation of orphan, abandoned and relinquished children in the country has asked the State Governments to take immediate step to put a ban on illegal adoptions of the children. In a letter written to the Chief Ministers the States, Chairman of the CARA, Shri J.K. Mittal has said that it had come to the notice that large number of adoptions are taking place without following the due procedure especially through hospitals/nursing homes or agencies not recognized by the State Governments/CARA and such adoptions are outside the purview of the existing in-country Guidelines, 2004. Citing the Supreme Court's directives in the matter of adoption of children, CARA has said it is mandatory that all nursing homes and hospitals which come across abandoned and destitute children or find such children abandoned in their precincts or otherwise shall immediately give information in regard to the discovery or find of such children to the social welfare department of the concerned Government or the collector of the district for proper and legal rehabilitation of the children. Shri Mittal has said while adoption is considered as the best alternative family rehabilitation for all orphan-abandoned/ surrendered children, all children homes and Child Welfare Committees may be directed to make family preservation efforts, such as; restoration of children to natural parents/guardians, prevention of abandonment on the ground of poverty or gender issues through various measures such as sponsorship and foster care etc. before adoption could be considered as the best alternative for rehabilitation of such children. Chairman of CARA, Shri J.K. Mittal has urged the State Government to initiate a time bound drive to recognize all unregistered agencies for in-country adoption as per the prescribed procedure so that adoptions could carried out legally and through recognized agencies. He has also asked the States to ensure that every child in these agencies is properly accounted for and list of those children which are declared free for adoption, are made available to the concerned State Adoption Cell and/or Adoption Coordinating Agency (ACA). Underlining the importance of due care of children, Shri Mittal has said that all children regardless of race, ethnicity, gender, medical limitations or other conditions deserve permanent loving homes, but only about 3,500 legal adoptions take place in the country annually which is a very small figure in comparison to number of children available for adoption in the country. Therefore, Panchayats and local bodies should be involved to identify orphan and destitute children so that such children can be placed with loving and caring family.

509. (30-4-2007) NEW DELHI : A festival for National Film Development Corporation (NFDC) films for Members of Parliament got underway today. The Minister of Information & Broadcasting and Parliamentary Affairs, Shri P. R. Dasmunsi inaugurated the retrospective wherein eight prominent NFDC films in different languages will be screened. The event opened with the screening of film 'Gandhi' (English) directed by Richard Attenborough. The other films included in the festival are: 'Agantuk' (Bengali), directed by Satyajit Ray, 'Jaane Bhi Do Yaaron' (Hindi), directed by Kundan Shah, 'Swara Mandal' (Hindi), directed by Rajan Khosa, 'Antarjali Yatra' (Bengali), directed by Goutam Ghose, 'Marupakkam'

(Tamil), directed by K. S. Sethu Madhavan, 'Shree 420' (Hindi) directed by Raj Kapoor and 'Mangamma' (Malayalam), directed T. V. Chandran. The screening will continue up to May 18, 2007. Speaking on the occasion, Shri Dasmunsi said that NFDC is being strengthened to play its role as a support base for good cinema. In the past, several film directors got a new lease of life in the career through the support of NFDC and came out with memorable films, he added. Secretary, Ministry of Information & Broadcasting, Smt. Asha Swarup in her remarks said that NFDC is the biggest production house with over 300 films in 15 different Indian languages to its credit. It also has film co-production agreement with 50 international organisations, she said. Members of Parliament from across the political spectrum, besides some members of the cast and crew of the inaugural film were present.

510. (30-4-2007) NEW DELHI : Shri Kamal Nath, Union Minister of Commerce and Industry, has called the market access made available to Indian mangoes recently by US and Japan as a major breakthrough that augurs well for Indian agro product exports. He hoped that Indian mangoes will gain popularity over the South American and Mexican varieties presently available in the US market on account of better taste, aroma and flavour. While giving away the APEDA (Agricultural Processed Food Products Export Development Authority) Annual Export Awards at a function here today, Shri Kamal Nath stated that agro exports are a thrust area for development and promotion. On this occasion, Shri Kamal Nath gave away the Golden Trophy to Allanasons Limited, Mumbai and awarded the silver and bronze trophies and certificates of merit to other exporters. He complemented all awardees for their excellent efforts to promote agro exports. Shri G.K. Pillai, Commerce Secretary and Shri K.S. Money, Chairman, APEDA also addressed the function. The Minister highlighted the need for infusion of new technology and capital in agriculture to enable India to harness the untapped potential in agro exports. "Cold chain infrastructure has been the missing link in the process of agriculture, post-harvest storage and transportation in India. Supply chain from production clusters to the markets needs to be strengthened including grading, pre-cooling, packaging, storage and marketing of fresh farm produce. The organized retail both in fresh and processed food products which has started taking shape in the metros and other large cities needs to be extended to other towns as well. The FDI by leading global players for strengthening the backward linkages and infrastructure including cold chain can provide a boost to processing and help in reducing wastage of fruits and vegetables. This will ensure better returns to the farmers for their produce", Shri Kamal Nath said. Shri Nath highlighted the importance of adhering to food safety and international standards for trading in food products. He complemented APEDA for encouraging the adoption of quality certification systems like ISO and HACCP amongst its registered exporters. "The Government has introduced an integrated food law, which is expected to help in making the Indian food industry more competitive in the global market. It intends to set up a single line of command from the present multi-level and multi-departmental control. There will be a single reference point for all matters relating to food safety and standards, regulations and enforcements", he said. Agro exports constitute about 9.3% of the total merchandise exports of the country. Total agro exports through APEDA in 2005-06 was Rs.17,918 crores compared to Rs.16,828 crore in 2004-05.

511. (30-4-2007) NEW DELHI : A Japanese Delegation led by Minister of Land Infrastructure and Transport Mr. Tetsuzo Fuyushiba called on Tourism & Culture Minister Smt. Ambika Soni here today. During their half-an-hour meeting both the leaders recalled long and traditional relations between India and Japan. The Tourism & Culture Minister Smt. Ambika Soni while mentioning the Indo-Japan Tourism Exchange Year 2007 stressed the need to bring more tourists into each other's country. She said that 90% of the package tour itineraries for Japanese tourists include Delhi-Agra (Taj Mahal)-Jaipur 'Golden Triangle'. Varanasi, Khajuraho, Ajanta and Ellora are the destinations also frequently visited by Japanese tourists. She said India is promoting Buddhist Circuit and a special train is also launched recently to cover major attractions of Buddhist sites in India. She said Japanese tourists can also take advantage of MICE and Golf Tourism in India. Recalling the assistance of JBIC (Japan Bank for International Cooperation) Smt. Soni said Ajanta-Ellora Conservation and Tourism Development Project is being successfully implemented and phased II is expected to be completed by 2009. The total expenditure on the Ajanta-Ellora work during Phase I was to be tune of Rs. 1275 million. For the Phase II development at Ajanta-Ellora the assistance is of Rs. 299.2 crores. She said a loan agreement for the development Buddhist Circuit in Uttar Pradesh was also signed with JBIC. This project will include improving infrastructure at Buddhist sites at Sarnath, Kushinagar, Kapilvastu, Sravasti and Sankisa. She said JBIC officials had expressed their keenness to start the project for infrastructure development on Buddhist sites initially in the states of Sikkim, Ladakh and Madhya Pradesh only. She said that to meet the growing room requirement in India, her Government is making efforts to build Budget Hotels in Public Private Partnership. Mr. Tetsuzo Fuyushiba said his country is committed to promote tourism and cultural ties between the two countries. He said from first of September, 2007 ANA will have seven flights a week to India and with increase of JAL flights from first October 2007, a total number of 12 flights will be available for passengers. Mr. Tetsuzo Fuyushiba urged New Delhi to make visa availability easy for tourists from Japan to India. Japan is one of India's top tourist generating market. In 2005 the figures of tourists arrival from Japan to India reached 102000. Outbound traffic from India to Japan in 2004 was 53000.

512. (30-4-2007) NEW DELHI : Union Finance Minister, Shri P. Chidambaram has approved 23 Foreign Direct Investment proposals recommended by Foreign Investment Promotion Board (FIPB) in its meeting held on 23rd April, 2007. The approval amounts to Rs. 351.4132 crore. The proposals relate to Ministries/ Departments, namely, Agriculture & Cooperation, Commerce, Food Processing

Industries, Information & Broadcasting, Information Technology, Industrial Policy & Promotion, Petroleum & Natural Gas, Railways, Shipping, Small Scale Industries, Telecommunications and Economic Affairs. The major investment proposals pertain to the Ministry/Departments of Commerce, Railways, Telecommunications and Economic Affairs.

513. (30-4-2007) NEW DELHI : In supersession of Press Note [F.No.17/3/97-NRJ] dated 31st l July, 1997 containing the guidelines for Indian Companies for mobilizing foreign investment through issue of preference shares for financial projects / industries, the following guidelines are prescribed with immediate effect: 1. Foreign investment coming as fully convertible preference shares would be treated as part of share capital. This would be included in calculating foreign equity for purposes of sectoral caps on foreign equity, where such caps have been prescribed. 2. Foreign investment coming as any other type of preference shares {non-convertible, optionally convertible or partially convertible) would be considered as debt and shall require conforming to ECB guidelines / ECB caps. Any foreign investment as non-convertible or optionally convertible or partially convertible preference shares as on and up to today (30/4/ 2007) would continue to be outside the sectoral cap till their current maturity. Issue of preference shares of any type would continue to conform to the guidelines of RBI/SEBI and other statutory bodies and would be subject to all statutory requirements.

514. (30-4-2007) NEW DELHI : Dr. Duvvuri Subbarao joined as Secretary, Department of Economic Affairs, Ministry of Finance, this afternoon. He belongs to the 1972 batch of the IAS (AP cadre) and topped the Civil Services Exam 1972. Prior to this assignment, he was working as Secretary to the Prime Minister's Economic Advisory Council. He has been appointed against the vacancy arising out of retirement of Finance Secretary, Shri Ashok Jha, IAS (AP.69) today. Dr. Subbarao has wide experience on issues in public finance and has held important posts in this area for the last 18 years. He has worked as Joint Secretary in the Department of Economic Affairs during 1988-1993 when economic reforms were initiated. He also served as Finance Secretary of Government of Andhra Pradesh 1993-98 and was actively involved in initiating fiscal reforms at the state level. He was lead Economist in the World Bank during 1999-2004 and worked on issues of public finance in countries of Africa and East Asia. While in the World Bank, he task managed a flagship study on decentralization across major countries of East Asia (China, Indonesia, Vietnam, Philippines and Cambodia). Dr. Subbarao studied at IIT Kanpur and was one of the first IIT products to join the civil services. Subsequent to joining the IAS, he did his MS in Economics from Ohio State University (1978) and was a Humphrey Fellow at MIT during 1982-83. He has a Ph. D in Economics from Andhra University.

515. (30-4-2007) NEW DELHI : The Competent Authority has appointed Shri P.K. Chakraborti to the post of Director (Pipelines), Indian Oil Corporation Limited (IOCL), with effect from the date of assumption of charge of the post on or after 1.8.2007 till the date of his superannuation, or until further orders, whichever event occurs earlier. Ministry of Petroleum and Natural Gas New Delhi: Vaisakha 10, 1928/April 30, 2007

516. (30-4-2007) NEW DELHI : The All India Consumer Price Index Number for Industrial Workers (CPI-IW) (base 2001-100) during March 2007 decreased by one point to stand at 127 (one hundred and twenty seven) points. The Rise/ Fall in index varied from centre to centre. The index during March 2007 decreased by 3 points in Sholapur centre. It decreased by 2 points in 8 centres, and 1 point in 17 centres, The index recorded the highest increase of 4 points in Labac Silchar and Siliguri centres. It increased by 3 points in Kodarma centre, by 2 points each in 5 centres and by 1 point in 18 centres. While in the remaining 26 centres the index remained stationary. The decrease of 3 points in Sholapur centre was the outcome of decrease in the prices of Rice, Wheat, Jowar, Arhar Dal, Onion, Garlic, Vegetable & Fruit Items, Electricity Charges etc. The increase of 4 points in Labac-Silchar centre was mainly on account of the rise in the prices of Rice, Fish Fresh, Pan Leaves etc. while in Siliguri centre the increase was mainly due to increase in the prices of Rice, Wheat Atta, Urd Dal, Masur Dal, Mustard Oil, Pork, Chillies Green, Vegetable & Fruit items, Cinema Charges etc.

517. (30-4-2007) NEW DELHI : According to the survey conducted by the National Sample Survey Organization (NSSO) in 2004-05, the total employment in both the organized and the unorganized sectors in the country was 459 million. Of which, 433 million are in the unorganized sector. The number of unorganized workers in urban and rural areas separately and State wise is not presently available. This was stated by the Minister of State (Independent Charge) for Labour and Employment, Shri Oscar Fernandes in written reply in Lok Sabha today.

518. (30-4-2007) NEW DELHI : The issue regarding rate of interest on Employees Provident fund (EPF) deposits has been deliberated upon by the Central Board of Trustees, Employees' Provident Fund in its meetings wherein no consensus was reached with regard to rate of interest. The issue is to be discussed again by the Central Board. The rate of interest on EPF deposits for the years 2003-04 and 2004-2005 was 9.5% whereas for the year 2005-06 it was 8.5%. However, the rate of interest for the years 2006-07 and 2007-08 has not yet been recommended by the Central Board of Trustees, Employees' Provident Fund. The rate of interest to be credited on EPF accounts in any particular year is determined in such a manner that there should be no overdrawal on the Interest Suspense Account as a result of debit thereto of the interest credited to members' accounts. The investments made are monitored by the Central Board and suitable recommendations are made from time-to-time for better return, safety and liquidity. This was stated by the Minister of State (Independent Charge) for Labour and Employment, Shri Oscar Fernandes in written reply in Lok Sabha today.

519. (30-4-2007) NEW DELHI : Over 19.88 lakh beedi workers are getting benefits under the Employees' Provident Fund Scheme, 1952. The Employees' Provident Funds & Miscellaneous Provisions Act, 1952 applies with its own force and the establishments fulfilling the condition of the applicability are required to comply with the provisions of the Act. Special drives are launched from time-to-time for coverage of coverable establishments avoiding compliance. Further compliance of the covered establishments is monitored regularly to ensure that the benefits under the Act and Schemes framed thereunder are extended to all eligible employees. With a view to restrict the activities of unscrupulous elements, strict vigil is kept on the functioning of all offices of Employees' Provident Fund Organisation. A full-fledged grievance redressal machinery already exists in the Organisation to redress grievances of the aggrieved member/employer. Whenever activities of unscrupulous elements are detected, appropriate action *e.g.* lodging complaints, disciplinary action etc. is taken against the persons concerned. This was stated by the Minister of State (Independent Charge) for Labour and Employment, Shri Oscar Fernandes in written reply in Lok Sabha today.

520. (30-4-2007) NEW DELHI : During the financial year 2006-07, Rs. 25,952.91 crore has been paid as fertiliser subsidy. Budget Estimates for the year 2007-08 is Rs. 22,451.01 crore. The subsidy on fertilisers is released to manufactures/importers to bridge the gap between the normative delivered cost of the fertilisers and the Maximum Retail Prices (MRP) at which they are made available to the farmers. The subsidy reaches the farmers in form of subsidized MRP. The Fertiliser Industry has agreed to work with the Department of Fertilisers to conduct study for finding alternate model of delivery of subsidy to the farmers. Fertilisers Association of India (FAI) has entrusted a study to Tata Consultancy Services Ltd. (TCS) to suggest a model for disbursement of fertiliser subsidy directly to farmers. The draft report of FAI is likely to be ready in April 2007. This information was given by the Minister of State for Chemicals & Fertilisers and Parliamentary Affairs Shri B.K. Handique in a written reply in the Lok Sabha today.

521. (30-4-2007) NEW DELHI : The Union Government has no specific proposal for development of sponge iron industry. However, Government has formulated a National Steel Policy under which sponge iron industry finds an important role. National Steel Policy envisages sponge iron production to 30 million tonne per annum by the year 2020 from the current level of about 13 million tonne per annum. Sponge iron like steel is completely deregulated industry. Therefore, initiative on quality improvement of the product rests with the entrepreneurs. Sponge iron products have a strong national market where these are used in melting furnaces for further value addition. Since the sector is deregulated, the sponge iron producers are free to explore national and international market for their products. This information was given by the Minister of State for Steel Dr. Akhilesh Das in a written reply in the Lok Sabha today.

522. (30-4-2007) NEW DELHI : In the draft National Pharmaceutical Policy, 2006 it has been proposed, inter alia, that one of the ways to make available cheaper drugs to people at large and to public health system could be to promote the production and marketing of generic drugs in the country. This may be achieved through preference of genetic drugs for public procurement and distribution and free of cost quality certification for generic drugs. This Policy was submitted before the Cabinet for its approval. The Cabinet considered the proposal in its meeting held on 11.1.2007 and has referred the matter to a Group of Ministers (GOM). A GOM has since been constituted. The first meeting of the GOM was held on 10.4.2007. No time frame can be given for finalisation of the pharma policy. The 74 bulk drugs specified in the First Schedule of the Drugs (Prices Control) Order, 1995 (DPCO, 95) and the formulations based thereon are under price control and their prices are fixed/revised by the National Pharmaceutical Pricing Authority (NPPA) in accordance with formula given in Para 7 of the DPCO, 95. Under Para 8 of the DPCO 1995, Government/NPPA is empowered to fix from time to time, retail prices of Scheduled formulations in respect of individual manufacturers. Under Para 9 of DPCO 1995, the Government is empowered to fix from time to time ceiling prices of Scheduled formulations and such ceiling prices will be applicable to all such packs including those sold under generic name and for every manufacturer of such formulations. At present Maximum Allowable Post Manufacturing Expenses (MAPE) is allowed @ of 100% on ex-factory price in respect of indigenously manufactured Scheduled formulations and not exceeding 50% of the landed cost for imported Scheduled formulations. Prices of non-Scheduled formulations are fixed by the manufacturers themselves keeping in view the various factors like cost of production, marketing/selling expenses, R&D expenses, trade commission, market competition, product innovation, product quality etc. The Government takes corrective measures where the public interest is found to be aversely affected. This information was given by the Minister of State for Chemicals & Fertilisers and Parliamentary Affairs Shri B.K. Handique in a written reply in the Lok Sabha today.

523. (30-4-2007) NEW DELHI : The Appointment Committee of the Cabinet has approved the appointment of Dr. D Subba Rao (IAS, AP cadre, 1972 batch) as the Secretary, Department of Economic Affairs (Ministry of Finance) in the vacancy arising on the retirement of Shri Ashok Jha today. Dr. Rao is at present the Secretary, Economic Advisory Council to the Prime Minister.

524. (30-4-2007) NEW DELHI : Ministry of Agriculture is implementing four watershed development programmes/schemes, namely, National Watershed Development Project for Rainfed Areas (NWDPRA), Soil Conservation for Enhancing Productivity of Degraded lands in the Catchments of River Valley Project & Flood Prone River (RVP & FPR), Reclamation of Alkali Soils (RAS) and Watershed Development Project in Shifting Cultivation Areas (WDPSCA) for development of degraded lands including soil & water conservation. In addition to these, Ministry of Rural Development is also implementing three area development programmes, namely, Drought Prone Area Programme (DPAP), Desert Development Project (DDP) and Integrated Wasteland Development Project (IWDP) which also have a component of land conservation. During tenth plan an area of 183.14 lakh ha. was covered against the target of 181.00 lakh ha under these three programmes. These Watershed Development Programmes have been found effective in conservation of degraded lands and sustaining agricultural production, besides helping in in-situ moisture conservation and ground water recharge in the watershed areas. This information was given in the Lok Sabha today by Shri Kanti Lal Bhuria, Minister of State for Agriculture in a written reply.

525. (30-4-2007) NEW DELHI : As estimated by the National Remote Sensing Agency (NRSA) in 2003, about 16, 469 ha of more land is engulfed by existing ravines every year. The villages situated within about 2 km range of Chambal river or its tributaries are under the grip of gully erosion. The Research Centre of Central Soil and Water Conservation Research and Training Institute (CSWCR&TI) located at Kota (Rajasthan), has developed technology packages for reclamation of Chambal ravines. With the application of this technology, about 3 lakh ha of Chambal ravine in M. P and about 1.4 lakh ha in Rajathan have been restored under various watershed/wastelands development programmes. This information was given by Minister of State in the Ministry of Water Resources Shri Jai Prakash Narayan Yadav to a question by Shri Ashok Argal in a written reply in the Lok Sabha today.

526. (30-4-2007) NEW DELHI : The progress under restructured Command Area Development and Water Management Programme has been satisfactory except for the new components of correction of system deficiencies up to distributaries of 150 cusec capacity and the renovation of minor irrigation tanks. For implementation of new components of correction of system deficiencies up to distributaries of 150 cusec capacity and the renovation of minor irrigation tanks, formation of legalized Water Users Associations is pre-requisite, which is taking time as several States have not yet enacted a new Participatory Irrigation Management Act or make amendments in the existing Irrigation Act to facilitate formation of Water Users' Associations. Projects under the restructured Command Area Development & Water Management Programme are continuing in all the states except in Goa where all CAD projects were completed prior to restructuring of the programme. The programme implementation is being monitored and reviewed periodically to ensure achievement of the targets. This information was given by Minister of State in the Ministry of Water Resources Shri Jai Prakash Narayan Yadav to a question by Shri Ranen Barman in a written reply in the Lok Sabha today.

527. (30-4-2007) NEW DELHI : There is an increase both in the area and production of horticulture crops which indicates a shift from traditional crops to horticulture including floriculture. National Horticulture Mission has been launched in the country during 10th plan with effect from 2005-06 for holistic development of horticulture sector duly ensuring horizontal and vertical linkages with the active participation of all the stake-holders. All the States and Union Territories of India are covered under the Mission except the eight North Eastern States including Sikkim and the States of Himachal Pradesh, Jammu & Kashmir and Uttaranchal which have been covered under the Technology Mission for integrated development of horticulture in the North Eastern States (TMNE). Under the Scheme, assistance is provided to the farmers for taking up various activities related to Horticulture and Floriculture such as area coverage, rejuvenation of senile orchards, protected cultivation, organic farming, promotion of Integrated Nutrient Management/ Integrated Pest Management and bee-keeping including setting up of Markets, Rural Mandis and Cold Storages.

528. (30-4-2007) NEW DELHI : Central Water Commission (CWC) is maintaining a Gauge & Discharge observation site on river Yamuna at Old Delhi Railway Bridge downstream of Wazirabad barrage since 1963. A study of observed data at the site does not suggest that there is any trend showing that water levels in river Yamuna are falling over the years during the corresponding periods of the year. River Yamuna is one of the main sources of water supply to Delhi. The water from River Yamuna is supplied to Delhi at Wazirabad barrage also. The full pond level at Wazirabad barrage is to be maintained as per the orders of Hon'ble Supreme Court dated 29.02.1996. The release of water in river Yamuna and canal network is regulated through Hathnikund Barrage (nearly 240 kms. From Delhi) and a regulator at Munak, both under the control of Haryana Irrigation Department. The water travels a long distance before reaching Delhi. Therefore there is a possibility of fluctuation of water level at Wazirabad barrage. As and when a fall in water level is reported by Delhi Jal Board, the Haryana Irrigation Department is requested to release more water for maintaining the pond level, so that the water supply to Delhi from river Yamuna is ensured.

529. (30-4-2007) NEW DELHI : The Government is providing subsidy for setting up organic fertilizers and biogas units. The financial assistance for setting up of mechanized compost plants of Rs. 50 lakhs for conversion of biodegradable municipal solid waste into city compost (organic fertilizer) is being provided under Centrally Sponsored Scheme of Balanced & Integrated Use of Fertilizers and Rs. 40 lakhs for setting up of fruits and vegetable waste compost units, Rs. 1.50 lakhs for vermiculture hatcheries and Rs. 20.00 lakhs for setting up of bio-fertilizer units under Central Sector Scheme of National Project on Organic Farming. In addition, under the Centrally Sponsored Scheme of National Biogas and Manure Management Programme of Ministry of New & Renewable Energy, financial assistance ranging for Rs. 2100 to Rs. 11700 for different regions of the country is being provided for setting up of family type biogas plants. This information was given in the Lok Sabha today by Shri Kanti Lal Bhuria, Minister of State for Agriculture in a written reply.

530. (30-4-2007) NEW DELHI : The Centre has provided assistance of Rs. 198.65 crore to the States in the last three years for setting up of cold storages.

A total of 28.39 lakh tonne cold storage capacity is likely to be created with the assistance. A Cold Storage Summit-2007 was held in March 2007, which has recommended that a task force may be created for large-scale argumentation of cold chain infrastructure in the country. The task force, involving the Ministries of Agriculture and Food Processing Industries, NABARD, APEDA etc., is expected to complete its work within three months of its construction. This information was given by Shri Kanti Lal Bhuria, Minister of State for Agriculture in written replies to questions in the Lok Sabha today.

531. (30-4-2007) NEW DELHI : Bawanthadi Project which is known as Rajiv Sagar Project in Madhya Pradesh is an Interstate project between the States of Madhya Pradesh and Maharashtra to provide irrigation benefits to both the States. The headwork comprises of dam on Bawanthadi river. Most of the villages affected and submergence is in the State of Maharashtra. The State Government of Madhya Pradesh has reported that 95% head works and 85% canal work (in Madhya Pradesh) have been completed up to March 2007 and total expenditure incurred up to March 2007 is Rs.298.9655 crore. The ultimate irrigation potential of the project in Madhya Pradesh is 29412 ha against which, no irrigation potential is created so far. Irrigation is a state subject and planning, execution, funding as well as priority of execution is within the purview of State Governments. However, in order to expedite completion of project, the project has been included in Accelerated Irrigation Benefits Programme in 2003-04 and total central assistance released under AIBP to Madhya Pradesh is Rs.54.1001 crore. The project was targeted for completion by June 2008. However its completion depends on completion of resettlement and rehabilitation works to be done by State Government and additional forest land clearance by the Union Ministry of Environment & Forest to be obtained by the State Governments. This information was given by Minister of State in the Ministry of Water Resources Shri Jai Prakash Narayan Yadav to a question by Shri Krishna Murari Moghe in a written reply in the Lok Sabha today.

532. (30-4-2007) NEW DELHI : Government of Punjab has informed that no area of land is being lost to Pakistan due to land erosion. As per information available with Government of Punjab, Pakistan has built some works to push the course of the river Sutlej towards Indian side. Government of Punjab has further informed that the course of river Ravi has shifted gradually towards India due to normal country slope and some works constructed by Pakistan in their territory and that there is no major diversion of the course of the rivers Ravi and Sutlej in the India territory. A Committee constituted by the Ministry of Water Resources visits vulnerable spots every year before and after monsoon in the border Districts and suggests counter remedial measures on these rivers and reviews the prevailing ground conditions and recommends flood control/anti erosion schemes to be executed by the State Government. Government of Punjab undertakes counter remedial measures from its own resources. Union Government is also providing financial assistance in the form of special loan and grant-in-aid as well as technical expertise to the Government of Punjab for undertaking the works. This information was given by Minister of State in the Ministry of Water Resources Shri Jai Prakash Narayan Yadav to a question by Shri Ramdas Athawale in a written reply in the Lok Sabha today.

533. (30-4-2007) NEW DELHI : Central Adoption Resource Agency (CARA), a nodal body of the Union Government in the matters related to rehabilitation of orphan, abandoned and relinquished children in the country has asked the State Governments to take immediate step to put a ban on illegal adoptions of the children. In a letter written to the Chief Ministers the States, Chairman of the CARA, Shri J.K. Mittal has said that it had come to the notice that large number of adoptions are taking place without following the due procedure especially through hospitals/nursing homes or agencies not recognized by the State Governments/CARA and such adoptions are outside the purview of the existing in-country Guidelines, 2004. Citing the Supreme Court's directives in the matter of adoption of children, CARA has said it is mandatory that all nursing homes and hospitals which come across abandoned and destitute children or find such children abandoned in their precincts or otherwise shall immediately give information in regard to the discovery or find of such children to the social welfare department of the concerned Government or the collector of the district for proper and legal rehabilitation of the children. Shri Mittal has said while adoption is considered as the best alternative family rehabilitation for all orphan-abandoned/ surrendered children, all children homes and Child Welfare Committees may be directed to make family preservation efforts, such as; restoration of children to natural parents/guardians, prevention of abandonment on the ground of poverty or gender issues through various measures such as sponsorship and foster care etc. before adoption could be considered as the best alternative for rehabilitation of such children. Chairman of CARA, Shri J.K. Mittal has urged the State Government to initiate a time bound drive to recognize all unregistered agencies for in-country adoption as per the prescribed procedure so that adoptions could carried out legally and through recognized agencies. He has also asked the States to ensure that every child in these agencies is properly accounted for and list of those children which are declared free for adoption, are made available to the concerned State Adoption Cell and/or Adoption Coordinating Agency (ACA). Underlining the importance of due care of children, Shri Mittal has said that all children regardless of race, ethnicity, gender, medical limitations or other conditions deserve permanent loving homes, but only about 3,500 legal adoptions take place in the country annually which is a very small figure in comparison to number of children available for adoption in the country. Therefore, Panchayats and local bodies should be involved to identify orphan and destitute children so that such children can be placed with loving and caring family.

534. (30-4-2007) NEW DELHI : The procurement of wheat in Rabi Marketing Season (RMS) 2007-08 which is presently in progress is 73.8 lakh tonnes as on

26.4.2007. The stocks of wheat in the Central Pool as on 31.3.2007 were 45.63 lakh tonnes. The Government has decided that action may be initiated by STC for import of one million tonnes of wheat in suitable tranches, by July, 2007 since there can be no compromise on food security. The Government is carrying out Minimum Support Price (MSP) operations for wheat through the Food Corporation of India (FCI) and State agencies in wheat producing states to ensure remunerative prices for farmers. In order to protect the interest of farmers the MSP of wheat announced for RMS 2007-08 is Rs. 750 per quintal which is Rs. 100 per quintal more than that announced for RMS 2006-07. A bonus of Rs.100 per quintal over and above the MSP is also being given in RMS 2007-08.

535. (30-4-2007) NEW DELHI : The Minister for State for Labour & Employment (Independent Charge), Shri Oscar Fernandes has greeted the workers on the occasion of May Day. In his May Day message Shri Fernandes has said that the Government is working for producing a world class work force to enable the workers to face stiff competition in the global markets. He said that from the current financial year, 300 Industrial Training Institutes (ITIs) will be upgrades each year under public-private-partnership (PPP) mode with the cooperation of the State Governments. Shri Fernandes said Rs. 750 crore have been kept aside for this purpose. Referring to the unorganised sector workers, who contribute about 60% to the country's GDP, the Labour Minister said that besides enacting a legislation for providing social security to these workers, the Government wants to effectively implement some of the important legislations enacted for their welfare. The full text of Shri Fernandes May Message is as follows: "On this day, which happens to be International Labour Day and which, symbolises the unity and solidarity of the working class, I extend to workers all over the country my warmest greetings and best wishes. It is the day of hopes and aspirations of the working class. It reminds us that Labour and capital can jointly contribute to the well being of the individuals and prosperity of the Nation. 2. After Independence, Government had initiated several important steps for improvement in the working conditions and welfare of the working class. However, much still remains to be done, particularly, for the workers in the unorganized sector, which provides the major chunk of employment in the country and contributes about 60% to our GDP. Some important legislations have been enacted to promote welfare of the workers in the unorganized sector. We want these to be implemented effectively. In addition, Government is actively considering to bring about a legislation for providing social security to workers in the unorganized sector. 3. In the present economic scenario of liberalization, privatization and globalisation, skill development has acquired immense significance so as to enable us to produce world-class work force that can face stiff competition in the global market. The Government through Directorate General of Employment & Training (DGE&T) continues to play a major role in the area of skill development through an effective vocational training system in the country. One of the steps taken is to upgrade 500 ITIs into the Centres of Excellence, for producing multi-skilled workforce of world standard. Accordingly, action has been initiated for upgradation 100 ITIs from domestic resources and 400 ITIs through World Bank assistance. 4. In his Budget Speech 2007-08, Hon'ble Finance Minister has announced that 1396 ITIs would be upgraded into centres of excellence in specific trade and skills under public-private partnership. Under the proposed scheme, the State Government as the owner of the ITI, will continue to regulate admissions and fees, the new management will be given academic and financial autonomy, and the Central Government will provide financial assistance by way of seed money. Once a tripartite MOU is signed among the three stakeholders, an interest free loan upto Rs.2.5 crore to each ITI for upgradation and revision of courses would be granted. The cooperation of State Governments has been sought to upgrade atleast 300 ITIs every year, beginning 2007-08, under the PPP mode for which Rs.750 crore has been kept aside. 5. Mention needs to be made of our efforts for elimination of child labour in hazardous employment. The National Child Labour Project (NCLP) has been extended to cover 250 districts. In addition a$40 million INDUS Project (Indo-US project) is in operation. The Government has banned the employment of children working as domestic servants and in tea-shops, restaurants, hotels and dhabas, etc. w.e.f. 10th October, 2006. 6. Government has approved the constitution of two Wage Boards one for the Working Journalists and another for Non-Journalists Newspaper Employees. 7. In accordance with the mandate given by the National Common Minimum Programme (NCMP), we continue to have consultations with social partners to obtain consensus for enacting new laws or bringing about changes in the existing laws as well as on other important policy issues. The industrial relations machineries of the Central and States are continuously at work so that industrial relations situation remains harmonious and peaceful. Both Employees' Provident Fund Organisation (EPFO) and Employees State Insurance Corporation (ESIC) are modernizing their system of operation to improve upon their delivery mechanism. Under the 'Rajiv Gandhi Shramik Kalyan Yojana', ESIC is providing unemployment allowance to the insured persons who have been rendered unemployed involuntarily due to the closure of the factory / establishment, retrenchment or permanent invalidity arising out of non-employment injury. Welfare schemes covering housing, health and educational facilities are being provided to beedi, cine and non-coal mine workers and their families. Similarly out of the cess collected, welfare schemes such as Group Insurance, Medical and Health Care, Scholarships, Pension etc. are implemented for construction workers. 8. With the promise that we would continuously pursue our efforts to promote the welfare of workers, I once again convey my best wishes on this auspicious day."

536. (30-4-2007) NEW DELHI : In the present scenario of globalization where national barriers are fast disappearing, where time zones have shrunk, we must embark upon a new global enterprise, chartering new areas of international collaboration in the true spirit of the Antarctic Treaty. This was stated by Shri Kapil Sibal, Union Minister for Science & Technology and Earth Sciences while inaugurating the XXX Antarctic Treaty Consultative Meeting (ATCM) which began in New Delhi today. Spelling out India's deep commitment in playing an active role in the domain of Antarctic science with the underpinning motto to preserve the pristine environment of the last frontier on earth, he urged the Antarctic Treaty Parties to cooperate in the scientific pursuit for the benefit of mankind. Shri Kapil Sibal in his inaugural address drew the attention of delegates to the role played by Antarctic Treaty in providing good governance and environmental stewardship in managing the continent of Antarctica, common heritage of mankind. The Antarctica Treaty which is devoted to science and peaceful use, is also the pre-cursor to the Space Treaty. The Minister stated that the International Polar Year 2007-08 has also brought countries together for the launch of a comprehensive science mission. Such a mission is not geared for economic gain, but it is, in fact, a long term campaign through which scientists hope to unravel the enigmas of nature and space best understood from a vantage point, like the Antarctica. He also impressed upon the need to give a fresh look at the growth of tourism in Antarctica, in the context of exploitation of the resources of this vast continent, as well as the imperative of protecting the Antarctica environment. He urged the delegates to develop a framework of regulation to contain tourism activity. The other issue, which needs to be addressed, he said, is the importance of the polar region in the context of global climate change and its impact on our environment and the human beings, going by the recent data and issues thrown up by the Inter-Governmental Panel on climate change.

537. (30-4-2007) NEW DELHI : The Ministry of Rural Development has sanctioned Rs. 40.95 crore to the State Government of Karnataka towards part payment of first instalment of funds against the provisional allocation of Rs.245.72 crore made for the Government of Karnataka under Accelerated Rural Water Supply Programme (Normal) of Rajiv Gandhi National Drinking Water Mission, during the year 2007-08. Under the Scheme, an amount of Rs.5.46 crore has also been released towards part of first instalment of ARWSP-DDP funds against provisional allocation of Rs.32.79 crore for the year 2007-08. Up to 15 per cent of funds released under this sanction may be utilized for Operation & Maintenance and up to 5 per cent of funds may be spent for taking sustainability measures. States have been requested to delegate powers for management of Rural Water Supply Schemes through the Panchayati Raj Institutions (PRIs) as per the Constitution of India. As such Operation and Maintenance of the completed RWS Scheme should be transferred to the PRIs. No expenditure shall be incurred on taking water quality problems form the present release, as there is a separate allocation for the purpose. This release is being made for execution/completion of schemes to provide safe drinking water facilities to rural habitations and schools under the Centrally Sponsored ARWSP. Priorities set in ARWSP guidelines and through other instructions issued from time to time shall be followed for coverage of rural habitations and rural schools.

538. (30-4-2007) NEW DELHI : The Ministry of Rural Development has sanctioned Rs. 46.96 crore to the State Government of Andhra Pradesh towards part payment of first instalment of funds against the provisional allocation of Rs.281.78 crore made for the Government of Andhra Pradesh under Accelerated Rural Water Supply Programme (Normal) of Rajiv Gandhi National Drinking Water Mission, during the year 2007-08. Under the Scheme, an amount of Rs.2.25 crore has also been released towards part of first instalment of ARWSP-DDP funds against provisional allocation of Rs.13.52 crore for the year 2007-08. Up to 15 per cent of funds released under this sanction may be utilized for Operation & Maintenance and up to 5 per cent of funds may be spent for taking sustainability measures. States have been requested to delegate powers for management of Rural Water Supply Schemes through the Panchayati Raj Institutions (PRIs) as per the Constitution of India. As such Operation and Maintenance of the completed RWS Scheme should be transferred to the PRIs. No expenditure shall be incurred on taking water quality problems form the present release, as there is a separate allocation for the purpose. This release is being made for execution/completion of schemes to provide safe drinking water facilities to rural habitations and schools under the Centrally Sponsored ARWSP. Priorities set in ARWSP guidelines and through other instructions issued from time to time shall be followed for coverage of rural habitations and rural schools.

539. (30-4-2007) NEW DELHI : Winner of this year's Abel Prize in Mathematics, awarded by the Norwegian Academy of Science and Letters and regarded as equivalent to a Nobel Prize in the discipline, India-born and US-based Professor Srinivasa S.R. Varadhan, acknowledged via e-mail a message of greetings and congratulations sent by Prime Minister Dr. Manmohan Singh, last month, and said "As I receive the award I am very aware that the early education I received in India from high school through college and doctoral studies at ISI, Calcutta, has provided me with the necessary foundation for success." "For this", Professor Vardhan adds, "I will always be grateful. I hope that I will continue to maintain my contacts and be helpful for the development of mathematical talent in India." Earlier, In a letter to Professor Varadhan, The Prime Minister, Manmohan Singh had said, "I hope your example will inspire a new generation of Indians to pursue the study of mathematics, a discipline to which Indians have made significant contribution since times immemorial. This is not just a personal honour for you but an honour for all Indians and people of Indian origin the world over. Please accept my sincere greetings and best wishes." Professor Varadhan is presently Frank J. Gould Professor of Science and Professor of Mathematics Courant Institute of Mathematical Sciences, New York University. He was a student of Madras University and has a doctoral degree from the Indian Statistical Institute, Kolkata. He was awarded the Abel Prize for his work on probability theory and in developing a unified theory of large deviations.

540. (30-4-2007) NEW DELHI : During the month of March 2007, the Ministry of Small Scale Industries and Agro and Rural Industries continued to implement its various schemes, programmes, etc. to assist the promotion and growth of small enterprises. Forty Entrepreneurship Development Programmes, 45 Motivational Campaigns and 30 Management Development Programmes were conducted by the SIDO field institutions in different States during the month. Altogether, 6475 persons took part in these programmes. NSIC conducted 52 Intensive Campaigns and 11 Marketing Promotion Seminars at various places in the country. The National Institute of Small Industries Extension Training (NISIET), Hyderabad conducted 77 training programmes for 1764 participants. The Indian Institute of Entrepreneurship (IIE), Guwahati conducted 31 training programmes for 1206 participants. The National Institute for Entrepreneurship and Small Business Development (NIESBUD), NOIDA conducted 17 training programmes for 424 participants. Under ISO-9000/14001 Reimbursement Scheme, an amount of Rs.0.88 crore was reimbursed to 190 SSI units and during the year 2006-07 an amount of Rs.12.80 crore has been reimbursed to 2797 units.

541. (30-4-2007) NEW DELHI : The Government has implemented National Rural Health Mission (NRHM) throughout the country with special focus on 18 high focus states which includes 8 Empowered Action Group (EAG) States (Bihar, Jharkhand, Madhya Pradesh, Chhattisgarh, Uttar Pradesh, Uttaranchal, Orissa and Rajasthan), 8 NE States, Himachal Pradesh and Jammu & Kashmir. The NRHM aims at improving the range and quality of hospital care, decentralization of programme to district level to improve intra and inter-sectoral convergence and effective utilization of resources. The NRHM further aims to provide overarching umbrella to the existing National programmes of Health & Family Welfare including RCH-II, Malaria, Blindness, Iodine deficiency, Filaria, Kala Azar, T.B., Leprosy and Integrated disease Surveillance. Further, it addresses the issue of health in a sector-wide manner addressing sanitation and hygiene, nutrition and safe drinking water as basic determinants of good health. The year 2005-06 was the formative year for the NRHM during which the institutional framework to operationalise the Mission was set up in all the States. The Mission envisages provision of quality health care to the entire population with special focus on the underserved sections. This information was given by the Minister of State for Health & Family Welfare, Smt. Panabaka in a written reply to a question in the Rajya Sabha.

542. (1-5-2007) NEW DELHI : India and Bangladesh today renewed the Protocol on Inland Water Transit and Trade which will remain in force up to 31st March, 2009. In this Protocol, which was originally signed in 1972 and is being renewed from time to time, inland vessels of both countries ply between Kolkata-Pandu, Kolkata-Karimganj and Rajshahi-Dhulian and Karimganj-Pandu. This inland water transit Protocol facilitates movement of inter-country trade and transit cargo. Secretary (Shipping) Shri A.K. Mohapatra who led the Indian delegation stated that India attaches the highest importance to its relations with Bangladesh and both countries have shared history and cultural heritage and have now shared aspirations. To fulfil these aspirations we must go through agreed instrumentalities and evolve united will, he said. He said that this Protocol has been instrumental in increasing the volume of trade by IWT between the two countries by almost 13 times in last 10 years. He also emphasized the need for long-term renewal of the Protocol. The important issues such as need for inclusion of additional stretches, additional Ports of Call, better river conservancy works etc. were also discussed during the meeting. Mr. Sheikh Enayetullah, Secretary, Ministry of Shipping, Govt. of Bangladesh who led the Bangladeshi delegation stated that though the renewal of the Protocol is being discussed after eight years, the movement of cargo on the Protocol Rules is functioning smoothly and volume of trade has grown significantly. He further stated that the two countries should exchange know-how for development of this mode for mutual benefit.

543. (1-5-2007) VIJAYAWADA: The Communist Party of India (Marxist) will organise several programmes and protests to bring pressure on the State Government to speed up the process of distributing land to the poor for building houses. Addressing newsmen on Monday, CPI (M) district secretary V. Umamaheswara Rao said Ministers Koneru Ranga Rao, Dharmana Prasada Rao and K. Jana Reddy had described, during their campaign in municipal elections, distribution of house sites and construction of houses for the poor as the top priority of the Government.

544. (1-5-2007) NEW DELHI : On the complaints of Mr. Ramesh Sippy and 4 other film distributors, the Monopolies & Restrictive Trade Practices Commission (MRTPC) passed an order here today, restraining the Multiplex Association of India and its members from carrying on the impugned restrictive trade practices and directed them to file an affidavit of compliance within four weeks. The complainants, the film distributors, had filed a complaint alleging that the Multiplex Association of India and its members are resorting to restrictive trade practices as defined under the Monopolies & Restrictive Trade Practices (MRTP) Act, 1969. The complainants have also filed an interim application seeking temporary injunction restraining the respondents from carrying on restrictive trade practice. It was alleged that certain clauses of the Multiplexes Association of India Terms agreement, 2007, (MAI Agreement), are restrictive in nature. As per the agreement Multiplex Chains shall negotiate terms with distributors on a national/regional basis and that no Multiplex Chains shall pay the distributors more than what has been agreed to in the MAI Agreement. It was alleged that the agreement is with the intention of forming a 'cartel' to pressurize the producers/distributors of films to accept the terms as dictated by the cartel of Multiplex Owners. It was also alleged that the agreement restricts the members from entering into agreements with the distributors unless the same terms are extended to other members.

545. (1-5-2007) NEW DELHI : Shri Arjun Singh, Human Resource Development Minister has said that among the institutions that contribute to the makeup of a public sphere in society, the media perhaps perform the most critical function.

While inaugurating the 'Media and its Responsibilities' Seminar here today the Minister said the media is rightly acknowledged as one of the important pillars of democracy. 'It is always interesting to study how the media report and interpret political events and issues, and how media itself influences the political processes and shapes public opinion' he said. Shri Arjun Singh said the face of Indian Media has been fast changing on account of growth of Internet, the phenomenal rise of Satellite & Cable networks, the continuing growth of regional press and blurring of lines between news and entertainment. This has obviously led to technological and commercial pressures and changes in professional practices for the media sector. Against this backdrop, it is important for small and medium newspapers to make efforts to occupy a special place for itself in media sector. The Minister said the small and medium newspapers are largely catering to information communication and entertainment needs of rural and semi-urban India. They draw their strength from being local. One needs to appreciate that people belonging particularly to rural areas possibly would not have access to mediums like internet and satellite and cable television. Their information requirement could either be met by Doordarshan, Radio or newspapers. Thus, the small and medium newspapers have a greater responsibility in dissemination of news among the rural people.

546. (1-5-2007) NEW DELHI : Japanese delegation led by H.E. Mr. Tetsuzo Fuyushiba, Minister of Land, Infrastructure and Transport, Government of Japan called on the Union Minister for Railways, Shri Lalu Prasad here today. Shri R Velu, Minister of State for Railways, Shri Ramesh Chandra, Member (Electrical), Railway Board and other senior officials were also present on the occasion. Welcoming the delegation, Shri Lalu Prasad said that the Indian Government was committed to implementing all elements of India-Japan Strategic and Global Partnership agreed to by the Prime Ministers of the two countries in December 2006. Which included comprehensive economic partnership. While appreciating Japan's support for the Dedicated Freight Corridors project, the Minister said that this project would open the doors for the Delhi-Mumbai Industrial Corridor project. He appreciated Japan's efforts to expedite the feasibility study on the Dedicated Freight Corridors expected in October this year. H.E. Mr. Fuyushiba thanked the Railway Minister for the warm hospitality and said that the feasibility study report on the Dedicated Freight Corridor project will be completed by October 2007 and will be a comprehensive one covering technology and maintenance issues. He assured the Railway Minister of Japan's full cooperation in ensuring implementation of the project. Shri Ramesh Chandra, Member (Electrical), Railway Board, in his welcome address, said that Dedicated Freight Corridor project was a flagship project for modernizing Indian Railways and looked forward to close cooperation with the Japanese Government.

547. (1-5-2007) HYDERABAD: The Communist Party of India (CPI) has asked the State Government to initiate works in the different infrastructure and irrigation projects only after suitably rehabilitating the people displaced by them. The party has demanded that the Government suitably amend the Relief and Rehabilitation Act, as the present law was not serving the interests of the displaced people. "There is a huge gap between the compensation paid by Government and actual market prices. This needs to be rectified," CPI MP Suravaram Sudhakar Reddy said.

548. (1-5-2007) NEW DELHI : The modern economic growth is driven by skills and knowledge that in turn promotes social development. Skilled human potential makes economy more productive, innovative and competitive. The level of employment and its quality pay a crucial role in the development process. Increase in quality of work has direct relation with productivity, which in turn is connected with skill availability of the workforce. Unfortunately, the skill availability and productivity of our workforce is one of the lowest in the world. As per 61st round of the National Sample Survey Organisation, out of 470 million working population, 11 million are openly unemployed, meaning that they did not get any work round the year. Given the country's size of population, it may not be significantly though the focus is on employment for all. But what is of concern is that 130 million workers, which is a large number are living below poverty level. These workers are no doubt employed but their quality of employment is poor and unable to bring them above the poverty line. The main reason being low income earnings and low level of productivity due to lack of skills. According to the National Sample Survey organisation (NSSO) Survey only 5% of the Indian Labour Force in the age group of 20-24 years have obtained vocational skills through formal institutes whereas the percentage in industrial countries is much higher, varying between 60% to 96%. The other bane of our work force is that while their educational attainment is very low on the one hand, 61% of those educated upto secondary level and beyond on the other hand are without any professional skills. This is because our general education system is not oriented towards attaining vocational skills. The mid term appraisal of the 10th Plan points out, "our education system is not generating sufficient supply of trained people especially those trained in skills that are in demand." Labour productivity of an Indian worker is $3.05 per hour while in most developed economies it is more than $30. Increasing pace of globalization and technological change provide both challenges and growing opportunities for economic expansion and job creation.

549. (1-5-2007) NEW DELHI : The Transport Minister of Singapore, Mr. Raymond Lim called on the Minister for Civil Aviation, Shri Praful Patel to discuss the civil aviation ties between the two countries. Welcoming the Minister, Shri Patel said that India gave highest importance to the relationship between the two countries. There were several sectors of cooperation between the two including civil aviation which were progressively growing. Commending the heartening growth in civil aviation ties between India and Singapore, the Civil Aviation Minister said that the number of flights between the two countries has seen a tremendous growth. Singapore has the highest number of flights to and from India. The Minister expressed his wish to take this cooperation even further. Speaking about the

ASEAN Open Skies, Shri Patel said that airport infrastructure is one of the constraints in making the Indian skies more open and liberalized. The Indian Government would also like to redefine the air traffic pattern within the country which till very recently had been concentrated between Mumbai and Delhi. The Government's recent efforts have been to redistribute air traffic patterns and make sure that other cities across the country also build up air traffic volumes effectively for an equitable distribution of economic development in the country. Shri Patel assured the Transport Minister that the Government would look at the ASEAN Open Skies issue meaningfully. He said it was just a question of time.

550. (1-5-2007) NEW DELHI : A 16-member US Financial Services and Industry Study Group led by Dr. David G. Blair, Professor of Economics, National Defence University, Washington called on the Union Minister for Railways, Shri Lalu Prasad here today. The delegation comprised of mid and senior level officers from the US Army, Navy and Air Force and Civil & Foreign Service officers. The discussions centred round the recent turn around in Indian Railways. The Minister informed the visiting delegation that Indian Railways is the lifeline of the country and there are more than 14 lakh railway employees. The Railways have broad guage, meter guage and narrow guage lines besides prestigious world heritage sites like Darjeeling Himalayan Railway, Nilgiri Mountain Railway etc. The Railways carry 16 million passengers and 2 million tonne goods every day and have a network of 63000 route km out of which 18000 km are electrified. Shri Lalu Prasad informed the delegation that the turn around had been possible because of strong determination and vision for the development of the railways, increase in occupancy of trains, more number of coaches etc. The increase in axle load resulted in increased loading capacity of goods trains. The passenger and freight traffic rates were rationalized and a flexible tariff policy was adopted for peak and non-peak seasons. The turn around in the railways has resulted in a surplus of Rs.20000 crore during the year 2006-07. The Minister informed the delegation that the mission of the Indian Railways is to construct Dedicated Freight Corridors, modernization of track and signals, manufacture of low weight wagons, extension of e-ticketing and online enquiry through out the country. He told the delegation that Public Private Partnership will play a vital role in the new container policy, logistics park, warehousing, railway connectivity with ports and developing world class railway stations etc.

551. (1-5-2007) NEW DELHI : It has been brought to the notice of the Ministry of Finance that certain organizations/other agencies are not accepting coins of lower denominations such as 25 paise on the plea that the same are not in circulation any more. It is clarified that Government of India have not stopped circulation of any coin of any denomination and coins of all denominations should be accepted by all and sundry.

552. (1-5-2007) NEW DELHI : Central Board of Excise and Customs (CBEC), Department of Revenue issued Notification no. 40/2007-Cus (N.T), here today notifying tariff values of edible oils and brass scrap (all grades) as shown in the Table below. The tariff values of six palm group oils and crude soyabean oil remain unchanged. However, tariff value of brass scrap (all grades) has been marginally increased.

553. (1-5-2007) NEW DELHI : Whereas it has come to the notice of the Government of India that Institutions and Universities, including Institutions Deemed to be Universities, are admitting students to technical education programmes long before the actual starting of an academic session; collecting full fees from the admitted students; and, retaining their school/institution's leaving certificates in the original; And Whereas, Institutions and Universities are also reportedly confiscating the fee paid if a student fails to join by such dates; And, Whereas, certificates in original are being detained by institutions and universities to force retention of admitted studentsv; And, Whereas the time-limit for students to join the courses /programmes is also being advanced in some cases unrealistically so as to pre-empt students/candidates from exercising other options of joining other institutions of their choice. Now, therefore, in exercise of the powers conferred in it by Section 20 (1) of the University Grants Commission Act and Section 20(1) of the All India Council of Technical Education Act, the Central Government hereby directs the UGC and the AICTE to instruct Institutions and Universities in the public interest to maintain a waitlist of students/candidates. In the event of a student/candidate withdrawing before the starting of the course, the wait listed candidates should be given admissions against the vacant seat. The entire fees collected from the student, after a deduction of the processing fee of not more than Rs. 1000/- (one thousand only) shall be refunded and returned by the Institution/ University to the student/candidate withdrawing from the programme.

554. (1-5-2007) NEW DELHI : The Central Adoption Resource Agency (CARA), a body of the Ministry of Women and Child Development, is organizing meet on adoption for its partner/associated agencies on 3rd and 4th May 2007 in Delhi. The Meet will be inaugurated by Smt. Renuka Chowdhury, Minister of Women and Child Development and will be attended by the senior officials of State Governments dealing with adoption matters, representatives from Placements Agencies, and Homes run by NGOs/State Govts. getting grant-in-aid from Central Government for running Shishu Greh Scheme, Adoption Coordinating Agencies and other associated agencies. The objective of the meet is to review issues related with adoption and to get feedback from the State Governments and adoption agencies for further rationalization adoption process. The meet will include sessions on adoption scenario in the States, implementation of Juvenile Justice Act particularly related to adoption matters, suggestions from States Govts./associated agencies about In-country Guidelines and Inter-country Guidelines, issue of child protection, preparation of Centralized Database and facilities for registration of prospective adoptive parents within the country etc.

555. (1-5-2007) NEW DELHI : Ministry of Women and Child Development is organizing a workshop on gender equality in Indian media here on 3rd May, the world Press Freedom Day. The workshop will be inaugurated by Shri P.R. Dasmunsi, Minister of Information and Broadcasting and will be presided over by Smt. Renuka Chowdhury, Minister for Women and Child Development. Inaugural session will also be addressed by Smt. Mrinal Pandey, Editor, Hindustan Times and Smt. Sushma Ramachandran, President, Women Press Club. Presentations will be made by the distinguished journalists which will include 'challenges before the news Media and gender equality' by Ms. Akhila Sivadas, 'the representation of women in print media' by Ms. Angana Parikh and 'the representation of women in electronic media' by Ms. Shelaja Vajpayee. It will be followed by panel discussions.

556. (1-5-2007) NEW DELHI : Central Water Commission (CWC) under Ministry of Water Resources is monitoring storage position of 76 important reservoirs spread all over the country, of which as many as 31 reservoirs have significant hydro-power benefits with installed capacity of more than 60 MW each. The combined live storage in these 76 reservoirs at the beginning of monsoon *i.e.* 1st June, 2006 was 22 per cent of their designed capacity and stood at 32 per cent of the designed capacity as on 26th April 2007. The present storage is 110 per cent of the last year's storage and 147 per cent of last 10 years average storage during the same period. Out of these 76 reservoirs there are presently 16 reservoirs where this year's storage is 80 per cent or less than the average of previous 10 years and in the remaining 60 reservoirs the storage is more than 80 per cent of the average of previous 10 years. In order to derive the best possible benefits from the available water, Central Water Commission is keeping in touch with the Department of Agriculture and Cooperation and providing information of the weekly storage position to the Crop Weather Watch Group for evolving suitable crop strategies and also appraising the situation to various Departments and Ministries involved in Water Resources Planning.

557. (1-5-2007) NEW DELHI : Dr. Christy Fernandez (IAS, Gujarat Cadre, 1973) has taken over as the Secretary, Ministry of Tourism w.e.f 01/05/07. He replaces Shri A.K. Misra who retired on superannuation on 30/04/07.

558. (1-5-2007) NEW DELHI : In order to ensure correct loading of aircraft and keeping the centre of gravity of the aircraft within limits at all times during flight, it has now been made compulsory that row numbers and seat numbers are allocated to all passengers travelling in a public transport aircraft. Office of the Director General of Civil Aviation has issued a Civil Aviation Requirement (CAR) under the provisions of Rule 133A of Aircraft Rules 1937 for compliance by all passengers transport aircraft operators. The allotment of specific seat numbers will ensure that the boarding of aircraft is carried out in a smooth and orderly manner and there is no confusion as to which seats passengers are required to occupy. In addition, such allocation of seat numbers will also facilitate quick head-count of passengers for tallying with passenger manifest entries as and when required. Furthermore, in the unlikely event of an aircraft accident or in the case of unlawful interference with the aircraft, the seat numbers allotted to individual passengers will assist follow-up action/investigation. Allotment of specific seat numbers will also help airline staff to properly position handicapped or physical infirm or aged passengers to convenient seats of ease of boarding, disembarkation or use of aircraft facilities etc.

559. (1-5-2007) NEW DELHI : The cumulative value of India's exports for the period April-March, 2007 was US $ 124629.48 million ($ 124.6 billion) or Rs.563800.06 Crore as against US $ 100606.92 million ($ 100.6 billion) or Rs.445657.97 Crore during the same period last year, indicating a growth of 23.88%, according to the provisional data for merchandise exports available from Directorate General of Commercial Intelligence & Statistics (DGCI&S). Exports during the month of March 2007 were valued at US $ 12583.58 million ($ 12.5 billion) or Rs.55400.45 crore compared with US $ 10906.21 million ($ 10.9 billion) or Rs.48511.93 Crore in March, 2006. The cumulative value of India's imports during April-March, 2007 was US $ 181368.26 million ($ 181.3 billion) or Rs.820568.13 Crore which was higher than imports at US $ 140237.65 million ($ 140.2 billion) or Rs.620826.68 Crore during April-March, 2006. Imports during the month of March, 2007 were valued at US $ 16382.94 million (Rs.72127.53 crore) compared with US $ 13811.65 million (Rs.61435.58 Crore) in March, 2006. Crude Oil imports were valued at US $ 4597.64 million in March, 2007 compared with US $ 4202.92 million in the corresponding period last year thus registering a growth of 9.39%. Crude Oil imports during April-March, 2007 were valued at US $ 57271.10 million which was 30.31% higher than Crude oil imports of US $ 43951.27 million in the corresponding period last year. Non-oil imports were estimated at US $ 11785.30 million during March, 2007 which was 16.55% higher than growth on non-oil imports of US $ 10111.47 million in March, 2006. Non-oil imports during April-March, 2007 were valued at US $ 124097.15 million which was 24.74% higher than the level of such imports valued at US $ 99481.88 million in April-March, 2006. The trade deficit for April-March, 2007 was estimated at US $ 56738.77 million which was higher than the deficit of US $ 39630.72 million during April-March, 2006.

560. (1-5-2007) NEW DELHI : India and Japan signed a Memorandum of Understanding for setting up Indo-Japan Joint Working Group on Urban Development. Shri S. Jaipal Reddy, Union Minister for Urban Development and Mr. Tetsuzo Fuyshiba, Japanese Minister of Land, Infrastructure and Transport inked the pact in New Delhi today. The first meeting of the Working Group is scheduled in June this year in Tokyo. The meeting is expected to discuss specific areas of cooperation in the field of water environment, urban development and urban transport. Speaking on the occasion, Shri Reddy said, Japan Bank for

International Cooperation has provided loan of over US $ 1.36 billion for Delhi Mass Rapid Transit System, MRTS project which is a shining example of Indo-Japanese Cooperation in urban transport. He said, "Japan is renowned for its advanced urban transport technologies in the field of Metro Rail, Mono Rail, Linear Metro and Maglev. Some of these are being introduced in India also. We would welcome technical collaboration with Japanese experts for setting up such systems in other metropolitan cities". The Minister stated that collaboration would also be required in the field of Intelligent Transport Systems and Traffic Information Centres as the government is promoting them in all cities having million plus population. Shri Jaipal Reddy said that if the momentum of economic growth were to be maintained, the challenges thrown up by large-scale urbanization would have to be addressed without delay. He stated that the total investment required in urban transport in India during the next five years is estimated at US $ 29.5 billion. He stated that the Japan Bank for International Cooperation, JBIC's assistance would be further required for the new corridors being sanctioned for Delhi Metro Phase II Project as well as for other Metro Projects like Kolkata and East-West Corridor. The Urban Development Minister said that other areas of collaboration could be integrated land use planning, safety certification mechanism and laying down parameters for Guided Urban Transit Systems, GUTS. The Japanese Minister, Mr. Tetsuzo Fuyshiba, who is heading a 17 member delegation said that Delhi Metro is the symbolic expression of goodwill between India and Japan. He stated that the agreement is not only a great step in the expansion of cooperation between the two countries, but also a step forward for building of world peace. During Prime Minister, Dr. Manmohan Singh's visit to Japan in December 2006, India and Japan agreed to establish a Strategic and Global Partnership involving political and diplomatic coordination on bilateral, regional and global issues. The two sides have also agreed to set up Joint Working Group in the fields of water environment, urban development and urban transportation.

561. (1-5-2007) NEW DELHI : The Ministry of Rural Development has released Grants-in-aid amounting to Rs. 64.31 crore as third/additional instalment of Central assistance to 21 districts of Maharashtra for the implementation of the Sampoorna Grameen Rozgar Yojana (SGRY) during the current financial year (2007-08).

562. (1-5-2007) NEW DELHI : The Ministry of Rural Development has released Grants-in-aid amounting to Rs. 2.26 crore as part of first instalment of Central assistance to 5 districts; Rs. 4.22 crore on account of release of 3rd/additional instalment to 6 districts and Rs.72.61 lakh as second instalment to 2 districts of Manipur for the implementation of the Sampoorna Grameen Rozgar Yojana (SGRY) during the current financial year (2007-08).

563. (1-5-2007) NEW DELHI : Surg Vice Admiral Yogendra Singh took over as Director General of Armed Forces Medical Services in New Delhi today. An alumnus of Armed Forces Medical College, Pune, he passed his MBBS in 1968 and was commissioned in Army Medical Corps on 27 Jan 1969. He did his advanced course in General Surgery from AFMC Pune in 1975-1977 and obtained MS degree in General Surgery from Pune University in the same year. As a young surgeon he was on deputation to Oman Armed Forces Base Hospital, from 1979 to 1982. For his meritorious service and dedication to duty as Surgeon at 153 General Hospital at Leh during the peak of Siachen conflict in 1986 he was awarded Vishisht Seva Medal. He has held may prestigious appointments both as a specialist and administrator. He is a Post Graduate teacher and examiner in Surgery at Pune and Delhi Universities. After commanding Medical Hospital Agra he was Deputy Commandant of the prestigious Army Hospital (R&R) Delhi. He then took over as Dean and Dy Comdt, Armed Forces Medical College, Pune on 16 Feb. 2004, the first alumnus of the college to do so where he was closely associated with the training of medical cadets and specialists. He took over the reins of Army Medical Corps Centre & School, Lucknow on 01 Dec. 2005 before moving on as Director General Medical Services (Navy) 01 Jun. 2006. He was appointed Honorary Surgeon to President of India on 06 Oct. 2006. The Flag officer is a keen sportsman with several achievements to his credit. He has had the rare distinction of representing the country twice in international athletics meet. He won the gold medal in the triple jump event at the Association of South East Asian Nations (ASEAN) Games at Colombo in 1970.

564. (1-5-2007) NEW DELHI : The performance of Indian Railways in respect of loading has gone up from 666.51 Million Tonnes during financial year 2005-06 to 728.41 Million Tonnes during financial year 2006-07, an increase of 9.29 per cent. Freight earnings have also gone up from Rs. 36286.97 crore during financial year 2005-06 to Rs. 41904.80 crore during financial year 2006-07, registering an increase of 15.48 per cent. Passenger earnings have also gone up from Rs. 15080.77 crore during financial year 2005-06 to Rs. 17160.12 crore during the year 2006-07, an increase of 13.79 per cent. Number of accidents in Railways have come down from 233 during financial year 2005-06 to 194 this year. The Diesel Locomotive Works (DLW), Integral Coach Factory (ICF) and Rail Coach Factory (RCF) produced 186 locomotives and 1251 & 1319 coaches respectively during financial year 2006-07 exceeding the target by 36 locomotives and 10 & 83 coaches. Rail Wheel Factory (RWF) produced 126126 wheels and 58259 axles during the same period compared to the target of 126080 wheels and 58723 axles while Chitranjan Locomotive Works (CLW) produced 150 electrical locomotives equalizing the target. The punctuality percentage of mail/express trains was 91.5% in Broad Gauge and 98.4% in Metre Gauge during financial year 2006-07 compared to 91.2% and 97.6% respectively during the same period last year.

565. (1-5-2007) NEW DELHI : The Prime Minister, Dr. Manmohan Singh, inaugurated the Institute for Studies in Industrial Development Campus here today. Speaking on the occasion, the Prime Minister said that 'it is only through rapid industrialization that we can find meaningful solutions to the problems of mass unemployment and underdevelopment. Therefore, we have to find ways and means to accelerate the process of industrialization and also to ensure that this process is sufficiently labour intensive.' Emphasising the need to address the concerns of those who may see themselves as losers in the in the process of industrialization, the Prime Minister said that 'we must learn to address their concerns and assuage them to the extent possible. Industrialisation ought to be a win-win process of social transformation and economic development', he added.

566. (1-5-2007) NEW DELHI : The Ministry of Rural Development has sanctioned Rs. 8.81 crore to the State Government of Punjab towards part payment of first instalment of funds against the provisional allocation of Rs.52.91 crore made for the Government of Punjab under Accelerated Rural Water Supply Programme (Normal) of Rajiv Gandhi National Drinking Water Mission, during the year 2007-08. Up to 15 per cent of funds released under this sanction may be utilized for Operation & Maintenance and up to 5 per cent of funds may be spent for taking sustainability measures. States have been requested to delegate powers for management of Rural Water Supply Schemes through the Panchayati Raj Institutions (PRIs) as per the Constitution of India. As such Operation and Maintenance of the completed RWS Scheme should be transferred to the PRIs. No expenditure shall be incurred on taking water quality problems form the present release, as there is a separate allocation for the purpose. This release is being made for execution/completion of schemes to provide safe drinking water facilities to rural habitations and schools under the Centrally Sponsored ARWSP. Priorities set in ARWSP guidelines and through other instructions issued from time to time shall be followed for coverage of rural habitations and rural schools.

567. (1-5-2007) NEW DELHI : The Ministry of Rural Development has sanctioned Rs. 15.99 crore to the State Government of Chhattisgarh towards part of first instalment of funds against the provisional allocation of Rs. 95.95 crore made for the Government of Chhattisgarh under Accelerated Rural Water Supply Programme (Normal) of Rajiv Gandhi National Drinking Water Mission, during the year 2007-08. the balance amount of first instalment will be released on receipt of AG report for 2004-05. Up to 15 per cent of funds released under this sanction may be utilized for Operation & Maintenance and up to 5 per cent of funds may be spent for taking sustainability measures. States have been requested to delegate powers for management of Rural Water Supply Schemes through the Panchayati Raj Institutions (PRIs) as per the Constitution of India. As such Operation and Maintenance of the completed RWS Scheme should be transferred to the PRIs. No expenditure shall be incurred on taking water quality problems form the present release, as there is a separate allocation for the purpose. This release is being made for execution/completion of schemes to provide safe drinking water facilities to rural habitations and schools under the Centrally Sponsored ARWSP. Priorities set in ARWSP guidelines and through other instructions issued from time to time shall be followed for coverage of rural habitations and rural schools.

568. (1-5-2007) NEW DELHI : The Prime Minister, Dr. Manmohan Singh, has greeted all countrymen on the auspicious occasion of Buddha Purnima. In a message, the Prime Minister said that Lord Buddha showed humanity the enlightened path of peace, non-violence and virtuous living. His eternal message continues to guide us to a society where spiritual and material salvation is possible for one and all. May Buddha Purnima usher in peace, prosperity and happiness for everyone, the Prime Minister added.

569. (2-5-2007) NEW DELHI : The Minister of Petroleum & Natural Gas Shri Murli Deora has emphasized the need for sustainable international oil prices stating that the high oil prices are neither in the interest of oil importing countries nor beneficial to the exporting nations. He was addressing the 2nd Ministerial Energy Roundtable of Asian Oil Producing and major Asian Oil Importing Countries, today at Riyadh. Referring to the three-fold increase in global oil prices between 2000 and 2006, Shri Deora pointed out that the high oil prices in the long run will adversely impact both oil producing and importing countries. The high oil prices leads to fall in demand by encouraging conservation & technological innovations and makes alternative investments for energy attractive besides putting strains on the resources of oil importing developing countries. He called for evolving appropriate policy reforms and practical measures to ensure that the prices remain stable and affordable in the long run. Further, the Minister reiterated India's commitment to the forum which was initiated in India in January 2005. Shri Deora also strongly supported the idea of greater inter-dependence, supplemented by cross investment in energy markets to promote shared interest of energy producers and consumers. The Minister called upon Asian countries to explore various opportunities for forging partnerships in oil and gas sector. This, he explained is required for optimum exploration of hydrocarbons, expansion and modernization of refining infrastructure, augmentation of regional oil and gas transport infrastructure and exchange of information and development of knowledge in Asia. On the sidelines of the Roundtable, Shri Murli Deora today met his Iranian Oil Minister Mr. Seyed Kazem Vaziri Hamaneh and Pakistani Petroleum Minister Mr. Amanullah Khan Jadoon to discuss cooperation in hydrocarbon sector including the Iran-Pakistan-India (IPI) Gas Pipeline Project. In the meeting with the Iranian Minister Shri Deora further discussed the vexed issue of the LNG contract as a follow up of their last meeting in Tehran. It may be recalled that Shri Deora had recently returned from his tour of Iran where he had discussed both IPI Gas Pipeline Project as well as the Indo – Iran LNG contract for 5 million tonne which was signed in June 2005 at Tehran. Shri Deora also had a bilateral meeting with Iraqi Oil Minister Mr. Hussain Al-Shahristani and raised the issue of moving forward with OVL's participation in Iraq's upstream oil sector. The Iraqi Minister invited IOCL and EIL to consider participation in the downstream sector of Iraq in particular for construction of Oil Refinery. Saudi Arabian Oil Minister Engineer Ali Al Naimi received the Indian Minister at Riyadh Airport yesterday and the two Ministers took the opportunity to discuss very strong bilateral relations between the two countries. Saudi Arabia is the largest supplier of crude oil to India. Shri Murli Deora is attending the 2nd Asian Ministerial Energy Roundtable in Riyadh. He is accompanied by a high level delegation comprising CEOs of ONGC, IOC, BPCL, HPCL & EIL.

570. (2-5-2007) NEW DELHI : The attention of the Government is drawn to the incident being broadcast by Star News involving a case of corruption in getting a job as loader through a cargo complex employee. According to the Bureau of Civil Aviation Security (BCAS), prima facie there appears to be no security breach as the cargo complex falls within the city side of the airport, an area controlled by the Delhi International Airport Ltd. (DIAL). Security of IGI Airport International Cargo Complex is the responsibility of DIAL. For the Cargo Complex, DIAL issues pass for entry only into the cargo complex building, and these passes do not allow for entry into the operational airside area of the airport. There is total segregation of the Cargo Complex from the airside operational area of the airport by means a steel chain link 12 ft high along the boundary. There is only ONE exit and ONE entry gate in this boundary, which is guarded by CISF. Access from International Cargo complex to airside areas is effectively controlled by CISF and all persons entering the airside areas even with authorised documents are subjected to screening and frisking before each entry. In this case, the person who obtained employment and a DIAL pass as loader does not seem to have gone beyond the chain link into the operational and vulnerable area of the airport and was shown to be within the cargo complex till where his entry was restricted. The current incident is more a case of malpractice involved to get a job as a loader through a Cargo Complex employee, rather than a case of a security breach, and appropriate authorities will look into it. In case there has been any security breach, it will be investigated thoroughly by CISF and BCA S. The issue needs to be seen in the above perspective so that unnecessary alarm is not generated as has happened in the instant case.

571. (2-5-2007) NEW DELHI : The annual Indo-German Consultation meeting for development cooperation shall be held in New Delhi tomorrow *i.e.*, 3rd May, 2007 to discuss the new projects for funding by the Government of Germany in 2007. The umbrella agreements for technical cooperation and financial cooperation in respect of projects committed in 2006 shall also be signed tomorrow by the Joint Secretary, Ministry of Finance, Mr. Kumar Sanjay Krishna from Indian side and Mr. Bernd Mutzelburg, the German Ambassador to India. The agreements entail German development assistance amounting to Rs.1450 crore (€ 240 million). German development cooperation is an important component of bilateral economic relations between the two countries. The two countries are doing well in improving the bilateral trade, which has already crossed the agreed target of $ 10 billion (to be reached in 2010) well in advance by 4 years in 2006 itself. The development cooperation portfolio supports a number of activities that promote investment in India particularly in infrastructure sector including a JWG on Infrastructure and

FC/TC support to various projects in power, road and railways sectors. The bilateral development cooperation with the Federal Republic of Germany has been an example of excellent bilateral cooperation, innovation and alignment of development priorities. The German development cooperation portfolio is closely aligned with our development guidelines as laid out in 11th Five Year Plan. In 2005, new priority areas of Indo-German development cooperation were mutually agreed upon, which focus on Energy (energy efficiency and renewable energy), Environmental Protection and sustainable use of natural resources and Economic Reforms (micro financing, cooperation, banking, SME financing). The Indo-German development cooperation has been historically important having the roots in the German FC support to Rourkela Steel Plant in 1958. Since then, it has led to development of longstanding and fruitful partnerships in health, infrastructure development, rural development, poverty alleviation, economic reforms, consumer protection, environmental protection, SME development and other relevant sectors. Germany is the pioneer in providing useful technical assistance to us in the important area of energy efficiency. In fact, the road map of the Bureau of Energy Efficiency (BEE) has largely been laid out with the German technical assistance. Germany is also supporting important power sector projects, both hydro and thermal, in the States of Uttaranchal, Andhra Pradesh and Madhya Pradesh. Recently, an Indo-German Energy dialogue to support the development cooperation has been launched by the two sides. Besides this, German technical assistance in the sphere of micro-financing through NABARD and creation of self-help groups under various German-assisted projects is worth being replicated. Recently, an important project for Revival of cooperative banking, which is based on the Vaidyanathan Committee Report, is also being supported by KfW. The German experience of efficient management of their natural resources is an important source of technical assistance for India under the "Natural resources management" umbrella project launched in 2005. Germany took the lead as the first development partner to support the projects in social security sector in the State of Karnataka. Likewise, the first externally-aided project on SME development and financing (SIDBI) is also being extensively supported by Germany.

572. (2-5-2007) NEW DELHI : The Department of Biotechnology (DBT), Ministry of Science & Technology, Government of India and the International AIDS Vaccine Initiative signed an agreement today to address a major obstacle in AIDS vaccine development: the design of candidate vaccines to elicit neutralizing antibodies against HIV. A new Indian Medicinal Chemistry Programme, co-sponsored and co-funded by IAVI and the Department of Biotechnology, will comprise top Indian and U.S. scientists tasked with accelerating the pace of AIDS vaccine discovery and developing creative concepts for the next generation of AIDS vaccines. Union Minister for Science and Technology and Earth Sciences Shri. Kapil Sibal said that vaccine research is so critical that the Health Ministry and the Science and Technology Ministry have joined hands to provide the effort the support it needs. India's Department of Biotechnology is delighted to be a part of the global search for an efficacious AIDS vaccine. This was stated by Dr. Maharaj K. Bhan, Secretary, DBT. He said only through these kinds of biotechnology ventures involving international collaborations and the sharing of scientific knowledge, can we hope to solve the complex biomedical problems of our times. According to Seth Berkley, CEO and President of IAVI, this new partnership will broaden ongoing efforts in India to find an AIDS vaccine. The Indian Programme will complement the work of IAVI's Neutralizing Antibody Consortium (NAC), a team of internationally recognized scientists working on the neutralizing antibody challenge. Researchers believe an ideal AIDS vaccine must evoke an antibody response that can block HIV from entering healthy cells, as well as reduce the amount of viral dissemination through a cell-mediated immune response to HIV-infected cells. Yet today, virtually all current vaccine candidates in the pipeline are based on cell-mediated immune responses alone, failing to target the second critical arm of the human immune system. The first component of the DBT-IAVI Programme will consist of a collaboration of principal investigators from different academic research laboratories to design novel HIV antigens. The investigators include Professor Virander S. Chauhan of the International Centre for Genetic Engineering and Biotechnology, New Delhi; Professor Raghavan Varadarajan of the Indian Institute of Science, Bangalore; Dr. Stephen Kaminsky of IAVI's AIDS Vaccine Development Laboratory, New York; and Dr. Philip Dawson of The Scripps Research Institute, California. IAVI and DBT may select additional principal investigators, contract researchers, or partners in India to participate in the Programme, and will discuss ways to build infrastructure for subsequent HIV/AIDS vaccine candidate evaluation.

573. (2-5-2007) NEW DELHI : Shri Kamal Nath, Minister of Commerce & Industry, will deliver a Special Address at the University College in Oxford, in response to an invitation from the University of Oxford on 3rd May, 2007. The Special Address, which is part of the University's Global Economic Governance Programme, will be on "India and the Future of the World Trade Talks". During his visit to the UK, Shri Kamal Nath is also likely to call on Prime Minister Tony Blair. On the bilateral front, he will hold discussions with Mr. Alistair Darling, UK Secretary of State for Trade & Industry and participate in the Indo-UK Joint Economic & Trade Committee (JETCO) review meetings. JETCO was established in September 2004 to further develop a strategic economic relationship and promote business-led vehicles to enhance bilateral trade and investment between India and the UK. Indo-UK trade has gone up substantially in recent years, with two-way trade between the two countries rising from a level of US $ 6.2 billion in 2003-04 to US $ 9 billion in 2005-06. India had a trade surplus with the UK in 2005-06 as India's exports to the UK surged to US $ 5.1 billion and India's imports from the UK stood at US $ 3.8 billion.

574. (2-5-2007) NEW DELHI : I am indeed delighted to participate in the inauguration of Poly Medical Clinic established by Wat Thai Kusinara Mahavihar at Kushinagar to commemorate the 2550th Anniversary Mahaparinirvana of Lord Buddha. My greetings to the reverent Monks, doctors, nurses, paramedical staff and distinguished guests. I congratulate Wat Thai Kusinara Charitable Trust for planning and creation of a large medical centre in this divine place. I am glad to see this hospital grow with facilities for admission in general medicines, orthopaedics, paediatrics, gynaecology, and chest diseases and many other specialities. A report on "Health Care in India" was prepared in consultation with leading doctors, medical technologists and healthcare providers in the country. The report brought out typical problems facing us for two decades in the health care and suggested possible solutions. The expert team has identified eradication of three major diseases namely, Tuberculosis, HIV and water-borne diseases by next decade; followed by cardiovascular diseases, neuro-psychiatric disorders, renal diseases and hypertension, gastrointestinal disorders, eye disorders, genetic diseases, accidents and trauma, which need our attention. There are two major issues involved. First, we have to augment our primary healthcare system in a big way, empower our secondary healthcare system and integrate both with the tertiary care centres. Second, we should see how the advancement in technology could be put to use to improve the health care system of the country. These two efforts will make modern medicine available and accessible to all the citizens of our country. The Poly Medical Clinic will be the first step towards providing quality healthcare to the people of Kusinara and the tourists coming to this place in view of its international importance. When I am with you, I would like to discuss my experience with mobile clinics in Hill Regions.

575. (3-5-2007) NEW DELHI : Nano Technology is a knowledge-intensive and "enabling technology" which is expected to influence a wide range of products and processes with far-reaching implications for national economy and development. The Government of India has approved the launch of a Mission on Nano Science and Technology (Nano Mission) with an allocation of Rs. 1000 crore for 5 years. The Department of Science and Technology will be the nodal agency for implementing the Nano Mission. Capacity-building in this upcoming area of research will be of utmost importance for the Nano Mission so that India emerges as a global knowledge-hub in this field also. For this, research on fundamental aspects of Nano Science and training of large number of manpower will receive prime attention. Equally importantly, the Nano Mission will strive for development of products and processes for national development, especially in areas of national relevance like safe drinking water, materials development, sensors development, drug delivery, etc. For this, it will forge linkages between educational and research institutions and industry and promote Public Private Partnerships. The Nano Mission has been structured in a fashion so as to achieve synergy between the national research efforts of various agencies in Nano Science and Technology and launch new programmes in a concerted fashion. International collaborative research efforts will also be made wherever required.

576. (3-5-2007) NEW DELHI : The Union Cabinet today gave its approval by accepting the recommendation of the Joint Committee that a Member of Parliament will be allowed to engage any number of persons either in Delhi or in his constituency for obtaining secretarial assistance within the total monetary ceiling of Rs.14,000/- per month and out of them at least one person should be computer literate and the certification by the Member about the computer literacy of such person would suffice. The Cabinet also gave its approval for making consequential amendments in the Members of Parliament (Office Expense Allowance) Rules 1988. The amendment would give required flexibility to the Members of Parliament in obtaining secretarial assistance.

577. (3-5-2007) NEW DELHI : The Union Cabinet today approved for India becoming a Member of the Hague Conference on Private international Law. The Hague Conference on Private International Law is an inter-governmental organization. The main purpose of the Conference is to work for the progressive unification of the rules of private international law by finding internationally agreed approaches to issues such as jurisdiction of courts, applicable law, and recognition and enforcement of judgements in a wide range of areas such as commercial laws, international civil procedures and matters relating to child protection, marriage and personal issues. At present, it has 65 Member States. The issues dealt with and the Conventions adopted by the Hague Conference are of great practical relevance to India in view of its large diaspora, increasing trade relations and travel abroad by Indian citizens. As a Member State, India would be entitled to participate in all the meetings and conferences. India would also have a role in deciding on the future work programme.

578. (3-5-2007) NEW DELHI : The Union Cabinet today approved for passing the Airports Economic Regulatory Authority Bill, 2007 in the Parliament. The AERA Bill, 2007 will enable setting up of Airports Economic Regulatory Authority (AERA), which will fix, review and approve tariff structure for aeronautical services and also will monitor pre-set performance standards at Indian airports. The Authority will not have regulation over Army and Paramilitary Airports.

579. (3-5-2007) NEW DELHI : The Union Cabinet today approved for moving the official amendments to the Constitution (One Hundred and Third Amendment) Bill, 2004 and the National Commission for Minorities (Repeal) Bill, 2004, in Parliament for consideration and passage. These amendments would infuse a greater sense of confidence amongst the minorities.

580. (3-5-2007) NEW DELHI : The proposed Bill for setting up the Airport Economic Regulatory Authority (AERA) received the clearance of the Union Government today. The Bill will now have to be passed by the Parliament. The prime objective of AERA will be to create a level playing field and foster healthy competition among all major airports (Government owned, Public Private

Partnership based, Private) encourage investment in airport facilities regulate tariffs of aeronautical services, protection of reasonable interest of users, operate efficient, economic and viable airports at notified airports. The Authority shall consist of a Chairperson and 2 persons to be appointed by the Central Government from amongst persons having adequate knowledge and professional expertise in aviation, economic law, commerce or consumer affairs. The member shall be whole time appointees. Whenever the Authority is deciding a matter involving a civil enclave in a Defence airfield, the Defence Ministry will be represented by an additional member on the Authority who will be nominated by the Ministry of Defence.

581. (3-5-2007) NEW DELHI : The Minister for Civil Aviation, Shri Praful Patel, today welcomed the exemption from customs duty on import of aircraft by non-scheduled operators and flying training institutions. It may be recalled that in the Budget of 2007-08 it was decided to impose import duties on aircraft – 3% customs duty, 16% counter-veiling duty and 4% additional duty of customs, on aircrafts imported for non-scheduled airlines, chartered operations and private imports by individuals and corporates. Welcoming the move the Minister said that this relief will help in promoting connectivity to the remote areas including the North-East and the islands and to the remote tourist destinations. It will help in the economic development of these areas as well as promote tourism. This decision will help in promoting the flying training institutions and help combat the severe shortage of pilots that the civil aviation sector is facing today. Institutes like the Indira Gandhi Rashtriya Uran Akademi (IGRUA) will substantially benefit from this decision. Further, the helicopter services operated by non-scheduled operators in Andaman and Nicobar Islands and Lakshadweep, North-East will also be benefited.

582. (3-5-2007) NEW DELHI : A blood and organ donation camp was organised at Base Hospital here today under the aegis of Army Wives and Welfare Association (AWWA). This Camp was basically organised to promote awareness among the all ranks regarding usefulness of donating blood and organs. The camp was inaugurated by Mrs. Vandana Oberoi, President Delhi Area AWWA. Major General KJS Oberoi, General Officer Commanding, Delhi Area alongwith other senior officers donated blood and pledged to donate organs. The camp was a huge success as nearly 220 personnel donated blood. About 130 army personnel and their wives pledged to donate their organs during this camp. Along with the blood and organ donation camp a health education campaign regarding blood donation and its benefits was also carried out during the camp.

583. (3-5-2007) NEW DELHI : The Bharatendu Harischandra Awards for the year 2004 & 2005 have been announced. These awards are given by the Ministry of Information & Broadcasting to promote original writings in Hindi on Journalism and Mass Communication.

584. (3-5-2007) NEW DELHI : A request is pending with Government to grant the Navratna status to Shipping Corporation of India (SCI). However, many areas of deficiency have been noticed in corporate governance of Shipping Corporation of India (SCI) which need to be removed in the interest of efficiency and transparency. SCI is taking corrective measures to ensure that its internal governance system achieves a level of efficiency and transparency that a company should desirably achieve before Navratna status is bestowed on it. The progress of SCI towards these reforms is being monitored regularly. This information was given by the Minister of Shipping, Road Transport and Highways, Shri T.R. Baalu in a written reply in the Rajya Sabha today.

585. (3-5-2007) NEW DELHI : Improving efficiency of the ports is an ongoing process and involves development of berths, deepening of channels, equipment upgradation and modernization of rail-road connectivity. Government of India has constituted an Inter-Ministerial Group (IMG) under the Chairmanship of Secretary, Department of Shipping to make recommendations for reducing the dwell time at Major Ports and to bring it in line with international standards. The IMG is in the process of finalizing the report. Except Paradip and Ennore Ports, Electronic Data Interchange (EDI) (between Ports and Customs Department) has been implemented in all the major ports including Visakhapatnam Port in Andhra Pradesh. The scope of EDI is being further enlarged. This information was given by the Minister of Shipping, Road Transport and Highways, Shri T.R. Baalu in a written reply in the Rajya Sabha today.

586. (3-5-2007) NEW DELHI : Some pirates had hijacked an Indian ship M.V. Nehm Tulah alongwith its 14 members crew on 1st April, 2007. As per reports received from the owners of the vessel, the vessel, cargo and all the 14 crew members have been released at around 1120 hours Indian Standard Time on 6th April, 2007. The crew comprising all Indian nationals are safe. The Government is not aware of any conditions attached to the release of the said vessel. The Directorate General of Shipping, Mumbai had issued a circular on 27th April, 2006 informing all concerned about the incidents of piracy and armed robbery against ships especially in the vicinity of the Somalian coast where incidents of piracy and attacks on ships have been on the rise. The Indian National Ship owners Association (INSA) and Federation of All India Sailing Vessels Industry Association have also been informed to convey to their members that they should keep away from the Somalian coast. Subsequently, the Directorate General of Shipping, Mumbai issued another circular on 8th January, 2007 drawing attention of the shipping fraternity and seafaring community of attacks against ships in Somalian waters. This circular also contained detailed guidelines to avoid such attacks and acts of piracy. This information was given by the Minister of Shipping, Road Transport and Highways, Shri T.R. Baalu in a written reply in the Rajya Sabha today.

587. (3-5-2007) NEW DELHI : There are 27 Shipyards in the country out of which 6 Shipyards are under the Central Government. The combined capacity of these yards is approximately 2,81,200 DWT and the maximum size of ship which can be built in Indian shipyard is 1,10,000 DWT. The order book position of Indian Shipyards is approximately Rs.14,000 crore. No proposal for setting up a Maritime Board for modernization of Shipyards is under consideration at present. This information was given by the Minister of Shipping, Road Transport and Highways, Shri T.R. Baalu in a written reply in the Rajya Sabha today.

588. (3-5-2007) NEW DELHI : BJP National Vice President Shri Mukhtar Abbas Naqvi today said that the BSP and Congress have both lost the semifinal match of the Uttar Pradesh elections. Shri Naqvi, who is the incharge of the BJP Election Management and Coordination Committee, said this in a meeting of the "Election War Room" while reviewing the six phases of the Uttar Pradesh elections as well as preparations for the forthcoming seventh phase. Shri Naqvi added that the final round match of the Uttar Pradesh elections is a direct contest between the BJP and the Samajwadi Party where the BJP will defeat the Samajwadi Party's "Tamancha, Tijori and Tushtikaran Raj" by a heavy margin of seats. Shri Naqvi said that the alliance of the BJP, Apna Dal and JD(U) has instilled confidence of good governance, security and prosperity among all sections. As a result of this, the "Vijay Rath" of the BJP alliance is on the path of forming a government in Uttar Pradesh with complete majority. Shri Naqvi further said that the minority community's extensive support for the BJP alliance is a clear indication of the fact that the conspiracy for their political exploitation by the "fraud secular brigade" stands completely exposed and that the muslims consider the BJP alliance as the guarantor for their economic, social and educational development. Shri Naqvi said that the results of the Uttar Pradesh elections will be responsible for bringing about revolutionary changes in the national political scenario and will also prove to be the "last nail in the coffin" for the Congress led central government. Shri Naqvi said that based on the analysis of the six phases of elections so far and indications gathered from various reports about the seventh phase, the BJP alliance is confident of winning over 200 seats in the state.

589. (3-5-2007) NEW DELHI : As per the Detailed Project Report (DPR), the Sethusamudram project is scheduled to be completed by November, 2008. There is no scientific evidence regarding the existence of any ancient man-made structure in the proposed Sethusamudram Ship Channel alignment. Representations against undertaking the project have been received. However, as per the scientific information available with the Project Authorities, there is no underwater construction in the project area. As per the information available no heritage site has been declared in the project area. Final selection of the alignment has been done keeping in view various aspects including the navigational, environmental and ecological considerations. This information was given by the Minister of Shipping, Road Transport and Highways, Shri T.R. Baalu in a written reply in the Rajya Sabha today.

590. (3-5-2007) NEW DELHI : Director General of Shipping is the regulatory body for seafarers training and is ensuring quality training. About 18000 officers and 20,350 ratings are either awaiting sea time training or under employed or in the process of getting sea time training. In view of shortage of Indian officers, the Government is considering a proposal to allow foreign officers to work on Indian ships subject to certain conditions in consultation with the shipping industry. This information was given by the Minister of Shipping, Road Transport and Highways, Shri T.R. Baalu in a written reply in the Rajya Sabha today.

591. (3-5-2007) NEW DELHI : The quality control of the construction of four laning works are monitored by Independent Consultants (who are generally International Consultants) appointed through International Competitive Bidding by National Highways Authority of India (NHAI) for supervision of the civil contract and who act as Engineer for administration of the contract. Quality standards for construction of the road is governed by "Specification for Road and Bridge Works" published by Ministry of Shipping, Road Transport and Highways/ Indian Roads Congress and these specifications are part of the Contract Agreement. Quality tests are regularly carried out at field laboratories by Supervision Consultants. Further, quality audits are also being carried out by NHAI. Whenever any deficiency or defects of not conforming to the technical specification in construction are found, remedial action is taken by the Engineer for rejection/ replacement/rectification of work/material as per provision of the Contract Agreement. Similarly, defects detected during defect liability period (which is normally 12 months from the date of completion of the project) are also rectified by the contractor as part of the obligations as per contract. This information was given by the Minister of State for Shipping, Road Transport and Highways, Shri K.H. Muniyappa in a written reply in the Rajya Sabha today.

592. (3-5-2007) NEW DELHI : On the recommendations of the Committee on Infrastructure, the Ministry of Shipping, Road Transport and Highways had constituted a Committee under the Chairmanship of Shri S. Sundar, former Secretary of the then Ministry of Surface Transport to deliberate and make recommendations for setting up an effective and dedicated agency for Road Safety and Traffic Management. The Committee submitted its report on 20.2.2007. The main recommendations of the Committee include creation of National Road Safety & Traffic Management Board through an Act of the Parliament. Enabling provision has been suggested in the report for creation of similar bodies at State level. The Committee has recommended earmarking of atleast 1% of the total proceeds of cess on diesel and petrol for road safety fund. The recommendations of the Committee have been circulated among the States/UTs and concerned Ministries/ Departments for their comments. This information was given by the Minister of State for Shipping, Road Transport and Highways, Shri K.H. Muniyappa in a written reply in the Rajya Sabha today.

593. (3-5-2007) NEW DELHI : The Road Safety Forum had suggested about uniform testing and grant of driving licenses all over the country. This Ministry has already developed a standardized software to facilitate issuance of smart card based Driving Licenses and Registration Certificates and given free of cost to all State Governments/UT Administration. The Proforma for issuance of license in Smart Card mode has already been prescribed by the Central Government and is applicable uniformly throughout the country. However, implementation of various provisions of Motor Vehicles Act, 1988 and Rules framed thereunder *i.e.* Central Motor Vehicles Rules, 1989 is the responsibility of the concerned State Government. The driving skill of the applicant seeking driving license is tested either by the Licensing Authorities or the applicant has to obtain a driving certificate (for non-transport vehicles) from any institution recognised in this behalf by the State Government. The issuance of driving license is already decentralized and the driving licenses are issued by concerned State Governments through RTOs. The Motor Vehicles Act, 1988 further empowers State Governments to make rules for appointment, jurisdiction, control and functions of the Licencing Authorities. However, the State Governments can recognise certain institutions to conduct the test of competence and issue driving certificates which enables the licensing authorities to issue driving licence. Any complaint regarding corruption at the testing centres is to be looked into by the concerned State Government. This information was given by the Minister of State for Shipping, Road Transport and Highways, Shri K.H. Muniyappa in a written reply in the Rajya Sabha today.

594. (3-5-2007) NEW DELHI : Some representations were received, especially during monsoon season, regarding repair and maintenance of certain highways/ bridges under National Highways Development Project (NHDP), which were duly attended to as part of maintenance to keep the highways/ bridges in traffic worthy condition. Wherever 4/6 laning works under NHDP are under implementation, to keep the existing roads in traffic worthy condition, the maintenance of existing roads are carried out by the Contractor/ Concessionaire as part of their obligations under contract/ concession agreement. In case of sections identified under NHDP where 4/6 laning has not yet started, the maintenance of existing roads are being carried out by NHAI, State Public Works Departments (PWDs)/ Border Road Organisation (BRO) through funds provided by the Ministry of Shipping, Road Transport and Highways. This information was given by the Minister of State for Shipping, Road Transport and Highways, Shri K.H. Muniyappa in a written reply in the Rajya Sabha today.

595. (3-5-2007) NEW DELHI : The Heritage Route from Ahmedabad to Dandi has been declared as National Highway No. 228 in June, 2006 and entrusted to the National Highways Authority of India (NHAI) on 31.10.2006 for development and maintenance. NHAI has been asked to take up the improvement works on this National Highway to minimum 2-lane NH Standards under Ministry's budgetary support. However, there is no separate allocation for NH-228. It is too early to give time frame for completion of the improvement works. This information was given by the Minister of State for Shipping, Road Transport and Highways, Shri K.H. Muniyappa in a written reply in the Rajya Sabha today.

596. (3-5-2007) NEW DELHI : Women should be provided all opportunities to contribute to the development of the society and they should be given due space to grow at par with men. Addressing a workshop on gender equality in Indian media organized by the Ministry of Women and Child Development here today on the world Press Freedom Day, Smt. Renuka Chowdhury, Minister for Women and Child Development said that gender justice and recognition to the potential of the women is must for the positive development of the society. Expressing concern over gender discrimination in various fields, she said that if given chance women could contribute better in many ways than their counterparts in the fields. Addressing the workshop, Shri P.R. Dasmunsi, Minister of Information and Broadcasting said that proper facilities at the workplace especially for the women journalists, considering their specific needs, should be ensured. He announced that equal opportunities would be provided to the women in Doordarshan and All India Radio in anchoring and news reading from 15th August onwards this year. Inaugural session was also addressed by Smt. Mrinal Pandey, Editor, Hindustan Times. She said that more representation of women at the management level in the newspaper industry is desirable. Smt. Sushma Ramachandran, President, Women Press Club raised the issue of better understanding of the needs of the women journalists, she said that in the recent past women journalists had come in a big way to contribute significantly in various forms of reporting. On the occasion, presentations were made by the distinguished journalists which included 'challenges before the news Media and gender equality' by Ms. Akhila Sivadas, 'the representation of women in print media' by Ms. Angana Parikh and 'the representation of women in electronic media' by Ms. Shelaja Vajpayee. It was followed by panel discussions.

597. (3-5-2007) NEW DELHI : The Ministry of Women and Child Development is working on a time bound package to remove procedural bottlenecks and systematic gap in the present adoption system to make it simple, quick and more transparent. This was stated by Smt. Renuka Chowdhury, Minister for Women and Child Development while inaugurating the National meet on adoption organized by the Central Adoption Resource Agency (CARA) here today. She said that lack of transparency across the adoption process and time taken to complete various formalities had made the programme confined to few pockets/cities. The total number of adoption is less compared to total number of orphan and abandoned children in the country. She said that working of the CARA would be revamped to show results both in qualitative and quantitative terms and adoption process would be made hassle free and less cumbersome through centralized database. The two-days' meet is being attended by the senior officials of State Governments dealing with adoption matters, representatives from Placements Agencies, and Homes run by NGOs/State Govts. getting grant-in-aid from Central Government for running Shishu Greh Scheme, Adoption Coordinating Agencies and other associated agencies. The objective of the meet is to review issues related with adoption and to get feedback from the State Governments and adoption agencies for further rationalization adoption process. The meet includes sessions on adoption scenario in the States, implementation of Juvenile Justice Act particularly related to adoption matters, suggestions from States Govts./associated agencies about In-country Guidelines and Inter-country Guidelines, issue of child protection, preparation of Centralized Database and facilities for registration of prospective adoptive parents within the country etc.

598. (3-5-2007) NEW DELHI : Dr. Dasari Narayan Rao, Minister of State for Coal informed the Rajya Sabha in a written reply today that to deal with the problems of fire, subsidence and rehabilitation in the leasehold area of Bharat Coking Coal Limited (BCCL) a Master Plan (updated July 2006) has been prepared. Under this, the existing 67 nos. of fires is proposed to be controlled/ extinguished by implementing 45 numbers of fire projects in 12 years time with a total investment of Rs. 2152.51 crore. A total of 595 sites are proposed to be resettled and the number of houses to be rehabilitated has been estimated at 98314. These include BCCL houses-44155, Non-BCCL houses(Authorised Private)-29444, Un-authorised (Encroachers)-23847 and Others (religious structures, schools, Post office etc.)-868. The houses from the endangered area are proposed to be rehabilitated in 4 to 5 satellite townships in non coal bearing areas along the periphery of Jharia Coalfield. The total investment has been estimated at Rs 4185.94 crore to be spent in 12 years time frame. Dr. Rao explained that the rehabilitation of BCCL houses would be the responsibility of BCCL. Rehabilitation of Non-BCCL houses from the endangered areas will be the responsibility of State Govt. of Jharkhand and necessary funds will be made available to State Govt. by BCCL. The Minister also informed that an authority namely Jharia Rehabilitation and Development Authority (JRDA) has been constituted by State Govt. under the Chairmanship of Commissioner North Chotanagpur for the purpose of rehabilitation of non-BCCL houses. A Demonstration Scheme for shifting of 3100 non-BCCL houses (un-authorized) is under implementation at Belgoria mouza where work is in progress for which a total fund of Rs. 16.4 crore has already been made available to JRDA till date. BCCL reported an accident due to caving-in of land *i.e.* subsidence, in which two houses collapsed at Kusunda Collieries area at 2.15 AM on 15.3.2007 (night shift of 14.3.2007) involving loss of life of ten persons and injuries to five persons. All the persons involved belonged to families of two BCCL employees. This subsidence occurred in old abandoned mined out area.

599. (3-5-2007) NEW DELHI : There are 27,82,293 elected representatives in Panchayats out of which 10,42,282 are women which constitute to 37.46 %. Article 243D of the Constitution provides that not less than one-third of the total number of seats in every Panchayat shall be reserved for women including Chairpersons in every Panchayats and such seat may be allotted by rotation to different Constituencies/ Panchayats at each level.

600. (3-5-2007) NEW DELHI : The total amount paid to the coal transportation companies owned by Ex-Servicemen (ESM) during the financial year 2005-06 is Rs. 536.88 crore. ESM companies are deployed in coal producing subsidiaries of Coal India Limited (CIL) except Eastern Coalfields Limited (ECL), Northern Coalfields Limited (NCL) and North Eastern Coalfields (NEC) for coal transportation work as per the Memorandum of Understanding between Director General Resettlement (Ministry of Defence) and Coal India Limited. The rate of coal transportation for ESM Company is fixed for different leads based on normative rates as per the recommendations of M/s Price Water House Coopers. However, in case of transportation done by civilian transport agency, the award of work is done through open tender and rate is recommended by Tender committee and approved by the Competent Authority. As the payment made to ESM Companies is based on normative rates, whereas payment made to civilian transport companies is based on tendered rate, the two rates are not exactly comparable. As such the question of excess payment made to Ex-servicemen Transport Companies does not arise. This information was given by the Minister of State for Coal Dr. Dasari Narayana Rao in a written reply in the Rajya Sabha today.

601. (3-5-2007) NEW DELHI : The Minister of State for Coal Dr. Dasari Narayana Rao informed the Rajya Sabha in a written reply today that coal companies have sufficient coal stock to meet the assessed demand of power plants. Off-take by power utilities from Coal India Limited sources during 2005-06 was as per the Annual Action Plan targets. However, he added, off take by power utilities from Coal India Limited sources during 2006-07 was less than the Annual Action Plan target by about 4% on account of non-materialisation of demand, infrastructural bottlenecks, unloading constraints, transportation constraints and reluctance in building up normative level stocks by power plants at their end. Dr. Rao also informed the House that power utilities have imported only about 10 million tonnes of coal during 2006-07 as against the target of 20 million tones.

602. (3-5-2007) NEW DELHI : The Minister of Overseas Indian Affairs, Shri Vayalar Ravi inaugurated the computerisation of Protector of Emigrant (POE) Office in New Delhi today. He announced that all the POE offices, which are functioning in Mumbai, Kolkata, Cochin, Hyderabad, Thiruvananthapuram, Chandigarh and Chennai will be computerized soon. He said that this will make immigration process more easy and transparent and also check the illegal immigration. The POE office at New Delhi is the first in the line and the pilot project of automation through computerization has been completed in this office. Mr. Ravi also said that Ministry is taking further steps to extend this automation to other POE offices shortly and link-up the same with the Ministry and also the Missions abroad and to the Immigration desks at the airports to organize faster delivery of such services. Also through the web, all information would be available to one and all uniformly and this could go a longway in ensuring transparency, he added.

603. (3-5-2007) NEW DELHI : The Minister of State for Communications & Information Technology, Dr. Shakeel Ahmad, informed the Rajya Sabha today, in a written reply to a question by Smt. Syeda Anwara Taimur that Bharat Sanchar Nigam Limited (BSNL) is planning to invest on WiMax infrustructure in 10 cities/ towns namely Bangalore, Chennai, Kolkata, Pune, Hyderabad, Ahmedabad for urban applications and Hissar, Pinjore, Rohtak and Panipat for rural applications. The Minister further stated that BSNL has finalised a tender for WiMax systems. The finalised rate for procurement was Rs. 1.92 crore. The equipment has been received and one system has already been installed at each of the ten selected cities/towns. Guwahati was not included in this phase of ten cities deployment.

604. (3-5-2007) NEW DELHI : The Minister of State for Communications & Information Technology, Dr. Shakeel Ahmad, informed the Rajya Sabha today, in a written reply to a question by Prof. Alka Balram Kshatriya and Smt. Shobhana Bhartia that the Government has decided to set up telecom-specific Special Economic Zones to make India telecom manufacturing hub. Dr. Ahmad further stated that the Government has granted approval for setting up of 'Export Promotion Forum' under the aegis of Telecom Equipment Manufacturers Association of India to promote export of telecom equipment and services. The Minister further stated that his Ministry has set a target of 500 million phone connections by 2010 and the Government is taking measures to facilitate all the operators to enhance their penetration. With the passing of the Indian Telegraph (amendment) Bill, 2006, it will be possible to provide USO support of provision of mobile services and broadband connectivity in rural areas. USO subsidy support scheme will be utilised for shared wireless infrastructure in rural areas with about 8000 towers by 2007. Measures are being taken to increase availability of spectrum including the release of substantial quantum from Defence.

605. (3-5-2007) NEW DELHI : Shri Abhishek Singhvi said that the Congress Party welcomes the Apex Court order directing more information, more detailed report, including specific report about the obstructions and transfer in respect of Geeta Johari, the IPS officer, regarding Gujarat events. The Court had simply differed its final decision till May 15 and we hope and trust that the court will take action, commensurate with the acts and omissions and guilt of the Gujarat government after ascertaining all the facts. Yesterday the Gujarat government tried to block off its police headquarters to the media. It is understandable because those who do dark deeds in the darkness of night do not want the disinfectant of sunlight. But no amount of obstructions or blocking can cover up the dark deeds of the governmental machinery in Gujarat or rather the absence of governmental machinery. As recently as April 27, the infamous P.C. Pandey, already structured for the Godhra events, issued a circular saying that the entire investigation by Rajneesh Roy, the police official who had arrested Mr. Vanzara and others, would be supervised by a new person, Shri O.P. Mathur. Clearly, the attempt is to control, guide and monitor the investigation itself. But this is only the detail, the larger issue is the real issue, Gujarat is a proud state and Gujaraties are a proud people, rightly so. But the Modi government has reduced it to a lawless government. It has raised the basic question, who will guard the guardians. It has become lawlessness by the state, for the state, of the state and the events make it clear that without full institutional state awareness, without state support, without state acknowledgment, such things could not have happened. Is it possible to rape a woman at the farm house of a sitting BJP corporator without some element of state assistance? Is it possible to liquidate that woman and then burn her with 300 to 400 kg. of wood brought on truck and cranes in the capital of Gujarat without awareness, knowledge and connivance? Is it possible to kill the only witness, Prajapati, to liquidate Mr. Sheikh, to claim in a written report to the Supreme Court that Sheikh was riding a motorcycle and firing in the heart of Ahmedabad where he was killed in an encounter? Please note two more things. The Gujarat government is today crying hoarse and shedding crocodile tears and expressing full cooperation did nothing for months. It is only when the Supreme Court gave them directions that even Ms. Johri's enquiries were allowed to go on but even those enquiries, as Ms. Johri's written report shows, were obstructed. What is worse, the Supreme Court asked for a report by the Additional Solicitor General of India. In a written report of this year, Mr. Subramaniyam has said that further related documents were not supplied to him and has in writing asked the Supreme Court to draw an adverse inference on the suppression of documents. So, it is the larger full picture which matters. It is this picture which shows that Gujarat is and has become a lawless state. Off course, no wonder, we find that here there is Katara, there it is Modi govt. and police lawlessness and no wonder the patriarch who presided over all this, Mr. Vajpayee, now wants to run away and retire from politics. Even he perhaps cannot stand the succession of BJP scandals one after the other or perhaps he is disillusioned by the fact that the President of the BJP talked of Mr. Advani in succession and not of Mr. Vajpayee. But whatever be the reason you are seeing here all the symptoms of a rotten, decaying, failed state. CBI enquiry is the minimum but much more so is required to cleanse the rottenness of the state of Gujarat under the Modi govt. To a question as to how Congress Party would react to connection of AP police with that of Gujarat police, Shri Singhvi said that of Gujarat police, Shri Singhvi said that do not fall into the old established trap of the BJP and Mr. Modi. A trap tried again and again by aggressing and deviating from the main issue. Who is the main culprit? The officers and the state of Gujarat where rottenness is there, where there is decay and no amount of deliberate finger-pointing to divert attention should be allowed to succeed. Secondly, when we from this podium strongly condemn and criticize such actions, we cannot draw boundaries. If anybody else is involved, off course he must be punished.

606. (3-5-2007) NEW DELHI : Minister for Tourism and Culture Smt. Ambika Soni informed the Lok Sabha today that there are 3667 monuments/sites which have been declared as of national importance. The State-wise list is at annexure.

There is no proposal to enact a new law for the preservation and conservation, maintenance of State-wise database of heritage sites and antiquities or for the utilization of funds from MPLADs. However, the Government has set up a National Mission on Monuments and Antiquities for preparation of a national database on monuments and antiquities. As the budgetary allocations for heritage conservation is not adequate, a proposal has been made to consider funding the renovation and maintenance of monuments out of MPLAD funds.

607. (3-5-2007) NEW DELHI : A large number of homeless people come from the categories of manual workers engaged in construction activities. To address the problems of housing and civic amenities of the homeless poor, Jawaharlal Nehru National urban Renewal Missions (JNNURM), launched on December 3, 2005, provides Additional Central assistance ranging from 50% to 90% of the project cost depending upon State/category of city. This was stated by the Minister of State (Independent Charge) for Housing and Urban Poverty, Kumari Selja in a reply to a question by Shri Mahendra Mohan in the Rajya Sabha today.

608. (3-5-2007) NEW DELHI : A number of airports have been taken up for upgrdation in the 10th Five Year Plan. The expenditure incurred as on 31st March 2007 for this purpose is:- Rs. 116.89 croes for the Northern Region, Rs. 3.9 crores for the Eastern Region, Rs. 58.33 crores for the North-Eastern Region, Rs. 80.32 crores for the Western Region and Rs. 101.87 crores for the Southern Region. This information was given by Shri Praful Patel, Minister for Civil Aviation in the Lok Sabha today. The airports that have been taken up for upgradation in the Tenth Five Year Plan are at Dehradun, Jaipur, Khajuraho, Kullu, Lucknow, Pantnagar, Srinagar and Udaipur in the Northern Region; Bhubaneshwar and Gaya in the Eastern Region; Agartala, Dibrugarh, Guwahati and Silchar in the North Eastern Region; Ahmedabad, Akola, Aurangabad, Belgaun, Diu, Goa, Gondia, Nagpur, Raipur, Pune and Vadodara in the Western Region; and Agatti, Calicut, Madurai, Mangalore, Mysore, Tirupati,. Trichi and Vizag in the Southern Region. The projects include construction of new runways, new international terminal complex, apron taxi-ways, terminal buildings, technical blocks cum control towers, drainage and rain water harvesting systems, re-carpeting of runways etc. While most of the projects are running as per schedule, there have been delays in respect of certain projects due to non-closure of airports by State Governments in view of assembly elections, inclement weather conditions, hostile law and order salutation etc. Most of these projects are likely to be completed by December 2007. Certain projects whose scheduled date of commencing is in 2008 are expected to be completed as per schedule.

609. (3-5-2007) NEW DELHI : The quality control of the construction of four laning works are monitored by Independent Consultants (who are generally International Consultants) appointed through International Competitive Bidding by National Highways Authority of India (NHAI) for supervision of the civil contract and who act as Engineer for administration of the contract. Quality standards for construction of the road is governed by "Specification for Road and Bridge Works" published by Ministry of Shipping, Road Transport and Highways/ Indian Roads Congress and these specifications are part of the Contract Agreement. Quality tests are regularly carried out at field laboratories by Supervision Consultants. Further, quality audits are also being carried out by NHAI. Whenever any deficiency or defects of not conforming to the technical specification in construction are found, remedial action is taken by the Engineer for rejection/ replacement/rectification of work/material as per provision of the Contract Agreement. Similarly, defects detected during defect liability period (which is normally 12 months from the date of completion of the project) are also rectified by the contractor as part of the obligations as per contract. This information was given by the Minister of State for Shipping, Road Transport and Highways, Shri K.H. Muniyappa in a written reply in the Rajya Sabha today.

610. (3-5-2007) NEW DELHI : Modernization work of Terminals in the Cochin, Kozhikode and Thiruvananthapuram Airports in Kerala are progressing in a time bound manner. Information regarding these airports was given by the Minister for Civil Aviation, Shri Praful Patel in the Lok Sabha today. At Cochin Airport, which is a private airport managed by Cochin International Airport Limited (CIAL), the modernization work of arrival Block of International Terminal Building has been completed whereas 70% work of its Departure Block has been completed. The modernization work is expected to be completed by March, 2008. As per the information furnished by CIAL, an expenditure of Rs. 43.60 crore (approx.) has been incurred so far. At Kozhikode Airport, expansion and modification of International and Domestic Terminals has been undertaken to increase peak hour capacity to 500 international arriving and 500 international departing passengers and 250 domestic arriving and 250 domestic departing passengers. The project cost is Rs. 89.48 crore. The New International Terminal Building is likely to be commissioned in May, 2007 and the expected date of completion of Domestic Terminal Building is September, 2007. At Thiruvananthapuram airport, construction of New International Terminal Building for 500 arriving and 500 departing passengers has been initiated. The project will be completed in two phases at an estimated cost of Rs. 245.58 crore, which includes New International Terminal Building, Apron and remote bay, Taxi-link, Approach road car parking and other civic amenities and associated works. The existing International Terminal Building is also being extended for 2 nos. of incontact bays alongwith apron strengthening and extension. An expenditure of Rs. 14.30 crore has been incurred and the work of Phase-I is likely to be completed by December 2008.

611. (3-5-2007) NEW DELHI : The number of air miss incidents has not shown any significant increase in the last few years and a number of steps are being taken by the Government for avoiding them. This information was given by Shri Praful Patel, Minister for Civil Aviation in the Lok Sabha today. The number of air-miss incidents per lakh movements for the last four years are 2.041 in 2003; 2.081 in 2004; 2.506 in 2005 and 2.559 in 2006. The marginal increase is due to substantial increase in Air Traffic Density in the past few years. Further, better surveillance mechanisms like installation of Airborne Collision Avoidance System/Traffic Collision Avoidance Systems on aircraft and increase in RADAR coverage are have enabled reporting and monitoring of every breach of minimum separation between flights/aircraft. Safety of aircraft operations and avoiding air miss incidents is ensured by making installation of Airborne Collision Avoidance System (ACAS) and Mode "S" transponder on aircraft with certified seating capacity of more than 30 or pay load capacity more than 3 tones mandatory. Apart from this, Airports Authority of India (AAI) has installed Automatic Dependant Surveillance and Controller Pilot Data Link Communication (CPDLC) at Delhi and Mumbai airports. Minimum Safe Altitude Warning (MSAW) system is also in vogue which provides radar warning to ATCs, enabling them to alert the pilots timely. Most of the busy airspace in the country has been covered by Mono Pulse Secondary. Surveillance Radars (MSSRs) installed at Major airports which provide information on aircraft altitude to ATCOs. Training procedure of ATC is amended and modernized. Further refresher courses and proficiency checks for controllers are being varied out regularly. Specific coordination procedures have also been framed for transfer of traffic from one unit to another. DGCA has also advised AAI to ensure strict compliance of Air Traffic Control procedures and instructions.

612. (3-5-2007) NEW DELHI : On the recommendations of the Committee on Infrastructure, the Ministry of Shipping, Road Transport and Highways had constituted a Committee under the Chairmanship of Shri S. Sundar, former Secretary of the then Ministry of Surface Transport to deliberate and make recommendations for setting up an effective and dedicated agency for Road Safety and Traffic Management. The Committee submitted its report on 20.2.2007. The main recommendations of the Committee include creation of National Road Safety & Traffic Management Board through an Act of the Parliament. Enabling provision has been suggested in the report for creation of similar bodies at State level. The Committee has recommended earmarking of atleast 1% of the total proceeds of cess on diesel and petrol for road safety fund. The recommendations of the Committee have been circulated among the States/UTs and concerned Ministries/ Departments for their comments. This information was given by the Minister of State for Shipping, Road Transport and Highways, Shri K.H. Muniyappa in a written reply in the Rajya Sabha today.

613. (3-5-2007) NEW DELHI : The Road Safety Forum had suggested about uniform testing and grant of driving licenses all over the country. This Ministry has already developed a standardized software to facilitate issuance of smart card based Driving Licenses and Registration Certificates and given free of cost to all State Governments/UT Administration. The Proforma for issuance of license in Smart Card mode has already been prescribed by the Central Government and is applicable uniformly throughout the country. However, implementation of various provisions of Motor Vehicles Act, 1988 and Rules framed thereunder *i.e.* Central Motor Vehicles Rules, 1989 is the responsibility of the concerned State Government. The driving skill of the applicant seeking driving license is tested either by the Licensing Authorities or the applicant has to obtain a driving certificate (for non-transport vehicles) from any institution recognised in this behalf by the State Government. The issuance of driving license is already decentralized and the driving licenses are issued by concerned State Governments through RTOs. The Motor Vehicles Act, 1988 further empowers State Governments to make rules for appointment, jurisdiction, control and functions of the Licencing Authorities. However, the State Governments can recognise certain institutions to conduct the test of competence and issue driving certificates which enables the licensing authorities to issue driving licence. Any complaint regarding corruption at the testing centres is to be looked into by the concerned State Government. This information was given by the Minister of State for Shipping, Road Transport and Highways, Shri K.H. Muniyappa in a written reply in the Rajya Sabha today.

614. (3-5-2007) NEW DELHI : The technical and procedural formalities for merging the two national carriers, Indian Airlines and Air India, is likely to be completed by July 2007. This information was given by Shri Praful Patel, Minister for Civil Aviation in the Lok Sabha today. The Minister also said that for the purpose of this merger, a new Company, National Aviation Company of India Ltd., (NACIL) has been incorporated on 30th March 2007 under the Companies Act, 1956. The complete merger is expected to be completed in a phased manner over the next two years. While the brand name of the merged airline was still under the consideration of the Government, the Minister said that the new airline, with more than 112 aircraft, having an international and domestic footprint would set fresh benchmarks for efficiency and reliability, thus benefiting the civil aviation sector in the country, specially the travelling public. The integration of the two airlines will lead to developing seamless connectivity network of regional operations, short to medium haul trunk operations, long haul operations resulting in an improved product through wider network coverage. The merger will also provide significant synergy for procurement. Further, the merger will result in creation of a much bigger airline, as compared to the nearest domestic competitor. The new entity will have strategic Business Units (SBUs) in the areas of Integrated Passenger Service, MRO, Ground Handling, LCC, Cargo and other related activities. The proposed SBUs will have nation-wide operations. In the answer to a separate question regarding the two national airlines, the Minister informed the Parliament that Air India and Indian Airlines have 38 and 74 aircraft respectively in their fleet including aircraft on lease. The average fleet age of Air India and Indian Airlines aircraft presently is 14.6 years and 16.2 years respectively. It may be recalled that the Government recently gave permission for aircraft acquisition to both the Companies – 68 for Air India and 43 for Indian Airlines.

615. (3-5-2007) NEW DELHI : Some representations were received, especially during monsoon season, regarding repair and maintenance of certain highways/ bridges under National Highways Development Project (NHDP), which were duly attended to as part of maintenance to keep the highways/ bridges in traffic worthy condition. Wherever 4/6 laning works under NHDP are under implementation, to keep the existing roads in traffic worthy condition, the maintenance of existing roads are carried out by the Contractor/ Concessionaire as part of their obligations under contract/ concession agreement. In case of sections identified under NHDP where 4/6 laning has not yet started, the maintenance of existing roads are being carried out by NHAI, State Public Works Departments (PWDs)/ Border Road Organisation (BRO) through funds provided by the Ministry of Shipping, Road Transport and Highways. This information was given by the Minister of State for Shipping, Road Transport and Highways, Shri K.H. Muniyappa in a written reply in the Rajya Sabha today.

616. (3-5-2007) NEW DELHI: After two rounds of meetings in Washington, D.C., between Foreign Secretary Shivshankar Menon and Under Secretary of State Nicholas Burns, India and the United States publicly claimed that considerable progress had been made in the crucial '123 agreement' on bilateral civil nuclear cooperation. But where U.S. State Department spokesman Sean McCormack sought to push the envelope by speaking of a "final agreement" by the end of May, Mr. Menon struck a more cautious note. "On the 123, we think we've made considerable progress forward and we now expect to welcome Under Secretary Burns later this month and we hope to finalise this as soon as we can." But he also acknowledged that the two sides "still have issues to settle."

617. (3-5-2007) NEW DELHI : A request is pending with Government to grant the Navratna status to Shipping Corporation of India (SCI). However, many areas of deficiency have been noticed in corporate governance of Shipping Corporation of India (SCI) which need to be removed in the interest of efficiency and transparency. SCI is taking corrective measures to ensure that its internal governance system achieves a level of efficiency and transparency that a company should desirably achieve before Navratna status is bestowed on it. The progress of SCI towards these reforms is being monitored regularly. This information was given by the Minister of Shipping, Road Transport and Highways, Shri T.R. Baalu in a written reply in the Rajya Sabha today.

618. (3-5-2007) NEW DELHI : Improving efficiency of the ports is an ongoing process and involves development of berths, deepening of channels, equipment upgradation and modernization of rail-road connectivity. Government of India has constituted an Inter-Ministerial Group (IMG) under the Chairmanship of Secretary, Department of Shipping to make recommendations for reducing the dwell time at Major Ports and to bring it in line with international standards. The IMG is in the process of finalizing the report. Except Paradip and Ennore Ports, Electronic Data Interchange (EDI) (between Ports and Customs Department) has been implemented in all the major ports including Visakhapatnam Port in Andhra Pradesh. The scope of EDI is being further enlarged. This information was given by the Minister of Shipping, Road Transport and Highways, Shri T.R. Baalu in a written reply in the Rajya Sabha today.

619. (3-5-2007) NEW DELHI : The commencement of the work for the project was inaugurated by the Hon'ble Prime Minister of India on 2-7-2005 and the work is in progress. The project involves dredging work mainly at two places namely Adam's Bridge and Palk Strait. As estimated, a total quantity of 82.5 million cubic metres is required to be dredged. The Dredging Corporation of India Ltd., Visakhapatnam has been entrusted with the dredging work of the project. The work at Adam's Bridge has commenced on 11-12-2006. There is no scientific evidence regarding the existence of any ancient man-made structure in the proposed Sethusamudram Ship Channel alignment. Some representations against undertaking the project have been received. However, as per the scientific information available with the Project Authorities, there is no underwater construction in the project area. This information was given by the Minister of Shipping, Road Transport and Highways, Shri T.R. Baalu in a written reply in the Rajya Sabha today.

620. (3-5-2007) NEW DELHI : Some pirates had hijacked an Indian ship M.V. Nehm Tulah alongwith its 14 members crew on 1st April, 2007. As per reports received from the owners of the vessel, the vessel, cargo and all the 14 crew members have been released at around 1120 hours Indian Standard Time on 6th April, 2007. The crew comprising all Indian nationals are safe. The Government is not aware of any conditions attached to the release of the said vessel. The Directorate General of Shipping, Mumbai had issued a circular on 27th April, 2006 informing all concerned about the incidents of piracy and armed robbery against ships especially in the vicinity of the Somalian coast where incidents of piracy and attacks on ships have been on the rise. The Indian National Ship owners Association (INSA) and Federation of All India Sailing Vessels Industry Association have also been informed to convey to their members that they should keep away from the Somalian coast. Subsequently, the Directorate General of Shipping, Mumbai issued another circular on 8th January, 2007 drawing attention of the shipping fraternity and seafaring community of attacks against ships in Somalian waters. This circular also contained detailed guidelines to avoid such attacks and acts of piracy. This information was given by the Minister of Shipping, Road Transport and Highways, Shri T.R. Baalu in a written reply in the Rajya Sabha today.

621. (3-5-2007) NEW DELHI : There are 27 Shipyards in the country out of which 6 Shipyards are under the Central Government. The combined capacity of these yards is approximately 2,81,200 DWT and the maximum size of ship which can be built in Indian shipyard is 1,10,000 DWT. The order book position of Indian Shipyards is approximately Rs.14,000 crore. No proposal for setting up a Maritime

Board for modernization of Shipyards is under consideration at present. This information was given by the Minister of Shipping, Road Transport and Highways, Shri T.R. Baalu in a written reply in the Rajya Sabha today.

622. (3-5-2007) NEW DELHI : As per the Detailed Project Report (DPR), the Sethusamudram project is scheduled to be completed by November, 2008. There is no scientific evidence regarding the existence of any ancient man-made structure in the proposed Sethusamudram Ship Channel alignment. Representations against undertaking the project have been received. However, as per the scientific information available with the Project Authorities, there is no underwater construction in the project area. As per the information available no heritage site has been declared in the project area. Final selection of the alignment has been done keeping in view various aspects including the navigational, environmental and ecological considerations. This information was given by the Minister of Shipping, Road Transport and Highways, Shri T.R. Baalu in a written reply in the Rajya Sabha today.

623. (3-5-2007) NEW DELHI : Director General of Shipping is the regulatory body for seafarers training and is ensuring quality training. About 18000 officers and 20,350 ratings are either awaiting sea time training or under employed or in the process of getting sea time training. In view of shortage of Indian officers, the Government is considering a proposal to allow foreign officers to work on Indian ships subject to certain conditions in consultation with the shipping industry. This information was given by the Minister of Shipping, Road Transport and Highways, Shri T.R. Baalu in a written reply in the Rajya Sabha today.

624. (3-5-2007) NEW DELHI : Northern Railway and Indian Institute of Technology, Delhi have joined hands to revamp security on rail premises. A team of experts led by Prof. D. T. Sahni from IIT, Delhi has been constituted to carry out security audit in the railways. The team surveyed the Delhi junction to study the density of passengers, movement of trains and the working of various security agencies to study the ground realities. Currently, the security arrangements on the Railway Stations in Delhi area have been strengthened by deploying 12 more trained dog squads for conducting frequent checks at railway stations. These highly trained dogs are assisting the RPF to carry out security checks of luggage and other packages. Door Frame Metal Detectors (DFMDs), Hand Held Metal Detectors (HHMDs) and CCTV cameras are being intensively used by security personnel at New Delhi, Delhi Jn. and Hazart Nizammuddin railway stations. A baggage screening machine is being commissioned by the Railways for ensuring smooth and speedy checking of baggage. In view of heavy rush of passengers, Northern Railway have deployed an additional fleet of 3 companies of Railway Police Special Force (RPSF) in Delhi area. Security arrangements at Platform No. 18 at Delhi Jn. have been made stringent, particularly for the departure of Attari Link Express, running between Delhi and Attari. This includes thorough and intense screening of luggage and passengers before the departure of the train. Coolies, Vendors and parking lot attendants have been sensitized towards the possibility of security threat on railway premises. They have been trained to identify such activity and report to the authorities in such eventuality. Public Address System, hand held loud hailers are frequently use by RPF to educate passengers against drugging, pick pocketing and baggage lifting by anti social elements.

625. (3-5-2007) NEW DELHI : In reply to a question regarding the number of Communities to know the status of Muslims before the constitution of Sachar Committee, The Minority Affairs Minister Shri A.R.Antulay has stated that a High Power Panel, known as the Gopal Singh Committee was constituted on 10th May, 1980 and it submitted its report on the Scheduled Castes, Scheduled Tribes, other weaker sections and minorities including Muslims. The report along with a statement indicating the comments of the Government on the recommendations made by this panel was lid on the table of the Lok Sabha on 27th August, 1990. Shri Antulay further informed that a High Level Commission, known as the Sachar Committee, has brought out the social, economic and educational status of the Muslim community of India. The report of the committee has been tabled in the Lok Sabha on 30th Nov., 2006. It is also available in the website. The recommendations of this Committee are under consideration of the Government. The Minister was replying to an unstarred question tabled in the Lok Sabha today.

626. (3-5-2007) NEW DELHI : In reply to a question regarding the recommendation to provide religion based reservation in admissions in the Educational Institutions and also in providing Government jobs, the Minority Affairs Minister Shri A.R.Antulay has stated that the National Commission for Religious and Linguistic Minorities, set up in October 2004, has, as one of its term of references, " to recommend measures for the welfare of socially and economically backward sections among religious and linguistic minorities, including reservation in education and Government employment". The Minister was responding to an unstarred question tabled in the Lok Sabha today.

627. (3-5-2007) NEW DELHI : The Minister of Minority Affairs, Shri A.R. Antulay informed the Rajya Sabha that the National Commission for Minorities has, in some of its annual Reports, made recommendations regarding the representation of the minority communities in police and paramilitary forces. He further informed that annual Reports of the commission, containing such recommendations, for the years 1997-1998, 2002-2003 and 2003-2004, alongwith the Action Taken Memorandum on the recommendations contained therein, have been Tabled in the Rajya Sabha on 11th and 18th December, 2006. The Minister was responding to an Unstarred Question in Rajya Sabha.

628. (3-5-2007) NEW DELHI : In reply to a question whether Government have any plan to offer special measures to generate employment among the tribal

Christians in the States of Jharkhand, Chhattisgarh, Orissa, Madhya Pradesh, Gujarat and Rajasthan, the Minister of Minority Affairs, Shri A.R. Antulay informed the Lok Sabha that besides, the Prime Minister's New 15-Point Programme for the Welfare of Minorities envisages earmarking of 15% of outlay for minorities, including tribal Christians, under three schemes related directly to employment generation, *i.e.* Swarnjayanti Gram Swarojgar Yojna (SGSY), Swarn Jayanti Shahari Rojgar Yojana (SJSRY) and Sampoorna Grameen Rozgar Yojana (SGRY). Under the National Rural Employment Guarantee Programme (NREGP), a total of 80 districts covered are in these six States. He further informed that as per Report No. 521 of the National Sample Survey (NSS) 61st round, the unemployment rate among Christians was higher as compared to that among the Hindus or the Muslims. The details are available on the web site of the Ministry of Statistics and Programme Implementation. The Minister was responding to an Unstarred Question in Rajya Sabha.

629. (3-5-2007) NEW DELHI : In reply to a question whether the directions have been given in the 15-Point programme about the 15% priority sector loan be given to the minority community, the Minority Affairs Minister, Shri A.R. Antulay has stated that instructions have been given to public sector banks to increase the flow of credit to the minority communities. Public Sector Banks have been advised to open more branches in the 103 districts where the proportion of the minority population to the total population is at least 25%. The flow of credit to minorities in these districts will be specially monitored. Besides, public sector banks have been advised to include enhanced lending to minority communities in the annual District Credit Plan formulated for each of these 103 districts. The instruction relating to special monitoring of credit flow to minorities in these 103 districts is contained in the letter of Government of India to the RBI dated 18.4.2007. this instruction as well as other instructions referred to above were reiterated at the meeting of the CMDs of public sector banks on 19.4.2007. The Minister was responding to an Unstarred Question in Rajya Sabha today.

630. (3-5-2007) NEW DELHI : The Minority Affairs Minister, Shri A.R. Antulay has stated that the Central Wakf Council has been given Central Grant of Rs. Rs.143.25 lakh in 2005-06 and Rs.206.00 lakh in 2006-07 respectively. Moreover, in order to provide sufficient funds to the Central Wakf Council enhanced provision for Grants-in-Aid to the tune of Rs.290.00 lakh has been made during the current financial year(2007-08). The Minister was responding to an Unstarred Question in Rajya Sabha today.

631. (3-5-2007) NEW DELHI : It has been decided to carry out pre-feasibility studies for one high speed corridor each in the Eastern, Western, Northern and Southern regions of the country. At the stage of implementation of these corridors, all alternatives including Public-Private Partnership will be considered. No section has been identified for construction of high speed corridor. This information was given by Shri R. Velu, Minister of State for Railways in a written reply to a question in Lok Sabha today.

632. (3-5-2007) NEW DELHI : RailTel, a Public Sector Undertaking under the Ministry of Railways, is planning to provide broadband services at select railway stations using Wi-Max technology under public-private partnership. Using this technology, it will be possible to provide broadband services and Voice Over Internet Protocol services at the railway stations as well as towns/villages in the vicinity of railway stations. The stations will become hot spot zones and any passenger with suitable laptop/other device will be able to access internet facility. The investment on infrastructure to provide these services would be made by the private partner. This information was given by Shri R. Velu, Minister of State for Railways in a written reply to a question in Lok Sabha today.

633. (3-5-2007) NEW DELHI : The area of railway land that has been encroached in Delhi amounts to about 40 hectares. There are about 27,000 encroachments on railway land in Delhi. The encroachments have come up over various years. Various steps have been taken for removal of encroachments, which also include action under Public Premises (Eviction of Unauthorised Occupants) Act, 1971. In the National Capital Territory of Delhi, railways have agreed to bear part cost of relocation of Pre-1998 encroachers located on Railway land in 'Safety Zone' and on land required for execution of sanctioned projects, as per the Resettlement and Rehabilitation policy of Delhi Government, which has the approval of the Ministry of Urban Development. Northern Railway have deposited over Rs. 11 crores with the Government of Delhi on this account, for relocating 'Jhuggies / Jhopries', to get encroachments removed from railway land. Regular chasing and meetings are done by railway officials with Delhi Government officials. All efforts are made by railway towards proper coordination with the Government of Delhi including seeking assistance of local police as eviction of encroachers can lead to Law and Order problems. This information was given by Shri R. Velu, Minister of State for Railways in a written reply to a question in Lok Sabha today.

634. (3-5-2007) NEW DELHI : Udhampur-Srinagar-Baramullah (292 km.) new line National project has been taken up to provide rail connectivity to Kashmir Valley. The section from Badgam to Kakapore including Srinagar has been completed and train services will be commissioned after inspection by Commissioner of Railway Safety and successful trial of DMU coach which are under transportation to Valley. Further the section from Udhampur to Katra, Quazigund – Kakapore and Badgam to Baramullah are targeted for completion in 2007-08. To provide rail services in Andaman and Nicobar Islands, an updating survey was carried out in 2002-03 for rail line between Port Blair and Diglipur. As per the survey report, the cost of 239 km long line was assessed at Rs. 867 crore with negative Rate of Return. In view of unremunerative nature of the project, huge throwforward of ongoing projects and scarcity of resources the project was not taken up. This information was given by Shri R. Velu, Minister of State for Railways in a written reply to a question in Lok Sabha today.

635. (3-5-2007) NEW DELHI : As per intelligence inputs, Indian Railways is a soft target for terrorists in Indian and a few cases of attack from terrorists and anti social elements on rail network have been reported over Indian Railways. 185 Railway Stations including 17 metro stations of 50 divisions over Indian Railways have been identified as sensitive where security systems are proposed to be upgraded.

636. (3-5-2007) NEW DELHI : Close on the heels of Prime Minister Dr. Manmohan Singh's call to focus on the role of small & medium enterprises (SMEs) in India's industrial development, national and international experts at an SME Cluster Conclave have emphasised the critical importance of SMEs in India's economic growth. At the SME Cluster Conclave organised by Confederation of Indian Industry (CII) in partnership with the Ministry of Small Scale Industries here yesterday, it was indicated by the Secretary, Ministry of Small Scale Industries & Rural and Agro Industries, Dr. Chandrapal, that government was proposing to increase financial assistance to existing clusters of Micro, Small and Medium Enterprises (MSME) upto as much as 80% of their financial requirements under the 11th Plan. Shri Jawahar Sircar, Additional Secretary & Development Commissioner, Ministry of SSI & ARI said that the Cluster Concept was India's answer to global competition. "To enable MSMEs to become competitive, the government is proposing to build a pool of consultants under its National Manufacturing Competitiveness Programme. These consultants would be deployed with a cluster of 8-10 companies for a period of one to one and a half years. The cost of these consultants will be borne by the government", he said. Participating in the Conclave, Mr. Philippe Scholtes, UNIDO Regional Representative in India, said that the United Nations Industrial Development Organisation (UNIDO) has proposed a 5-year country Strategy for India, of which cluster development would be an integral part along with programmes aimed at upgrading technological capability and building up of social capital in the country's industrial sector. He also referred to the interesting new experiment of Twinning of Clusters as in the India-Italy Cluster Development Cooperation and said that UNIDO was also exploring new applications of Industrial cluster based approaches focusing on corporate social responsibility and poverty alleviation in micro enterprises. On behalf of the National Manufacturing Competitiveness Council (NMCC), Shri Rajeev Ranjan, Chief (Joint Secretary)/NMCC, stated that the National Strategy for Manufacturing drawn up by NMCC had been accepted by the government for implementation and that enabling SMEs to achieve competitiveness was one of the key elements of this strategy He further indicated that Strategy had identified the following areas for priority action viz., textiles & garments, food processing, IT hardware & electronics, leather & footwear, automobiles & auto-components and chemicals & petrochemicals including pharma. Other speakers included Mr.

Jamil Ashraf, Executive Director, Sandhar technologies; Mr. H.P. Kumar, Chairman & Managing Director, NSIC; Mr. Rakesh Rewari, Deputy Managing Director, SIDBI; and Mr. S. Sandilya, Chairman, CII Economic Affairs Committee & Chairman, Eicher Group

637. (3-5-2007) NEW DELHI : At present, there is no shortage of coaches to run the scheduled services. Works have been approved for augmenting capacity of RCF (Rail Coach Factory), Kapurthala and ICF (Integral Coach Factory), Chennai from 1000 coaches per year to 1400 coaches & 1500 coaches per year, respectively. Apart from augmenting the existing capacity, there is also a proposal to set up a new coach factory, to meet the projected increase in demand. This information was given by Shri R. Velu, Minister of State for Railways in a written reply to a question in Lok Sabha today.

638. (3-5-2007) NEW DELHI : Bharat Heavy Electricals Limited (BHEL) has secured an order from M/s Grand Paroisse, France for supply and supervision of Erection and Commissioning of a Compressor Package for a Urea Plant in France. BHEL has recently commissioned 600 MW Western Mountain Power Plant in Libya, the largest power plant commissioned by BHEL overseas.

639. (3-5-2007) NEW DELHI : Planning and execution of Railway projects for expansion of the network is done in an integrated and need based manner keeping the national perspective in view. Geographical boundaries of a State, per se, do not form a criterion for determining Railway investments, especially in a scenario where many Railway projects span across more than one State. However, a number of new line projects have been taken up throughout the country which on completion would add to the route kilometres in various States. This information was given by Shri R. Velu, Minister of State for Railways in a written reply to a question in Lok Sabha today.

640. (3-5-2007) NEW DELHI : The subject of electoral reforms is presently under consideration of the Department Related Parliamentary Standing Committee on Personnel, Public Grievances, Law and Justice. As such the Committee was requested to give its recommendations on the proposal of the Election Commission to disqualify a person from contesting election against whom charges have been framed by a competent court for certain serious criminal offences. The Committee has presented its eighteenth report on the subject to the Rajya Sabha/laid on the Table of the Lok Sabha on March 15, 2007. It has been inter alia mentioned in the said report that the Committee is constrained to disagree with the aforesaid proposal as the proposal is a major departure from the law for the time being in force, which provides that if a persons is convicted for an offence and the court gives a judgement convicting him, then such a person shall be disqualify for contesting elections. But the Committee has recommended that proclaimed absconders under section 82 of the Criminal Procedure Code be disqualified from contesting polls. The Government has not taken any decision on the recommendations of the Committee so far. The subject of electoral reforms is presently under consideration of the Department Related Parliamentary Standing Committee on Personnel, Public Grievances, Law and Justice. As such the Committee was requested to give its recommendations on the proposal of the Election Commission to disqualify a person from contesting election against whom charges have been framed by a competent court for certain serious criminal offences. The Committee has presented its eighteenth report on the subject to the Rajya Sabha/laid on the Table of the Lok Sabha on March 15, 2007. It has been inter alia mentioned in the said report that the Committee is constrained to disagree with the aforesaid proposal as the proposal is a major departure from the law for the time being in force, which provides that if a persons is convicted for an offence and the court gives a judgement convicting him, then such a person shall be disqualify for contesting elections. But the Committee has recommended that proclaimed absconders under section 82 of the Criminal Procedure Code be disqualified from contesting polls. The Government has not taken any decision on the recommendations of the Committee so far. This was stated by the Minister of Law and Justice, Shri H. R. Bhardwaj in a written reply in the Rajya Sabha. MLD/LK/L&J-27(RS-amendment in representation of peoples' act)(3.5.07) This was stated by the Minister of Law and Justice, Shri H. R. Bhardwaj in a written reply in the Rajya Sabha.

641. (3-5-2007) NEW DELHI : The life of a Railways bridge is not based on its age but on physical condition as ascertained by inspections. Railways have a well-laid down system of multi-tier inspection of bridges. Railway undertakes repair, rehabilitation/rebuilding of bridges on the basis of their physical condition as ascertained during inspections and not on the basis of age. Few bridges which may show signs of deterioration of physical condition indicating need for rehabilitation are classified as distressed bridges. These, however, are neither unsafe nor dilapidated bridges. Based on such identification of bridges, allotment of funds is made annually to carry out their repair, rehabilitation/rebuilding duly prioritizing the works as per requirement. In 2001-02 to clear the backlog of replacement of such identified Bridges on Indian Railways, 2370 bridges were sanctioned for repair/rehabilitation/rebuilding at a cost of Rs. 1530 crore (net) under Special Railway Safety Fund (SRSF). Apart from SRSF, additional funds are also made available annually in Railway Budget to undertake repair/rehabilitation of fresh accruals of Bridge works under Depreciation Reserve Fund (DRF).

642. (3-5-2007) NEW DELHI : A budget provision of Rs. 65 crore was made in respect of central share of the assistance for development of infrastructure facilities for the judiciary for the financial year 2006-07. Release of funds to the States/UTs is made on the basis of furnishing of Utilization Certificates (Ucs) by the recipient entities in respect of the funds released to them earlier. On the basis of the Utilization Certificates furnished by these entities and on the basis of proposals received from a few states, an amount of Rs,. 50.19 crore, including

Rs. 2 crore in respect of Family Courts, was released to the States/UTs in the financial year 2006-07. Except for the unutilized provision in respect of States in the North Eastern Region, the unutilized portion of the budget provision for the year 2006-07 stands surrendered. This was stated by the Minister of Law and Justice, Shri H. R. Bhardwaj in a written reply in the Rajya Sabha.

643. (3-5-2007) NEW DELHI : As per available information 39.7 thousand cases in the Supreme Court, 39.9 lakh cases in the High Courts and 2.63 crore cases in the Subordinate courts were pending as on December 31, 2006. With a view to reducing pendency in the courts, Government has taken steps to increase the judge strength from time to time and has extended the term of central assistance to Fast Track Courts for a period of five years beyond March 31, 2005 *i.e.* upto March 31, 2010. Other measures like grouping of cases involving common question of law and application of Information and Communication Technology in the courts have also been taken. Tribunals like Central Administrative Tribunal, State Administrative Tribunals, etc. have been set up to dispose of cases in different areas. Government has encouraged alternative modes of disposal which include mediation, negotiation and arbitration. The Government proposes to establish Gram Nyayalayas in the rural areas to provide speedy justice and reduce pendency. This was stated by the Minister of Law and Justice, Shri H. R. Bhardwaj in a written reply in the Rajya Sabha.

644. (3-5-2007) NEW DELHI : The External Affairs Minister, Shri Pranab Mukherjee in a written reply to an unstarred question informed the Rajya Sabha today that officials from the Government of India and the Government of the United States have held three rounds of talks on the 123 Agreement from June 12-14, 2006 in New Delhi; March 25-27, 2007 in New Delhi; and April 16-19, 2007 in Cape Town, South Africa. The Indian team was led by Dr. S. Jaishankar, currently High Commissioner of India in Singapore, and included other officials of the Ministry of External Affairs and representatives of Department of Atomic Energy and Prime Minister's Office. The U.S. team was led by Mr. Richard Stratford, Director of Office of Nuclear Energy, Safety and Security, Bureau of Nonproliferation in the U.S. Department of State. India has maintained that our obligations and commitments would be those that we undertake in the bilateral cooperation agreement and that we expect that to reflect the commitments of July 18 Joint Statement and March Separation Plan. The process of negotiating the 123 Agreement is ongoing. Progress has been made on some issues. The final arrangements on various aspects of nuclear cooperation will emerge only after the Agreement has been concluded.

645. (3-5-2007) NEW DELHI : The External Affairs Minister visited Japan on 22-23 March, 2007 at the invitation of the Foreign Minister of Japan. The two Ministers initiated the first Ministerial-level Strategic Dialogue between the two countries. They exchanged views on ways to enhance cooperation on regional, multilateral and global issues, and reiterated their readiness to cooperate in the process of community building in the Asian region. Both sides also discussed ways to strengthen bilateral relations through the implementation of understandings and agreements contained in the Joint Statement signed by the two Prime Ministers in December 2006. During the visit, the two sides agreed on the modalities for the High Level Energy Dialogue and the Bilateral Consultation Mechanism on High Technology Trade. Government are regularly monitoring progress on the implementation of understandings reached with Japan in the fields of defence and security, economic cooperation, science & technology & people-to-people exchanges. The above information was given by the External Affairs Minister, Shri Pranab Mukherjee in written reply to a question in the Rajya Sabha today.

646. (3-5-2007) NEW DELHI : Border Roads Organisation (BRO) have constructed 1710 Kms, 1581 Kms and 1910 Kms of road in 2004-2005, 2005-2006 and 2006-2007 respectively. Presently, BRO is engaged in the construction/improvement of 525 roads of operational importance and agency works sponsored by other Ministries. Works on the sanctioned road projects are progressed as per priority accorded to it by Army or sponsoring agencies and availability of budget each year. The above projects are in various stages of construction.

647. (3-5-2007) NEW DELHI : The average training costs vary from service to service and stream to stream ranging from Rs. 0.302 crores to Rs. 10.35 crores. Certain domestic problems relating to inheritance of property, need to look after ailing parents, family business, serious illness of wife requiring officer's presence at home, possibility of breakup of conjugal life if the officer continues in service, etc. are considered as compassionate grounds, depending upon the circumstances of each case. The Indian Air Force has agreed to allow officers in the age group of *54* years and above to join the national carrier. A Memorandum of Understanding has been signed between IAF and Air India on 5th April, 2007. This is to facilitate a second carrier option to the retiring IAF officers and also reduce the requirement of expatriate pilots for the national carrier. The exit of the officers being sponsored would not affect the operational status of the Air Force as these officers would have already served their useful tenure as pilots. The officers being sponsored are generally those who are superannuating within a year or so. Hence, this would neither lead to shortage of pilots in the IAF nor any loss incurred on their training. This information was given by the Defence Minister Shri AK Antony in a written reply to Shri Badiga Ramakrishna and Shri Eknath M Gaikwad in Lok Sabha today.

648. (3-5-2007) NEW DELHI : A Letter of Request has been issued to the Government of United States in December, 2006 indicating the requirement of C-130J transport craft for the Air Force. However, no contract has been concluded for purchase of the aircraft. This information was given by the Defence Minister Shri AK Antony in a written reply to Shri Rabinder Kumar Rana in Lok Sabha today.

649. (3-5-2007) NEW DELHI : The soldiers deployed in notified Counter Insurgency Operations are entitled for Special Compensatory Counter Insurgency Allowance (SCCIA) at the rates which range from Rs. 1500 to Rs. 3900 per month subject to the fulfillment of laid down conditions. The Civilians as well as Defence Service Personnel working in Border Roads Organisation (BRO) and Civilians of Military Engineer Services (MES) are not entitled to SCCIA since they are not actually involved in the conduct of counter insurgency operations. However, the Defence Service Personnel of MES are entitled for SCCIA. It may be added that Civilian employees of BRO and MES working in some specified districts in Jammu & Kashmir are, however, entitled to certain incentives/special benefits as per order issued by Department of Personnel & Training. This information was given by the Defence Minister Shri AK Antony in a written reply to Shri Jasubhai Dhanabhai Barad in Lok Sabha today.

650. (3-5-2007) NEW DELHI : Presently there is a total shortage of 14165 officers in the Armed Forces. The Army has a shortage of 11238 officers, whereas the Navy and the Air Force have a shortage of 1399 and 1528 officers respectively. Several steps have been taken by the three Services to fill up the vacant posts. All officers including those in Short Service Commission (S SC) have been made eligible to hold substantive rank of Captain, Major and Lieutenant Colonel and equivalents after 2, 6 and 13 years of reckonable service respectively. The tenure of SSC Officers has been extended to 14 years in the three Services. Besides, the Armed Forces have undertaken sustained image projection and publicity campaign to create awareness among the youth on the advantages of taking up a challenging and satisfying career. Candidate-friendly recruitment procedures to attract more number of candidates and a focused publicity drive in various institutions to attract potential candidates have been undertaken. Awareness campaigns, participation in career fairs and exhibitions, advertisements in print and electronic media, motivational lectures in schools, colleges are also some of the other measures in this direction. This information was given by the Defence Minister Shri AK Antony in a written reply to Shri Thawarchand Gehlot and Shri SK Kharventhan in Lok Sabha today.

651. (3-5-2007) NEW DELHI : The Minister of Tourism and Culture Smt. Ambika Soni informed the Lok Sabha today that the Ministry of Tourism has 13 India Tourism Offices in various countries abroad and 20 India Tourism Offices in India. The total strength of officers and staff in Overseas India Tourism Offices is 59 and in domestic India Tourism offices it is 247. In a written reply she said, Ministry of Tourism regularly reviews the functioning of India Tourism Offices both in India and abroad to ensure effective marketing of India Tourism products as well as liaison & coordination with State Governments/ Union Territories and all stakeholders.

652. (3-5-2007) NEW DELHI : The Minister of Tourism and Culture Smt. Ambika Soni informed the Lok Sabha today that the Archaeological Survey of

India has identified 46 centrally protected monuments in Delhi for repairs, upgradation, illumination, provision of amenities, environment development, etc. in view of the Commonwealth Games. In a written reply she said there are 21 monuments on the World Heritage List in India. Of this, Qutb Minar and Humayun's Tomb are in Delhi.

653. (3-5-2007) NEW DELHI : The Minister of Tourism and Culture Smt. Ambika Soni informed the Lok Sabha today that the Ministry of Finance in their budget proposal 2007-08 has proposed income tax holiday for hotels for a period of five years. The incentive is available for hotels in the 2, 3 and 4-star category which would complete construction between 1-4-2007 upto 31-3-2010. The incentive is only available in NCT Delhi, districts of Gurgaon, Faridabad, Ghaziabad and Gautam Budh Nagar. There is subsidy assistance available for 1 to 3 star category hotels and subsidy to Large Revenue Generating projects under the scheme of the Ministry of Tourism. In a written reply she said, the Ministry of Commerce and Industry (Department of Industrial Policy and Promotion) have announced packages for the hill States of Jammu & Kashmir, Sikkim, Himachal Pradesh and Uttaranchal by way of concessions under Excise Duty, Income Tax Exemption and Investment Subsidy etc. for certain identified thrust industries, including Eco-Tourism industries set up in these States. The Ministry of Tourism under its various schemes provide financial assistance for the development of rural tourism and pilgrim centres. Under the North East Industrial and Investment Promotion Policy (NEIIPP), 2007, hotels (not below 2 star category), adventure and leisure sports including ropeways are eligible for all incentives.

654. (3-5-2007) NEW DELHI : It is indeed a welcome development that importance of continuing the dialogue process, by holding roundtable conference, initiated last year in February by Prime Minister Dr. Manmohan Singh has not only been accepted but appreciated with an air of optimism. Evidently, those keen on solving problems of Jammu & Kashmir (J& K) recognize importance of holding such discussions periodically. The second roundtable conference was held last year in May. Achieving success at level of convincing participants of the importance of this process is in itself a major development. In this context, among those who participated in the third roundtable conference last week (April 24), chaired by Prime Minister, were Home Minister Shivraj Patil, J&K Chief Minister Ghulam Nabi Azad, former Chief Minister Mufti Mohammad Sayeed, Mehbooba Mufti (People's Democratic Party), Omar Abdullah (National Conference), Bhim Singh (Panther Party), Agnishekhar (Panun Kashmir), Yusuf Tarigami (Communist Party of India-Marxist) and Bharatiya Janata Party representative. Separatist groups, including both factions of Hurriyat Conference, had refused to participate in the talks. During his address, opening the conference, expressing hope that they would participate in near future, the Prime Minister said: "I am impressed by the representative character of all people taking part in this roundtable. There are others who have decided not to join the dialogue. I hope they too join this process and contribute to the resolution of issues which affect the people of J&K."

655. (3-5-2007) NEW DELHI : The Minister of Tourism and Culture Smt. Ambika Soni has said that Ministry of Tourism extends Central Financial Assistance to State Governments/ Union Territories under its scheme "Product/ Infrastructure Development for Destinations and Circuits" including Tea Tourism Circuits for the projects prioritized in consultation with them. In a written reply in the Lok Sabha today she said, the amount allocated for the year 2007-08 for the scheme "Product/ Infrastructure Development for Destinations and Circuits" is Rs. 460.00 crore for project proposals to develop tourism products including tea tourism.

656. (3-5-2007) NEW DELHI : The guidelines for National Programme of Nutritional Support to Primary Education (commonly known as Mid-Day Meal Scheme) was formulated in September 2004. The same was revised in June 2006. The existing scheme covers children studying in classes I-V in Government, Local Body and Government aided schools and Education Guarantee Scheme (EGS) and Alternative and Innovative Education (AIE) Centres. Considering the nature of hilly and difficult terrain, the Scheme provides central assistance to transport food grains at a higher rate of Rs. 100 per quintal (as against Rs. 75 per quintal to other States) in the case of eleven Special Category States which include Uttarakhand and Himachal Pradesh.

657. (3-5-2007) NEW DELHI : Jawahar Navodaya Vidyalaya (JNU) and Kasturba Gandhi Balika Vidyalaya (KGBV) are the only two residential schooling programmes, under the Ministry of Human Resource Development. For admissions in JNVs, seats are reserved for children from SC and ST communities in the district in proportion to their population in the concerned district but not less than the national average of 15 per cent for SC and 7.5 per cent for ST candidates. In KGBV, 75 per cent of the seats are reserved for girls from SC, ST, OBC and minority communities. There is no proposal to increase the reservation percentage. This information was given by the Minister of State for Human Resource Development Shri M.A.A. Fatmi in a written reply in the Rajya Sabha.

658. (3-5-2007) NEW DELHI : State-wise allocations are not made under the Centrally Sponsored Schemes/Projects administered by the Ministry. Grants are, however, released to the State Governments keeping in view the proposals received, availability of resources and progress of utilization of funds earlier released under each scheme. Following is the statement indicating the amount released during 2005-06 to the State Government of Bihar under various Centrally Sponsored Schemes administered by the Ministry of Human Resource Development..

659. (3-5-2007) NEW DELHI : As per Selected Educational Statistics, 2004-05, the Gross Enrolment Ratio (GER) in Rajasthan is 102.67 for class I-VIII, which compares favourably to the national level GER of 93.54. It is better than GER of 16 States/UTs. The GER is 105.16 and 96.33 for SCs and STs respectively in Rajasthan for class I-VIII and is 95.65 and 86.10 for SC and ST girls, respectively. The drop out rate in Rajasthan is 56.59 per cent for class I to V and 73.87 for class I to X. Data is unavailable for Rajasthan. Government of India is assisting Rajasthan for implemention of the Sarva Shiksha Abhiyan programme for promotion of elementary education, under which an outlay of Rs. 1599.99 crores has been provided for 2007-08. This information was given by the Minister of State for Human Resource Development Shri M.A.A. Fatmi in a written reply in the Rajya Sabha.

660. (3-5-2007) NEW DELHI : Ministry of Human Resource Development in collaboration with National AIDS Control Organisation (NACO) has launched an educational programme, known as Adolescence Education Programme (AEP) which is being implemented by all the States and Union Territories of the country. The Programme is aimed at the following learning outcomes: (i) to make the learners aware of the major concerns, *i.e.* process of growing up during adolescence, HIV/AIDS and drug (substance) abuse; (ii) to inculcate in them positive attitude regarding these concerns; and (iii) to help them acquire life skills so that they avoid risky situations like HIV infection and drug abuse and develop healthy and responsible behaviour. This information was given by the Minister of State for Human Resource Development Shri M.A.A. Fatmi in a written reply in the Rajya Sabha.

661. (3-5-2007) NEW DELHI : According to the information furnished by Indira Gandhi National Open University (IGNOU), any university set up by the Act of Parliament/State legislature or deemed to be university can offer distance education programme subject to the fulfillment of norms and guidelines laid down by the Distance Education Council (DEC) and other apex bodies. DEC in its meeting held on March 23, 2007 had resolved that it would not insist on territorial jurisdiction to be followed by institutions in offering programmes through distance mode and on that matter universities should be governed by their own Act and Statutes. A list of the universities including deemed universities running distance education courses is annexed. IGNOU has informed that DEC does not maintain the details of the courses offered by these universities.

662. (3-5-2007) NEW DELHI : Fifty-Fifty ratio will be ensured between male and female anchors of Doordarshan and All India Radio by 15th August this year. This was stated by Minister of Information & Broadcasting and Parliamentary Affairs, Shri P. R. Dasmunsi while inaugurating a 'Workshop on Gender Equality in Indian Media' today. The Minister said the step would be a beginning towards ensuring parity for women in the field of Media. Shri Dasmunsi said that freedom of the Press is guaranteed but the same is not the case as regards the freedom of journalists, most of whom are in the private sector. He felt that the condition of women journalists in India, especially those in their early career, is far from satisfactory. The Minister advocated proper facilities at all work place considering specific needs of women who have to take care of their familial obligations along with their job/career. The Workshop has been organised by the Ministry of Women and Child Development on the occasion of World Press Freedom Day.

663. (3-5-2007) NEW DELHI : The Ministry of Rural Development has sanctioned Rs. 30.23 crore to the Gujarat Water Supply and Sewerage Board, Gandhinagar of the State Government of Gujarat towards part of first instalment of funds against the provisional allocation of Rs. 181.44 crore made for the Government of Gujarat under Accelerated Rural Water Supply Programme (Normal) of Rajiv Gandhi National Drinking Water Mission, during the year 2007-08. Up to 15 per cent of funds released under this sanction may be utilized for Operation & Maintenance and up to 5 per cent of funds may be spent for taking sustainability measures. States have been requested to delegate powers for management of Rural Water Supply Schemes through the Panchayati Raj Institutions (PRIs) as per the Constitution of India. As such Operation and Maintenance of the completed RWS Scheme should be transferred to the PRIs. No expenditure shall be incurred on taking water quality problems form the present release, as there is a separate allocation for the purpose. This release is being made for execution/completion of schemes to provide safe drinking water facilities to rural habitations and schools under the Centrally Sponsored ARWSP. Priorities set in ARWSP guidelines and through other instructions issued from time to time shall be followed for coverage of rural habitations and rural schools.

664. (3-5-2007) NEW DELHI : The Ministry of Rural Development has released first instalment of the Central share amounting to Rs. 25.00 lakh to the DRDA Pondicherry in Pondicherry towards Part Payment of first instalment of funds under the 'Swarnjayanti Gram Swarojgar Yojana' (SGSY) during the year 2007-08. The amount should be utilized on the Programme as per approved guidelines of SGSY. The funding pattern will be 75:25 by the Centre and the State. The State Government should release its share within one month of the date of release of the Central assistance. Under SGSY, assistance is given to the poor family living below the poverty line for taking up self-employment. It actively promotes group approach by organising the rural poor into Self-Help Groups.

665. (3-5-2007) NEW DELHI: A survey by CNN-IBN-Indian Express has predicted that the Bahujan Samajwadi Party led by Mayawati is poised to get 103-109 seats out of 292 seats, for which polling has been held so far in the Uttar Pradesh Assembly elections. If the same trend continues, the BSP is likely to emerge the biggest party with 145-155 seats in the 403-member House, says the post-poll survey. After the first five phases, Mulayam Singh's Samajwadi Party is projected to get 75-81 seats, followed by the Bharatiya Janata Party and its allies with 65-71, the Congress with 19-23 and others 17-21. If the same trend as seen in the survey continues, the SP is expected to get 100-110 seats, followed by the BJP and its allies with 90-100 and the Congress and others with 25-30.

666. (3-5-2007) NEW DELHI : The Ministry of Rural Development has released part payment of first instalment of Central share of funds amounting to Rs. 5.07 crore under the 'Swarnjayanti Gram Swarojgar Yojana' (SGSY) during the year 2007-08 to 14 DRDAs of Kerala.

667. (3-5-2007) NEW DELHI : The Ministry of Rural Development has released first instalment of the Central share amounting to Rs. 12.51 lakh to the 2 DRDAs of Goa, viz. North Goa (Rs.8.83 lakh) and South Goa (Rs.3.68 lakh) towards Part Payment of first instalment of funds under the 'Swarnjayanti Gram Swarojgar Yojana' (SGSY) during the year 2007-08. The amount should be utilized on the Programme as per approved guidelines of SGSY. The funding pattern will be 75:25 by the Centre and the State. The State Government should release its share within one month of the date of release of the Central assistance. Under SGSY, assistance is given to the poor family living below the poverty line for taking up self-employment. It actively promotes group approach by organising the rural poor into Self-Help Groups.

668. (3-5-2007) NEW DELHI : Close on the heels of Prime Minister Dr. Manmohan Singh's call to focus on the role of small & medium enterprises (SMEs) in India's industrial development, national and international experts at an SME Cluster Conclave have emphasised the critical importance of SMEs in India's economic growth. At the SME Cluster Conclave organised by Confederation of Indian Industry (CII) in partnership with the Ministry of Small Scale Industries here yesterday, it was indicated by the Secretary, Ministry of Small Scale Industries & Rural and Agro Industries, Dr. Chandrapal, that government was proposing to increase financial assistance to existing clusters of Micro, Small and Medium Enterprises (MSME) upto as much as 80% of their financial requirements under the 11th Plan. Shri Jawahar Sircar, Additional Secretary & Development Commissioner, Ministry of SSI & ARI said that the Cluster Concept was India's answer to global competition. "To enable MSMEs to become competitive, the government is proposing to build a pool of consultants under its National Manufacturing Competitiveness Programme. These consultants would be deployed with a cluster of 8-10 companies for a period of one to one and a half years. The cost of these consultants will be borne by the government", he said. Participating in the Conclave, Mr. Philippe Scholtes, UNIDO Regional Representative in India, said that the United Nations Industrial Development Organisation (UNIDO) has proposed a 5-year country Strategy for India, of which cluster development would be an integral part along with programmes aimed at upgrading technological capability and building up of social capital in the country's industrial sector. He also referred to the interesting new experiment of Twinning of Clusters as in the India-Italy Cluster Development Cooperation and said that UNIDO was also exploring new applications of Industrial cluster based approaches focusing on corporate social responsibility and poverty alleviation in micro enterprises. On behalf of the National Manufacturing Competitiveness Council (NMCC), Shri Rajeev Ranjan, Chief (Joint Secretary)/NMCC, stated that the National Strategy for Manufacturing drawn up by NMCC had been accepted by the government for implementation and that enabling SMEs to achieve competitiveness was one of the key elements of this strategy He further indicated that Strategy had identified the following areas for priority action viz., textiles & garments, food processing,

IT hardware & electronics, leather & footwear, automobiles & auto-components and chemicals & petrochemicals including pharma. Other speakers included Mr. Jamil Ashraf, Executive Director, Sandhar technologies; Mr. H.P. Kumar, Chairman & Managing Director, NSIC; Mr. Rakesh Rewari, Deputy Managing Director, SIDBI; and Mr. S. Sandilya, Chairman, CII Economic Affairs Committee & Chairman, Eicher Group.

669. (4-5-2007) NEW DELHI : The Union Minister of External Affairs, Shri Pranab Mukherjee today said that secure and sustainable energy sources are vital for ensuring India's high economic growth rate and enable it to address the developmental challenges of the poorest of its citizens. "We need to tap all sources of energy and keep our options in this regard open. It is an appreciation of this need that is at the heart of the India-US civil nuclear understanding and the larger energy dialogue which focuses on oil and gas, coal, power, energy efficiency, renewable energy and new technologies", Shri Mukherjee said while delivering the Inaugural Address at a Conference on the subject 'Business in and between India and the US-Legal and Regulatory Framework', organised by the Indo-American Chamber of Commerce, here.

670. (4-5-2007) NEW DELHI : Shri Kamal Nath, Minister of Commerce & Industry, has said that India is disappointed with a Paper on Agriculture circulated at a Special Session of the World Trade Organisation (WTO) in Geneva on 30 April, 2007 "because while the concerns of all the developed countries have been taken fully on board in a spirit of mutual accommodation, the sensitivities of developing countries with millions of resource poor farmers, have been left effectively unaddressed". India strongly feels that any outcome of the Doha Development Round, which tends to perpetuate the structural flaws and distortions in agriculture trade and does not address the sensitivities of the agriculture of the developing countries and LDCs, will run counter to the Doha mandate and risk another failure of the recently resumed negotiations, Shri Kamal Nath warned. In a statement issued in London today on his return from Oxford, the Minister said that India is specially disappointed to note that the Paper by the Chair of the WTO Committee on Agriculture suffers from a serious imbalance in terms of the suggested way forward. While it proposes that effectively, the Overall Trade Distorting Support (OTDS) of one of the major agricultural subsidisers could remain at least 50% above its actual levels of subsidies disbursed last year, it also suggests indirectly that the market access commitments of the major group of developed countries could remain at levels proposed in July, 2006 at the time of the breakdown of negotiations or could even be reduced effectively from that level by using liberal flexibilities Such a step would also lead to the impairment of the reduction commitments to the high tariff regimes of another group of developed countries. Side by side, "the Paper proposes stringent norms and low numbers for the Special Products (of agriculture) of developing countries and LDCs, which are required to protect their food security, livelihood security and rural development needs. It also leaves the question of removal of subsidies relating to cotton by a major developed country, which has caused serious problems to many African LDCs, largely unanswered", the Minister said. "India will work together with the G-20, G-33 and G-90 group of developing countries to put forward a common response to the proposals and options presented in the Paper", Shri Kamal Nath said.

671. (4-5-2007) NEW DELHI : May 7 to 11, 2007 will be historic days for India in the celebration of 150 years of its First War of Independence that had claimed thousands of freedom fighters in 1857 for the cause of their motherland. The commemoration of the days will also cast a new light on the hidden pages of the history of India's freedom struggle. The UPA government has organized a yearlong programme across the country to pay tributes, particularly, those who gave a kick-start to the initial momentum to free the country from the clutches of the British rule. According to majority of the historians, the revolt by Sepoys against their British masters in Meerut (Uttar Pradesh) in May 1857 is considered to be the First War of Independence of India. The fact remains that the events in Meerut gave an instant inspiration to the people to launch a revolt against the century-old despotic rule of the British.

672. (4-5-2007) NEW DELHI : Government of India have announced the sale (re-issue) of "7.49 per cent Government Stock, 2017" for a notified amount of Rs. 6,000 crore (nominal) through a price based auction using multiple price method.. Government of India have also announced the sale (re-issue) of "8.33 per cent Government Stock, 2036" for a notified amount of Rs. 4,000 crore (nominal) through a price based auction using multiple price method. The auctions will be conducted by the Reserve Bank of India, Mumbai Office, Fort, Mumbai on May 11, 2007 (Friday). Up to 5% of the notified amount of the sale of both the stocks will be allotted to eligible individuals and Institutions as per the Scheme for Non-Competitive Bidding Facility in the Auction of Government Securities.

673. (4-5-2007) NEW DELHI : The Government has also taken up schemes for application of Information and Communication Technology in the Indian courts through comprehensive computerisation of District and Subordinate Courts of the country and for development of infrastructure facilities for the judiciary as part of implementation of judicial reforms in the country. The First National Judicial Pay Commission also known as Shetty Commission had in its report presented on 11.11.1999 stated that the expenditure in our country in terms of GNP was relatively low. As per that report it was not more than 0.2% in our country whereas in the USA it was 1.4%, in the UK it was 4.3% and in Singapore it was 1.2%. This was stated by the Minister of State in the Ministry of Law and Justice, Shri K. Venkatapathy in written reply in Lok Sabha today.

674. (4-5-2007) NEW DELHI : After the Supreme Court Judgement of October 6,1993 in the Supreme Court Advocates-on-Record & Anr. Vs. Union of India, read with the Advisory Opinion of October 28, 1998, the entire process o[f] initiation of proposal for appointment of a Judge of a Supreme Court lies wit[h] the Chief Justice of India and for the appointment of a Judge of a High Court with the Chief Justice of that High Court. Government has been periodicall[y] reminding the Chief Justices of High Courts, the Chief Justice of India and th[e] Chief Ministers of the States to initiate proposals for filling up all vacant post[s] of judges in the High Courts.

675. (4-5-2007) THIRUVANANTHAPURAM: Leader of the Oppositio[n] Oommen Chandy has said that the attempted assault on Thursday on a delegatio[n] of Congress leaders who visited Munnar to inquire about encroachments an[d] unauthorised constructions clearly shows the involvement of CPI(M) leaders i[n] the widespread land grab in the district. Taking strong exception to the inciden[t] in a statement here, Mr. Chandy pointed out that the assault took place when th[e] KPCC delegation, led by the former MP Thalekkunnil Basheer, was visitin[g] encroached areas near the S.N. Lodge at the heart of Munnar. The assault als[o] showed that the Chief Minister's visit to Munnar to inquire about the issue wa[s] nothing but a farce. Although the Chief Minister ordered stoppage of unauthorise[d] constructions in the area, there had been no let up in the construction activities.

676. (4-5-2007) NEW DELHI : No State Government except Gujarat has formall[y] written to the Central Government for launching Evening Courts. The Governmen[t] of Gujarat after the Evening Courts were launched in that State requested th[e] Central Government for a special grant of Rs. 5 crore. Administration of Justic[e] being primarily a State subject and also because there is no scheme in this regar[d] for giving central assistance, the request of Government of Gujarat has not bee[n] agreed to. The matter of introduction of shift system in subordinate courts, amon[g] other things, was discussed in the Conference of Chief Ministers and Chief Justice[s] of High Courts held in New Delhi on April 8, 2007. In that Conference all State[s] had welcomed the introduction of shift system in subordinate courts and promise[d] to work in that direction. It was decided in that Conference that evening/mornin[g] courts be set up, wherever found feasible, and appropriate cases including thos[e] involving petty offences be transferred to such courts. Either retired Judicia[l] officers be re-employed or serving Judicial Officers be given suitable incentive to preside over these courts. Government has requested the State Government[s] to take action on the above mentioned decision, as also on the other decision[s] of the Conference, in consultation with their respective High Courts. The governmen[t] has also requested the Chief Justice of the High Courts to take action in consultatio[n] with the State Governments. This was stated by the Minister of Law and Justice, Shri H. R. Bhardwaj in written reply in Lok Sabha today.

677. (4-5-2007) NEW DELHI : Workers employed in agriculture are to receiv[e] higher Variable Dearness Allowance (VDA) with effect from April 01, 2007. According to the Chief Labour Commissioner (Central) the new rates of VDA calculated on six monthly average of Consumer Price Index for Industrial Workers reaching 382 from 361 as on 31-12-2006 (base (2001=100) would be as under in 'A', 'B' and 'C' areas.

678. (4-5-2007) NEW DELHI : The Railway Budget for 2007-08 includes 43 new proposals for developing 48 freight terminals over Indian Railways out of which 16 freight terminals were handling more than 15 rakes per month. These 16 freight terminals are Ahmednagar, New Mulund, Balabhgarh, Gonda, Barbil, Noamundi, Lakshmibai Nagar, Saharsa, Danapur, Sukinda Road, Yamuna Bridge, Sanvardam, Sankaval, Gosalpur, Mandideep and Mandi Govind Garh.

679. (4-5-2007) NEW DELHI : It has been decided to carry out pre-feasibility studies for one high speed corridor each in the Eastern, Western, Northern and Southern regions of the country. No sector has been identified for construction of high speed corridors. This information was given by Shri R. Velu, Minister of State for Railways in a written reply to a question in Rajya Sabha today.

680. (4-5-2007) NEW DELHI : Accidents at unmanned level crossings is not a routine feature. Most of the accidents take place due to negligence of road users while crossing the unmanned level crossings. However, it is a fact that a number of demands for manning of unmanned level crossings are being received from time to time. The problem can be partially addressed by replacing unmanned level crossings with road under bridges. Ministry of Railways has decided and delegated powers to Zonal Railways to provide 'Limited Height Subways' of cost upto Rs. 50 lakhs in replacement of manned / unmanned level crossings where such construction is technically feaible and the State Government agrees to close the level crossing. This policy is also applicable for manned /unmanned level crossings falling over North Western Railway including Rewari-Sadulpur, Sadulpur-Bikaner, Jaipur-Ringus-Luharu, Phulera-Ringus-Rewari, Ratangarh-Degana and Udaipur-Himmatpuri routes. Construction of Road Under Bridges in lieu of existing level crossings shall be duly considered with due undertaking from the State Government. This information was given by Shri R. Velu, Minister of State for Railways in a written reply to a question in Rajya Sabha today.

681. (4-5-2007) NEW DELHI : Toilets in all passenger coaches of long distance trains have been provided with Water Closet (WC). Presently these discharge the waste on track. In order to improve sanitation at station areas, controlled Discharge Toilet Systems (CDTS) are being progressively introduced in coaches. The control discharge toilets prevent discharge of waste on the tracks when the train is stationary or moving at low speeds, thereby helping to make the stations and nearby areas relatively cleaner. The waste is, however, eventually discharged on tracks away from station areas.

682. (4-5-2007) NEW DELHI : IRCTC has signed Memorandum of Understanding (MoU) with Bharat Petroleum Corporation Limited (BPCL) to sell railway tickets through internet (e-tickets) from their petrol pump / retail stores. This facility has already started at 36 locations in Bangalore, Bhubaneshwar, Chennai, Hyderabad, Kolkata, Mumbai, New Delhi and Pune. This information was given by Shri R. Velu, Minister of State for Railways in a written reply to a question in Rajya Sabha today.

683. (4-5-2007) NEW DELHI : Indian Railway Catering and Tourism Corporation (IRCTC) has initiated an exercise on audit of food safety standards in its base kitchens and pantry cars. The food safety audit is also done for stalls on railway platforms, kiosks and food plaza joints. Imparting training to the catering staff is an on-going process. IRCTC is conducting training programmes regularly for both departmental as well as private licencees' staff working in kitchens and on running trains through reputed agencies viz. Indian Tourism Development Corporation and Training Institute of Railways at Kishan Ganj. This information was given by Shri R. Velu, Minister of State for Railways in a written reply to a question in Rajya Sabha today.

684. (4-5-2007) NEW DELHI : The Rajya Sabha was today informed that the Group of Ministers on the Bhopal Gas tragedy has not taken a decision to declare the rest 20 wards of Bhopal as affected by the gas tragedy. Giving this information in a written reply in the house today, the Minister of State for Chemicals & Fertilisers and Parliamentary Affairs Shri B.K. Handique said it was decided in the meeting of the Group of Ministers held on 11th May, 2005, that the Government of M.P. would furnish detailed information with related data on morbidity, mortality and other parameters required for declaring the remaining 20 wards also as gas affected. This would be analyzed and the approximate requirement of additional funds worked out in consultation with the Office of the Welfare Commissioner. The matter would then be placed before the Prime Minister, through the Chairman of the GoM. In compliance with the decision taken by the GOM, the Government of MP was requested to furnish the detailed information with relevant data vide this Department's letter dated June 16, 2005 followed by subsequent reminders. The State Government of Madhya Pradesh has not furnished the desired information, as yet. The names of the Ministers included in this Group as per the Office Memorandum issued by the Cabinet Secretariat dated November 10, 2006, are i) Shri Arjun Singh, Chairman, ii) Shri A.R. Antulay, iii) Shri Ram Vilas Paswan, iv) Shri Sis Ram Ola, v) Shri Kamal Nath vi) Shri H.R. Bhardwaj, vii) Shri Oscar Fernandes, viii) Smt. Renuka Chowdhury, ix) Shri Suresh Pachouri and x) Permanent invitee Minister-in-charge of the Department of Bhopal Gas Tragedy, Relief and Rehabilitation, Government of Madhya Pradesh.

685. (4-5-2007) NEW DELHI : The Chief Minister of Punjab Shri Prakash Singh Badal called on the Union Minister of Shipping, Road Transport and Highways, Thiru T.R. Baalu here today and discussed various issues relating to development of highways in the State. Thiru Baalu informed the Chief Minister that a sum of

Rs. 304 crores has been sanctioned by the Ministry under Central Road Fund Scheme (CRF) so far. On the basis of the present status of utilization, an estimated sum amounting to Rs. 30 crores could be further sanctioned to the State. On Chief Minister's request for four laning of NH-64 from Patiala to Sangrur, Thiru Baalu said that the Ministry has already sanctioned consultancy services for four-laning of NH-64 from Km.0-45 (Zirakpur to Bahadurgarh) and the work has been awarded. The execution is proposed to be taken up on BOT basis. Shri Badal requested Thiru Baalu to consider four-laning of the remaining portion of Patiala to Bhatinda section also. The Chief Minister requested for additional fund for Domoria Bridge which was sanctioned under CRF for Rs.26.11 crores with Ministry's share of Rs.20.11 crores. The Minister asked the officers of the Ministry and the State Government of Punjab to find out avenues as to how the funds could be made available. Shri Badal requested that the remaining portion from Talwandi Bhai to Ferozepur on NH-95 may also be included in the project under NHDP-III. The Minister assured that he would ask the officials to look into it. The Ministry officials said that on Pathankot-Jalandhar section NH-1A, there is a problem of land acquisition. Thiru Baalu urged the State Chief Minister to direct the State PWD to help in expediting the land acquisition.

686. (4-5-2007) NEW DELHI : National Manufacturing Competitiveness Council will launch on Monday in New Delhi, the Post Graduate Program for Executives for Visionary Leadership in Manufacturing. The Visionary Leaders for Manufacturing Program (VLMP) aims to provide skill based training to transform potential middle-level managers in the Indian manufacturing industry into visionary leaders. These leaders would implement principles of manufacturing excellence in their organizations and promote innovation to make Indian Industry a global leader in the world of manufacturing. The programme will provide an opportunity for India's best and brightest mid-career professionals who are dedicated to manufacturing, to develop them into future visionaries those who can guide the manufacturing sector in a strategic way. The programme aims to have a proper balance of theoretical inputs and practical training to develop a high degree of leadership skills which would enable Indian companies convert manufacturing into a competitive weapon. This programme proposes to bring together the cutting edge expertise of the Indian Institutes of Technology and the Indian Institutes of Management that which can be delivered under the stewardship of the National Manufacturing Competitiveness Council (NMCC), Government of India. With a world focus on India as an alternative to China in the manufacturing sector it will be necessary to bring a quantum change in the quality of human resources in the manufacturing sector of the country. India is on the growth path but for the growth story to continue there is a pressing need to enhance the quality of leaders that we have in the manufacturing sector. The growth could get severely affected due to a shortage of leaders capable of thinking ahead and building on visions. Recognizing these pressing needs to develop Visionary Leaders, the Government of India proposes to launch a training Program on the lines of the "Leaders for

Manufacturing" programme of the MIT. As part of the protocol signed by the Prime Ministers of India and Japan, the Government of Japan is actively supporting various initiatives of the Indian academia and industry in the area of manufacturing and design. The function will be presided by Dr. V. Krishnamurthy, Chairman, NMCC, Government of India which will be attended by the leading industry and academic partners and the members of media. The organizers have also requested the President of Confederation of Indian Industry to deliver a key note address on the perspective of the manufacturing sector on various transformations and current demands in the manufacturing sector in India. The organizers have also invited the Ambassador of Japan in India, Mr. Yasukuni Enoki to grace the occasion as a guest of honour and deliver speech on the Indo-Japan Collaborations and the perspective of the Government of Japan.

687. (4-5-2007) NEW DELHI : Securities and Exchange Board of India has informed that all listed companies are not required to maintain a minimum public shareholding of 25%. However, of the companies required to do so, 240 are non-compliant. The listing agreement provides a mechanism for enabling non-compliant companies to graduate to the level of compliant companies. If a company, however, fails to do so within the permissible time, its shares are liable to be delisted in terms of the delisting guidelines and it is liable for penal actions under the securities laws. This information was given by Shri Pawan Kumar Bansal, Minister of State in the Ministry of Finance in reply to a question raised by Shri Subhash Sureshchandra Deshmukh in Lok Sabha today.

688. (4-5-2007) NEW DELHI : With a view to facilitating the promotion and development of bamboo and bamboo processing related industries, the Small Industries Service Institute (SISI), Cuttack, with the support of the National Mission for Bamboo Application (NMBA), organised an Entrepreneurs' Meet on 28 February 2007. Thirty four serious entrepreneurs participated in it. A special emphasis was laid on entrepreneurs having closed saw mills to enable them to convert their units into bamboo-based enterprises. The SISI at Cuttack intends to work in close collaboration with NMBA to develop the bamboo sector by (i) organizing exposure visit of 7 entrepreneurs to Nagaland and Ratnagiri, and (ii) to conduct Entrepreneurship Development Programmes (EDPs) of bamboo based industries, in the current year. The SISI at Cuttack intends to work in close collaboration with NMBA and Orissa Bamboo Development Agency (OBDA) to develop Micro, Small and Medium Enterprises (MSMEs) based on bamboo through organizing Entrepreneurship and Skill Development Programmes, preparation of project reports, conduct of exposure visits, etc. This information was given by the Minister of Small Scale Industries and Agro & Rural Industries, Shri Mahabir Prasad in a written reply to a question in Rajya Sabha today.

689. (4-5-2007) NEW DELHI : A meeting of the Consultative Committee of the Ministry of Home Affairs was held here today to discuss the issue relating to the

Draft National Policy on Criminal Justice. The Home Minister, Shri Shivraj Patil presided over the meeting. Taking part in the deliberations, the members of the Parliamentary Consultative Committee welcomed the Government's attempt to draft the National Policy on Criminal Justice. The members made certain suggestions during their presentations. The Drafting Committee of National Criminal Justice Policy will take into account these suggestions while finalizing the draft policy paper. The members present at today's meeting included Dr. P.C. Alexander of the Rajya Sabha and S/Shri Nikhil Kumar, Mohanbhai Delkar and Sarbananda Sonowal of the Lok Sabha. The Ministers of State for Home, S/Shri Sriprakash Jaiswal and S. Regupathy and the Union Home Secretary, Shri Madhukar Gupta were among those who participated in the meeting.

690. (4-5-2007) NEW DELHI : The Ministry of Women and Child Development has taken up number of initiatives to ensure easy access to the lending operations of Rashtriya Mahila Kosh (RMK) for empowering of women through micro financing. Lending has been recently decentralized through 38 nodal agencies in various States. A special package for marginalized women group of North-East region has been launched. This was informed by the Minister of Women and Child Development, Smt. Renuka Chowdhury to the Members of the Parliamentary Consultative Committee attached to the Ministry while briefing about the activities of RMK, a National Credit Fund under the Ministry. Underlining the importance of low interest lending to the Self Help Groups (SHG) of women, Smt. Renuka Chowdhury said that RMK had been asked to expand its credit programme to cover at least 20 lakh Self Help Groups and to include disaster management package in case of droughts, floods and other natural calamities. She informed that during 2006-07 about 5.83 lakhs women benefited with the lending at low interest rate from RMK without collateral and these included mostly poor women in rural and semi urban areas. It had resulted in improved earning capacity and better living standards. The Minister said that the Government had also decided to organize workshops and training programmes for SHG of women to upgrade skill, technology and packaging of their products. Replying to the concern expressed by the Members of the Committee, the Minister accepted that RMK established to address the cause of poor women in alleviating poverty and promoting empowerment is now in clash with the commercial objectivities adopted by the private sector banks and other non-Government fund providers who had jumped in to the sector recently in a big way. Still, the Government is actively considering to further reducing the lending rate of RMK because most of its finance is directed towards women from the poorer and marginalized sections of the society, she said. Participating in the discussions members suggested uniform regulations for all micro finance lending institutions. They were of the opinion that the Government should ensure cap on interest rate in the proposed Micro Financial Sector (Development and Regulation) Bill, 2007 which is under consideration in the Parliament. They also suggested for taking up awareness programme about the lending operation of RMK in a big way. The meeting was attended by Ms. Supriya

Dutt, Ms. Viplov Thakur, Ms. P. Satidevi, S/Shri Francis Fathome and Luxminarayan Sharma (all Members of Parliament).

691. (4-5-2007) NEW DELHI : Steel Authority of India Limited (SAIL)'s Corporate Plan envisaged a tentative investment of Rs. 37,000 crore towards expansion and modernization. The schemes of individual steel plants are getting firmed up based on composite feasibility reports. Eventually investment and proposed capacity is slated to go up compared to targets earlier envisaged. The tentative project investment based on feasibility reports will be known only after firming up of schemes by all the plants and their approval by SAIL Board. The share of alloy and special steel plants in the overall investment is tentatively about Rs.2200 crore. To improve its market presence in the alloy and special steels market, SAIL has drawn out expansion plans for its special steels plants at Alloy Steel Plant (ASP), Salem Steel Plant (SSP) and Visvesvaraya Iron Steel Plant (VISL). After implementation of the expansion plan, the total production of saleable steel from these units will increase from a level of around 4.5 lakhs tonnes during 2006-07 to around 10 lakhs tonnes of saleable steel. This information was given by the Minister of State for Steel Dr. Akhilesh Das in a written reply in the Rajya Sabha today.

692. (4-5-2007) NEW DELHI : The public sector banks who have implemented Core Banking Solutions (CBS) propose to install ATMs at major/ selected Railway Stations subject to approval of Railway authorities and Reserve Bank of India. Location of ATMs would depend upon specific site clearance by Railway Authorities. There is no separate target for installation of off-site ATMs at railway stations for the current year. However, any request received from banks for installation of off-site ATMs at railway stations during the current year would be examined by RBI in terms of the extant Branch Authorization Policy guidelines. This information was given by Shri Pawan Kumar Bansal, Minister of State in the Ministry of Finance in reply to a question raised by Shri Rajnarayan Budholiya in Lok Sabha today.

693. (4-5-2007) NEW DELHI : 114 companies stand identified as vanishing companies with issue size of approximately Rs. 799.31 crores. Prosecutions have been filed against 107 companies and their promoters/directors u/s 62/63, 68 and 628 of the Companies Act, 1956 and against 94 such companies for non-filing of Statutory Returns. In addition, FIRs have also been filed against 102 companies and their Promoters/ Directors for the offences punishable under Sections 420, 406, 403, 415, 418 & 424 of the Indian Penal Code (IPC). A large number of investors have suffered due to the vanishing companies. The exact number of these investors is not ascertainable, in view of frequent change by way of transfer of shares etc. A Central Coordination and Monitoring Committee, co-chaired by Secretary, Ministry of Company Affairs and Chairman, SEBI has been set up to look into issues relating to vanishing companies and their promoters and to monitor the progress of action against them. Besides taking action against these companies and their promoters/directors under the Companies Act and the Indian Penal Code, the Ministry has implemented an e-Governance project under which the identity of authorised directors and professionals is established in a secure manner. Securities and Exchange Board of India (SEBI) has also amended the SEBI (Disclosure and Investor Protection) Guidelines to enforce higher disclosure requirements pertaining to promoters of companies, besides taking punitive action in a number of cases. SEBI has also debarred 100 companies and 378 directors u/s 11B of the SEBI Act from raising money from the Capital Market in any form, for a period of five years. SEBI has amended the existing Clause 49 of the Listing Agreement, which seeks to strengthen the disclosure requirement in particular pertaining to promoters and also providing for monitoring of utilisation of funds raised from the public. This information was given by Shri Prem Chand Gupta, Minister of Company Affairs in reply to the questions raised by Shri Braja Kishore Tripathy in Lok Sabha today.

694. (4-5-2007) NEW DELHI : An understanding has been reached between the Reserve Bank of India (RBI) and the State Bank of Pakistan (SBP) on granting permission for opening two branches of banks from India and Pakistan in each other's country, on a reciprocal basis. The specific banks to be permitted to open the branches would be mutually agreed upon by RBI and SBP keeping in view their respective regulatory policies and procedures. RBI has proposed to SBP the names of State Bank of India and Bank of India for opening their branches in Pakistan. Habib Bank Ltd., National Bank of Pakistan and United Bank Ltd. from Pakistan have evinced interest in opening their branches in India. In the meeting of Governor, RBI with the Governor of State Bank of Pakistan held on 26.09.2006, it was agreed that the licences to the banks for opening of their branches in each other's country would be given on reciprocal and simultaneous basis. This information was given by Shri Pawan Kumar Bansal, Minister of State in the Ministry of Finance in reply to a question raised by Shri Bapu Hari Chaure and Shri Sanjay Dhotre in Lok Sabha today.

695. (4-5-2007) NEW DELHI : The Minister for Civil Aviation, Shri Praful Patel shall receive the inaugural flight of the national carrier Indian from Delhi to Surat in Gujarat on 6th May, 2007. He will also flag off the inaugural flight from Surat to Delhi the same day. This will be Surat's first air link to the national capital. Indian Airlines will also be the first carrier to provide air connectivity to this city after a long time. This flight is expected to provide a much needed air link between two important cities and facilitate business travel and others. It will also fulfil a long time demand from the people of the region. The new flight will operate with brand new Airbus A-319, offering seats in both Executive and Economy class. It will be a direct flight between the two cities operating on daily basis. Meanwhile the Airports Authority of India has upgraded the Surat Airport for operations of wide-bodied aircraft like B-737-800, AB321 keeping in view the overall growth of the aviation in the domestic sector and the increased traffic flow. This is being done at a cost of Rs. 68.81 crore.

696. (4-5-2007) NEW DELHI : The Comptroller and Auditor General (CAG) of India Shri VN Kaul has proposed functional autonomy for internal auditors to various Ministries and Government Departments. The suggestion is part of six recommendations made by a task force constituted by the CAG to strengthen internal audit in the Government of India. Delivering the keynote address at a day-long seminar on internal audit in New Delhi today, Shri Kaul disclosed that the task force had submitted its report to the Finance Ministry in November last year. He hoped the Ministry would soon take a decision to undertake reforms in the internal audit of Government. While seeking independence for internal auditors from the administrative setup, the CAG said that they should directly report to the Secretary in the Ministry or to the heads of various departments and agencies. The other measures include widening of the mandate of internal audit to suggest steps to improve efficiency, formulation of risk based audit plan, adoption of international benchmark auditing standards, computerisation to detect fraud and corruption and implementation of auditors' suggestions. Senior officers of Indian Defence Accounts Service, Indian Civil Accounts Service, Indian Audit and Accounts Service and Indian Railway Accounts Service attended the deliberations. Speaking on the occasion, the Secretary (Defence Finance) Shri VK Misra pointed out the need to review the periodic internal audit certificate and reduce the large expenditure at the level of service headquarters and lower formations. Shri Misra said this is necessary to make optimum use of funds for modernisation of Defence Forces and maintain high serviceability levels when there were constraints of reducing fiscal deficit in the Union Budget. In his introductory remarks, the Controller General of Defence Accounts Shri Jnan Prakash pointed out that of the 97,000 crore rupees Defence Budget for the current financial year, the capital outlay for modernization and acquisition of weaponry and other equipment stood at nearly 44 % while there was a need to make proper utilisation of the huge revenue expenditure. The Deputy CAG Shri CV Avadhani and Shri Harish Dua, President of the Delhi Chapter of the Institute for Internal Auditors, USA were among those who spoke in the seminar.

697. (4-5-2007) NEW DELHI : The Government has taken a number of initiatives to alleviate the sufferings of the farmers including small and marginal farmers. From Kharif 2006-07, farmers are being provided crop loan up to Rs. 3 lakh at 7% rate of interest. Keeping in view the importance of flow of credit to agriculture, in particular to the smaller borrowers who may not have the necessary assets as collateral, banks have been advised to waive margin/security requirements for agricultural loans up to Rs. 50000/-. The Government has also announced a package for revival of cooperative credit structure. A major effort has been initiated for diversification of agriculture. National Horticulture Mission has been launched for ensuring end-to-end approach with backward and forward linkages covering research, post harvest management, processing and marketing. Other initiatives taken by Government include expanding the area under irrigation, improved water management with watershed development and rain harvesting and establishment of National Rain-fed Area Authority. National Agricultural Insurance Scheme is being implemented with the objective of protecting the farmers against the crop losses occurring on account of natural calamities. This information was given in the Rajya Sabha today by the Minister of State for Agriculture, Shri Kanti Lal Bhuria in a written reply.

698. (4-5-2007) NEW DELHI : Shri Kamal Nath, Union Minister of Commerce and Industry, has cautioned against attempts to move the current Doha Round negotiations in the World Trade Organisation (WTO) from an unconditional delivery of the development dimension of the Round to conditionalities which would hinder such an outcome. Delivering a Special Address at the University of Oxford (University College) last evening, the Minister deplored that although development was enunciated as the centrality of the Round, "some are seeking to weave it in a mesh of ifs and buts". Highlighting India's concerns in agriculture, Shri Kamal Nath strongly emphasised the need for a safety net to protect the interests of farmers in developing countries like India. "Even the window of Special Products and the Special Safeguard Mechanism that was devised in the July Framework as a means of safeguarding livelihood security and rural development needs – even this is being sought to be tied up in knots so as to render it ineffective. Low-income or resource-poor rural households have little ability to absorb price fluctuations and a flood of subsidized imports of agricultural products. If developing country governments are not able to provide a safety net – a safety net for livelihoods, mind you, not for corporate profits – then it would be the surest recipe for social disaster and instability", he said. Referring to concerns on industrial tariffs, Shri Kamal Nath warned that unrestrained tariff liberalisation can have disastrous effects on a country's industrial economy. "The former Trade Minister of Zambia told me that his country actually experienced de-industrialisation after its membership of the WTO. The harsh truth is that the most vulnerable in any re-adjustment are women and artisans, small scale industries run by local entrepreneurs and those that are located in geographically disadvantaged pockets of the country. Flexibilities in the application of a NAMA formula remain an inviolable essential to ensure balanced regional and sectoral development", he stressed.

699. (4-5-2007) NEW DELHI : The Minister of State (Independent Charge) for Labour and Employment, Shri Oscar Fernandes has said that the Government proposes to make Plantation Labour Act, 1951 more stringent to ensure welfare and safety of workers. Addressing the meeting of the Parliamentary Consultative Committee attached to his Ministry here yesterday evening, Shri Fernandes said that eleven changes including incorporating a new chapter are proposed for amending the Act. He said safety precautions should be made part of the Act particularly in handling of agro-chemicals specially insecticides and herbicides. He said it is also necessary to amend the Act to enable the Central Government to prohibit, restrict or regulate employment of women and children below 14 years for handling hazardous chemicals in plantations. Shri Fernandes said that the basic approach to changes in the Act should be to increase the competitiveness of the plantation industry and to build on the capacity of the workforce employed in this sector. The Labour Minister also referred to proposed amendments in the Employees' Provident Fund and Misc. Provisions Act (EPF & MP Act) to secure compliance and to arrest the default by establishments. He said that his Ministry is aware of the default by some establishments and the amount of arrears outstanding is around Rs. 2,500 crore which is a little over one per cent of the total progressive collection. The Minister said that one of the measures taken by the EPFO to curtail default and improve service delivery is embarking on a total computerisation process. Its aim is to identify the default immediately on its occurrence and also to provide service delivery on anywhere, anytime basis. He said the project is now at a critical stage and the trial run in the pilot offices is already on. It will be soon replicated in all the field offices of the EPFO, he added. Participating in the meeting, the Members of Parliament, Shri Gurudas Dasgupta and Shri Dawa Narbula welcomed the proposed amendments in the Plantation Labour Act and the EPF and MP Act. They said that these Acts should be implemented more effectively particularly in tea gardens where they alleged that the Plantation Act is not being implemented. They also said that managements of plantations are committing default by not depositing EPF deductions of the employees which they said is a serious offence. Shri Gurudas Dasgupta said that the default is maximum in Jute and Tea industry. He said that the non-payment of the employees share to Employees' Provident Fund should also be made punishable with imprisonment like the non-payment of employees share. Shri Fernandes said that the Ministry would look into these issues. The Labour Secretary, Smt. Sudha Pillai told the meeting that V.V. Giri National Labour Institute has undertaken a study for strengthening of labour laws. Earlier, the meeting, which was also attended by senior officials of Labour and Commerce Ministries, condoled the death of sitting member of the Parliamentary Consultative Committee, Shri Chittabrata Majumdar who died in February this year. In a condolence resolution, it was stated that in Shri Majumdar's passing away the country has lost a prominent trade unionist and able parliamentarian. The meeting observed one minute's silence in honour of late Shri Majumdar.

700. (4-5-2007) NEW DELHI : The country is expecting bumper production of sugar. In order to ensure that over production of sugar does not lead to a situation of mounting cane price arrears, the Central Government on 24th March, 2007 have decided as under: (i) to provide export assistance to defray the internal transport and freight charges, marketing and handling charges at the flat rate of Rs.1350 per ton on export of domestically manufactured sugar from sugar factories situated in the coastal States and at the flat rate of Rs.1450 per ton from sugar factories situated in other than coastal States. Exports made under Open General License (OGL) only (and not under 'advance license') on or after 19th April, 2007 and upto 18th April, 2008 or till further orders, whichever is earlier, would be eligible for this assistance. The estimated cost of export assistance is Rs.205 crores. The amount so received is to be used for cane price payment. (ii) to create a buffer stock of 20 lac tons for a period of one year (01.05.2007 to 30.04.2008) under which interest charges, insurance and storage charges for the quantity taken as buffer will be reimbursed to sugar factories. The cost of this subsidy is estimated to be Rs.378 crores for one year. Further, banks would provide additional credit of Rs.420 crores on creation of 20 lac tons of buffer. Thus, Rs.798 crores would be available with sugar factories to pay cane price to sugarcane farmers, for the sugar season 2006-07 including the cane price arrears of previous sugar seasons. The buffer subsidy and the additional credit are to be used exclusively for the payment of cane price. This information was given in the Rajya Sabha today by the Minister of State for Consumer Affairs, Food and Public Distribution, Dr. Akhilesh Prasad Singh in a written reply.

701. (4-5-2007) NEW DELHI : The Parliamentary Consultative Committee attached to the Ministry of Civil Aviation met here today. It was chaired by the Minister for Civil Aviation, Shri Praful Patel. The Members congratulated the Minister on the progress of the civil aviation sector. They also congratulated the decision of the Government to merge the two national carriers Air India and Indian Airlines. Besides the Members discussed other issues like connectivity to the various parts of the country, the working of the two national airlines as well as that of the private carriers, the working of the private airport operators and proliferation of institutes providing training for various aviation related employments and their sanctity. A number of Members of the Committee expressed concerns about reported security breach at airports. Replying to the concerns of the Members, the Minister for Civil Aviation assured them that the Ministry would seriously consider all aspects of the issues and apprehensions raised, take a comprehensive review together with the Ministry of Home Affairs and plug all possible loopholes in the security arrangements at the airports. Regarding the proliferation of aviation training and institutes in the metros, the Secretary, Ministry of Civil Aviation, Shri Ashok Chawla assured the Members that the Ministry would look into the matter to see whether any policy in this regard or any legal intervention was required. At today's meeting it was decided that a special meeting of the Members of the Consultative Committee would be held with the private airport operators to review the progress of their work and their future plans. Members of Parliament who were present at the meeting were: S/Shri Madhu Goud Yashki, Sachin Pilot, Santosh Gangwar, Tapir Gao, Ratilal K. Verma, Ashok Argal, Ramswaroop Koli, Sumitra Mahajan, Santosh Bagrodia, Tarlochan Singh, Dinesh Trivedi and Dr. Farooq Abdullah.

702. (4-5-2007) NEW DELHI : The Minister of State in the Ministry of Rural Development, Smt. Suryakanta Patil in reply to a question in Lok Sabha today stated that according to the programme guidelines, the State Governments, Union Territory Administration, District Rural Development Agencies/Zila Parishads have been allowed to have a limit of 10% as Opening Balance of the available funds with them, to maintain continuity of the programmes. As reported by the States, under SGRY, 267 districts in the year 2004-05, 245 districts during 2005-06 and 28 districts during 2006-07 utilised more than 90% of the available funds. The expenditure figures of 2006-07 are provisional and position may improve, when complete information for all schemes is received. Under IAY, 311 districts in year 2004-05, 280 districts in 2005-06 and 261 districts in 2006-07 utilised more than 90% of the available funds. Under SGSY, 331 districts in the year 2004-05, 443 districts in 2005-06 and 25 districts in 2006-07 utilised more than 90% of the available funds.

703. (4-5-2007) NEW DELHI : In reply to a question whether some States have not finalised the BPL list till date, the Minister of State in the Ministry of Rural Development, Smt. Suryakanta Patil informed the Lok Sabha today that the States of Andhra Pradesh, Assam, Bihar, Goa, Gujarat, Haryana, Himachal Pradesh, Jammu & Kashmir, Karnataka, Kerala, Maharashtra, Manipur, Meghalaya, Mizoram, Nagaland, Orissa, Rajasthan, Sikkim, Tamil Nadu, Tripura and West Bengal have not yet finalized the new BPL list on the basis of BPL Census, 2002. After the vacation of stay by the Hon'ble Supreme Court on 14.2.2006, the matter has been taken up with the States/ Union Territory Administrations at different levels to finalise the BPL list expeditiously after ensuring transparency and redressing the Public grievances, if any. The States and UTs have been advised to complete the exercise possibly by June, 2007, the Minister informed further.

704. (4-5-2007) NEW DELHI : The Swaranjayanti Gram Swarozgar Yojana (SGSY) is a credit-cum-subsidy scheme. While subsidy is only a minor and enabling component, Credit is a critical component of the scheme that envisages involvement of the banking sector. The banks, however, have generally not been able to meet the credit disbursement targets under the scheme. The matter has been regularly taken up with the RBI and the Ministry of Finance at various levels. These measures have resulted in a credit mobilisation of 77% of the target during the financial year 2006-07.

705. (4-5-2007) NEW DELHI : Close on the heels of Prime Minister Dr. Manmohan Singh's call to focus on the role of small & medium enterprises (SMEs) in India's industrial development, national and international experts at an SME Cluster Conclave have emphasised the critical importance of SMEs in India's economic growth. At the SME Cluster Conclave organised by Confederation of Indian Industry (CII) in partnership with the Ministry of Small Scale Industries here recently, it was indicated by the Secretary, Ministry of Small Scale Industries &

Rural and Agro Industries, Dr. Chandrapal, that government was proposing to increase financial assistance to existing clusters of Micro, Small and Medium Enterprises (MSME) upto as much as 80% of their financial requirements under the 11th Plan. Shri Jawahar Sircar, Additional Secretary & Development Commissioner, Ministry of SSI & ARI said that the Cluster Concept was India's answer to global competition. "To enable MSMEs to become competitive, the government is proposing to build a pool of consultants under its National Manufacturing Competitiveness Programme. These consultants would be deployed with a cluster of 8-10 companies for a period of one to one and a half years. The cost of these consultants will be borne by the government", he said. Participating in the Conclave, Mr. Philippe Scholtes, UNIDO Regional Representative in India, said that the United Nations Industrial Development Organisation (UNIDO) has proposed a 5-year country Strategy for India, of which cluster development would be an integral part along with programmes aimed at upgrading technological capability and building up of social capital in the country's industrial sector. He also referred to the interesting new experiment of Twinning of Clusters as in the India-Italy Cluster Development Cooperation and said that UNIDO was also exploring new applications of Industrial cluster based approaches focusing on corporate social responsibility and poverty alleviation in micro enterprises. On behalf of the National Manufacturing Competitiveness Council (NMCC), Shri Rajeev Ranjan, Chief (Joint Secretary)/NMCC, stated that the National Strategy for Manufacturing drawn up by NMCC had been accepted by the government for implementation and that enabling SMEs to achieve competitiveness was one of the key elements of this strategy He further indicated that Strategy had identified the following areas for priority action viz., textiles & garments, food processing, IT hardware & electronics, leather & footwear, automobiles & auto-components and chemicals & petrochemicals including pharma. Other speakers included Mr. Jamil Ashraf, Executive Director, Sandhar technologies; Mr. H.P. Kumar, Chairman & Managing Director, NSIC; Mr. Rakesh Rewari, Deputy Managing Director, SIDBI; and Mr. S. Sandilya, Chairman, CII Economic Affairs Committee & Chairman, Eicher Group.

706. (4-5-2007) NEW DELHI : The Union Minister for Shipping, Road Transport & Highways Thiru T. R. Baalu discussed the initiatives of the Central Government on the Shipping, and Road Sector Development in Kerala with the Members of Parliament belonging to the State here last evening. The senior officials from the Ministry of Shipping, Road Transport & Highways, NHAI, and Team Leaders of various Projects briefed the participants on the progress of various projects in the State. Also the Chairmen of the Inland Waterways Authority of India (IWAI), Cochin Port Trust and Cochin Shipyard Ltd. were present in the meeting. Making a Presentation on the Inland Waterways in Kerala, it was pointed out that the progress on developing the National Waterway-3 is slow as issues pertaining to reclamation of the waterway are not being resolved. It was pointed out that removal of fishing nets/stakes from fairway, removal or relocation of cables, pipelines etc. for widening of canal on Alappuzha-Kollam stretch and handing over entire requisite land for Mullackal (Alappuzha) terminal are the necessary tasks to accomplished to make the waterway fully operational. Thiru Baalu asked the Kerala MPs to impress upon the State Government to expedite the work on these issues. The Status and pace of implementation of various projects under North-South Corridor (Phase II) and Projects under NHDP III were discussed at length. The development of other National Highways in Kerala being improved under the Central Road Fund Scheme was also deliberated upon. The participating Ministers and MPs brought out the problematic issues pertaining to their respective areas and sought to know the status of various projects.

707. (4-5-2007) NEW DELHI : Shri Arjun Singh, Minister for Human Resource Development has said that gradual growth of Jamia, from a small institution in the pre-independence India to a Central University located in New Delhi – offering integrated education from nursery to research in specialised areas is a story of dedication, conviction and vision of the people, who worked against all odds and saw it growing step by step. Shri Singh was inaguarating the Noam Chomsky Complex at Jamia Millia Islamia Premises here today Those present on the occasion included, Shri F.T. Khorakiwala, Chancellor; Prof. Mushirul Hasan, Vice Chancellor, Jamia Millia Islamia, and Members of the University Court, Executive Council, Academic Council and Faculty & Staff of the University.

708. (4-5-2007) NEW DELHI : The products of Soft Drinks are covered under the Standards of Carbonated Water, prescribed under the PFA Rules, 1955. The standards for carbonated water under the PFA Rules do not prescribe any limits for total pesticide residues. However, water used in the manufacture of carbonated water is required to conform to the standards of Packaged Drinking Water, wherein the limits for Pesticide Residues has been prescribed. Water comprises approximately 88% of most carbonated drinks. The analysis of the informal samples of carbonated water were collected by the State Governments as per the direction of the Ministry of Health and Family Welfare during August – September, 2006, and were analyzed by the Central Food Laboratories for pesticide residues. As per the analysis reports, none of the samples exceeded the permissible limits prescribed for pesticides residues in Packaged Drinking Water. States/UT Governments are the implementing authorities under the PFA Act. They have been advised to ensure regular sampling and testing of soft drinks to ensure that quality standards are maintained. Rule 43-A of the PFA Rules, 1955, provides that there shall be no advertisement of any food which is misleading or contravening the provisions of PFA Act 1954 or the Rules made there under. Violation of any provisions of the PFA Act 1954 and Rules made there under attracts penal action under the said Act. This information was given by the Minister for Health & Family Welfare, Dr. Anbumani Ramadoss in a written reply to a question in the Rajya Sabha.

709. (5-5-2007) NEW DELHI : Agricultural Minister Shri Sharad Pawar today re-affirmed government's support to the agribusiness sector. Shri Pawar said that the government has taken a number of steps for creating an enabling environment for investment in agribusiness. Policy and regulatory measures have been taken for strengthening forward and backward linkages and reforms in the marketing sector have been given high priority. On Centre's initiative, majority of States have already amended their APMC Acts to allow direct transaction between buyers and sellers outside the regulated agricultural markets. Financial institutions have been permitted to fund contract farming schemes. Taxes on processed food have been reduced. A number of Agricultural Export Promotion Zones have been established. FDI is allowed in food processing and single brand retailing, the Minister informed. The Agriculture Minister was speaking at the inauguration of the workshop on 'Contract Farming: Methods and Experiences' being held as part of the Indo-US Knowledge Initiative on Agriculture. The Initiative was announced in July 2005 during the visit of Indian Prime Minister to the US. The workshop is being held to share experiences of experts and farmers of the two countries in contract farming. The Minister emphasised that the demand for high-value and processed food products is rising and will continue to rise because of booming economy, rising incomes, growing urbanization and changing consumer preferences. In addition, globalisation offers an opportunity to access the world market. He expressed happiness that realizing the enormous untapped opportunities in the Indian agribusiness sector, a number of business houses locally and from abroad have started entering it. Shri Pawar, however, cautioned about concerns and apprehensions about contract farming, such as exclusion of small farmers and the likely adverse impact of contract farming on food security. The government's main concern is how benefits of emerging opportunities reach the producers, especially the smallholders, he said. Since the small farmers face problems relating to credit, technology, inputs and market access, Shri Pawar suggested that agribusiness firms should integrate farmers in their supply chains through institutions such as cooperatives, producers' associations and contract farming. 'We are encouraging farmers to form grass-root level associations/informal cooperatives owned and managed by farmers themselves and/or producer companies,' he said. Asking the American and Indian participants in the workshop to come out with models of contract farming that are relevant to Indian realities, Shri Pawar mentioned that case studies of some successful models indicate that contract farming, if well managed, benefits the farmers in terms of assured market, reduced marketing and transportation costs, access to improved technology and quality inputs, and sharing of production and price risks. Agriculture Secretary, Dr. P.K. Mishra, called for removing the constraints of the present contract farming: issues relating to enforceability of contract and dispute resolution, and high transaction costs. He also stressed that for contract farming to succeed, trust was as much important as the formal contract. Industries could build such trust by bearing social responsibilities, he said. DG (ICAR), Dr. Mangla Rai, said that besides increasing net income of the producer, contract farming has the potential to infuse new technologies, quality inputs and investment into agriculture.

710. (5-5-2007) NEW DELHI : The Union Minister of Youth Affairs & Sports Shri Mani Shankar Aiyar has called upon the youths to uphold the ideals of national integration, secularism and unity in diversity to carry forward the message of martyrs of First War of Independence 1857. Addressing a function on the eve of National Youth Rally from Kranti Park, Meerut to Red Fort, Delhi, Shri Aiyar said events during the first war of independence in 1857 for the first time made Indians that they belong to one nation. The Governor of Uttar Pradesh Shri T.V. Rajeshwar listing the events which led to 1857 revolt against British rule said during that period people from far-flung areas participated in the uprising with just one goal in mind to get rid of the oppressive rule of the British. A book "Meerut 1857 Sanjhi Shahadat ke Kuch Phool" was also released on the occasion. A cultural programme was also presented by NYKS Cultural team and TIRANGA Group of Artists. The historic rally will be flagged off in full patriotic fervour on 7th May, 2007 from Meerut. It will reach Red Fort, Delhi on May 11th 2007 via Modinagar, Muradnagar & Ghazibad. The rally will be flagged off by Shri Mani Shankar Aiyar. More than 30,000 participants will take part in the 4 day event.

711. (5-5-2007) NEW DELHI : The Prime Minister, Dr. Manmohan Singh received a telephone call from President George Bush this evening. The two leaders discussed matters pertaining to the agenda of the G-8 Outreach Summit due next month. The Prime Minister conveyed India's commitment to work with other countries to deal with the problems of climate change and global warming. He said that the problems of environment cannot be solved by perpetuating poverty in developing countries. The two leaders discussed the Clean Development Mechanism and agreed that the emphasis has to be on greater energy efficiency and the development of new technologies. The two leaders also emphasized the importance of a successful conclusion of the Doha Development Round of multilateral trade negotiations. The Prime Minister said that India has a strong vested interest in the successful functioning of a multilateral trading system, and that India would like the Doha Round to adhere to the original understanding that it will be a development round. The Prime Minister said India would like to work with all like-minded countries to make a success of Doha negotiations. The two leaders expressed happiness at the strengthening of the bilateral relations and reviewed developments pertaining to negotiations on bilateral civil nuclear cooperation. They also discussed other regional matters. The President invited the Prime Minister to visit the United States again. The Prime Minister accepted the invitation and said mutually convenient dates will be worked out.

712. (5-5-2007) NEW DELHI : The outstanding balance of 11.90 per cent Government Stock, 2007 and 11.90 per cent Government Stock, 2007 (MSS) is repayable at par on May 28, 2007 and no interest will accrue thereon from the said date. The redemption of security amounting to Rs.6,000 crore issued under

Market Stabilization Scheme (MSS) would be met out of balances available in MSS Account. In the event of a holiday being declared on May 28, 2007 by any State Government under the Negotiable Instruments Act, 1881, the Loan will be repaid by the paying offices in that State on the previous working day. To facilitate repayment of the Loan on the due date, holders may tender the securities, duly discharged, at the Public Debt Offices, Treasuries/Sub-Treasuries and branches of State Bank of India and its Associate Banks (at which they are enfaced/registered for payment of interest) 20 days in advance of the due date for repayment. Full details of the procedure for receiving the discharge value may be obtained from any of the aforesaid paying offices. Department of Economic Affairs, Ministry of Finance.

713. (5-5-2007) NEW DELHI : Government of India have announced the sale (re-issue) of "7.55 percent Government Stock, 2010" under Market Stabilization Scheme for a notified amount of Rs. 2,000 crore (nominal). The Government Stock will be sold through price based auction using multiple price method. The auction will be conducted by the Reserve Bank of India, Mumbai Office, Fort, Mumbai on May 9, 2007 (Wednesday). Up to 5% of the amount notified for the sale of stock is reserved for allotment to eligible individuals and Institutions on non-competitive basis as per the Scheme for Non-Competitive Bidding Facility in the Auction of Government Securities. Bids in the prescribed form obtainable from the Regional Director, Reserve Bank of India, Mumbai Office (Public Debt Office), Fort, Mumbai-400 001 and RBI website www.rbi.org.in should be submitted to that Office on May 9, 2007. The NDS members should submit competitive as well as non-competitive bids in electronic format using Primary Market Operation (PMO) module of NDS. All bids should be submitted by 12.30 P.M. The result of the auction will be announced on May 9, 2007 and payment by successful bidders will be during banking hours on May 10, 2007 (Thursday). Department of Economic Affairs, Ministry of Finance.

714. (5-5-2007) NEW DELHI : Minister of State for Defence Shri MM Palam Raju has called upon the captains of industry and commerce to utilize the vast skilled managerial talent of ex-servicemen population to sustain the growth of a booming economy as well as helping the ex-servicemen in their resettlement efforts. Inaugurating the 4th Independent Director's Course for Senior Defence Officials at ASSOCHAM House here today, Shri Raju said that majority of the Armed Forces personnel are retiring at a time, when their family liability is at its peak. There is therefore, a dire need to provide them with a second career in the civil sector. As these personnel are imbued with virtues of integrity of highest order, dedication and management skill, they could do wonders in corporate sector if they are taken into it and given a little orientation in corporate governance, he remarked. Welcoming the participants to the programme, past President ASSOCHAM Shri Govind Hari Singhania said that the Indian industry as a whole is undergoing rapid changes. According to one estimate 3000 to 4000 independent directors would be needed to comply with SEBI's requirement. He hoped that this training would enable the participants to acquire necessary know-how about corporate governance and help them in overcoming different challenges. Maj Gen Harwant Kishan, Director General Resettlement in his address highlighted the growing shortage of experienced managers in industries. He said that DGR in association with Confederation of Indian Industry (CII), FICCI and ASSOCHAM is organizing various training programmes, seminars and workshops etc. to create awareness in the corporate sector about the vast reservoir of trained and multi-discipline human resource available in the form of ex-service personnel who could be gainfully employed in civil sector. About fifty senior officers of the rank of Brigadier to Lt. Gen are attending this one-week specialized course which would be over on May 12, 2007.

715. (5-5-2007) NEW DELHI : In the Press Release entitled "Agricultural Workers To Receive Higher Variable Dearness Allowance from April" issued on May 4th, 2007, the Variable Dearness Allowance per day for semi skilled/unskilled supervisory worker in Area 'C' may be read as Rs. 10.01 in place of Rs. 9.01. Accordingly the rate of VDA as mentioned in Column 'C' in Table 2 of the above said release for semi-skilled/unskilled supervisory workers may be read as 107.00+10.01 = 117.01

716. (5-5-2007) NEW DELHI : In reply to a question whether the Government have plans to enhance the corpus of the National Minorities Development and Finance Corporation in view of the recommendations made in the Sachar Committee Report for the economic upliftment of minorities, the Minority Affairs Minister, Shri A.R. Antulay informed the house today that the authorized share capital of NMDFC has been raised from Rs.500 crore to Rs.650 crore during 2004-05. The budgetary allocation for equity contribution by Central government has been raised from Rs.18.29 crores in 2006-07 to Rs.70 crores during 2007-08. The Minister informed that the Reserve Bank of India was requested to include "minority communities" under priority sector lending in RBI's Master circular on Lending to Priority Sector dated 3.7.2006. RBI, vide its letter dated 24.4.2007, has intimated that they propose to include the following at item No.(iii) under paragraph No.2.2 of their Master Circular on Lending to Priority Sector as follows: "(iii) loans granted to specified minority communities under (a) to (i) above will be reported separately". Shri Antulay further informed that instructions have been given to public sector banks to increase the flow of credit to the minority communities. Public Sector Banks have been advised to open more branches in districts with a substantial proportion of the minority communities and the flow of credit to minorities in these districts will be specially monitored. This information was given by the Minister in reply to a question in the Rajya Sabha today.

717. (5-5-2007) NEW DELHI : The Minister of Minority Affairs, Shri A.R. Antulay informed the Rajya Sabha today that the reports in the media on the

NCAER Study have come to the notice of Government. The reports are based on tabulations obtained from one of the income surveys conducted by NCAER for the year 2004-05 and are based on the result of a multistage, stratified, random sample.

718. (5-5-2007) NEW DELHI : The Minority Affairs Minister, Shri A.R. Antulay has stated that the National Commission for Minorities (NCM) had recommended that, as a separate religion, Jains deserve to be notified as a minority community. However, in its Annual Report for 1997-98, the NCM stated that the demand of Jains for minority status is one view point prevailing in the community and recommended that the Government must through its own resources ascertain the broad consensus on this issue keeping in view all dissenting voices. The Minister stated that as per Census 2001, the total population of Jains is 4,225,053, which is 0.4% of the total population of the country. The Jain community is spread through out India except in the Union Territory of Lakshadweep. Shri Antulay further informed that a Civil appeal was filed by Bal Patil & Another seeking issuance of a direction to the government to notify Jains as a minority community. In accordance with the recommendation of the Standing committee on Social Justice & empowerment, Government has examined the implications of the judgment in this case and is proposing official amendments to the constitution (One Hundred and Third amendment) Bill, 2004. The Minister was replying to an Unstarred Question in Rajya Sabha today.

719. (5-5-2007) NEW DELHI : Traditional Forest Dwellers (Recognition of Forest Rights) Act, 2006 seeks to recognise and vest certain rights over forest land in forest dwelling Scheduled Tribes and other traditional forest dwellers who have been residing in such forests for generations but whose rights could not be recorded to ensure (a) tenurial security, providing them relief against the physical and psychological alienation from land belonging to them; (b) livelihood, in terms of agriculture and ownership of minor forest produce, including right to collect, use, and dispose the same; and (c) traditional and customary rights. This was stated by Shri P.R. Kyndiah in a reply to a question by Shri B.K. Hariprasad in Rajya Sabha today. He further state that as per the Act, the Gram Sabha has been designated as the authority to initiate the process of determining the nature and extent of individual or community forest rights or both that may be given to the forest dwelling Scheduled Tribes who have been in occupation of forest land prior to 13 December, 2005 and to other traditional forest dwellers, who have been in occupation of forest land for three generations prior to 13 December, 2005, he added.

720. (5-5-2007) NEW DELHI : The Government provides Rajiv Gandhi National Fellowship to tribals students for taking up higher studies. Fellowships are provided through the University Grants Commission to ST students to pursue M.Phil. and Ph. D courses, in any university/institution recognized by the University Grants

Commission (UGC). Up to 667 such fellowships may be awarded annually. This was stated by Shri P.R. Kyndiah in a reply to a question by Shri Ravula Chandra Sekar Reddy in Rajya Sabha today.

721. (5-5-2007) NEW DELHI : The Government of India, Ministry of Environment and Forests have notified the Hazardous Waste (Management and Handling) Rules, 1989 which was amended in 2000 and 2003. The E-wastes are regulated under these rules. Industrial and medical units are not the only generators of E-wastes. The users of electrical and electronic gadgets users also generate E-waste. According to an assessment made in a study commissioned by Central Pollution Control Board to M/s IRG South Asia (Pvt.) Ltd., New Delhi, the estimated total generation of electrical and electronic wastes in the country is about 1,46,000 tonnes per year. The study also revealed that approximately 29,000 tonnes of E-waste is generated in the four Metro cities in the country. According to the Hazardous Waste (Management and Handling) Rules, 1989 as amended in 2003, the residues and wastes generated from the operations in electronic industry are considered as hazardous wastes and are listed at Sl. No. 31 of Schedule 1 of these rules. Further, as per the provisions of these rules Electrical, and Electronics Assemblies are covered under Categories A-1180 and B-1110 in Schedule 3 which are applicable for import and export of hazardous wastes. The import of wastes under this category are only permitted for direct reuse and not for recycling or final disposal. The Central Pollution Control Board (CPCB) has undertaken a study for the preparation of "Guideline Document for Environmentally Sound Recycling of E-waste" for the State Pollution Control Boards and Pollution Control Committee of the Union Territories and the industries for handling E-waste. This information was given by the Minister of State in the Ministry of Environment and Forests, Shri Namo Narain Meena in a written reply to question by Shri Girdhari Lal Bhargva and Shrimati Kiran Maheshwari:

722. (5-5-2007) NEW DELHI : The first stretch of the Dahej – Panvel – Dabhol pipeline from Dahej to Surat of 100 km. length was commissioned today by Shri Murli Deora, Union Minister of Petroleum and Natural Gas, with the gas-in at Dahej. Shri Dinsha Patel, Union Minister of State for Petroleum and Natural Gas, Dr. U D Choubey, Chairman and Managing Director, GAIL (India) Limited, Shri D N Narsimharaju, Joint Secretary, Ministry of Petroleum and Natural Gas, Shri Santosh Kumar, Director (Projects), GAIL and other senior officials of the Ministry of Petroleum and Natural Gas and GAIL were also present on the occasion. Shri Deora along with other dignitaries also inspected the pipeline laying work at Surat which had faced some difficulties. Close on the heels of the gas-in into the first stretch of the Dabhol-Panvel – Dabhol pipeline, decks have been cleared for the resumption of the work on a 12 km stretch of the pipeline in Chourasiya Taluka in Surat district with the active support from the Gujarat Government and the Union Ministry of Petroleum and Natural Gas. GAIL is laying 30" diameter, 576 km long Dahej – Panvel – Dabhol pipeline at an estimated investment of Rs. 3200 crore. The pipeline has a design capacity of 12 MMSCMD and will carry R-LNG from Petronet LNG Limited's LNG terminal at Dahej to Dabhol. The pipeline on completion, will supply natural gas to the Dabhol Power plant of Ratnagiri Gas and Power Private Limited (RGPPL), and thus help in revival of the power plant. Being a project of national importance for revival of Dabhol power plant, the project is being monitored regularly by Empowered Group of Ministers and Ministry of Petroleum and Natural Gas to ensure expeditious completion of this project. The interstate gas pipeline would link the two important gas markets of Gujarat and Maharashtra. Currently, the gas market in Gujarat has access to 5 different gas supply sources namely, (a) the South Bassein fields; (b) Panna-Mukta Tapti Field; (c) Lakshmi fields; (d) Dahej RLNG and (d) Shell RLNG. On the other hand, the Maharashtra market has access to gas supplies from only the Bombay High Fields, which is fast declining. Once the DUPL project is commissioned, the Gujarat and Maharashtra markets shall be interconnected. The pipeline will also enable supply of natural gas to various cities and towns and industries in areas falling enroute to the pipeline such as Vapi, Valsad, Navsari etc. The project is being executed in five spreads with the deployment of heavy construction equipment. Approximately 222 km long stretch of the pipeline is covered in Gujarat state and the remaining 354 km long stretch of the trunk line passes through Maharashtra. At Dahej terminal, the gas will have throughput of 92 kg per sq. centimetre pressure for gas to reach Dabhol. The pipeline traverses through 33 river crossings including 1 km wide stretches on Narmada and Tapi rivers. The project also involved 16 crossings by Horizontal Direction Drilling (HDD) method. The project execution team also had to overcome 310 km of rocky and steep hilly terrain. An amount of approximately Rs.100 crore has been disbursed to the farmers of the land as compensation. The construction activities commenced in May 2006, which faced intervening monsoon and RoU related issues. The commissioning activity of the first stretch started from 17th April 2007. The entire project is expected to be completed by the end of May 2007 within the approved cost of Rs. 3200 crore and the gas supply to the Dabhol Power Plant is expected by June end.

723. (5-5-2007) NEW DELHI : The scheme of Conditional Cash Transfer with Insurance Cover includes cash transfers to the family of the girl child based on the fulfillment of four important conditionalities viz. birth and registration of the girl child, immunization, retention in school and delaying marriage beyond 18 years of age, has been included in Annual Plan 2007-08, as a Central Sector Scheme. This was stated by Smt. Renuka Chowdhury, Minister for Women and Child Development in a reply to a question by Smt. Shobhana Bhartia and Prof. Alka Balram Kshatriya in Rajya Sabha today.

724. (5-5-2007) NEW DELHI : Health being a State subject, the data in regard to doctor-patient ratio in various State Government Hospitals is not maintained centrally. The doctor-patient ratio, varies from case to case depending upon various factors like the type of disease, nature of specialization, type of patient-care required *i.e.* indoor/outdoor. According to the Medical Council of India, the allopathic doctor-population ratio at present works out to 1:1722. The patient nurse ratio also depends on various factors like type of patient care provided and nature of specialization etc. and varies from 5:1 to 19:1. The policy of recruitment of nurses depends upon the number of sanctioned position in a hospital and nursing qualification prescribed for the recruitment of nurses. This information was given by the Minister of State for Health & Family Welfare, Smt. Panabaka Lakshmi on 4th May, 2007 in a written reply to a question in the Rajya Sabha.

725. (5-5-2007) NEW DELHI : Government has approved a scheme for computerization of district and Subordinate Courts in the country, the first phase of which is to be completed by 2007-08 at an estimated cost of Rs. 442 crore. An amount Rs. Rs. 187.05 crore has been released upto March 31, 2007 to the National Informatics Centre, which has been entrusted with the task of implementing the scheme in the various courts in the States/Union Territories. This was stated by the Minister of State for Law and Justice, Shri K. Venkatapathy in a written reply in the Rajya Sabha.

726. (5-5-2007) NEW DELHI : Paediatric TB is of concern as it is a reflection of the prevalence of sputum smear positive pulmonary tuberculosis and the extent of transmission of TB infection in the community. 6 to 8% of all new TB cases reported under the programme are of paediatric age group (0 to 14 years). In the year 2006, the percentage of paediatric cases reported at national level and Orissa State was 6% and 4% respectively. The State wise details about paediatric cases (0-14 years) registered under the programme during year 2006 is given at Annexure-I. As paediatric TB is a reflection of extent of transmission of TB infection in the community, detection and cure of adult tuberculosis will prevent the transmission of TB infection and hence reduce the burden of paediatric tuberculosis.

727. (5-5-2007) NEW DELHI : On the basis of the requirement/request received from the State Governments, the quota of Notaries is enhanced from time to time. During 2007, on the request of the State Government of Uttar Pradesh, the maximum number of notaries to be appointed by the State Government of Uttar Pradesh has been enhanced by 50%. Requests from the State Government of Gujarat and Rajasthan have also been received for enhancement of quota of Notaries. The proposal for enhancing the quota of Notaries to be appointed by the State Government of Gujarat and Rajasthan, by 50% is under active consideration of the Government. This was stated by the Minister for Law and Justice, Shri H.R. Bhardwaj in a written reply in the Rajya Sabha.

728. (5-5-2007) NEW DELHI : As per available information upto April 8, 2007, more than 62,000 cases have been reportedly disposed by the evening courts in Gujarat. Under article 235 of the Constitution, administration of justice is a State subject and the State Government in consultation with its concerned High Court decides all matters concerning operations and setting up of courts. It is for the other State Governments to consider the practice of holding Evening Courts initiated in the State of Gujarat and to emulate/replicate the same in the State with or without modifications. The State Governments have to take a decisions in this regard in consultation with their respective High Courts. This was stated by the Minister of State for Law and Justice, Shri K. Venkatapathy in a written reply in the Rajya Sabha.

729. (5-5-2007) NEW DELHI : The Bharatiya Janata Party condemns CPM for its insensitivity towards the welfare of people and its callous attitude exhibited by their both governments in Kerala and West Bengal. The Court's strictures about brutal killings by CPM cadres in Nandigram and callous attitude of Health Minister of Kerala are cases in point. This exposes not only double speak of CPM but also bares hollowness of their slogan for posing as a pro-poor party. The CPM thus is a party of authoritarian rule, which has scant regard for either the welfare of the poor or for court's directions. The Bharatiya Janata Party is extremely concerned over the tragic death of at least 38 infants at the State-run Sree Avittam Tirunal (SAT) Hospital, Thiruvanantpuram in Kerala, on account of hospital-acquired infections during past four months. Responding to a petition filed by BJP leader Pongumood Vikraman, the Hon'ble court in Kerala has directed the authorities to file a culpable Homicide case against State Health Minister Smt P.K. Sreemathy and seven others under sections 304 and 34 of the Indian Penal Code. The CPM government totally ignored to take steps to cleanse the labour room even after the seriousness of the matter was brought to the notice of the Health Minister. The blunt refusal of the Health Minister Ms. Sreemathy to own up the responsibility for the infant deaths and failure of the CPM government to initiate corrective measures shows gross negligence, insensitivity and unaccountability of the Marxist government in Kerala towards the people's welfare. The Hon'ble Calcutta High Court also recently observed that the CPM government in West Bengal denied the people of Nandigram, of their fundamental rights to life and liberty guaranteed under Article 21 of the Constitution. The Advocate general of West Bengal in his status report submitted to the Hon'ble Calcutta High Court candidly stated that the CPM cadres are directly involved in the brutal killings of innocent farmers at Nandigram. These incidents clearly establish the fact that the Marxists governments in both West Bengal and Kerala are anti-people and apathetic towards public welfare.

730. (5-5-2007) NEW DELHI : An in-depth study of the great rebellion of 1857 will reveal that its known heroes are too well known, its unknown heroes are not known at all while its lesser known heroes are only vaguely remembered as footnotes of the textbooks of history. Now when the nation is celebrating the 150th year of its First War of Independence it is time to remember the un-remembered and pay our homage to all those soldiers, peasants, artisans, landlords and scholars who made a common cause with the rulers and the chiefs to overthrow th foreign rule from the Indian soil. It is the participation of the common man whicl gives this great upheaval a popular, a patriotic character making it a nationa upheaval, unique in the annals of world history. More than a lakh of soldiers fel in the various battles and became martyrs. The number of civilians who lai down their lives to free their motherland from the British barbarism is not exactly known. Although the rebellion was widespread in regions such as Delhi, Avadh Rohilkhand, Bundelkhand, areas around Allahabad, Agra, Meerut and the whole of western Bihar, it is estimated that in Avadh alone 150,000 people were killed, making it a glorious chapter in the history of Indian people. The revolt produced many legendry heroes such as Mangal Pandey, Rani of Jhansi, Tantia Tope, Nana Sahib, Begum Hazrat Mahal of Lucknow and Kunwar Singh of Jagdishpur who have been a source of inspiration to the succeeding generations in their struggle for Independence. At the same time the upheaval produced men and women of rare valour who are not so well known such as Bakht Khan, the Commander-in-chief of rebel armies, Rao Tula Ram of Rewari, Raja of Ballabhgarh, Nawab of Jhajjar, Shazada Firuz Shah, Abdul Samad of Badli, Saadat Khan of Indore, Virangani Jhalkari of Women's Regiment of Jhansi, Amar Singh of Jagdishpur, Pir Ali of Patna, Udmi Ram of Libaspur (Delhi) and thousands of Gujjars and Jats and Rangars and Meos of Rohtak, Hissar, Gurgaon and Karnal who joined the rebels of their free will to see their country free from the most inhuman rule of the world history.

731. (5-5-2007) NEW DELHI : Sex ratio in India has declined over the century from 972 in 1901 to 927 in 1991. The sex ratio has since gone up to 933 in 2001. In contrast, the child sex ratio for the age group of 0-6 years in 2001 is 927 girls per thousand boys against 945 recorded in 1991 Census. As far as worldwide sex ratio is concerned, it is 1.01 male (s)/females as in 2006. Some of the reasons commonly put forward to explain the consistently low levels of sex ratio are son preference, neglect of the girl child resulting in higher mortality at younger age, female infanticide, female foeticide, higher maternal mortality and male bias in emuneration of population. Easy availability of the sex determination test and abortion services may also be facilitating the process which may be further stimulated by pre-conception sex selection facilities. The Government has taken a number of initiatives to implement the Pre-Conception and Pre-Natal Diagnostic Technique Act (PC&PNDT) and to spread awareness on the issue through Information, Communication and Education (IEC). They include amendment of PC&PNDT Act in 2003 to make it more comprehensive, more frequent visits of National Inspection and Monitoring Committee (NIMC), setting up of National Support and Monitoring Cell (NSMC), sensitization through Members of Parliament, publication of handbook on the Act, Annual Report on the Act, Frequently Asked Questions (FAQ), involvement of District Magistrate, launching of "Save the Girl Child" campaign etc.

732. (5-5-2007) NEW DELHI : Total number of government allopathic doctors in the country are 73557. There are 22273 numbers of doctors at Primary Health Centres (PHCs) in position in rural areas as on March 2006. As on 1.1.2007, total numbers of beds available in the rural government hospitals are 132475 and 340308 beds are available in urban government hospitals including Community Health Centres (CHCs). 75.3% of PHCs and 92.4% of CHCs are located in government buildings. As on March 2006, about 7.5% of the PHCs were without a doctor, about 38.9% were without a lab technician and about 17.7% were without a pharmacist. In the CHCs, overall about 54.5% of the sanctioned posts of the specialists were vacant. The National Rural Health Mission (NRHM) envisages strengthening health care delivery in the rural areas by strengthening physical infrastructure, manpower, medicine availability etc. at Sub-Centres PHCs and CHCs. Sustainable quality care with accountability and people participation is proposed to be achieved through a management structure called Rogi Kalyan Samittees/Hospital Management Committees. To take care of continuous local needs, the Health Centres have been provided with Untied grant. For taking health care to the door steps of the public especially in under served areas, Mobile Medical Units (MMUs) have also been provided under NRHM. This information was given by the Minister of State for Health & Family Welfare, Smt. Panabaka Lakshmi on 4th May, 2007 in a written reply to a question in the Rajya Sabha.

733. (5-5-2007) NEW DELHI : Under Pradhan Mantri Swasthya Suraksha Yojana (PMSSY), it has been decided to set up six new AIIMS like Institutions, each in the States of Bihar (Patna), Chhatisgarh (Raipur), Madhya Pradesh (Bhopal), Orissa (Bhubaneshwar), Rajasthan (Jodhpur) and Uttaranchal (Rishikesh). The estimated cost for setting up each institute is Rs. 332 crore based on CPWD plinth area rates. Under PMSSY, it has also been decided to strengthen 13 existing Medical College Institutions in terms of infrastructure and equipments. List of institutions being upgraded can be seen in the **Annexure.** An outlay of Rs. 120 crore has been approved for upgradation of each medical college institution. Out of this, the Government of India is investing Rs. 100 crore for each institution and the State Government's share is Rs. 20 crore and subsequent recurring, maintenance and manpower costs. In respect of SVIMS, Tirupati, the TTD trust is bearing half of the cost *i.e.* Rs. 60 crore and the GOI share is only Rs. 60 crore. Likewise, in respect of IMS (BHU) Varanasi, which is a GOI institution, Rs. 20 crore is being provided by Ministry of Human Resource Development.

734. (5-5-2007) NEW DELHI : Shri Arjun Singh, Minister for Human Resource Development will inaugurate National Seminar on '1857-Renaissance of Indian Languages' tomorrow. The Central Institute of Hindi, Ministry of HRD, Govt. of India in collaboration with the National council for promotion of Urdu is organizing this seminar from the 8th of May till the 10th of May, 2007. Chairman of National Book Trust, Shri Bipin Chandra, will be presiding over the function. The key note address will be delivered by Shri, Sabysachi Bhattacharya, Chairman, Indian

Council for Historical Research. The welcome address will be given by the Vice-Chairman, Kendriya Hindi Shikshan Mandal, Prof. Ram Sharan Joshi and Prof Shambhunath, Director, Central Institute of Hindi will be presenting the theme of the seminar. Prof. Ali Javed, Director NCPUL will propose a vote of thanks and the programme will be compered by Prof. Shrish Chandra Jaswal, coordinator of the seminar. Prominent scholars like Prof. Kamala Prasad, Prof. Imtiaz Ahmed, Shri, Sudeep Banerjee, Shri. Prabhash Joshi, Prof. Purushottam Aggarwal, Shri. Nadir Ali Khan, Prof. Iqbal Hussain and Prof. Iktedar Alam Khan will participate in the seminar. The aim of this national seminar is to highlight the role of 1857 in the renaissance of India. The conference also aims at evaluating the effect of the renaissance on the modern developments in the Indian Languages. The purpose is to find out how the northern Indian Languages, especially Urdu, Hindi, Punjabi, Kashmiri, Dogri, Rajasthani etc. were struggling with the problems of self-identity in the process of their modernization and to explore how communicability and interrelationship was being established due to the cultural and linguistic interaction among the different Indian Languages. The main sessions of the seminar are: 1857 and Indian Renaissance (8th May); 1857 and Urdu (9th May); 1857, secularism and Urdu-Hindi interrelationship (9th May); Modernization and the question of linguistic identity (10th May); globalization and new challenges before Indian Languages (10th May) and 1857 & North Indian Languages Media (10th May). The valedictory session will be on '1857 and the media of northern Indian Languages.' Shri. Chandra Kant Tripathi, Registrar, Central Institute of Hindi will present a vote of thanks.

735. (5-5-2007) NEW DELHI : The Brahmaputra Board has prepared the Master Plan of the Main Stem of Brahmaputra (Master Plan Part 1), Barak and its tributaries (Master Plan II) and identified 52 numbers of tributaries under Master Plan (Part III). So far, Government of India has approved the Master Plan Part-I, Part-II and 34 Sub-basin Master Plan under Part-III. Further, 3 numbers of Sub-basin Master Plans have also been completed. The total cost involved in the implementation of the schemes recommended in third part of the Master Plan, based on 2004 price level, is estimated to be around Rs. 11674.00 crores. The expenditure incurred on the works recommended in the earlier Master Plans I & II was Rs. 52.78 crores. The two schemes recommended in part III of the Master Plan and implemented during Xth plan are (i) protection of Majuli Island and (ii) Anti-erosion works Kusiabil area near Dimapur in the river Dhansiri (S), for which outlays of Rs. 41.28 crores and Rs. 2.64 crore were provided during Xth Plan. As against this, the actual expenditure was Rs. 20.55 crores and Rs. 1.74 crores respectively. The balance expenditure on these works will spill over to XIth Five year Plan. This information was given by the Minister of State for Water Resources, Shri Jai Prakash Narayan Yadav in response to a question by Dr. Arun Kumar Sharma in the Lok Sabha today.

736. (5-5-2007) NEW DELHI : The Government of India had constituted a Task Force for flood management/erosion control in August, 2004 to look into the recurrent floods in Assam and some other neighbouring States, under the chairmanship of Chairman, Central Water Commission. The Task Force submitted its report on 31.12.2004. The Task Force recommended a number of Flood Management schemes/works amounting to a total of Rs 4982.10 crore. It included works of Rs. 316.14 crore under immediate, works of Rs. 2030.15 crore under Short Term-I and works of Rs, 2635.81 crore as Short Term-II category, to be implemented during next six months, 2 years and 7 years respectively. The state governments were, however, required to prepare detailed project reports of the schemes and process them for approval as per the guidelines of the Planning Commission and get them techno-economically cleared by appraising agencies for taking them up for implementation. The report of Task Force was circulated to various Ministries/Planning Commission and the State Governments. Based upon the recommendations of the Task Force, two on-going schemes during X plan under central plan, namely, "Critical Anti Erosion Works in Ganga Basin States" and "Critical Flood Control and Anti Erosion Schemes in Brahmaputra and Barak Valley" were upwardly revised to Rs 1150.68 crore and Rs 830.14 respectively. However, considering very little time left in the X plan period, these schemes were sanctioned for Rs. 305.03 crore and Rs. 225 crore respectively with a suggestion that the scheme for balance works may be proposed during XI plan period. Accordingly, remaining works recommended by the Task Force have been included in the proposals of XI Plan. This information was given by the Minister of State for Water Resources, Shri Jai Prakash Narayan Yadav in response to a question by Shri Sugrib Singh, Shri Anwar Hussain and Shri Kishanabhai V. Patel in the Lok Sabha today.

737. (5-5-2007) NEW DELHI : Five Decisions Support Systems are proposed to be developed by National Institute of Hydrology. 5 Decision Support Systems (DSS) are in the areas of (a) Surface Water Planning; (b) Integrated Operation of Reservoirs; (c) Conjunctive Surface Water and Ground Water Planning; (d) Drought Monitoring Assessment and Management; and (e) Water Quality to be integrated into one comprehensive system during implementation of Hydrology Project-II with a view to address the various issues related to Integrated Water Resources Development and Management. This information was given by the Minister of State for Water Resources, Shri Jai Prakash Narayan Yadav in response to a question by Dr. Raghuveer Singh Koshal in the Lok Sabha today.

738. (5-5-2007) NEW DELHI : Water quality at western Yamuna canal meets the desired water quality standards. Pollution Control Research Institute (PCRI), Haridwar, is carrying out water quality monitoring and analysis under Yamuna Action Plan. It is being conducted at Yamunanagar upstream, Yamunanagar downstream, Panipat downstream and Sonepat upstream once a month for the laid down core parameters. The monitoring results are being submitted by PCRI to the Ministry of Environment and Forests on a regular basis. To abate pollution in the river Yamuna, Yamuna Action Plan (YAP) Phase-I has been implemented at an estimated cost of Rs. 715 crores. 15 towns have been covered under YAP-I. A total of 269 Schemes of pollution abatement were completed including 38 sewage treatment plants having treatment capacity of 753. 25 million litres per day. Out of this 401.25 mld. is in Uttar Pradesh, 322 mld is in Haryana and 30 mld is in Delhi. The YAP Phase-II is being implemented at an estimated cost of Rs. 624 crore. Under this phase, sewage treatment plants in Delhi and Uttar Pradesh and interception and diversion of sewer lines in Haryana will be taken up. This information was given by the Minister of State in the Ministry of Environment and Forests, Shri Namo Narain Meena in a written reply to question by Shri Ramdas Athawale in the Lok Sabha today.